From Arctic Ocean to Tropical Rain Forest

MAMMALS
in North America

Wildlife Adventure Stories
and
Technical Guide

by Robert E. Wrigley

Wildlife Paintings
by
Dwayne Harty

HYPERION PRESS LIMITED
in cooperation with the
Manitoba Museum of Man and Nature

Design by A. O. Osen. Transparencies
produced by Henry Kalen, Ltd.,
typesetting by the Manitoba Museum of
Man and Nature, printed and bound by
D. W. Friesen & Sons, Ltd.

Printed in Canada

ISBN 0-920534-33-3

Hyperion Press Limited wishes to thank
the Manitoba Arts Council and Canada
Council for their continued support of
publishers in Canada. Special thanks are
given to the Zoological Society of
Manitoba and the Manitoba Museum of
Man and Nature for their support of this
book.

Canadian Cataloguing in Publication Data
Wrigley, Robert E.

   Mammals in North America

   Bibliography:
   ISBN 0-920534-33-3

1. Mammals - North America - Juvenile literature.
I. Harty, Dwayne, 1957-   II. Manitoba Museum of
Man and Nature.   III. Title.

QL715.W74 1986 j599.097 C86-098031-6

Contents

Preface

I dedicate this book to the two women of my life — my mother Eva and my wife Gail — for nourishing my interest in nature. Even before I could walk, my mother wheeled me, almost daily, through the extensive Buenos Aires Zoo in Argentina to experience firsthand the wonders of the animal world. These early impressions — of Julio the camel, a hippopotamus, storks, and others — remain with me to this day. Later, at my home in St. Lambert, Quebec, no creature was too repulsive to be allowed in my room or the basement, for my mother would not refuse me any chance to learn. Not without some fear on her part, she let me keep an alligator, many kinds of snakes including a mature boa constrictor, an iguana, salamanders, frogs and toads, local and tropical fish, mice, guinea pigs, as well as the more common pets. Escapees and unanticipated offspring in my collection were only a few of the events she put up with. Such is the love of a mother.

During these childhood and early teenage years, books on keeping animals as pets were quite scarce, and I could find little information on the native animals that I came into contact with during my daily romps in the nearby woods, swamp, and along the St. Lawrence River. When I did find a helpful book, it was like opening up a treasure. I read and reread the pages until I had the words and pictures memorized.

Today there are hundreds of good books on animals of North America and other parts of the world, and excellent wildlife films and television shows attract an ever-increasing audience. And yet I have never come across that special source of information I was searching for as a youngster — a book that entered the daily lives of animals, both large and small; one that described facts about the wonderful creatures that most people don't even know exist in their country. I have tried in the following pages to write that book. I hope that both young and adult readers will enjoy these accounts and illustrations and learn to value their fellow mammals, for we have much to learn from and about them.

The idea for the present volume arose while I was working on several story-coloring books on small and large mammals, published by Hyperion Press Limited of Winnipeg. The owners of Hyperion, Dr. Marvis Tutiah and Ms. Arlene Osen, encouraged me to consider writing a comprehensive book for student and adult readers, combining educational stories about animals with detailed factual information, illustrations, and distribution maps. I express my sincere thanks to them both for advice and the chance to write the book I have always been looking for. I was also permitted to enlist the artistic services of Dwayne Harty, a close friend who had recently illustrated two other books for me — *Manitoba's Big Cat: The Story of the Cougar in Manitoba*, and the first volume of the *Large Mammals* coloring books. He accepted the challenge to paint the 115 species of mammals in this volume, perhaps not fully realizing at first the mammoth task involved. With artistic skill, wildlife experience, and great dedication he has succeeded in capturing the essential nature and story of each animal with accuracy and charm. I deeply appreciated his full commitment to the project, which included meeting with me, often on a weekly basis, for two years to examine specimens and other source materials, and to work out the many details of each painting. We were also able to travel together on a whirlwind trip throughout the western United States to observe mammals in nature, zoos, aquaria, and museums, and to sketch the mammal specimens we collected on the way.

I must thank my secretary, Mrs. Evelyn Billington, for typing and editing several drafts of the manuscript. Her eagerness and thoughtful advice about each account made them more fun to write. The manuscript was typeset by Linda Jackson, Linda Lindsay, and Sheila Proteau and proofread by Valerie Hatten and Paulette Gendre. Betsy Thorsteinson painted the beautiful dioramas of prehistoric life. The maps were prepared by David Hopper, Eric Crone, Alan Einarson, and Teri McIntyre (all staff of the Manitoba Museum of Man and Nature). Dr. Robert Seabloom (University of North Dakota) and Dr. Rick Riewe (University of Manitoba) kindly agreed to review sections of the book and offered many helpful suggestions. Dr. Sydney Anderson (American Museum of Natural History) responded to my request for literature from Mexico and Central America, and Dr. William Pruitt Jr. (University of Manitoba) made available his Russian texts and translations. I am grateful to Dr. Donald Hoffmeister and Dr. Charles Kendeigh (both of the University of Illinois) for providing me with my first introductions to the wonderful scenery and wildlife of the southern United States, the Mexican border, and the southern Appalachians. Likewise, Dr. Phillip Youngman (National Museums of Canada) offered me the opportunity to study in the western Canadian Arctic for two months. My fifteen years with the Manitoba Museum of Man and Nature have allowed me to pursue mammalogy not only in Manitoba but in many areas of North America. During this period I have been fortunate to have the help and company of assistant curators Jack Dubois and Herb Copland. Although I have included in this book my own experiences and research from the Atlantic to the Pacific coasts, the Canadian Arctic to the Yucatan jungle of Mexico, I have obviously drawn heavily from the work of hundreds of other mammalogists and naturalists, many of whom are listed under "Additional Reading".

My family — Gail, Mark, and Robert — patiently listened to the animal stories and put up with mountains of books and papers on our dining room table. As this project drew to a conclusion, my dear wife Gail passed away, so unexpectedly. Over our twenty-two years together, she was frequently at my side while studying mammals in forests, mountains, prairies, and deserts. My early training in field mammalogy was centered at her cottage at South Bolton, in the beautiful rolling hills of southern Quebec. She never tired of checking traplines with me day or night, or recording endless data from specimens while on visits to numerous museums. During the past several years of researching and writing this book, she sustained my interest and inspired me to persevere with the task by her enthusiasm and comments, shared over tea and her baking. I hope her great love of nature and devotion to teaching children shine through these pages, for this is really her book too.

Introduction

Mammals may be distinguished from other groups of animals by a number of characteristics, but the two main ones are a body more or less covered with hair (though hair is greatly reduced in some forms like the whales) and mammary glands in the female which nourish the young — a feature so important that it gave rise to the group's name, Class Mammalia. Many kinds of mammals have become familiar to us from pictures, films, or by actually viewing them in the wild or at a zoo. Other species, especially the small or secretive ones, make every effort to stay out of sight, and we may pass right by them without realizing their presence. In addition there are those mammals that live in remote regions where few people have the opportunity to visit. Mammalogists (biologists specializing in the study of mammals) observe or collect these animals and preserve specimens as dry skins and skeletons, or in alcohol, for detailed examination and reference in museum collections. Mammals are particularly fascinating to study because of their many amazing adaptations of body form and behavior patterns, and perhaps because we most easily identify with them, for they are our closest relatives among all the earth's creatures.

North America is the third largest land mass on earth, covering about 23.5 million square kilometers (8.7 million square miles). It measures 6 960 kilometers (4,325 miles) east to west, and 8 160 kilometers (5,070 miles) north to south. The shape and topography of North America have been anything but constant over the millenia. For much of its early history it was part of one immense land mass called Pangea, which subsequently (200 to 300 million years ago) broke up into a number of continental plates that are still drifting apart to this day. Over the ages, sudden or gradual movements of the crust have resulted in volcanism and uplifting of massive rock formations into mountain ranges, some of which were higher than the recent Himalayas. During quieter periods, persistent forces of erosion (water, wind, heat, and cold) once again leveled the higher ground and carried the sediments great distances to low-lying regions. At other times North America was invaded by vast seas, some so extensive as to divide the continent into east and west halves.The migration of the poles, the presence of mountains, volcanic dust, solar outbursts, and perhaps other factors have profoundly affected the climate. Parts of the landscape have experienced extensive glaciation, temperate and desert conditions, as well as tropical heat and humidity. All of these events and environments have helped mold the nature and course of evolution of life on the ancient land mass we now call North America.

Closely correlated with the changing climate was the evolution of the continent's plant life. Abundant fossil evidence suggests that three main floras dominated North America over most of the recent geological period called the Tertiary (within the last 65 million years). The Arcto-tertiary Flora covered the northern part of the Northern Hemisphere and was divided into two units — the more northern or boreal one (with pines, spruces, and willows) became arctic tundra, boreal forest, and montane forest, while the temperate unit (maples, oaks, and birches) became deciduous forest. The southern half of North America supported the Neotropical-tertiary Flora consisting of tropical and subtropical plants with thick evergreen leaves as occur in the tropical evergreen and tropical deciduous forests of today in Florida, Mexico, and Central America. The Madro-tertiary Flora appears to have originated on the high Mexican plateau from small trees, shrubs, and grasses of the latter flora, in response to increasing aridity. This flora spread northward into the American southwest and Great Basin regions, giving rise to desert, grassland, shrubland, and woodland communities. The grassland region of North America, so prominent today, is of mixed origin and is relatively recent. The arctic ice cap formed as late as three million years ago in response to the cooling of the earth's climate. Consequently, the arctic community of plants

Selected animals found in the Boreal Coniferous Forest and Arctic Tundra zones along the edge of the Pleistocene glacier

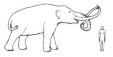

American Mastodon
Mamut americanum

Wooly Mammoth
Mammuthus primigenius

Giant Bison
Bison latifrons

Stag Moose
Cervalces scotti

Jefferson's Ground Sloth
Megalonyx jeffersoni

Woodland Muskox
Symbos cavifrons

Short-faced Bear
Arctodus simus

Saber-toothed Cat
Smilodon

Dire Wolf
Canis dirus

Giant Beaver
Castoroides ohioensis

Selected animals found in the Transition Forest and Grassland zones of the northern Great Plains during the Pleistocene

Columbian Mammoth
Mammuthus colombi

Western Bison
Bison antiguus occidentalis

Yesterday's Camel
Camelops hesternus

Shasta Ground Sloth
Nothrotheriops shastensis

American Lion
Panthera (Leo) atrox

Scott's Horse
Equus scotti

Large-headed Llama
Hemiauchenia macrocephala

Mexican Wild Ass
Equus (Assinus) conversidens

Leidy's Peccary
Platygonus vetus

Bone-eating Dog
Borophagus diversidens

Paintings by
Betsy Thorsteinson,
Manitoba Museum of Man and Nature

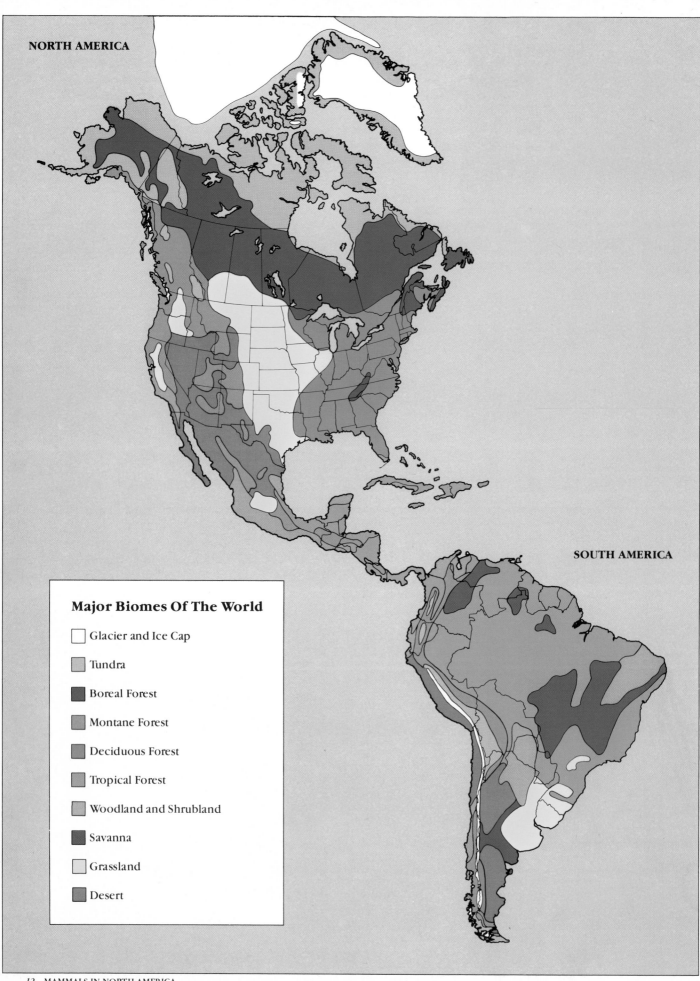

SOUTH AMERICA

Major Biomes Of The World

- Glacier and Ice Cap
- Tundra
- Boreal Forest
- Montane Forest
- Deciduous Forest
- Tropical Forest
- Woodland and Shrubland
- Savanna
- Grassland
- Desert

and animals is probably the youngest in the world. Inhabiting these vastly different habitats and environments were fascinating sequences of mammal faunas and other forms of animal life. The two accompanying dioramas show selected animals found in the arctic tundra-boreal forest and transition forest-grassland communities during the Pleistocene ice age.

North America now encompasses Arctic, Temperate, and Tropical climatic zones, and the whole spectrum of moisture conditions from rain forest to some of the driest deserts on earth. Two major geographical regions of animal life also spread across

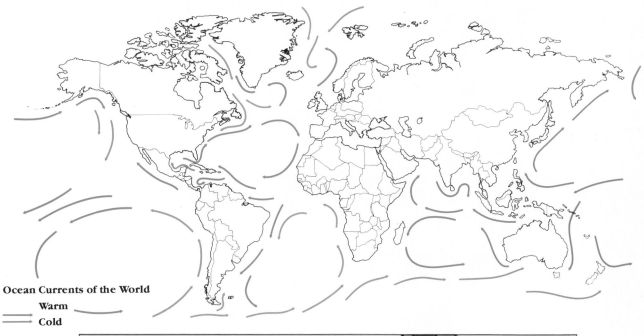

Ocean Currents of the World

Warm

Cold

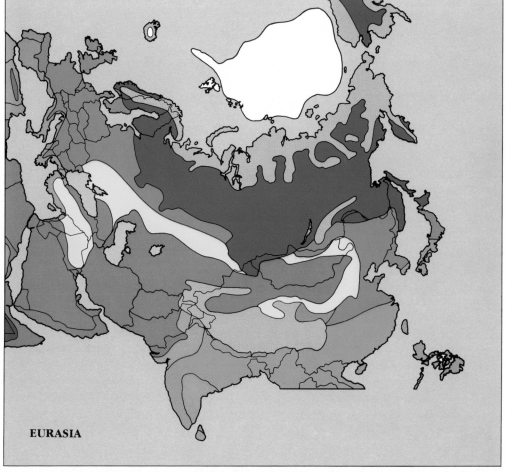

EURASIA

the face of the continent — the Nearctic Realm extending from the arctic south to California, northern Mexico, and Florida; and the Neotropical Realm which continues south to include much of Mexico, the West Indies, Central America, and all of South America. Eurasia is known as the Palearctic Realm, and because of its similarities in fauna and flora with the Nearctic, the two are grouped together as the Holarctic Realm.

Ecologists also recognize a number of major plant and animal communities around the world, called biomes. These are usually based on the dominant type of vegetation (e.g., Grassland Biome) or water body (e.g., Arctic Marine Biome), and are shown in simplified form for North America, South America, and Eurasia on the previous pages. Certain biomes may be present on two or more continents due to similar conditions of climate. More interestingly, they may also share some of the same animals and plants as a result of earlier connections between the continents. During the last three million years North America exchanged numerous mammal species with Eurasia over the Bering land bridge (between Alaska and Siberia), and with South America over the Panamanian land bridge. These relatively recent exchanges and consequent similarities in plant and animal life between North America and these two continents have led to considerable debate over whether some mammals (e.g., beaver and wolverine) represent one, two, or more species on different continents. As new information accumulates on hereditary relationships of North American mammals, certain species may be found to contain several distinct species (short-tailed shrew), while groups of different-looking animals are sometimes discovered to be a single species (caribou).

Mammals may be restricted to one biome (collared lemming of the Tundra Biome) or range through many biomes (coyote). Often, mammals that live along watercourses or in the mountains extend into several biomes. I have grouped selected species of mammals into eleven chapters based on the biomes where they are most typically found, recognizing that these animals may be present in other biomes and habitats as well. The major characteristics of the biomes are described at the beginning of each chapter, in terms of vegetation, animal life, climate, and topography.

Each account in this book begins with a story which attempts to reveal in an entertaining way the nature of the animal's experiences and how it is adapted to and copes with its environment and with other creatures in the community. The accompanying illustration shows the animal's physical features, posture, facial expression, and the vegetation and terrain of its home. The following section covers more detailed information outlining the scientific name (common names are sometimes inconsistent), family and order, measurements, color, distribution, status, diet, reproduction, growth, and remarks on form, habits, and personal anecdotes.

Distribution maps depict the natural range of each species in North America, including recent range extensions achieved by the animals themselves, although in some cases these may have been influenced by the effects of humans on the landscape. Introductions into new regions, as well as range reductions due to habitat destruction, overharvesting, poisoning, etc., are not shown on the maps, but these facts are mentioned in the text. Distribution maps of South America and Eurasia are also provided for those species whose ranges extend onto these other continents, for this adds an interesting dimension about the animals that is often omitted from other books. It is important to realize that these maps indicate the areas where species may be found in appropriate habitats; however, the animals do not necessarily occur everywhere within these zones.

There are a surprisingly large number of species of mammals native to North America (from the Arctic and Greenland to Panama) — approximately 855 — only 115 of which are described briefly in this book. A complete checklist is provided which graphically illustrates the incredible diversity of mammal life in this region. For more detailed information on life history, habits, and distribution of mammals I have also included a list of national, regional, and state/province/territory books and papers for Canada, the United States, Mexico, Central America, and the West Indies. Unfortunately, few popular books in English are presently available from these southern countries. Much of this additional reading can be found in local libraries, museums, and universities.

Mammals of the
Cold Oceans

Oceans and seas cover over 70 percent of the earth's surface. They are mainly cold dark environments with only the upper few hundred meters (yards) lit and warmed by the sun's rays. It is a restless world near the surface, with currents driven by the prevailing winds and by the rotation of the earth on its axis, as well as by the twice-daily tides powered by the immense forces of attraction of the moon and sun. Ocean water is a solution of inorganic compounds (most of which have been washed in from land) and a suspension of organic particles. One kilogram (2.2 pounds) of salt water in the arctic averages 34 grams (1.2 ounces) of salt; 37 grams (1.3 ounces) in the tropics. There are also minute traces of nitrates and phosphates — nutrients essential for plant growth.

The arctic region is cold because of the low angle of the sun. Ice and snow contribute to the frigid conditions over most of the year by reflecting up to 90 percent of the solar radiation back into space, so that only 10 percent is absorbed by the surface. Unlike Antarctica, whose ice cap rests mainly on land, the arctic's permanent and seasonal ice sheets are largely over water; the North American shore of the Arctic Ocean is bordered by fast ice for 9 months of the year. During the brief summer, displaced sea-ice (derived from either the edge of the arctic pack or from land-fast ice) is carried great distances by powerful sea currents such as the Subarctic Current off Alaska, East Greenland Current, Labrador Current, and offshoots of the Gulf Stream. High arctic waters are dilute, cold (generally at the freezing point of sea water which is -2 °C or 28.4 °F), and biologically poor, since they are cut off from sunlight by ice for most or all of the year. Low arctic and north-temperate oceans are warmer (reaching 4 °C to 10 °C or 39.2 °F to 50 °F at the surface in summer), richer in dissolved nutrients, and are exposed to the sun during summer — all the necessary ingredients for photosynthesis of plants. While arctic waters are not as biologically productive as antarctic waters, upwhellings of nutrients from the bottom in some regions result in incredible blooms of plankton — tiny drifting plants and animals that form the basis of marine food chains. The flushing of this fertilizer from the depths to the surface occurs as a result of turbulence (from major currents meeting or from gales) and from the turnover of cool and warm layers in spring and late summer. Surprisingly, in spite of the cold, these waters are far richer in plankton mass per unit volume (although not in variety of species) than most tropical and south-temperate seas whose surface waters are low in nutrients.

In contrast to land, most marine plant life consists of phytoplankton — microscopic single or chains of cells such as diatoms and dinoflagellates. Amazingly, these tiny plants are responsible for producing about 70 percent of the earth's oxygen. Minute drifting animal life called zooplankton, such as crustaceans, arrowworms, jellyfish, and larvae of fish, sea urchins, and star fish, actively or passively collect algal cells for food. They spend bright days below 20 meters (65.6 feet) depth, then rise to upper levels to feed at night. Plankton is eaten by larger animals like fish and squid which, in turn, support larger fish, seals, whales, and birds. Dead organisms and wastes from the upper levels of the sea continually rain down to the floor to nourish anemones, sponges, clams, and other detritus collectors, which are fed upon by deep-sea fish, narwhals, and walrus. In autumn, the unavailability of nutrients and the spreading ice create conditions unsuitable for phytoplankton, and they cease photosynthesis, decline in abundance, and form spores. With little to eat, the zooplankton become scarce and the survivors sink into deep water to rest. Whales, walrus, some seals, and marine birds migrate to ice-free waters, while ringed seals and polar bears center their activities during the long dark arctic nights along pressure cracks in the pack-ice or the few extensive areas (called polynya) of water kept open by strong winds or currents.

Typical herbivores of the Cold Oceans Biome are copepod crustaceans, sponges, sea urchins, sea cucumbers, clams, and bowhead whale. Carnivores are represented by jellyfish, arrowworm, arctic cod, capelin, herring gull, oldsquaw duck, king eider, black guillemot, ringed and harp seals, walrus, killer whale, white whale, narwhal, and polar bear.

Polar Bear

A black nose suddenly appeared out of a snowbank, followed by a huge white head. Arousing from a temporary winter den, the large male polar bear decided to desert the coast and strike out onto the ice in search of seals. For three weeks this king of the arctic had been forced to bed, since Baffin Bay was frozen fast, leaving few open leads in the ice where he could hunt. Stiff limbs were stretched, and a yawn blew out a puff of white haze in the −40°C (−40°F) air. A particularly bright wave of northern lights distracted him for a few seconds, then his big floppy feet and long legs began to carry him eastward onto the bay ice. At midday, a faint light from the hidden January sun appeared on the southern horizon, but most of the time the bear traveled by the eerie reflected light of the moon and stars.

A week later he finally caught a whiff of seal. His keen nose directed him for over a kilometer (0.6 mile) upwind to a spot where the stench of seal was very strong. Stalking slowly and then pouncing through the ringed seal's snow den, the bear swiped at the prey with its clawed paw, but the frantic animal slipped down through the hole in the ice. The bear knew from experience there was no point in waiting for the seal to return, so he threw his head aloft in frustration and moved on.

Several days later, the bear detected the odor of the sea and marine life. Strong currents had opened a long crack in the ice and numerous seals, beluga whales, and a few narwhals were swimming from one end to the other. The bear slipped quietly into the icy water and began paddling with his front feet towards the dark shapes on the far edge of the ice. Holding his breath, the bear dove under water and without warning, exploded in a big wave right up beside a sleeping seal. One stroke of the powerful paw killed the eighty-kilogram (176-pound) ringed seal instantly. The hungry polar bear ripped the skin and blubber off the carcass and downed mouthfuls of the fatty

material. In half an hour only a few muscled bones were left. His stomach full, the hunter proceeded to wash the fat and blood from his face and paws. Then he climbed atop a jagged mound of snow and ice where he surveyed the barren wastes using his nose, eyes, and ears. The other seals and whales had all retreated to the far end of the open water. Only an occasional muffled breath from surfacing whales broke the polar solitude. With a slight wind ruffling the big bear's coat, he descended headfirst down the hill. In the shelter of a sculptured snowdrift, the animal circled into position, lowered itself with feet tucked under its body, and promptly fell asleep. Particles of snow drifted onto his fur, making the bear almost invisible against the landscape.

As spring approached, the current plucked free large pans from the rotting pack ice, which began to drift southward. The bear swam between the ice floes, pursuing seals that were present in the thousands, basking on the ice or diving for fish and shrimp. By April the bear had drifted far down to the Labrador coast. One afternoon he paced impatiently back and forth over an ever-shrinking raft. The increasingly warm air caused him to pant heavily. His huge chest heaved and his dark blue tongue hung out one side of his jaw. Perhaps he smelled land or maybe caught sight of the shore, for suddenly the white hulk did a spectacular belly flop into the sea and began "dog-paddling" through the waves in a westward direction. The strong current swept him still farther southward, but finally, after eight hours of swimming and floating, his feet touched the rocky shore of Labrador. The bear had drifted sixteen hundred kilometers (994 miles) in two months. It would be a long walk back home to Baffin Island.

POLAR BEAR

Scientific name *Ursus maritimus*

Family Bears (Ursidae)

Order Carnivores (Carnivora)

Total length males 225 cm (89 in);
females 190 cm (75 in)

Tail length 12 cm (5 in); 9 cm (4 in)

Weight 550 kg, maximum 800 kg
(1,213 lb, maximum 1,764 lb);
285 kg (628 lb)

Color The coat is white when newly grown, but becomes faded and stained to yellow or gray.

Distribution and Status The polar bear occurs along the arctic coasts and islands of North America, Greenland, and the Soviet Union. The range closely follows the distribution of polar sea ice, which shifts position from summer to winter. This species has been recorded as far north as 88° N, and as far south as James Bay, Newfoundland, Iceland, and the Pribilof Islands of Alaska.

There are 6 major populations of polar bears in the Arctic (with little movement between them), 3 of which lie in North America — western Alaska, northern Alaska, and the Canadian mainland and islands. Overharvesting in the past had reduced numbers to a dangerously low level. Under an international agreement, the killing of these magnificent animals has now been restricted, with hunting quotas limited mainly to native people (the worldwide harvest is about 1,000 per year). Concentrated efforts are underway to study this species on its home grounds. Although it is difficult to obtain an accurate count, there are probably not more than 20,000 polar bears living in the wild at present. The polar bear and brown bear *(Ursus arctos)* are believed to have originated from a common ancestor during the Pleistocene, about 2 million years ago.

Food This maritime bear feeds mainly on seals, particularly ringed, bearded, harp, and hooded seals. Walrus, whale, carrion, sea birds, fish, crabs, and even grass, berries, and seaweed are devoured. Occasionally a polar bear catches a caribou.

Reproduction and Growth Females come into heat for brief periods from March to June, and an individual may mate with several males, which often fight over the privilege of her company. In early winter she retires to a maternity den in the snow, which may be located from 3 to 60 km (2 to 37 mi) inland. Following an arrested period of growth, the one to 4 embryos develop to a weight of 0.6 kg (2.2 lb) and are born blind and sparsely haired, from November to January. The family emerges from the den in March or April. The cubs are weaned at 2 or 3 years of age, and reach sexual maturity at 5 or 6 years. Females produce a litter every third year, from about age 4 to 20, and both sexes may live to 30 years in the wild.

Remarks The polar bear is characterized by an unusually long neck and a rounded nose. The feet are broad, enabling the bear to stalk quietly over any terrain, and to swim with ease. Hairs on the soles provide some insulation and traction on snow and ice. With a thick fur coat and layer of blubber, the polar bear suffers less from winter cold than from summer heat. When confined to land because of the disintegration of the ice pack, the bear spends most of its time sleeping in as cool a place as possible. In Hudson Bay, this means digging through the moss and sedge to reach the cold permafrost. At home in the water, the bear swims leisurely at 6.5 km (4 mi) per hour for long distances; swims of 65 km or 40 mi are known. Modern capture-mark-release techniques, including satellite tracking, have shown individual bears making remarkable journeys of over 1 000 km (621 mi) over sea, ice, and coastline.

Polar bears are fun to watch in the safety of a zoo, but it is quite a different matter to encounter them in the wild. On a boat trip up the coast of Hudson Bay I counted 13 bears in 2 days. We approached some so closely in the water that our guide touched them with a paddle. Since we could not always carry a rifle for protection during our investigations, we were always looking over our shoulder for a patch of white on the green tundra. I still remember the sick feeling in the pit of my stomach when 2 large bears appeared from nowhere, only 50 m (164 ft) from our tent. I knew they could easily outrun and outswim us, and the nearest dwarf spruce to climb was far south at treeline. Lucky for us, the bears moved on.

The town of Churchill, Manitoba proudly calls itself the polar bear capital of the world, and for good reason. The town lies directly in the path of a major migration route for the bears as they await the formation of ice on the Bay each autumn. There are also several winter maternity denning areas to the southeast. Generally it is subadults or mothers with cubs that enter the townsite, driven away from the points of land by aggressive males, as well as being attracted by the smell of human food. Wildlife officials and townspeople have cooperated in a program of alerting the public and of trapping problem bears. Instead of killing the animals or flying them out in helicopters, most bears are simply maintained in holding cages until the ice forms. They are then released unhurt to continue their lives on the sea ice. Several recent cases of humans being mauled and killed indicate just how serious this long-term problem is for both people and the bear population. Fortunately for the bears, they have become a major tourist attraction, bringing millions of dollars annually into the local economy. Special "tundra buggies" creep over the frozen tundra, offering visitors close-up glimpses of these stately lords of the arctic.

POLAR BEAR

WHITE WHALE

Scientific name *Delphinapterus leucas*
Family White Whale and Narwhal (Monodontidae)
Order Toothed Whales (Odontoceti)
Total length males 4.2 m, maximum 6 m (13.8 ft, maximum 20 ft); females 3.9 m (12.8 ft)
Weight 1.5 t, maximum 2 t (3,307 lb, maximum 4,409 lb); 1.3 t (2,866 lb)
Color Calves are a slate-gray color for the first year and become progressively paler. At age 10 no trace of gray remains. This species is also called "beluga," a Russian term for "whitish," referring to the white skin of adults.
Distribution and Status This is a small shallow-water whale that lives year-round in the cold arctic waters of North America, Europe, and Asia. Populations occur as far south as James Bay, the Gulf of St. Lawrence, and Nova Scotia. A few individuals have appeared over 1 000 km (621 mi) up rivers, occasionally entering lakes. Migratory movements are largely controlled by ice conditions. Aerial surveys are thought to be relatively accurate, for white whales are easily seen against the dark water and they congregate by the thousands while migrating along specific courses. The world population is believed to number around 30,000, with about 14,000 in eastern Canada and Greenland, 5,000 in the Beaufort Sea, and 4,000 in Alaskan waters. This species seems to be limited to waters with temperatures under 15°C (59°F).
Food White whales feed on fish such as capelin and char, squid, marine worms, and the larger shrimps found in the plankton. They devour about 25 kg (55 lb) of food per day. The mouth, studded with an average of 32 teeth, opens widely, and the head can bend to a surprising degree — both useful adaptations for catching fast-swimming fish.

Reproduction and Growth Mating occurs in shallow estuaries in spring and summer, and after a period of 14 months, one (occasionally 2) 1.2-m (3.9-ft)-long young is born, usually in June. The female continues to nurse her offspring for 20 months. Females become sexually mature at 5 years of age, males at 8. Young are produced every second or third year. The life span is 50 years or more.
Remarks The white whale used to be an important resource to the Inuit. The skin was eaten fresh or cooked *(muktuk)*, and made into leather for boots or a covering for boats *(umiak)*. Whale oil was eaten or burned for cooking and light, while the meat was eaten by people and dogs. Several thousand whales are still taken each year, though an equal number are lost by sinking. This species is easily hunted for it frequents shallows and estuaries to feed and to rub off old layers of skin on gravel bars. Mercury levels in the meat prohibit marketing in North America.

I will never forget my first sighting of these whales. Flying low over the west coast of Hudson Bay in a single-engine Otter bush plane, I looked out the tiny window to view the estuary of the Seal River. There, in the shallows, were about 400 white whales, scattered singly or in small groups like grains of rice against the muddy shallow bottom of the Bay. I could pick out the small gray babies swimming alongside their mothers. Our research team, sitting here and there among the gas cans, food boxes, and equipment, burst forth with whoops and a flurry of picture-taking at such a magnificent sight.

On several occasions since then, we have viewed these gentle sea mammals at close range while we were drifting in the current at the mouth of the Churchill River on Hudson Bay. At any one time we could see dozens of white backs arching out of the choppy water.

By positioning ourselves in the way of a feeding pod, the whales surfaced all around us, blasting breaths of air. It became quite a challenge to focus the cameras on the spot where we thought each whale would surface again. Sometimes the white torpedoes passed right under our small craft. I recall vividly a baby whale surfacing for air about 10 m (32.8 ft) away and looking astonished at our sudden appearance. It whistled in surprise and quickly disappeared in the icy dark depths.

The white whale story was based on an actual incident at Churchill. I remember feeling sorry for the captured young whale as I observed it cruising endlessly around in its tank. I heard later that this individual and several others made the trip to Sea World in San Diego. Many years passed before I had the opportunity to visit this aquarium. There, only a meter (yard) away behind the glass, was a white whale about the right size of my old friend. The creature stayed close by, observing me watching it, and making a most remarkable variety of "expressions" with its flexible head and neck. I finally departed, thankful that this arctic visitor was being cared for so well.

KILLER WHALE

Scientific name *Orcinus orca*
Family Dolphins (Delphinidae)
Order Toothed Whales (Odontoceti)
Total length males 8 m, maximum of 10 m (26.3 ft, maximum 32.8 ft); females 7 m, maximum 9 m (23 ft, maximum 29.6 ft)
Weight 6 t, maximum 9 t (6.6 tons, maximum 9.9 tons); 4 t, maximum 6 t (4.4 tons, maximum 6.6 tons)
Color The color and pattern of this species are distinctive. It is shiny and black above, with white extending from the chin and belly to 3

Continued on p.24

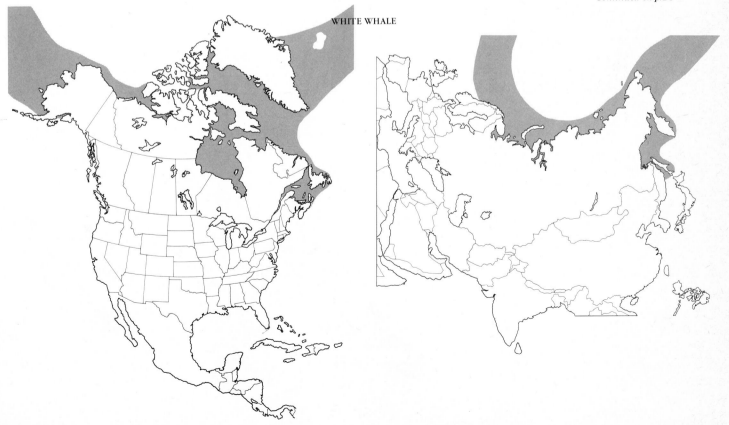

WHITE WHALE

White Whale

In the northern part of the bay, sea currents and tidal forces had kept a long narrow lead of water open in the ice sheet all winter long. Narwhals and white whales were attracted to this breathing hole from great distances, as such openings in the ice were few and far between. The whales dove repeatedly to chase fish, while others grubbed in the muddy bottom for worms. As the ice melted back into sculptured icebergs, the white whales joined additional small herds migrating into the bay and they all headed southward along the rocky coastline. Four-meter (13.1-feet) tides, produced by the tugging of the moon's gravity, left twelve-kilometer (7.5-mile)-wide flats of mud and rock exposed several times each day. While feeding for char along the shore and estuaries of rivers, the whales had to be careful they were not left stranded when the tide ran out to sea. Marauding polar bears would quickly take advantage of such a situation. The usually peaceful world of the shallow sea was alive with a myriad of sounds — whistles of whales calling to each other and locating food, and moans and thuds as ice masses the size of a house ground over the rocks and collided with each other.

Dozens of char flashed their silvery sides as they dashed behind a large gray boulder. Through the clear water appeared a subadult white whale in hot pursuit. Exhibiting surprising agility the whale followed the school's every sharp turn and sprint until the fish began to tire. With a rapid series of up-and-down strokes of its tail flukes, the whale overtook the school. Then, with a quick sideways lunge of its flexible neck, the whale caught a good-sized char in its jaws, the numerous peg-like teeth preventing its escape and then crunching through the soft flesh. Slowing to cruising speed, the white predator jostled the fish in a head-on position and swallowed it whole. The whale arched upward toward the surface for air, tumbling transluscent fish scales in its wake.

As the whale continued on its way through some twisted ribbons of kelp, it detected a harsh whirring sound that grew increasingly louder until it began to cause the animal pain. Suddenly the intensity dropped off, and looking up, the whale saw a boat passing slowly overhead. The herd squealed a warning and glided away, but the whales were no match for the screaming engines that roared around them. Two boats succeeded in rounding part of the herd into the shallows, where the white backs were forced clear of the water. Men jumped overboard, grabbed onto the thrashing subadult whale, and tied several strong ropes around its body. The other whales heard its distress call but were powerless to help, and they fled to deeper water. The men towed the whale away to a nearby port where the captive animal was carried on a stretcher to a large pool. Around and around it swam, its fearful-looking eyes scanning the many interested onlookers. Repeatedly it called for help from its herd-members but there was none to hear.

Two days later the whale was hoisted onto a special supporting structure and into a plane. In ten hours the white whale was released into its new home at an aquarium. Within weeks it lost its fear of the people who fed and trained it, and it soon learned to perform and enjoy tricks, much to the amusement of thousands of visitors. The white whale's constant "smile," friendly nature, and intelligence gave all observers a new appreciation of sea mammals.

Killer Whale and Harbor Seal

On a windless evening at high tide, a number of harbor seals were sleepily basking on ice floes, while out of sight below the surface others twisted gracefully through the water, snapping up big shrimps in their dog-like jaws. The peaceful scene glowed yellow in the light of the setting sun, giving no indication of the violent events that were about to take place. Farther along the coast a ten-meter (32.8-foot)-long, black shadow cruised under the icebergs, forcing its massive frame through the frigid water. The "wolf of the sea" — a giant, male killer whale — was on the hunt. A few hundred fish and squid were not enough to satisfy his enormous appetite. Every five minutes or so the whale rose to blow out stale air and take in fresh air through the single nostril situated on top of his head. Although still some distance away, a number of the seals caught sight of the whale's black dorsal fin sailing across the surface. As the two-meter (6.6 foot)-high structure approached, the seals instinctively realized they were in trouble. Of all creatures of the world's seas and shores, the killer whale is the most dreaded. No animal is safe from attack, particularly when a pack of killer whales appears on the scene.

The seals panicked and shot off like rockets, hoping to out-distance the oncoming whale. Rapid up and down strokes of the powerful tail flukes propelled the whale's huge body to a speed of fifty-five kilometers (34.2 miles) per hour, which soon brought it into close range. Darting left and right the seals then tried to dodge the whale, but he was too swift. With a lightning-fast motion he crunched down on one seal with his sharp, interlocking teeth and released it. Without losing the momentum of his charge he flipped another seal completely out of the water with his nose and knocked it unconscious with a tremendous smash of his broad tail. Then he flipped the heavy body of the seal two meters (6.6 feet) into the air with his jaws and deftly caught it again.

For the next twenty minutes the whale bit and tore the seal carcasses into large chunks and swallowed them whole. Then his large shiny black head rose slowly straight up into the air, exposing the flippers, and the hunter looked around for other seals, several of which had taken refuge on a pan of ice. He made his way over to the ice without surfacing and began cruising around in circles. His beeping calls told him that no seals had dared re-enter the water. After ten minutes he began to tire of this waiting strategy. Without surfacing for air the whale dove down into the murky depths. Just when the seals thought the terrifying creature had left, he came charging upward at incredible speed, throwing his heavy body against the ice pan. The impact snapped a section of ice and knocked a seal into the water. In a flash the seal raced towards land — the only avenue left to flee. The whale recovered his balance and with echolocating beeps, quickly determined where the seal was heading. About fifty meters (164 feet) off shore the whale pulled up alongside the seal and cut off its path of escape. Each time the exhausted seal tried a new direction of retreat, the whale blocked its way. As if playing a game, the killer whale took its time circling and sizing up its prey. The seal just bobbed in the whirlpool, its nostrils flaring widely for air, its panic-stricken, glazed eyes staring at the whale's black dorsal fin slicing the surface like a knife.

An excruciatingly slow minute passed and still no attack. Meanwhile the waves had pushed the two mammals still closer to land, which gave the seal courage to try for the rocks one more time. Leaping out of the water past the whale's tail flukes, the seal literally flew through the air, and on reaching the shallows it hunched along as fast as it could over the rocks. The black and white rubbery body of the whale came crashing through the waves, and reaching right up on dry land its jaws snapped shut on the seal's hind flipper. Half out of the water, the whale attempted to refloat its chest by arching its back. Rolling back and forth for fifteen seconds, the stranded whale finally eased off the algae-covered rocks with the aid of a big wave. The squirming seal secure in its jaws, the hunter slid silently backwards underwater, leaving only the excited gulls as witnesses to the grim scene.

KILLER WHALE *continued from p.19*

lobes which spread beneath and onto the sides of the tail region. A spindle-shaped patch also occurs behind each eye. The underside of the tail flukes is white and a gray saddle is present behind the high dorsal fin. It has been reported that each individual whale can be identified by its characteristic eye patch, gray saddle, and dorsal fin.

Distribution and Status This species is probably the most widely distributed marine mammal in the world and may appear in any ocean; on occasion it swims far up rivers. The main populations (and perhaps these remain separate) are found in the northwest Atlantic (near Iceland), northeast Pacific (Vancouver to Alaska), southwest Atlantic (Argentina), tropical eastern Pacific (Mexico), and Antarctic waters. Killer whales are year-round residents in some areas and migratory in others, depending on the movements of prey and ice conditions. They generally prefer cool coastal waters but occasionally appear in deep waters over 780 km (435 mi) out to sea. The species is still common but has declined from hunting. Over 1,000 were taken in 1979 by the Soviet whaling fleet.

Food Killer whales eat almost any sea creature they come across, including seals, walrus, polar bears, ducks, penguins, fish (such as salmon, herring, and shark), squid, and occasionally the larger whales (white, gray, humpback, sei, minke, and even the blue whale). They usually hunt in family groups along the continental shelves where food is most abundant. The whale's 50 or so peg-like teeth are used to grasp slippery prey, or to bite out mouthfuls of flesh from large animals. Whether attacking fish, seals, or a whale, killer whales demonstrate cooperative hunting strategies.

Reproduction and Growth Killer whales have a relatively low reproductive rate related to a low death rate, since no other creatures but people regularly prey on them. Some accounts state May to July as the mating season, while others note September (in the Northern Hemisphere). The courting couple break from the surface in graceful arcs, roll over, and smack the water with their fins. The bull inserts his long penis in the female's slit while he floats belly-up beneath her. A single calf

(rarely twins) is born 16 months later (generally in the autumn), measuring 2.5 m (8.2 ft) in length and weighing 180 kg (396.8 lb). Weaning occurs at about 2 years of age, but the calf generally stays close to the female until she gives birth again, perhaps a decade later. Adults become sexually mature around 16 years old when they are about 5 m (16.4 ft) long. Estimates of longevity are from 50 years to a century.

Remarks This legendary sea mammal is a stocky, blunt-nosed member of the dolphin family and not actually a whale. The flippers are relatively large and the tall dorsal fin is erect, pointed, and up to 2 m (6.6 ft) long in males, shorter and curved backwards in females. The body is supported by 52 massive vertebrae and there are about 44 sharp, curved teeth in the jaws, each about 12 cm (4.7 in) long but partially covered by the gums. The upper and lower teeth neatly interlock when the jaws close. An adult devours an average of 45 kg (99.2 lb) of food per day but occasional gorgings are just amazing — one male was reported to have 13 porpoises and 15 seals in its digestive tract at one time.

Recent studies have shown that these whales live in closed family groups or pods, generally numbering from 8 to 20 individuals, but sometimes more. Composed of bulls, cows, and young, these units travel, hunt, and play together, seldom spreading out for more than 2 km (1.2 mi), and communicating with a complicated language of beeps, chirps, screams, and whines. A transient whale sometimes travels with a pod, but this individual is thought not to be fully accepted by the group. On rare occasions, and probably related to an abundant source of food, hundreds or even 2000 killer whales may be seen together. When migrating, these animals can easily cover 100 km (62.1 mi) in a day. Normal cruising speed is 10 to 13 km (6.2 to 8.1 mi) per hour but bursts of 55 km (34.2 mi) per hour are possible. Dives of 300 m (984.3 ft) have been observed and one individual has been found entangled in a cable at a depth of 1 000 m (3,280.1 ft). The frequency or maximum limit of such deep dives is unknown, but it appears the animal cannot hold its breath longer than 21 minutes. The killer whale often makes 5 short dives of 10 to 30 seconds, surfacing to

breathe in between, then remains below for about 4 minutes.

Killer whales are subject to predation only by people, but surprisingly the species rarely attacks humans unless provoked. Strandings are rare occurrences and usually involve a single male; however, mass strandings have been reported, such as on Vancouver Island in 1955. The "demon dolphin" has proven to be a highly intelligent, trainable creature and has learned fairly complex routines within only 2 months of capture. Individuals can be gentle and even playful in captivity but they eventually succumb to various infections. I have observed about six killer whales in a number of aquaria and still find it difficult to believe that such an enormous animal can propel itself so fast through the water and hurl its bulk clear into the air. The resulting splash always surprises unsuspecting onlookers, and the whale is not beyond spitting a mouthful of water on a visitor, just for fun.

I was once sent a photograph of a large killer whale which had entered Hudson Bay and then found its way through Chesterfield Inlet to freshwater Baker Lake — an inland distance of over 250 km (155.3 mi). Such an occurrence was almost unbelievable, yet there was the evidence. The local Inuit killed the unfortunate animal, probably in fear for their safety, but the whale was likely hunting only fish and harbor seals. As I added the photo to my file I suddenly remembered the trips I and several colleagues had been on in small motor boats along the same shore of the Bay. We had been so busy watching polar bears and white whales that we never even thought that killer whales could have been in these waters.

HARBOR SEAL
Scientific name *Phoca vitulina*
Family Hair Seals (Phocidae)
Order Carnivores (Carnivora)
Total length males 155 cm (61 in); females 148 cm (58.3 in)
Tail length 108 cm (42.5 in); 100 cm (39.4 in)
Weight 87 kg, maximum 170 kg (191.8 lb, maximum 374.8 lb); 66 kg, maximum 142 kg (145.5 lb, maximum 313.1 lb)
Color The color and pattern of harbor seals are remakably variable, ranging from grayish-

KILLER WHALE

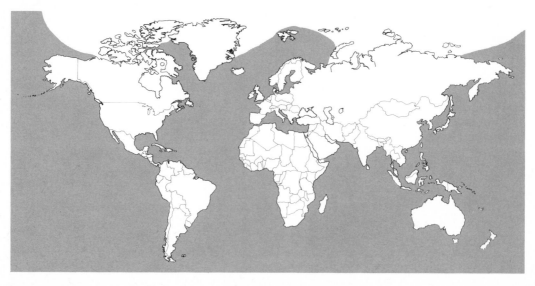

white to dark brown. The underside is much lighter than above, and both areas are heavily marked with rings, spots, and streaks. The larga pup is white while the harbor seal pup is colored like the adult, its white "lanugo" coat being shed before birth.

Distribution and Status The harbor seal has one of the largest distributions of any seal, including both temperate and arctic waters. In the North Atlantic, it is found from Portugal north to the Barents Sea (Soviet Union), the islands of Iceland and Spitsbergen, southern Greenland, around Baffin Island and into Hudson Bay, and as far south along the east coast as Florida. In the west, it occurs in the Beaufort Sea (Canada), Chukchi Sea (Alaska and Siberia), and south along the Pacific coasts and islands to Baja California, Japan, and China. Geographic variation in this widespread seal has led to the naming of several species and subspecies. Recent evidence suggests that the western populations (except those of the Aleutians and west coast of North America) are a distinct species called the larga seal *(Phoca largha)*.

The harbor seal lives year-round along marine coastlines, tidal flats, estuaries, and swift-flowing rivers, and hauls out on ice floes, rocks, islands, and reefs. The larga seal, in particular, migrates offshore in the autumn to live along the pack ice and floes for the winter. Harbor seals frequently move up rivers to lakes where they may stay or return to the sea; for example, along the eastern and western coasts of Hudson Bay, the Columbia River (290 km or 180.2 mi inland), and the American River near San Francisco (210 km or 130.5 mi).

The world population of harbor seals has been estimated at nearly one million, over half of which are larga seals. Hunting, pollution, and disturbance have caused declines in certain areas such as eastern Canadian and Washington coasts. There are five other close relatives — the ribbon seal *(Phoca fasciata)* which lives along the pack ice from Alaska to Japan; ringed seal *(Phoca hispida)* of Arctic waters; harp seal *(Phoca groenlandica)* in Baffin and Hudson Bays, south to Nova Scotia and east to northwestern Siberia; Caspian seal *(Phoca caspica)* of the Caspian Sea; and the Baikal seal *(Phoca sibirica)* found in deep Lake Baikal in the south-central region of the Soviet Union.

Food Fish make up the bulk of the seal's diet; smaller fish are eaten whole while underwater, while larger ones are taken to the surface and bitten into pieces (heads discarded). Particular species include hake, mackerel, cod, capelin, and smelt. Many of its favorite fishes, like salmon and herring, are commercially important, and so the seal comes into conflict with local fisheries. This seal is also the final host of a roundworm which also infects the fish, thereby reducing its value for human markets. In addition to fish the harbor seal devours squid, octopus, clams, crayfish, crabs, and shrimp-like crustaceans, the latter being important food for newly weaned pups. Sea water is only ingested accidently and the animal obtains fresh water mostly from its food.

Reproduction and Growth While males are ready to mate from March to November, females come into heat from one to 9 weeks following nursing of the previous pup. The exact time of mating varies considerably according to location and is likely timed to maximize the survival of the young. No harems are formed and each seal may mate a number of times, usually from late July to September. The pair engage in active foreplay such as rolling and jumping out of the water, and the female often bites the male's neck and shoulders, leaving him bleeding. The embryo ceases development for 1.5 to 3 months. After a gestation period of about 10 months, the single pup (rarely twins) is born on shore, generally in May to July, but from February to September at extreme localities; for example the larga seals give birth from February to April.

The pup weighs about 11 kg (24.3 lb) and loses its soft silvery coat before birth (harbor seal) or soon after (larga seal), revealing a shorter and spotted coat. At first the pup can only float in the shallows, often whimpering loudly for its mother, but after one week it can dive and crawl ashore. The mother suckles the pup either onshore or in the water, and is so devoted to its care that she will carry it to safety on her back or dive with the pup in her teeth if danger threatens. The two are quite playful. The pup nurses for about one month, then begins to feed on small crustaceans. Males become sexually mature at 3 to 6 years, females at 2 to 5 years. Males continue growing until 10 years old, females about 7. Around 88 percent of females give birth each year. The life span in captivity is 33 years, though probably few survive to this age under natural conditions. Caspian seals are reported to have lived up to 50 years in the wild.

Remarks The seal's fur is stiff and only one cm (0.4 in) long, with an even shorter underfur. Insulation from the cold is achieved mainly by the thick blubber. The skin and extremities are allowed to cool in frigid weather, thereby conserving heat deep within the body. At over 30°C (86°F), the animal begins to overheat, and if it cannot find a cooler site, blood vessels expand in the skin and flippers which helps rid the body of excess heat. These seals are not very vocal but do make grunts and growls to express their moods. They may use a clicking sound to assist in locating prey while underwater, where they hear about as well as humans in air. Seals have been known to dive to depths of 300 m (984.3 ft) and to distances up to 400 m (1,312.3 ft). They exhale before diving and continue to blow out bubbles as the tiny sacs or alveoli in their lungs collapse under the pressure. They can hold their breath for up to 23 minutes but most dives are only 6 minutes in duration. When diving, the heart slows from 85 to 15 beats per minute and blood is shunted to the vital organs such as the heart, brain, lungs, and kidneys. The muscles are able to continue working because of the high concentration of myoglobin (an oxygen-binding protein) in the blood. Harbor seals spend about an equal amount of time in water as on land, and when hauling-out grounds are not conveniently nearby, they sleep on the sea bottom, rising to breathe every six minutes or so. Their main predators are humans, killer whales, and polar bears. The animal provides the Inuit with food, clothing, fuel, and materials for household articles.

HARBOR SEAL

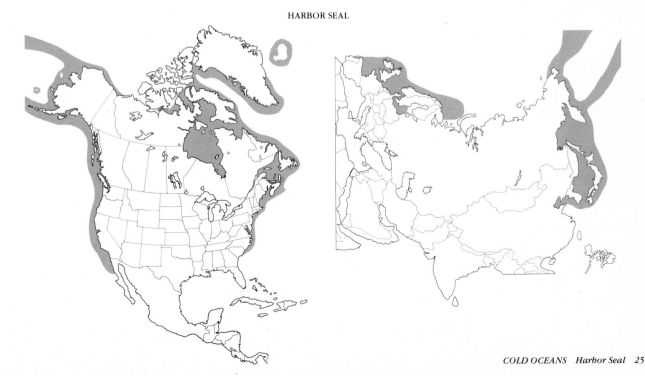

Bowhead Whale and Narwhal

Two Inuit children were jumping from rock to rock along the shore, oblivious of the fog rolling in off the sea. Suddenly the laughter stopped as they spotted something white in the gray water. Afraid it might be a polar bear they were about to run home when they realized it was a herd of whales. *"Tugalik, tugalik"* they shouted, following the grayish-white narwhals as they passed by. Every forty seconds or so, the nine whales surfaced together to breathe, emitting whistle-like blows of air. A magnificent large male showed off its long spiraled tusk above the dark water. Below, some whales were chasing polar cod, while others routed on the bottom for flatfish. The bull ripped through the sediment with its worn tusk, stirring up the mud and hopefully something to eat. Gliding past the excited children on shore, the narwhals continued on their southward migration.

Several kilometers (miles) away, a massive shape rose slowly out of the choppy sea, its black color contrasting with the white icebergs. A double spray shot up suddenly above the bowhead whale's head and hung there in the fog for some time. Cruising for fifteen minutes with its arched mouth open, long rows of baleen plates swept quantities of plankton from the water like an enormous broom. The huge whale hugged the edge of the ice pan and drifted off to sleep again.

Over the next few days the air grew so cold that wisps of water vapor began to escape from the sea's surface. The herd of narwhals encountered several noisy ships and the shy animals retreated from their traditional course. The next evening a north wind blew the ice toward shore, cutting off their route. They became trapped in an ever-shrinking circle of ice. A week passed before the bull narwhal decided to leave the herd in the hope of locating open water. For half an hour it swam under the ice before hearing a familiar sound. It had found the bowhead, also distressed at being caught by the ice.

The whales' prison was a one-hundred-and-fifty-by-eighty meter (492 by 262 feet)-stretch of water kept open by strong offshore currents. The bowhead swam back and forth, sometimes leaping completely into the air before landing with a tremendous splash. The narwhal followed like a puppy, keeping up a constant chatter of whines and clicks. There was little food here for the bowhead, but it didn't need to eat, for it had grown fat from feeding all summer. The narwhal devoured an occasional fish that wandered by.

The two whales continued the same dull routine through the long dark arctic winter. Then one day in early spring, a strange sound reached their sensitive ears through the water. They poked their heads inquisitively above the surface into the sunlight and their tiny eyes spotted an Inuit hunter approaching with his dog team. The father of the two children walked over on the crunchy snow and stood at the edge of the ice, watching as the whales retreated to the opposite side. He would need help to kill and retrieve the narwhal, and he thought how much meat and *muktuk* the bowhead would provide for his village if the men could return in their boats in a few days.

Several days later six men crept up on the channel from different directions, hoping to shoot and then harpoon the narwhal before it could sink. As the narwhal rose slightly out of the water to breathe, rifle shots shattered the still air and resounded underwater. The terrified whales swam under the ice at full speed, right under the father's feet. With the greenish light from the channel growing ever fainter, the whales soared away into the darkness. Twenty minutes, then half an hour passed, as the two animals frantically scanned the sculptured roof of ice with their powerful sound waves. They began to weaken from lack of oxygen in their muscles, but they persevered together. Finally, in danger of suffocating, the bowhead swerved upward and sent its massive bulk crashing headfirst into the ice pack. Triangular plates of rotting ice, one meter (3.3 feet) thick, lifted and fell backwards as the black snout and white chin emerged into the fresh air. After recovering from the tremendous concussion and breathing their fill of air, the two companions continued their battle for survival. This time the narwhal located the edge of the pack ice, and the two sea mammals seemed to express relief from their long ordeal with several spectacular leaps and splashes amid the hovering gulls and terns.

BOWHEAD WHALE

Scientific name *Balaena mysticetus*
Family Right Whales (Balaenidae)
Order Baleen Whales (Mysticeti)
Total length 15 m, maximum 20 m
(49 ft, maximum 66 ft)
Weight 90 t, maximum 110 t
(99 tons, maximum 121 tons)
Color The bowhead is black except for a creamy-white chin (sometimes with a necklace of black spots), and occasionally gray is present on the tail, flippers, upper lip, and eyelids.
Distribution and Status The bowhead is a whale of the arctic and subarctic seas, clinging to shallow shorelines or the edge of ice floes over deeper water. Its former range may have been continuous from the East Siberian Sea east through Alaskan and Canadian waters to the Barents Sea of western Soviet Union. It regularly ventured as far south as central Hudson Bay and the Gulf of St. Lawrence. There are now 4 remnant populations, the largest occurring in the Beaufort Sea (in summer) and Bering Sea (in winter). Another inhabits the Sea of Okhotsk north of Japan, and the third in Baffin Bay (in summer) and Labrador Sea (winter). Small numbers still live in the once-great breeding grounds between Greenland and the Barents Sea.
Food Other than an occasional fish, marine worm, and mollusc scooped from the sea bottom, the bowhead concentrates its feeding on microscopic crustaceans, mainly copepods, which swarm in surface waters during the summer. When the open-mouthed whale collects a sufficient weight of the organisms among its baleen fibers, the great arched jaws close and the tongue wipes the meal into the esophagus. About 700 baleen plates attach to the upper jaw and are the longest of any whale, averaging 3 m (9 ft) but sometimes reaching 4.5 m (15 ft). Cruising at 6 km (3.7 mi) per hour, the animal can collect 100 kg (220 lb) of food in a hour.
Reproduction and Growth Mating is believed to occur in April and May during the spring migration northward. Courting lasts for hours and involves much rolling and twisting of their great tadpole-like bodies. The pair couples belly to belly horizontally, or while treading vertically, their heads sometimes rising out of the water. After 12 months development, a calf (rarely twins) is born measuring 4 m (13 ft) long. The young is weaned by one year, at which time it has doubled in length. Females become sexually mature at a length of 12 m (39 ft) and reproduce once every 2 years.
Remarks Bowheads and other whales are descended from land animals, and although highly evolved for a totally marine existence, they still retain some vestiges of their terrestrial ancestors. For example, small remnants of hind limbs and the pelvic girdle lie in the muscle of the tail region, unattached to the skeleton. Also, the lips and snout have rows of short white bristles of hair. This whale has an enormous head (up to 40 percent of the body length) and the first 7 vertebrae are joined into a single rod to help support the weight and movement of the high arched jaws. The brain is tiny for such a large creature and weighs only 3 kg (6.6 lb), while one testicle alone may weigh 50 kg (110 lb).

Intensive hunting as early as the 12th C in Europe and during the 18th C in North America depleted these slow-swimming and valuable whales to alarmingly low numbers. There may not be more than 3,000 left, even though only Inuit hunters have been allowed to hunt them since 1935.

NARWHAL

Scientific name *Monodon monoceras*
Family White Whale and Narwhal (Monodontidae)
Order Toothed Whales (Odontoceti)
Total length males 5 m, maximum 6.2 m
(16.4 ft, maximum 20.3 ft);
females 4 m, maximum 5.1 m
(13.1 ft, maximum 16.7 ft)
Weight 1.6 t, maximum 1.8 t
(1.8 tons, maximum 2 tons);
1 t (1.1 tons)
Color A calf narwhal is a dark blue-gray and becomes lighter as it grows older. Adults are pale gray or white below and heavily marked with gray blotches on the upper side, particularly dark on the head. Old narwhals are almost white.
Distribution and Status The narwhal is the northern-most cetacean (whales and dolphins), spending much of its life near the ice pack, whether in deep water or in fiords and bays. It avoids extensive shallow waters such as those around Alaska and adjacent Canada. Traditional migration routes exist which are timed by ice conditions in spring and autumn. Distribution may once have been continuous around the Arctic Circle, but the whale is now absent from many seas. The main population (over 10,000) occurs in the eastern Canadian arctic, especially in Baffin Bay. The world population is estimated at over 22,500. Occasionally one shows up in the waters off Alaska. Southern records have been noted at Newfoundland, England, Holland, West Germany, and Japan. For a period following the Ice Age, this species lived in the Gulf of St. Lawrence.
Food The diet consists of fish (particularly polar cod, halibut, flounder, skate, and sculpins), squid, octopus, molluscs, and shrimps. These animals are crushed by the jaws and swallowed whole, since the narwhal has no functional teeth.
Reproduction and Growth Mating takes place in early April, and following the unusually long growing period of 14.5 months, a single (twins are rare) 80-kg (176-lb), 1.5-m (5-ft) calf is born, generally in June or July. The nursing period lasts up to 20 months. Narwhals produce young no more frequently than every third year. Sexual maturity is thought to occur from 4 to 7 years for females, 8 to 9 for males. The maximum life span is 40 years.
Remarks Narwhals are social animals, often traveling in groups of 6 to 20 with a bull in charge. Several thousand have been reported together during migration. Females and young enter fiords and come closer to shore than adult males. This species with its up-turned mouth seems to display a perpetual smile, and often swims on its side or upside-down. It can dive to depths of 366 m (1,200 ft). There is only one pair of teeth in the upper jaw — both imbedded in the gums of the female, but in the male the left one grows through the lip into a 2- to 3-m (6.6- to 9.8-ft) long, right-spiraling tusk. Occasionally 2 tusks appear in the male, and one or 2 in the female. The tusk cannot be referred to as canine or incisor; it consists of dentine covered with a layer of cement, but no enamel. The function of this unusual tooth is not known with certainty, but fighting, courting, feeding on the sea bottom, radiating excess body heat, and even echolocation have been suggested. It is probably a "secondary sex characteristic" used in establishing dominance rank, and in jousts during the mating season. Broken tusks and scars on the heads of males are common.

Narwhals have long played an important role in the life of the Inuit. The whales are shot and harpooned in open water or when trapped in the ice. Over 1,000 were killed in just 2 leads in one year (1915) off Greenland. Narwhals are still hunted under quota by native people, particularly for the ivory tusk, but more than half of the animals killed sink and are lost. There is still concern that kill rates are higher than reproductive rates, and water pollution from northern development may become a serious problem and affect their numbers in the future. Other causes of mortality are predation by the killer whale, Greenland shark, polar bear, and walrus, and suffocation when accidently trapped or stranded. Although narwhals can break through 18 cm (7 in) of ice with their heads (and sometimes several individuals cooperate in doing so), they cannot always extricate themselves from some ice conditions. As the breathing hole shrinks in size, the stronger whales push aside the weaker ones. Narwhals have never survived for long in aquariums, unlike their close relative the white whale or beluga.

RINGED SEAL

Scientific name *Phoca hispida*
Family Hair Seals (Phocidae)
Order Carnivores (Carnivora)
Total length 136 cm (53.5 in)
Weight 90 kg, maximum 101 kg
(198 lb, maximum 223 lb)
Color This seal's coat is brownish-black on the back, broken by white rings with black centers. The underside is creamy-yellow with black spots. The pup's coat is soft and white.
Distribution and Status The ringed seal inhabits the land-locked ice and offshore ice floes in the polar regions of North America, Europe, and Asia. It also extends into the adjoining seas of Japan, Okhotsk, and Baltic, as well as several inland lakes in Finland and the Soviet Union. In North America it reaches as far south as James Bay and Newfoundland. This is the most abundant arctic seal, with estimates as high as 7 million.
Food Shrimps, crabs and other crustaceans, and fish, such as polar cod, capelin, sand lance, and smelt, are favorite foods. The seals slow their food consumption in early spring and eat nothing from June to early July — the reproductive and molting periods. They spend the time basking on the ice.
Reproduction and Growth Males are ready to breed from March to May, during which period they smell strongly of musk. They mate with one or more females while the latter are still nursing last year's pups. The embryo enters a resting stage until August, and the pup is born the following March or April (total development period of 11 months). Nursing continues for 4 to 6 weeks, often terminating when the den collapses during the break up of the ice. Females become sexually mature at 6 to 8 years, males 7 to 9. This species has survived in captivity for 15 years, but a much longer life span is probable, perhaps up to 50 years.
Remarks This smallest North American seal is so streamlined in body design that it slips through the water with a minimum of

resistance. It has been known to dive as deep as 100 m (328 ft), and can hold its breath for over 20 minutes while swimming strenuously. The furred hind flippers face backward and provide propulsion in water and on land, where the animal hunches along, caterpillar-like. Insulation against the arctic cold is achieved more through the thick layer of blubber than by the fur coat. In late autumn, blubber may account for up to 40 percent of the animal's weight, which reduces to under 25 percent by spring. The large eyes are able to adapt to both low and high light densities in both air and water. Eyesight is important in finding landmarks while migrating, avoiding predators, and searching for food in the upper sea levels and on the bottom. The senses of smell and hearing are also well developed. On land, the ringed seal communicates by whining, moaning, and growling, while high- and low-pitched barks, as well as yelps and chirps have been recorded underwater. The seals often slap their flippers on the surface

of the water when approached, perhaps warning other seals in the area.

Although sometimes seen in loose groups, the ringed seal is mainly solitary. This habit, and its often inaccessible haunts along the pack ice, have protected the species from the overexploitation suffered by many of its relatives. In fact, its numbers at present are probably close to original levels. Its main predators are polar bear, killer whale, and the Inuit, with walrus and arctic fox taking an occasional pup. This seal has traditionally been a mainstay of the Inuit economy, providing food, clothing, fuel, leather, and other necessities. A potential threat to the ringed seal is oil spillage from tankers and drill sites. Floating oil damages the seal's eyes and kidneys, reduces the insulation of its fur (especially important in the pup), and poisons and reduces its living food resources in the sea.

On a recent trip to Hudson Bay, our field crew attempted to collect several ringed seals for specimens. It was not easy to approach

them, for these animals are hunted by the native people and have become wary of approaching boats. After obtaining the necessary permits, our plan was to shoot an animal with a rifle, and then speed over to the carcass so we could harpoon it before it sank. Bobbing up and down on the waves in our boat, we missed the first shot, then kept circling in hopes of seeing another black head poking above the surface. The mouth of the Churchill River was alive with hundreds of white whales surfacing to replenish their air supply, then disappearing below to chase fish. After a chilling half-hour we spotted what seemed like a bloated carcass of a ringed seal floating in the water. The rifle was put away and we prepared to haul the seal aboard. Suddenly the seal's head popped up in astonishment and quick as a flash the animal dove underwater! It had been so sound asleep that it hadn't heard the engine or voices.

BOWHEAD WHALE ◻   NARWHAL ◻

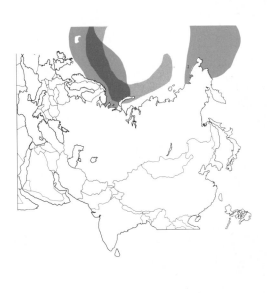

RINGED SEAL

Ringed Seal

The short arctic summer ended with a blasting snowstorm. As the temperature dropped, ice began to form along the rugged shorelines of islands. The coming of winter transformed the land into a cold white desert overnight, yet below the ocean's surface little had changed. The ringed seals arched through the water like torpedoes, gliding long distances with each flap of the tail and flippers. They were feeding on large shrimps and small fish such as polar cod. Because of the plentiful food that abounds in arctic waters during summer, the seals were fat and sleek. The thick layer of blubber kept them warm in the coldest water. Every few minutes a rounded seal head broke the still surface of the water to breathe. The big dark and wet eyes looked around through the mist, before the animal slipped straight down again.

As weeks passed the sea ice spread out from land, and as it steadily thickened, the seals continually clawed the ice around their breathing holes to keep them open, just wide enough to allow the animals to haul out onto the ice. After several snowstorms, the drifts covered the holes over, and the seals hollowed out dens where they could rest out of the water. A female ringed seal maintained five breathing holes all winter, most of them along a crack in the ice formed by the current. Her snow den was three by one meters (9.8 by 3.3 feet) in size, and in time became coated with ice on the inside from frozen condensation. All winter she lived alone in a world of darkness, for the dim light of the short arctic days could not penetrate the deep layer of snow and ice. In April she gave birth to a single white-haired pup within the den. Though the water below and the air above the den could have frozen the unprotected young, the air within the den was relatively warm from the mother's body heat.

The female no longer ate, and she spent most of the time nursing and sleeping beside the pup. The pup's fluffy fur began to fall out in only two weeks, and by six weeks it was completely replaced by a new coat — dark gray on the back and silver on the belly, with traces of the rings so typical of its mother.

As time passed, the pup created tunnels in the snow by scratching with the claws of its foreflippers. The smell of seal from the den carried for great distances in the crisp, clean arctic air, and eventually reached the keen nostrils of a large polar bear. Hunting seals was its favorite pastime, and within minutes it strode up to the roof of the den. The broad black nose thrust its way into the snow with a snort, as the bear prepared for an ambush. A powerful blow by the forelimbs broke through the ceiling and the two seals awoke in a fright. Brilliant sunlight streamed into the den. As the bear charged with its great mouth open, the mother seal managed to push her pup into the plunge hole, and she followed, but not before the bear's teeth tore open the web of her hind flipper. The bear stared down at the dark water, hoping the seals would have to return to breathe, but they were already nearing another hole a safe distance away.

Walrus

It was unusually warm for a summer day in the arctic. Though the herd of about one hundred walruses took advantage of the slight sea breezes by hauling out on the rocky peninsula, the heat was causing them problems. The huge creatures lay on their backs like grotesque sunbathers, tusks up, waving their flippers as fans, but this did little to cool the tempers of those underneath who were being squashed or poked. During the day the herd usually slept peacefully, snoring loudly and using each other as pillows. Only a few sentries remained on the alert. But today they were all awake with roaring bellows and restless kin turning over, fighting, and taking to the water to cool off. Their brown skin turned pink as the blood vessels in their skin dilated to cool their massive bodies. Patches of smeared blood from tusk wounds stained the chests of a number of bulls. Until recently, land-locked ice and huge plates of sea ice provided easily accessible refrigerated beds to rest on, but spring break-up forced the herd to land.

One sentry let loose a loud whistling alarm call, and a hundred hunching hulks lunged for the sea, tripping and stumbling over each other. The water churned for several minutes before all of them made it safely. Treading water, the animals extended their round heads as high as possible and looked fearfully around, trying unsuccessfully to determine the cause of their retreat. In an hour most of them were back on their rookery, dozing again.

One cow chose to join a bull on a nearby cake of ice, and by hooking-her tusks on the slippery surface and thrusting with flippers and hindquarters, she managed to ease her bulk onto the white platform. In spite of her weighing over three-quarters of a tonne (0.8 ton), she was dwarfed by the impressive bull who stared down at her with his bloodshot eyes. They tolerated each other for a few minutes, then the cow seemed to decide it was time to depart. Their raft was drifting too far away from the herd in any case. Poised on the edge of the ice, the cow's weight tipped the pan slightly, causing the bull to lurch in a most undignified manner. She chest-flopped into the sea, leaving the bull snorting with head held aloft, impatient to be left alone again.

The cow now headed out offshore to the clam beds. Inhaling a deep breath and expelling it, the walrus dove downward. Powered by strokes of the foreflippers, and steering with the hind flippers, her brown form glided straight downward. The increasing water pressure collapsed the animal's flexible chest wall and lungs, while oxygen-rich blood shifted from the muscles to the brain and heart. The pupils of her eyes opened widely, allowing her to see in the fading light. The walrus finally reached the dark bottom at a depth of eighty meters (263 feet), and occasionally pulling forward with the tusks she began to poke among the rocks and mud with her whiskered snout. A dozen clams were quickly uprooted and the walrus then used her front flippers to gather the clams into a pile. Taking several in her mouth at a time, she bit down and sucked out the soft feet and siphons of the clams, swallowed them whole, and then spit out the shells. Having eaten the parts of about forty clams in eight minutes, the walrus headed to the surface for air. Again and again she returned to the depths until her belly was full with forty-five kilograms (100 pounds) of flesh from about three thousand clams. She had also swallowed some sand, rocks, and pieces of shell. Twisting leisurely as she rose from the dark depths the walrus was a picture of grace, such a contrast to her awkward movements on land. In no hurry to return to the grumpy horde on shore, she inflated the spacious air sacs in her neck and floated off to sleep.

WALRUS

Scientific name *Odobenus rosmarus*
Family Walrus (Odobenidae)
Order Carnivores (Carnivora)
Total length males 3.5 m (11.5 ft);
females 3 m (9.8 ft)
Weight 1 200 kg, maximum 1 600 kg
(2,646 lb, maximum 3,527 lb);
850 kg (1,874 lb)

Color The new-grown hair is silver colored but it soon turns to a reddish-brown similar to the color of the folded, bumpy, and scarred skin which shows through the sparse coat. When cold, the walrus' skin becomes pale due to the constriction of blood vessels in the skin. However, when overheated, the animal turns a remarkable pink color as the capillaries expand within the skin to assist in heat loss. Pups are a slate gray.

Distribution and Status The walrus is found along the pack ice and arctic coasts where clams are abundant on the continental shelves, generally in waters less than 18 m (60 ft) deep. Many herds migrate north and south each year, following the ice. Several centuries of persecution have destroyed many southern populations. In the 16th and 17th centuries huge colonies were found as far south as Sable Island off Nova Scotia and the Magdalen Islands in the Gulf of St. Lawrence. Some individuals were even reported to have reached New York City and Massachusetts. During the Pleistocene Ice Age, walruses extended south to California, North Carolina, and France. There are presently 4 main isolated groups, occurring from east Greenland to the Kara Sea of western Soviet Union (about 2,000); eastern Canadian Arctic and Hudson Bay to west Greenland (about 10,000); the Chukchi and Bering seas of Alaska (about 3,000); and the Laptev Sea of eastern Soviet Union (about 140,000).

Food Walruses depend mainly on clams, but also eat crabs, sea cucumbers, fish, and occasionally seals, though it is not known how frequently seals are killed by walrus. The animals fast during the spring breeding season, and males continue to eat little in the summer.

Reproduction and Growth Unlike many other seals that haul out on shore in packed herds, the walrus is not territorial and does not form a harem during the breeding season. The bulls mate with the cows from December to March, but embryos cease to develop at an early stage and resume growth in May. The calf (twins are rare) is born the following May and weighs up to 68 kg (150 lb). It is nursed from the mother's 4 mammae and closely protected for 2 years. If danger threatens, the calf clings to the mother's neck and is enveloped in her front flippers. In the sea she may carry the calf on her back. Males become sexually mature at 6 years of age, females at 4. Walruses may live to 20 or 30 years in the wild and 40 years in captivity. Age is determined by the rings and wear on the tusks.

Remarks The walrus' family name "Odobenidae" means "those that walk with their teeth." Though this is not really the case, the walrus does use the 600-cm (2-ft)-long tusks for hooking onto the edge of the ice floe as the animal hauls itself out of the water. The tusks are also used occasionally for pulling itself along the sea bottom when feeding, for protection against polar bears and other walruses, for killing and opening up seals, and for keeping some breathing holes in the ice. The tusks are composed of dentine (the enamel wears off the tip at an early age) and continue to grow throughout life, faster when the animal is young, then slower in old age, so that they finally wear down to stubs. Maximum length is one m (3.3 ft) and weight, 5 kg (11 lb). The tusks are considerably larger in males, and tusk size appears to be directly related to dominance.

The walrus' square head with heavily whiskered muzzle is attached to the bloated body by a rather short neck. The eyes are tiny and the ear openings are covered by folds of skin. It is quite probable that this species is able to navigate in the dark sea depths and under the ice by echolocation. The skin becomes thicker with age (males up to 5 cm or 2 in) and along with the attached blubber (up to 15 cm or 6 in) may account for more than a third of the animal's total weight. The long foreflippers have five webbed digits and bare but rough surfaces for traction on ice and rocks. The hind limbs can be turned forward to enable walking on all four limbs. A thick penis bone or baculum (reaching 63 cm or 25 in) has become a sought-after souvenir for some northern visitors.

Walruses are highly gregarious and are not often seen on their own. They are quick to defend other threatened members of their herd, and angry bulls have been known to kill polar bears and attack boats. Predators are few, mainly the killer whale, polar bear, and people, but death from fighting among themselves, or accidental crushing of the young, are other factors that reduce their numbers.

WALRUS

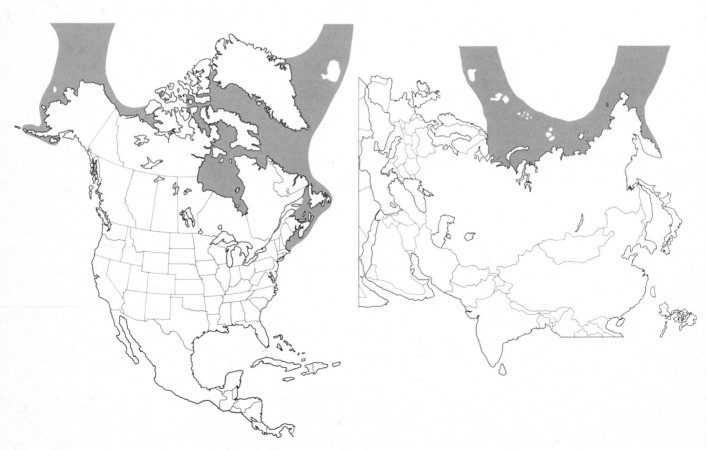

Mammals of the
Tundra

Tundra is a treeless landscape of high latitudes and elevations, dominated by a low cover of vegetation. The following three types of tundra are generally recognized — sedge-grass on moist organic soil, heath-moss on moist acid soil, lichen-moss on thin soil or rock; fell-fields of barren soil and rock, and polar or alpine desert with perpetual snow and ice also occur here. Geographically, this biome may be arctic tundra (barren-ground, coastal, and island tundra of the arctic in North America and Eurasia) or alpine tundra (mountain tops of ranges like the Rockies and Andes, or high plateaus such as in Tibet).

Arctic tundra experiences extremely cold winters with a mean monthly temperature in January of -34°C (-29.2°F), and cool summers with a July mean of 7°C (44.6°F). The frost-free period ranges from 0 to 60 days from north to south. Annual precipitation is usually under 10 centimeters (3.9 inches) but can reach 20 centimeters (7.9 inches) at some eastern locations. Snowfall is light but it drifts and packs from wind action, and covers the ground for much of the year. The air relative humidity is high and the evaporation rate is low, since cold air cannot hold much moisture. The subsoil is permanently frozen (permafrost) to great depths (up to 600 meters or 1968.5 feet), limiting plant roots and impeding soil drainage so that vast regions are covered in lakes and wet muskeg. The upper layer of soil is subjected to alternate freezing and thawing, which slows plant succession and pushes rocks and gravel to the surface into regular patterns. Summer days and winter nights are long, each reaching 24 hours in the far north. The sun's rays are weak because of their oblique angle, but what little solar radiation is available is absorbed by soil and plants, creating a microhabitat at the surface which may be as high as 22°C (40°F) higher than the air one meter (3.3 feet) above. Tundra plants are perennials, and many are fuzzy (arctic poppy) or cushion-shaped (moss campion) to help conserve heat.

Alpine tundra, surprisingly, may inflict more severe living conditions on plants and animals than the arctic tundra. With a low annual temperature, summer minima and maxima may fluctuate as much as 32°C (57.6°F) in a single day. Precipitation is high but runs off rapidly, while snow depths reach an astounding 18 meters (59.1 feet) in some regions. In spite of a generally high evaporation rate, periods of fog are common. Winds are strong and solar radiation intense. Daylength is more regular than in the arctic. Alpine tundra is often found as isolated pockets on rugged terrain. The soil is rocky and unstable, except in meadows, and permafrost is absent. The lower limit of alpine tundra ranges from 120 meters (393.7 feet) above sea-level in Alaska, 3 050 meters (10,006.6 feet) in the Sierra Nevada of California, and 3 650 meters (11,975.1 feet) in Mexico. Alpine plants are generally small perennials, which undergo limited growth each summer.

Common herbivores (eaters of plants) of the Tundra Biome include caribou, arctic hare, collared lemming, snow goose, and rock ptarmigan. Major carnivores (eaters of animals) are arctic fox, ermine, snowy owl, arctic loon, and parasitic jaeger. Reptiles and amphibians are absent.

Collared Lemming

In the soft, reddish-orange light of the evening sun, the lichen-crusted boulders and patches of bearberry, arctic willow, and saxifrage on the gently rolling tundra hills were ablaze with warm reds, yellows, and greens. Several arctic terns flew by on stiff wings, on their way back to some distant lake. As the afternoon breeze finally died away, something was moving about on top of a hill. It was a collared lemming in its beautifully colored, rusty-brown coat, highlighted by a black stripe down the back. The pudgy little rodent had short legs, a stubby tail, and its eyes and ears were almost hidden in the luxurious fur. Scurrying between the boulders, it stopped now and then to nibble on leaves. There were plenty of rocks to hide under, as well as old lemming holes, in case an ermine, arctic fox, or snowy owl suddenly appeared. After foraging over a distance of about twenty meters (66 feet) the lemming ran down the hillside to drink from a small creek that ran through the sedge and moss meadow. It didn't hesitate to use the worn trails that abounded through the wet sedge, even though they belonged to its neighbor, the brown lemming. The two rodents usually just ignored each other.

As the autumn days grew shorter, the strangest things began to occur to the lemming. Unconscious of the fact, its eyes relayed the message of decreasing periods of daylight to its brain, which in turn sent messages to several internal glands and organs to begin preparation for winter. White hairs started to grow out through the rusty-brown fur on its sides. Within a week, the long white hair spread onto its back and belly. Day by day its coat turned whiter, until in early October the animal looked like a round puff of cotton blowing over the greenish-brown tundra. Then something even more bizarre happened — the claws and pads on the third and fourth fingers began to lengthen; in fact they grew so big that the lemming almost tripped over them. But as the autumn blizzards covered its home with heavy drifts, the claws were found to be exceptionally useful in digging tunnels through the snow. And when the lemming lay flat and still on a snow bank, the white coat seemed to disappear against the white crystalline blanket.

In spite of the longer fur coat, the lemming frequently felt chilled in its underground nest, since the cold winter winds blew the insulating snow cover off the hills and into the valley. So the collared lemming moved downhill and constructed a new nest of shredded sedge leaves inside a moss hummock, and lined it with the soft fibers of cotton grass. Here it occasionally bumped into the brown lemming as they tunneled under the moss on the hard floor of permafrost, or on the ground surface, or through the maze of runways in the packed snow. Then one January night, in the pitch black of the burrow, this female collared lemming detected the alluring scent of a male of her own kind. She became extremely excited and commenced to track him down. Led by her sensitive nose and feeling the way with whiskers, she finally found the spot where the male had penetrated her burrow system. Appearing agitated she blocked the opening with snow and returned to her nest. About an hour later, she awoke with a start as the male cautiously entered her nest chamber. In a flash she attacked, squealing and biting at the intruder, and sending him back home oozing blood from a shoulder wound.

Over the next few weeks, the persistent male returned repeatedly, each time receiving a somewhat better reception, until they actually slept in the same nest together. Not long after, the pair were ready to mate even though it was the dead of winter. By the end of February, ten brown youngsters were running through the tunnels and digging in the snow. When the snow melted in late April, the family had grown to fifty. The famed population explosion of lemmings had begun, and the whole tundra community of plants and animals would be affected.

COLLARED LEMMING

Scientific name *Dicrostonyx torquatus*
Family Voles and Lemmings (Arvicolidae)
Order Rodents (Rodentia)
Total length 145 mm (5.7 in)
Tail length 15 mm (0.6 in)
Weight 75 g (2.6 oz)

Color In summer, the upperparts are a grizzled brownish-gray with a black stripe running from nose to tail. The sides, ears, and belly are rusty-brown. A light gray collar is often present. In winter, the whole body is covered by extremely long white hair, with the gray bases showing through in places. These lemmings are the only rodents that develop a white coat in winter.

Distribution and Status The collared lemming is the northern-most rodent and lives on the coastal and barren-ground tundra from northern Greenland south to Manitoba, and westward through the Northwest Territories to Alaska. It also occurs in alpine tundra on mountain tops in the Yukon and Alaska. It is known as well in the tundra regions and arctic islands of the Soviet Union. A closely related species, the Labrador collared lemming *(Dicrostonyx hudsonius)* is found east of Hudson Bay in Quebec and Labrador. Recent evidence suggests *Dicrostonyx torquatus* may actually represent 9 different species, but considerably more research is needed to sort them out.

Food The summer diet includes the fleshy bases, leaves, fruit, and heads of such plants as sedges, grasses, cotton grass, mountain avens, mushrooms, willows, birches, cranberry, and other dwarf creeping shrubs. During the winter bark, buds, and roots are added. Carrion is eaten when food is scarce. Mosses are only ingested accidentally. Pieces of plants are frequently hoarded in underground or surface pantries.

Reproduction and Growth In years of good snow cover, relatively mild weather, and abundant food, lemmings may breed during the winter months. However, when these conditions are poor, or when the animals have been overcrowded, breeding is restricted to the warm months or may cease altogether. Usually the lemmings are capable of mating from March to August, and 2 or 3 litters are born from April to September. The female carries the young for 19 to 21 days (a week longer if already nursing) and often mates again soon after giving birth. The offspring, averaging 5 but ranging from one to 11, are reared in an underground nest or inside a hummock of moss. They suckle milk from the female's 8 mammae and develop quickly, beginning outside excursions to eat plants as early as 16 days. The young can grow from 4 to 56 g (0.1 to 2 oz) in 40 days. Sexual maturity is reached at 4 weeks for females and 7 weeks for males. Since the father lemming remains close to the family, it frequently breeds with its daughters. The life span of most lemmings is about one year, although some may reach 2 or 3 years.

Remarks Lemming populations often increase to high levels over large regions, resulting in overgrazing of the vegetation and stress from crowding and fighting in defense of territories. These peaks seem to occur at intervals of 3 to 5 years, and greatly affect other animals such as arctic fox, ermine, and snowy owl which rely on them for food. One year the rodents may be running all over the tundra, and then they vanish for the next several years. Densities fluctuate from 0.6 to 400 per ha (0.2 to 161.9 per a), but 15 to 40 per ha (6.1 to 16.2 per a) are more usual peaks. No satisfactory explanation has yet been discovered for these fluctuations, but weather conditions, nutrients in the plants, and factors relating to reproduction and survival under stress of crowding, appear to be important. These animals do not commit suicide, as the myth states, but they do die off quickly in large numbers from drowning, fighting, starvation, disease, and predation. The collared lemming is an excellent swimmer, buoyed up by air trapped between the hairs; however, numbers of them sometimes drown in attempting to swim large bodies of water, obviously not realizing the distance due to their poor vision.

These rodents are active anytime during the day or night, throughout the year. While they occasionally make long exploratory excursions, most of the time is spent on a home range averaging 2 ha (4.9 a). When the animals are crowded, this range shrinks to only 0.2 ha (0.5 a). The lemming seeks the cover of rocks and shallow burrows, generally less than one m (3.3 ft) long and 15 cm (6 in) deep. There are many of these escape burrows and nesting sites present within the home range of each lemming, some excavated by the recent inhabitant, others dug by previous generations. Nests are located in a chamber at the end of the tunnel, or in winter, may be placed on the ground surface but under the snow, or actually inside a drift.

Locating this species can be most frustrating at times. I have walked many kilometers to find a site where runways and droppings indicated there might be lemmings present, only to find empty traps on my return the next day. Yet, on other occasions, they have appeared in traps set behind the tent with no more cover than a few rocks and low heath-moss vegetation. They are rather attractive little mammals, reminiscent of a hamster, but care must be taken in handling them for they are aggressive in defending themselves and can inflict quite a bite.

COLLARED LEMMING

ARCTIC HARE

Scientific name *Lepus arcticus*
Family Rabbits and Hares
Order Rabbits, Hares, and Pikas
(Lagomorpha)
Total length 650 mm (25.6 in)
Tail length 65 mm (2.6 in)
Weight 4.5 kg, maximum 5.4 kg
(10 lb, maximum 12 lb)

Color In the high arctic this hare remains pure white all year (except for the tiny black ear tips and yellow-stained fur on the bottom of the feet), while farther south on the barren grounds, a gray coat with black-tipped guard hairs is worn in the summer. The young are gray.

Distribution and Status The arctic hare occurs on the tundra and forest-tundra from the Mackenzie Delta and northern Greenland south to northeastern Manitoba and Newfoundland, including all the large arctic islands. It is the most northern land mammal, extending onto the polar ice north of land (83°10'N). The arctic hare and Alaskan hare *(Lepus othus)* are considered by some mammalogists to be just subspecies of the blue or mountain hare *(Lepus timidus)*, which lives on the tundra and in the boreal coniferous forest of Eurasia. Hares and rabbits were long thought to be, or closely related to, rodents — but it is now known that the resemblance (particularly the teeth) is only superficial and mainly related to similar eating habits. They are actually closer in origin to ungulates like deer. The similarity of hares and rodents is an example of what is known as convergent evolution, and illustrates the power of natural selection in molding unrelated groups of animals of comparable lifestyle into a somewhat common body form.

Food Arctic hares are fond of most kinds of arctic plant leaves, berries, twigs, and even roots. Particularly important are grasses, saxifrages, willows, crowberry, cranberry, and seaweed. They are also known to devour carrion.

Reproduction and Growth The lengthening hours of daylight trigger the beginning of the breeding season in April and May. The female signals her willingness to mate through her odor and posture. Most females bring forth a single litter of about 5 young (range of one to 8) in June but some have a second or third litter in August in the southern parts of the range (e.g., Newfoundland). The embryos require a relatively long time to develop (about 50 days) and consequently the young are born at an advanced stage — fully haired and weighing around 100 g (3.5 oz). The surface nest of moss or grass, sheltered by boulders or shrubs, is soon abandoned. This large hare is fully grown by autumn and breeds for the first time the following spring. Most live for only a year or two, but maximum longevity may be up to 12 years.

Remarks Arctic hares provide a beautiful example of camouflage, as their white coats blend in with the snow. In summer, the gray pelage merges with the dark boulders. With ears laid back and the body flattened, they remain motionless for long periods of time in the hope that no predators can see them. Individuals of northern populations are remarkably gregarious, sometimes congregating in the hundreds and even thousands in communal feeding areas. They also leap up and bound along on their hind feet more than do their southern relatives on the mainland. Home ranges extend from 4 to 20 ha (10 to 49 a) and there is great overlap among individuals. Only the vicinity of the nest is defended by the female. In areas where the arctic hare has little contact with people, it can be approached within a few meters. Where hunted however, it is hard to spot and if discovered will bound away at speeds up to 40 km (25 mi) per hour while yet some distance from the observer.

The major predators are gray wolf, arctic fox, red fox, ermine, snowy owl, gyrfalcon, and rough-legged hawk. Starvation is also an important cause of death. The incredibly dense and silky fur, composed of both underfur and guard hairs, provides excellent insulation against the frigid arctic environment. The fur is kept groomed by constant licking and rubbing with the paws, and by rolling in the snow or sand. The ears of the arctic hare (of the tundra), snowshoe hare (boreal forest), white-tailed jackrabbit (grassland), and antelope jackrabbit (desert) show a marked and progressive increase in length related to the need to conserve or radiate body heat. The arctic hare has excellent vision and the large eyes are adapted not only to twilight and nighttime but also to the long bright days of summer. Watching several arctic hares graze on the low tundra vegetation north of Churchill, I was astonished to see their size. They were 3 times the weight of the snowshoe hares that lived in the nearby forest-tundra.

ARCTIC HARE

Arctic Hare

In the long arctic night, fierce bitterly cold winds swirled and tumbled snow crystals over the ground, rounding their edges and packing them into every nook and cranny. Within hours the thin snow cover was stripped from the ridge tops and deposited in the low areas of the tundra. Though it was not actually snowing, the blowing particles made it impossible to see — an arctic "white-out." Snug in their beds hollowed out from under the crust of snow, seventy-five white arctic hares lay sleeping, some together, others by themselves. The storm raged for two days before it blew itself out, allowing the animals to come out of their shelters. The late risers could hear the muffled sounds of digging and the pounding of big feet on the surface, as other hares warmed up their stiff muscles. The lazy ones simply extended their long hind legs backward and stretched out in a perfect push-up position, but a few were so excited to be out again that they dashed about in circles, sometimes executing a complete change in direction during a spectacular leap.

Hungry after their long detention, the hares worked their way up the ridge where the drifts were shallow. With blows from the front feet and rapid scratching with the claws they broke through the crust and scooped away the loose snow. Sensitive noses poked into the holes, attempting to detect the odors of the hares' favorite food plants. Sharp, projecting front teeth cut off twigs and buds of frozen cranberry, willow, saxifrage, and grass which grew only several centimeters high. Any portion of the plants extending above the snow had been blasted off by the abrasion of the wind-blown snow crystals. While most of the hares grazed over the ridge in the bright moonlight, several took turns watching with their large, yellowish-brown eyes over the vast whiteness of the valleys and hilltops. As if some invisible signal was given, every hare suddenly turned in the direction of a shadow stealing toward the colony. A lone white arctic wolf, who had gone without eating for three weeks, caught the hares' scent from over a kilometer away.

The hares froze in whatever position they were in, as the white ghost with lowered head and slanting eyes came up the ridge, taking advantage of boulders and snowdrifts to help conceal its approach. When it stalked within thirty meters (98.4 ft), the nearest hares could not hold their places any longer and they turned and retreated toward the rest. Then all frenzy broke loose. Every hare straightened up onto its long hind limbs and bounded off like a kangaroo down the side of the hill. The wolf immediately broke into a gallop after the hopping throng, checking each hare for a slight limp or unbalanced move — telltale signs of a slow or weak individual. The hares raced across the valley on all fours like rockets, scattering in several directions. Every few seconds they bounded up again on their hind feet to obtain a better view of their pursuer. While the wolf ran at peak bursts of fifty kilometers (31 miles) per hour on the hard crust, it was left behind by the speedier hares. At a distance, they regrouped and headed at a slower pace to the safety of the next ridge.

It was June before the sun strengthened sufficiently to push the air temperature past the magic melting point for most of the day. As if saddened to see the snow disappear, the hares lay flat on their bellies or on their sides to sunbathe beside the last patches of white. With the trails through the snow all vanished, the animals switched to routes worn clear of most vegetation and loose gravel by generations of hares. Each hare periodically rubbed its nose glands on nearby twigs or rocks, leaving a scent message for others. In addition, the anal glands under the tail deposited a musk on the ground every time a hare sat down, communicating its presence and sexual state. Should this be insufficient to attract attention, the animals produced another perfume from cheek glands which they rubbed all over their head and body with their front feet. A number of hares could frequently be seen following the trails in single file, checking for scents and adding fresh ones.

Almost every female appeared to be swollen with young, and one by one they went off by themselves to give birth. One yearling female had never bred before and she hesitantly hollowed out a depression in the sedge and moss between some rocks. The next day the form held three precious gray hares. While the new mother was away foraging, a white and brown-speckled hunter swooped up the hill and landed on one of the rocks. The snowy owl stared down at the unprotected babies with an intense glare, then looked all around, its neck turning smoothly one hundred and eighty degrees in each direction. When the mother returned an hour later, the nest was bare. She anxiously searched the vicinity for five minutes, then gave up and returned to the other hares on the hillside. She would soon be pregnant again.

Arctic Fox

It was early June on the west coast of Hudson Bay. A huge mass of brilliant white ice groaned as the incoming tide eased the eroded sculpture over polished black boulders. Not far away, snuggled in a den deep within the sandy beach ridge, a white fox whimpered softly as she pushed the fifteenth brown-haired pup from her birth canal. Attentively, she licked each squirming newborn dry and devoured the afterbirths, retaining vital nutrients needed to nourish her family. Clean-up completed, she nestled the sleepy pups in her long belly fur. Several weeks under the warming sun transformed the tundra from a white desert into a flooded marsh. The father fox was kept busy hunting and adding constantly to the food cache of voles and lemmings, which the mother converted into a rich milk for the rapidly growing pups. By early July, fifteen brown bodies came tumbling out of the den each day, barking, biting, kicking, and pouncing on every butterfly and spider unfortunate enough to catch their attention. The adults, now in their brown and yellow summer coat, had to travel farther and farther afield to hunt lemmings. Although summer should have seen an increase in the numbers of these rodents from spring breeding, they were instead becoming scarcer — a sign of an impending lemming crash. The half-grown foxes scrounged all available eggs and fledgling birds, then resorted to berries and insects. Several years of high lemming populations had permitted a corresponding buildup of foxes, but with the disappearance of their major food item, the tundra could no longer support all these carnivores.

As the autumn days shortened and the weather cooled, white hairs began to poke through their brown fur. When snow finally covered the landscape the foxes could find only an occasional arctic hare or ptarmigan to eat. To hunt these prey required more energy than the food provided and the white hunters began to lose weight. Driven by hunger, several of the fox family traveled out onto the pack ice where they cleaned up the oily remains of seals killed by polar bears. Others headed westward onto the barren grounds to search for scraps of caribou left by wolves. But most of the foxes, by the thousands, pushed southward along the coastal tundra and into foreign territory — the boreal forest. Numbed into an instinctive obsession to keep traveling, the foxes ignored every hardship and kept on the move. Short limbs and dainty paws, suited for running on the packed tundra snow, floundered in the fluffy, bottomless snow cover of the forest. Windblown lakes and rivers, plus an occasional snowmobile trail, aided their solitary journeys, averaging over fifteen kilometers (9.3 miles) per day.

The father fox was one of the throng to penetrate deeply into the spruce forest. It had been six weeks since his tail last wagged in the direction of the bay. Through most of this period he had seldom paused to eat, taking only a few meadow voles or a spruce grouse which he captured while the bird slept under the snow. For a few hours each day he rested in shelters quickly hollowed out of a snow bank.

One night the fox was jolted awake by the deep-throated calls of wolves. With rounded ears and tail held low, the fox sneaked away under tree branches bent down with great pillows of snow. It was -46°C (-51°F) and clear all night, yet the fox did not need to shiver nor turn up its internal thermostat to keep warm. All that filled his mind was the overpowering urge to keep running, but where he did not know. His attention was suddenly arrested one morning by another arctic fox stretched out in the snow. Its body was frozen solid and tied to a steel chain. The fox whimpered and pranced around the lifeless form for a minute. Then overcome by starvation, he ate his fill and moved on.

A few days later the arctic fox came to a frozen lake so large that it reached to the horizon, unbroken by any tree or hill. This bleak terrain of frozen packed snow was just like his tundra home and he sometimes covered thirty kilometers (18.6 miles) in a day. For over a week he followed the shoreline, finding nothing to eat. On reaching the southern end of the lake, bordered by patches of mixed woodland, his leg muscles were shaking and cramping. This little traveler, no bigger than a house cat, had now run an incredible one thousand kilometers (621 miles) from the barren grounds to the edge of the prairie. His keen nose led him to an uplifted piece of ice where he found a goose carcass frozen in the ice. He gnawed frantically at the rock-hard bird and scavenged enough meat to fill his belly. As he curled up to sleep amid the goose feathers, he looked up to see a familiar sight — a snowy owl flapping slowly on its broad wings down the shore. Both tundra wanderers were so far from home. Would the fox be able to find its way back like the owl when the urge would come to travel north?

ARCTIC FOX

Scientific name *Alopex lagopus*
Family Wolves, Foxes, and Dogs (Canidae)
Order Carnivores (Carnivora)
Total length males 90 cm (35.4 in);
females 82 cm (32.3 in)
Tail length 32 cm (12.6 in); 29 cm (11.4 in)
Weight 3.5 kg, maximum 9 kg
(7.7 lb, maximum 19.8 lb);
3 kg (6.6 lb)
Color There are two color phases of the arctic fox. The more common one is a short brown and gray coat worn from July to November, which is replaced in winter by long, dense, white fur. The blue phase is dark bluish-gray or chocolate brown in summer and bluish-gray to bluish-black in winter. This blue phase is controlled by a single hereditary gene and is most frequent in populations of foxes that live along shorelines with open water in winter. One hundred percent of the foxes are blue phase in Iceland, 90 percent in the Pribilof Islands of Alaska, 50 percent in Greenland, and only one percent in the rest of Alaska and Canada. The pups are a brown color.

Distribution and Status This diminutive fox lives mainly within the Arctic Circle — on the arctic and alpine tundra and ice-covered seas of North America, Europe, and Asia. An isolated relict population has been reported in the Altai Mountains of Mongolia. Despite its small size, it is a great traveler and has reached all the major arctic islands by crossing the pack ice. Individuals have ranged out onto the polar icecap as far as 800 km (497 mi) north of land in the Soviet Union. During southward migrations into the boreal forest, they have been known to reach the southern regions of Manitoba and Ontario, and to drift on ice pans as far south as Newfoundland and Nova Scotia. There is only the single species in the genus *Alopex*, but some mammalogists prefer to include the animal in the genus *Vulpes*, like many other kinds of foxes. The red and arctic fox may have shared a common ancestor *(Vulpes alopecoides)* about 2 million years ago.

Food Lemmings and voles are the fox's staple food, but at times of need it will eat any animal it can find, dead or alive. Ringed seal pups, arctic ground squirrels, bird eggs and young, hares, insects, fish, and other marine animals (crabs, sea urchins, and clams) are relished. Its sense of hearing is so keen that it can hear lemmings under deep snow, while its nose can smell carrion from 50 km (31 mi) away in the clean arctic air.

Reproduction and Growth Arctic foxes are monogamous, meaning that each mates only with one other individual during a particular breeding season. Some pairs remain together for life, although one or 2 additional females may live within the male's home range and act as helpers in raising the young. The female comes into estrus or heat for 12 to 14 days from February to April. After mating the couple prepares a den which likely has been used by generations of foxes. Development of the young inside the female requires 52 days before birth, generally in May or June. The number of young varies considerably with the degree of fitness (based on age and adequate food supply) of the female. Generally a litter consists of 6 to 12 offspring, but can range from 2 to an astonishing 25. When starving a female may not breed at all, thereby improving her own chances of survival. The haired

pups weigh around 57 g (2 oz) and are weaned in only 2 to 4 weeks. Both parents feed and care for the pups until they are abandoned in the autumn. Sexual maturity and first breeding occurs at 10 months. Most of the young foxes perish before reaching 6 months and few survive more than 2 years in the wild. Captives have lived as long as 15 years.

Remarks The arctic fox is a beautiful creature with short rounded ears, sharply tapering snout, and luxurious dense fur. Even the soles of the feet are protected from the cold by long hairs. As is mentioned in the arctic hare account, there is a fascinating correlation in the length of the extremities in related species that live under contrasting environmental conditions. Ear length, for example, progressively increases in size from the arctic fox (tundra), red fox (forest, tundra, and grassland), swift fox (grassland), to the kit fox (desert) — likely adaptations for the conservation or radiation of body heat. The arctic fox exhibits remarkable characteristics for life in the cold. With excellent fur insulation the fox does not increase its internal production of heat (metabolic rate) until the temperature drops below -50°C (-58°F), shivering begins at -70°C (-94°F), and captive individuals have survived experimental conditions of -80°C (-112°F).

The arctic fox makes the most extensive journeys of any land mammal in the whole world. The above story was based on a report turned in to me of a young male fox that had actually migrated from the barren grounds west of Hudson Bay all the way to the edge of the prairie in Manitoba, almost to the North Dakota border. This individual is estimated to have traveled about 1 000 km (621 mi) — the longest inland trek ever recorded for the species in North America. Even more surprising is a similar southward penetration of 2 000 km (1,243 mi) up the Amur River to Komsomolsk in the Soviet Union. Moving in the opposite direction a captive fox from Aberdeen Lake, District of Keewatin, escaped near Ottawa, Ontario and 2 years later was trapped on the Belcher Islands of Hudson Bay, 1 120 km (696 mi) to the northwest, while apparently heading homeward. There are dozens of other remarkable records of long-range movements for this species, particularly within the arctic region. For example, one fox was trapped, radio-collared, and released on Banks Island and trapped at Repulse Bay (Northwest Territories) 250 days later — a straight-line distance eastward of 1 530 km (951 mi). Stamina and homing abilities of this tiny fox seem beyond belief — like the annual migration of the arctic tern from the arctic to antarctic regions. While starvation or overcrowding trigger some of the journeys, the full explanation for wanderlust in the fox is far from known.

As might be expected with a species subjected to uncertain food resources, home ranges vary tremendously in size, from 860 to 6 000 ha (2,150 to 14,820 a). Urine, droppings, and scent are deposited on tufts of grass, moss hummocks, and boulders to announce the animal's tenure on a piece of land. I was unable to find information on population estimates, but it is known that fox numbers fluctuate drastically over large regions, and are often correlated to the 3- to 4-year cycle of lemmings — their major food supply. The animals may be active anytime of the day and night, during any season, but increased activity has been

noted during the night. No type of terrain, water body, or stretch of ice seems to act as a barrier.

The main den is generally a network of tunnels covering an area of around 30 sq m (324 sq ft) and with 4 to 12 entrances. Some dens have been used for centuries and have been remodeled and extended to many times the normal size. Other resting dens are located over the home range, often several kilometers apart. Selected sites include almost any well-drained esker, ridge, bank, or pile of rocks.

One warm summer afternoon I was walking along a high rock- and pond-strewn esker near the Manitoba-Northwest Territories border. Spectacular views of the tundra on all sides and a refreshing breeze would have made it a hiker's paradise were it not for the more than 500 black flies striking me constantly in the face and hands. In a sandy depression I discovered the large tracks of a wolf, which led over to 2 small den entrances in the bank. Peeping into these arctic fox tunnels, as the wolf had done, I saw a grotesque toothy skull staring back at me. It turned out to be a skeleton of an enormous pike, no doubt picked clean by the family of foxes. I could not understand how an animal as small as an arctic fox could have dragged this big fish up the esker from the nearest lake, 2 km (1.2 mi) away.

ARCTIC GROUND SQUIRREL

Scientific name *Spermophilus parryii*
Family Squirrels (Sciuridae)
Order Rodents (Rodentia)
Total length 400 mm (15.8 in)
Tail length 120 mm (4.7 in)
Weight 800 g (28.2 oz)
Color The upperparts are brownish-gray, grizzled with black- and white-tipped hairs. A band along the back is darker, with white spots. The tail tip is black, while the head, belly, and feet are orangy-brown. This attractive and complicated color pattern blends in well with the sand and lichen-covered rocks often found where these animals live.

Distribution and Status This northernmost member of the squirrel family lives in alpine meadows and shrubby thickets, arctic tundra, and adjacent forest-tundra woodland, from the west shore of Hudson Bay west through northern British Columbia and Alaska to the northeastern part of the Soviet Union. It occurs from sea level to elevations of over 1 100 m (3,600 ft). For hibernation it must find well-drained sites that are free of permafrost, such as ridges and riverbanks of sand, gravel, or sandy clay. Its close relative, the long-tailed souslik *(Spermophilus undulatus)* of the mountains of southern Soviet Union, northern Mongolia, and China, was long thought to be the same species.

Food The diet includes the leaves, stems, roots, and berries of many kinds of tundra plants like sedges, bearberry, cranberry, willows, and saxifrages, but vetches (of the pea family) are especially sought after. Mushrooms, insect larvae, caribou antlers, birds' eggs, and the meat of dead animals are also eaten when available.

Reproduction and Growth Arctic ground squirrels are ready to mate within days of emerging from hibernation in May when there may still be a heavy cover of snow. All females of the colony become pregnant by the end of May and 25 days after mating, an average of 7 young (range of 4 to 12) are born in a deep underground den that is lined with moss and hair. The babies crawl around the entrance in late July, are weaned at 5 weeks, leave the nest at 6 weeks, and are almost full grown when they retire for the winter in September. The young of the year are forced to the edge of the colony or farther away, and many do not survive the 7-month deep sleep because they may freeze, be flooded out, or run out of fat or stored food. The average life span is 3 years, but potentially may be as high as 8.

Remarks The arctic ground squirrel is a robust animal with short legs, a brush-like tail, and a rounded profile characterized by a blunt nose and eyes situated high on the head. Its whole life seems to consist of annual periods of reproduction, fattening, and hibernation. In early September the obese adults begin to enter torpor but some individuals, particularly young of the year, are still out in October trying to add to their fat reserves that will see them through the long winter sleep. The nest is generally located about one m (3.3 ft) below the surface and is lined with dried vegetation and fur. The animal curls up in a tight ball and its body temperature falls from 36.4° C to around 4°C (97.5°F to 40°F). Except for short arousals every couple of weeks, the squirrels are in a state of suspended life for 7 months until their world becomes habitable once more. Depending on the region and the weather, the squirrels emerge from late March to early May, the males appearing a week or so before the females. They sometimes must dig their way out through the snow to see if conditions are suitable. Poor weather sends them below until the sun shines.

Although the growing season is short, the squirrels take advantage of the extra-long summer days, and are active for up to 17 hours in a 24-hour period. This species is almost always found in colonies, sometimes numbering in the hundreds of individuals. Each squirrel forages over a home range of around 4 ha (10 a) and occasional forays can reach 1 550 m (5,085 ft) from the burrow. Males are known to defend territories of around 2 ha (5 a) from other males, but females freely overlap the territories of males. The burrow system often descends no deeper than one m (3.3 ft), however it may consist of 21 m (68 ft) of tunnels with toilet, food storage, and nest chambers, along with half a dozen openings to the surface. Arctic ground squirrels become tame around campsites and cabins, and soon learn to beg for a handout. The Inuit collect them for food and clothing, while others fall prey to ermine, grizzly, gray wolf, arctic and red foxes, gyrfalcon, and snowy owl.

Flying into a remote and little-studied region is a thrilling experience for biologists, for one can never tell what fascinating plants and animals might occur there. Of course, a hypothetical list of possible species is drawn up and double-checked, but there are always surprises, especially on the tundra. As our plane circled around a little cabin on the shore of Hudson Bay, I had one thought on my mind. Would arctic ground squirrels be found this far south? There were no records for the Manitoba coastline, the nearest being at Eskimo Point to the north in the Keewatin District, discovered there in the year 1900. I thought to myself, if they are here, I'll probably have to walk great distances to locate them.

The plane succeeded in landing on the primitive sand runway with only 10 m (33 ft) to spare before dropping off into the sea, and our much-relieved field crew quickly unloaded the gear and began carrying it along a trail to our new home. Sweating under the heavy load, and cursing the clouds of swarming black flies, I heard an unfamiliar whistle and glanced up to see what looked like a sandy-colored woodchuck perched on top of a huge boulder. Suddenly there were over a dozen members of the welcoming committee, all lined up along the trail right to the cabin door. Arctic ground squirrels! I couldn't believe my eyes and good fortune. I often think back to this occasion when I am experiencing problems in locating other mammal species.

Several years later, I came across another colony of these squirrels in a sandy area farther north along the coast. About 50 could be counted at a time, as they ran from burrow to burrow. I was unable to outrun them, for they were fleet of foot and always kept within range of a nearby burrow. Since we saw 3 polar bears in the area, I figured all the slowpokes had long been eliminated. The adults can put up quite a fight, as I found out when I live-trapped a number of them in the Yukon and at Tuktoyaktuk on the Beaufort Sea. They backed against the cage wall, shrieking and snapping viciously with their long incisor teeth. I was astonished to see how fat these arctic fellows can become by autumn. They could almost turn around inside their skin. I could well understand why this energy-rich animal is so sought after by predators.

ARCTIC FOX ▢   ARCTIC GROUND SQUIRREL ▢

Arctic Ground Squirrel

The morning sun began to warm up the southern slope of the sand and gravel ridge, tempting open hundreds of dazzling yellow arctic poppies. As far as the eye could see, dozens of arctic ground squirrels stood motionless at their den entrances, looking much like bowling pins. They seemed to be taking turns watching for trouble, while other individuals crept half hidden among the low vegetation, nibbling at willow and sedge leaves. This colony had awakened from hibernation in the cold ground only three weeks ago in May, and the squirrels were obviously enjoying their two favorite pastimes — eating and sunning. Several of the animals climbed up onto large gray boulders splashed with bright orange, red, and black lichens. They stretched out on their bellies on the warm rocks, half closing their eyes in contentment. One big male drew its head backward and yawned, exposing two pairs of chisel-sharp incisor teeth. A few individuals had already started their spring molt and looked odd with the front half of the body in new orange-brown fur and the back half in ragged grayish-brown.

As the day grew on, the colony became a hive of activity, with the squirrels continually moving in and out of the maze of tunnels and pausing to emit piercing "keek-keek" calls. Females were carrying mouthfuls of soft plants and tufts of caribou fur to line their nests, for they were becoming heavy with young. One male, who was recovering from a strenuous week of chasing and mating with females, decided to go on an exploring expedition. His short legs carried him along the ridge top and in an hour he was half a kilometer (0.3 miles) away from the colony, yet he could still faintly hear the other squirrels calling to each other. Once off the ridge the squirrel crawled down through a tangle of low willow shrubs covered in fuzzy catkins, then past a series of mossy hummocks, and finally out onto the low sedge flats. The ground here was saturated from meltwater, and a number of extensive ponds forced the squirrel along narrow bridges of drier land. Since the vegetation in this area had not been visited by any other squirrels, the male reveled in a sea of choice leaves. Neither wet feet nor an occasional swim could deter him, for this little sunworshiper was full of the exuberance of life. His seven months of confinement in the depths of the cold dark ground were over for this year.

The ground squirrel was so busy sniffing all sorts of new odors and filling his belly that he was unaware of a huge brown form galloping towards him. When the squirrel finally looked up, the grizzly was only twenty meters (66 feet) away. With a flick of his tail the squirrel dashed off in the direction of home. The two splashed through the water then bounded up the side of the ridge. Down between some rocks squirmed the squirrel, as the big bear came puffing up to the spot. With a swipe of its clawed paw the bear tumbled the rocks down the hillside and the chase was on again. For a whole terrifying minute the squirrel managed to keep away from those claws and teeth. But while the squirrel was quicker in dodging, the bear finally ran it down. Within ten minutes the bear had finished its snack, and its appetite whetted for squirrel meat, it began moving swiftly toward the colony. No ambush this time, as the alert squirrels gave a series of alarm calls and quickly disappeared underground. The bear rushed up and in frustration tore up the sandy soil with powerful strokes of its forearms. Thrusting its broad black nose into a burrow, it could smell the squirrels down there somewhere. Fifteen minutes and five deep craters later, the grizzly gave up with a snort and wandered away in a foul mood. In a few minutes, every tunnel entrance was filled by a little head with bright black eyes, wondering if it was safe to come out yet. Soon the frightening episode was forgotten and life went on as usual in the colony. Then one warm afternoon in July, eight baby squirrels crawled out on the surface mat of crowberry for the very first time. The offspring of the dead male had come to take its place.

Ermine and Brown Lemming

Snowflakes tumbled from the heavens all night long, building up the second snowfall of the season to a depth of fifteen centimeters (5.9 inches). Soon the wind would blow across the sedge-moss meadow, tumbling and shattering the delicate crystals and packing their remains into a hard layer. But this new fluffy snow cover was full of air spaces and too soft to support animals. Puff! Two shiny black eyes popped out of the white blanket, blinking in the dazzling morning sunlight. In an instant they were gone and the scene was quiet and peaceful again, with no hint that a deadly hunter was on the prowl. Two meters (6.6 feet) from the hole the ermine burst out again, its head twisting from side to side as the animal considered where to go next. Caught in its autumn molt, patches of brown fur still lingered along the back, ruining an otherwise snow-white coat. Another week and the brown would be gone.

The ermine alternated bounding with tunneling, as its elongated body snaked across the valley. From a distance only the black-tipped tail could be seen, which perhaps would distract a snowy owl or arctic fox during an attack. The ermine left its tracks over the crest of a ridge, and half jumping and sliding down the other side, it stopped suddenly, as if it had bumped its pink nose into an invisible wall. There between its paws lay a single black pellet on the snow, only a centimeter (0.4 inches) from a little round hole.

Hidden, but not far away, a brown lemming was working diligently on its new nest — a ball of dry sedge lined with caribou hair and a few downy feathers recycled from an old underground den. Now that snowdrifts had built up in the lee of the ridge, the lemming instinctively decided to move from a summer subterranean nest, situated above the cold permafrost, to warmer snow-insulated quarters on the ground surface. Day or night meant nothing to the lemming in its snow-covered dark world. It continued to use certain old trails to favorite feeding sites, but now it began to construct additional tunnels through the snow while exploring for new food sources. Droppings were usually deposited in a separate toilet chamber. Occasionally the hamster-like rodent even dug its way through the snow to the surface, sometimes leaving a black dropping at the edge of the tunnel.

The ermine became very excited when its keen nose located the fresh scent, and its movements shifted to double speed. Frantically it waded through the snow, pausing repeatedly to listen and to push its nose into the white flakes. At one point it stood straight up on its hind legs to see whether its prey was attempting an escape over the snow from some hidden burrow. Down periscope, the little submarine shot under the surface again. It was dark, moist, and warmer down here, and the odor of lemming grew strong. The ermine's ears detected faint scratching sounds, and seconds later it broke into the lemming's tunnel. In the faint light the terrified lemming could see the weasel's flashing eyes. Racing along another tunnel as fast as its short legs could carry it, the lemming was grabbed by the rump and it spun around chattering and biting with its large yellow incisor teeth. But the ermine was quicker and its jaws closed on the rodent's neck. The two animals tumbled in a ball, the ermine grasping its prey with its forelimbs and kicking with its hind feet. The lemming squealed, struggled as best it could against its more powerful adversary, then went limp with its black eyes bulging from the pressure of the weasel's embrace. For fifteen seconds longer the weasel held on, its head buried in the long soft lemming fur. Finally it released its jaws, but continued to sniff the warm body. Shaking off the snow that had collapsed around them during the tussle, the ermine dragged its heavy prey forty meters (131.2 feet) through the snow to its den on the gravel ridge. Pausing to rest beside some snow-covered grasses, it lapped up a few drops of blood. Here, under a boulder, lay the frozen bodies of six other lemmings, safely stored for a time when food might become scarce.

This hunt successfully completed, the ermine stood up on its hind legs, looked around, then in a flash bounded away once more over the white sea of snow. Its urge to hunt still not satisfied, it again began to track its favorite quarry. Circling around in one spot, it arched its tubular back and deposited a black tapering dropping beside the trail, then dove down out of sight. That afternoon, the clawed white paws of a larger carnivore strode up and stopped on either side of the dropping. The black nose of a wolf thrust into the open tunnel, sniffing in a musky odor that promised food.

ERMINE

Scientific name *Mustela erminea*
Family Weasels (Mustelidae)
Order Carnivores (Carnivora)
Total length males 275 mm (10.8 in);
females 230 mm (9.1 in)
Tail length 75 mm (3.0 in); 55 mm (2.2 in)
Weight 80 g, maximum 206 g (2.8 oz,
maximum 7.3 oz); 55 g (1.9 oz) European male ermine can reach 320 g
(11.3 oz)

Color In summer the upperparts are chocolate brown, the undersides white, and the tip of the tail black. In snowy parts of the range, the ermine molts into a white coat (except for the black tail tip) in winter, a process that requires about 3 weeks. The fur often becomes stained a bright yellow on the hind quarters by a secretion from the anal glands.

Distribution and Status Grasslands, meadows, marshes, bogs, river banks, forests, tundra, and farmlands are all home to this adaptable little hunter. It extends up mountainsides to elevations of 4 000 m (13,123 ft) but avoids dense coniferous forest. Water is an essential part of its habitat, so it does not live in desert areas. It occurs over an enormous range (the largest of any weasel) including almost all of Canada, the United States south to northern California, New Mexico, Iowa, and Virginia, and even the northern half of Europe and Asia from Spain to northern China and Japan. It has also been introduced to New Zealand from Britain. There are 15 other species in the ermine's genus *Mustela*, which occur throughout North and South America, Europe, and Asia. It is closely related to the long-tailed weasel *(Mustela frenata)* and least weasel *(Mustela nivalis)*; the ranges of all 3 overlap in central North America. The ermine evolved in Europe and it spread from Asia over the Bering land bridge into North America within the last several hundred thousand years.

Food Mice and shrews are the mainstay of the ermine's diet, but almost any animal it can overpower may be eaten, including pocket gophers, ground squirrels, chipmunks, hares,

birds and their eggs, frogs, snakes, and even fish, insects, and earthworms. It will pursue chipmunks into the trees and fish in the shallows. Its wide distribution and abundance are due in large part to the animal's ability to change from one food source to another when certain kinds of prey become scarce. Occasionally this weasel resorts to feeding on poultry. Weasels are seldom found far from some source of water and usually drink many times each day.

Reproduction and Growth Ermine are polygamous, meaning that each may mate with a number of individuals rather than pairing with just one partner. The testes of the male enlarge as early as April in response to increasing daylight, while the female comes in estrus (heat) for several periods from April to August, the first occurring within days after giving birth. The male enters the range of a female, and following much excited chasing and rigorous struggle, he subdues her in the typical jaw hold on the nape of her neck. The larger male may drag the passive female until he is ready to mount her from behind. Coupling lasts from 2 to 20 minutes and is repeated numerous times (sometimes 5 matings within an hour) over several days. The male may also breed with his spring-born daughters at this time, so that almost all females are pregnant by the end of summer. The fertilized eggs enter a resting phase until triggered to resume development in March or April (stimulated indirectly by increasing daylight). Strangely, the least weasel and the black-footed ferret *(Mustela nigripes)* do not exhibit this arrested growth phase of embryos as in the ermine and long-tailed weasel. Four weeks later, in April or May, an average of 6 (range of 4 to 18) babies are born, 278 to 283 days after conception. The nest chamber is situated in a renovated burrow of some other mammal, a tree hollow, stump, or rock pile. The newborn weigh 2 g (.07 oz) and are blind and naked. A fine coat of white hair soon develops, accentuated by an unusual mane or ruff of dark hairs, the function of which is unknown. The ears and eyes

open at 5 weeks and solid food is eaten by this time, although nursing continues for 7 to 12 weeks. Mice are first captured when the rapidly growing weasels attain their full complement of teeth at 2.3 months. Females are sexually mature at 3 or 4 months while males first breed at one year. Most ermine live for an average of 2 years, some may reach 7 years in the wild, and captives have survived for 10 years.

Remarks The male ermine is almost twice the weight of the female, which may be an adaptation to lessen the competition between the sexes for food. The female is able to live on more abundant smaller prey, and can enter animal burrows too small for the male, while the male can tackle large prey like rabbits, which the female could not handle. Large males may also outcompete small males in breeding with more females — a selection process favoring larger size. The body is extremely elongated with short legs. The head is pointed and has rounded ears. The soles of the rounded feet are well insulated by fur during the winter in snowy regions. The skull is long with a fairly large braincase and the jaws contain 34 teeth with sharp edges designed for shearing flesh.

The eyes are prominent but apparently vision is not well developed, for the animal frequently fails to notice prey almost in front of its nose. The senses of hearing and smell first locate the presence of prey, whose movements then trigger an attack (a hunting strategy similar to that of snakes). The ermine is known for its aggressiveness and will readily attack an animal much larger than itself. With a strong instinct to kill, the ermine will destroy more individual prey than it can eat at one time, but it usually caches the extra carcasses for future use. This species is one of the major checks on the numbers of rodents. A powerful musk is discharged from the anal glands when the animal is irritated or frightened. Several calls have been reported — a trill when searching or playing, a screech when startled, and a squeal when attacked. The ma-

ERMINE BROWN LEMMING

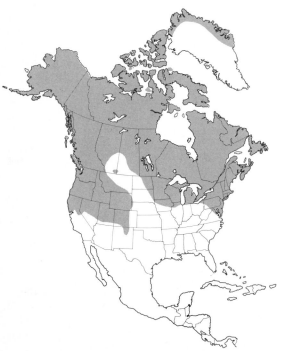

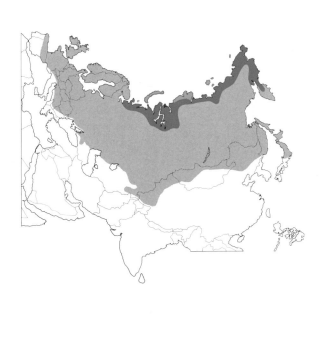

jor predators of ermine are the coyote, wolf, bobcat, hawks, owls, and snakes.

It is surprising that this species is so successful in cold regions for the following reasons — its long thin body and short coat (even in winter) result in double the heat loss from the body than a compactly built animal, and it is unable to coil up in a ball to lessen exposure of its surface when resting as can most other species of small mammals. However, these serious limitations are overcome by being able to increase its production of body heat 4 times its basal rate, being able to catch and eat prey one-quarter of its weight per day to meet this high energy demand, and by lessening its exposure to the cold air by remaining under the snow and sleeping in a thick, fur-lined nest. It is unable to hibernate.

Active mostly at dusk and dawn, this weasel can appear anytime. Often it will be active for 10 to 45 minutes (sometimes up to 4 hours) and then rest. It follows a circuit of trails, traveling from 1.3 to 8 km (0.8 to 5 mi) each 24-hour period. A series of dens are used for shelter such as a tree hollow, crevice under rocks, snow cave, or an abandoned burrow of another animal. Home ranges vary from 2 to 10 ha (4.9 to 24.7 a) for females and 8 to 34 ha (19.8 to 84 a) for males, the larger ranges occurring when mice are scarce. The range is extended into trees when feeding on young birds and squirrels, and into shallow water when pursuing fish. Males are known to wander widely, especially during the breeding season, and consequently are trapped 3 times more often than females. One male was found to have traveled a remarkable 37 km (23 mi) straight-line distance in 7 months. The animal is solitary and defends its territory against individuals of the same sex by a threat display and aggression if necessary. Males are dominant to females except when the female is pregnant. The population density of ermine fluctuates widely depending on prey abundance, but averages one per 10 ha (24.7 a) in good habitat, with a range of one per 17 ha (42 a) to one per 50 ha (120 a).

BROWN LEMMING

On the tundra, I once followed an ermine for some distance as it investigated old lemming holes on a gravel ridge. It loped along almost like a speedy giant inchworm, with its long slender back hunched up. I watched another one repeatedly dart out to nibble on a road-killed collared lemming which seemed too heavy for it to carry away. In the Yukon, I chased yet another into a brush pile, and as it popped its head out again, its eyes glowed (from the tapetum area of the retina) with a mysterious green color which I have never seen again in any animal.

BROWN LEMMING
Scientific name *Lemmus sibiricus*
Family Voles and Lemmings (Arvicolidae)
Order Rodents (Rodentia)
Total length 150 mm (5.9 in)
Tail length 22 mm (0.9 in)
Weight 70 g, maximum 113 g
(2.5 oz, maximum 4.0 oz)
Color The brown lemming's coat is a reddish-brown color, particularly bright on the rump and more grayish on the head, shoulders, and underparts. The feet are silvery. The winter coat is considerably longer and grayer, but there is no molt into a white pelage as occurs in the collared lemming. The juvenile fur is dull reddish-gray.
Distribution and Status This lemming dwells on the arctic tundra from Alaska to Hud-

Brown lemming

son Bay in the Northwest Territories, including the lower arctic archipelago from Banks Island to Baffin Island. In the east, the range sweeps south almost to the Manitoba border. In the west, the lemming inhabits alpine tundra and subalpine woodland, surprisingly reaching central British Columbia and Alberta in the Coast and Rocky Mountain ranges at elevations of 1 800 to 2 500 m (5,906 to 8,202 ft). Favored habitats are wet sedge-grass tundra or alpine meadows and the edges of ponds and watercourses, but sometimes it appears in sphagnum bogs, subalpine woodland, and talus slopes. Dry gravel ridges and lichen-moss sites (often preferred by the collared lemming) are usually avoided.

The brown lemming also occurs along the narrow strip of arctic tundra and adjacent islands in the Soviet Union, from the White Sea to Bering Strait and Kamchatka Peninsula. Four other species of the lemming genus *Lemmus* are found from Scandinavia east to Kamchatka, and as far south as the Himalayas, Mongolia, and China. The most famous is the Norway lemming *(Lemmus lemmus)* notable for its spectacular population cycles and migrations, and its beautiful coat of yellow and black.
Food The brown lemming is a direct competitor of caribou for tundra vegetation such as sedges, grasses, cottongrass, mosses, lichens, bearberry, saxifrages, and buttercup. Willow catkins, roots, bark, bulbs, and many kinds of berries also help appease this rodent's ravenous appetite. Bulbs may be stored underground, but grass and sedge are cut and left on site for later use, or are carried back to be eaten near the den. A lemming will not refuse carrion, even if it is another lemming.
Reproduction and Growth Generally the breeding season lasts from June to September — the snow-free, growing season of arctic plants. Adult females raise 3 litters during this period, while young of the year produce one or 2. During optimal conditions of temperature, snow cover, and food availability, lemmings continue to breed throughout the winter, resulting in a great build-up in the population. The gestation period is 23 days and the average number of young per litter is 7 (range of 4 to 9). The nest is located in a grass-lined underground den, often situated under a boulder, or in winter, is likely placed on the surface under the snow. The pink infants weigh about 4 g (0.1 oz) and nurse from the mother's 8 nipples. Their eyes open at day 11, they are furred at day 12, and begin eating vegetation at day 13, which results in a rapid increase in growth. At around 3 weeks the youngsters often play near the burrow entrance. Lemmings are known to have lived 14 months in the wild.
Remarks The brown lemming resembles a stocky meadow vole, but with shorter tail and limbs. The fur, remarkable for its length and softness, traps an insulating layer of air between the hairs, providing protection from heat loss and great buoyancy when swimming. The eyes are small and the ears are hidden in the fur. The front claws are thick and sharp, except for the thumb claw which is flat. Fur and bristles keep the soles of the feet from contacting the cold substrate.

As with most other arctic creatures, the brown lemming is active for periods during the day as well as night. Through the long

Continued on p. 54

Caribou

The bull caribou stood motionless beside a yellow thicket of willows, exhausted from three weeks of clashes with other bulls and from mating with over a dozen cows. Drained of his strength from the rut, he had lost twenty-five kilograms (55 pounds) of fat reserves, built up over the summer and autumn. Amid grunts, sneeezes, belches, and the sharp clicking of hooves, thousands of cows, calves, yearlings, and bulls filed past, but he ignored them all. The urge to fight and mate had finally passed. Wearily his legs began to move, keeping pace with the herd as it foraged, rested, and traveled up to thirty kilometers (18.6 miles) a day. Through the mountain passes and across the tundra valleys the animals streamed, ever onward toward the open forest where they would spend the winter. Within a week the bull's antlers fell to the ground and he began to keep company with other bulls. Then one day in December they drifted off from the main herd. It would be next June, back on the tundra calving grounds, before the bulls would meet up with their herd again.

The bull's winter coat had now grown to its full thickness and rich coloration. The long guard hairs, tapering at both ends, captured a dead air space, which along with the wooly underfur kept its body warm even at -45°C (-49°F) and while swimming through ice water. As the temperature fell and the snow deepened, the bachelors continued foraging for lichens, willow, and cranberry. The bull could smell particular plants under half a meter (1.6 feet) of snow by plunging its haired snout into the white powder, or by sniffing the air vents where saplings and trees poked through the snow cover. By day the caribou slept out on frozen lakes where they could watch for wolves. Confident of their ability to escape an attack, they did not even bother to stand up until the wolf pack approached within two hundred meters (656 feet). Since most of the wolves followed the main herds, concentrating their hunting on calves and cows, the bulls, being more dangerous quarry, were usually left alone.

In late January, a fierce windchill sucked the heat from every living boreal creature, causing the caribou to lay side by side in a bed of snow. The temperature in their legs dropped to 10°C (50°F), which slowed down heat loss from the limbs. But neither cold nor wolves were the caribou's greatest winter hardship; it was starvation. With sedges and grasses of the meadows and lake shores buried deeply under snowdrifts, the herd had to rely mainly on lichen and heath plants growing under jack pine and spruce trees on the hillsides. The animals' hooves, no longer worn flat by abrasion on rough gravel, grew sharp rounded edges which were useful in poking through the crust and shoveling away the snow. At the bottom of the feeding crater, the caribou could reach down and graze on the sparse vegetation.

At sunrise and sunset, and sometimes throughout the night, the herd of bulls left the lake in single file and entered the woodland to feed. In order to eat about six kilograms (13 pounds) of food, each caribou had to forage for twelve hours and dig over one hundred craters in the snow. As the winter months passed by, the animals grew thin on their starvation diet. Fat stored under the skin, around the belly organs, and in the bone marrow, was used up to keep the animals warm and to provide the energy to travel several kilometers each day to new feeding grounds where the snow cover was uncrusted and less than sixty centimeters (23.6 inches) deep. In a few areas of mature forest the caribou stood up on their hind legs to pull off strands of black or yellow lichens draping down from the branches of tamarack and spruce.

By March, the animals had lost so much weight that the outlines of their ribs and hip bones could be seen under the faded and worn hides. The strongest bull pushed its weaker companions out of their feeding craters, saving himself the work of digging his own. With the health of several bulls reaching a critical condition, the forage situation began to improve as warming temperatures melted away the snow cover on exposed ridges. And yet, rather than wait for the snow to disappear completely and to take advantage of the accessibility of food, the herd began its long leisurely trek back through the spruce woodland to the barren grounds. The endless tracts of the summer range would once more resound with the clicking of thousands of hooves.

BROWN LEMMING *continued from p. 51*
frigid winter, it seldom travels on the surface of the snow where it would be exposed to cold air and predators, and perhaps become lost. People have reported following lemming tracks for great distances on the snow, and a few have been found as far as 35 km (21.8 mi) out on the sea ice or on glaciers. For an animal with such a reputation for traveling, the lemming has an unexpectedly small home range. Generally under 35 sq m (376.8 sq ft), the range may shrink to only 5 sq m (53.8 sq ft) under crowded conditions.

While North American lemmings are not as famous for migrations as the Norway lemming, they do exhibit impressive fluctuations in numbers over wide regions on a 2- to 5-year basis. Perhaps the lemming migrations in Scandinavia are just more noticeable because the animals are funneled past human settlements by the intricate topography of mountains and fiords. The brown lemming often occurs in colonies and becomes quite quarrelsome when other individuals appear in its runways. The crowding problem worsens as litter after litter are added to the population over the summer and right through the winter during a population outbreak. By spring, the lemmings are in a high state of agitation from continually searching for or defending a home area. Then the spring thaw hits suddenly, flooding their burrows and further reducing habitable ground. The rodents are seized by a powerful urge to disperse and the massive exodus begins. Both night and day their brown bodies can be seen scurrying over the tundra and swimming over ponds and rivers. Lemmings by the thousands are drowned after becoming exhausted, or are snatched up by eager foxes, wolves, weasels, bears, owls, gulls, jaegers, and even fish. Mortality is particularly high for young and old lemmings, since they are less able to defend a suitable space. Females breed less, litters are smaller, and infant survival is low throughout the summer. From the constant chewing of millions of little lemming teeth over the winter, spring, and summer the vegetation may be severely overgrazed. These factors combine to decimate the lemming population and for the next few years hardly a lemming can be found over great regions of the tundra, with dire consequences to arctic carnivores.

When I was a student at the University of Illinois I received a phone call from the Curator of Mammals at the National Museums of Canada. He was putting the final touches on a book on the mammals of the Yukon, and asked me if I would join his assistant on an 8-week field trip to the Yukon and Mackenzie districts to obtain specimens and information on a number of specific mammals. Since it meant postponing my own research for the summer, I had to give this offer some serious thought. Within a few minutes, however, I realized I couldn't pass up the opportunity.

The itinerary proved just how fortunate I was to be on the expedition, for each week we flew by helicopter or float plane, drove, or canoed into some of Canada's most spectacular country. From the wet tundra and "pingos" (hills of ice raised by frost action) of Tuktoyaktuk to rocky peaks and snow packs of the Richardson Mountains, it was an experience of a lifetime. The final week we spent on the crest of Haeckle Hill, just north of Whitehorse in the Yukon. Our main task here was to collect the brown lemming in a fantasy-

like landscape of green alpine meadows, dwarf wind-sculptured spruce, and orange and yellow lichen-painted rock faces, all looking down on a vast expanse of valley forest and talus slopes that stretched away as far as the eye could see. After setting up the tent I was excited to find the tunnels and thick (but old) pellets of lemmings in the mat of alpine tundra, and I quickly set row after row of mouse traps. The following morning I jumped from the tent and raced over the rough ground to the waving red flagging tapes that marked the lines. Two months of hiking all day through sodden muskeg and up mountain-sides had built up leg muscles that felt like they could carry me anywhere. The brisk breeze just lifted my spirits higher. Working along the lines, hoping to discover the reddish color of my first brown lemming in a trap, all I found was mouse brown and shrew gray. The legendary creature of "boom and bust" population must have now been in the latter stage. I couldn't find a single specimen anywhere. To make matters worse, it turned cold over the next few days and began to snow, though it was only mid-August. We busied ourselves taking blood samples from arctic ground squirrels and processing other small mammals. Descending the hill again later in the week while on our way home, I glanced over to some bushes. The only known specimen of the brown lemming from these parts had been found mummified in the top of this type of bush. Though our efforts failed to produce the brown lemming, we had been fortunate in finding most other species over the past 2 months. It was time to return to university life, but I still have hopes of returning to the tundra, only the next time during a "lemming high".

CARIBOU

Scientific name *Rangifer tarandus*
Family Deer (Cervidae)
Order Even-toed Ungulates (Artiodactyla)
Total length males 180 cm (70.9 in);
females 165 cm (65 in)
Tail length 18 cm (7 in); 15 cm (5.9 in)
Weight 110 kg, maximum 318 kg
(242.5 lb, maximum 701 lb);
80 kg (76.4 lb)

Color The caribou is basically a brown animal with a white neck, belly, and rump, and a dark line along the sides. The northern-most populations are gray and white while the woodland race is dark brown. The calf's coat is reddish-brown with a dark stripe extending from the neck to the tail.

Distribution and Status Caribou occur throughout the tundra and boreal forest regions of North America, Greenland, Europe, and Asia, extending from high arctic islands to formerly as far south as Idaho, Michigan, Nova Scotia, and the northern regions of Mongolia and China. The animal is known as reindeer in the Old World, where it was domesticated about 3,000 years ago. Population sizes and ranges of most herds have been greatly reduced, particularly in southern areas. It is gone from Prince Edward Island, Nova Scotia, New Brunswick, and the Queen Charlotte Islands of British Columbia. A herd of less than 2 dozen still exists in northern Idaho and Washington. Large herds of domestic reindeer have replaced the wild animals in regions of Scandinavia, Siberia, Alaska, and northwestern Canada. Reindeer have been introduced in Iceland, Spitzbergen, Scotland, and South Georgia Island in the South Pacific.

This primitive member of the deer family evolved in Europe about 440,000 years ago and crossed into North America over the Bering Land Bridge before the last (Wisconsinan) Ice Age. Formerly numbering 3.5 million in North America, recent estimates are around 1.03 million divided into 30 separate herds. Certain subspecies or groups are quite distinct in appearance and habitat, and consequently have been given common names. For example, Peary caribou (numbering only 13,000) are small, pale-colored animals of northern arctic islands (now disappeared from northwest Greenland). Barren-ground caribou (the most abundant) are medium size and occur across the continent and adjacent islands on sedge-grass, heath-lichen, and shrub tundra. Most migrate (up to 1 000 km or 621 mi) into the forest-tundra woodland for the winter. Woodland caribou (43,000 estimate) are a large, dark race which remain in the boreal forest of spruce, fir, pine, and birch, or in the western mountains inhabit alpine meadows and subalpine forest in the summer and move about 2 000 m (6,562 ft) down into valley forests and bogs for the winter.

Food Caribou graze on lichens, grasses, sedges, horsetails, low broad-leaved plants, willow and birch twigs, and mushrooms. The diet becomes more restricted in winter, consisting mainly of lichens. Lichens are largely water and are low in protein. Caribou are able to utilize nitrogen from urea (a waste product eliminated in the urine) circulating in the blood to form certain amino acids — the building blocks of protein. The animals also graze on antlers and bones lying on the ground, which serve as a source of minerals. Even birds' eggs and lemmings are devoured when available. Radioactive fallout, like Cesium-137, has become increasingly concentrated in the food chain from lichens to caribou and other animals and man.

Reproduction and Growth Woodland caribou bulls may gather harems of a dozen cows, but bulls in the larger herds of barren-ground caribou mate as the cows are moving by on their southward migration. The cows come into heat several times at intervals of about 11 days during October and early November. While pursuing a female a bull frequently clashes with other bulls or pauses to thrash shrubs with his antlers. As his energy ebbs he concentrates on tending one female. Mating is a single swift act occuring at dusk or dawn. Females in poor physical condition do not come into heat (estrus) and postpone breeding until the following year. About 230 days after fertilization (generally mid-May to early July), the single (rarely twins) fawn is born, as the female wanders off from the herd. Almost all births in a population occur within 10 days. The young can walk within minutes and run with the mother in several hours. For the first few days the calf nurses for a minute about every 18 minutes. The calf develops rapidly, growing from 6 to 48 kg (13.2 to 105.8 lb) in 5 months. Caribou grow little fat if at all during the winter when food is scarce. The weaning process begins by the end of July and is completed by October. A strong cow-calf bond improves the survival of the young animal. Females may breed as early as 1.5 years but most do not until 3.5 years of age. They reach full size by 4 years, while males require 6 years. The average life span is only 4.5 years in the wild, with a maximum record of 13 years, but captives have been known to reach 20 years.

Remarks Caribou have a distinctive shape with a heavy body and rectangular head. But even more noticeable are the spectacular pair of antlers present on bulls as well as cows. Even calves grow spikes. The long main beam curves backward then upward while the flattened single (rarely 2) right brow tine extends vertically to protect the face. Those of the bulls begin to grow in March or April, reach a length of up to 1.3 m (4.3 ft), and are shed during or after the rut in autumn. A bull in poor physical condition may drop its antlers early and consequently loses its dominance and sex drive. Females' antlers are under 0.5 m (1.6 ft) in length and are kept until spring. They are used to defend newborn calves and to gain the best forage sites. The cleft hoof is large and rounded with soft pads which offer sure footing on rock, gravel, and spongy ground. These pads shrink and the hoof becomes sharp edged in winter, providing a useful shovel for digging and also ensuring a non-skid surface for travel on ice. The large dew claw increases the support area of the hoof. There are 34 teeth present in the jaws which show considerable wear on the grinding surfaces in animals approaching 10 years of age. A series of scent glands, with which the animals identify and keep track of each other should they become separated, are located in front of the eye, on the lower legs, between the hooves, and at the end of the tail. A caribou has relatively poor vision, moderate hearing, and a keen sense of smell which detects both food sources and predators.

Caribou are great travelers, averaging 19 to 55 km (11.8 to 34.2 mi) each day during annual migrations which may cover from 500 to 1 000 km (310.7 to 621.4 mi) from summer to winter grounds. They often cover 500 km while foraging during summer, averaging a speed of 7 km (4.4 mi) per hour. When need be a caribou can gallop at speeds of 60 to 80 km (37.3 to 49.8 mi) per hour, swim long distances at 11 km (6.8 mi) per hour, and climb over treacherous terrain. At certain times of the year, especially during migration, large numbers of herds unite into concentrations of up to 19,000 animals per sq km (0.4 sq mi).

It has been estimated that a wolf kills and devours an average of a dozen caribou each year. Other important predators are the grizzly, wolverine, lynx, black bear, coyote, golden eagle, and raven. Calves and weak adults are most susceptible to attack, as well as to death from cold wet weather. Additional mortality factors are trampling, drowning, and other accidents. Biting and blood-sucking flies harass caribou all summer, causing considerable mental and physical stress. The decline in many caribou herds has caused great concern and controversy among native people, wildlife managers, and conservation organizations. Overhunting, predation by wolves in particular, habitat degradation especially by uncontrolled fires, and a parasitic worm introduced by contact with deer have all been factors in the plummeting numbers and range reductions of caribou. In the 1940s, one study found that the annual caribou kill totaled around 100,000 animals, but this has been greatly reduced in recent years. The fight to save the dwindling herds continues.

The annual migration of tens of thousands of caribou between the tundra and open forest is among the most spectacular events to be found in nature. It may take days for a large herd to pass through an area, to the sound of grunts and clicking and pounding hooves. The urge to reach their destination sometimes has tragic consequences, as occurred in the autumn of 1984 in northern Quebec. Thousands of animals attempted to cross a river at a traditional point, but the river was swollen and treacherous from recent heavy rains (and perhaps additional excess water released from a hydro dam). For days, caribou persisted in entering the water, even though drowning animals and carcasses floated by in full view. When the situation was discovered by native people and the wildlife service there was really nothing they could do but drag thousands of carcasses out of the water and try to save some of the meat. An estimated 10,000 caribou perished in a couple of days. The whole sad incident reminded me of lemmings which occasionally drown in huge numbers when migrating. Instinctive behavior, although wonderfully adaptive under normal circumstances, can lead to inappropriate actions by animals in unusual situations.

On a boat trip up the west coast of Hudson Bay we sighted a lone caribou bull standing on a rocky point, trying to find a cool sea breeze to blow away the black fly menace. We put to shore that afternoon at high tide and began our studies of tundra plants and animals. Our guide, always anxious to trail caribou, told us excitedly of a small herd he had just discovered. Several of us followed him and began stalking closer for a better look. From rock to rock we crept, trying to stay downwind and out of the caribou's sight. From a distance, the shimmering summer heat rising from the gray and black tundra boulders made it difficult to see the animals. All of a sudden, our herd of caribou began squawking loudly, jumped into the air, and flew away! Our embarrassed guide stood up and I chuckled to myself as a flock of sandhill cranes soared noisily overhead.

CARIBOU

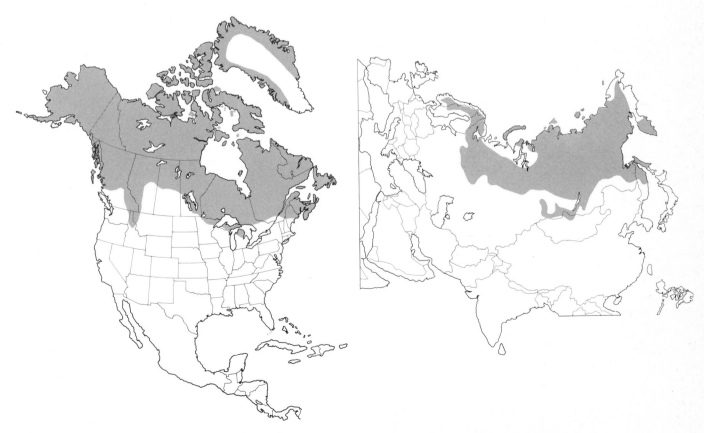

Muskox

With the first frosts of August, patches of brown and yellow vegetation spread among the gray boulders, replacing the green mantle of the arctic summer. The sun rode lower in the southern sky and the days grew shorter. In late afternoon, shaggy brown beasts appeared in single file on the top of a distant tundra hill — muskoxen, on their way to the valley to graze on sedges and forbs. Every so often an animal stopped to shake its head and coat to rid itself of mosquitoes swarming around the exposed lips and eyes. Without any boulders nearby, one itchy individual rubbed itself vigorously against the only other available object, another muskox. Amid this pastoral scene, two calves splashed about in a creek and then started playing "king of the mountain," both attempting to retain a position on top of a peat mound. On the next hill three white wolves sat watching the herd, their eyes gazing intently, their muscles tensing in anticipation of a chase.

The muskoxen spread out over the green valley to feed as two bulls, which had recently joined the herd, began hooking their horns into the peat. With mounting aggression, they closed the distance between them until the two animals stood only ten meters (33 feet) apart. With lowered heads, the bulls rubbed their eye glands with an outstretched foreleg. Then, without warning, they roared and charged at a forty-kilometer (25-mile)-per-hour gallop. The gap separating them closed rapidly until their flattened horns crashed together with a loud heavy thud which rolled over the hillside to the wolves' keen ears. While one bull held its ground, the other backed off and stood there, swinging its massive head from side to side. The rest of the herd resumed grazing as if bored with the duel. The head-swinging bull charged again, trying to overpower or gore its combatant. Although they had traveled together peacefully all summer, hormones in their blood had dramatically changed their mood. The two powerful animals were now contesting the right to dominate the herd and to mate with all the cows. With the second crushing impact, the charging bull fell backwards to its knees, staggered to its feet, and walked slowly away as if stunned.

Meanwhile, the wolves had taken advantage of the fight's distraction and the spread-out herd and were stalking a cow and her calf. With their keen eyesight the two muskoxen spotted the white predators and quickly ran toward the others, the calf bleating as it tried to keep up with its mother. Hooves flying and long hair streaming in the breeze, the dozen muskoxen galloped shoulder to shoulder back up the hillside. Displaying remarkable agility, the clumsy-looking animals negotiated the rocky slope with ease, their hooves resounding on the stones. Reaching the summit they stood in a straight line behind the victorious bull, heads lowered toward the attackers. The wolves approached silently and cautiously, testing the situation, almost as if they were just curious. One wolf darted too close to the line, and the second bull charged for several meters, sending the wolf scurrying out of range. Several wolves tried approaching from the rear, but the herd closed ranks, with heads facing outward, protecting the three calves within the tight circle. For half an hour the wolves dashed in and out, searching for a weakened animal, hoping the herd would stampede. As the wolves circled ever closer, trying to cut an animal off from the group, both bulls and cows took turns at short charges which drove the predators back again. At each charge, the muskox herd shifted forward to protect the rear of the exposed animal. Suddenly a wolf leapt to the shoulder of a charging cow, burying its teeth into her thick fur and hide. The cow whirled and threw off her attacker, while another cow butted it away. The bitten cow panicked, and began to run away, but in an instant the lead bull cut her off and forced her back into position.

As darkness fell, the moonlight reflected off both polished horns and bared teeth. The muskoxen stood their ground patiently against the wolves, just as their ancestors had done for thousands of generations. Finally, the wolves strode off on their long stiff legs, knowing their chance would come again in the weeks ahead. An hour later, as deep mournful howls carried across the barrens, the muskoxen still held their formation.

MUSKOX

Scientific name *Ovibos moschatus*
Family Cattle, Sheep, and Goats (Bovidae)
Order Even-toed Ungulates (Artiodactyla)
Total length males 245 cm (96.5 in);
            females 200 cm (78.7 in)
Tail length 14 cm (5.5 in); 10 cm (3.9 in)
Weight 340 kg, maximum 410 kg
            (750 lb, maximum 904 lb);
            180 kg (397 lb)

Color The coat is dark brown with lighter brown areas on the legs, muzzle, and middle of the back. The horns are yellowish-brown.

Distribution and Status This tundra species is found in moist meadows and willow-birch thickets in valleys in summer and windswept plateaus and ridges in winter. Adapted to an arid and cold environment, it is generally absent from regions with a mean annual snowfall in excess of 50 cm (20 in). The muskox once inhabited the arctic tundra from Alaska to Manitoba on Hudson Bay, including most large arctic islands and the northern coast of Greenland. For centuries these animals were killed off faster than they could breed, and they are presently found on only half their former range. The species has recently begun to increase in numbers and to expand into formerly occupied areas. There are approximately 45,000 muskoxen now living in the Northwest Territories — up from a 1967 estimate of 10,000. The muskox died out on the tundra of the Soviet Union after the last Ice Age (perhaps as recently as 2,000 years ago), but it has been reintroduced there on the Taimyr Peninsula and Wrangel Island, and in Norway, Sweden, Iceland, Spitzbergen, Alaska, and several antarctic islands. A recent introduction to the tundra region of northern Quebec has resulted in a population of 148 which is expanding its range rapidly.

The closest living relative is the golden takin *(Burdorcas taxicolor)* — a goatlike animal of the Himalayas. The muskox evolved on the Siberian tundra about 3 million years ago and emigrated across the Bering land bridge around 110,000 years ago. Two populations became separated during the Wisconsinan glacial advance. One survived south of the glacier in the northern United States as far south as Kansas, while the second lived in a northern ice-free refugium on Ellesmere Island and Greenland.

Food Muskoxen are both grazers and browsers, feeding on grasses, sedges, and forbs, as well as such shrubs as willow and crowberry. A herd wanders slowly through river valleys and meadows, eating only some of the available supply of plants. Feeding this way, the animals do not overgraze the range and it can be used again in the near future. During the winter months, the herd moves to hilltops and other exposed areas where the wind blows the vegetation free of snow. Extensive regions of tundra are unsuitable for muskoxen because of lack of proper forage.

Reproduction and Growth The mature bulls join the herd of cows, young bulls, and yearlings during midsummer, and the rut occurs through August and early September. The bulls smell strongly of musk at this time, which gives rise to the species' name. One or occasionally 2 calves are born 8 months later, between late March and early June, when wintery conditions (down to -40°C or -40°F) may still be present. The 12-kg (26.5-lb) calf stands in less than an hour and seeks shelter in the long coat of the cow where it nurses from 4 mammae. Green plants are nibbled as early as one week, but nursing continues for up to a year and a half. In areas of poor to average forage, cows give birth only once very 2 years, but annually on good range. Following a severe winter, females may not come into heat at all in autumn. Female muskoxen become sexually mature at 2 years old if well nourished (one year in captivity), 4 to 5 years if in poor condition. Males begin breeding after 5 years. Individuals may live 23 years in the wild and 25 years in captivity.

Remarks The muskox is kept warm, even in the coldest weather, by its magnificent coat which reaches full development at the end of the third year. The dense soft undercoat is the insulating layer, while the long guard hairs (which may reach the ground) break the wind, help shed moisture, and protect the underfur from wear. Only the lips and the nose pad are left unhaired. The hooves have sharp rounded edges and rough pads for sure footing on snow and ice. The horns, present in both sexes, are not shed like antlers, but have a bony core and continue to grow throughout life. They start growing at an age of 4 weeks and reach full size in 6 years. In males, the bases of the horns become wide and almost touch each other on the forehead. The ears and tiny tail are hidden in the fur, while the eyes are protected by the downward and forward-sweeping horns. The neck and legs are noticeably short. The large humped shoulders support the animal's heavy head.

Muskoxen have excellent senses of hearing and sight. They don't hesitate to swim across wide stretches of water and solitary individuals have been seen to enter a lake and remain there to escape attack from wolves. The species is gregarious, generally numbering 15 to 20 in winter herds and 10 in summer. A group of 100 has been reported, representing a temporary merging of several herds. The bulls are often solitary or keep to small bachelor herds from spring to the autumn rut, but sometimes remain with the cows and young for much of the year. During the breeding season one dominant bull will aggressively drive away his competition for the right to lead and mate with all the adult cows of the herd. A cow will assume control of a herd in the absence of a bull.

When unharassed, muskoxen move at a slow deliberate pace, covering one to 10 km (0.6 to 6.2 mi) in a day. They remain bedded down during severe arctic storms. Sometimes a herd moves long distances over the sea ice to colonize another island. Usually the summer and winter ranges are less than 80 km (50 mi) apart. In winter, the animals paw craters in the snow to reach their food, but icing and deep snow conditions often result in decreased feeding activities leading to a net loss of energy. In fact, for 6 to 7 months of the cold season, muskoxen continually lose weight and must regain their health and body fat content during the brief summer. Below a temperature of -40°C (-40°F) individuals must increase their heat production, in spite of wearing one of the best insulating coats in the animal world. Yearlings suffer the most during initial winter periods, for they are no longer nourished and protected by their mothers, and are outcompeted by the adults at the best feeding sites.

Over countless ages the muskox has provided northern people with meat, hide, fur, sinew, and horn (for utensils and bows). Other mortality factors include starvation (whole herds may succumb), wolf and grizzly predation (often as high as 50 percent of the muskoxen in a region), and accidents such as drowning, falling, and fighting. Though circle formation of a herd provides considerable defense against wolves, it is a poor strategy for human hunters. With dogs holding a herd at bay, native people were able to advance within easy range for kills with spear or bow and arrow. Later, the use of firearms wiped out whole herds. The Canadian government placed a ban on hunting in 1917, and numerous populations have since been reestablished. In 1969, the Northwest Territories government opened the first muskox hunt to the Inuit of Grise Fiord on Ellesmere Island, and elsewhere a quota system is now in place. However, northern

MUSKOX

development and resource extraction have resulted in new problems for muskoxen. Harassment by people in aircraft, on all-terrain vehicles, and on foot cause stampedes away from the few areas of optimum habitat, sometimes leading to the death of weakened animals and abandonment of calves not strong enough to keep up. Recently muskoxen have become economically important in some regions as a trophy animal, as a tourist attraction, and for wool sheared from captive animals. I have never been fortunate enough to study these majestic creatures in the wild, only in zoos. However, several of my friends have recounted their observations of muskoxen in the high arctic. One of them, a photographer, approached a herd too closely and was charged by a bull. Luckily, he retreated in time and the bull chose not to pursue him.

GRAY WOLF

Scientific name *Canis lupus*
Family Wolves, Foxes, and Dogs (Canidae)
Order Carnivores (Carnivora)
Total length 180 cm (70.9 in)
Tail length 45 cm (17.7 in)
Weight males 50 kg, maximum 80 kg
(110 lb, maximum 176 lb);
females 45 kg, maximum 55 kg
(99 lb, maximum 121 lb)
Color Most wolves are a mixture of tan, brown, and gray, darkest along the back and white below. Black and even white coat colors occur, the latter most frequently in the arctic.
Distribution and Status The gray wolf displays one of the most extensive distributions of any land mammal. It is native to most of North America, with the notable exception of Baja California, southeastern United States (perhaps displaced by the closely related red wolf, *Canis rufus*), coastal Mexico, and Central America. The largest wolves are in the northwest part of the continent, the smallest in southeastern Canada and in Mexico (averaging 35 kg or 77 lb). The gray wolf formerly occurred throughout most of Europe and Asia north of the tropical forest. Typical habitats of this adaptable carnivore include the tundra, coniferous and deciduous forests, grasslands, and semidesert. From old historical accounts it appears that the wolf was quite common and feared by the early settlers of North America. Shooting, trapping, and poisoning for centuries have severely reduced the numbers and distribution of this species, so that most are now found in fairly remote country. Recent estimates are around 50,000, from the high arctic to Mexico. The wolf is classified as endangered in the United States (except in Alaska and Minnesota) and is also protected in Mexico. Its status is classified in a variety of ways in Canadian provinces. Occasionally government hunters are called in to reduce the wolf population due to pressure from big-game hunters and outfitters. Such political action causes quick reaction by conservationists who view wolf predation as a part of nature that should not be interfered with.

The wolf line is believed to represent an early stage of development in the family, originating from fox-like animals about 4 million years ago (in Pliocene times). These small wolves eventually crossed from North America into Asia over the Bering land bridge and evolved into the gray wolf, which later reinvaded North America. Living alongside the modern wolf species was the giant of the family — the dire wolf *(Canis dirus)* which occurred from Canada to South America. It became extinct only 8,000 years ago, probably as a result of the disappearance of the large herbivorous mammals it depended on as prey.

The gray wolf's closest relatives in North America are the red wolf, found in the southeastern United States from Texas and Kansas to Pennsylvania, and the coyote, all 3 of which may interbreed to form hybrids. The domestic dog probably arose from a south-Asian wolf about 15,000 years ago. Viewing the modern breeds of dogs, it is astonishing what has been achieved by selective breeding.
Food Wolves concentrate their hunting efforts on large mammals such as deer, elk, moose, caribou, sheep, muskox, and goat. Many other animals are taken as available, including beaver, foxes, ground squirrels, hares, mice, birds' eggs, fish, and insects. A wolf's digestive system is adapted to handling large amounts of meat at a single meal, commonly 2 to 6 kg (4.4 to 13.2 lb), but up to 9 kg (19.8 lb). Such heavy meals can be consumed several times in one day. When food becomes scarce, a wolf can usually fast for up to 2 weeks without much harm.
Reproduction and Growth Certain pairs of wolves develop a close bond and remain together for life, but lone individuals may also pair off during the breeding season. Depending on the latitude, females become receptive from January to April, with the period of heat (estrus) lasting 5 to 7 days. During the mating act, the penis swells inside the female's vagina and the 2 animals remain locked together, just like dogs, for up to 30 minutes. Around 63 days after fertilization, an average of 6 young (range of one to 11) are born blind and helpless. Their eyes open at 2 weeks and the quickly growing pups begin to play outside the den at 3 weeks, and are weaned as early as 5 weeks. The female generally remains close to them for 2 months, the family being fed by the pack. About this time the wolves abandon the den and frequent a new site called a rendezvous area, providing access to water and plenty of room for the pups to romp and develop their skills in running, hunting, and play fighting. A strong social attachment to other pack members is formed during this period. In the autumn, the pack leaves this second home of trails and beds, and wanders widely over the home range. By 10 months of age, the subadults have grown to full size and participate in bringing down large prey. Both sexes reach sexual maturity at 2 years, but most breed for the first time at 3 years. While 10 years is old for a free-ranging wolf, captive individuals have survived for 18 years.
Remarks Wolves are adapted physically for running long distances, often required to locate their prey. They walk on their toes (digitigrade) — 5 on the front foot (the dew claw does not reach the ground) and 4 on the hind foot. Unlike almost all cats, the claws are rather straight and unretractable. The beautiful fur coat is composed of long guard hairs and a dense short underfur. An extended period of molt occurs in the spring, when the animal appears rather slim without the full winter coat. There are 42 teeth in the heavily built skull, with long canines and special shearing cheek teeth (carnassials) formed by the sharp-edged fourth upper premolar and lower first molar. Powered by strong muscles the jaws rip out large pieces of flesh from the downed prey, and the chunks are swallowed whole.

Wolves usually rest in the shade during the day, for any activity in the warm sun causes overheating and panting. Hunting activity most often begins in late afternoon and the pack may wander over 30 km (18.6 mi) in search of food. One pack was reported to have traveled a remarkable 72 km (44.7 mi) in 24 hours. Most prey are discovered by their scent; chance encounters and tracking are less successful hunting strategies. The wolf's keen nose can pick up airborne scents of prey from distances as far as 3 km (1.9 mi). Individuals position themselves to stalk within close range, then rush in an attempt to overtake large animals before they can gain top speed and escape. Actual attacks are directed at the prey's shoulder, flank, or rump. Once severely wounded, most big animals enter a state of shock and stand still until pulled down by the pack. If the moose, elk, or caribou puts up a brave fight with kicking hooves and sparring antlers, the wolves may lose heart and give up. In pursuing fleeing animals, the wolves often give up the chase within one km (0.6 mi) unless their trained eyes detect signs of weakness, in which case the pack persists until they are either successful or become exhausted.

The range of a wolf pack varies with the season, density of prey, size of the pack, and type of terrain. Some populations are migratory on the tundra or on mountainsides, following their main prey or avoiding deep snow. Densities range from a high of one wolf per 8 sq km (3 sq mi) but average fewer than one per 26 sq km (9.6 sq mi). Most packs consist of around 8 individuals (often related), including the dominant pair of breeders, pups, and additional adults who breed as well. Packs have been seen as large as 36 members, but perhaps this represents a temporary union of several packs. The leadership role of the dominant male is critically important to the well-being and even the survival of the pack. Every member holds a certain level or status in the group, often exhibited when feeding, mating, or reserving space. Studies have shown a complex system of communication among wolves involving voice (howls, growls, whimpers), sight (baring teeth, lowering ears, elevation of the tail), and smell.

While cross-country skiing in the boreal coniferous forest (taiga), I once came across a most gruesome sight — a deer kill. A pack of wolves had brought down the deer and eaten everything except for a few pieces of hide and the long bones, which lay scattered and broken all over. The ground was flattened with deep paw prints, and hair and blood stained the white snow. As I stood there in astonishment, I recreated the savage scene in my mind. It was several years later before I saw my first wolves. Boating down a remote river near the Keewatin District, I looked up momentarily from watching for rocks under the water and noticed 2 large dogs following us along the nearby barren esker. Suddenly it dawned on me that they couldn't possibly be dogs. One wolf was gray, the other pure white. As the 2 bounded effortlessly over the sandy hills, I felt lucky to have witnessed such secretive and spectacular animals. The next day I caught sight of the white wolf walking along the edge of the lake where I had set my trapline for small mammals. Its coat stood out boldly against the dark spruce — a most impressive sight. At another location, in southern

Continued on p.64

Gray Wolf

Way off in the distance, a thin line of eight animals snaked across the tundra meadow, around a pond, and up a ridge. The last individual lagged behind and finally stopped in the evening shadows, panting heavily from exertion. The pack of wolves returned to the exhausted straggler, nudging her with wet noses and impatient pleas to continue the hunt. The time was early May and the female was obviously heavy with pups. After some apparent exchange of messages, the others continued on their way, their flagging tails disappearing over the top of the ridge. The female rested for a minute, then backtracked, pausing only to lap up a drink of water. An arctic loon skirted around to the opposite end of the pond, keeping a watchful eye on the wolf.

The wolf's destination lay about ten kilometers (6.2 miles) to the south, in a small grove of stunted spruce protected in the lee of a prominent hill. Although she had not visited this spot since last spring, she strode directly to her traditional den site which was tucked under the cover of several enormous lichen-covered boulders. Looking cautiously over her shoulder to ensure she was not being followed, she promptly disappeared into the dark tunnel. Her keen nose picked up the scent of other creatures that had recently sought refuge there — red-backed voles, a snowshoe hare, and an ermine. With stiff-legged strokes of her front and hind limbs she set to work renovating and cleaning the den. Intermittent sprays of sandy soil and dust flew out the entrance and from deep inside came a sneeze followed by a loud snort. Tired from the strenuous day, the wolf trotted up on top of the den and lay down on the cool moss. In a minute she was asleep with chin resting on her forepaws, but her nose and ears continued to monitor every scent and sound.

A week later, a steady two days of rain drenched the landscape and the musty odor of lichen and soil permeated the humid air. Dry inside the den, the wolf was in labor. Pup after pup appeared from her birth canal and she licked each one clean in turn. Before an hour had passed, eight blind, floppy-eared, and whimpering babies lay curled at her belly. In about one week, the pups' eyes opened, and soon after, eight balls of brown wool began playing around the entrance to the den, wandering ever-farther outside into their fascinating new world. The wolf pack returned periodically to bring the mother an arctic hare, some mice, or lemmings, but she clearly yearned to join her mate and the others on their nightly forays. Then one evening she could resist no longer, and leaving the pups in the care of another female, she ran with the pack to feed on a caribou kill about twenty kilometers (12.4 miles) away. In the ensuing weeks, the pups began to be weaned from a diet of milk. The father wolf and occasionally the other pack members regurgitated half-digested meat for the pups to devour.

One afternoon the dozing wolves heard the approaching drone of a float plane, which soon roared over the den site, sending them scurrying for cover under the spruce boughs. The next day, two fishermen left their camp for a walk and spotted the gnawed bones and hare's feet scattered around the den. They soon realized it was an active den and began looking down the entrance. The father wolf allowed himself and the others to be seen, and drew the men away from the family that had taken refuge underground. The female prepared to move her offspring, obviously nervous about being discovered. For sanitary reasons she had already planned a move to a second den. When it was dark she grasped a pup by the back with her mouth and carried it off into the night, returning a half hour later for the next youngster. The other members of the pack returned the next morning to find the den empty. This situation caused great concern and much tail wagging, as the animals searched around and around, looking for clues. The fresh scent of the mother wolf's trail soon gave the answer, and the pack bounded off to rejoin their companions.

Wolverine

In the early-morning darkness, a single closed flower of mountain avens jostled in the wind atop a gravel esker. As the sun finally rose to spread its warmth and light over the rolling tundra landscape, the flower opened its yellow petals and began tracking the sun across the blue sky. The start of another beautiful day was also heralded by a chorus of trills from longspurs, the buzzing of black flies conducting their warm-up exercises, and the slow, grazing approach of several caribou. All life seemed to bustle into activity, as if not wanting to waste a precious moment of the short growing season. When a caribou cow reached the top of the esker, the bright flower caught her attention, and she strode over to the matted plant and nibbled it.

Just then, the caribou became aware that she was being watched by several wolves, about three hundred meters (984 feet) away. Perhaps in nervousness or anticipation of being pursued, the cow relieved herself of a dozen black pellets, which showered down on the remains of the mountain avens. For two days the wolves shadowed the cow, waiting their chance, for they realized they could not outrun her. When the ambush and savage kill finally occurred, the whole dramatic scene was over within two minutes. The three wolves ate their fill, kicked lichen and moss over the carcass, and trotted off in single file, planning to return for another meal in a few days. But there would be little left to feed on, for the hot carcass was soon discovered by a wolverine. The stocky black and cream-striped animal rushed up to the caribou remains as if it hadn't eaten for a month. With great powerful jaws and teeth, the wolverine tore out chunks of muscle and belly organs, swallowing them whole. Half an hour later, the animal had devoured so much food it could hardly walk. Ambling over to the shade of a big boulder, the wolverine flopped down to digest the meal. With hundreds of black flies desperately trying to penetrate its shaggy coat, the satiated scavenger licked the blood and grease off its face, and with a paw, wiped the sticky caribou hair from its mouth.

The following day the wolverine consumed the rest of the flesh and began extracting marrow by cracking apart the long bones with its molars. Holding the slippery white leg bone with its wide front paws, the animal closed its beady eyes, angled the shaft between the back molars, and with muscles bulging on the sides of the head, clamped down and shattered the thick bone. Snorting, licking, and swallowing, as if in great haste, the wolverine literally cleaned up the whole carcass, leaving only hair and broken bones scattered over the ground.

No sooner had the wolverine curled up to sleep when the wolves bounded up the esker, eager to claim their hard-earned prize. With noses to the ground, the agitated wolves quickly figured out what had happened. In seconds one of the wolves discovered the concealed thief, and deep throaty growls warned the wolverine that it was in serious trouble. The wolves were not fond of wolverines even on neutral terms; the raiding of their food supply drove them to attack at fever pitch. The wolverine arched its back hard against the boulder and growling menacingly, bared its fangs. The wolves repeatedly feinted and drove in to bite, each attacking from a different angle. One wolf succeeded in clamping down on the wolverine's front left paw as the defender was distracted for a split second. The wolverine countered by a savage bite to the wolf's head, and the two spun apart. With one of the pack bleeding, the wolves circled around, sizing up the situation. Realizing their foe was not worth risking their further injury, the wolves departed, leaving the wolverine panting heavily and licking its wounded paw.

During the next week, the wolverine nursed the damaged foot and remained in seclusion in a nearby den, hidden among some rocks. Bones were broken and bacteria from the wolf's mouth infected the open wound. Able to walk only on three limbs, the wolverine weakened from blood poisoning and lack of food. By the time the tundra took on its autumn cloak of russet colors, the animal was still experiencing difficulty in walking. With food as scarce and temporarily available as it was in this environment, the wolverine needed to be fit to successfully forage over an enormous home range. Sometime in late winter, while sleeping in a snow bank, the wolverine's heart ceased to beat. Later, its soft tissues provided food for an arctic fox and insects, and its bones were gnawed by lemmings for calcium. The following summers, the mountain avens plant grew stronger and produced dozens of flowers, fertilized by the last remains of the wolverine. Energy from the sun had flowed from plant to herbivore to carnivore, and nutrients from the soil had returned full cycle.

GRAY WOLF *continued from p. 59*
Manitoba, one wolf successfully communicated its feelings concerning my trapping activities within its home range. The animal deposited a remarkably large pile of droppings on my equipment!

WOLVERINE
Scientific name   *Gulo gulo*
Family   Weasels (Mustelidae)
Order   Carnivores (Carnivora)
Total length   males 100 cm (39.4 in);
          females 90 cm (35.4 in)
Tail length   23 cm (9.1 in); 22 cm (8.7 in)
Weight   males 25 kg, maximum 32 kg
          (55.1 lb, maximum 70.4 lb);
          females 18 kg, maximum 22.4 kg
          (39.7 lb, maximum 49.3 lb)

Color   The wolverine is covered in glossy black and dark brown fur, short on the head, longest on the tail. The forehead and ear tips are grayish-brown, and 2 broad brown or yellowish stripes run from the shoulders, along the sides, to the base of the tail. There are often whitish spots on the throat and belly.

Distribution and Status   The wolverine is a creature of alpine and barren-ground tundra; subalpine, mountain, and boreal coniferous forests; and deciduous forests on occasion. It was formerly found over a remarkably large region — from Alaska to California, Ellesmere Island to Pennsylvania. In Eurasia it was known from Norway to Romania, eastern Siberia to northern China. Its range and numbers have been greatly reduced on both continents, and the animal is now present only in remote regions. There are still small populations in the mountains of the western United States. The North American population was long thought to be a distinct species *(Gulo luscus)*, but it is probably no more than a subspecies of the Eurasian wolverine.

Food   This powerful animal is omnivorous, but is noted most for its scavenging role in nature. It devours berries and small animals, including birds' eggs and nestlings, insects, fish, frogs, mice, ground squirrels, marmots, beaver, and porcupine. It has been known to attack and kill elk, moose, caribou, and sheep, particularly young, sick, or crippled individuals. It also specializes in cleaning up carrion of these large mammals, plus that of whales and seals along the arctic coast. In some regions it takes advantage of wolf and bear kills, and may follow the migrating caribou herds for this purpose. Its massive molars and powerful jaw muscles enable the wolverine to crack open long bones for marrow — a habit which has given rise to the nickname "hyena of the North."

Reproduction and Growth   The wolverine leads a solitary life, the 2 sexes coming together for only a short courtship. Females come into heat for one period of several days from March to October, though usually in summer. A male will attempt to mate any female (generally one to 3) that occurs on his territory. Following fertilization the embryos cease development until January — a process called delayed implantation. About 5 weeks later (February to April), 3 (range of 2 to 6) young are born, after a total gestation period of 7 to 9 months. Each weighs about 100 g (3.5 oz). The den may be dug underground in a snowbank, rocky crevice, or beneath a fallen tree. The youngsters' eyes open at 4 weeks, when the babies are covered in fuzzy cream-colored hair. They suckle milk from the mother's 4 mammae until 10 weeks of age, by which time they can swallow regurgitated food from the mother. The offspring become independent the following winter, when they have learned to hunt, cache food, and defend a territory. Females are sexually mature at one year, males at 14 months, but most do not breed until their second or third year. Life expectancy in the wild is unknown, but they have survived over 17 years in captivity.

Remarks   The stout wolverine has a reputation of toughness and great endurance. It gallops with an awkward rolling gait on short legs and wide fur-lined feet. Capable of running for hours without stopping to rest, a wolverine may cover over 50 km (31 mi) in one day, and wander over a home range of 2 000 sq km (740 sq mi) in the course of a year. These animals generally respect each other's territory which is marked in numerous places by droppings, urine, scent from the anal glands, and scratches on tree trunks. It climbs and swims well, and frequently caches food in trees, snow, or in the soil. Population densities of one individual per 200 to 500 sq km (74 to 185 sq mi) have been recorded. Never a common species, the wolverine has fared poorly in its contacts with humans. Disturbance from resource development, heavy trapping pressure, habitat and food depletion, along with a low reproductive rate have made the wolverine one of the rarest and most isolated creatures of North America.

GRAY WOLF ▢   WOLVERINE ▢

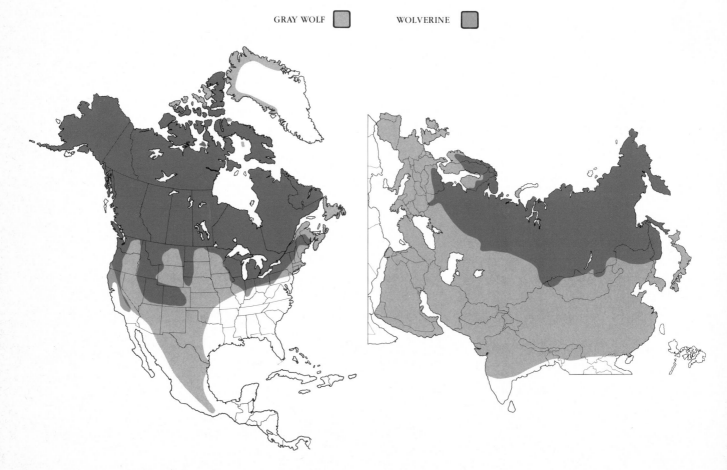

Mammals of the
Montane Forest

Mountain slopes of temperate and tropical regions are clothed in numerous types of needleleaf and broadleaf forests. With increasing elevation, the temperature drops an average rate of 1.8°C per 333 meters (3.2°F per 1,092.5 feet). In addition, higher elevations generally receive more rain and snow, a higher relative humidity, and greater winds than those below. These factors result in the formation of successive layers of communites, each adapted to a particular elevational zone. For example, climbing up the Santa Catalina Mountains of Arizona one would pass through ponderosa pine-silverleaf oak forest at 2 000 meters (6,561.7 feet), Mexican white pine forest at 2 500 meters (8,202.1 feet), white fir-Douglas fir forest at 2 700 meters (8,858.3 feet), and alpine fir-Engelmann spruce forest at 3 000 meters (9,842.5 feet). Constant heavy mist and drizzle form a cloud forest at 900 to 2 700 meters (2,952.8 to 8,858.3 feet) in areas from northeastern Mexico to Panama. Montane forest types occur at different elevations and contain different species of plants and animals on cooler and moister north-facing slopes versus hotter and drier south-facing slopes of the same mountain. Herb and shrub layers are frequently sparse and snow accumulates to many meters' depth in protected spots.

Nearby mountains may exhibit vastly different plant and animal communities depending on the direction of air masses. The western slopes of the Cascade and Coast mountains in British Columbia have cool summers, 200 centimeters (78.7 inches) of precipitation, and a frost-free period of over 200 days, due to the Japanese ocean current that warms and drenches the Pacific coast. This tall, shady rain forest consists of western hemlock, western red cedar, Sitka spruce, yellow cypress, Douglas fir, and many other species. To the east, in the rain-shadow side of tall mountains, lies the dry yellow pine forests of the Okanagan Valley, where the summers are hot, annual precipitation averages less than 38 centimeters (15 inches), and the frost-free period is about 140 days. Mountainous regions often have steep slopes and thin, rocky, well-drained soil. Conifers are adapted to these conditions, with their shallow root systems.

In the United States and Canada, two major units are recognized. The Pacific Coniferous Forest extends from British Columbia to California and boasts the tallest living tree — the coastal redwood at over 106 meters (347.1 feet). The Cordilleran and Rocky Mountain Coniferous Forest is characterized by yellow pine, the bristlecone pine — the oldest living thing at an age of up to 8000 years — and the giant sequoia — the world's most massive organism. The Montane Forest Biome is sometimes combined with the Boreal Forest Biome under the Coniferous Forest Biome. Mammals living at high elevations develop large lungs and heart, and their blood contains additional red blood cells and hemoglobin — all adaptations to the thin air.

Common herbivores are the mountain sheep, mule deer, American elk, golden-mantled ground squirrel, porcupine, pine siskin, and spruce grouse. Carnivores and insectivores include the grizzly, black bear, cougar, red-breasted nuthatch, and mountain bluebird. The mountain pine beetle, spruce budworm, ants, and butterflies are abundant.

American Shrew-mole

All afternoon a heavy mist drifted through the coastal forest of giant redwoods and Douglas fir — among the biggest living things ever to inhabit the earth. At the base of a colossal fir, and hidden under gracefully arching ferns, the brown soil shuddered slightly as a little black creature burrowed its way along, just below the surface. Suddenly a black scaly palm with long claws reached out and pushed aside the debris. Then out popped a long pink snout with the nostrils opening on each side. This strange nose worked its way up and down and sideways for a few seconds before the rest of the shrew-mole emerged completely. Resembling either a big shrew or a tiny mole, the animal began moving slowly over the ground. "Tap-tap-tap," its nose poked among the leaves and needles, as the shrew-mole shuffled along on its front knuckles. Only a white patch of skin was visible where the eyes should have been, and no ears extended through the fur. Even a neck was lacking, as the front limbs appeared to grow right out from the sides of the head. Guided by the thin snout and a barrage of whiskers, the animal investigated everything it encountered, perhaps searching for an insect or spider to eat. Finally contacting an enormous fallen log draped in a sheath of green moss, the shrew-mole couldn't resist the temptation to explore it to its end.

A gentle breeze ruffled the shrew-mole's sleek coat and water droplets began to condense on the hair tips. Finding nothing of interest in its three minutes of rambling, the creature dug down in the loose peaty soil and promptly disappeared, the thick, bristly tail being the last to slip down the hole. Tired from its adventure, it curled up for a ten-minute nap, but even in sleep the animal continued to twitch nervously. The long whiskers, which lay in contact with the soil, began to vibrate ever so slightly. Some bigger creature was coming this way. The shrew-mole awoke with a start, but remained motionless in its short burrow. All was quiet for awhile, then a scraping sound became progressively louder until a big coast mole burst into the tunnel. The shrew-mole froze in fear as the mole perceived its presence. Angered by the discovery that its territory had been invaded by this musky-smelling shrew-mole, the coast mole snapped its long jaws which were lined with an impressive array of sharp teeth, and shoved at the shrew-mole with its spade-shaped, clawed hand. An exchange of high-frequency whistles quickly informed the little traveler that it had strayed too far. Retreating as fast as possible, the shrew-mole backed out of the open hole and onto the surface again, whereupon it scrambled with surprising agility into the branches of a low shrub. Loath to leave the security of its burrow system, the coast mole was content to block the open passageway and to continue on its way below ground. After shaking for ten minutes in the shrub, the vanquished shrew-mole completely forgot about the incident, backed down, and went below for another snooze.

Such encounters on the forest floor were frequent, involving not only these two species but also Trowbridge and Pacific shrews. The ground was honeycombed with their burrows which were extended continually as the insectivores searched for worms and grubs. Each took advantage of this subway system, not differentiating or caring whether the tunnels were of their own construction or not. Nips, pushing, and twittering generally solved the soil war and serious injuries were rare.

AMERICAN SHREW-MOLE

Scientific name *Neurotrichus gibbsii*

Family Moles, Shrew-moles, and Desmans (Talpidae)

Order Insectivores (Insectivora)

Color The coat is black or dark gray, interspersed with silver hairs.

Total Length 120 mm (4.7 in)

Tail Length 40 mm (1.6 in)

Weight 10 g (0.4 oz)

Distribution and Status The shrew-mole is found along the humid Pacific coast at elevations from sea level to 2 500 m (8,202 ft) from extreme southwestern British Columbia south through the Coast and Cascade Mountain ranges to central California. It can be quite common in the moist crumbly soil of ravines and river banks in deciduous, coniferous, and mixed forests. In the south it is a typical inhabitant of the majestic redwood and Douglas fir forests, while farther north it dwells in wet forests of western hemlock, western red cedar, and Sitka spruce. The shrew-mole occasionally extends into relatively dry yellow pine forest. This is the smallest of the 7 North American moles, and is most closely related to 2 species of Japanese shrew-moles *(Urotrichus)* which inhabit mountain forests and grassland.

Food This mouse-sized mole can eat more than its own weight in worms, insects, and spiders overnight. Some vegetable matter is also accepted, and even an occasional salamander. Digestion is so rapid that food passes through its system in little more than half an hour.

Reproduction and Growth Living in a mild climate, the shrew-mole breeds once or twice a year from February to November. Most pregnancies have been recorded in the spring (March to May). The developmental period of the embryos is unknown but is probably around 22 days. A litter consists of one to 4 pink young, each averaging 26 mm (1 in) long and weighing 0.7 g (.03 oz). The nest is generally underground or in a stump and is lined with a bit of leafy material. The female nurses the offspring with milk from her 8 mammae. Most likely the young reach sexual maturity at one year of age, and survive 2 or 3 years.

Remarks As the name implies, this little mole looks like a cross between a shrew and a mole. The front limbs are not modified into outward-facing shovels as in other moles, although the claws are long and flattened for digging. Five toes are present on the short front and hind feet. There are no external eyes or ears, but the animal can probably detect the difference between day and night and it reacts to sounds. Vibrations reaching the animal through the soil are picked up by sensitive hairs and nerves distributed on the head, tail, and body. Vocal communication is achieved through a faint twittering and perhaps high-frequency calls as in shrews. The tail is ringed with rows of scales and is bristly, thick, and constricted at the base. The long thin skull has 36 sharp teeth for cutting up prey into pieces small enough to be swallowed.

The shrew-mole digs through the loose soil with alternating strokes of the front limbs. The excess soil is packed along the sides of the burrow and is not dumped on the surface into a mole hill. Also, the exit holes are left open, which is most unusual for moles. Perhaps this habit is related to the greater surface activity of the shrew-mole; the creature can more easily find its way back into the tunnel system. Burrows are shallow (under 30 cm or 11.8 in), since most of the mole's prey inhabits the upper soil layer. This seems to be a relatively social insectivore, with individuals frequently using each other's tunnels. The shrew-mole does not hibernate but is active day and night, interrupted frequently by short rest periods. It forms part of the diet of hawks, owls, raccoons, skunks, and snakes.

I first came across this strange small mammal in the dripping wet forests of British Columbia. As I set a trapline I felt as tiny as an ant under the towering hemlock, cedar, spruce, and fir. Logs as high as 2.5 m (8.2 ft) blocked my way along the ravines, so I had to crawl under or walk around them. The next morning I discovered that 10-cm (3.9 in)-long slugs had set off some of the traps, however numerous Cascade deer mice had been caught as well as 2 shrew-moles. It is one thing to learn about an unusual animal from a picture or film, but to have the chance to examine it firsthand was really exciting. Years later I was fortunate to collect several more specimens along the edge of a beautiful forest of redwoods in California. These primitive-looking creatures, the huge ancient trees and fantastic growth of ferns, and the misty air gave me a feeling of stepping back into prehistoric times.

GRIZZLY BEAR

Scientific name *Ursus arctos*

Family Bears (Ursidae)

Order Carnivores (Carnivora)

Total length 200 cm (78.7 in)

Tail length 8 cm (3.2 in)

Weight males 260 kg (573.2 lb); females 170 kg (374.8 lb) Northern bears are much larger: 453 kg, maximum 780 kg (998.7 lb, maximum 1,719.6 lb); 320 kg, (705.5 lb)

Color The grizzly is usually some shade of brown, but can vary from almost white to brownish-black. There may also be different color patterns, such as light patches on the throat, back, and head. Cream-tipped guard hairs give some bears a frosted appearance. The hair is not glossy like that of the black bear.

Distribution and Status The grizzly, or brown bear as it is sometimes called, formerly covered half of North America west of Hudson Bay, Minnesota, and Texas. It ranged from the arctic coast as far south as central Mexico. While now mainly restricted to mountain meadows, subalpine forests, and the tundra, it used to be common on the prairies. The animal is presently found from Alaska east over the barren grounds to Hudson Bay, and south in the Rockies to Idaho. There are only 1,000 grizzlies left in the United States south of the Canadian border, down from 100,000 in the 19th C. Only 30,000 are left in western Canada and Alaska. Its distribution in Europe and Asia has also decreased tremendously (100,000 remain), although it used to occur over the entire forested region from the British Isles to Japan and from northern Siberia to north Africa, the Himalayas, and China. The grizzly was a relatively recent immigrant to North America, crossing the Bering land bridge at the end of the Ice Age. In fact, it was confined to ice-free areas of Alaska until the glaciers melted back, freeing the bear to expand its range over the western interior of the continent. Fossil records are known from as far east as Ohio and Kentucky. There are 5 other species in the genus *Ursus* including the polar bear and black bear of North America and 3 species found throughout Asia.

Food This bear, like most members of its family, is omnivorous, meaning it eats a wide variety of both plants and animals. Over 200 kinds of plants have been recorded in the diet, with favorites being pine nuts and cranberries. On emergence in the spring, the grizzly survives on its fat until plants start to grow. It grazes on grass and other herbs, and then turns its attention to berries in the summer and fungi and seeds in the autumn. Insects, mice, ground squirrels, marmots, and plant roots are dug from the ground, fish are snapped out of the

AMERICAN SHREW-MOLE

waters with the jaws, and big mammals such as elk, deer, moose, mountain sheep and goats, and caribou are actively hunted or scavenged if found dead.

Reproduction and Growth Grizzlies pair up for several weeks to a month prior to the breeding season of May to late July, but both sexes may mate with other individuals, even in the same day. The mating act varies from 10 to 60 minutes. The embryos cease development until October or November, so that they may be born from 180 to 266 days later, usually in February (January to March) while the female is hibernating in the winter den. The average litter is 2 (range of one to 4) and the young are the size of kittens and weigh about 0.5 kg (1.1 lb). At first blind and naked, they do not appear out of the den until 4 months old and then begin to eat foods other than their mother's milk. Weaning occurs from one to 2 years. The female aggressively defends her offspring, particularly from large male grizzlies that would likely kill and devour the cubs if found alone. Females often begin to mate at 3.5 years of age, but generally don't produce their first litter until 5.5 years. They give birth every second or third year up to age 25. Males begin to mate from 3 to 6 years of age. Grizzlies have lived 30 years in captivity, but 6 to 10 years is common for wild animals.

Remarks The grizzly is the largest and strongest land-dwelling carnivore in North America. A few individuals, particularly from the Alaska coast, may reach over three-quarters of a t (0.8 ton). Throughout their wide range grizzlies vary so much in size, color, and even shape of the face, that they were once thought to represent many species. This animal has a thick body, highest at the

shoulders, and an almost unnoticeable tail. The claws are remarkably long, up to 15 cm (5.9 in), but they wear down each summer from walking and digging in rocky ground. Thick pads on the feet cushion the animal's heavy weight, and allow it to stalk with hardly a sound. Though clumsy looking, the animal can gallop at speeds approaching 60 km (37.3 mi) per hour — far surpassing the fastest people and quick enough to overtake large mammals on rough terrain. The grizzly relies most on its keen sense of smell in detecting food and other animals (including people) that may be nearby. Its hearing ability is less developed than the large animals it hunts, and its eyesight is poor.

While generally leading a solitary life, grizzlies are sometimes seen in groups of over 100 when attracted to acorns, fish, or some other abundant food. Population density averages one per 20 sq km (7.4 sq mi) but may range from one per 1.5 to 150 sq km (0.6 to 55.5 sq mi). The animal may be active any time of the day or night, but often beds down during the middle part of the day. This bear is quite a traveler and can easily cover 25 km (15.5 mi) in 24 hours. While most bears find sufficient food resources to maintain themselves in a home range of 50 to 600 sq km (18.5 to 222 sq mi), others forage over 2 600 sq km (962 sq mi) in their lifetime. Surprisingly, the grizzly is not territorial over denning and resting sites or food resources. Even an aggressive bear at a carcass will defend it only as long as it is hungry. These bears put on over 100 kg (220.5 lb) of fat in the autumn and enter a deep sleep from late October to early May in the north, though animals formerly living in the southern range remained active all year.

Human interests of hunting, recreation, ranching, agriculture, and resource extraction brought inevitable clashes with grizzlies, much to the detriment of the animal. This huge, unpredictable predator and people are clearly incompatible as evidenced over the centuries in Eurasia as well as in North America right up to the present time. There have been a number of terrible maulings and deaths of people whose only mistake was to camp, hike, or work within grizzly range. Experts on bear behavior have repeatedly pressed for improved public education and the separation of recreation and commercial interests from areas frequented by grizzlies.

While camping on a remote lake in the Yukon, a colleague and I unknowingly walked within 10 m (32.8 ft) of a large grizzly that was napping in a thicket. It was only after we climbed part way up the mountainside and sat down to catch our breath that we saw the giant animal emerge from the thicket beside the lake and move across the alpine tundra at a remarkable speed. The grizzly stopped to scratch its belly by bending down an 8-cm (3.2-in) aspen sapling with its chest, and then moving back and forth over the stem and branches. Unconcerned by our presence, the bear remained in the valley during our week-long stay. The powerful creature was never far from our thoughts as we went about our research. I cannot say I slept well, knowing that the bear might be a short distance from my head, with only canvas separating us. Occasional bouts of sudden snoring by my companion certainly added to the tension.

GRIZZLY BEAR

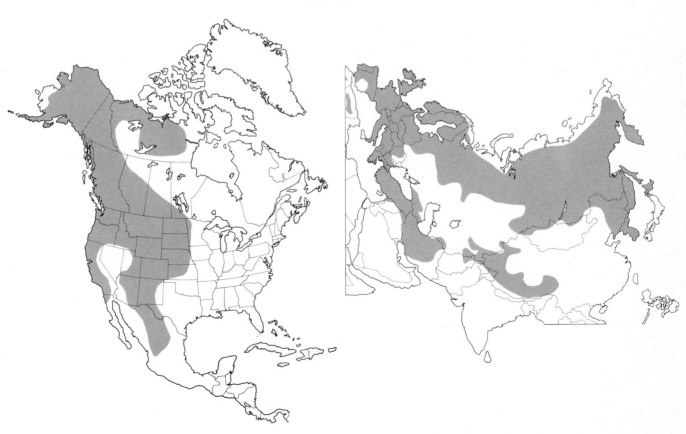

Grizzly Bear

The two-year-old grizzly finally broke its long winter sleep and crawled out of its underground den. Located on the mountain's north slope, the area surrounding the den was still covered with snow. The young bear would now lead a solitary life, for his mother had abandoned him and his sister the previous autumn. Moving at an unhurried pace toward the valley below, as if still half asleep, the animal came across a steep slope which he slid down on his furry rump. Next he found a sunny spot to soak up the sun and rest his shaky leg muscles. With the massive head lying on his front paws, he drifted into slumber, snoring loudly. Two days later the grizzly reached the valley where only patches of snow remained. He was hungry after the six-month sleep, but there wasn't much to eat. For the next month the bear would have to live mainly off his body fat and an occasional meadow vole. With the warming temperature and longer days, grass and other plants began to grow, and the bear nipped off buds and leaves with his front incisor teeth and tongue. Since his stomach was unused to such green food, the meals passed through him rather quickly.

One evening a breeze carried such an exciting scent that the big bear rose up majestically on his hind feet. His rubbery keen nose then led him on a two-kilometer (1.2-mile) search for the carcass of a moose that had died in late winter. The bear used his long pointed canines for grabbing onto the carcass and he dragged the heavy animal by backing up slowly into a secluded thicket. Bracing himself while standing directly over the animal, the bear ripped open the thick hide with his front teeth so he could reach the liver. The sharp premolars on the upper and lower jaws cut off hunks of flesh like a pair of scissors, while the flattened back molars worked them into softened pieces ready for swallowing. Each night the bear returned to feed on the moose, being careful to cover it with brush before leaving. This helped protect the smelly remains from other scavengers and the hot sun. The grizzly was always hungry and couldn't even pass up mice, insects, grubs, or ants that he uncovered by raking the grass and soil with his long claws, or by flipping over rocks with an outward swipe of his paw. His favorite snack was the fat hoary marmot, but he had to work hard at digging the animal out of rock piles.

By late spring, the grizzly had wandered about ninety kilometers (56 miles) from the den. His worn winter coat began to itch terribly and the animal rubbed his sides, back, and belly against boulders and white aspen trunks to scratch off loose patches of fur that he couldn't reach with his claws. Gorging all summer, the big brown bear gained over a kilogram (2.2 pounds) per day and continued to grow in size and strength. Even the black bear ran from his path as he roamed over the mountain meadows. But big as he was, he couldn't resist acting like a cub again every once in awhile. When no one was looking he galloped around in circles, rolled over on his back and kicked the air, then rocked back and forth while holding his hind feet with his front claws.

Throughout the autumn the grizzly spent most of his time looking for food. He frequently joined several other bears that gathered in the open forest to feed on a bumper crop of whitebark pine nuts. These oil-rich seeds were quickly converted into fat, which was clearly evident when the animal tried to run. When he charged another grizzly that came too close, ripples ran down his thick hide of skin and blubber. In October, after months of molting and regrowth, the fur coat regained its full pile and insulating qualities. With the shortening days, cooler weather, and disappearance of reliable food sources, the animal became progressively sleepier. Day by day he moved higher up the mountainside forests and into the subalpine zone where he somehow found his old den. Over twice as heavy as he was when he departed the previous April, the bear squeezed into the rocky cavern to begin his marathon six-month dormancy. His body processes slowly tuned down over the next two weeks. Heart rate and breathing dropped to almost one-half speed, and his body temperature fell by 5°C (9°F). The grizzly would remain in this state of suspended life until his mountain home became hospitable once more.

Dwayne Harty

Cougar

"You're crazy! Cougars don't live anywhere near these parts. Must have been a coyote or something." That "something" was, in Mrs. Kowalski's mind, a big cat — a very big cat. She had lived all her life on the valley farm and knew each wild animal on sight. The creature she saw last night was no coyote, deer, or bear. A terrible painful scream had awakened her and quite shaken, she drew back the kitchen curtains to view the yard. The moon cast an eerie glow over the surrounding buildings, but all now seemed quiet. She watched nervously for a minute, her heart pounding. Maybe the scream was part of a bad dream. Just as she was about to draw away from the window, some large animal moved in the shadows by the fence. A tingle ran up her neck and she swallowed hard as she strained to see the intruder. A round head with piercing yellow eyes appeared through the fence, then a long lean body. Stepping cautiously out into the light beside the haystack was an enormous cat! It moved slowly like a pale ghost, gliding without a sound on powerful legs that bulged at the shoulders. A thick rope-like tail dragged along just clear of the ground. Though still frightened, Mrs. Kowalski had to admire the majesty of her visitor. It sniffed the ground, than sat upright and looked around, flicking the black-tipped end of the tail back and forth like a giant house cat.

"But what is it doing here and why did it scream?" she thought to herself.

The dog at her side suddenly became aware of the cougar's scent, and it began to growl and the hair rose up on its back. Bark-bark!

At the sound of the dog, the cat whirled around and bolted three meters (9.8 feet) over the fence and disappeared in a flash. When she had calmed down, Mrs. Kowalski then feared for the safety of the cattle in the pasture. She went to the truck and then drove it along the road, honking the horn and flashing the lights.

The next morning she was simply amazed by the size of the tracks in the mud and the distance the creature had cleared in one jump. She called to warn the neighbors, but they didn't take her too seriously. Within a week, no one laughed at her any longer. On several nearby farms a dog was dead with a slash to its neck, a calf had been killed and partly eaten, and a horse was badly scratched right through the thick hide along the neck and rump. The local people banded together and with the help of dogs they tried to hunt the cougar down, but the big cat was nowhere to be found. Some said it was just a transient animal passing through the area. Others continued to wonder at the large rounded tracks that appeared in the snow every now and then.

It was not until the following spring that the mysterious cat showed itself again. Farther down the forested valley a farmer was cultivating his field when he noticed some creature stretched out in a freshly turned furrow. Every once in awhile the animal flopped over from side to side, as if scratching an itch on its back. The farmer continued his rounds on the tractor, once passing within fifteen meters (49.2 feet) of the animal which he was now convinced was the legendary cougar. At this close range the big cat sat up, curled back its whiskered upper lips, and snarled. Rising onto its hind legs the cougar swung its body away from the tractor and walked unconcernedly toward the woods. Fascinated by this incredible event the farmer turned off the machine and watched the animal stride away. Pausing briefly, the cougar then glanced toward the woods and growled, whereupon three spotted kittens emerged. The youngsters had been waiting obediently but impatiently under cover until their mother signaled it was safe to come out. With spring in their stocky legs and mischief on their pug little faces the kittens bounded after the adult, two of them intent on capturing the swinging black tip of her tail while the third leapt up and ricocheted off her thigh. The family finally disappeared among the trees.

The news of this most recent sighting spread rapidly throughout the valley. It seemed everyone had theories or questions on where the cougars had come from, why were they living here, and if they were dangerous to people and livestock. A conservation officer was called in to provide some answers and relieve the mounting tension in the community. At a meeting he explained that improved habitat conditions and mild winters over the last few years had resulted in an increase in the deer population. This ready source of prey and adequate forest cover must have encouraged several dispersing cougars to take up residence in the valley. He went on to explain that the cat's main foods were deer, elk, rabbits, ground squirrels, and mice, and that generally only when starving would they kill livestock. With a government offer to compensate for any such losses and the knowledge that cougar attacks on people were extremely rare, life soon returned to normal.

COUGAR

Scientific name *Felis concolor*
Family Cats (Felidae)
Order Carnivores (Carnivora)
Total length males 240 cm (94.5 in); females 205 cm (80.7 in)
Tail length 88 cm (34.7 in); 78 cm (30.7 in)
Weight 80 kg, maximum 136 kg (176.4 lb, maximum 299.8 lb); 50 kg (110.2 lb) The smallest cougars live in the tropics.
Color Adult cougars are brown (darker along the back) and white or pale brown on the underside. The muzzle, tip of the tail, and behind the ears are black. The young have a spotted coat which is replaced at 6 months of age.
Distribution and Status The cougar or mountain lion is capable of living in a remarkable variety of habitats from desert, swamp, and grassland to hardwood, evergreen, and tropical forests, from sea level to alpine treeline at 3 350 m (10,990.8 ft). The cougar has one of the most extensive ranges of any land mammal in the world, reaching the Yukon Territory and New Brunswick in the north to southern Argentina in the south. After centuries of being hunted as a feared and hated predator, the cougar had become restricted by the mid-1900s to remote, often mountainous regions of the west and the dense forests of Florida. A more enlightened view of predators brought some protection, and along with increases in deer populations the big cat has begun to recover much of its lost territory. There are thousands of reliable sight records and a number of specimens taken in the eastern part of the continent where the species was long thought to have been eliminated forever. From southern Canada to Louisiana, Oklahoma to Pennsylvania, this magnificent mammal is making an astonishing comeback.

The cougar is found only in the New World, and first appears in the fossil record in the early Pleistocene, about 2 million years ago. Recent studies suggest that the cougar and the cheetah of Africa and Asia may have arisen from a common ancestor in North America. There are approximately 37 species of cats distributed over every continent except Australia and Antarctica. However there is disagreement over their relationships at the genus level, some authorities recognizing only 2, others up to 19, most around 4 genera.

Food The cougar's favorite and most important prey is deer which it captures by ambush or by blinding speed after stalking within close range. A deer is eaten every one to four weeks, depending upon their availability. Almost any animal it can catch is devoured, from elk and moose to mice and insects. Porcupines, skunks, beaver, rabbits, domestic animals and grass are taken more frequently when white-tailed or mule deer are scarce. In the southern regions of North America red brocket deer, jackrabbits, and armadillos are prevalent in the diet.

Reproduction and Growth When cougars are ready to mate, they scream loudly to attract one another, hence the numerous reports of blood-curdling calls. The female comes into heat for 8 to 11 days in a 23-day cycle. One or more males follow the female for days, during which time the males may engage in savage fights to determine dominance and courting rights. The successful suitor mounts the female from behind and grasps the back of her neck in his powerful jaws, no doubt to protect himself. The sex act requires less than a minute

and then the two generally go their own ways. From 82 to 98 days later, an average of 3 (range of one to 6) young, each weighing around 350 g (12.4 oz), are born in a rocky den or under the cover of a thicket or fallen tree. Amazingly, births may occur any time of the year but most frequently from June to September — the period most advantageous to the survival of the young. Male cougars are driven away, for they would likely kill and devour even their own offspring. The mother feeds the kittens from her 6 teats and teaches them how to hunt and survive. For some unknown reason the cougar, as well as other cats, are not the most careful parents and cub mortality is relatively high. They are weaned to meat around 2 or 3 months, and remain as a family for one or 2 years. Generally a litter is produced every second year, but healthy females with plenty of food can reproduce each year. Sexual maturity is reached at 2.5 years for females, 3 years for males, and the maximum life span is 19 years in captivity.

Remarks Finely tuned by natural selection over a period of several million years, this large edition of the domestic cat is marvelously adapted for a predatory way of life. After a patient stalk to within close range of the prey, the cougar's great maneuverability and rapid acceleration enable it to run down deer before they attain their full speed. The impact of the cat's hard, muscular body often breaks the deer's neck. Directing the attack at the prey's head and neck with a powerful grip of the forearms, the sharp retractable claws, and 2.5-cm (1-in)-long canine teeth, the cougar can bring down a bull elk over 6 times its own weight. Yet it is nimble enough to pounce on a grasshopper or mouse scurrying through the grass.

With a narrow, long, and low torso and large padded feet the cougar slips through dense cover without a sound. Since the forelimbs are heavier and shorter than the hind legs, the animal walks with the hindquarters held higher than the rest of the body. The cat is capable of incredible physical feats — covering 13.7 m (45 ft) in one bound, leaping 5.5 m (18 ft) into a tree, and 3.7 m (12.1 ft) vertically while carrying a deer carcass in its jaws. Jumping from a tree, changing direction abruptly, or racing over rough terrain, the cougar moves smoothly and swiftly, balancing itself by swinging its long, heavy tail from side to side. The head is rounded and appears too small in comparison to the rest of the body. Short rounded ears, bright yellow eyes, and a variety of facial expressions combine with vocalizations to express emotions ranging from contentment and alertness to rage and fear. The coarse coat is surprisingly short considering the intense cold the cat experiences in some regions. The cougar swims well but doesn't appear to enjoy the water. It may be active anytime of the day or night, but is least so at midday.

In good habitat population densities may reach one per 35 sq km (13 sq mi). Home ranges vary widely, from 40 to 650 sq km (14.8 to 240.5 sq mi). Following the seasonal movements of prey, a cougar's range may shift to adjacent areas from summer to winter. The home ranges of individuals overlap considerably, except those of adult males, but the animals avoid each other, leaving their personal marks by depositing urine, scent, and droppings on a small mound of leaves and soil scraped up by the front limbs. Shelter of rocks, thickets,

or trees is sought wherever the cat happens to be, for there is no main den. Although cougars lead solitary lives, they will not remain long in a region unless others live nearby. They are capable of traveling great distances in search of new territory — a 2-month-old kitten tagged in Wyoming was found 2.5 years later in Colorado, a straight-line distance of 483 km (300.1 mi). These animals are masters at staying out of sight if they want to, and yet at other times, they will sit by the side of a road and watch cars go by without any apparent concern. This species occasionally attacks people, particularly in British Columbia and California. The animals are generally found to be young individuals recently forced away by their mother, or old ones in a poor state of health from starvation.

During the early 1970s, a concerted effort was made by a colleague of mine in Manitoba's wildlife branch to locate and record cougar sightings from this region of the midwest. At that time, the nearest cougars were generally believed to be 1 200 km (745.7 mi) to the west in the Rockies. In spite of considerable skepticism by officials and naturalists in the area, several hundred convincing sightings were accumulated. Then, on Christmas Day, 1973, several farmers went to check on a disturbance near the corral on their treeless farm not far from Winnipeg — a city of half a million people. Shooting in the dark at what they thought was a wolf or coyote near a butchered cow, the men were astonished to find a cougar dying in the snow. The first authentic record of the animal in the province, and perhaps a specimen of the endangered eastern cougar, had finally turned up in the most unlikely of places — on the edge of the prairie. With support from other people and organizations, I was ultimately able to recover the carcass of the 2-year-old cat for the Manitoba Museum. The animal was placed on public display, followed by the publication of several papers and a book based on our findings. This species quickly gained legal protection in the province and attracted wide public interest and support for its conservation.

PIKA

Scientific name *Ochotona princeps*
Family Pikas (Ochotonidae)
Order Rabbits, Hares, and Pikas (Lagomorpha)
Total length 190 mm (7.5 in)
Tail length tail insignificant
Weight 190 g (6.7 oz)
Color The pika is grayish-brown above, and whitish on the belly and feet.
Distribution and Status The pika occurs in scattered colonies on open mountain slopes and alpine meadows from elevations of 90 to 4 100 m (295.3 to 13,451.4 ft) from central British Columbia south to California and New Mexico. A close relative — the collared pika *(Ochotona collaris)* — lives farther north in Alaska, the Yukon and Northwest Territories, and northern British Columbia. Some scientists believe they are both the same species, while others group these 2 with the northern pika *(Ochotona alpina)* from Siberia, Mongolia, and Japan. A recent study described the 3 species as distinct.

About 18 or 19 species of pikas are presently recognized in the single genus *Ochotona*, all but 2 of which are found in mountains, plains, and deserts of Asia. The family is believed to have split from the rabbit family during the Oligocene (37 million years ago), with south-central Asia as the center of evolution. The order of rabbits and pikas was once thought to be most closely related to rodents, but more recent evidence suggests closer ties with even-toed ungulates (Artiodactyla).

Food The pika selects a menu of many kinds of plants, including grasses, sedges, broad-leaved species, and even woody shrubs, which the pika climbs to browse on twigs and buds. From June to October, the pika makes repeated forays (15 an hour) into adjacent meadows, and returns with mouthfuls of vegetation which are piled on top of its hay stack, up to 60 cm (23.6 in) high. There may be one or 2 main stacks, usually exposed to the drying sun, or a number of smaller ones hidden among the rocks. The cured material forms the bulk of the animal's food supply from November to May, although additional plants are reached by tunneling through the snow.

Reproduction and Growth Pikas are solitary throughout most of the year, but pair briefly during the breeding season. Mating occurs in spring and summer, so that 2 litters are produced. The embryos develop for 30 days before birth and the average number of young is 3 (range of one to 6). Some litters are born as early as March, but most appear from May to July. The 9-g (0.3-oz) young are born in a grass-lined nest under the rocks and soon commence to nurse from the mother's 6 nipples. The babies are well developed, covered in hair, and able to crawl within hours. They begin to nibble on green plants in 2 weeks and become quite playful. Weaning occurs at around 30 days when the offspring are driven away by the mother to fend for themselves. This rapid development is in tune with the short growing season of their alpine home. Pikas breed as yearlings and have a life expectancy of 5 years, but a few reach 7 years.

Remarks The pika has a blunt head with rounded ears, a negligible tail, and a thick coat of long fluffy hair. The short limbs have 5 toes with friction pads and heavily furred soles. The large incisor teeth resemble those of rodents, but there is a second pair of tiny upper incisors behind the first. A third pair of incisors is present at birth and is soon shed. A total of 26 teeth are present in the adult. Strangely, there is no scrotum, the testes lying internally and in front of the penis (as in marsupials).

Pikas are most active in the early morning and evening, but occasionally are out at night or on cloudy days. They do not hibernate and have been seen sunning themselves at temperatures as low as -17°C (1.4°F). Highly territorial, pikas live separately and inflict wounds on others that enter to raid their portion of meadow. Territories are marked by rubbing rocks and plants with scent from the cheek glands, and by sharp, brief calls. An average density in a talus slope would be 15 pikas per ha (6.1 per a), with a range of 4 to 24 per ha (1.6 to 9.7 per a). Unlike its long-legged relatives, the hares, which outrun predators, the short-legged pika seldom strays far from the cover of rocks. Predators include hawks, owls, eagles, weasels, red foxes, coyotes, and cougars.

These cuddly looking creatures are seldom seen by people because their habitats are isolated high in the mountains and generally far from roads and trails. Their ability to throw their voices is remarkable. I once stood for 20 minutes in a light rain trying to spot a pika in a pass in the Rockies. It sounded like there must have been at least 50 pikas calling above me on the rocky hillside. Although I couldn't see them, I'll bet there were only 6 or so individuals sitting motionless on the rocks, sending their bleats in every direction.

COUGAR   PIKA

Collared Pika

Pika

Pika

High in the Rocky Mountains patches of stunted trees, mosses, and grasses ran down the gray mountainsides like green stains. At the valley edges shattered rocks lay in huge piles, settling there after being plucked by erosion and gravity from the towering cliffs above. The sharp and loose ground cover made any animal crossing difficult, yet there were strange sounds coming from this rugged terrain. All of a sudden a little fluffy animal popped up on top of a boulder and sat there motionless for about ten minutes. It looked like a tiny rabbit with guinea pig ears. Finishing its rest and surveillance, down it scampered among the rocks, only to appear again where the slide met a grassy slope. The pika proceeded along a well-trampled trail through the grass until it encountered a patch of wildflowers. Cutting several with its large incisor teeth, the animal then munched away with a rolling motion of its jaws, drawing in the stems and leaves till they disappeared inside the cheeks. Some yellow pollen from a flower dusted the pika's face, causing its nostrils to open and close several times until a sneeze blew the irritating powder away. Next, the pika bent forward and picked up in its mouth three soft, dark-green pellets that had just passed from its digestive system. They were swallowed without being chewed.

Having satisfied its hunger, the pika collected a mouthful of grass and was halfway to its home in the rocks when it came nose to nose with another pika. The interloper must have realized it was not on its own territory, for it fled with great agility, closely pursued by the owner. "Bleat-bleat" they both called as the chase entered the rock slide. From the sounds of the skirmish below, the second pika was bitten sharply for its indiscretion. The first pika retraced its steps, gathered the cuttings that lay scattered on the ground, then ran back to its rocky den to add the new material on top of its private stock of hay. The mound of grass and broad-leaved plants was drying in the sun and would be fed on by the pika over the long winter. Having just completed its fourteenth excursion for hay during the morning and evening hours, the pika was exhausted. It settled down on a rock to watch the sun go down, calling periodically in answer to other pikas on nearby territories. Although the air began to chill rapidly, the rock felt comfortably warm on the animal's belly and feet.

Farther down the slope, the "bleat-bleat" calls had aroused the interest of a young cougar as it made its way around the edge of the rock slide. Stealthily it crept forward, careful not to expose its approach. With lowered ears and straining eyes the hungry cat peered over a boulder, surveying the tumble of rocks above. "Bleat-bleat!" The sounds seemed to come from various directions, but no animals were visible. The cougar shuffled its feet to steady itself as it waited for something to appear. Then suddenly the cougar was surprised to see a grayish rock roll up the hillside. The big cat sprang into action, bounding after this unusual prey. Swinging its long tail for balance, the cougar quickly closed the gap, and at the last second the little round animal dropped to safety in a crevice between the rocks. Alarm bleats of other animals echoed off the cliff, then all was quiet. The confused cat sniffed the pile of hay and black droppings. It had just encountered its first colony of pikas.

Golden-mantled Ground Squirrel and Columbian Ground Squirrel

High in the Rocky Mountains an old trapper followed an overgrown trail marked by blazes of cut bark on the pine trees. He was preparing his trapline for the winter season. Since there were no roads to his cabin, not many human visitors came his way. But he was not alone because he had two animal friends that saw him off each morning and welcomed him home in the evening. The first was a golden-mantled ground squirrel which resided under the woodpile. A rich golden-brown, with two black-edged white stripes running down the back, it resembled an overgrown chipmunk. The old man chuckled when he fed peanuts to his bold friend, for its cheek pouches bulged so widely with nuts that it looked as if it had the mumps. The rodent even tried to whistle thanks with its mouth full, though not very successfully. Off it ran with its tail held high, only to disappear into the woodpile.

Once underground, the squirrel emptied the nuts into a special chamber used only for storing food. It would need these supplies in early spring when there would be little to eat among the traces of snow. It protected its food caches and the vicinity of its burrow as if its very life depended on them each time another golden-mantled ground squirrel or chipmunk invaded the area. The warm summer days were spent sunning while perched on a log or boulder, feeding on fungi, green plants, and insects, and satisfying its curiosity about every object and movement in its surroundings. Once in awhile it stopped to lick or scratch its beautiful fur coat or to engage in a luxurious dust bath. Unlike the chipmunks in the nearby woods, the mantled ground squirrel seldom climbed into bushes and shrubs while foraging, preferring to work over the ground surface, the herb layer, and underground for its food. Wherever it traveled it left a faint personal scent from a gland situated between the shoulders. The golden-mantled ground squirrel was careful not to leave physical signs of its presence that might attract weasels or foxes; it used a toilet chamber underground and scattered the earth from the tunnels so that no mound was visible.

Not quite so fastidious was a neighboring Columbian ground squirrel. This much larger and speckled character had dug its home under the old man's cabin, and every sunny day it was sure to be found lying about on top of the mound at its burrow. As it roamed about the one-hectare (2.4-acre) meadow on its well-defined trails in search of green plants, it was never far from "plunge holes" — hidden tunnels into which the animal dashed if it sensed danger from a predator. Once underground, only weasels or badgers could threaten it. This individual liked to keep in touch with others of its kind in the nearby horse pasture, where loud, high, "chip-chip-chip" calls could be heard coming from the colony all day long. It was from this area that the ground squirrel had dispersed as a youngster late last summer. When it answered back, it chirped so hard that its tail flicked and its body jerked right off the ground. On warm summer afternoons when it felt adventurous, the rodent occasionally ran over to greet its neighbors, kissing each one in turn with its broad snout. In cold windy weather, it spent much of the day excavating a two-meter (6.6-foot) deep tunnel and nest-chamber off the main tunnel system where it would spend the winter in deep sleep.

With these two performers to keep him company, the old gentleman was seldom lonely. By sitting quietly and watching, he learned how these and other creatures made their living and survived in their mountain home.

GOLDEN-MANTLED GROUND SQUIRREL

Scientific name *Spermophilus lateralis*
Family Squirrels (Sciuridae)
Order Rodents (Rodentia)
Total length 290 mm (11.4 in)
Tail length 100 mm (3.9 in)
Weight 235 g (8.3 oz) Fat individuals may weigh up to 350 g (12.4 oz).

Color This attractive and complicated color pattern camouflages the rodent with the forest floor, especially in the autumn when brown and yellow leaves fall to the ground. The centre of the back is frosted gray, and on each side there is a long white stripe edged in black. The head, shoulders, and rump are a warm golden-brown. The underparts are creamy-white or pale yellow with gray showing through. The tail is black with a pale yellow border.

Distribution and Status This species is found on mountains and foothills from British Columbia to New Mexico, and the California coast to Colorado. In the south, a number of populations are isolated on mountain ranges surrounded by desert or plains. The animal is common in open forests of pine (yellow, limber, lodgepole), Douglas fir, Engelmann spruce, and aspen; sagebrush flats; and sometimes extends above treeline into alpine meadows and rock slides. It reaches an elevation of 4 300 m (14,107.6 ft) on certain mountain peaks. It is a common rodent, similar to the many western chipmunks in its attraction to the cover of logs and rocks, especially in logged areas. This ground squirrel has 2 close relatives in North America — the Cascade golden-mantled ground squirrel *(Spermophilus saturatus)* from the Cascade Mountains of eastern British Columbia and Washington, and the Sierra Madre golden-mantled ground squirrel *(Spermophilus madrensis)* found in the Sierra Madre Mountains in Chihuahua, Mexico. The three groups of animals look much the same and probably arose fairly recently through evolution from a single ancestral species.

Food Nuts, seeds, berries, leaves, flowers, fungi, and insects form the diet. Some of their favorite plants include pine and fir seeds, gooseberry, serviceberry, rose hips, lupine, fireweed, grass, strawberry, and dandelion. These animals spend many hours each day locating and then caching food deep underground or in shallow hiding places. They also relish animal material in the form of grasshoppers, caterpillars, beetles, and butterflies.

Reproduction and Growth The short breeding season begins in April, and extends to July (in areas with a short summer). One litter of around 5 (range of 2 to 8) babies are born about 28 days after mating. The young are first seen above ground in July, at which time they begin to add green vegetation to their diet of mother's milk (from 8 to 10 mammae). Soon after they disperse. They become sexually mature the following spring. This species seldom lives more than 4 years in nature, but captives have lived a surprising 11 years.

Remarks The golden-mantled ground squirrel is one of the most admired and characteristic mammals of the mountains. It is anything but shy around campgrounds and other sites where it repeatedly comes into contact with humans. At first a person might confuse it with a chipmunk, but its body is much stockier. The fur is soft, dense, and splashed with warm tones and bright stripes. It is active only during daylight hours, avoiding midday heat, cold and damp mornings, and rainy and windy weather. The home range is usually under one ha (2.5 a) but individuals will undertake excursions of over 300 m (984.3 ft) to reach some new source of food. Populations average one or 2 per ha (0.4 to 0.8 per a). Females with young are particularly protective of their homesite, but all individuals become upset when competitors show up near their dens and caches.

These ground squirrels construct numerous short burrows under brush piles, logs, or rocks, and are used for escape, rest, and food storage. Most are around 25 cm (9.8 in) deep and 35 cm (13.8 in) long. The main burrow, complete with a deep (below the frost line) hibernating chamber lined with dry leaves and bark fibers, may extend for 3 m (9.8 ft).

The hibernation period runs from September to April in the north and on mountain tops, and from November to late March in the south and at low elevations. The actual date of entrance is largely determined by the physiological preparedness (e.g., abundant body fat) of the animal and by cold weather. Juveniles are the last to disappear, adult males the first to emerge. Arousals occur every 5 to 16 days, with the frequency higher for adult males and for all squirrels at higher den temperatures. Requiring about 20 minutes of shaking and yawning to awaken, the squirrels remain active for a few hours to 24 hours — time to urinate, drink, and adjust various internal processes. While protected by frozen ground the squirrels are safe from predators (e.g., red fox, coyote, weasels, skunk, grizzly, black bear, and hawks), but many succumb to lack of adequate fat reserves or freezing temperatures in the burrow.

My first introduction to this charming animal occurred unexpectedly at a place called Hope Slide in British Columbia. Several decades ago a large piece of the mountainside came loose without warning and slid into the valley below, wiping out the small town of Hope and a beautiful lake. While I stood there in awe, reading the road sign and viewing the devastation still evident today, a golden-mantled ground squirrel popped out of the rocky rubble and perched, full of life and energy, on top of a gray boulder — one which had been plucked from the mountain over 1 000 m (3280.8 ft) above. The squirrel seemed to symbolize the rejuvenation of living things in the face of such natural disasters.

GOLDEN-MANTLED GROUND SQUIRREL

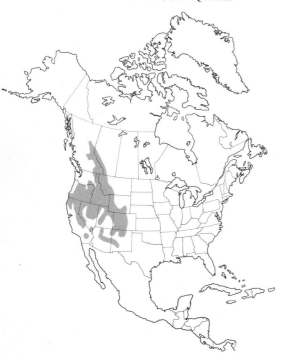

COLUMBIAN GROUND SQUIRREL

COLUMBIAN GROUND SQUIRREL

Scientific name *Spermophilus columbianus*
Family Squirrels (Sciuridae)
Order Rodents (Rodentia)
Total length 350 mm (13.8 in)
Tail length 100 mm (3.9 in)
Weight 500 g (17.6 oz) Fat individuals may weigh 682 g (24.1 oz)
Color The upperparts are grizzled light brown and black, the shoulders and sides frosted gray, the face, limbs, and belly rusty-orange, and the tail black with a pale orange border.
Distribution and Status This common ground squirrel is found in the central Rocky Mountains, from central Alberta and British Columbia south to Idaho and Oregon. It lives in open areas where the ground is light (sandy or loam) and easy to dig, and avoids packed or clay soils. The animal appears in many habitats including sagebrush and grassy plains at 230 m (754.6 ft) elevation, through grassland — spruce forest foothills, open pine flats, old burns, rocky slopes, streambanks, subalpine forest glades, and alpine meadows up to 2 700 m (8,858.3 ft). It also invades grainfields, pastures, and hay meadows.
Food This species dines on hundreds of kinds of plants such as ragweed, dandelion, lupine, strawberry, currant, gooseberry, serviceberry, glacier lily, camas, and wild onion, as well as cultivated crops (clover, wheat, oats, rye, barley, potatoes, carrots, and lettuce). Roots, bulbs, stems, leaves, flowers, seeds, and fruit are eaten. Animal material in the form of insects (grasshoppers, caterpillars, cicadas, beetles), mice, and dead fish and other carrion is not refused when available.
Reproduction and Growth The males are the first to emerge from hibernation, sometimes digging up through the snow. They are sexually developed at this time and mate with the females when they appear in April. At high elevations where spring comes later, the breeding season begins in May. After 24 days' development, about 4 (range of 2 to 7) naked and blind babies are born in a nest chamber below ground. Weighing only 9 g (0.3 oz) at first, they grow hair at 19 days, their eyes open at 22 days, they begin to appear on the surface at 25 days, and the diet changes from milk to plants at 30 days. There is only time for one litter a year. Though juveniles become full grown by hibernation time in autumn, they do not breed until the following spring. Some have lived 8 years in captivity, while few survive more than 4 years in the wild.

Remarks This is a large and attractively colored ground squirrel with relatively short ears and legs, and short, fine fur. Eyesight and hearing are keenly developed and are relied on to detect predators such as weasels, badger, coyote, red fox, bobcat, cougar, black bear, grizzly, eagles, and hawks. The rodent often occurs in extensive colonies where it leads a surprisingly sedentary life. Overlapping home ranges are only 0.4 to 0.7 ha (1 to 1.7 a) and an excursion of 150 m (492.1 ft) from the den is exceedingly rare. Males 4 years and older appear to be dominant over all other groups and can become territorial.

Burrows in hilly country are situated most often on south-facing slopes which allow early snow melt and good drainage. In level areas, one or more drains are added to the burrow system near the grass-lined nest to carry away excessive water. During the summer a deeper hibernating chamber is dug or cleaned out. The animals become extremely fat by feeding throughout the day. Perhaps due to drought and parched vegetation, some adults commence hibernation in late July and early August, while youngsters, needing more time to grow and fatten, retire in September and early October. Periodic arousals occur from 10 to 19 days throughout the winter torpor. Since little or no food is stored, the animals live off their fat. In areas with a short cold period, they emerge from late February to March, while in the north and high mountains, they appear in the snow from late April to June. Most Columbian ground squirrels hibernate for 7 to 8 months of the year.

Anyone traveling from the foothills to the mountains in the central Rockies will have an excellent chance to see these colorful squirrels standing in alert position, hunched over eating, or leaping through the grass. When approached, they dive for the cover of their dens with a warning "chur-r-r" call. Half a minute later their brightly colored faces appear at the entrance to see whether it is safe to come out again. They can become a serious pest in agricultural areas. For example, one female and her brood ate or destroyed 23 kg (50.7 lb) of wheat in 130 days, each eating up to 17 percent of their body weight in greens per day. Over 1 200 were trapped in an 80-ha (197.6-a) pasture where they were estimated to be eating as much food as 12 sheep.

BUSHY-TAILED WOODRAT

Scientific name *Neotoma cinerea*
Family New World Mice and Rats, Gerbils, and Hamsters (Cricetidae)
Order Rodents (Rodentia)
Total length 420 mm (16.5 in)
Tail length 215 mm (8.5 in)
Weight 400 g (14.1 oz). Some races are considerably smaller, weighing only 270 g (9.5 oz).
Color The upperparts are grayish-brown with numerous black hairs along the middle of the back. The undersides and feet are white. As in most members of this family, the tail is gray above and whitish below.
Distribution and Status This woodrat occupies a large region of western North America, from Alaska and the Northwest Territories in the north to California and New Mexico in the south, and from the west coast east to the Dakotas. Its elevational range extends from sea level to alpine treeline at 4 500 m (14,763.8 ft) elevation. Suitable habitats are desert scrub, sagebrush, pine forests, and spruce-fir forests — a remarkable range for a rodent. Favorite sites are canyons, cliffs, and talus slopes where the animal can hide in caves or crevasses in the rocks. Abandoned buildings and mines are used as well. About 20 species of woodrats have been described from Canada south to Central America. They are frequently common and form an important part of the mammal fauna in numerous forest, woodland, shrubland, grassland, and desert communites.
Food This species is vegetarian, selecting leaves, roots, bark, buds, fruit, and seeds from hundreds of kinds of broad-leaved herbs and deciduous and coniferous trees and shrubs. Frequent choices are cherry, aspen, rose, willow, raspberry, currant, fireweed, snowberry, and cacti. Twigs and needles of western white pine, Engelmann spruce, alpine and Douglas fir, and junipers are important fare.
Reproduction and Growth The breeding season extends from February to August, during which 2 litters are born in the south (usually April and July) and only one in the northern range (in June). Four (range of one to 6) babies, each weighing 13 g (0.5 oz), are born after 32 days development. The young hang on to the mother's 4 nipples with great vigor, even when she runs away from the nest due to some disturbance. The young soon develop a gray coat, the eyes open at 15 days, and they become active outside the den in 21 days. At one month they are weaned and soon depart. Adult weight is attained in 8 months. Both sexes first breed the following spring as yearlings. Most woodrats live only 2 or 3 years, however captives have survived for 8 years.
Remarks This animal looks like a deer mouse grown to the size of a squirrel. The fur is long and soft, and the bushiness of the tail is best developed in adult males. One notices the large eyes, naked ears, and the long whiskers on the nose. Altogether it is a rather handsome creature. Its most notable behavior is its habit of collecting items for its nest structure, which gives it the nickname of packrat or traderat. The presence of woodrats is often obvious in an area, due not only to the large domed den of sticks, but also to the nearby urine-stained rocks and piles of black droppings. The animal is careful not to foul its living quarters, though it cannot do much about fleas and other external parasites that accompany it in the nest. There are usually separate chambers for sleeping and food storage. In winter a covering of snow insulates the nest from the cold air. *Continued on p. 84*

Golden-mantled ground squirrel

Columbian ground squirrel

Bushy-tailed Woodrat

As evening fell in the Rocky Mountains, a squirrel-like animal with a pointy nose awoke in its nest, then stretched its hind legs, one at a time. For the last month this male woodrat had been living with his mate in a nearby rock pile, but she had driven him away following the birth of their young. Now that he was back at his old abandoned home, it was time to start repairing the one-meter (3.3-foot)-high structure. It needed a new lining of soft leaves and shredded bark, and several tunnels had to be cleared of fallen debris. This heap of sticks and rocks leaning against a rock wall was the woodrat's castle — where he ate, slept, stored plant cuttings, and escaped from predators. It was such a choice site it had been used by generations of woodrats, since it offered both restricted access on the rugged slope as well as a deep crack in the ground where the rodent could retire in winter. Worn runways leading to the bases of trees or trailing off through the underbrush revealed the woodrat's personal highways. About ten meters (32.8 feet) from the nest was the animal's latrine, stained white and black from decades of use. Cached neatly among the fallen slabs of rock were mounds of plant cuttings, mainly willow, aspen, and pine, which were drying for use as winter forage. The animal was evidently quite fastidious as a homemaker, for everything had to be in its proper place. In spite of preferring a solitary existence, he didn't seem to mind that a deer mouse had also taken up residence within the den. For the last two years the woodrat's curiosity and love of hoarding had urged it on a never-ending search over the rocky slopes and valley floor for unusual items to add to the nest. The collection now included a bottle, a horseshoe, an empty tin can, pine cones, and several nice bones, but still lacked that special something to crown his creation.

Before setting to work on the renovations the woodrat decided to find something to eat. He ran nimbly down the hillside and eventually came to a cabin. Climbing up the rough-hewn logs he peered in the window and observed the miner finishing his dinner by lantern light. Although the cabin smelled wonderfully enticing, the woodrat was afraid to enter. Perhaps on the way home it would be quieter

and darker. So he rambled off in the dark through the nearby meadow, guided by his big black eyes and the long touch-sensitive whiskers on his wrists and snout. The aroma of ripe raspberries stopped him in his tracks, but no sooner had he pulled over a cane and gobbled down the tart fruit, when he heard a rustling in the leaves. Every muscle tensed and his brain flashed a message to flee. Turning around, he spotted another woodrat with his mouth full of the red pulp. The two animals faced each other, teeth chattering. The resident woodrat drummed its large hind feet, then began to attack. Rather than fight, the second animal backed off, leaving the bigger male to claim this berry patch as his own, which he confirmed by rubbing his belly scent glands on the wet humus. This musky smell would last for weeks, informing other woodrats that they had better stay clear, for this area was already claimed by one who would defend his territory to the death.

With adrenalin flowing it took the woodrat ten minutes to calm down before he was able to finish his dinner. A quick wash was always appropriate after a meal, and sitting back on his haunches he stroked forward with moistened paws from behind his big ears, over his closed eyes, and down to his wet nose. On the way home, the woodrat detected the sweet aroma of horses and he picked up an interesting dried piece of manure in his teeth to add to the nest. As he arrived at the cabin he noticed it was now dark and quiet except for the occasional snore, so the rodent squeezed under the door. Jumping up on a table, the woodrat almost tripped over a most unusual item — just the shiny thing it had been looking for. The rat dropped the manure, picked up his new treasure, and headed for home. The next morning the miner, still half asleep, reached over to the table for his false teeth and was shocked to find instead the woodrat's present.

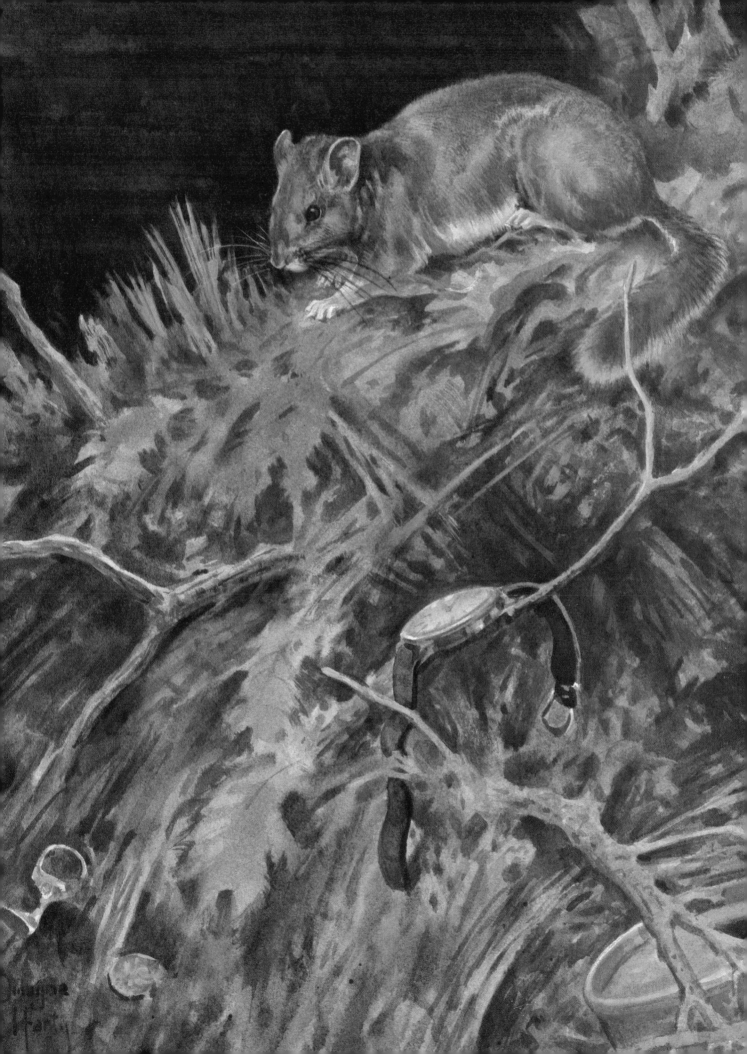

BUSHY-TAILED WOODRAT *cont. from p.81*

Outside the breeding season the bushy-tailed woodrat lives alone and is intolerant of other individuals of its own kind or other related species. The home range is only around 0.3 ha (0.7 a) and may overlap with that of an adjacent resident which sometimes results in aggressive encounters with much squealing and biting. Scars and stub tails are common among woodrats. Sometimes these animals wander quite far from their regular paths and their tracks have been seen 200 m (656.2 ft) from the den. They are swift runners as well as agile climbers in trees and rocks. Although mainly active after dark and before dawn, they are occasionally out on cloudy days. Woodrats do not hibernate but subsist on plants stored in and around the den, and by foraging. Population densities generally range from one to 6 per ha (0.4 to 2.4 per a). Woodrats are preyed upon by coyotes, foxes, wolves, martens, weasels, skunks, rattlesnakes, owls, and hawks.

The first specimen of the bushy-tailed woodrat that I had the chance to examine was one that turned up in Winnipeg, Manitoba — far east of its range. It seems this individual took a liking to a boxcar somewhere in the Rockies and then hitched a train ride across the prairies to downtown Winnipeg. On a recent trip to collect material for this book, we found one of these woodrats living among the lava outcrops and sand dunes at a picturesque desert spot along the Colorado River in Washington. The animal's fur was full of white volcanic ash (drifted in from Mount St. Helens) that lay 5 mm (0.2 in) deep on the ground. Artist Dwayne Harty soon went to work on a drawing of the woodrat's features, which formed the basis of the portrait appearing with this account.

I have collected about half a dozen species of woodrats in the southwest. Once their large nests are located it is an easy task to secure specimens. They are such strong animals that mouse traps frequently fail to hold them, and one may lose quite a few traps that woodrats drag away. These creatures construct their incredible nests out of whatever material is handy, and I have come across some formidable structures built entirely of cholla cactus. It is remarkable that the owner can dash through the tunnels without being impaled. It is always fascinating to examine what treasures woodrats have collected. I once found a golf ball on the top of one den, which may not have been so unusual but for the fact that is was far out in the Sonoran desert of Arizona.

AMERICAN ELK
Scientific name *Cervus elaphus*
Family Deer (Cervidae)
Order Even-toed Ungulates (Artiodactyla)
Total length males 230 cm (90.6 in); females 200 cm (78.7 in)
Tail length 15 cm (5.9 in); 14 cm (5.5 in)
Weight 325 kg, maximum 590 kg (717 lb, maximum 1,300 lb); 225 kg (496 lb)

Color This large deer is light brown or reddish-brown, darker on the head, neck, belly, and legs. The large rump patch may be creamy-buff, yellow, or even light orange, fading to white in winter. Newborn are light brown with areas of cream-colored spots which disappear by August.

Distribution and Status The American elk has an extensive range in North America, from northern British Columbia east to Quebec and south to California, Texas, and South Carolina. It inhabits lowland and alpine meadows (elevation of 0 to 2 286 m or 7,500 ft), marshes, prairie, aspen parkland, eastern deciduous forest, and western coniferous forest. At the turn of the century the elk's range had been drastically reduced in populated and agricultural regions and the total population on the continent was estimated at only 41,000. Several subspecies—the eastern and the Merriam elk—became extinct. The development and application of wildlife management measures have resulted in protection of the stock as well as reintroductions into almost all suitable habitat. Presently the species numbers almost one million in the United States and Canada. Surviving subspecies are quite distinctive in form and have been given common names—Tule, Rocky Mountain, Roosevelt, and Manitoba elk.

BUSHY-TAILED WOODRAT

In the Old World this species is called the red deer and it occurs from the British Isles and north Africa east to the Soviet Union, China, and the Himalayas. It has also been introduced to South America and New Zealand. The species originated in Eurasia and reached North America over the Bering land bridge during a glacial period over 130,000 years ago. Some populations crossed back again during subsequent interglacial periods. There are 10 other species in the genus *Cervus* including the fallow deer *(Cervus dama)* of the Mediterranean region, the spotted deer *(Cervus axis)* of India, and the sambar *(Cervus unicolor)* of southeast Asia.

Food The American elk is a grazer in the summer, feeding mostly on grasses, sedges, broad-leaved herbs, and mushrooms. During winter in snowy regions, it digs through the snow with its sharp hooves to reach grasses, and also browses the twigs, bark, and buds of deciduous trees and shrubs such as aspen, willow, red-osier dogwood, mountain maple, and chokecherry. When food is scarce, the needles of Douglas fir, juniper, and pine are eaten. Elk compete with cattle and sheep for forage — a concern of livestock producers.

Reproduction and Growth The rut, or mating season, begins in late August, shortly after the velvet has been shed from the male's antlers. Triggered by decreasing day length, females come into heat up to 4 times from September to November, until they become pregnant. One or rarely 2 calves are born about 8.5 months later, from mid-May to mid-June. The mother and calf live alone for the first 20 days, the youngster spending most of the time hidden. It weighs 13 to 18 kg (28.7 to 39.7 lb) at birth, can stand within hours, and milk in-

cisors and premolars have already erupted. By 3 days it gains the strength to follow its mother and on a diet of rich milk it doubles its weight by 2 weeks. Grazing begins at 4 weeks but nursing continues until 3 months of age at which time the coat has lost its white spots. Both sexes can breed as yearlings. A full set of 34 adult teeth is not attained until the age of 3 years. Elk may live up to 26 years in captivity but few survive to half this age under natural conditions.

Remarks American elk are almost always found in groups. Herds of several dozen (sometimes up to 400) females and their calves forage during the summer months, leaving the males to form their own bachelor herds of up to 6 animals. In the fall, a dominant male gathers a harem of up to 15 females along with their calves, while young males remain nearby. Following the rut the males depart, leaving the harems to merge into large winter herds, sometimes numbering up to 1,000 animals, and generally supervised by a mature female. Individuals move from one herd to another, so that a particular herd consists of different animals over time. American elk feed mainly at dusk and dawn, and retire to grassy beds during the day and night to chew on their cuds and to sleep. In some regions they may make extensive migrations (up to 90 km or 56 mi) from summer range to winter range, moving to lower valleys when snow is deep at high elevations. Average densities are 3 to 9 per sq km (per 0.4 sq mi). There are no individual home ranges, since the herd wanders widely.

Elk can swim well and often play in the shallows. They are surprisingly quick for such large animals and can gallop at 48 km (30 mi) per hour. Antlers occur only in the male and

first appear as 3-cm (1.2-in)-long nubbins on top of the calf's head. The bull's antlers begin to develop in April or May, are fully formed by August, and are rubbed free of the velvet shortly afterwards. Each antler grows to 100 to 160 cm (39.4 to 63 in) in length, develops around 6 points, and weighs up to 6.6 kg (14.6 lb). The major causes of death for elk are hunting by people, predation by cougars, wolves, black bears, and grizzlies, and from accidents (drowning, falls), disease, and fighting.

My most memorable sighting of these beautiful animals was at daybreak in the Carberry Sandhills of Manitoba — the very spot where the famous naturalist and storyteller Ernest Thompson Seton was inspired to write his *Trail of the Sandhill Stag.* At daybreak, I walked quietly over a hill and met face to face with 8 magnificent elk, standing elegantly with their long necks in a layer of morning haze. They had been nibbling on ears of corn and acted as if I had caught them red-handed. With nervous agitation, they trotted off with heads held high to the golden aspen woods, leaving deep tracks and black droppings on the sand.

On another occasion a bull elk interrupted my checking a trapline in northern California. He stared at me rather menacingly for a few moments while I glanced around for the nearest climbable tree. Then, growing bored with my interruption of his breakfast hour, the huge creature drifted off into the woods, in the direction of my line. I wisely waited for some time before intruding on his territory, especially since it was the rutting period when elk can become quite aggressive.

AMERICAN ELK

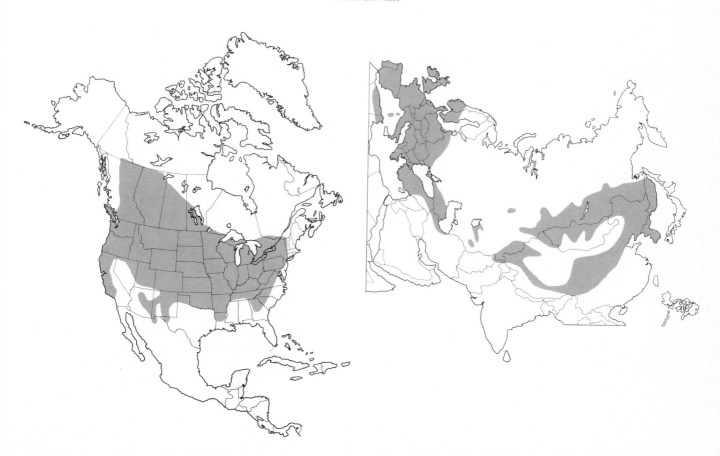

American Elk

A four-year-old elk rose from his bed in the sedges and walked slowly towards some willows, leaving a pile of rounded black droppings on the trail. Fully rested and with a surge of energy flushing through his muscular body, he began to thrash his long branched antlers against the stems. Last April two bony knobs had appeared on the top of his head. Over the summer, the knobs grew rapidly into a long main beam with six branches or points. The spongy antlers turned hard by August as blood vessels in their fuzzy skin supplied calcium and other minerals extracted from the animal's food. The heavy structures were now rubbed clean of skin and polished to a lustre from being whipped against saplings and shrubs. Though this stag had preferred the company of other males during the summer, he now felt a strong urge to join the herds of cows and their yearling calves, for the autumn rut or mating season was underway. Becoming increasingly restless, the bull roamed widely, occasionally pausing to roll over in wet holes or wallows and smudging its brown- and cream-colored coat with black mud. For several years he had eagerly attempted to court females, but larger males had always driven him off. Now that he had reached the prime of his life, he was ready to take on any rival.

At daybreak and sunset the bull's clear, bugling call and coughing grunts pierced the crisp autumn air. He stamped back and forth in full view of five cows, and when they ignored him, he trotted up to them with a great show of bravado, his majestic antlered head held high. The threat worked. Several groups of cows ran together, and in half an hour he was in control of a harem of fifteen animals. Over the next week, two other large bulls approached the herd, but they quickly retreated when the herdmaster charged. It seemed that the possession of the harem automatically gave him an advantage in out-bluffing the outsiders.

Early one morning another powerfully built bull entered the clearing where the herd was quietly feeding. With head extended he bellowed a challenge, his moist breath turning to mist in the cool air. While the cows took notice of the concert from the edge of the clearing, the two bulls became increasingly more aggressive as the distance separating them diminished. They tested each other's determination by rising on their hind legs and jabbing with vicious kicks of the front legs. Downward thrusts of the hard pointed antlers came close to striking each other's shoulders and head, but they caught the blows with their antlers like prizefighters. At one period in the struggle, their antlers locked and the strain was evident by their bulging neck and leg muscles, and by the heavy snorting. A look of wild fury and confidence exuded from their glaring eyes. Pushing and twisting with heads lowered almost to the ground, the two giants tore up the sod with their sharp hooves. The knocking of antlers rang through the forest. For fifteen minutes neither had the upper hand. Then the outsider, backing up under the momentum of a charge, lost his balance slightly on a section of exposed bedrock, and he used the opportunity to suddenly break free and trot off. Breathing deeply, the herdmaster walked back on shaking legs to reclaim his harem. Only now did he become aware of pain coming from several bruises on his neck and shoulders. The challenge was over for the moment, but there would be other rounds to come over the next few weeks. He was kept so busy defending and mating with his cows that he had no time to rest or eat. By the end of October he was exhausted and thin, while the cows were sleek and fat — in much better condition to face the long winter ahead. But he had successfully and unknowingly completed his most important task in life — fathering the next generation.

Mountain Beaver

Chewing sounds were coming from a dense thicket of blackberries and salmonberries growing along the steep banks of a creek. The shrubs quivered, then parted, and out crawled what looked like a giant brown mouse. This strange animal, called the mountain beaver, had just finished an early morning snack of juicy plants and now sat on its haunches to wash its face and ears with its paws. It sensed the dropping air pressure signaling an approaching storm, but rain was of no concern to this moisture-loving creature. The mountain beaver bent over a crystal clear pool for a drink, then ambled down the rocky creek bed and disappeared into a hole in the bank that was only big enough to allow the passage of its fat rounded body. The burrow ran just below the surface and opened up here and there under logs and ferns. Well-worn runways in the undergrowth and leaf litter revealed where the heavy animal had traveled repeatedly to reach new feeding areas. Hikers on a nearby pathway, who had never seen or even heard of a mountain beaver, were left wondering what animal could have made all these signs.

The mountain beaver knew its home range so well, both above and below ground, that it could easily find its way without using its tiny eyes. Guided by touch-sensitive whiskers on the head and by its own musky scent, the animal was at home anywhere in the maze of trails and tunnels. Active mainly at night for several hours at a time, it cut ferns and other soft green plants and piled them neatly on the ground to dry. Later, this crop would be cached below ground for winter use, since it would be more difficult to travel far in snow tunnels to reach these areas. The animal had also carefully prepared a nest chamber filled with ferns and lined with soft plant material. A nearby drain carried off excess water from torrential downpours that occurred now and then. It had taken two years to prepare its living quarters and memorize the home range, and the big rodent was quite comfortable and secure in its familiar surroundings.

The mountain beaver liked to forage for a couple of hours and then retire for a snooze, maintaining this sequence of activity and rest whether it was night or day in all seasons. One afternoon its slumber was broken by strange vibrations in the ground, and a bad smell reached its nostrils through the open tunnels. Afraid of the noisy monster outside, the rodent began to shake, grind its teeth, and whimper while sitting in its bed. Suddenly the animal and its nest were picked up by an enormous steel shovel, carried across a clearing, and dumped down the bank. Unhurt but terrified, the mountain beaver dug itself free, squealed, and ran as fast as its short legs could carry it along the creek channel, where it sought refuge in another mountain beaver's den. It was safe here for a while, but the neighbor was not overly friendly and growled repeatedly. The next day the outcast retraced its steps back home and tried to locate some familiar landmark, but the site had totally changed. Secret trails, tunnels, den, and food stores were all gone, and the area was covered with gravel. This part of the forest would now be used for the temporary shelters of people. A busy campground was no place for a nervous mountain beaver who needed quiet and seclusion. Rising on its hind feet for one last look around, the puzzled creature turned away and waddled off down the creek in search of new quarters.

MOUNTAIN BEAVER

Scientific name *Aplodontia rufa*
Family Mountain Beaver (Aplodontidae)
Order Rodents (Rodentia)
Total length 350 mm (13.8 in)
Tail length 25 mm (1 in)
Weight 1.2 kg, maximum 1.8 kg
(2.7 lb, maximum 4 lb)

Color The dense dark-brown coat is formed of a thick underfur and long sparse guard hairs. It is slightly grayish on the belly and a white patch is present under the ears. The young have grayish fur the first year.

Distribution and Status The mountain beaver occurs in the Coast and Cascade Mountains from southern British Columbia to northern California (as far south as San Francisco Bay), and the Sierra Nevada Mountains of northwestern California and adjacent Nevada. Although its recent range is quite restricted, one million years ago it ranged over most of the western states. The animal prefers stream banks and moist sites in forests and meadows from sea level to treeline up to 2 957 m (9,700 ft). Newly logged areas with new succulent growth are particularly attractive sites. The mountain beaver is the only living member of a primitive family of rodents native only to North America. It likely survived to this day because of the relatively constant and favorable conditions of its west coast environment. The species is still quite common in some regions.

Food This species spends much of its nightly active periods munching on tender green plants such as sword and bracken fern, grass, forbs such as skunk cabbage and nettles, and shrubs like salmonberry, red huckleberry, red alder, ocean spray, and willow. It actually devours less than half the plants it cuts and stores because much of it turns moldy and decays. During the winter it burrows under the snow or climbs into trees for bark, leaves, and buds of trees such as bigleaf maple, hemlock, fir, and cedar. It also nibbles on dried vegetation stored underground from the summer-time. It has been known to eat its own green droppings, obtaining extra nutrients during the food's second passage through the digestive tract.

Reproduction and Growth Like most underground animals that are subject to relatively low predation, the mountain beaver has a low rate of reproduction. Males are ready to mate from late December to March and aggressive individuals are the most successful breeders. Females come into heat for a short period in February or March. Four weeks following fertilization of the eggs (late February to April) 2 to 6 babies are born in an underground den. Each weighs about 27 g (one oz), hair develops by day 7, and the eyes open at day 10. The offspring nurse from the mother's 6 nipples and grow at a rapid rate. Weaning occurs at 8 weeks when they emerge from the tunnels for the first time. By autumn they are almost full grown and depart on their own course, generally taking up residence from 100 m to 2 km (328.1 ft to 1.2 mi) away from their mother's home. These animals do not breed until 2 years old. The average life span is 5 years but some reach the ripe old age of 10 years.

Remarks Considering its many adaptations for an underground life (short strong limbs and long claws for digging, tiny eyes and ears, small tail, and tubular body), it is surprising that this creature can climb into bushes and the lower branches of trees to a height of 7 m (23 ft) to reach leaves and bark. It swims well and frequently crosses creeks and walks through flooded tunnels. The movement of loose soil is handled much like a pocket gopher — pushing it ahead with the front feet, shoulders, and chest, and sometimes shoving it along with the head. The burrow system may extend for 100 m (328.1 ft) with an opening every 6 m (19.7 ft) or so. Tunnels descend usually no deeper than 1.2 m (3.9 ft) and end in 5 kinds of chambers — nesting, feeding, refuse (debris or decayed food), toilet, and earth (excess earth and stones). The home range of moun-tain beavers is remarkably small, ranging from .03 to 0.2 ha (.07 to 0.5 a). Most activity occurs within 25 m (82 ft) of the nest site. A number of individual home ranges may overlap, but only the burrow system is defended. Average densities are 6 to 9 animals per ha (2.4 to 3.6 per a) and may reach as high as 75 per ha (30.4 per a) in choice sites. The species seems to occur in colonies even though each individual prefers to live on its own. In fact, many adults, particularly males, are scarred from fighting their territorial disputes.

The mountain beaver has 22 teeth which fortunately continue growing throughout life. A non-growing set would soon wear away with abrasion from soil incidently taken in with plants. Large amounts of food must be consumed because of its fairly low nutritional value. The digestive tract is large and may account for almost half the weight of the animal. Living under relatively constant conditions of temperature and moisture has resulted in some unusual features of the animal's body functions (physiology). It begins to overheat at an air temperature of only 29°C (84.2°F) and dies within a few hours at 32°C (89.6°F). The relatively primitive kidneys are unable to concentrate urine, therefore considerable water must be taken in either by eating moist foods or by drinking. The limited ability to regulate body temperature and the need for moisture in both food and in the air of the burrow system probably limit the mountain beaver's distribution to cool areas of high rainfall (up to 350 cm or 138 in). Though typically found on wet secluded mountain slopes, it sometimes invades people's vegetable gardens. Damage and loss of conifers by foraging mountain beavers has been estimated in the millions of dollars annually, so trapping programs have been put in place to destroy the animals. When out of its burrow the unwary mountain beaver is easily captured by skunks, mink, foxes, coyotes, cats, and owls.

I have not yet met this unusual character in the deep woods of the western mountains, but

MOUNTAIN BEAVER

MOUNTAIN GOAT

I shall continue to look for it. The animal's haunts among the tall stately trees, steep banks leading to clear brooks, spongy damp soil, and still humid air make the search well worthwhile. One develops the feeling that this kind of forest has always been here — a perfect place for the world's most ancient living rodent.

MOUNTAIN GOAT
Scientific name *Oreamnos americanus*
Family Cattle, Sheep, and Goats (Bovidae)
Order Even-toed Ungulates (Artiodactyla)
Total length males 180 cm (70.9 in);
females 148 cm (58.3 in)
Tail length 12 cm (4.7 in); 11 cm (4.3 in)
Weight 85 kg, maximum 136 kg
(187.4 lb, maximum 300 lb);
62 kg (136.7 lb)
Color Mountain goats have long creamy-white fur with scattered brown hairs on the back and rump. The winter coat appears yellowish by spring. The lips, nose, eyes, horns, and hooves are black. The kid has a grayish-brown stripe along the back.
Distribution and Status Mountain goats are native to the Rocky, Coast, and Cascade mountain ranges at elevations of 1 500 to 3 400 m (4,921.3 to 11,155 ft) from Alaska and the Yukon south to Oregon and Idaho. The range is not continuous and is restricted to alpine meadows, talus slopes, and exposed outcrops of rock supporting a rich growth of forbs and stunted subalpine fir-beargrass at treeline. This goat has been introduced to several Alaskan islands, the Olympic Peninsula of Washington, Montana, Colorado, Nevada, Utah, and the Black Hills of South Dakota. Remote and rugged terrain make accurate census-taking of mountain goats especially difficult, and total estimates vary from about 50,000 to 100,000. In spite of the name "mountain goat," this animal is not really a goat but a member of the goat-antelope tribe, related to the chamois *(Rupicapra)* of European mountains and the goral *(Naemorhaedus)*, serows *(Capricornis)*, and takin *(Budorcas)* of Asia. Its ancestor crossed the Bering land bridge sometime in the mid-Pleistocene and survived the last Ice Age in the western mountains of the United States.
Food Mountain goats feed on grasses, sedges, rushes, ferns, mosses, lichens, broad-leaved plants such as lupin, vetches, cinquefoil, and low shrubs like huckleberry, currant, and bearberry. When these types of plants are largely unavailable in winter the animals eat more buds and twigs of shrubs and trees such as willow, subalpine fir, and ponderosa pine. The goats will travel long distances to reach salt licks which provide sodium and other minerals.
Reproduction and Growth The rutting period is from October to early January, during which period the males join the small herds of females. A male becomes possessive and will fight other intruding males with swipes of its horns. They do not butt heads as do sheep. The females come into heat for 2 or 3 days, and 180 days after fertilization, usually one young is born from mid-May to mid-June. Twins are uncommon and triplets are rare. Females likely have difficulty raising more than one offspring at a time. The 3-kg (6.6-lb) newborn is up and walking in a few hours despite its precarious location and footing. Nursing occurs every few hours from the mother's 2 teats. The kid begins to nibble green food as early as the second day and as

it grows larger, it must kneel down to reach the mother's udder, wiggling the little tail in contentment. The horns begin to sprout from the skull within only days of birth, reaching 3 to 6 cm (1.2 to 2.4 in) by September, when the youngster is completely weaned. It remains with its mother for 2 summers, but is kept at a distance once a new kid is born. Females breed at 2.5 years of age and yearling males participate in the rut but probably don't breed until 2 years old. The maximum recorded life span of females is 18 years, and 14 years for males.
Remarks A mountain goat perched on a cliff or ledge is a striking looking animal with its high shoulders, long bearded face accentuated by the pair of black horns, and a beautiful white coat. A dense underfur and guard hairs, which can reach 18 cm (7.1 in) in length, offer excellent insulation from chilling winds. The animals seem to avoid having their fur drenched from rain or wet snow, for they seek shelter under conifers or in caves during heavy storms. An annual molt occurs in May and the ragged-looking goats rub off patches of matted hair against rocks and trees. They frequently dig dry wallows in summer and spend hours rolling in the dust; in winter they roll in the snow. This habit is thought to relieve irritation from insects or matted fur, and also helps dry up excessive oil on the hair.

Unlike the pronghorn, the mountain goat's horn is not shed but continues to grow over a bony core until it reaches a length at maturity of about 23 cm (9.1 in). These sharp weapons can cause injury to other goats and potential predators, but they are most often used in threat displays rather than in serious fights. Two male antagonists stand side to side and thrust their horns at each other's rump.

Vision and smell are important senses in detecting the approach of predators. Goats can see a moving animal while it is still several kilometers away; however, the goat seems to have difficulty making out or interpreting stationary objects. Individuals generally feed in the morning, rest during mid-day, then feed again from late afternoon to the evening, males traveling about one km (0.6 km) in an hour, females 0.5 km (0.3 mi). Sometimes foraging continues throughout the night but they do not travel far. Billies wander either singly or occasionally within a small herd over a home range of 2.8 to 22 sq km (1.0 to 8.1 sq mi) while a herd of nannies ranges over 5 to 24 sq km (1.9 to 8.9 sq mi). The home ranges of the two sexes overlap and they often feed in the same meadow but at different times. The social tendencies vary among individuals and change during the year. Groupings with as many as 27 females and 14 males have been reported in meadows or at natural salt licks which are visited a number of times each year. Movements from summer to winter range average only 3 km (1.9 mi) but may extend up to distances of 11 km (6.8 mi). Population densities have been recorded at levels of 0.7 to 3 goats per sq km (1.9 to 8.1 per sq mi). The solitary habits of males and the aggressive nature of females help ensure that the population is spread out, particularly during the winter when food and preferred sites are in short supply. In severe winters up to half of the young may perish from starvation and exposure. Cougars, bobcats, bears, coyotes, eagles, parasites, avalanches, and accidental falls take their toll. Hunting pressure for this trophy animal has also been severe, but now

populations are carefully managed and have remained quite stable. The mountain goat is fully protected in the Yukon Territory, but may be hunted in most other regions. It is a most difficult species to maintain in captivity.

Although I have seen mountain goats through binoculars a number of times, on one occasion I chanced to wander within 80 m (262.5 ft) of them. My colleague and I had been dropped by helicopter above treeline in the Mackenzie Mountains of the Yukon. While looking among the broken rocks for patches of moss where the rare singing vole *(Microtus miurus)* might be found, I was thinking more of grizzlies, for their big tracks were common in the melting snow and mud. As I made my way across the treacherous alpine rock field and came over a rise, there stood a family of 6 goats, all staring at me and wondering where on earth I had come from. After half a minute I started to approach slowly at an angle for a closer look, but the herd spooked and took off over the rocks at an astonishing speed. I could not imagine how they were able to traverse such rough terrain at top flight without stumbling and breaking a leg, for I had to take each step with great caution. I was so excited to see these splendid creatures that my heart must have been beating as fast as theirs.

Mountain Goat

The billy, or adult male goat, had spent the summer alone in the high rugged reaches of the mountain. His solitude was complete on this sunny afternoon, except for an eagle that glided by and the wind that ruffled his long coat and beard. Lying on his side at the shaded edge of a sheer cliff, he raised his head periodically to survey the subalpine forest and valley below. Several kilometers downslope something was moving and his keen black eyes picked out the form of a coyote. Satisfied that he was safely out of range, the goat brought up into his mouth his recent meal of grass and mountain bluebells, and chewed the soft mush over again with a contented look on his face. Several hours later and fully rested, the goat rose up on his front legs and while sitting, kicked the wet soil and moss onto his belly and sides, staining the white fur brown. He was feeling an urge to join the small herd of nannies (females) that lived on the same northeastern slopes during the summer.

He finally stood up on all fours, leaving the five-centimeter (2-inch)-deep bed he had so carefully prepared that morning. He then shook his body vigorously and bit at the dense wool on his shoulder before proceeding downslope. In a graceful leap he confidently landed on another precarious ledge of rock three meters (10 feet) away, oblivious to the possibility of a tumble to the rocks three hundred meters (984.3 feet) below. The pliable pads swelling under the hooves seemed to cushion the shock of the animal's weight and to grasp onto the wet surface like glue. Walking stiff-legged, the muscle-bound appearance accentuated by the hump on the shoulders, the goat picked his way over the outcropping of rocks, pausing to nibble here and there on his favorite greens.

Several days later this billy goat located the nursery band in an alpine meadow. He approached slowly, grunting and stopping to rub the scent gland found behind each horn on nearby bushes and grass. One of the two nannies, who was the leader of the group, did not receive the newcomer kindly. Each time he came too close she jabbed at his side and flanks with her sharp horns. Were it not for the thick skin on his sides he might well have been badly wounded. The two kids began to butt each other in imitation, and even climbed on each other's back. Folding their necks over each other they then tried to force the other to its knees by exerting downward with all their might. Still ready for more fun, the youngsters jumped up a boulder and took turns

playing "king of the mountain." All these games would someday develop into serious goat behavior related to survival and reproduction.

The billy continued his courtship unsuccessfully for a week, standing alone for long periods and hardly bothering to eat. Approaching a nanny from the rear, he flared his nostrils, flicked his tongue in and out, and tapped her flank with his front leg. When this brought no results, the billy kicked her so hard that she jumped forward. She frustrated him again by leaning so tightly against a rock wall that he was unable to mount her. He then tried stretching low on bended knees in front of her, which stimulated her to wet the ground slightly. Encouraged by the action and the aroma, the billy pulled back his upper lip as he strutted behind the nanny and gave her yet another kick, this time landing his front hoof between her haunches. This correct sequence appeared to be what the nanny was waiting for, as she then permitted her suitor to mount several times. The same day he successfully mated with the second nanny and having satisfied his urge, soon lost interest in them and returned to his solitary life

Within several weeks, storms buried the goats' food supply under a meter (3.3 feet) of snow. The herd made its way to lower elevations on the southwest slopes of the mountain where the temperatures were slightly warmer and the snow cover was shallower. Each kid followed its nanny closely on the slippery slopes, their large oval hooves with sharp edges and friction pads helping to gain adequate footholds in the snow. Floundering in a drift, a kid bleated until its mother returned to its side. The goats' long fleece offered excellent insulation from the cold winds down to -20°C (-4°F), but temperatures seldom plummeted this low. Snow now became the dominant factor controlling the herd's activities. Depth, crusting, and moisture content dictated whether they moved up or down a slope, or selected one particular area over another. Only the severest of storms forced the animals into the subalpine fir forest or into one of several caves. Lying in beds in the snow the goats almost vanished in the dazzling whiteness. They were generally able to browse on shrubs and saplings and to paw little craters to reach other plants lying dormant at ground level. The mountain goats passed the winter peacefully, since no cougar, grizzly, or coyote ventured into their high-altitude home.

Mountain Sheep

Amid a chorus of baas, barks, whistles, and neighs the rancher and his dogs rounded up the several hundred domestic sheep and drove them down into the valley pastures, for winter had arrived early in the mountains. Way up on the white slopes, he could barely make out groups of brown animals browsing where the wind had blown off most of the season's first snowfall. The sounds of the roundup faded away, leaving the mountain sheep in much preferred solitude. Sometimes in sight of each other the band of seven rams remained apart from the main group of twelve ewes and lambs.

Throughout the winter the bands appeared to wander at random below elevations of thirty-three hundred meters (10,826.8 feet). They moved at a steady pace, covering a half to three kilometers (0.3 to 1.9 miles) in a day. Actually they were carefully selecting certain pasture to forage where the snow was not excessively deep or encrusted by ice, yet thick enough to protect the juiciness of the low vegetation from the drying winds. They pawed the snow away to reach their favorite plants and also clipped the buds of shrubs and trees as they walked by.

During the month of May the sun ate away at the white cloak of snow covering the mountain slopes until only patches remained in the shadows of rock piles and cliffs. Standing majestically, a sentinel mountain sheep surveyed the valley below while the other rams grazed on grass, noisily nipping off and chewing the stems. One, then the others, lay down to rest, first preparing the bed by pawing the ground before bending the front and then the hind legs. The distant rumbling of an avalanche from a higher peak brought the band members quickly to their feet and ready to run across the rocky slopes to a stand of fir trees if falling snow and rock came their way. With keen eyes and ears they soon perceived they were in no danger, and the animals bedded down once more.

Later that afternoon, two of the rams became restless and began a test of their strength and dominance. The younger aggressive ram approached the leader with lowered head, and shoulder to shoulder they kicked out with their forelegs. The struggle became more heated as the two pushed and shoved, demonstrating their boldness and courage. Finally they walked ten meters (32.8 feet) past each other, whirled around, and charged. Reaching an astonishing fifty-four kilometers (33.6 miles) per hour the two combatants rose up on their hind feet at the last second and their thick brown horns collided with such force that the sound of the blow echoed through the mountains. They paused for a moment, as if to determine whose head hurt the most, then the ram with the smaller horns casually turned his white rump toward the leader and began to feed — a sign of submission. Then everything was serene once more, as if the challenge had never occurred. All six rams were aware of their status within the herd, but they frequently tested each other in hopes of climbing higher in rank. The thick skull and massive horns absorbed the force of the blows and so injuries were rare. The dominant ram would be able to mate with most of the ewes as each came into heat in November.

By late summer several of the lambs and adults became ill and died of pneumonia. The local game manager determined that the problem was caused by a parasite called lungworm — an infection picked up from the domestic sheep that grazed the lower slopes. The worms had laid eggs in the domestic sheep's lungs, and upon hatching they migrated up the windpipe and down the digestive tract. The larvae passed out in the animal's droppings and entered snails, where they continued to develop. The life cycle was completed when the mountain sheep accidently ate the snails while grazing on grass. The worm had then been transferred from the ewes to their unborn lambs.

The game manager mixed a worm poison into a mash of fermenting apples, which the mountain sheep could not resist eating. The herd was saved from the lungworm infection but the manager realized the problem was worsened by overcrowding of the range by both domestic and wild herds. In addition to limiting the grazing of the domestic sheep he considered opening the hunting season on mountain sheep and protecting predators such as cougars and wolves. These steps would help reduce and disperse the mountain sheep over the range, resulting in a healthier herd.

MOUNTAIN SHEEP
Scientific name *Ovis canadensis*
Family Cattle, Sheep, and Goats (Bovidae)
Order Even-toed Ungulates (Artiodactyla)
Total length males 170 cm (66.9 in);
               females 140 cm (55.1 in)
Tail length 11 cm (4.3 in); 10 cm (3.9 in)
Weight 125 kg, maximum 143 kg
          (275.6 lb, maximum 315.3 lb);
          80 kg (176.4 lb)
Color The animal is light brown, darker on the face, chest, and legs. The muzzle, belly, back of the legs, and rump patch are white. The dense coat is formed of brittle guard hairs, white at the base and brown on the tips. The thick underfur or fleece is gray.
Distribution and Status Mountain sheep, formerly known as bighorns, range from central Alberta and British Columbia as far south as northern Mexico. West to east these sheep occur naturally from the central regions of the Pacific states to the Dakotas. This species inhabits grassy mountain slopes and plateaus, foothills with bluffs, and desert badlands, but its numbers have been drastically reduced to less than 45,000 animals due to a century of excessive hunting, disease, and habitat destruction. The animal is now found in only a fraction of its former territory, often in isolated locations. Numerous introductions of herds have been made in formerly occupied areas. A close relative — the Dall's or stone sheep *(Ovis dalli)* — occurs farther north in alpine meadows in British Columbia, the Yukon and Northwest Territories, and Alaska. Both species evolved from ancestors that immigrated from Siberia within the last several million years. About 7 or 8 species of *Ovis* are presently recognized, mostly occurring in Europe and Asia, but their relationships are still controversial.
Food Almost two-thirds of the diet is grass and sedge, although many kinds of other herbs

are accepted as well. Some important plants are wheatgrass, bluegrass, brome grass, fescue, cinquefoil, fireweed, clover, and horsetail. In the desert, on poor range, or in winter, sheep resort to browsing on forbs, shrubs, and trees such as sage, Douglas fir, willow, bearberry, rose, mountain mahogany, desert holly, Russian thistle, and prickly pear. This species has suffered from competition for food with livestock in many areas of its range. While moisture is easily obtained by most mountain-dwelling sheep from pools, snow, or succulent forage, those individuals living in deserts or badlands must have access to water, for 14 days is about the longest period they can last without drinking.
Reproduction and Growth The rut or breeding season is mainly in November and December in northern populations, and from July to December in the south. Most of the mating is done by the dominant males, usually characterized by the largest and heaviest horns. These individuals are attractive to the ewes, who actively rebuff rams less well endowed. The males strut around stiff-legged, engaging in terrific head-on battles to secure the courting rights to each female. No harem is gathered however, and usually only half the females become pregnant. The embryos require 6 months to develop before birth in May or June in the north, January to June in the south. Single lambs (weighing 4 kg or 8.8 lb) are the rule, though twins occasionally appear in herds on excellent range. Within weeks the lambs form into bands, returning to their mothers periodically to suckle. A young female remains with its mother's group, while a male leaves when 2 to 4 years of age to join a herd of rams. Exceptional individuals become sexually mature at 1.5 years old but 2.5 years is more common for females. Young males must compete with older rams for a chance to breed and may not be successful un-

til 7 years old. Life expectancy is 10 to 12 years with a maximum of 20 years for rams and 24 years for ewes.
Remarks Male mountain sheep protect themselves and determine their rank in the herd with their broad curving horns which average 110 cm (43.3 in) in length. Those of the females are considerably smaller and only slightly curved. Following the first winter, horn growth is rapid in both sexes. The heavily ridged structure reaches full size in 4 or 5 years, and the animal can be aged by counting the rings that form during the rut. The horny sheath grows over a bony core arising from a thickened area on top of the skull, which helps protect the brain from concussion during clashes. The tip of the horn is worn away from repeated impact with the opponent's horns. Surprisingly, the horns are largest in the smaller desert sheep — perhaps an adaptation to increase heat loss from the body. Rocky Mountain, California, and desert bighorns are common names given to subspecies that vary considerably in size and color.

Mountain sheep are not territorial and follow traditional routes from summer to winter ranges; some herds occupy as many as 7 separate areas during the year, each one to 32 km (0.6 to 19.9 mi) apart. They move up to 16 km (10 mi) in the course of a day and bed down for the night. Home ranges average under 16 sq km (5.9 sq mi) and densities of 2 to 23 per sq km (5.4 to 62 per sq mi) are common. Gregarious animals, they sometimes gather in herds of over 100 individuals. These stocky animals are heavy but sure-footed, with independently moveable sections of the hoof, each backed by a rubbery pad and a scent gland in between. While the young are born with a full set of "baby" teeth, the adult set of 32 teeth does not fully erupt until the age of 4. Sight is well developed and far more important in detecting predators than either hearing or smell. It is almost impossible to approach sheep without being seen. The major causes of death are starvation, drought, disease, accidents, and predation by humans and wolves, rarely by eagles and grizzlies. The band will huddle in a tight circle, facing outward, if threatened and surrounded by wolves.

During a summer vacation to the Alberta Rockies, my family visited the majestic Columbia Icefield. The snow in the middle of summer was too much to resist, and soon we were sliding down the hillside and throwing snowballs. One of the boys noticed several brown animals making their way along the edge of the road some distance below. The mountain sheep, obviously familiar with bothersome tourists, continued to graze peacefully as we pulled up in the car. Viewing these rugged mountain creatures at such close range was quite an experience, not only for our family but for a number of other people who also stopped to watch.

MOUNTAIN SHEEP

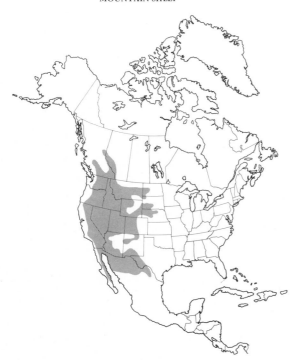

MULE DEER

Scientific name *Odocoileus hemionus*
Family Deer (Cervidae)
Order Even-toed Ungulates (Artiodactyla)
Total length males 170 cm (66.9 in);
females 160 cm (63 in)
Tail length 18 cm (7.1 in); 17 cm (6.7 in)
Weight 100 kg, maximum 215 kg (220.5 lb, maximum 474 lb); 50 kg, maximum 72 kg (110.2 lb, maximum 158.7 lb). Size varies greatly over the range, with the largest animals in the north.

Color The summer coat is thin and reddish-brown, becoming thicker, longer, and grizzled-brown in winter. The forehead, ear edges, and chest are blackish-brown. The tail is white or brown with a white tip. The rump patch and belly are white. The fawn is reddish-brown with rows of white spots on the upper parts. The adult pelage grows in around 86 days of age.

Distribution and Status The mule deer is native to the western half of North America from southern Alaska, the Yukon and Northwest Territories, and Manitoba south to Baja California, the highlands of central Mexico, and western Texas. Over such a large area the mule deer is capable of living in remarkably different types of habitat — from alpine meadow; desert scrub; arid plains; prairie; chaparral; woodland; boreal, mountain, and coastal coniferous forests; and temperate and tropical deciduous forests. Climatic extremes vary from -60°C to 50°C (-76°F to 124°F).

The deer family is believed to have originated in Eurasia and reached North America about 10 million years ago. Mule deer and white-tailed deer *(Odocoileus virginianus)* evolved on this continent, the former in the rugged and often arid terrain of the west, and the latter in the more moist deciduous forests of the east. Over its vast range, the mule deer has been divided into 7 subspecies or geographic races, several of which are so distinct in appearance and behavior that the use of common names has persisted for the 2 main groups — mule deer and black-tailed deer (along the west coast). Other close relatives include the marsh deer *(Blastocerus dichotomus)* and pampas deer *(Ozotoceros bezoarticus)* of South America. Four species of tiny brocket deer *(Mazama)* occur throughout South America, with 2 species reaching as far north as Panama and Mexico.

There were perhaps 5 million mule deer in North America prior to European contact. Since that time, hunting, habitat loss, land development, overbrowsing by domestic stock, and climatic factors have all acted to greatly reduce deer populations. The greatest decline (to about 500,000) occurred in the late 1800s, but by the 1940s numbers had increased dramatically, beyond the capacity of the land to support them. After alarming declines in the 1960s and 1970s, populations have recently stabilized at a higher level, although the species is still absent from parts of its former range in the east and Mexico. Fluctuating trends in mule deer numbers seem to occur independently of the attempts of biologists to manage the herds. Recent population estimates are about 2.5 million, with 0.5 million killed annually by hunters.

Food The diet of this animal varies greatly depending on where it lives. Over 800 kinds of plants have been listed, including grasses, herbs, shrubs, and both deciduous and coniferous trees. The deer is primarily a grazer in

summer. Selection is often based on high nutritional value of particular plants. During late spring and summer the deer has access to plenty of nourishing food from new plant growth, and it builds up fat reserves. During winter, when plants are dormant or covered with snow, a deer often cannot maintain its weight, especially when it has to eat relatively poor forage like sagebrush and juniper. Favorite winter foods are aspen, willow, red-osier dogwood, huckleberry, Douglas fir, and western cedar. The survival of the deer is dependent on the quality of food plants and the ability of the deer to reach it, particularly in winters with deep snow. In the desert, summer or autumn drought may cause a serious depletion of forage.

Reproduction and Growth The rut occurs from October to December in the north, November to January in the south, although most mating takes place in November and December. The bucks engage in terrific battles using their forked antlers and powerful neck muscles, which increase in size at this time of year. The dominant bucks become exhausted from defending their does from other persistent bucks. The doe's cycle extends from 22 to 28 days and she comes into heat for 24 to 36 hours. From 183 to 218 days (average 203) after mating, 2 (range of one to 4) spotted fawns are born, each weighing 5 kg (11 lb) or less. Depending on when the female mated, births occur from March to November, though usually in June or July. The fawns are hidden in a thicket for the first month and visited and nursed about every 4 hours. They nibble on plants after a few days, are able to run at 3 weeks, and are weaned at 4 months. Frequently only one in 4 fawns lives to be one year old. Sexual maturity is attained at 1.5 years of age and the average life span is 4 years, although some survive to 10 years in the wild. Does have reached 22 years and bucks 16 years in captivity.

Remarks The mule deer is distinguished from its white-tailed relative by its long ears, smaller rounded tail, stockier build, large gland (metatarsal) on the lower hind legs, and forked antlers on the male. The antlers grow over the summer (up to 1 cm or 0.4 in per day), they are polished by rubbing in August and September, and fall off from January to February but sometimes as late as April. This deer is also more sociable than the white-tail and forms mixed herds, particularly in winter when they may even be seen grazing with pronghorns and elk. The main activity periods are early morning and evening to several hours after dark, but when the deer needs food it may be out anytime.

The mule deer is known for its high-bounding gait, landing on all fours. It can reach the astonishing speed of 60 km (37.3 mi) per hour, cover 8 m (26.2 ft) in a single jump, and clear a 2-m (6.6-ft) fence. The body can be turned completely in the opposite direction during a single bound. Undisturbed, the deer walks normally and can trot and gallop. A deer can move through snow less than 30 cm (11.8 in) deep by wading or jumping, but greater depths and crusting decrease mobility; 50 cm (19.7 in) of snow virtually eliminates deer from an area. Seasonally, a mule deer remains in a fairly small home range with short daily movements if sufficient forage and cover are nearby. Ranges of 40 to 100 ha (98.8 to 247 a) have been reported in summer, and up to 300 to 2 100 ha (741 to 5,187 a) in winter. In mountainous regions, the animals migrate to winter range at lower elevations with less snow for distances of several to 160 km (99.4 mi). This species generally does not defend a territory; however, some highly dominant bucks may keep other males away by aggressive encounters during the rut. The carrying capacity of various habitats for mule deer varies considerably with such factors as vegetation,

Continued on p.100

MULE DEER

Mule Deer

In the late afternoon a red squirrel paused while opening a cone to watch a small flock of songbirds darting among the stately boughs of fir and hemlock. Warm drafts, rising up the mountainside from the valley below, battled through the cool autumn air. Down on the forest floor, three mule deer does and a buck directed their huge antennae-like ears towards a rumbling sound off in the distance. Within a minute a car rounded the curve and lurched to a halt as several excited heads popped out of the windows to watch the deer. The graceful animals standing in the sunlit glade were a majestic sight. The parents and children quietly got out of the car and walked slowly toward the deer, which followed their every move with their large dark eyes. The deer were used to the odor, sight, and sounds of people, for this area was a national park. They allowed the family of admirers to approach within two meters (6.6 feet) before revealing their nervousness by flicking their black-tipped tails and moving cautiously away into the forest. Being so close to this wildlife was the highlight of the family's vacation, and it would be a long time before they would forget the incident. They all agreed it was quite a different experience than seeing captive deer in a zoo.

Several weeks later the animals had wandered twelve kilometers (7.5 miles) away near the border of their home range and outside the park boundary. One of the does had just entered a period of heat and her urine deposits greatly excited the buck. He bent low to sniff in the scent, curled his lips, and arched his neck. With increasing arousal he walked over to a shrub and thrashed his polished antlers across the branches till the bark peeled off. In an early morning drizzle, the deer began browsing on blackberry bushes at the forest edge, when their shiny moist nostrils began to flare open. The smell of people wafted in on the breeze. They looked all around and listened carefully, but nothing seemed to be moving. They showed mild alarm by a peculiar stiff-legged walk. Unlike white-tailed deer, which would have bolted from the scene to hide in dense bush, the mule deer cautiously moved into the open, relying on their eyes, ears, and nose to provide information on any possible danger. Since they were familiar with the presence of humans, the animals were more intent on locating the intruders than retreating. Then, amid a terrible crack like thunder, one of the does tumbled to the ground, while the buck felt a searing pain in his shoulder. He staggered but regained his balance, and all but one of the deer bounded off, striking the ground with all four feet at once. As the sound echoed away through the hills the deer stopped to look back, shocked and perplexed at what had just happened. They kept expecting the downed doe to rise and join them, but she lay still in a crumpled position in the grass. With their hearts pounding and legs shaking in fright, they lay down to rest for a minute under some dense shrubbery. A trickle of crimson blood dripped down the buck's brown fur onto the yellow aspen leaves. Just as they were calming down, their ears picked up the sound of footsteps. Quietly the deer rose and retreated with lowered heads to a secluded spot where no one could follow them.

MULE DEER *continued from p. 97*

cover, terrain, water, and climatic conditions. Population estimates are one per sq km (2.7 per sq mi) in prairie, 5 per sq km (13.5 per sq mi) in mountain forests, 16 per sq km (43.2 per sq mi) in foothills, and 30 per sq km (81.1 per sq mi) in chaparral. Concentrations on winter range may reach 40 per sq km (108.1 per sq mi), and up to 200 per sq km (540.5 per sq mi) in black-tail populations of mule deer on the west coast.

Mule deer have 32 teeth (no upper incisors or canines) which wear down over the years of grinding food. The eruption and degree of wear of the teeth can be used to age individuals with considerable accuracy. The stomach is 4-chambered and harbors bacteria and other simple organisms which assist in digestion of plant material. The hairs of the deer's coat are tubular, brittle, and filled with air pockets — a feature that offers insulation from the cold and buoyancy while the animal is swimming. While usually silent, mule deer communicate by whistles, snorts, coughs, grunts, bleats, barks, and roars. Important predators include people, coyotes, cougars, wolves, lynx, bobcats, black bears, grizzlies, and eagles.

While walking carefully on a hillside of broken rock in west Texas, I looked up in time to see a herd of 7 airborne mule deer, as they seemed to fly over the ridge using their strange 4-legged jump. Perhaps on rough terrain, better footing is achieved if all feet come down at once rather than in pairs as is the habit of white-tailed deer. Mule deer may become remarkably tame in parks where they learn to lose their fear of people. In national parks of California and Alberta, I have had deer thrust their heads through the open car window in search of a handout. On another occasion, a young buck approached my family so closely that we decided we had better back away down the trail — I had read that people have been kicked by seemingly friendly mule deer.

Mammals of the
Boreal Forest

Circling the Northern Hemisphere lies a broad band (about 800 kilometers or 497 miles wide) of northern coniferous forest or taiga composed of spruce, fir, pine, and larch. At its northern extent, this boreal forest merges with tundra, the trees becoming widely spaced and stunted. On its southern border, boreal forest joins with montane coniferous forest in the west, characterized by Douglas fir, yellow pine, and Engelmann spruce. On the northern plains it forms a transition with the grasslands as aspen and oak parkland, while to the east it merges with the deciduous forest as mixed forest. Large tracts of boreal forest also extend farther south at high elevations in the New England States and also around the Great Lakes. White spruce and balsam fir are found in areas with deep soil and good drainage, jack pine on rocky and sandy well-drained sites, and black spruce and tamarack in wet situations. In Siberia, larch is often the dominant tree, occurring north to the treeline. Boreal forest may become tinder dry in summer, which results in widespread forest fires. Paper birch, trembling aspen, and balsam poplar often grow first in these burns or other disturbed moist sites, to be replaced later by conifers. Sedge, sphagnum or feather moss, and lichen are common on the forest floor, while shrubs such as alder, willow, and Labrador tea are prevalent where conditions are wet or not too densely shaded by the trees. However the herb layer is rather sparse, giving the ground a barren appearance. The air is calm within the forest because the dense coniferous boughs dissipate the wind. Boreal forest soils are thin, gray, infertile, and acid from the slowly decomposing conifer needles and other plant material. Most of the soil of this region was scoured away and deposited in the south by immense glaciers, 1.6 kilometers (one mile) thick, leaving a landscape of low relief and with countless lakes, bogs, outcroppings of bedrock, and glacial till (sand and gravel).

Precipitation varies between 25 and 125 centimeters (9.8 and 49.2 inches) per year. The ground often seems dry because the dense tree branches catch much of the rain, where it soon evaporates. In winter, snow commonly accumulates to a depth of over one meter (3.3 feet), and may reach 5 meters (197 inches) in the east, which profoundly affects animals that must wade through or live on or under the snow. Its insulative properties protect hibernating or active creatures from the frigid air above. Mean monthly temperatures reach -30°C (-22°F) in winter to 20°C (68°F) in summer. The growing season or frost-free period lasts from 60 to 120 days in various regions.

The main problems of boreal animals are finding enough food to eat and staying warm in a winter climate that may fall to -51°C (-60°F) — a full 84°C (150°F) below their body temperature. Many creatures, like bats and numerous birds, migrate south to warmer regions.

Common herbivores are the moose, caribou, snowshoe hare, red squirrel, spruce grouse, red crossbill, green-winged teal, and gray jay. Carnivores and insectivores include the gray wolf, fisher, lynx, raven, arctic loon, gray owl, black-backed three-toed woodpecker, and masked shrew. Garter snakes and several species of frogs are found here as well. Certain species of insects are abundant, particularly the biting flies (mosquitoes and black flies) and grubs that feast on the bark and leaves of conifers.

Masked Shrew

A light rain dampened the floor of an aspen forest, each drop of water forming a little round jewel on the golden aspen leaves. The air was heavy with a musky but sweet autumn odor of decaying vegetation. Scarcely noticeable, a sharp tiny nose appeared from under a fallen leaf. Quivering faster than the eye could follow, a masked shrew shot out from its underground nest. Although no worn trail was evident, the creature dashed along its customary runway, invisibly marked by secretions from glands on its sides and anal region. The lingering odor warned all other shrews that might pass this way that this area was already occupied by one highly aggressive tenant. The shrew jolted to a stop and stretching backward, began chewing frantically on its rump, perhaps itchy from some tiny mites that threaded their way through the hairs. A dry leaf came tumbling down from the treetops and landed with a sharp sound only a short distance away. It might as well have been a clap of thunder, for the nervous shrew reacted by leaping into the air. Its legs were already flailing by the time it came down, and the frightened creature disappeared under a stump.

Ravenous after an hour's sleep, the shrew reappeared and darted here and there, thrusting itself into the spaces between the rotting leaves. Suddenly its sensitive nose picked up the scent of a large black beetle, and the tiny hunter became highly excited. The shrew's eyesight was so poor it had difficulty locating the prey. The beetle soon realized it was being followed and it scurried away over the ground, tumbling over twigs. The shrew closed in, using its ears and nose to keep on the trail. Squeaking and twittering at a high frequency, the echoes bounced off the moving beetle and back to the shrew's ears. Using this effective radar system the shrew dashed toward its prey. As soon as the shrew's hairy snout touched the beetle's back, its jaws snapped quickly and the battle was on. Rolling over and over, the two tiny animals pushed and kicked. Several times the insect broke away, but the shrew never gave up. Finally the shrew's sharp and protruding incisors penetrated the hard-shelled beetle, and its movements slowed. Rolling the prey over on its back, the victor nibbled away at the soft undersides while the beetle's hooked legs continued to kick aimlessly in the air. The shrew ate so fast and noisily it seemed desperate to finish, and in less than a minute only the legs and wings of the beetle were left. The exhausted hunter gave a shake of its body, and with its nose twitching it headed off for home.

On its way it kept stopping without apparent reason, as if it had forgotten to do something. Hunching up its back in a most remarkable show of flexibility, the shrew attacked a section of moss likely kicked up previously by a moose. Ripping a piece free the little animal carried off its prize to a hole in the ground and disappeared. The tunnel led to a circular woven mass of sedge leaves and moss. The shrew dropped its cargo, plowed right through the wall, and seconds later its pointy head popped back out again. Grasping its prize moss in its mouth, it dragged it all the way into its nest. The structure quivered as the owner circled around inside, then all was quiet. Exhausted from the hectic proceedings, the shrew promptly fell asleep once again.

MASKED SHREW

Scientific name *Sorex cinereus*
Family Shrews (Soricidae)
Order Insectivores (Insectivora)
Total length 100 mm (3.9 in)
Tail length 40 mm (1.6 in)
Weight 5 g (0.2 oz)
Color The coat is light or dark brown, and is pale underneath. The grayer winter coat is remarkably long for such a small creature, reaching 10 mm (0.4 in) on the rump.
Distribution and Status The masked shrew is a common dweller of bogs, meadows, thickets, deciduous and coniferous forests, prairie, and the tundra. It reaches its greatest abundance in the coniferous forest zone, often outnumbering all other species of small mammals. Although favoring moist sites, it sometimes appears in quite dry habitats. It occurs from the Atlantic to the Pacific coast and from Georgia and New Mexico north to the Arctic Ocean. It has also been introduced successfully in Newfoundland.

During the Pleistocene Ice Age this species crossed the Bering Land Bridge into Asia, and now occurs in northeastern Siberia and the Kuril Islands. The masked shrew may actually represent several very similar species. For example, the prairie shrew *(Sorex haydeni)* of the northern Great Plains, and the barren-ground shrew *(Sorex ugyunat)* of the tundra, have recently been raised to full species status from former subspecies (geographic races) of the masked shrew. No one is sure how many species of *Sorex* exist and estimates range from 49 to 64, including many found in Eurasia. Presently from 31 to 37 species have been described in North America, some of which are extremely rare and localized. No doubt some of these will be combined into single species, while others will be separated. Obviously much work remains to be done on the study of shrew relationships.
Food Shrews eat an incredible number of insects, including many kinds that injure trees. Worms, snails, spiders, other lower animals, carrion, and some vegetation are also present in the diet. Shrews are well known for their

relatively huge appetite, and may consume over their own body weight in one day. They must feed often just to maintain their body temperature and internal processes.
Reproduction and Growth When a female is ready to breed, she secretes a scent from the genital area that male shrews locate and follow. Only during the brief courtship is the male permitted to approach, since at other times she would attack him instantly. Following the rapid mating act, the resulting embryos require about 20 days to develop before birth. Females have one to 3 litters of 2 to 11 young from April to September in the north, March to October in the south. The newborn suckle from the female's 3 pair of mammae for several weeks. The young are almost full grown at one month, when they leave the nest. Young of the year may be identified by the abundance of hair on the tail. Second-year shrews have almost naked tails. Spring-born individuals are capable of breeding later in the summer. While most of these tiny mammals perish within a year, a few lucky ones survive 2 years.
Remarks Although this bundle of energy is widespread and common, it is seldom seen by people. It tries to remain hidden from birds of prey, foxes, and weasels by running under logs or thick grass. The short and delicate limbs are too weak to dig through heavy soil, gravel, or frozen ground, so the shrew lives in the leaf layer or uses the burrows of other small animals. Male shrews have scent glands along their flanks that release a musky, yellowish liquid. This scent is rubbed off on trails and tunnels, identifying the owner's home range and perhaps attracting females. Day and night through all seasons, the masked shrew keeps up such a hectic pace that it reaches old age by the end of one year. A heart rate up to 1,200 beats per minute has been recorded.

One of the most unusual things about these fascinating small mammals is the long, flexible snout that is constantly poking and bending in all directions. Underneath is a battery of 32 miniature but impressive teeth, tipped (for some unknown reason) with red. The

middle upper incisor has become a large, double-pronged pincer, while the cheek teeth exhibit w-shaped, sharp-edged cusps for chopping up insects. The first set of teeth is actually shed before birth. Shrews hunt their prey over a home range which may be quite variable in size — from 400 to 1 000 sq m (4,300 to 10,764 sq ft). Numbers often average 10 per ha (per 764 sq ft), but can reach as high as 100 per ha.

There are several species of shrews found in the same area as the masked shrew that are difficult to tell apart (e.g., pygmy, vagrant, smoky, and dusky shrews) without checking the teeth. In view of this problem I was once handed a dead shrew found beside one of our traps. I carefully opened its mouth to examine the teeth, and suddenly they clamped shut on my finger, causing me to jump in surprise. No harm done, but since then I am more careful when I pick one up, for it may not be dead and only have fainted from fear.

Were it not for the insulating cover of snow, the masked shrew would not be able to inhabit frigid regions of the north and mountainsides. When cross-country skiing, I have often come across the tiny trail of a masked shrew in the snow. The footprints and tail marks are smaller and closer together than those of a mouse, and the shrew is so light it barely sinks into the fluffiest snow. The trail generally leads to a hole where the shrew reenters its subnivean (under the snow) world or to some cover such as a log or the base of a shrub. Why it comes to the surface where it is exposed to cold air and predators, no one knows.

HOARY BAT

Scientific name *Lasiurus cinereus*
Family Smooth-faced bats
   (Vespertilionidae)
Order Bats (Chiroptera)
Total length 140 mm (5.5 in)
Tail length 60 mm (2.4 in)
Weight 25 g (0.9 oz)
Color This attractive bat appears to be a mixture of colors but is basically brown with a frosting of white which is why it is called hoary. The hairs are actually banded with 4 colors — a gray base, then yellow, brown, and silver on the tips. The muzzle and edges of the ears are black while the bare flight membranes are blackish-brown. The young are silvery-gray.
Distribution and Status This species has one of the largest ranges of any New World mammal and extends from southern Canada to central Mexico on this continent and throughout a wide corridor in South America, from Columbia and Venezuela to central Argentina and Chile. Perhaps it is displaced in southern Mexico and Central America by other kinds of bats with similar habits. It also thrives on Hawaii, the Galapagos Islands, and Bermuda. It is such a strong flier that when blown off course it has turned up in remarkably distant places from its usual range. Examples are Fort Resolution and Bear Island in the Northwest Territories of Canada, Iceland, Orkney Islands, Cuba, Guatemala, southern Mexico, and on ships out in the Atlantic.

Although generally associated with boreal and mountain coniferous forests, it also frequents mixed and deciduous forests as well. Over its broad distribution it occurs in dozens of distinct forest types. The forest edge, open glades, orchards, and watercourses are par-

MASKED SHREW

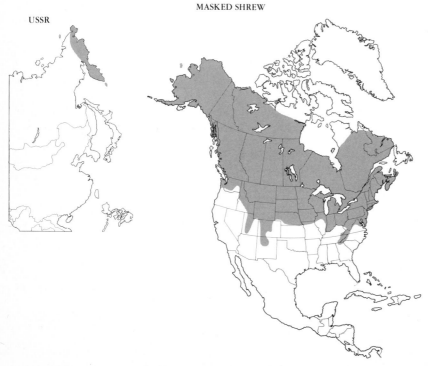

USSR

ticularly attractive sites. It is generally described as rare in most regions but this may be due to its late-night appearance. In some areas, like the northern prairies, it is one of the most common species of bats.

From October to March most of these bats winter in the southwestern United States (especially California) and Mexico (and perhaps Guatemala), with fewer numbers in the central and southeastern United States. From April to June, solitary or waves of hoary bats migrate to the rich feeding grounds of northern regions. For some unexplained reason females predominate in the north and east, while males are more common in the west during the summer months. The first arrivals reach Canada in early June. Some bats in mountainous regions simply migrate upslope to reach coniferous or mixed forest. A return migration occurs from late August to early October. The methods of navigation used during these incredible journeys are still unknown, although visual cues from the position of the sun and stars, topography, and magnetism have been proposed.

Up to 10 species of *Lasiurus* have been described from North and South America and the West Indies, but several of these may be just subspecies. A recent list of world mammals recognized only 7 species, including the widespread red bat *(Lasiurus borealis)*, seminole bat *(Lasiurus seminolus)* of the southeastern United States, and the northern yellow bat *(Lasiurus intermedius)* from New Jersey to Honduras.

Food   Night-flying insects such as moths and beetles are eaten in large numbers, often totaling 30 percent of the bat's weight each night. It may on occasion capture and eat a smaller bat. Water is sipped while skimming the surface.

Reproduction and Growth   Mating is presumed to occur mainly in the autumn (from late August) but possibly continues during migration and the following spring. Sperm is stored and nourished within the uterus of the female until her eggs are released in late February or March. The length of time of em-

bryonic development is unknown but approximates 85 days. Usually 2 (range of one to 4 — a most unusual number for any species of bat) young are born between May and July, generally mid-June in Canada. The baby bats appear rump-first which reduces the chance of the delicate wings becoming entangled in the birth canal. Each weighs about 4.5 g (0.2 oz). The mother licks them clean and then devours the afterbirth. The young alternate bouts of nursing from the mother's 4 mammae and sleeping while clutching onto the hair of her breast and back. They seldom fall even at this tender age, for they hang onto the nipple with their tiny milk teeth and to the fur by their big thumbs and claws of their hind feet. She leaves them hanging onto a branch or inside a tree hollow while foraging. They are anxious to greet her on her return and noisily climb aboard for warmth and milk. She repeatedly grooms them by licking their faces and membranes and combing their fur with the claws and bristles of her hind feet. The silvery-gray babies grow rapidly, their eyes open at 12 days, and they can fly and chase insects at only 4 weeks. The family hunts together for a period after weaning but drifts apart in August. Females may produce young at one year of age, while males first mate during their second autumn. The average life span is 7 years in the wild and up to 14 years in captivity.

Remarks   The hoary bat is one of the largest species of bats to be found in North America. One might surmise it to be of northern distribution based on its long, dense, silky coat and the fact that fur extends onto the wings and the top surface of the tail membrane, all of which are bare or scantily haired in most other bats. It has a pug face, bright black eyes, and short rounded ears. The mouth contains 32 teeth featuring impressive canines for biting and sharp-edged cheek teeth for cutting insect bodies. Like the red and silver-haired bats *(Lasionycteris noctivagans)* this species is described as a tree bat, since it is usually found roosting in the outer branches at heights of 3 to 12 m (9.8 to 39.4 ft), sometimes on the bark (where its colors blend in with the tex-

tured, lichen-crusted surface), or in a tree cavity. Only rarely has it been reported in a building or cave. While lacking color vision, as in other bats, it apparently sees better in light than do cave-dwelling species, a fact probably related to its bright roosts. In spite of this, however, the hoary bat is one of the latest bats to begin flying each night, which explains why it is seldom seen on the wing. Its flight pattern is direct and fairly high, frequently within 7 to 15 m (23 to 49.2 ft) above the ground. It is solitary with exceptions of a mother with offspring, and during migration when dozens may travel together. Sometimes it is active throughout the whole night, while at other times it hunts for a few hours after dark and again before dawn. Animals known to prey on hoary bats are owls, hawks, raccoons, snakes, and cats. Occasional individuals carry rabies so a bat should never be touched or approached too closely to risk being bitten and infected.

On a warm summer evening, I once sat down in the grass of an apple orchard in Quebec to watch a couple of little brown bats go through their maneuvers in pursuit of moths. On fluttering wings the bats paused, then swooped swiftly before continuing on their patrol, back and forth, from one end of the orchard to the other. My eyes strained to catch their return against the last light on the horizon, when a really large bat soared past. I jumped to my feet in surprise, being unaware that bats of such size existed in eastern Canada. On checking a field guide in the library the following day, I concluded I must have been introduced to my first hoary bat.

Each summer someone delivers a hoary bat family in a bag to the Museum, or calls to ask advice on what to do about bats stranded on the ground. In most cases, the female has been blown from her perch and cannot take flight due to the weight of her attached young — hence the idea for the story. On some occasions we kept the bats in captivity for a few days, offering them insect food and water until they regained their strength. The bats made quick work of meal worms, chopping them up noisily with their sharp teeth. When disturbed the mother buzzed and clicked and opened her pink mouth to reveal an impressive array of teeth. I later placed each family on a branch outside just before dark and they were gone by morning.

HOARY BAT

Hoary Bat

March winds swept the rocky hillside of pine-oak forest in a northern area of Mexico. Awakened by the swaying trunk, a silver-frosted and brown bat stretched and yawned inside a tree cavity. It was impatient for the last light of the setting sun to fade away on the western horizon. Climbing on its hind feet and thumbs to the edge of the hole, it peered outside, blinking as if the light hurt its big black eyes. Dark enough at last it leapt into the air and swooped away on delicately framed wings spread over forty centimeters (15.8 inches) wide. Tonight was a special time because this female hoary bat was beginning a long journey north to the aspen parkland of Saskatchewan. Why it suddenly felt so restless to travel, and how it knew which way to go were questions well beyond the primitive animal's capability to deal with. Yet, the power of instinct and an uncanny ability to navigate would lead the little creature twenty-four hundred kilometers (1,491 miles) to its place of birth. Flying through the night at twenty kilometers (12.4 miles) per hour, it darted to catch an occasional moth in midair or descended to sip water from a lake as it skimmed over the surface. During daylight hours the bat rested amid the leaves of trees, but each night brought it closer to home. Inside the female's womb, three baby bats had started to grow, the result of her mating the previous autumn.

In late May, after traveling for two months along the eastern outliers of the Rocky Mountains, the hoary bat finally arrived at a familiar place. She fluttered back and forth over a sixty-meter (197-foot) stretch of the river until she was certain this was her traditional hunting grounds. For six years she had spent the summer months at this site. The tallest trees of the canopy were her landmarks and she knew every trail and glade in the surrounding forest of white spruce and aspen. Exhausted after her long journey she hovered over an aspen tree about ten meters (32.8 feet) high, landed on the end of a branch, and crawled in among the shiny green leaves. Hanging from her hind feet she drifted off to sleep for the day, swaying gently in the rustling boughs. As soon as it was dark she dropped from her roost and began patrolling the river for insects. Periodically emitting an intense high-frequency scream, she scanned the air pathway until echoes indicated a large moth was ahead at a distance of three meters (9.8 feet). She banked to the left to intercept the swiftly moving prey when suddenly another bat snatched it away and tumbled past out of view. The hoary bat wheeled around in hot pursuit. She soon picked up the silver-haired bat on her radar system and began to close in. The silver-haired bat heard her aggressive transmissions from behind and dropped the moth. With great agility the intruding bat attempted evasive action by turning and diving. The hoary bat was swifter but its large size did not permit as great maneuverability. Like star-fighter jets the two bats swept around a turn in the river and past a startled boy sitting on the bank. On another occasion the hoary bat might have captured and eaten the smaller bat, but once outside her territory she turned around and headed for home.

Several weeks later the hoary bat gave birth to three young. The large offspring nestled in her long fur and it was difficult to distinguish them among all the folded wings and legs. Each evening, when it was time for her to forage, she pried her resisting babies off her and onto a branch so that she could hunt unencumbered. When she returned, the three quickly crawled back on board and sought a free nipple to nurse. At two weeks of age the rapidly growing youngsters weighed more in total than the mother. Then one evening a terrible storm hit the area with strong winds and driving rain. Soaking wet, the bats were torn from the roost and they fell in a ball to the forest floor. The mother was unable to leap into the air with the baby bats clinging to her, so she just lay on the grass, trying to protect them with her wings and body. It seemed likely they would be killed by a passing dog, cat, or other predator.

The next morning the boy was out for a walk and spotted the pile of wet fur in the grass. Buzzing, clicking, and displaying her sharp teeth, the mother bat attempted to defend her family. The boy carefully lifted the bats up with a forked stick and placed them on the rough bark of a tree. As he watched quietly from a distance, the upset bats finally settled down to sleep. That evening the bat loosened her grip from the perch and loaded with young she managed to flap her way to the safety of a tall tree. Over the following month the boy occasionally caught sight of the bat family while they pursued insects over the river. As if to reward him for his kind deed the female returned to the same site for several more years to show off her new babies.

Snowshoe Hare

A subadult snowshoe hare sat resting under a jack pine log. Though her eyes were closed, her nose twitched every so often. Both long ears moved to face different directions like radar receptors, feeding information on all forest sounds to the hare's brain. If some odor, bird song, or insect call wasn't quite right, the eyes opened, just to be certain there was no danger. The hare could never relax completely, for there were too many animals in the forest that liked to eat hares, such as the great-horned owl, red fox, fisher, and especially the long-legged lynx. Since the hare's parents and four brothers and sisters had all disappeared over the summer, she alone patrolled the runways of her territory each evening, nipping clear the vegetation as she passed. Killing frosts soon made scarce many of her favorite plants. She ripped off some leaves of wild strawberry with her large front teeth. The leaves slowly disappeared into the sides of her mouth as her jaws rocked back and forth, the cheek teeth grinding the plant into a green paste. Occasionally the hare paused during the meal and rose up on hind feet to look around, just in case some animal was trying to sneak up on her. Shortly after, the hare bent downward and proceeded to eat several of her own soft green droppings. She would gain added nutrients by passing the material through her digestive system twice. Hopping from front feet to hind feet, the hare sought the cover of a shrub thicket to rest once again.

As the days of autumn grew shorter, a wonderful change began to take place. Snow-white hairs appeared throughout the hare's grayish-brown coat. By the time snow blanketed the forest floor she had turned completely white, except for the black tips on the ears. When standing still she blended so well with the snow that a lynx once crept by within two meters (6.6 feet) and failed to detect her presence. The hairs on her hind feet grew into thick pads, and when she spread her long toes she could bound over the snow on her "snowshoes" and scarcely sink in. At night when the moon shone clearly through the crisp winter air, she abandoned all caution and dashed here and there, sending the soft flakes flying. Someone seeing all her tracks the next day would think a dozen rabbits had played tag.

The winter months passed slowly and the hare slept most of the day and night under snow-covered bushes and logs. The deep snow greatly curtailed her movements and she spent considerable time trampling down trails through the fluffy white stuff. These narrow open runways allowed her to reach food supplies with a minimal of trail-breaking, and also provided escape routes if ambushed by predators. With snow burying most of the food plants found on the forest floor, the hare turned her attention to the buds, twigs, and bark of shrubs and low trees. She stood up on her hind feet to nibble on all accessible browse, and with each snowfall she was able to reach higher and higher up the shrubs. Wherever she paused to rest, a few wood-filled droppings marked the depression in the snow, revealing the contrast in her diet from summer to winter.

Springtime came unusually early, signaled not only by the rapid melting of snow but by the arrival of the first migrant birds. It was the breeding season for the hare. Inside her body, many kinds of changes were occurring in response to the lengthening days, preparing her to court, mate, and produce a family. But there were no males of her species in the area. Restlessly she searched all corners of her home range, not really aware what was driving her or what she was looking for. The disappearance of the snow lowered her back to the forest floor, where she once again had access to broad-leaved plants. It also left here out of phase as far as her white camouflaged coat was concerned. She now stood out in stark contrast to the greens and browns of the vegetation. Then, one evening, as she nibbled on some new green shoots of sedge, she heard a rustling sound on the far side of the bog. Her ears trained forward, her eyes bulged, and her heart doubled its pace in fright. The hormone adrenalin shot into her blood system from glands, in preparation of a frantic flee for life. In a frozen position she waited, one excruciating minute after another. Suddenly she saw a white hare hop out from behind a dwarf black spruce. The two animals rose ever so hesitantly on their hind legs and gazed across the clearing at each other.

SNOWSHOE HARE

Scientific name *Lepus americanus*
Family Rabbits and Hares (Leporidae)
Order Rabbits, Hares, and Pikas
(Lagomorpha)
Total length 480 mm (19 in)
Tail length 48 mm (1.9 in)
Weight 1.5 kg (3.3 lb)
Color In summer the upperparts and feet are light brown mixed with black hairs, and the belly is grayish-white. In winter, the new guard hairs come in white, although a brown underfur shows through faintly. The edges of the ears are black. Young hares are gray.
Distribution and Status The snowshoe hare inhabits thickets and deciduous and coniferous forests, with recent burns and willow and alder swamps being favored habitats. It often extends into clearings, but quickly retreats to woody cover if danger threatens. It is widespread across the continent, from treeline in northern Canada and Alaska, through the northern United States, and south in the mountains to California, New Mexico, and North Carolina. It has been introduced in Newfoundland and Anticosti Island. The snowshoe hare closely resembles the European hare *(Lepus capensis)* which has been released and is living wild in Ontario and New England. There are 19 to 22 species of hares and jackrabbits (genus *Lepus*) found in North and South America, Eurasia, and Africa.
Food This hare eats hundreds of kinds of plants, including grasses and sedges as well as broad-leaved species such as clover, dandelion, jewelweed, and ferns. When snow covers its green food, the hare concentrates more on the bark and buds of shrubs and saplings like birch, larch, rhododendron, mountain maple and willow, and the evergreen needles of fir, cedar, spruce, and jack pine.
Reproduction and Growth Mating begins in late March while there may still be plenty of snow in the woods. The female is followed by one or more males and chasing, hopping, and urinating are all part of the courtship. Competing males may fight fiercely by boxing and kicking with the hind feet. After 37 days, one to 8 (average 4) haired young are born in a grassy nest. They are able to hop around in only several days. The mother hides her family beneath some cover and returns to nurse them for about 10 minutes at sunset. There are 4 pairs of mammae to provide milk. The mother hare mates again soon after giving birth and produces 2 to 4 litters before the end of September — perhaps up to 20 babies in one season. The young reach adult size by 5 months but the majority do not breed until the following year. Most hares perish before one year of age; however the maximum life span exceeds 5 years.
Remarks The snowshoe hare is characterized by its long ears and well developed hind limbs, features that are used to good advantage in detecting and outrunning predators at speeds up to 40 km (25 mi) per hour. People think of hares as quiet creatures but they scream when frightened or hurt, click when nervous, whine when mating, and grunt when angry. They also signal danger by drumming with the hind feet. The snowshoe hare is active in the evening, for periods through the night, and in the early morning hours. It is a solitary creature, the female even leaving the young stashed separately under cover and only visiting them briefly to nurse. The nest or form hardly deserves this description, for it is little more than a depression in the leaves or ground. No tunnel is excavated in the soil, but vacant burrows are sometimes used for cover. The home range averages around 10 ha (24.7 a), but when food is scarce, individuals wander up to 8 km (5 mi) away.

Internally, the hare is unusual because of the sizeable caecum or pouch connected to the large intestine, with a capacity 10 times that of the stomach and functioning in the digestion of woody food. It produces the special droppings, rich in vitamins and proteins, that the hare ingests. Also, during the breeding season, the testes descend into a sac or scrotum which lies in front of the penis instead of behind, like most other mammals. There are 28 teeth in the jaws, the first pair of incisors, above and below, forming an efficient clipping organ. Strangely, a second pair of tiny incisors is present in the upper jaw behind the first pair.

The snowshoe hare is an important animal of the northern forests, since it is usually common and many other mammals (lynx, bobcat, cougar, mink, wolf, coyote, red fox) and birds of prey (great-horned and barred owls, goshawk, raven) rely on it as a main source of food. Every 10 years or so these hares become incredibly abundant over extensive regions, at which time they do considerable damage to the forest by eating the bark from shrubs and young tress. Numbers may increase from 2 to 400 per sq km (0.4 sq mi), although most fluctuations are not this drastic. Rather suddenly, the hare population drops to low levels again as the animals stop breeding and many of them die from stress, disease, and predation. The factor controlling this spectacular cycle is a major unsolved mystery of nature, but it seems clear that a complex interaction with the vegetation is involved.

Both the summer and winter coats camouflage the hare so well that I have unknowingly walked within 2 m (6.6 ft) of them before they dashed away. In winter, the animal avoids the cold temperatures and wind chill by snuggling under a snow-covered bough or log. While walking a trail in the Yukon, I spotted a tiny gray hare sitting motionless on the moss, hoping I hadn't noticed it. It refused to budge and remained "frozen" while I examined it closely and took pictures. I was careful not to touch the baby hare for fear that its mother might abandon it because of my scent. Its great beauty of form and vulnerability in such a hostile environment impressed me.

FISHER

Scientific name *Martes pennanti*
Family Weasels (Mustelidae)
Order Carnivores (Carnivora)
Total length males 100 cm (39.4 in);
females 82 cm (32.3 in)
Tail length 35 cm (13.8 in); 31 cm (12.2 in)
Weight 3.8 kg, maximum 9 kg
(8.4 lb, maximum 19.8 lb);
2.2 kg (4.9 lb)
Color The fur is dense, glossy (coarser in the male), and dark brown to black in color. Adults have lighter hairs on the face, neck, and shoulders.
Distribution and Status The fisher is typically an inhabitant of mature spruce forest, though it is also found in mixed deciduous-coniferous forest, cedar swamps, poplar or alder forests, and stands of young trees on old burns. It is absent from the open spruce-tamarack woodland south of the treeline across Canada. The range formerly extended southward in the Appalachians to Tennessee and North Carolina but shifted to the northern states in the early 1800s. The animal is still found as far south as Utah in the Rockies and California in the Sierras. Populations have been wiped out by overtrapping in large parts of the southern range, but better management, reintroductions, and natural recovery have returned the animal to many former regions. The fisher is closely related to the American marten *(Martes americana)* and 5 other martens distributed throughout Eurasia.
Food Important foods of the fisher are snowshoe hare, red squirrel, porcupine, red-backed vole, deer mouse, and shrews. Other mammals are eaten in smaller proportions

SNOWSHOE HARE

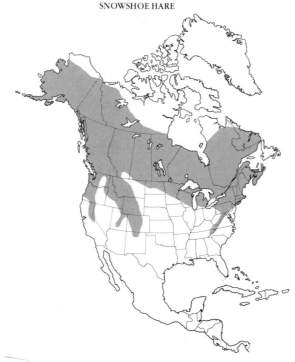

along with birds, fish, frogs, insects, fruits, and nuts. Carrion of moose, deer, caribou, and beaver is also accepted when available.

Reproduction and Growth Although solitary for most of the year, adult fishers begin to seek each other's company in the breeding season, commencing in late February and March, and lasting in some areas into May. Mating occurs within 10 days after the female gives birth. Amid loud yowls, the male grasps the back of the female's neck in his jaws and they remain coupled for about 4 hours. Then a remarkable thing happens — the embryos become dormant after only 15 days growth and remain so for the rest of the spring, summer, autumn, and most of the winter. Then, with the increasing period of daylight in February and March, a hormone (called prolactin) in the female triggers the embryos into renewed growth. Thirty days later, she gives birth to about 3 babies (range of one to 6) high up in a tree hollow. The male does not assist in raising the family and is, in fact, busy in search of other females in heat. The young are slow to develop, with eyes opening at 7 weeks, eating meat at 9, running at 10, and climbing at 12 weeks. Both sexes are mature at one year, but it is questionable whether many males breed successfully until 2 years old. Fishers live up to 7 years under natural conditions but have reached 10 years in zoos.

Remarks The fisher has a number of adaptations that permit it to hunt effectively on the ground and in the trees. Foot pads and retractable claws give good traction, and the big feet, heavily furred in winter, help the animal to stay on the surface of the snow. The ankle is remarkable for rotating 180°, which allows the animal to descend tree trunks head first, hanging by the hind feet much like a tree squirrel. Round patches of coarse hair on the central hind foot pads are associated with glands, which mark the trail with the fisher's personal scent. The animal bounds from front to hind feet when traveling over its home range of 20 sq km (7.7 sq mi). The long bushy tail assists in balance while chasing squirrels through the trees or when jumping and twisting in pur-

suit of a zigzagging snowshoe hare. Movement of the prey seems to trigger the fisher to attack. Although fishers are adept at killing porcupines, this animal is relatively safe if it protects its head in a tree crevice or sits on a tree limb with its back and quills aimed toward the fisher.

The male's skull develops high crests of bone on the top and back for the attachment of the big jaw muscles. The great size difference between the sexes appears to offer several advantages—the larger-sized male can overpower a wider variety of prey, while the smaller female requires less food to support her body during the reproductive period of her life. Adult fishers are occasionally attacked by cougars and wolves, and younger animals are killed by other predators such as hawks and owls.

LEAST CHIPMUNK

Scientific name *Tamias minimus* (formerly *Eutamias*)
Family Squirrels (Sciuridae)
Order Rodents (Rodentia)
Total length 220 mm (8.8 in) (some races are smaller — 198 mm or 7.9 in)
Tail length 100 mm (4 in)
Weight 45 g (1.6 oz)
Color The least chipmunk has a beautiful orangy-red and gray coat marked on the sides of the face by 3 black and white lines. Along the back are 5 brownish-black lines, the inner 3 separated by 2 gray lines, the outer by whitish lines. The underparts are white and the tail is orangy-brown.

Distribution and Status This species has the largest range of any chipmunk in North America and occurs from such far-distant places as the Yukon to western Quebec in the north, and south to Wisconsin, New Mexico, and California. Throughout this broad region it inhabits widely different environments, including spruce and pine forests, mixed deciduous-coniferous forest, aspen grove, alpine shrub up to 3 200 m (10,448.7 ft) elevation, and down onto sagebrush plains. Wherever it occurs, however, the least chip-

munk seems to maintain a preference for the forest edge or bushy vegetation.

Food Like the other 22 species of chipmunks on this continent, the least chipmunk eats seeds, nuts, berries, fungi, other vegetation, and insects such as grasshoppers, caterpillars, and beetles. Cactus and wild rose fruits are eagerly sought after along the edge of the plains, while pinyon nuts and hazelnuts, and the seeds of conifers are a mainstay in the diet of the woodland and forest dwellers.

Reproduction and Growth The breeding season begins as early as March in warm regions, peaking in April over most of the range, and continues at a lower rate into May. The animals are generally ready to mate within a few weeks of their appearance from hibernation, and engage in noisy and lively chases over the ground and up into the lower branches of trees. After 28 to 30 days of development, usually 5 or 6 (range of 3 to 9) young are born in warm underground quarters amid a nest ball of shredded bark or grass. Though their eyes don't open until 4 weeks, they are fully independent by 2 months, having learned from their mother how to forage for food and hide from danger. There is only one litter produced annually. A few litters have been reported in summer, but these are probably from females who lost their first young, or who were mated late in the season. The average life span is 3 years, however captive individuals have lived to 6 years.

Remarks This rodent begins storing nuts and seeds as they ripen in late summer. Food items are stuffed into the internal cheek pouches and carried underground where they are stored in the hibernating chamber. The animal, which has grown fat from eating oil-rich seeds, enters progressively deeper sleeps each night as its body processes slow down. In cold regions the chipmunk disappears below ground before the snow falls, usually by early November. The burrow is blocked by a plug of earth and the chipmunk curls into a tight ball, nose thrust into the belly fur and tail wrapped around the body. Its temperature falls to a degree or two above that of the nest;

Continued on p.114

FISHER

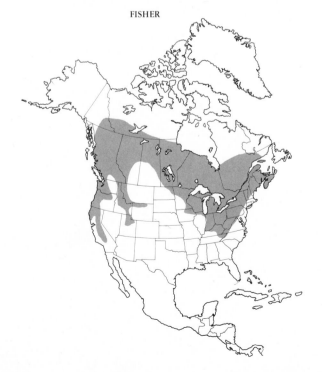

LEAST CHIPMUNK

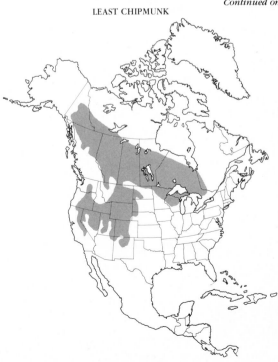

Fisher and Least Chipmunk

For countless generations, hunter and hunted had lived together in balance in a northern tract of pine and spruce forest. The fisher relied upon a dozen kinds of small animals as well as carrion of large mammals to provide its basic food needs for growth, energy, and reproduction. When the fisher's main prey species of snowshoe hare or porcupine became abundant, the fisher concentrated on them since they provided more energy for the effort of capture than rarer, smaller, or harder-to-catch prey. In turn, each species susceptible to attack by the fisher had developed various physical and behavioral adaptations to avoid predation. Because of this relationship, there was enough food to support the fisher and its family throughout the year, but not one prey species was wiped out by overhunting.

One of these prey species was the least chipmunk, which happened to live along the edge of the forest where the fisher passed every week or so. For three years these two individuals had been involved in a game of hide-and-seek, though it was anything but play for them. The fisher knew there was a chipmunk nearby because its scent lingered on stumps, logs, and thickets where the little rodent roamed in search of fruits, seeds, and insects. But the chipmunk was seldom around when the fisher bounded onto the scene. By being active only during the daytime, the chipmunk was safely underground in its burrow when the fisher usually appeared on its nightly rounds. Also, the chipmunk liked to venture out into the open burned-over areas, where blueberries and weed seeds grew in abundance. Perhaps for fear of wolves, the fisher felt insecure without trees around to climb, and so it generally avoided the chipmunk's favorite sites.

The chipmunk had two close calls, however, which made its heart pound in fright. While nibbling on the gills of a mushroom held in its front paws, the chipmunk was startled by the sudden explosive bark of a red squirrel. Before it could scamper for cover, it glanced up to see the squirrel leaping through the air from one spruce to another, the big black fisher right on its tail. Up and down the branches and trunks they raced, ripping claws sending a shower of needles and bark to the ground where the chipmunk cringed in terror. With a flick of the tail and a trilling alarm call, off it shot to its den entrance, which was hidden strategically under a log.

Later that fall the least chipmunk was working late in the evening, harvesting nuts in some hazel bushes, when it heard a crunching noise in the dry fallen leaves. Stopping in midaction as if instantly frozen solid, the chipmunk, with bulging eyes, watched its old enemy bound up to the bushes. The fisher rose on its hind feet, then thrust its pointy snout upward, straining to see, smell, or hear the something that was hiding among the stems. Once more on the verge of panic, the chipmunk fortunately managed to stay put, its white belly blending in with the evening sky and its orangy-brown sides disappearing among the shriveled leaves. Being color-blind, the fisher could only make out shades of gray in the bushes. Since nothing moved, the fisher concluded there was nothing there to eat after all, and it rambled off to check for porcupines. Two mintues later, the shaken chipmunk descended with short jerky movements to the ground and sneaked away to its den. Soon it would be safely underground for the winter, not knowing or caring that the fisher's paws left fresh tracks in the snow only a meter (3.3 feet) above its cold hibernating body.

Least chipmunk

Dwayne Harty

LEAST CHIPMUNK *continued from p.111*

if the nest temperature falls below 0°C (32°F), the animal will usually arouse or else it will freeze to death. The nest is made of soft insulating materials like hare fur, feathers, or silky plant fibers. Under this nest are thousands of nuts and seeds which are fed upon by the chipmunk during its periodic arousals. About half an hour of shaking and shivering occurs before its temperature rises to normal levels. In warmer parts of the range some individuals may remain active all winter or come out periodically during mild spells. Most emerge from hibernation by early April.

Chipmunks have characteristic chirping calls which serve to communicate with neighbors and to announce the presence of foxes, coyotes, weasels, hawks, and other predators. It is almost impossible to sneak up on a least chipmunk, for it is keenly aware of any movement or unusual sound. After the animal's initial retreat, it is fun to sit quietly and out-wait the little character. It generally cannot stay put for more than a minute or two, and soon comes out to pursue its activities. Chipmunks often become bold around campgrounds and cottages, and their charming appearance and entertaining antics have made them one of the most popular forms of wildlife.

I was once attempting to photograph a least chipmunk but it kept shifting to the opposite side of a tree trunk. Using an old squirrel-hunter's trick, I threw my hat on the far side of the trunk, and when the chipmunk came scurrying around to my side, click!

PORCUPINE

Scientific name   *Erethizon dorsatum*
Family   Porcupines (Erethizontidae)
Order   Rodents (Rodentia)
Total length   100 cm (39.4 in)
Tail length   17.5 cm (6.9 in)
Weight   7 kg, maximum 18 kg
(15.4 lb, maximum 39.7 lb)
Color   The shaggy coat is generally black or dark brown with black and white banded quills. However, the race dwelling on the prairies is a beautiful combination of black and yellow.

Distribution and Status   The porcupine is widespread on the continent, from the edge of the tundra from Alaska to Labrador, and south to northern Mexico (Sinaloa to Coahuila). For some unknown reason it is absent from the southeastern United States and most of California. Although mainly confined to forests, the species extends out into grassland, desert, and tundra by way of forested stream banks or patches of shrubby vegetation. Mixed deciduous and coniferous forest seems to be the preferred habitat over much of the range.

There are about 12 living species of New World porcupines, arranged in 5 genera. The family evolved in South America and invaded North America only about 3 million years ago, leaving 4 recent survivors outside the southern continent. The North American porcupine *(Erethizon)* has adapted remarkably well to cold climates, whereas the Mexican and Rothchilds' prehensile-tailed porcupines *(Coendou)* are restricted to tropical climates. The fourth species, the Antillean porcupine *(Sphiggurus pallidus)* from the West Indies, became extinct in the mid-1800s, and the remains of only 2 specimens are known. It is unclear whether *Erethizon* originated in

South America or evolved from a species of *Coendou* living in southern North America.
Food   In summer the diet includes leaves, catkins, nuts, berries, and roots of many kinds of plants, but in winter the animal resorts to the inner bark, buds, and needles of trees. Pines, hemlocks, and maples are favorites. Any antler or bone the animal finds in its travels is avidly gnawed on for its mineral content.
Reproduction and Growth   Males search for receptive females from October to January. The estrous cycle lasts about one month, and occurs repeatedly until pregnancy is achieved. When in heat (which lasts for 8 to 12 hours), the female joins the male on the ground in an unusual courtship of rising on their hind feet, boxing, pushing, and grunting. Finally the male sprays her with urine and mounts her from behind, apparently avoiding quills. The single young (twins are rare) is born from April to June (occasionally as late as August) in a remarkably advanced stage of development after growing in the womb for 205 to 215 days. The 450-g (15.9-oz) youngster's eyes are open, teeth have erupted, quills are in place, and it is capable of walking and climbing within days. Although it continues to nurse from the female's 6 mammae for up to 2 months, it begins to nibble on plant material by 2 weeks. Infant mortality is extremely low, since it can manage on its own and defend itself at an early age. It wanders away to become independent by autumn. Some become sexually mature at 16 months, while others mate for the first time the following year. Individuals reach full size in their fourth year and may survive for a decade in the wild.
Remarks   The porcupine has a thickset body with short limbs and a blunt face. The ears and tail are almost hidden among the long guard hairs. A dense underfur adds protection from cold weather, particularly important in its northern range. The feet are heavy and adapted for climbing, with 4 strong claws on the front and 5 on the hind foot, and creased, naked pads on the soles for traction on smooth bark. It is a sure-footed, if rather slow climber, resembling in some ways the sloth of the

tropical forest. Although its sense of sight appears to be limited, hearing and smell are keen.

One of North America's largest rodents, the porcupine is noted most for its protective quills or stiff hairs on the upperparts — up to 30,000 on a large animal. A sheet of muscle lying under the skin contracts and raises the quills. These sharp and barbed quills are about 7 cm (2.8 in) long, pull out easily on contact, and are replaced in half a year. Animals that attack porcupines often depart with painful reminders of the encounter as the quills work their way through their flesh at about one mm (0.04 in) per hour. The cougar, fisher, wolverine, bobcat, lynx, and great-horned owl are adept at killing and devouring porcupines without becoming pricked too badly, but occasionally they fall victim if quills penetrate a vital organ or cause infection. I once examined a cougar carcass that had numerous quills imbedded in its cheeks and forearms, apparently not causing any major problem in these tissues.

The porcupine is mainly a loner, preferring its own quiet company in a tree. Males are known to fight violently and scream during the breeding season, often resulting in wounds and imbedded quills. Several individuals may feed together for a while or den up in a hollow of a tree in winter. Porcupines often return to, or remain in, a single tree to feed, sometimes causing considerable damage or death by stripping the bark, hence their notorious reputation in the forest industry. One estimate placed the damage caused by each porcupine at $6000; however, in other studies it was thought to be insignificant. The animal also has the bad habit of chewing human articles, particularly if they are salty from handling, such as paddles and axes. Control by bounty, poisoning, hunting, trapping, and introduction of fishers have not had a major impact on the animal.

Porcupines eat much woody material consisting mainly of cellulose — a difficult substance for animals to digest. A long digestive tract of over 8 m (26.2 ft) and a large side pocket called the caecum house special

PORCUPINE

bacteria that break down cellulose into carbohydrates of use to the porcupine. The animal's enormous and ever-growing incisor teeth are worked by powerful cheek muscles, and cut easily through the tough outer bark to the nutritious inner layer or cambium. The lips fold in behind the incisors to keep the mouth free of wood and bark chips. There are a total of 20 teeth.

I once followed the trail of a porcupine through deep snow in Quebec, which connected its feeding station to the hollow base of a large tree about 100 m (328.1 ft) away. Huge piles of thick woody pellets showed that generations of porcupines had used this winter shelter. Most traverse a home area less than 12 ha (29.6 a) in their whole life, but some extend their activities over 100 ha (247 a). Daily movements in summer are about 120 m (393.7 ft), much less in winter when snow hinders movement. Dispersing individuals or those changing home ranges may travel 8 to 10 km (5 to 6.2 mi) and one subadult male is known to have moved 31 km (19.3 mi) in 66 days. Population density often averages 10 per sq km (3.7 per sq mi) in good habitat and may reach as high as 37 per sq km (13.7 per sq mi).

On another occasion I was surprised to find a porcupine browsing contentedly in a dwarf jack pine on the edge of the tundra, but even more amazed to come across others living in one-m (3.3-ft) shrubs occupying the bottom of a prairie draw or coulee in Saskatchewan. For one who always related porcupines with trees, I must admit these prairie dwellers looked completely out of place in the sea of grass and shrubs. Such broad assumptions about an animal's habits are frequently incorrect when only populations from part of the range are studied.

My most unusual anecdote about this species occurred in Quebec, when I was out at dusk collecting bats along the edge of a majestic beech-maple forest. I had succeeded in shooting and retrieving a hoary bat, then decided to follow my trapline with a flashlight to see what interesting mice might have been active in the first few hours of darkness. A handsome deer mouse paused briefly in the light before continuing on its way in a brush pile. Halfway down a steep hillside, I was jolted by the most hideous wail imaginable. Standing there alone in the darkness, shivers ran up my neck, and I tried to compose myself. As a budding scientist I thought I should be able to figure out this clue. Could it be a bobcat? My heart was still pounding when I decided to investigate further by moving toward the area where I thought the call had come. Suddenly the same piercing wail again shattered the stillness of the night. That was enough for me. Swallowing my pride, I quickly headed off in the opposite direction. Sometime later I read that porcupines are capable of emitting such cries when communicating with each other. I chuckled to myself when remembering my fearful reaction to the call of a love-sick porcupine. Unexpectedly this animal is capable of uttering quite a variety of calls, including grunts, coughs, moans, whines, wails, and teeth chattering.

RED SQUIRREL
Scientific name *Tamiasciurus hudsonicus*
Family   Squirrels (Sciuridae)
Order   Rodents (Rodentia)
Total length   315 mm (12.4 in)
Tail length   125 mm (4.9 in)
Weight   200 g (7 oz)
Color   The red squirrel is white underneath and a beautiful reddish-brown above, the 2 colors being separated by a black line along the sides. In winter this line fades, tufts of hair grow on the ears, and a rusty-red band appears on the back. The tail molts only once a year, in the autumn.
Distribution and Status   This is a widespread and common rodent occurring in many kinds of coniferous, mixed, and in some places deciduous forests. Typical habitats are spruce-fir, lodgepole pine, jack pine, black spruce, and bur oak forests. It is found throughout most of Canada (south of the treeline) and the northern United States, reaching as far south in the mountains as North Carolina and Arizona. It is closely related to the Douglas' squirrel *(Tamiasciurus douglasi)*, and may in fact, represent a series of subspecies of the red squirrel. Douglas' squirrel lives mostly in humid mountain forests from southern British Columbia to California. A third isolated population in the San Pedro Martir Mountains of Baja California has recently been described as a new species *(Tamiasciurus mearnsi)*.
Food   The red squirrel owes much of its success to its ability to extract the seeds from the hard cones of conifers, and to accept a wide variety of items such as seeds, fruit, buds (such as white spruce, juniper, pines), sap, bark, mushrooms, and any animal material it comes across, such as birds' eggs and fledglings, insects, and carrion.
Reproduction and Growth   There are 2 mating seasons throughout most of the range (February to March and June to July) but only one (April to May) in the far northern regions of Canada and Alaska. With the lengthening periods of daylight, the testes of the males enlarge and descend into the scrotum. The female comes into heat for only one day, dur-

ing which she permits one or more adjacent males to enter her home range and mate. The mating chases are spectacular and noisy. Then she drives away all other squirrels and proceeds with her maternal duties on her own. After 35 days, one to 8 (average of 5) babies are born in a tree or underground nest. The newborn are blind, naked, and weigh only 7.5 g (0.3 oz). Development is rather slow, with the first coat of hair at 3 weeks, tooth eruption at 4 weeks, eyes opening at 5 weeks, weaning at 8 weeks, and dispersal at 18 weeks. They breed for the first time the following spring at an age of 10 months. While few survive more than 2 years, there are cases of individuals living 9 years in the wild and 10 years in captivity.
Remarks   It is hard to imagine the boreal coniferous forest without the red squirrel, for this saucy character or its sign always seems to be present, no matter how scarce other creatures become in a region. I was astonished to find squirrel sign in pockets of dwarf spruce huddled in the protection of an esker many kilometers north of treeline on the tundra. With tree stands so limited and far apart, I found it hard to believe that this forest dweller could have crossed such great distances of open sand, tundra, and low arctic shrubs to reach such places. Here and at other treeline sites, I have tried in vain to collect a few specimens. I heard them call but the little rascals were extremely wary and took refuge underground, unlike their southern kin who boldly climb the nearest tree and chastise any intruder.

The red squirrel leads a solitary life and is aggressive toward its own kind and even other members of the squirrel family. This behavior and its strong sense of territoriality are likely related to the survival value of keeping competitors away from food supplies and caches, so essential during periods of food shortage. The home range averages 1.5 ha (3.8 a) and populations range from 0.5 to 7 per ha (0.2 to 2.8 per a). Numbers have been known to fluctuate drastically, which can usually be traced to the success or failure of the cone crop in the forest. One squirrel may harvest and store

Continued on p.120

RED SQUIRREL

Porcupine

Perched amid the gently swaying branches of a ten-meter (32.8-foot) birch was a black ball of fur that resembled a bear cub. A soft spring rain began to fall and the pitter-patter of the drops striking the animal's hunched-over back and the surrounding green leaves caused it to waken. The sleepy face that slowly appeared was that of a porcupine. For the last eight hours the female had slept peacefully while wedged in the angle between the white trunk and a limb. She began to move forward at a slow pace, carefully grasping the smooth bark and side branches with her claws and rubbery foot pads. As she approached a sprig of tender leaves she rose up on her flat hind feet, braced herself with her stubby tail, and reached out to draw the meal to her mouth. Without warning she flinched in response to a sharp pain that shot across her abdomen. She hunched over once again, moaning from time to time as the pain returned then subsided. She had experienced these cramps before but could not know they were the result of her having mated over seven months ago.

Instinctively she backed down the tree and waddled across the forest floor toward her nearest den — a rotted-out hollow log. Within the hour she gave birth to a miniature copy of herself, complete with a black coat of hair and white quills. After licking her new offspring clean, the two animals curled up together and slept. Several hours later, in the middle of the night, the young porcupine awoke and began to whine because it was hungry. The exhausted mother positioned herself so that her baby could nurse from a nipple projecting from the thin growth of hair on her underside. For the next week the mother remained in or near the den, but by the second week she left the youngster on its own while she went off to forage and regain her strength.

For the first time in its short life the little fellow was all alone. Two bright eyes shone through the bundle of black hair and prickles, huddled under the cover of a tall pine. The two-week-old porcupine leaned hard against the rough bark for security, whimpering in a low voice and anxiously awaiting the return of its mother. It was now turning light again, and the youngster was frightened and hungry.

A scuffle in the nearby leaves caused it to lurch and it stood up on its hind feet and glanced over its shoulder, expecting to see the dark form of mother. But an unfamiliar odor reached its nostrils. A red fox, out hunting for a meal, had detected the calls of the porcupine and came prancing in to investigate. Instinctively the porcupine turned its back to the fox and tucked its head against the tree, hoping the big creature would go away. Around and around, then in and out the fox weaved, taking a whole minute trying to figure out what sort of creature this was.

Amid the excited investigation, the hair and white quills rose slowly on the youngster's back, and its teeth began to chatter. Since this potential prey seemed harmless and almost immobile, the fox became bolder and extended its pointy snout for a closer sniff. At the faintest touch of its long guard hairs, the porcupine jerked its tail upward, jamming a dozen sharp quills into the predator's nose and throat. The suddenness of the tail movement and the sharp pain from the quills caused the fox to leap almost a meter (3.3 feet) into the air. Yowling loudly, the fox dashed away, stopping periodically to rub its nose with a paw and its chin on the ground. It would be some time before the quills worked their way out, and much longer before the fox would forget about porcupines. Not many kinds of animals could defend themselves so well at such an early age.

Upset by the encounter and still feeling threatened, the porcupine remained huddled against the tree for another twenty minutes. Although it had never climbed before, it reached up with its front legs and sunk its sharp claws into the bark. With as much speed as a turtle, it proceeded to inch its way shakily up the trunk. Using all its remaining strength the porcupine managed to reach the first branch, where it locked its padded and naked soles around the limb and drifted off to sleep. When it awoke some time later, it was nose to nose with its mother.

Red Squirrel

There were not many places quieter than the old pine woods, especially in the autumn when the songbirds had flown south. On the forest floor, green moss and white lichens, sprinkled with old yellow pine needles, muffled the footsteps of a moose as it passed by. There really wasn't much to eat in the sparse undergrowth, for the soil was thin, dry, and rocky, and the tall straight pines shut out most of the sunlight. It seemed only the wind played here, gently swishing through the outstretched branches far overhead. The restful scene was suddenly shattered by a loud "chur-r-r," ending in a number of bird-like chirps. But no animal appeared and all was silent again except for the faint pitter-patter of something falling through the trees. The king of the pine woods — a red squirrel — was dining on pine seeds, and dropping the husks. At a height of thirty-five meters (115 feet), the little red and white creature dashed over the swaying branches as if they were familiar highways. After a fearless leap from one tree to another, the animal stopped suddenly as if frozen, leaving only its bushy tail curled and jerking over its back. With its big black eyes ringed in white, the squirrel was surveying the borders of its territory to ensure that no other squirrel had entered. It moved along a branch in quick short jumps, pausing to stamp its hind feet, scent the bark with its mouth glands, and to let out a long churring call to announce its presence. Other nearby squirrels answered. In squirrel language, these messages meant "stay away," "come closer," or "danger is near." Homeowners had to be particularly diligent to keep out all those interloping young of the year who were dispersing through the forest in search of a place of their own.

This was a busy time of the year for the squirrel. In addition to the daily routine of eating, grooming, and scolding, it concentrated on collecting and then hoarding food underground for those winter days when it would be too cold or stormy to venture out. Bounding along a log, the saucy harvester came across a patch of yellow mushrooms. It decided to eat one, and breaking off and holding the cap between its hands, it rapidly nibbled the white flesh. The squirrel cut the stems of several others with its teeth and carried them away, one at a time, to secret places in the woods. Each little treasure was wedged into the branches of trees or under the rough pine bark. Did the animal somehow know that fresh mushrooms had to be dried in the air before storing them below ground to prevent them from spoiling? The squirrel then bounded to the crown of a tree and began cutting the tough green pine cones that hung in dense clusters near the end of the short limbs. As each cone was gnawed free, the animal threw it to the forest floor. Patches of sticky pine gum began to build up in the corners of its mouth and paws, but there was no time to pull them off. Down the tree it scampered to find the cones and carry them in its mouth to the den, which was located at the base of the largest pine in the area. The litter of old cones was piled half-a-meter high around the tree, showing that many generations of squirrels had called this tree their home. Overhead was the squirrel's summer nest of grass and leaves, built in the angle of two branches, while under roots of the old pine, numerous holes in the ground revealed where the squirrel would spend much of the winter once the snow came.

Although the red squirrel was normally active only during the daylight hours, this evening it continued to harvest cones long after dark. One cone stubbornly refused to break free, and the squirrel began pulling extra hard with its mouth and front limbs. Without warning the stem broke with a snap, sending the creature and cone reeling backward into the air. The animal clutched frantically for branches but it dropped all the way to the ground, landing with a thud on the spongy, needled floor. The red and white body bounced with the impact and then lay still. A few seconds later, its legs started to twitch and its chest refilled with air. The stunned squirrel regained its feet and staggered away, deciding that was enough work for one night.

RED SQUIRREL *continued from p.115*
literally hundreds of spruce, fir, and pine cones in tree hollows, underground chambers, in crevices on the open ground, or in wet sites, which retards the cones from opening and dispersing their seeds for months or even years. Foresters often raid these cone piles to obtain seed for tree plantations. The squirrels may slow forest regeneration by cropping almost all available cones produced in a year. Gnawing and stripping bark and clipping conifer buds can also cause considerable damage to timber.

While this species is mainly active in the morning and evening, it is sometimes out anytime of the day, and occasionally even on a moonlit night. Excessively hot afternoons or cold (-32°C or -26°F) winter weather forces it to remain in bed. A deposit of brown fat located under each armpit provides emergency quick energy and heat if the animal is stressed by severe cold. Despite its finely tuned senses of sight and hearing, and its amazing speed and agility, the red squirrel falls prey to the marten, fisher, red fox, bobcat, lynx, and red-tailed hawk. Several million squirrels are trapped for their fur each year. One of their neatest tricks is to gnaw a branch of the sugar maple in spring and hang upside-down by all 4 feet to catch the dripping sap. I once kept a red squirrel in a cage for study, but it was always so nervous and wild that I would not recommend keeping it for a pet.

NORTHERN FLYING SQUIRREL
Scientific name *Glaucomys sabrinus*
Family Squirrels (Sciuridae)
Order Rodents (Rodentia)
Total length 310 mm (12.2 in)
Tail length 150 mm (5.9 in)
Weight 125 g (4.4 oz)
Color The upper body is grayish-brown, the gliding membrane, feet, tail, and face are gray, and the undersides are white.
Distribution and Status This species occurs across the continent in coniferous, mixed, and deciduous forest, including white spruce-balsam fir, hemlock-yellow birch, beech-sugar maple, green ash-box elder, yellow pine, Douglas fir, Engelmann spruce, and redwood. It does not quite reach the northern treeline as does the red squirrel. Within the forests that clothe the major mountain chains the flying squirrel inhabits increasingly higher elevations towards the south. In fact the southern-most populations are isolated from the main range — evidence of a northward expansion of the range following the last Ice Age. For example, these relict populations occur in the Sierra Nevadas of southern California, the Rockies of Utah (up to 3 140 m or 10,302 ft), and in North Carolina, Tennessee, and West Virginia in the southern Appalachians. Numbers are highest in old forests. Its smaller cousin, the southern flying squirrel *(Glaucomys volans)*, is found south and east of Minnesota and down through Central America. There are over two-dozen other kinds of flying squirrels distributed throughout Europe and Asia, but 2 Old World species in particular (genus *Pteromys*) are almost identical in habits and appearance to their New World relatives. The ancestors of the northern and southern flying squirrel are unknown, but it is likely that the species split from the rest of the North American squirrel line at an early date. They may not even be closely related to the recent tree squirrels.
Food Nuts, fruit, buds, catkins, sap, bark, fungi, lichens, insects, young birds and eggs, and even carrion are eaten. Food is cached underground for use in winter.

NORTHERN FLYING SQUIRREL

Reproduction and Growth These squirrels mate in late March or April. The act takes about 15 seconds and is repeated several times. The female utters a chirring sound while the male whines. After a development period of 37 days, one to 6 (average 4) young are born in a tree hollow or a bark or moss nest constructed in the branches. The nest is often lined with soft fur or plant down for comfort and insulation, for like most baby mammals, the newborn squirrels cannot maintain their body temperature at a high enough level for proper growth. Each weighs 5 g (0.2 oz) and is blind and naked, but the gliding membrane is present. The mother provides warmth from her body and nourishment from 8 mammae. The offspring are clothed in fur at 18 days, the eyes open at 25 days, they can crawl out of the nest at 7 weeks, weaning occurs at 8 weeks, and the first glides are attempted at 12 weeks. By the autumn, they can leap and glide as well as their parents. A few adult females produce a second litter in August. The young breed for the first time the following spring at 9 months of age. Captives have survived 12 years but this age may never be attained in wild individuals, since few live more than 4 years.
Remarks The northern flying squirrel is a beautifully formed woodland creature, with a charming face, big black eyes, incredibly soft fur, and fascinating habits. Unfortunately, few people ever have the opportunity to see this animal even though they are commonly found in forested parks and in back yards in some cities. Its claim to fame is the elastic membrane with which it glides at a speed of around 2 m (6.6 ft) per second for distances up to 40 m (131 ft) and even 90 m (295 ft) downhill. The flattened tail increases the gliding surface of the animal by as much as 25 percent. On landing at the base of a tree, the squirrel scampers to the crown and catapults itself off again. When not in use, the membrane folds neatly against the sides of the body. Gliding is a convenient way to travel quickly over the 2-ha (4.9-a) home range. It also spends time on the ground where it can run at speeds up to 13 km (8 mi) per hour. The species is sociable among its own kind, although a female may on occasion chase away others from its nest of young. Home ranges of several squirrels overlap and they commonly feed in the same tree without much apparent fuss. Up to 9 have been found in a communal nest in winter — an obvious advantage in heat conservation. (When one holds a live squirrel or prepared specimen in the hand, one quickly feels the sensation of heat which builds up rapidly from the insulative quality of the fine fur). Densities of 0.5 to 10 per ha (0.2 to 4.1 per a) have been recorded. The main activity periods are the first 2 hours after dark and for an hour and a half before sunrise. There is no hibernation period in winter, but the squirrels remain cuddled in their nest for days during cold, windy weather. Predators include owls, hawks, martens, lynx, red fox, gray wolf, and short-tailed weasels.

The first flying squirrel I ever examined was one I trapped in a majestic hemlock-yellow birch forest in Quebec where I used to wander in the summers. I had noticed claw marks on a birch tree and fresh bites out of a fungus growing about 2 m (6.6 ft) high on the trunk. A trap nailed to the tree produced a beautiful specimen the next morning. The fur was long, soft, and seemed to heat my fingers. On another occasion, I opened a wood duck nest box placed high in a tree, only to find a family of flying squirrels inside. The mother looked up at me with her big black eyes as I gently closed the lid. At one time, I kept a young southern flying squirrel as a pet. Sitting on my head or shoulder, it swayed from side to side, judging the distance before leaping off and gliding to another person across the room. It could change direction and land so lightly on its shock-absorbing legs that we hardly felt it.

While in Illinois, a fellow student showed me how to catch flying squirrels alive. We walked through an oak-hickory woodlot until we located a round hole in the side of a tree trunk. My friend then proceeded to club the tree with a baseball bat, and to my astonishment, a flying squirrel shot up the tree, then glided away to the base of another tree about 15 m (49 ft) away. The following day we returned and took up our positions with me batting the tree trunk, and my friend standing behind the landing tree, armed with a big butterfly net. The procedure worked beautifully as the little glider was plucked out of the air at the last second with a quick sweep of the net.

Many years ago, my family and I had just settled down to sleep in a cottage on the edge of the boreal coniferous forest when we heard something bounce off the roof. A minute later a creature scampered over the shingles. Suspecting a flying squirrel, we went quietly outside and shone a flashlight into the trees. Faint calls were coming from the crowns and an occasional acorn fell to the ground. There must have been a number of flying squirrels feeding up there. Suddenly one took flight and glided away, its eyes and white belly reflecting in the beam of light. We couldn't have been more excited with this show than if we had witnessed a display of fireworks. Later, while lying in bed, we chuckled each time a squirrel or acorn landed on the roof.

MOOSE
Scientific name   *Alces alces*
Family   Deer (Cervidae)
Order   Even-toed Ungulates (Artiodactyla)
Total length   250 cm (98.4 in)
Tail length   12 cm (4.7 in)
Weight   males 450 kg, maximum 596 kg (992.1 lb, maximum 1,313.9 lb); females 350 kg, maximum 490 kg (771.6 lb, maximum 1,080.2 lb)
Color   The moose's coat is blackish-brown or reddish-brown in summer and somewhat grayer in winter. The underparts and lower legs tend to be lighter in color. The calf is reddish-brown and unspotted.
Distribution and Status   The moose is found in coniferous and mixed forests (with a snow cover in winter) across Canada and the northern United States as far south as Utah, Wisconsin, and Pennsylvania. It also occurs throughout northern Europe and Asia from Scandinavia and the Ukraine east to Siberia, Mongolia, and northern China; in the Old World this animal is known as elk. It frequents shrubby areas like the shores of lakes and rivers, forest glades, and recently burned, logged, or flooded sites. Spruces, tamarack, balsam fir, trembling aspen, and maples are common trees found in typical moose habitat, interspersed with thickets of willow, alder, and dwarf birch. Moose are found from sea level to subalpine elevations.

During historic times moose seem to have expanded their range northward in the boreal coniferous forest (particularly north of Lake Superior) and into the forest-tundra woodland. Occasional individuals wander out onto the tundra in the Northwest Territories. A population has been introduced successfully in Newfoundland. This species was almost wiped out in southern regions such as the United States by 1900, but with protection it has returned to both eastern and western ranges. Estimates in the 1970s were one million each in North America and in Eurasia.

The earliest known moose was *Alces gallicus* which inhabited European savannas from late Pliocene to mid-Pleistocene times (4 to 1.5 million years ago). It was similar in size to the modern moose but its antlers had longer beams spreading to 3 m (9.8 ft). A larger and perhaps direct ancestor of the modern moose was *Alces latifrons* from northern Eurasia, Alaska, and the Yukon. It lived from the mid- to late-Pleistocene (within the last 1.5 million years) and developed more palmed antlers. Another relative, the stag moose *(Cervalces scotti)*, was common in boreal habitats during this period. The modern moose first appeared in the fossil record of Europe about 200,000 years ago and did not reach North America (over the Bering Land Bridge) until late Wisconsinan times (about 20,000 years ago). It is therefore a relatively recent arrival to this continent, although it was previously thought that this species reached North America during a much earlier time (Illinoian glaciation).
Food   The huge animal browses on the twigs and leaves of many kinds of plants, particularly red-osier dogwood, willows, viburnum, low-bush cranberry, trembling aspen, balsam poplar, hazel, cherries, and maples. Grasses, water lilies, and other marsh plants are also relished in summer. To reach these, the animal lowers its head underwater or actually dives in deep water (to 5.5 m or 18 ft), remaining below for up to one minute. Since moose have no upper front teeth, twigs are snapped off and bark is peeled with the upper lip and lower incisors. An average of 20 kg (44.1 lb) of forage is eaten per day, but this rises to 29 kg (63.9 lb) in spring and 59 kg (130.1 lb) in autumn.
Reproduction and Growth   The mating season or rut lasts from early September to November but peaks from late September to early October. No harem is gathered; usually a bull courts a cow until mating is achieved, then he departs in search of another. Both sexes sometimes gather in loose groups of up to 30 individuals during the breeding season, so a high percentage of the female population is impregnated. Males often wallow in mud holes and become aggressive during the rut. Their necks and shoulders swell in size, and

Continued on p.126

MOOSE

Northern Flying Squirrel

As the big red sun slipped below the horizon, the day shift of forest animals retired for the evening and the night shift began to stir in their beds. That noisy red squirrel disappeared into its leaf nest just as the bright black eyes of a flying squirrel appeared in a rounded hole three meters (9.8 feet) up in a hollow tree. She would not venture out for another hour, until it was really dark. This was going to be an important night in the life of this three-month-old juvenile. Although she had become quite agile in leaping from branch to branch, the delicate little creature had yet to build up its nerve for the first glide. Down the trunk she came, playing tag with her brothers and sisters, all chirping back and forth like birds. Nearing the base of the tree, the squirrel prepared for a practise glide to the ground. Its head bobbed side to side, trying to judge the best place to land. But then another squirrel jumped on her from behind, and off they scampered, round and round the tree, using their long, clawed hands and feet as hooks to cling onto the rough bark.

Some time later the mother and father squirrels descended to the forest floor, followed slowly by the six young. Here they spent twenty minutes searching under logs and moss for gleaming white insect grubs and yellow mushrooms. For the next two hours the group drifted apart, some foraging on the ground while the others headed back into the trees. It was midnight before they all returned with full bellies to their tree hole.

About four in the morning the family became active again, and the young squirrel made its way to the top of a fir tree. Her large eyes seemed to bulge out of her head as she searched the branches for cones. As the young animal cut a cone free with her sharp incisors and proceeded to nibble out the seeds, a shadow moved across the moonlight. A great-horned owl glided in on silent wings and with deadly talons stretched out. Without hesitating the flying squirrel instinctively shot out into space, narrowly escaping the owl's attack. As if by magic, the squirrel's arms and legs extended outward, spreading taut the loose folds of skin that ran from wrist to heel. Like a paper airplane she glided away through the dark. Her limbs and feather-like tail shifted position back and forth as the squirrel tried to maintain balance in midair. Down, down she glided for twenty-five meters (82 feet), narrowly missing collisions with several branches. Although she would have preferred to alight on the trunk of a tree, there were none in the flight path. As she approached the ground her tail jerked up and she brought her landing gear of four limbs into frontal position. The curve of her belly and the folded membranes turned the squirrel into a perfect parachute as she slowed speed, then crashed to the ground with a bounce and somersault. Not the best flight and landing, but at least that owl was nowhere in sight. The squirrel quickly ran to the base of a nearby fir and huddled there to recover from its terrible experience. After calming down for five minutes the squirrel made its way back on the ground to the nest tree, guided by the calls of its family. How was the little creature able to execute such a complicated maneuver so well without practise?

Moose

On a cool evening in June, a commotion arose near the rocky shoreline and parts of two massive dark creatures were just visible through the dense shrubbery. Instead of quietly browsing side to side, as the two moose had done for a whole year, the cow suddenly became aggressive towards her large calf. Not understanding this reversal of motherly attention, the yearling kept returning after each retreat from the cow's charges and kicks. Finally it decided it had better wander off and the cow moved directly to a secluded spot. She laid her swollen belly on the cool carpet of moss for a few minutes but she was unable to find a comfortable position. Up on her long legs, she stood still for awhile then settled down again, folding at the knees. Then it began. The life that had started growing inside her uterus two hundred and forty days ago was about to enter into the boreal world.

The birth took only fifteen minutes and ended with a big gelatinous mass being squeezed out onto the ground. For this experienced cow it was her twenty-fifth newborn. Then the contractions began again and a stillborn young and the placentas (after-births) were passed. She managed to regain her shaky legs and instinctively attended the moving youngster. With great care and dedication she licked her baby clean of membranes and fluid, and it was almost dry by the time she lay down to recuperate. The following evening she nudged the youngster onto its feet for the first time, its wobbly legs threatening to collapse like sticks at any moment. Several weeks passed before it was able to walk without falling down periodically. Patiently the mother stayed by its side, rubbing and comforting with her great soft nose and tongue-bathing the youngster several times a day. A bond was formed between the two animals during these early days that would last for a year. The yearling moose returned to keep them company for a few weeks, but with a new calf the center of its mother's attention, the older individual soon departed forever.

About a month later the cow was bedded down amid some spruce trees, quietly chewing her cud and pausing occasionally to flick water droplets from her erect ears. At her side the calf lay sleeping. A strong gusty wind and frequent rains had restricted the animals' movements for several days. The cow moose relied on her keen nose and ears to detect any signals of danger, but these senses were not effective during the stormy weather. She swung her huge head in the direction of a falling branch, obviously nervous over the safety of the calf. As rain trickled down the coarse brown hairs of her side, muscles tensed and twitched in her thighs. She stood up suddenly and moaned to her calf, which awoke and struggled sleepily to its feet. Something wasn't quite right. The cow sniffed and sniffed the air for odors, while the long ears honed in on every new sound. An expression of alarm appeared over her long horse-like face as she picked up a faint scent. In an instant she knew what it meant, and she quickly eliminated about eighteen large black pellets. Quietly she led her calf off downwind. Though she could step over mounds of moss and fallen trees, the youngster's legs were still too short, and it had to go around the obstacles, sometimes tripping over branches.

Meanwhile four wolves had discovered the warm beds and pranced excitedly around the black pellets. The race was on. The cow moose knew they were being pursued and her big eyes filled with terror as she glanced back over her shoulder. The wolves bounded with graceful ease over the rough terrain as if springs energized their long legs. The distance between predators and prey began to close. The mooses' sides heaved from exertion, forcing out loud bursts of hot used air from their lungs. Normally the cow could have kept the wolves at a distance with powerful kicks, but she knew she could not defend both herself and her offspring. There was only one route for escape — the lake — if only they could reach it in time.

The calf stumbled on its stilt-like legs and banged its chin on the ground, but regained its footing and trotted along as quickly as it could. Keeping close watch on the calf, the cow ran into a hard branch, gouging out a piece of flesh from her front leg. Ten seconds later the wolves went wild over the drops of warm fresh blood. Breaking through the dense alder thicket and cattails the two moose splashed into the shallows, just as the pack was about to overtake and surround them. Without looking back, the moose swam through the lily pads and into deep water, breathing heavily through their flared nostrils. The wolves ran back and forth along the shore yelping frantically to each other. The pack leader waded in up to his belly then gave up the chase. The calf had never swum far before, yet made good progress behind the cow. As the calf was close to exhaustion, the cow's feet touched the muddy bottom of the far shore. Then they shook the water off in a mist of droplets and disappeared into the dark forest.

MOOSE *continued from p.121*

sparring, pushing matches, and occasionally battles follow to determine dominance rank and right to mate nearby cows. Females are far from passive and actively search out males by bawling or moaning — a call imitated successfully by moose hunters. Females frequently become intolerant of each other during this time. The estrous cycle extends for 20 to 22 days. Females are receptive to males for 7 to 12 days, and the actual period of heat lasts for one day.

In late May to early June, 240 to 246 days after conception, one or two calves (triplets are rare) are born, each weighing about 14 kg (30.9 lb). On nutritious feeding grounds cows give birth to twins at a frequency of up to 28 percent (higher in Sweden). Labor lasts about 15 minutes and the calf is on its feet in one day. About 150 liters (39.6 US gal) of milk are provided by the cow from 4 mammae until weaning of the young in September. The calf grows one kg (2.2 lb) per day during the summer and weighs around 60 kg (132.3 lb) by October. Both sexes become sexually mature their second year (10 to 18 months) and cows reproduce annually until 18 years old. Maximum longevity recorded for this species is 27 years, but few survive in nature past 10 years.

Remarks The moose is the largest living member of the deer family. It is noted most for its palm-shaped antlers (in the male only), massive body, exceptionally long legs, broad overhanging muzzle, and the "bell" or flap of skin hanging from the throat. The head is horse-like and contains 32 teeth with the premolars and molars having numerous hard ridges for grinding plant food. Its eyesight is surprisingly poor but is compensated by acute senses of hearing and smell. While generally silent, bulls "croak" loudly during the rut (sound traveling over 3 km or 2 mi), cows moan, both have been heard to whine, and under stress they bellow. In spite of its large size a moose can attain speeds up to 56 km (34.8 mi) per hour and move through dense forest without making a sound. These ungainly looking creatures can sometimes be quite playful, particularly the calves, running in circles, splashing through the water, chasing, and mock fighting. When threatened, females fight and defend themselves with blows of the front feet, while males also use the antlers. Particular positions of the head and antlers are quickly recognized as threat signals by other individuals. Antlers begin to grow from nubbins on the skull each April and are fully formed by September. Yearlings' antlers are only knobs and larger sets are developed from ages 8 to 13 years. Maximum spread and weight are 205 cm (80.7 in) and 35 kg (77.2 lb). The skin which nourishes the antler bone dies and is rubbed off in the autumn. Antlers fall off in December or January and are often gnawed on by rodents for calcium. To grow an annual set of such immense bony structures is truly a remarkable feat of metabolism.

Moose are active at any time but peaks occur at dusk and dawn. A number of beds may be used during the day and night. An individual deposits about 15 to 20 pellet groups per day—indicative of its prodigious appetite. Moose have evolved in snowy regions and their long legs generally carry them over average snowfalls. However, movement becomes impeded at depths over 60 cm (23.6 in) and over 90 cm (35.4 in) may be critical in restricting both traveling and feeding. In some areas (particularly in the east), moose "yard" under conditions of deep snow, using beaten trails to reach food much like snowshoe hares. This species often moves from one home range in summer to another in winter where forage, snow quality and depth, and forest protection from the weather are more conducive to survival. These movements may occur in both flat and mountainous country and may be only several km (few mi) to 180 km (111.9 mi). Home ranges are often remarkably small for such big animals; usually within 2.2 to 17 sq km (0.8 to 6.3 sq mi). Ranges are larger in summer than in winter, but sometimes a moose ranges widely (300 sq km or 111 sq mi) even in winter. While most moose spend their entire lives in the same area, there are always a few others that develop wanderlust and travel long distances. Moose are not known to be territorial.

Population densities average from 0.1 to 1.1 per sq km (0.3 to 3 per sq mi), although a concentration of 200 per sq km (540.5 per sq mi) has been reported. Habitat destruction, hunting, starvation in severe winters, and predation by wolves, black and grizzly bears (mainly on calves) are important factors controlling numbers of moose in an area. From Manitoba eastward, a parasitic worm, contracted from white-tailed deer, destroys the mooses' brains and has become a serious problem in areas where both species occur. Wolf-control measures are frequently requested by hunting organizations in order to maintain adequate moose populations. One estimate indicated that a ratio higher than one wolf to 20 moose results in a declining moose population.

The moose is generally a loner, although they may group together at certain times of the year, particularly in autumn and winter. I was astonished on one occasion in autumn to see 3 bull moose with magnificent antlers standing nose to nose in an aspen thicket, as if they were discussing the rigors of the upcoming rut. The idea for the story of the swimming cow and her calf came from an observation in the Mackenzie River area of the Northwest Territories. I watched anxiously as the 2 animals swam for 20 minutes and I worried that the calf was not going to make it to the other side of the lake. There are similar cases where people have seen the cow dive and come up under a calf, supporting it long enough for it to regain its strength. However, in other cases the cow underestimated its calf's endurance and it drowned.

Moose sometimes do the strangest things, such as running along a road for a kilometer in front of a car instead of turning off into the forest. Not infrequently, they turn up on main streets of towns and even large cities such as Winnipeg. Though a few people in North America have semi-trained an orphan moose by feeding it when young, the Russians have actually domesticated it for use as a draft animal and for meat, hides, and milk.

While working for the Quebec Wildlife Service as a student biologist for a summer, I had numerous occasions to observe moose. Several technicians were old hands at calling in bulls to close range by imitating the love call of a cow. I remember sitting hunched down behind some dwarf birch in a spruce bog with one of these fellows, as he grunted through his cupped hands for just the authentic sound that he assured me would be irresistible to any bull within hearing range. I had my doubts as we developed leg cramps and it was becoming cold with the fading light, but I wasn't supposed to hit any of the hundreds of mosquitoes and black flies swarming over us for fear of giving away our position. Just as I was wishing the technician would give up for the night, he pointed slowly to the far end of the clearing and there it stood, in all the magnificence that only a bull moose can muster.

A few weeks later, I came closer to a moose than I ever care to again. The study involved trapping moose in a spruce-pole stockade and then anesthetizing, measuring, marking, and releasing them. My task was to assist the veterinarian. When we arrived at the trap I peered in to see an exhausted cow that had pawed up the ground into a thick layer of mud. Her nostrils flared open with each labored breath and her big brown eyes were full of fear. In 10 minutes she was down with the drug, and I held her huge head in my lap. Everything was proceeding as planned, up to the point of resetting one of the 2 heavy trap doors. Without the least warning the cow swung her neck free of my grasp and kicked violently in an attempt to regain her feet in the quagmire. What a scene! Three men scrambled up the 3-m (9.8-ft) walls with an ease that would have impressed a chimpanzee, while the veterinarian and I bolted toward the only open door. Mud sucked on my rubber boots with such force that I felt I was running in one of those slow-motion dreams. With visions of being run over and stomped on by a third of a tonne of moose, I just dodged past the exit and fell to one side as the moose stumbled out right behind me. She was so groggy from the drug that she swayed from side to side like a drunkard and disappeared down the road. Once we calmed down, my French Canadian friends and I burst into laughter. Another day we were called upon to collect the carcass and perform an autopsy on an unfortunate moose that had been struck by a speeding car on the highway. I shall never forget the incredible size of the stomach packed full of at least 50 kg (110.2 lb) of plant material.

HEATHER VOLE

Scientific name *Phenacomys intermedius*
Family Voles and Lemmings (Arvicolidae)
Order Rodents (Rodentia)
Total length 140 mm (5.5 in)
Tail length 35 mm (1.4 in)
Weight 30 g (1.1 oz)
Color The coat of the heather vole is long, soft, and grayish-brown in color. The nose, ears, and rump may have a touch of orange. The underparts are gray.
Distribution and Status The heather vole is generally a rare species found in the boreal and mountain forests from Quebec to the Yukon and south to California, Utah, and New Mexico. It may turn up in a variety of habitats from mature, damp, coniferous and mixed forests; woodlands of spruce, pine, fir, and hemlock; shrubby borders of forests; and even mountain meadows and patches of heath. However, the highest populations are located in birch and willow thickets near the northern treeline. It occurs from sea level to 2 195 m (7,201.4 ft) elevation.

There is a possibility that the heather vole may consist of several species instead of just one. It also has two close relatives — the white-footed vole *(Phenacomys albipes)* and the red tree mouse *(Phenacomys longicaudus)* — from Oregon and California. These latter two species are considered a different genus *(Arborimus)* by some mammalogists.
Food This vole devours the fruit, seeds, and green leaves of low heath shrubs like dwarf

birch, blueberry, cranberry, soapberry, crowberry, and bearberry, as well as mushrooms and herbs such as baked apple, fireweed, and cinquefoil. It does not seem very interested in grasses or insects. In winter the bark of willow, birch, and heath plants become important in the diet.

Reproduction and Growth Two or 3 litters of usually 5 (range of 2 to 8) young are born between May and September. The babies develop for 19 to 24 days within the female and weigh 2.4 g (0.08 oz) at birth. They nurse from the mother's 8 mammae, their eyes open at 14 days, and they are weaned at 17 to 21 days. Females mature sexually at 4 to 6 weeks and may produce one or 2 litters during the summer, but males do not breed until the following spring. The babies are on their own at the age of one month. Most heather voles survive for only one year, but a few live to 2 or even 3 years.

Remarks This little short-tailed vole closely resembles the meadow vole, and it takes a trained eye to identify it. In most southern parts of its range it is among the rarest of small mammals, but it can become quite common along the northern periphery of its range. The home range is believed to be about 0.8 ha (2 a) and one marked individual was found to have traveled 185 m (607 ft). The animal does not hibernate but remains active under the snow, generally constructing its nest within the insulating snow cover in winter. These grass nests and latrines can be found in the springtime when the snow melts. It also clips and caches twigs in piles here and there, to be eaten at a later date. Predators include the ermine, red fox, marten, owls, and hawks.

Years of intensive collecting with my assistants in southern Manitoba had produced only a dozen specimens, but several trips to just south of the treeline changed my mind about the rarity of this mammal. We trapped about 70 of them in dry, open, black spruce forests and in rock outcrops overgrown with thickets of willow and dwarf birch. It is really exciting to go to a place where a "rare" animal is common, for there is a great opportunity to learn new things about its life history and habits.

SOUTHERN RED-BACKED VOLE
Scientific name *Clethrionomys gapperi*
Family Voles and Lemmings (Arvicolidae)
Order Rodents (Rodentia)
Total length 135 mm (5.3 in)
Tail length 34 mm (1.3 in)
Weight 26 g, maximum 42 g
(0.9 oz, maximum 1.5 oz)

Color The upperparts are rusty-red, paler on the sides and cheeks. The undersides and feet are grayish white. An interesting color variation occurs in this species in which all the red pigment is missing from the fur. The animal appears black on the back and dark gray on the sides. Both dark and red animals may be born in the same litter. Though extremely rare or unknown in the south, the dark phase becomes common at the northern edge of the range, so that half the population may be dark. The 2 color forms look more like different species than siblings.

Distribution and Status The red-backed vole occurs from the Pacific to Atlantic coasts, from the treeline in northern Canada, south to the northern states, with southward extensions in the Rocky Mountains to Arizona and New Mexico, and in the Appalachian Mountains to Georgia and North Carolina. It is found in a great variety of habitats, including coniferous and deciduous forests and woodlands, spruce bogs, rock slides, shrub thickets, and pockets of shrubs on the edges of the prairie and tundra. Occasionally it extends out into grassland and marsh.

There are 7 species of *Clethrionomys* found throughout vast regions of northern North America and Eurasia. The northern red-backed vole *(Clethrionomys rutilus)* lives in shrub thickets on the mainland tundra of not only North America but from Scandinavia to Siberia as well. The California red-backed vole *(Clethrionomys californicus)* is restricted to coniferous and mixed forests of northern California and Oregon.

Food This vole devours a great number of leafy green plants, seeds, fruits, and nuts. Fungi are dominant in the diet in late summer and autumn. During the winter such a variety is unavailable, so it resorts to seeds and leaves of evergreen heaths, and the buds, twigs, and bark of stems and roots of shrubs and trees. Though insects are only eaten in small numbers, the vole will readily nibble on the flesh of a dead animal, even of its own kind. The vole continues to actively forage under the snow, for it does not store much food or lay on thick layers of fat.

Reproduction and Growth Few native mammals can match the red-backed vole's ability to breed. The reproductive season is long, from March to October, during which time 3 or 4 litters averaging 6 (ranging from 2 to 11) young are produced. Litters tend to be larger (7) in northern regions than in the south (3). On occasion the animals breed even under the snow. The nest is underground or in a stump. The young are born about 18 days after the mating act. They weigh 1.9 g (0.07 oz), hair appears at 7 days, and their eyes open at 9 to 15 days. The mother provides milk from 8 mammae until her offspring are 17 to 21 days old. They leave home when 3 or 4 weeks old. The young females are sexually mature in 3 months and can give birth at 4 months. Spring-born males can also breed by mid-summer. The average life expectancy is only one year, but some individuals reach 2 years. Related species have survived 5 years in captivity.

Remarks This vole is one of the most abundant and widespread mammals in North America, and owes this success to its high breeding rate (up to 25 young per year) and ability to adapt to a wide range of habitats, as long as there is shrub or forest cover. It apparently needs to drink about 22 cc (0.7 fl oz) of water a day — 10 times as much as a deer mouse in the same habitat. We often found that we had to trap and remove dozens or even hundreds of red-backs before we could catch the rarer species. Yet, on occasion, the population may drop to such low levels that they seem to have all died off or stopped breeding. Estimates of 2 to 74 per ha (0.8 to 30 per a) have been reported. The size of the home range can vary widely from season to season and from place to place. Extremes of home ranges are 0.01 to 7.6 ha (0.03 to 18.8 a) and may change from 1.4 ha (3.5 a) in summer to 0.2 ha (0.5

Continued on p.132

HEATHER VOLE

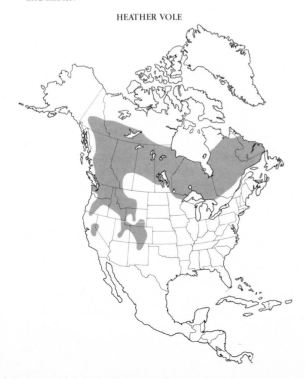

SOUTHERN RED-BACKED VOLE

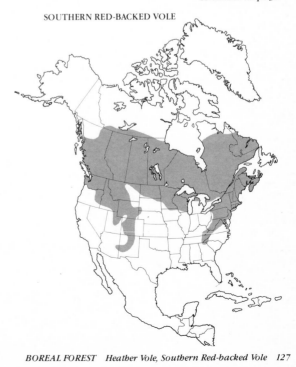

Heather Vole and Southern Red-backed Vole

Flying over the northern boreal forest in a helicopter, the research team of a geologist, botanist, and zoologist remarked on the unusual landscape. Half the ground area in view was under water — an endless weaving array of lakes, ponds, and creeks that sparkled in reflected sunlight. Around each watercourse stretched a thin border of light green sedge. Next to the sedge and on drier soil, a stunted black spruce and tamarack forest sprung up, the trees growing widely spaced in dark green and red sphagnum moss. Then out of the moss rose hills of pink and gray bedrock, covered here and there with a thin rug of white lichens, shiny bearberry, and birch and willow shrubs. The geologist explained how the glaciers of the last Ice Age had leveled the hilly terrain, and with the soil permanently frozen, the water had nowhere to drain. The botanist pointed out how the plant communities changed from the water's edge to the rocky bluffs. These plants were the same as those that grew in the area eight thousand years ago, just after the glacier retreated. The zoologist was anxious to find out what mammals were living in such a seemingly harsh environment that was free of snow for only three summer months.

After landing and setting up camp, the zoologist set up many rows of live traps to catch small mammals. Over the next three days she caught, earmarked, and released forty mice. There were four different kinds and she identified them as the meadow vole, northern bog lemming, southern red-backed vole, and heather vole.

"How was it," she asked, "that all four mice could live together in the same area?"

As the live-trapping study continued, she noticed that the meadow voles were largely restricted to the wet sedge border, the bog lemmings in the adjacent damp shrub zone, the red-backed voles in the spruce-moss open forest, and the heather voles up on the dry rocky hilltop under shrubs. Each species of mouse appeared to have its own preferred habitat.

The zoologist then studied the red-backed and heather voles in detail. The red-backed vole, as its name suggests, had a rusty-red stripe down the back. It was active anytime during the day or night, scurrying along on its short legs through runways sunk deeply in the moss. Its trail generally disappeared under the roots of a spruce tree, which concealed an underground nest of moss. While the red-back was extremely common, the heather vole was rare. This she discovered was due partly to fewer and smaller litters produced during the short breeding season. The heather vole was grayish-brown, with a touch of orange on the ears, snout, and rump. It preferred much drier conditions up on the rocks, and its runways and nests were not easily discovered down in the crevices between the boulders and through the mat of lichen, blueberry, and bearberry that crept over the ground. Active mainly at night, the heather vole cut three-centimeter (1.2-inch)-long twigs of birch and willow and gathered them into neat piles for winter food.

When the zoologist placed the two mice together in a cage, the red-backed vole was almost always the aggressor, chattering its teeth, biting, and chasing the shyer heather vole into a corner. The more she studied the two voles the more differences she discovered in their diets, habits, and behavior. Perhaps these characteristics were the reasons all four voles were able to live side by side without overcoming each other. By the end of the study all four voles were found to be quite distinctive, each with its own "personality," in spite of their being so similar in appearance.

As the helicopter shuddered into the air with the heavy load of equipment and the scientists, then moved away from the study site, the zoologist looked down at the beautiful landscape of rock, water, and autumn colors of the vegetation. It seemed hard to believe that such a complex community of plants and animals coexisted in such an apparently barren environment.

Northern Bog Lemming

It hadn't rained for over a month and even the mossy bogs in the low-lying areas between the pink granite outcrops had dried out. The gurgling creek was silent and no longer fed the pond with life-giving water. As the pond grew smaller, flat green lily pads were left stranded on the black mud. The surrounding spruce and pine forest was so dry that the ground cover of white and gray lichens turned to powder underfoot. People were warned by rangers to be careful with matches and camp fires. But one afternoon the sky turned hazy as white smoke drifted in from somewhere. An approaching roaring sound and the thickening smoke, hurled around by the strong wind, frightened the birds, moose, and hares and they ran off in all directions. The air grew terribly hot and treetops burst into flames, which quickly spread down to the ground. By evening, when the fire had passed, the lush green forest had turned into black poles amid a layer of gray ash. Many thousands of animals and plants perished as the fire, smoke, and intense heat swept over them, for they didn't know which way to flee. Yet miraculously a few creatures managed to survive. The sedges surrounding the lake shore were still green at the base, and a few hummocks of moist sphagnum moss in the bog had escaped.

After dark, a small brown mouse with a stubby tail poked its head out of the moss to look around. This bog lemming had avoided the choking smoke and killing heat by descending deeply underground in the saturated peat. The area had been its home for over a year, and several times a day it used to scamper down to the pond to eat the tender white bases of sedge leaves. The passing of countless little feet had sunk a trail into the moss and low shrubs, marked here and there by neat piles of green droppings and cut sections of sedge. Numerous tough roots had been cut and removed to make way for the underground tunnel system. But now the trails and protective covering of low shrubs had vanished and the ground was too hot to walk on. For a week the bog lemming lived inside the moss hummock, nibbling on the bark of bog laurel and the rootstocks of a few grasses. Eventually it gained the courage to run over the bare ground to the pond edge for a drink and to eat the sedges. On returning to its nest the little creature had to clean off the ash dust and mud from its fluffly fur and scaly feet.

Finally the rains came, and green sprouts popped through the gray mud from the roots of plants that had somehow remained alive. The bog and forest communities were starting to recover from the fire, as they had done countless times over the ages. The bog lemming found additional fresh greens to eat as new plants appeared from fire-resistant seeds buried in the ground or from other seeds that the winds carried in. Investigating the pond shore under the cover of overhanging sedges, the bog lemming met a few jumping mice, water shrews, and tiny masked shrews — all survivors of the fire's devastation.

One evening, while dashing along a trail to avoid being exposed any longer than necessary, the female bog lemming detected a fascinating scent along a section of the runway. Instinctively she knew there was a male of her own kind somewhere in the bog. Excitedly she thrust her sensitive nose this way and that, attempting to determine which way the visitor had gone. About ten meters (32.8 feet) farther along she almost ran into the male bog lemming, busily washing his face and combing his fur with his claws. Quivering with anticipation, the two rodents made their acquaintance using their noses, eyes, and little squeaks. The female recognized the scent on the trail as coming from the male's flank glands, marked by a thin blaze of white hairs. She turned and ran back to her nest hollowed out of a mound of sphagnum, making sure that she was being followed by her suitor. Soon there would be young bog lemmings burrowing through the expanding moss hummocks. But it would be a century before the forest matured again and regained all its former complement of plants and animals.

a) in winter when mobility is severely curtailed by snow.

These animals are shy and excitable and try to bite if touched. Sometimes they die of shock just from being handled. They are solitary in nature; several are found in the same nest only when mating, raising young, or huddling to keep warm. Though their legs are short, these little mice can move quickly — running at 1.8 m (5.9 ft) per second and jumping 20 cm (7.9 in). They climb occasionally into shrubs and trees (a nest was found at a height of 6.1 m or 20 ft), and are good swimmers as long as their coat remains water repellant and buoyant. This species is active anytime, but more so at night except in winter when it may become more diurnal under the snow. Each period of activity lasts about one or 2 hours, then it retreats to a nest of grass or moss about 10 cm (3.9 in) in diameter, hidden under a log, the snow, or underground. Food caches are sometimes found along its trails or inside burrows. The two most stressful times for the vole are the autumn freeze (especially without an insulating cover of snow) and spring thaw, when the creature is exposed to extreme cold and/or wet conditions. Many forest predators such as foxes, cats, skunks, weasels, and birds of prey rely heavily on red-backs as their main source of food.

NORTHERN BOG LEMMING
Scientific name *Synaptomys borealis*
Family Voles and Lemmings (Arvicolidae)
Order Rodents (Rodentia)
Total length 130 mm (5.1 in)
Tail length 20 mm (0.8 in)
Weight 30 g, maximum 50 g
　　　　　(1.1 oz, maximum 1.8 oz)
Color The long hair of the bog lemming is grizzled brown on the upperparts and gray on the underside. The rounded ears are edged with a rusty-orange color. The feet are black and the tail is bicolored.
Distribution and Status This species is generally rare but widespread from the southern edge of the arctic tundra from Alaska to Labrador and as far south as Washington, Minnesota, and Quebec. An isolated section of the range occurs in the Appalachian Mountains running from the Gaspé region of Quebec to New Brunswick, Maine, and New Hampshire. This strange distributional pattern developed as the range of the bog lemming shifted northward following the retreating glaciers, leaving the Appalachian populations behind in this elevated area.

Over much of its range the northern bog lemming is highly localized in cool sphagnum bogs, but it has also been reported in moist black spruce-horsetail forest, dry black spruce-lichen woodland, hemlock-beech forest, subalpine meadows, alpine tundra, weedy bluegrass fields, and surprisingly, dry hills of sagebrush. It is usually absent from apparently suitable habitat, and may be present in an area for a time and then disappear.

The northern bog lemming has only one other near relative — the southern bog lemming *(Synaptomys cooperi)*. The 2 resemble each other so closely that the cheek teeth must be examined to make a positive identification. The ranges of the 2 overlap in several regions, with the southern species occurring from Manitoba to Quebec and south to Kansas and South Carolina. It lives in fields, wet meadows, bogs, and moist forests and can be fairly common at times.

Food Though acid bogs are one of the poorer habitats in which to find food, the bog lemming is able to live on the sedge, grass, broad-leaved plants, berries, mushrooms, and the underground fungus Endogone. Most of the diet is vegetation, supplemented with an occasional snail or insect. Its teeth are like miniature horse teeth, with numerous ridges of hard enamel useful in grinding down rough plants like grass and sedge.
Reproduction and Growth The northern bog lemming begins to mate in April and the first litters appear in May, 23 days after fertilization. A second litter is produced, and perhaps a third in southern areas, before the end of August. The number of young per litter averages only 4 (range of one to 8), which partially explains why this species is relatively rare. The young are born naked and weigh about 3.7 g (0.1 oz). The nest is generally situated underground or inside a mound of sphagnum. Hair appears at day 6 and the eyes and ears open at 10 days. Nursing continues from the female's 4 pairs of teats (only 3 pairs in the southern bog lemming) until 16 to 21 days. Both sexes may begin to breed before the age of 6 weeks. Life expectancy is unknown but few individuals live more than one year and probably none more than 3 years.
Remarks Bogs are fascinating places to explore because of the unusual plants and animals that live there. Insect-eating plants (pitcher plants and sundews), high mounds of green and red sponge-like sphagnum moss, and dwarfed and gnarled black spruce and tamarack draped in lichens give the impression of an ancient, fairy-tale setting. Running between the mounds anytime during the day or night, summer or winter, one can sometimes find the bog lemming — a tube-shaped mouse with its eyes, ears, feet, and tail almost hidden in its long soft fur. The first feature that suggests this creature is not a meadow vole is the short tail, reduced almost to a stub. Checking the yellowish-orange and chisel-sharp upper incisors, a groove near the outside of the tooth is apparent, unlike the smooth surface of the vole's tooth. The fur of the bog lemm-

ing has a characteristic color and texture as well, but a trained eye is necessary to recognize the distinction.

The home range is remarkably small, generally within the range of .08 to 0.2 ha (0.2 to 0.5 a). Males tend to wander more widely than females. Population density may rise to 35 per ha (14.2 per a) but is generally close to 6 per ha (2.4 per a). Only the area in the vicinity of the nest is defended against other bog lemmings and small mammals. The main predators are the ermine, red fox, owls, and hawks.

In spite of both bog lemmings being quite rare over most of their range, the southern bog lemming was one of the first species that I encountered during my first introduction to trapping small mammals. My main job while working the summer for the Quebec Wildlife Service was to conduct a habitat survey in preparation for a reintroduction of woodland caribou. Actually this wasn't as exciting as it sounded, for most of the time I sat on the ground picking lichens and heath plants from within a one-m (3.3-ft)-diameter metal ring thrown at random in the spruce woodland. The heat and clouds of black flies were a severe test to one's patience and endurance, as anyone who has worked in the northern bush can attest. It was with keen interest therefore, that I looked forward to the evening diversion of fly fishing for speckled trout and setting traps for small mammals. I set my very first trapline back and forth through a sedge meadow and was rewarded, with great excitement on my part, with 8 southern bog lemmings, 18 masked shrews *(Sorex cinereus)*, and in some nearby willow shrubs, 2 pygmy shrews *(Microsorex hoyi)* and a woodland jumping mouse *(Napaeozapus insignis)*. The identification and preparation of these little creatures took me some time to complete, but I will never forget the experience — like a youngster catching a first fish.

I and my associates have found the northern bog lemming to be extremely rare along the southern edge of the range, but becoming more common in the central and northern

NORTHERN BOG LEMMING

regions. We have collected about 75 specimens in Manitoba, including one individual on the coastal tundra on the west side of Hudson Bay which was a northern range extension for this species.

In one particular bog in eastern Manitoba our field crew collected 24 bog lemmings — an exceptional number. Since we were about 100 km (62.1 mi) northwest of the known range of the southern bog lemming, I presumed they were all the northern species. It was half a year later, when the skeletons were cleaned and when the teeth were checked, that I found out we had collected both species in the same place. Studying wildlife can lead to such unexpected surprises and new discoveries.

LYNX

Scientific name *Lynx canadensis*
Family Cats (Felidae)
Order Carnivores (Carnivora)
Total length 90 cm (35.4 in)
Tail length 10 cm (3.9 in)
Weight 10 kg, maximum 20 kg
(22 lb, maximum 44 lb)

Color The lynx is basically brown with dark guard hairs, the underparts lighter with dark spots. The edges of the ears and tufts, stripes on the face and cheek ruffs, and the tip of the tail are all black.

Distribution and Status The lynx is found right across North America in boreal and mountain forests from the edge of the tundra south to Oregon, Colorado, and Indiana. Typical forests and swamps include white spruce-white birch and black spruce-tamarack. It has declined significantly or disappeared along the southern boundary from New Brunswick and Prince Edward Island to the northern great plains. The only area south of the Canadian border with traditional population levels is in the remote Rockies of Montana, Idaho, and Washington. During peaks in abundance, strays occasionally travel south to formerly occupied regions, but there is little opportunity for reestablishment. Some mammalogists consider the

American lynx to be the same species as the Eurasian lynx *(Lynx lynx)*, which lives in the taiga or boreal coniferous forest from Scandinavia and Europe to eastern Siberia and China. Its closest relatives are the bobcat *(Lynx rufus)* of warmer regions of North America, the Spanish lynx *(Lynx pardina)* of Spain and Portugal, and perhaps the caracal *(Lynx caracal)* of southwest Asia and northern Africa. Even the genus *Lynx* is lumped into *Felis* by some scientists, arguing that since members from each genus are capable of mating and producing hybrid offspring, they must be too closely related genetically to be placed in separate genera.

Food Lynx hunt at night or when the sun is low for many kinds of mammals and birds, but by far the most important food item is the snowshoe hare. A lynx eats an average of one hare every 2 or 3 days, but when hares are in the low part of their 10-year cycle, the cat depends on mice, squirrels, the young of deer, caribou and sheep, or grouse, ducks, and songbirds. They will also accept carrion of moose, caribou, and deer. When hare populations crash, many lynx starve and their numbers drop to low levels within a year or 2.

Reproduction and Growth Though usually solitary, lynx pair up when the female comes into heat from March to early April. During this season, lynx make rather scary-sounding screams in the night, which probably serve in announcing their presence and in locating each other. The scent left by the female may attract several suitors which occasionally become involved in fights. At the peak of courtship, the male mounts the female and grabs her neck in his jaws — a protective move typical of all cats. The mating act is accompanied by yowling, and the 2 part company shortly afterwards. The embryos require about 65 days to develop before birth. Most litters are born from late May to June in a den consisting of a hollow log, stump, or cave. An average of 3 (range of one to 5) young are born blind, with fuzzy gray fur, and weighing around 200 g (7 oz). Their eyes open at about 14 days and weaning occurs at 12 weeks;

however, some kittens continue to supplement solid food with milk until 5 months of age. They remain with their mother, learning survival skills, until the spring. Females may begin to breed when one year old, while males require 2 years to reach sexual maturity. Lynx have survived for 21 years in captivity; usual and maximum longevity in the wild are unknown.

Remarks A lynx gives the appearance of being a powerful animal, with its stern gaze and large face and paws. However, one would hardly recognize it after a swim. The animal is really a thin, long-legged, and timid creature, but beautifully adapted to a life in the northern snowy forests. The fur is soft, long, and luxurious, which explains why people are as fond of a lynx coat as a lynx is. The paws are large, densely furred, and leave a track almost the size of a cougar. When walking, the hind paws are placed in the exact spots just vacated by the front paws, thereby assuring good footing. The limbs are relatively long — an advantage in attaining a burst of speed in hunting and in wading through deep soft snow. Like other cats, the lynx moves on its toes and keeps its sharp claws retracted until needed to grasp prey, climb trees, or gain added traction on slippery ground. The animal is a good swimmer, but much prefers to walk around a watercourse than swim across. It is built for short-range attacks and has poor endurance, which might be expected by the small size of the rib cage and lungs. When pursued by some other creature, the lynx seeks refuge in a tree rather than trying to outrun its antagonist. A daily cruising distance while hunting averages from 5 to 19 km (3.1 to 11.8 mi).

The home range of this species is quite variable in size, depending on such factors as prey abundance, types of cover and terrain, and sex (males range considerably farther than females). Studies have produced estimates from 10 to 300 sq km (3.7 to 111 sq mi). Home ranges overlap widely, but sometimes those of females are fairly distinct. Rather than aggressively protecting their territories, the animals simply avoid contact with each other, assisted by a system of trails marked frequently (around 30 times per km or 0.6 mi) by urine, droppings, and scent from the anal glands. This odor can be quite strong and in places is easily detected by the human nose. Populations fluctuate widely in response to the 10-year cycle of the snowshoe hare — the main source of food. One study found a low of 2 and a high of 10 lynx per 100 sq km (37 sq mi). Following the rapid decline in the hares the lynx population falls as a result of starvation of kittens and a reduced production of young by females. The years of 1971 and 1972 were peaks in the hare and lynx populations in central Canada and adjacent United States. During these years I recall seeing a dozen or more snowshoe hares while driving down a remote road each evening, and heavy browsing of trees and shrubs was evident. Trapping of lynx in those two winters was unusually good, and I received a report of one trapper collecting 45 lynx in one season. While trapping and starvation appear to be the major causes of death, predation by wolves and accidents are also contributing factors.

Once, when I and several field assistants were working in an open spruce forest near the treeline, I heard a strange noise and my colleague approached looking rather pale and shaken. He informed me that he had just smell-

Continued on p.136

LYNX

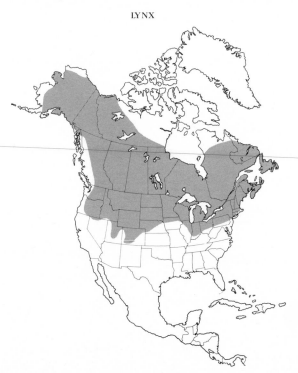

Lynx

A mother lynx and her two kittens had just settled down under a spruce tree after a busy night hunting snowshoe hares. One kitten opened wide its pink mouth several times, trying to remove a bit of hare fur caught in the corner of its jaw. Unsuccessful, it swiped the tickling tuft away with its paw and the fur sailed away on the breeze. Usually the kittens could not have resisted chasing after it, but they were just too tired. A leaping, dodging hare was more than they could cope with, so it was still up to the mother, using all her speed and experience, to bring down their favorite prey. Only their twitching stubby tails seemed to have any energy left. At last the three dozed off in the warm air, the two kittens curling up and using their mother as a pillow. Although the adult's eyes were closed, her ears moved every once in awhile, checking out any unusual sound.

Around ten o'clock in the morning both ears shifted in the same direction and the black eyelids parted to reveal her golden-yellow eyes. Something was coming their way, but what? A low drone of voices and the snapping of branches underfoot revealed there were several people nearby. She was instinctively distrustful of people and always made every effort to stay hidden from sight. She mewed quietly to the kittens and they obediently scrambled up the trunk, showering their mother with flakes of gray bark. She bent low on her long legs and appeared to flow like a pale ghost through the underbrush. The wide furry feet made no sound on the green feather moss and alder twigs on the forest floor. Lying silently under the cover of a thicket, and ready to take flight in an instant, she watched two hikers pass by within twenty meters (66 feet). When she was sure all was safe, she called to her kittens and in seconds they came bounding over to greet her.

It was time to move her family to a more secluded part of the home range and she guided them off in single file through the woods until they came to a gravel road. Suddenly she spotted a spruce grouse and immediately began her stalk. So intent was her concentration on the bird that she ignored the rumble of an approaching car. As it braked, the two kittens bolted in fear, and one of them leapt onto the road, where it was struck by the bumper. The two hikers jumped out of the car to see the back sides of two other lynx disappearing into the forest. They bent over to examine the struggling kitten and saw its hind leg was broken. Wrapping the hissing and kicking bundle in a blanket, they drove to a zoo in the next city, where the veterinarian applied a splint.

For the next six weeks the kitten hobbled around in an outside pen, hidden away from the public. It called and called for its mother, but only a strange lynx answered from a nearby pen. At first it was too frightened to accept any of the strange-smelling meat, but hunger finally forced it to eat. Over the following month the little lynx continued to grow rapidly and its leg soon healed. One day the zoo staff decided it was time to release the wild cat before the weather turned too cold. Driving to the approximate area of the accident, they opened the box and out slinked their patient, as fit as ever. Not knowing where it was or what to do, it scrambled up the first spruce tree it encountered and remained there for an hour. During the next several nights the young lynx caught and devoured six mice, but it still came out second best in pursuit of a hare. Then, in a dusting of snow, it came across a familiar scent and the rounded paw marks of two cats. Cautiously at first, and then in mounting excitement, it bounded off in their direction, its feet kicking high into the air.

LYNX *continued from p.133*

ed a strong cat-like odor when something exploded from under a nearby spruce tree. Shocked at first that he might have inadvertently wandered too close to a polar bear or wolf, he was most relieved to catch sight of a lynx bounding away. On another occasion in a national park, we drove past a lynx so intent on stalking a spruce grouse standing by the side of the road, that the cat completely ignored our presence.

A friend notified me that a lynx took up residence under his cottage and on several occasions he spotted the animal sitting along a path. Later that year, during the duck-hunting season, my friend left a pile of ducks on the wharf while he carried his gear back to the cottage. On returning to the wharf after each trip he noticed that one or two ducks were missing. From the cover of some vegetation he was surprised to see the lynx sneak out from the bushes and make off with yet another duck.

Mammals of the
Inland Waters

The Inland Waters Biome consists of a variety of freshwater communities. Water is over 800 times denser than air and contains less oxygen. It may be relatively free of dissolved solids, or contain high levels of silt which affects clarity and light penetration. Waterbodies in the north freeze over in winter, while in some regions they are subject to high temperatures, flooding, or drying up. Animals that live, feed, and seek shelter in water reveal special adaptations in body form, function, and behavior in dealing with this medium. Many other types of animals regularly visit watercourses to drink and feed on aquatic plants and animals.

Moving waters, such as rivers, streams and creeks, are conduits that empty into lakes or directly into the sea. They generally carry more oxygen than standing waters, and are ever changing in speed of flow, temperature, and clearness. Plants are mainly restricted to sites protected from the current; algae coat rocks while other plants develop holdfasts to prevent being swept away. Typical plants are cattails, rushes, pickerelweed, and arrowhead. Lining watercourses or floodplains are many kinds of forests such as cottonwood-willow on the plains, black spruce-tamarack in the north and west, willow-elm-hackberry in the east, water tupelo-red maple in the southeast, and Mexican rubber tree, palmetto, apompo, and zapotebobo in the south. Small animals seek refuge under stones while larger kinds are active swimmers. Typical species are water strider, bass, bullhead, snapping turtle, water shrew, river otter, mink, dipper, wood duck, and blue heron.

An estuary forms where a river enters the sea, the denser saltwater slipping underneath the outflowing freshwater. Estuaries are formidable environments for organisms, for they must contend with variation in salt content and suspended materials, as well as with water movements due to current, tide, and wind. In tropical eastern America, estuaries and deltas support mangrove swamps which are inhabited by creatures from the sea, river, and land. Found here are crabs, oysters, snails, ants, tarpon, kingfisher, green heron, white ibis, and raccoon.

Standing waters are lakes, ponds, marshes, bogs, fens, and swamps. Oxygen content is generally lower than in moving waters, and temperature gradients are significant. Lake water is divided into an upper warm and lower cold layer, while shallow waterbodies display a gradual temperature change with depth. These waterbodies are reservoirs destined to be filled in by sediments, and eventually to be covered by vegetation, although this process may take hundreds or thousands of years. Young lakes are deep, low in nutrients, and support few life forms (and named oligotrophic). In time they become shallower from debris building up on the bottom, richer in nutrients, and contain abundant life (eutrophic). In old age they turn into an acid bog or swamp, rich in organic matter, low in oxygen, and with a lower abundance of life (dystrophic). Standing waters have particular habitats, each with characteristic plants and animals. These are found in the shore or litteral zone, and the lemnetic zone in open water. Neuston are organisms living at the surface film, nekton are mobile forms like fish, plankton are small drifting life, and benthos are bottom dwellers such as crayfish. Pond plants include water lily, fanwort, arrowhead, bulrush, bur reed, and cattail, while on shore grow phragmites, sedge, or grass. Muskrat, mink, yellow warbler, snails, leopard frog, marsh hawk, mallard, and painted turtle are common inhabitants. In the boreal zone, ponds are edged with sphagnum moss, sweetgale, leatherleaf, sedge, Labrador tea, pitcher plant, and speckled alder, and eventually are invaded by black spruce and tamarack. Here lives the swamp sparrow, beaver, meadow vole, and moose. The Florida Everglades are a sea of tall saw-grass and spike-rush, with drier hammocks of sweetbay and live oak, and are home to the round-tailed muskrat and alligator. In the east are baldcypress swamps with swamp tupeio, waterlilies, bladderwort, golden club, and yellow-eyed grass. This is the habitat of the swamp rabbit and ivory-billed woodpecker. In brackish and salt marshes are saltwater cord grass, salt reed-grass, saw-grass, spike grass, and glasswort. Found here are the salt marsh grasshopper, water snake, greater scaup duck, and rice rat.

Water Shrew

It was a beautiful morning in the marsh, the rising sun banishing till nightfall the heavy layer of mist that hung low over the water. Several large dragonflies, clinging on bent legs to sedge stems, began warming up for a day of chasing mosquitos by fluttering their long transparent wings. It was still dark along the muddy pathways hidden under the cover of dew-soaked vegetation. Dozens of little tracks in the wet smelly mud, an occasional green dropping, and plant cuttings revealed that it had been a busy night in the small mammal world. Who had passed here a few hours before? A meadow jumping mouse cutting sedge stems to reach the seeds or a meadow mouse carrying grass for bedding? Perhaps a musky least weasel on the trail of both mice? Two eyes flashed at the end of the trail; something was coming this way. A sleek black creature with a constantly quivering pointy nose and a long tail sped by, stopping suddenly to sniff a pond snail. The water shrew deftly turned it over in its paws and with tweezer-like front teeth, it extracted the soft body from the spiraled shell. "Snap-snap-snap" worked the shrew's jaws, while its beady black eyes closed with apparent pleasure. The meal was finished in only a few seconds and the next two minutes were spent grooming the fur and removing some mud sticking to its toes.

Continuing along the trail and squeaking all the while, the shrew reached the edge of open water where it paused, directing its whiskered mouth into the liquid. Scooping up a mouthful, it raised its head while swallowing. Then a most amazing thing happened. Instead of wading in and swimming, the shrew actually dashed over the surface, as if the pond were covered by a transparent film of ice. Although its legs were going too fast to be seen, air bubbles trapped under the hairs on its big feet kept the shrew above the water for two meters (6.6 feet) before the animal disappeared with a plop amid expanding concentric ripples. The shrew was hoping to surprise a fish, pollywog, or insect larvae. Trapped air in the shrew's fur made it look like a silver bullet in the brown water as it paddled with all four legs to reach the bottom. A flattened leech slithered by in search of a host on which to attach its suction-cup mouth. The shrew did not give chase for it was almost out of breath. As soon as it stopped swimming the animal shot up to the surface like a cork. It then paddled directly to a nearby half-submerged log which was a favorite resting spot between dives. Climbing up,

droplets of water trickled off its dry coat. Next it shook itself into a blur and groomed its fur with the claws and bristles on its hind feet. Finally it grabbed the base of its long tail in its hands and mouth and licked it clean, right to the very end. The sun had now climbed above the trees and most creatures of the night had retired long ago.

The shrew had just completed its fur-dressing routine and was about to return to its den when its keen ears heard a high-pitched twittering. In a flash the shrew whirled around to see another water shrew, quite likely a brother or sister, sitting on the middle of the log. Never one to welcome a visitor, whether a relative or not, the water shrew emitted a sharp warning note. The two creatures squeaked back and forth for a few seconds, separated by only thirty centimeters (12 inches). When neither gave way, the original shrew showed its mounting anger by rising up on its hind feet, opening its mouth to reveal rows of red-tipped sharp teeth, and issuing a shrill threat in shrew language. Realizing a slashing and kicking attack was imminent, the intruder remained on all fours, turned, and ran off into the dense growth of sedge and grass. The excited shrew vented its pent-up energy by nibbling its belly fur in several places and scratching its ear with the claws of a hind foot.

Although the shrew's eyesight was limited, it noticed a fat black pollywog break the surface for air. Instantly the shrew dove in and gave chase. Aware that it was being pursued, the larval amphibian rapidly whipped its broad tail from side to side, propelling its rounded body between green chains of pond weed, then down into the cool soft muck on the bottom. The streamlined shrew followed its every move, homing in using its eyes and the vibration-sensitive whiskers of its snout. The hunter bit down hard into the soft swollen belly of the tadpole, and grasping the slippery prey firmly in its elongated jaws, the shrew bobbed to the surface with its prize. Paddling back to the old log, the shrew displayed its ravenous appetite by devouring the whole creature in only one minute. Highly active for an hour the shrew was now exhausted. Traveling down a familiar trail through the sedge and under a log, the water shrew arrived at a soggy den entrance in the bank. Once underground, it thrust its nose into a ball of shredded plants, turned around a few times, then promptly fell asleep.

WATER SHREW
Scientific name *Sorex palustris*
Family Shrews (Soricidae)
Order Insectivores (Insectivora)
Total length 150 mm (5.9 in)
Tail length 75 mm (3 in)
Weight 15 g (0.5 oz)
Color This beautifully colored shrew is black with a scattering of silver hairs above and silvery-gray below. The tail is bicolored as well. Perhaps this color pattern helps the shrew avoid detection by large fish such as pike or trout, which would no doubt like to eat it. Looking up at a swimming shrew, as would a fish, the silver belly blends with the light at the surface. Looking down on land, as would an owl, the shrew's black back blends in with the mud or shadows. The black color absorbs the moonlight instead of reflecting it as would a light color, making the shrew difficult to see.
Distribution and Status The water shrew is seldom found far from the open water of a river, creek, or pond. It is most abundant in sedge-grass marsh and alder-willow shrubs but it also occurs in a variety of coniferous and mixed forests, bogs, and swamps, from sea level to subalpine habitats. For example I have found the species in heath-moss and sedge-moss bogs, black spruce-tamarack swamp, white spruce-aspen forest, spruce-fir-birch forest, white cedar forest, and elm-maple-ash forest. A particularly choice place is the vicinity of a beaver dam where a creek empties into a lake. This big shrew occurs from Alaska to Labrador in the boreal coniferous forest zone, south to the edge of the prairies and extending southward at higher elevations in the Coast, Rocky, and Appalachian Mountains to California, New Mexico, and Pennsylvania. Its closest relative is the Pacific water shrew *(Sorex bendirii)* which lives from southwestern British Columbia to northwestern California. Eurasia is home to 3 species of Old World water shrews *(Neomys fodiens, anomalus,* and *schelkovnikovi)* which although placed in a different genus are very similar in appearance and habits to the 2 New World water shrews.
Food Insects make up most of the diet, particularly larvae found in water such as beetles,

mayflies, caddisflies, and stoneflies. Snails, leeches, fish, eggs, tadpoles, salamanders, and practically all small soft-bodied creatures are eaten by these ever-hungry shrews. Some hoarding of food is practised. Water shrews require almost one g (0.04 oz) of food per g of body weight per day.

Reproduction and Growth Water shrews develop their breeding organs in January and February (probably not until March in northern extremes of the range) and mating starts in late February and March. Mating may stimulate the release of eggs in the female and the embryos develop for about 20 days before birth. Two or 3 litters of 4 to 8 (average 6) young are born between April and August. The young nurse from the female's 6 mammae and leave the nest when they are two-thirds grown. A small percentage of females breed during their first summer, but most water shrews do not reproduce until their second year. The average life span is 1.5 years; however, a few survive to 3 years.

Remarks This is one of the largest shrews on the continent and it exhibits a decided preference for water while seeking prey. The well groomed fur resists wetting and traps pockets of air which help insulate the body against heat loss in cold water. The insectivore has even been seen swimming under the ice, although such excursions are no doubt of short duration. Stroking rapidly with all 4 limbs, the shrew may run on the surface for up to 5 seconds before submerging to intermediate levels or the bottom, where it remains for less than 48 seconds before bobbing up again for air. On land the water shrew travels the runways under vegetation and along the mud or sand shoreline, guided by its eyes, whiskers, and scent deposited during each passage by the anal glands. At times I have been able to detect this musky odor while setting traps. Some of its underground tunnels are filled part of their length with water, but eventually they lead to a dry nest of leaves in a chamber in the bank or under a log or tree root. A high relative humidity in the environment is necessary in maintaining its health. The soft black droppings of this shrew can be seen on its trails or

docks and are not formed into a regular-shaped pellet like those of mice and voles that live in the same vicinity.

The water shrew leads a solitary life-style except when a pair comes together to mate, or a mother caring for her young. A strange procession has been seen in this and several other species of shrews in which the mother leads her offspring in single file, each holding onto the tail of the sibling in front with the mouth. This unusual chain appears to be a method of moving the family around without losing offspring which may become easily disoriented during their first month. When two adults meet they are generally aggressive — squeaking and sometimes grappling and biting with their sharp teeth until one retreats. Since these shrews are closely tied to water, their home ranges tend to be elongated affairs, extending along 20 to 60 m (65.6 to 196.9 ft) of shoreline. Activity occurs mainly at night, especially just after dark, but they do emerge during the day as well, particularly on cloudy, rainy days. A frequent schedule for this and other shrews is alternating one-half hour of foraging with one hour of sleep. Its main predators are weasels, mink, otter, snakes, and large fish such as pike, trout, and bass. This is one of my favorite small mammals because of its interesting habits and the magical places it lives — tumbling creeks lined with ferns, logs, and boulders in the woods, and sedgy borders of small rivers and ponds. If ever there was a well dressed little creature stepping out for the night life it is this immaculate fellow dressed in a tuxedo-like coat.

Several years ago our museum field crew was joined by a curator from the National Zoo of the Smithsonian Institution, who wished to capture water shrews alive. He planned to study their echolocation abilities and to maintain them on display — perhaps for the first time in any zoo. He arrived at the airport laden with special traps, cages, and several bags of meal worms for shrew food. The next day we reached our camp in Precambrian Shield country on the Manitoba-Ontario border. Marshy creeks and small rivers wound their way between pink granite outcroppings which were covered in black spruce and jack pine forest. For the next 3 days we set hundreds of traps, which needed checking at midnight and at daybreak, for the captive shrews would perish within a few hours from exposure, stress, and lack of food. Each of us spent many solitary cold and wet hours running the lines by lantern light, all the time hoping the bait of peanut butter and bacon fat had not attracted the attention of black bears, which had become quite a problem in the area. We also had to be careful not to trip and fall into the water. On the drives back to camp we were kept awake by the excitement of spotting several woodland creatures — caribou and a red fox along the edge of the road. Eventually we were rewarded by 12 specimens of water shrews in the traps.

WATER SHREW

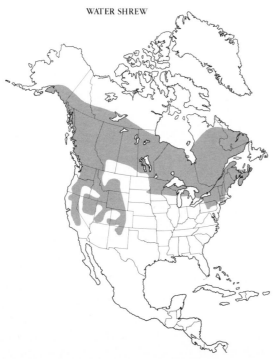

MUSKRAT

Scientific name *Ondatra zibethicus*
Family Voles and Lemmings (Arvicolidae)
Order Rodents (Rodentia)
Total length 550 mm (21.7 in)
Tail length 240 mm (9.5 in)
Weight 1 kg, maximum 2 kg
(2.2 lb, maximum 4.4 lb)

Color The upperparts are reddish-brown or dark brown, while the underparts are grayish-brown. The tail and the feet are black.

Distribution and Status The muskrat's range is extensive, reaching from northern Canada and Alaska south to the northern edge of Mexico. It is absent from desert areas lacking permanent rivers, all but the southern fringe of the barren-ground tundra, and the southeastern Atlantic coast. Although it used to live in Florida during the last Ice Age, it has been replaced there by the round-tailed muskrat *(Neofiber alleni)*. Almost any body of water (fresh or brackish) lined with sedges, reeds, cattails, and grasses may be home to a family of muskrats. The level of a marsh, estuary, river, lake, slough, ditch, or pond must not be too deep to support water plants, yet deep enough to prevent freezing to the bottom in winter. A thick layer of humus on the bottom allows easy digging of plants for food. This species has escaped from fur farms and is living in the wild over much of Europe, Scandinavia, the Soviet Union, and in parts of China, Japan, and southern South America.

Food This aquatic animal devours a wide variety of plants living under or emerging from the water. Favorite foods are the roots, bulbs, tubers, stems, and leaves of sedges, cordgrass, bluestem, cattails, reeds, burreed, bulrush, rushes, arrowhead, rice, water lilies, duckweed, and pondweed. Muskrats also like clams, fish, salamanders, turtles, crayfish, and snails. They do not store food for winter and when starving will even eat their lodge, nest, and other muskrats.

Reproduction and Growth In warm southern regions the muskrat breeds year-round, peaking in winter, and produces up to 6 litters. In cold northern areas, the breeding season is restricted from April to August and only 2 litters are born during this time. The female comes into heat for 30-day periods, but it is the curtailed sexual activity of the male that controls breeding. Each may mate with several individuals and the act lasts about 5 minutes. The gestation period ranges from 22 to 30 days. The number of young in a litter ranges from one to 11, and litters average larger in the north (7) than in the south (5). The newborn are blind, naked, and weigh 21 g (0.7 oz). Fur appears in one week and the eyes open at 2 weeks. The female nurses from 8 mammae. If she must move the litter she carries each one in her mouth above water. The young muskrats start eating plants after 3 weeks and are on their own at a month. Most mature sexually at one year of age, but some southern females become pregnant at only 6 months. Muskrats are fortunate if they live 3 or 4 years, but a few have survived for 10 years in captivity.

Remarks The muskrat resembles a huge vole with a number of aquatic adaptations. A rather stocky animal it has an unusual vertically flattened tail and large hind feet with partial webbing and a fringe of stiff hairs which increase the area of thrust against the water while swimming. The sparsely haired feet and tail radiate excess body heat but rapidly lose heat when in cold water or air. Critical chilling (hypothermia) is avoided by increasing the production of heat before entering frigid water, by climbing out periodically in push-ups or the den, and by huddling with other individuals. The heart rate actually drops from 200 to around 30 beats per minute when the animal submerges in cold water — lessening the circulation of warm blood to the animal's skin. Exposure to heat and cold is moderated by the great amount of time spent in the den. In areas with some topographical relief, the muskrat hollows out a den 3 to 15 m (9.8 to 49.2 ft) into a bank and with entrances below the usual water level. In flat regions like marshes and estuaries the animal builds a lodge of aquatic vegetation, about one m (3.3 ft) high and with a dry interior. The thick layer of plant stems (many with insulating air cells) and a cover of snow help to keep out the cold so that the interior of a lodge may be -9°C (15.8°F) while the exterior air temperature is -39°C (-38.2°F). To reach food sources in other parts of the marsh, the muskrat builds push-ups in the ice where it can pause to breathe or eat. In summer, when marshes often shrink in size from evaporation or drainage, the muskrat digs water-filled channels in the mud so it can still reach the sedge zone without having to expose itself to predators.

The muskrat's thick luxurious coat is responsible for the animal being the most important furbearing species on this continent; about 18 million pelts were sold on the North American markets from 1975 to 1977. The dense underfur and long guard hairs keep the muskrat warm and dry in cold air and icy water. The species receives its common name from the musk glands at the base of the tail that are used to add scent to its lodge, feeding platforms, and trails through the marsh. Individuals identify each other and their territories by this odor. The home range averages 61 m (200.1 ft) in diameter in a marsh and 183 m (600.4 ft) along the banks of a watercourse. Most feeding occurs within 15 m (49.2 ft) of the den, but the animal may travel as far as 457 m (1,499.3 ft) to reach new sources if food is scarce. While most young take up residence only 8 m (26.3 ft) away from their mother's den, others disperse greater distances; one tagged individual showed up an amazing 13 km (8.1 mi) away from home. Depending mainly on the availability of nutritious food and climate, muskrat populations are subject to great variations in numbers, with some evidence of a 10-year cycle. Most studies have found between one and 87 animals per ha (0.4 to 35.2 per a) but occasionally as high as 150 per ha (60.7 per a). At such high densities the muskrats literally devour most of the surrounding vegetation — an event known as an "eat-out." It requires several years for the plants to recover, with dire consequences to the muskrats, for they starve, disperse, and succumb to predators or exposure; and stress-related diseases and fighting (even cannabalism) are rampant. The results are low productivity in the waterbody and few muskrats for some years. I have skinned muskrats and found many terrible abscesses — the consequence of their aggressive nature.

This species is subject to an incredible number of parasites and diseases related to the animal's abundance in a relatively closed system like a marsh. Other causes of death are trapping, floods, drought, freezing, starvation, pollution, and predation by mink, raccoon, foxes, coyote, owls, hawks, alligators, and large snakes and fish.

As a child, I spent many glorious days playing in the forests and wetlands not far from my home in southern Quebec. Though the marsh has long since been replaced by a housing development, I still recall seeing my first muskrat there. Standing silently on the bank and taking in all the sounds of red-winged blackbirds, leopard frogs, crickets, and other noisy marsh life, I noticed something stirring up the green film of duckweed about 30 m (98 ft) away. Then a v-shaped wave began coursing around the marsh and headed my way. To my great excitement, it approached closer and closer, and I just caught sight of a muskrat as it swam into the bank under my feet. I had been standing upon its den. I raced home to tell my family and friends of my great discovery.

During a recent spring thaw, I spent an enjoyable morning watching the break-up of ice on a small river in Manitoba. The season was

Continued on p.144

MUSKRAT

Muskrat

The prairie marsh was a busy place in the autumn, much too noisy for the old scarred muskrat as it sat on a feeding platform chewing on the cattail stem in its paws. Hundreds of honking geese took off like airplanes on a runway, heading out for dinner in the grainfields. Several flocks of ducks whipped by in close formation overhead, while other ducks kept bobbing up unexpectedly from dives to the marsh bottom. Perhaps the muskrat knew that the coming winter would soon send all these splashing birds south and his world would be quiet again. Noise and bright light just added to his already nervous nature and so the animal spent over eighty percent of his time concealed in his lodge.

During the evening a light rain began to drift in around him and the sedges and cattails bowed gently to a pushy breeze. The muskrat liked cool rainy weather — a perfect time for a cruise around his home, just to check things out. He slipped into the dark water with only eyes, nose, and the top of his head showing. Paddling strokes of his big webbed hind feet and side to side sweeps of the tail carried the muskrat along at five kilometers (3.1 miles) per hour in a v-shaped wave through the floating green pondweed. With a forward roll the animal disappeared without a sound. A stream of bubbles followed his course underwater and his now-streamlined body took on quite a different appearance than his hunched-over posture on land. The muskrat was in its true element. Although he could remain below for twenty minutes and swim fifty meters (164 feet) before surfacing for air, he didn't have far to go before locating some tasty white stems and roots. Using his sharply clawed front feet he dug away the brown peaty muck and then gnawed several plants free with his large front incisors. Folds of cheek skin formed a perfect seal behind these teeth so that no water or debris entered his mouth. With two sections of plants tucked in his jaws he rose to the surface and headed for the closest feeding platform. When he climbed out, the water ran off his oiled coat, leaving it almost dry.

After munching down the tender juicy plants, the muskrat's next stop was his defecation post — the end of a partially submerged log where he left ten black oval droppings. Just as he circled past the far end of the marsh, the muskrat detected a dark shape on one of his platforms. With all the instincts of protecting his family and territory, the muskrat headed straight for the intruder. The newly arrived muskrat had been crowded out of its own marsh and was hoping to stay here for the winter. Emerging from the water, the resident muskrat gave off a strong scent of musk from glands at the base of his tail, which served as a warning that this marsh was already occupied by his family. The two muskrats chattered their teeth for a minute as they glared at each other, then clashed into a biting and kicking ball of fur. As most often happens, the home animal fought more fiercely, and it sank its long chisel teeth into its opponent's shoulder. The bleeding outsider staggered back in the mud, regained its feet, and disappeared into the night. The resident muskrat calmed itself by grooming its fur with its tongue and hind feet, then proceeded to its cone-shaped house to rest.

Early next morning the muskrat emerged through an underwater exit, and just as he was about to take a breath at the surface, he bumped his head on the thin layer of ice that had formed around the edge of the marsh. A few more strokes carried him to open water, but he had to lunge up and climb over the ice to reach a feeding site. The animal waddled onto the flattened vegetation, shook off the cold water, and reached for a stem with its mouth. Without warning a steel trap banged shut around its neck. The muskrat jolted backward into the water in shock, snorting loudly in an attempt to breathe. The animal's body and limbs arched and thrust violently underwater, and air bubbles swirled to the surface. The trapper had set the trap so that the muskrat would drown quickly. A minute later, the muskrat lay exhausted on the mud bottom, unable to hold his breath much longer. Bringing forward his powerful hind legs, the creature gave one last mighty push with all four feet, and the steel bars reluctantly slipped over his head. Two hours passed before the trapper returned to check his line and on reviewing the evidence he wondered how a lowly muskrat could have outsmarted him. It was only hunger that finally drove the muskrat out of his house three nights later. From now on he would be careful to test for human scent or steel before leaving the safety of the water.

MUSKRAT *continued from p.141*
well advanced and only remnants of snow drifts were left in hollows protected from the sun. Several crows flapped by, adding their cawing chorus to the thuds, cracks, and tinkles of colliding ice pans. Then I noticed a brown object, which I had formerly taken for a stump, begin to move on the edge of the shore ice. It was a muskrat, its beautiful brown fur glistening in the sunlight. As I watched through binoculars, the animal washed its face and sides with strokes of its front limbs, pausing to scratch its flanks with its large hind feet. This task completed, the muskrat launched itself into the 0°C (32°F) water, arched its back to keep its head above water, then swam to a particular spot. Here it rolled forward into a dive and disappeared into the silt-filled water. For 15 seconds I surveyed the swift current, trying to guess where the animal would resurface. Suddenly it popped up at the edge of the ice, climbed out, then proceeded to gnaw on a short black stick it had somehow found on the bottom. When I departed 20 minutes later, the muskrat was still diving for its breakfast. I wondered whether it and several other nearby muskrats had been flooded out of their dens, and how they managed to find food and shelter at this most difficult time of year.

Standing on the high banks of the Mackenzie Delta in the Yukon, I could see why this region is so famous a producer of muskrat fur. As far as the eye could see was a maze of sedge, shrubs, and open channels. I and a colleague spent a week there collecting mammals in the vicinity of a post called Reindeer Station. A young native boy befriended us and assisted with the trap line. He would drop over anytime, since even at 11 pm or 2 am it was still light. We asked him what he was having for lunch one afternoon as he prepared to depart, and he announced "rat and bannock." Apparently his family had skinned hundreds of muskrats and preserved the carcasses for future meals by placing them in a pit hollowed out of the permafrost. I cannot say the "rats" looked very appetizing but they were obviously quite nourishing considering the health of the children.

BEAVER

Scientific name *Castor canadensis*
Family Beavers (Castoridae)
Order Rodents (Rodentia)
Total length 104 cm (40.9 in)
Tail length 44 cm (17.3 in)
Weight 20 kg, maximum 50 kg
(44.1 lb, maximum 110.2 lb)

Color The beaver's coat is a chestnut or dark brown color, somewhat lighter on the undersides. Long, shiny guard hairs poke through a dense layer of wavy underfur. The young are reddish-brown.

Distribution and Status The beaver is found from the edge of the arctic tundra south to northern Mexico. It is rare or absent in arid areas of the American southwest and in the Florida peninsula. Distribution in alpine and arctic tundra is limited by ice freezing to the bottom of watercourses and by lack of woody food. Rivers, streams, creeks, lakes, and ponds are all suitable habitats for beavers, but watercourses subjected to extreme flooding or drying out are avoided. If left unmolested, this animal does not mind living close to people, and it may occur within the rivers of even large cities. The European beaver *(Castor fiber)* is a close relative (differing in cranial and chromosomal features) and has hybridized with the North American beaver following introduction of the latter species to Finland and the Soviet Union.

The 2 modern species of beavers were contemporaries of several giant species during the Pleistocene Ice Age. *Castoroides* of North America weighed about 360 kg (793.7 lb) and became extinct only 10,000 years ago. When Europeans arrived in the New World, there were an estimated 60 million beavers. Heavy trapping pressure over several centuries for this most valuable of furbearers (for felt hats and coats) seriously depleted populations in all corners of the range. Regulation of the harvest in the 1900s and reintroductions have resulted in a remarkable comeback, and indeed the beaver has become a nuisance in some areas—flooding roads and pastures, killing ornamental trees, damaging dikes and irrigation systems, and affecting fishing. These are minor problems when compared to its value as a highly visible wildlife species and the great variety of plants and animals that come to live in beaver-created habitats.

Food The beaver feeds on bark, twigs, leaves, and buds of shrubs and trees that are generally under 40 cm (15.8 in) in diameter. Over much of the animal's range, aspen is the favorite food, though many other trees are eaten as well, such as balsam poplar, willow, white birch, maple, cottonwood, and ash. In the southeast, sweetgum, loblolly pine, ironwood, and sweetbay are important. An average meal consists of about 600 g (1.3 lb) of woody material. The beaver is able to digest around 30 percent of this cellulose, with the assistance of bacteria in the intestine, and by reingesting the soft feces. However, the beaver does not live on woody food alone. Pondweed, algae, water lily, sedge, grass, ferns, acorns, fungi, skunk cabbage, stinkweed, giant ragweed, and many other aquatic and land plants are relished. For beavers living in ice-free regions winter poses no special problems, but in the north the animals are sealed in the darkness of their lodge and pond by ice. They subsist on rootstalks of aquatic plants and the bark of branches, specially dried in the autumn to the proper moisture level before felling and storing on the pond or river bottom.

Reproduction and Growth Beavers may pair for life or they may mate with several partners over the years. The breeding act occurs in the den, in the water, or on land. Southern beavers mate from November to January, while northern ones wait until January to March. The single annual litter of 3 or 4 (range of one to 9) kits are born 100 to 107 days later, inside the den. The kits weigh 0.5 kg (1.1 lb), are covered in fur, and have the eyes open. In fact, they are so well developed at birth that they are capable of swimming at only 13 hours. They suckle about 9 times a day from the mother's 4 mammae and are fully weaned at 60 days. The father and 2-year-old offspring are forced out of the den while the kits are young. If the den or dam is threatened, the mother carries her offspring in her mouth to another den. Health, environment, and social factors all influence the timing of a young female's first mating, which may occur from 1.5 to 4 years of age (generally 3). There is often considerable inbreeding. Beavers begin the nightly chores of dam and lodge repair as one-year-olds, and disperse or are forced out of the colony at age 2. Adult weight is reached at 5 years, though the animal continues to grow slowly throughout life. Beavers in the north cease growing in the winter period. Individuals have lived up to 24 years under natural conditions, but this is rare.

Remarks Everyone is aware that the beaver's life is closely tied to water, which it leaves only when necessary to reach new food sources. The ears and nostrils are able to close tightly and a transparent membrane protects the eyes when swimming underwater. The lips form a seal behind the large chisel-like incisors, so that the animal can chew without having water, mud, and chips enter the mouth. The unusual flat scaly tail acts as a rudder while swimming, a prop when the animal sits up, and also smacks the water or ground to communicate an alarm situation. It is difficult to determine the sex of beavers when alive because the sex organs, anal (castor) glands, anus, and oil glands all empty into a common

BEAVER

pocket called a cloaca. Scent from the castor glands is deposited on piles of mud and debris which serves to identify each individual and to mark the colony's territory. This thick, liquid musk is used as a base in the perfume industry and is also used by trappers to entice furbearers.

There are 20 teeth including 4 stout, ever-growing incisors and 16 cheek teeth, with numerous edges of enamel, which surprisingly do not grow throughout life. The beaver's coat must be groomed daily to keep it in good shape. The animal positions its tail forward to expose the cloaca, and withdraws oil on a front paw. This waterproofing and conditioning oil is spread diligently through all the fur, which is then combed by the hind feet, particularly with the 2 sets of inside toes which have special split and serrated nails.

Beavers are social creatures typically found in a family colony consisting of a dominant female, an adult male, several yearlings, and 3 or 4 kits. A colony may occupy a km (0.6 mi) of stream. Beavers are mainly active for periods during dusk, night, and dawn, but it is not unusual to see them out on cloudy days or even sunning themselves. Beavers swim with the webbed hind feet in unison when cruising, but switch to powerful alternating strokes when speed up to 8 km (5 mi) per hour is required. While generally submerging for only 2 or 3 minutes at a time, it can remain under for 15 minutes and travel 0.8 km (0.5 mi). It waddles or gallops awkwardly on land.

Beavers are fascinating animals to watch, although a spotlight and patience are required for night viewing. I remember watching kits on a creek shore strip willow bark and whimper loudly all the while. As I set a trapline one afternoon for small mammals around another creek, the resident beaver displayed its concern at my presence by slapping its tail on the water 48 times. My favorite observation involved a big beaver who watched and circled impatiently while 2 national park officials cleared out the dam blocking a road culvert. As soon as the men drove away, the beaver arrived with a mouthful of branches. When I returned one hour later, the culvert pipe was blocked again with a masterpiece of woven wood and mud construction.

MEADOW VOLE
Scientific name *Microtus pennsylvanicus*
Family Voles and Lemmings (Arvicolidae)
Order Rodents (Rodentia)
Total length 165 mm, maximum 197 mm
(6.6 in, maximum 7.9 in)
Tail length 44 mm, maximum 64 mm
(1.8 in, maximum 2.6 in)
Weight 42 g, maximum 75 g
(1.5 oz, maximum 2.6 oz)

Color The coat varies geographically and within a population from yellowish-chestnut to brownish-black, with numerous black-tipped hairs. The underparts are silvery-gray and the feet are grayish. The tail is slightly bicolored, darker on the top. The winter pelage is darker, as are immatures, which also have black feet and tails.
Distribution and Status The meadow vole's range extends from the southern edge of the arctic tundra through the zones of deciduous, coniferous, and montane forests to the grasslands region. The southern limits are Washington, increasingly higher elevations in the Rockies south to New Mexico and Chihuahua, Mexico, and eastward to Kansas

and Georgia. In fact, the meadow vole has by far the largest distribution of any of the 24 or so species of *Microtus* in North America. It is found predominantly in grasses and sedges, to a lesser degree in shrub thickets, and occasionally in woodlands and forests. It is often the most abundant mammal in meadows, moist and dry prairie, old fields, freshwater and salt marshes, sphagnum-heath bogs, swamps, and grainfields. Any substantial area of dense grass and herbs will likely harbor this vole. Optimum habitats are moist and the mouse is not afraid to get its feet wet or to swim to reach parts of its home range. There are about 24 other close relatives found throughout Eurasia, including the field vole *(Microtus agrestis)* which is physically indistinguishable from the meadow vole, but has a different number of chromosomes. Modern voles first invaded the New World across the Bering land bridge about 2 million years ago. The meadow vole appeared in the fossil record 0.5 million years ago and gave rise to a number of other species.
Food The diet is composed of a large number of the green plants available to the vole, but grasses such as bluegrass, brome, and bluestem, as well as sedges always predominate. Favorite forbs are clover, bushclover, golden rod, ragweed, beardtongue, and dandelion. Seeds, fungi, carrion, and sometimes insects are accepted as well. Large caches of seeds and bulbs have been found in their tunnels in autumn, but not all voles seem to bother to store food for winter use. During the cold months, shoots, seeds, roots, and bark are eaten and such stripping may kill shrubs and trees at the forest edge or in orchards. Voles cause enormous losses of grain, root crops, and fruit, and they utilize forage needed for domesticated animals. There is no ignoring the fact that meadow voles are successful competitors of humans.
Reproduction and Growth When a female comes into heat her odor attracts a number of male suitors in the vicinity. She rebukes and bites some males, but actively pursues the one of her choice. The couple mates repeatedly, each bout lasting only a few

seconds, and these acts result in the eggs being released from the female's ovaries about 12 to 18 hours later. The gestation period is only 21 days, and the 4 to 6 (range of one to 11) babies are born within one-half to 7 hours. The placenta (or afterbirth) is eaten by the female, thus retaining valuable nutrients at this critical time. The baby voles are pink, hairless, weigh about 2 g (.07 oz) each, and have their eyes and ears closed. They become furred at 4 days and begin to squeak. Developing rapidly on milk from the mother's 8 mammae, the mice's eyes and ears open at 8 days and weaning occurs at 14 days. The juveniles leave the nest and disperse at 4 weeks of age, and mortality is so high that only half to three-quarters of the litter is left alive by this time. They attain adult size by about 12 weeks.

The meadow vole is one of the most prolific breeders of all mammals. One captive female produced 83 young in 17 litters in one year! Generally, wild females have 3 or 4 litters per year — if they live that long. Surprisingly, young females are capable of starting a family at an age of 3 or 4 weeks and delivering at 6 or 7 weeks when only half grown. Males mature later at 7 weeks after they have dispersed, thereby reducing the chances of inbreeding with siblings.

The breeding season extends from April to September in the northern part of the range, March to November in the south. Occasionally breeding continues throughout the winter under the snow. I found one nest full of pink babies in the grass of a road bank, though it was a freezing cold October day in Manitoba.
Remarks The meadow vole is a stout-bodied rodent with short limbs and tail, small beady black eyes, a blunt nose, and rounded ears which barely show through the long fur. It makes numerous trails through the vegetation, nipped clear by the teeth and flattened by the repeated passage of their tubercled feet. Here and there are little piles of grass or sedge stems, about 3 to 6 cm (1.2 to 2.4 in) long, indicating where the vole sat to eat a meal. Though occasional droppings are seen on the runways, most are deposited in large piles in several toilets situated at the ends of side trails.

Continued on p.148

MEADOW VOLE

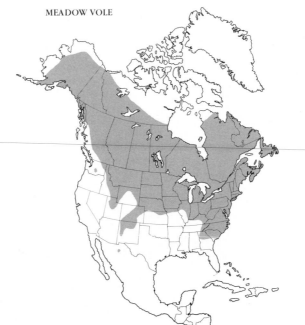

Beaver and Meadow Vole

Just before dark, air bubbles began popping at the pond's surface. Was this just swamp gas escaping from the murky bottom or was there some animal moving through the tea-colored water? A flat head appeared suddenly, sending a miniature wave washing to the shore. The beaver circled the pond slowly, watching, listening, and sniffing for anything unusual. Satisfied, it then paddled to the dam, crawled out on the pile of stripped saplings, and shook its head. Rubbing its eyes with its clenched paws, the beaver seemed confused. For over two years this young male had lived peacefully in the lodge with its parents, siblings, and yearlings, but it had now been chased out of its home by its mother. The colony numbered ten, and with a new litter expected any day, the mother beaver let the two-year-olds know it was time to leave. The young beaver sat there whimpering at being rejected.

Just then, two meadow voles ran out of the lush green sedges and over the beaver's scaly flat tail. In the heat of their courtship, the voles never even saw their towering relative the beaver, and they skittered across the dam as if it were their personal highway. Perhaps it was becoming too crowded around here! The beaver climbed down the dam, turned its back to the home pond, and slipped silently into the cool water. The animal swam downstream, passing familiar landmarks and smells, then entered foreign territory. By morning it had traveled a full four kilometers (2.5 miles) before putting to shore and falling asleep in a tangle of alders. During the next three days and nights the beaver investigated each tributary entering the stream, but mud patties laced with beaver scent lined the shores, telling all creatures that these waterways were occupied by beaver colonies.

After one week the beaver still had not found a suitable place to live. It was nervous at being away from home and exhausted from the twenty-kilometer (12.4-mile) trip, during which time it had scarcely paused to eat. Upon investigating the far reaches of a creek, it came nose to nose with another beaver, busy plastering a new dam with mud. The traveler could tell by the other animal's odor that it was a female. She did not seem to mind his sudden appearance, so after a sniffing, nudging, and grunting introduction, he began to follow her around as she showed off her pond and various construction projects.

The female beaver had arrived at this site a year ago, when a creek ran through a dense forest of aspen and spruce. Taking advantage of boulders in the creek bed, she had woven cut branches into a two-meter (6.6-foot) thick dam, weighed down with rocks and sealed with mud and trapped debris. As the water crept higher and higher into the surrounding forest, she had raised the level of the dam and extended its length to twenty-five meters (82 feet). At least eighty trees had been felled for food and construction, and several hundred other trees stood drowned and leafless, victims of the rising water. Sunlight flooded down on the pond where a dark forest floor had existed for a century.

As summer progressed, the two beavers enlarged a burrow the female had excavated into the side of the creek bank. Two underwater tunnels led upward to a sloping platform just above the waterline where the animals dried off and ate their meals. The floor was covered with strips of bark. Adjacent to this chamber was another more elevated room used as sleeping quarters. In the autumn, the beavers constructed a cone-shaped pile of branches above the den. When this lodge had reached a height of two meters (6.6 feet) they plastered the sides with mud, which they carried tucked between their front paws and chin. Then a small hole was chewed through the den roof reaching up to the lodge, allowing fresh air to reach the beavers inside. Their home renovations were finally finished.

Within two years the beavers had changed their surroundings from forest and creek to a pond whose shore was lined with bullrushes, sedges, and grasses. Soon pondweed, cattails, willows, and other marsh plants would arrive from seeds carried in by the wind, water, and on visiting ducks' feet. This new habitat quickly attracted a host of animals which found marshes to their liking — including meadow voles. No sooner had the green border of sedge formed at the edge of the pond, when these little brown mice showed up and began clearing trails through the dense stems. They dug extensive networks of burrows through the soft soil and discovered that, instead of having to swim, they could cross the pond and creek by scampering over a dam that happened to be situated at just the right place. As the pair of beavers sat on the shore, contentedly munching on aspen bark, they often saw their tiny neighbors going about their business.

MEADOW VOLE *continued from p.145*

The nest of shredded grass and other plant fibers is about 15 cm (5.9 in) across and is situated underground or on the surface, usually concealed in a tussock of grass or under some object. Most of the vole's life is spent curled up in the nest.

As soon as snow becomes too deep to wade through, the rodent begins to develop an extensive tunnel system on the ground's surface, occasionally leading to a ventilation or exit shaft to the top of the snow cover. From here one can often see tiny tracks and black pellets — evidence of the vole's occasional excursion in the cold winter air. I have seen these tracks end in a patch of disturbed snow, with the wing imprints of a bird of prey clearly visible on either side. Certain birds, like the great gray owl, can actually hear a vole moving deep under the snow, and with long thrusting talons it snatches up the vole and gulps it down whole (later coughing up the bones and hair). Generally safe under the snow, the vole huddles with several other meadow voles in its well-insulated nest. Interestingly, the rodent stops growing in winter, redirecting limited energy resources to maintaining body heat. It requires about 10 calories a day to live.

Grass and sedge are built of tough cellulose cell walls and abrasive particles of silica. In addition these plants are often coated with a thin layer of gritty soil. The meadow vole has adapted to the considerable wear on the teeth in grinding this fare by having ever-growing incisors and cheek teeth. This vole has been known to eat its own weight in vegetation within 24 hours, though generally one-third its weight would be the norm. The large caecum and colon of the intestinal tract harbor bacteria and other microorganisms that digest plant material far more efficiently (65 to 90 percent) than the vole's system alone. The animal will also reingest certain of its droppings, thereby capturing vitamins and nutrients that would otherwise be lost.

This vole lives at a fast clip and is active for periods every day and night, though most activity occurs at dusk and dawn. Seldom walking or hopping, it dashes along the trails from one shelter to another, sometimes swimming across a creek or climbing into a low bush. It is a relatively aggressive creature, especially during the breeding season or when numbers are high — which often occurs at a frequency of 2 to 5 years. Common densities are 20 to 128 voles per ha (8.1 to 51.8 per a) but estimates of over 1,000 per ha (404.9 per a) have been recorded. Particularly during these population outbreaks many voles are eaten by literally dozens of kinds of carnivores including large mammals (wolf and badger), small mammals (ermine and short-tailed shrew), birds (hawks, owls, and gulls), snakes, turtles, amphibians, and fish. Voles may be running all over the ground one year and be almost absent from the area a year later. Whatever the cause of these eruptions, it serves to disperse the voles to new, distant unoccupied habitats. There they set up a home range of 150 to 3 000 sq m (180 to 3,600 sq yd). When traversing the area they are able to orient themselves by the sun, and they mark favorite passageways and their territory with scent from both anal and flank glands.

MARSH RICE RAT

Scientific name *Oryzomys palustris*
Family New World Rats and Mice, Gerbils, and Hamsters (Cricetidae)
Order Rodents (Rodentia)
Total length 250 mm (9.8 in)
Tail length 120 mm (4.7 in)
Weight 50 g, maximum 80 g (1.8 oz, maximum 2.8 oz)
Color The upperparts are grayish-brown with numerous black hairs, while underparts and feet are white.
Distribution and Status The marsh rice rat is located from southeastern Kansas to New Jersey, and south to eastern Texas and Florida. There is some question whether populations of rice rats that occur in Mexico and Central America are this species or another *(Oryzomys*

couesi). Favorite habitats are marshes and swamps with plenty of grass and sedge, but the rats also invade meadows, rice fields, streambanks, sedge- and shrub-covered dunes, and open forests. Dry sites are avoided. This rat can become quite abundant in some areas such as in the Atlantic and Gulf coastal marshes. Formerly it occurred much farther north than at present, for fossils have been identified in many sites from Iowa to Pennsylvania. Rice rats *(Oryzomys)* play an important role in the ecosystems of many temperate and tropical regions for there are approximately 59 species distributed widely throughout southern North America, South America, the West Indies, and even the Galapagos Islands. Several closely related species of West Indian giant rice rats *(Megalomys)* reach 70 cm (27.6 in) in total length but became extinct during historical times from habitat destruction, predation from introduced feral species like the mongoose, and from volcanic explosions.

Food The rice rat eats the leaves and seeds of many kinds of green plants, mainly grasses, sedges, and planted rice (from which it is named). It is also fond of fungi, fruit, fish, clams, crabs, snails, insects, turtles, birds and their eggs, and carrion.

Reproduction and Growth The marsh rice rat is capable of producing young at any time of the year over most of its range. In the north breeding is usually restricted to the warmer months from April to September, while few litters are produced during the hot, dry summers in the south. A mature female may produce 3 to 7 litters in a year, each averaging 5 young (range of 2 to 6). The development period of the embryos is 25 days. The newborn weigh around 3.7 g (0.1 oz), are covered in fine hair, and begin to crawl around in a few days. The mother nurses from 8 teats and comes into heat within 10 hours after giving birth, with a 7-day cycle thereafter until pregnancy occurs again. The youngster's eyes open at 8 days, solid food is taken at 11 days, and weaning and independence are achieved at only 20 days when weighing about 23 g (0.8 oz). Full size is reached at 4 months but both sexes become

MARSH RICE RAT

Meadow Vole

sexually active by 50 days; some females breed as early as 40 days. The average life span is half a year and few individuals surpass one year.

Remarks With the long, scaly, sparsely haired tail and pointy snout, this species looks similar to the introduced brown rat that invades buildings. It is an expert swimmer on the surface and underwater. Like a muskrat, it often constructs feeding platforms with cuttings and by bending down the vegetation. Surrounding these platforms are discarded pieces of crab and snail shells. In areas subjected to flooding or tides, the nests are situated above the water level. Populations undergo great fluctuations in numbers during some years — thought to be related to weather (especially rainfall) and nutrition. The animals customarily lose weight during winter in the northern regions. Densities range from 0.1 to 50 per ha (0.04 to 20.2 per a) but average 4 per ha (1.6 per a). Home ranges overlap and extend up to 80 m (262.5 ft) across, covering an area of 0.3 to 1.3 ha (0.7 to 3.2 a). Individuals are primarily nocturnal, but they may be active for periods during the day as well. The marsh rice rat's main competitors are the meadow vole in the north and the cotton rat in the south. Important predators are barn and barred owls, marsh hawk, raccoon, red and gray foxes, mink, long-tailed weasel, striped skunk, snakes, and large fish.

STAR-NOSED MOLE

Scientific name *Condylura cristata*
Family Moles, Shrew-moles, and Desmans (Talpidae)
Order Insectivores (Insectivora)
Total length 200 mm (8 in)
Tail length 75 mm (3 in)
Weight 50 g (1.8 oz)
Color The coat is black, somewhat paler on the undersides.

Distribution and Status This eastern mole is found from Labrador west to Manitoba and south to Georgia. It is a semiaquatic species, preferring moist soft soils and avoiding dry, gravel, or heavy clay ground. Typical habitats include meadows, bogs, swamps, alder-willow thickets, and deciduous and coniferous forests. The star-nosed mole has 30 other relatives in its family, distributed throughout North America (total of 7 species) and Eurasia (24 species). Its range overlaps considerably with the hairy-tailed mole *(Parascalops breweri)*. The star-nosed mole is quite common in some areas and highly local or absent in others in spite of suitable habitat. It often appears to occur in small colonies.

Food The diet consists of worms (particularly earthworms), insects, crustaceans, mollusks, leeches, fish, salamanders, and a limited amount of vegetation and seeds. Many of these items are obtained underwater. Moles are voracious eaters, generally eating one-third to one-half their weight each day, and occasionally as much as double their weight.

Reproduction and Growth It is unclear what factors signal the onset of the breeding season, but in January the testes of the males begin to enlarge, and the tails of both sexes swell with fat. Mating reaches its peak in February and March, at which time the testes and associated glands may account for 10 to 14 percent of the male's weight. Following mating, the vagina of the female becomes plugged to prevent any loss of sperm. A nest of dry grass or moss is prepared in a chamber often situated on high ground or in a stump, which reduces the threat of flooding and consequent loss of the young. After developing for around 33 days, an average of 5 (range of 2 to 7) offspring are born, usually from March to May, but occasionally as late as June. The baby moles are naked, with wrinkled skin, tiny folded tentacles, and weighing only 1.5 g (.05 oz). They gain weight quickly from nursing on the mother's 4 pair of mammae and soon begin foraging on their own. By one month they weigh around 33 g (1.2 oz) and shortly thereafter leave the nest. Adult size is attained by late summer and sexual maturity at 10 months (the following spring). The maximum life span is not known but probably some survive 3 years.

Remarks The star-nosed mole is one of the most unusual-looking mammals on the con-tinent. In addition to the constantly moving ring of tentacles, there are no apparent eyes or external ears. Actually, tiny black eyes are present, hidden in the fur, but they function only to inform the animal whether it is in light or dark. In spite of the long nose, the mole has a poorly developed sense of smell and seems to have trouble locating food only a short distance away. It is the touch-sensitive tentacles and whiskers that function in foraging and navigating. The jaws are armed with a surprising number of 44 sharp-edged teeth. The broad hands are turned outwards and have 5 digits with stout claws. Unlike most other moles, which have a coat of uniform length, the star-nosed mole's is somewhat differentiated into longer hairs and shorter underfur — probably an adaptation to living under colder conditions than the other North American species. The coat lies in any direction and is waterproof. There are 2 annual molts, in spring and summer, and a sharp line is apparent separating the fresh fur from the old. The scaly ringed tail is used in feeling the sides of the tunnels, as a rudder while swimming, and as a fat-storage organ.

These moles are active anytime during the day or night, below ground or on the surface. They do not hibernate but continue their excursions through the soil, snow, and water. Were it not for the insulating quality of the snow cover, moles and other small mammals would not be able to survive the severe cold and deep frosts in the northern sections of their range. The home range averages 0.5 ha (1.3 a) and typical population levels are 2 to 5 per ha (0.8 to 2 per a). Two kinds of tunnels are constructed—shallow ones for feeding and traveling, and deeper ones leading to the living quarters. In the spring, when the moles begin to enlarge their tunnel systems, large piles of soil up to 15 cm (6 in) high are pushed out onto the surface. In bogs, the mole uses the little highways between the mounds of moss along with shrews and mice. When moles are out of their tunnels they are caught by skunks, foxes, raccoons, coyotes, snakes, owls, and occasionally by big fish.

STAR-NOSED MOLE

Marsh Rice Rat

Splash, splash! A grayish-brown animal with a long scaly tail disappeared around a curve in a trail that weaved along the muddy floor of the salt-grass marsh. Five minutes later, the splashing could be heard again, only this time an abundantly whiskered, rat-like head appeared. Obviously this was one creature that didn't mind wet feet. It had to swim, kicking strongly with the powerful hind legs, to reach all corners of its home range. In fact it frequently dove underwater and foraged along the bottom for ten meters (32.8 feet) at a speed of fifty-five centimeters (21.7 inches) per second, while searching for clams, crabs, and fish. On emerging the rice rat spent a full eight minutes combing and drying its fur —a necessary routine to maintain water repellency of its coat. Grooming, feeding, and resting activities centered around platforms of bent-over grass or inside a nest of woven grass, an abandoned muskrat lodge, a renovated wren's nest in a clump of reeds, and a burrow in the nearby wooded hummock.

From the green droppings left on the trail it was clear that the rice rat ate marsh grass, and here and there little piles of seed hulls indicated where it had paused for a snack of sedge seeds. On other warm evenings the rice rat explored the nearby meadow and open forests where the oaks were draped with long strands of gray Spanish moss and fan-bladed palmetto palms shaded the ground. The rat had to watch out for the tangles of thorny vines, and if it stopped too long to rest, dozens of red ants began to bite and hang on its tail and toes. No doubt about it, the rice rat felt safer and more comfortable in the cool water and thick grass.

Late one afternoon, what looked like a piece of black rope silently twisted its way through the grass stems, pausing every few meters to test the air with a thin forked tongue. It was a poisonous snake — a water moccasin — hunting for something warm to eat. As the thick-bodied reptile reached the rice rat's trail it stopped suddenly and its tongue curved down and began to quiver. Coated with scent from the rice rat, the tongue was withdrawn and inserted into a smell-sensitive pouch in the roof of the snake's mouth. The snake now realized the scent was fresh. Its body flowed slowly into a coil with the frightful-looking head on top.

As the last glow of the sun silhouetted the oak forest, the marsh rice rat descended from its nest in the reeds and dashed down the trail, intent on reaching some distant feeding site. It knew this route so well it didn't have to watch where it was going. Without warning a flash of white struck the rice rat on the hip, and with the sharp stabbing pain the rodent squealed and thrashed violently among the weeds, stirring up the muddy water. In an instant the rat regained its feet and raced through the marsh and up onto a grassy hill. Retreating under some vegetation the wet animal crouched down, panting and licking its wounds. But within minutes the rat was unable to move its hind feet, and it lay down with its sides heaving.

Back in the marsh, the water moccasin uncoiled, and with tongue flicking excitedly, it glided along the rat's path. Twenty minutes later the patient hunter reached the warm dead body of its prey. The snake investigated the rat until it located its snout, which it proceeded to engulf in its gaping jaws. Within minutes the tail slipped down the reptile's white throat. The next morning thousands of red ants stormed over the spot, but there was nothing left to eat.

Star-nosed Mole

A gray jay glided from the top of a stunted black spruce to a bare tamarack pole, then paused to survey the frozen swamp. Snow was piled on the branches of spruce and fir, and formed rounded caps on the tops of stumps and moss hummocks. The reflection of the midday sun on the snow created a dazzling bright scene. As the jay departed, uttering its song in the dry frigid air, the swamp was once more left in total silence. Not even the snow revealed any telltale tracks of passing animals. Where had all the creatures gone that abounded in this lively place last summer?

One meter (3.3 feet) below ground, a black figure moved stealthily along a dark, humid corridor. Its tiny eyes were of no use down here, their guiding function being replaced by bunches of touch-sensitive whiskers on the long snout, forehead, hands, and tail. Short but powerful arms and spade-like hands and claws ripped into the peat and stringy moss as the star-nosed mole forced its way through the soil. Its amazing nose, fringed with twenty-two pink and pointed tentacles, were kept in constant motion feeling for that slight twitch reaction of some uncovered prey — perhaps a worm or insect grub. For half an hour it persevered, sweeping its way along with alternate strokes of the forelimbs. But its efforts went unrewarded, and tiring from the heavy efforts the mole curled up and fell asleep.

Some time later it awoke with a start as it sensed the vibrations of an approaching creature. It turned out to be the mole's mate, and they greeted each other by fondling each other's tentacles. Since neither had eaten for almost twenty-four hours, the two were ravenous. The first mole pushed its way past the other and scrambled down the tunnel with such enthusiasm that the second mole decided to follow. This way and that, the tunnel led past roots, the bases of trees, and an occasional rock. The two eventually encountered water, yet without hesitation they entered the flooded tunnel which soon exited into a river. In single file the two moles paddled along, their noses groping along the muddy bottom. Their eyes could detect the light that filtered down through the ice where the wind had blown the surface clear of snow. It was during one of their trips to the surface, to breathe from a bubble of air trapped under the ice, that these two black objects caught the attention of a red fox. Through the ice cover the little plump moles seemed an enticing afternoon snack for the fox, but how to reach them? With nose to the hard cold barrier, the fox traced their every move. First it tried scratching the ice with its front paws, and when that failed it pounced again and again, hoping to smash its way through. When all attempts proved futile, the frantic fox ran around in circles, whimpering, as the moles swam by only five centimeters (2 inches) from its nose.

Oblivious to the drama above them, the moles finally located what they were looking for — several large dragonfly larvae buried in the mud. It was time to return to land, for they were becoming chilled in the cold water. With each carrying a larva in its elongated jaws, and tentacles folded over the nostrils, the moles somehow found the submerged tunnel entrance without apparent difficulty. When they reached a dry spot, the two hunters sat back and devoured their meal. When they had finished every last tidbit and licked clean their tentacles, the moles traveled directly to their nest chamber and fell asleep together inside a ball of moss and sedge. In less than half an hour the larvae were completely digested and the nutrients were carried by the blood system throughout their bodies. Fats formerly destined to provide the dragonflies with a spring burst of energy now became deposited in the moles' tails. The swelling of this appendage marked the onset of their breeding season, even though the world above was still locked in the icy grasp of winter.

Dwayne
Harty

Mink

As soon as the round red sun slipped below the horizon of the northern lake, the air chilled noticeably. With the drop in temperature a thin layer of dew condensed over the surrounding vegetation of stunted black spruce, pink-flowered Labrador tea shrubs, and mounds of red and green sphagnum moss. The last forlorn call of a red squirrel was soon lost in the moist atmosphere. Then all was quiet except for the gurgling sounds of the peat-stained water swirling over and around boulders in the shallows of the river draining the lake. Not far from the eroded bank some dark figures began to stir at the entrance of a burrow tucked neatly under a fallen tree. A female mink slipped down to the gravel shore, tested the air, stretched her stiff muscles, and crouched low to drink. Seconds later seven young mink came tumbling out of the hole, jumping and splashing through the shallows. They nipped and wrestled, then chased each other around the rocks, impatient for excitement after the long boring day beneath the ground. They were eight weeks old now, and greedily devoured red-backed voles and fish that their mother carried back to the den each night. Increasingly exhausted from single-parental duties, the mother had recently begun taking her offspring on nightly excursions in search of food. As the family proceeded downstream, the young followed the adult mink in single file, the procession resembling a moving snake as it twisted and wound around obstacles.

Suddenly the water in a pool began to churn with the frantic splashing of several fish that had been attracted close to the shore by flies alighting on the surface. The mother was an expert at fishing and she dove quickly underwater, all four feet paddling rapidly. With the grace of an otter she pursued and lunged at a fish and caught it in her powerful jaws. Meanwhile, frenzy broke out among the youngsters as they bounded along the shore and tried to catch a fish each time one broke the surface and flashed its shiny belly in the moonlight. While the young mink had attempted to catch fish before, none had yet been successful due to the lack of necessary skill and strength. But each passing night of running, swimming, and wrestling increased their prowess as hunters and their permanent set of thirty-four sharp teeth were now growing in. Clawed and partially webbed toes and soft friction pads on the toes and soles grappled for traction on the wet, slimy, algae-covered rocks. In their great excitement the mink emitted a musky secretion which drifted over the rapids and into the surrounding woods.

Finally, a grayling fish darted too close to shore and became stranded. Seeing its chance, one little mink pounced on top of the slippery prey and bit down on the head with all its might. A flap of the tail knocked the mink off balance, but it bravely held on with its sharp teeth. Using all its strength it tugged and tugged backwards on its short stubby legs, trying to pull its prize out of its element. A minute later both prey and predator lay exhausted on the shore, breathing heavily from exertion. Long after the fish had ceased struggling, the youngster still maintained its grip, as if the fish might escape back into the river at any second. The mink twitched excitedly, having captured its own food for the first time.

With two fish landed safely the family split into two camps to feed. While the mother was resigned to share her fish, the successful youngster evidently wanted no one else mooching on its hard-earned meal. It became so aggressive, snapping and baring its teeth, that it was soon left to dine alone. The little mink was exhibiting the first glimpses of self-sufficiency and independence. Family life was drawing to an end, and by autumn, each mink would take up residence along a separate section of shoreline. Kinship forgotten, they would chase each other away whenever they happened to meet. By spreading out over many kilometers of habitat, each member increased its chances of hunting success and in turn, its survival.

Dwayne
Horty

MINK

Scientific name *Mustela vison*
Family Weasels (Mustelidae)
Order Carnivores (Carnivora)
Total length males 530 mm (20.9 in);
females 500 mm (19.7 in)
Tail length 170 mm (6.7 in); 150 mm (5.9 in)
Weight 2 kg, maximum 2.3 kg (4.4 lb,
maximum 5.1 lb); 1 kg (2.2 lb)
Color Mink range from chestnut brown to almost black and are paler on the underparts. White patches are usually present on the chin, chest, belly, or anal region.
Distribution and Status The mink is found from the southern tundra regions of Alaska and Canada south to California, Texas, and Florida. It occurs in many kinds of wetlands including the borders of streams, lakes, and ponds, in freshwater and marine marshes, and in swamps, sloughs, and ditches. Dense vegetation is preferred which may consist of sedge-grass, shrubs, or forest such as cypress-tupelo in the south (Louisiana) or black spruce-tamarack in the north (Ontario). It is quite common in good habitat and has been introduced, deliberately and by accident, to Ireland, Britain, Germany, Scandinavia, and the Soviet Union. An almost identical species, the European mink *(Mustela lutreola)*, occurs from France to eastern Siberia. Another relative, the sea mink *(Mustela macrodon)*, formerly inhabited the Atlantic coast and islands from New Brunswick to Massachusetts, but was exterminated by people around 1880. A large reddish-brown species reaching 1.2 m (3.9 ft) in total length, it apparently fed on fish and mollusks along the edge of the ocean. Not one specimen was preserved and only skeletal fragments and teeth have been discovered, mostly in excavated middens of native people. A total of 16 recent species have been described in the genus *Mustela*, with representatives from North and South America, Europe, Asia, and Africa.
Food Mink accept almost any small animal as part of their diet, which may include muskrats, mice, rabbits, birds (songbirds and waterfowl) and eggs, fish, frogs, snakes, crayfish, worms, crustaceans, and insects.

Reproduction and Growth The breeding season runs from late February to early April, during which time the male wanders widely in search of one or more mates. The female is receptive every 7 to 10 days. When a pair meets they commence a vigorous courtship, emitting a chuckling call. The male is considerably larger and grasps the female by the back of the neck in his jaws, then adjusts his body to mate from behind. If she is not ready she breaks away and a fierce fight often ensues. Eventually she submits and the two animals remain connected from a few minutes to several hours, with short bursts of active thrusting broken by long rests. The male's penis is 5.6 cm (2.2 in) long and contains a supporting rod of bone named the baculum. The female's eggs are released one to 3 days following mating and the fertilized eggs enter a resting period. While the actual developmental (gestation) time is only 30 days, pregnancy lasts from 40 to 75 days. An average of 5 young (range of 2 to 10) are born in April or May in a den. They weigh 10 g (0.4 oz), are sparsely covered in fine white hair, and receive nourishment from their mother's 3 or 4 pairs of mammary glands (not all may be functional). Their eyes open, fur is present, and control of body temperature is achieved by 5 weeks. Weaning to solid food occurs a week later and they leave the den and begin hunting by age 7 or 8 weeks. The offspring disperse by autumn. Females reach adult size by 4 months and reach sexual maturity at 12 months, while males, being larger, require 10 and 18 months, respectively. Mink may continue to breed for 7 or more years. They have been known to reach the age of 10 years in captivity; however, few survive more than 3 or 4 years in the wild.
Remarks This species is well known because of the popularity of its lustrous fur, yet relatively few people are able to identify the animal on sight. It exhibits the basic weasel form of a long thin body, bushy tail, and short sturdy legs. The head is pointed and somewhat flat, the eyes are prominent, and the rounded ears are almost hidden in the fur. Like other members of its family, the mink possesses well-developed musk glands at the base of the tail

which are used to mark the territory. The dense underfur keeps the animal's body warm even in icy water, while the long well-oiled guard hairs help protect the coat from wear while rubbing against rocks, branches, and snow. The periods of molt in spring and autumn are triggered by the change in day length and by temperature.

Mink spend about 90 percent of their active time hunting — on land, along the shore, over ice, or underwater. An excellent swimmer the animal can descend to a depth of 6 m (19.7 ft) and reach 30 m (98.4 ft) before surfacing for air. In the warm parts of the year this species is mainly active from dusk to dawn, but in winter it more frequently comes out during the day. Extreme weather is avoided (there is no hibernation period) by retiring to dens which may number from 2 to as many as 22 scattered over its home grounds. Selected sites include rock piles, beneath tree roots or a fallen log, within an expropriated muskrat or beaver lodge, or a burrow dug within a bank — up to 3 m (9.8 ft) long and one m (3.3 ft) deep. Females generally occupy about one to 2.8 km (0.6 to 1.7 mi) of shoreline, males 1.8 to 5 km (1.1 to 3.1 mi). Home ranges have been calculated at 8 to 20 ha (19.8 to 49.4 a) for females, and up to 800 ha (1,976 a) for males. One male was found to have dispersed 45 km (28 mi) when food was scarce. Population density has been reported at one mink per 2.4 to 61 ha (5.9 to 150.7 a), but usually is under one per 27 ha (66.7 a).

The adult animal leads a solitary life except for the brief mating period. The only significant predator of the mink is people, although it occasionally falls prey to red and gray foxes, coyote, wolf, fisher, alligator, and owls such as the great-horned owl. A few are also hit by cars. It is a host to numerous parasites and succumbs to a variety of diseases. A more recent threat is the accumulation of toxic pollutants such as PCBs, dieldrin, and mercury, obtained by eating aquatic prey like fish.

The mink has long been an important fur-bearer in spite of its short-haired fur going out of style from time to time. While many are trapped, most of the mink appearing on the market

MINK

LITTLE BROWN BAT

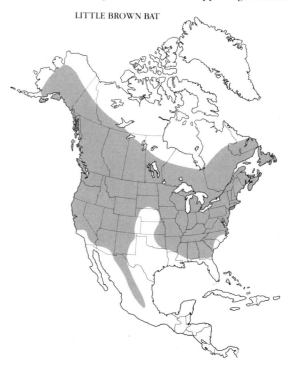

are raised on farms — as many as 21 million (most from the Soviet Union) in some years. Selective breeding has resulted in a number of beautiful color varieties. Eastern Canada has the reputation for producing the highest quality wild mink pelts, but the largest ones are from western North America.

Each time I walk through a marsh or along a stream I keep an eye open for mink. They are interesting to watch because of their hunting activities and agile movements. The winter offers the best opportunity to study mink because one can follow their tracks in the snow to see what they have been up to. Since their legs are so short, their belly often leaves a furrow in the snow. One time a colleague and I took a break from trapping small mammals to fish for grayling and lake trout in a northern waterway. Suddenly a family of mink appeared out of the spruce woods and along the shore. My friend remained motionless and the mink, in single file, ran right past his feet, not realizing he was there.

LITTLE BROWN BAT
Scientific name *Myotis lucifugus*
Family Smooth-faced Bats
(Vespertilionidae)
Order Bats (Chiroptera)
Total length 90 mm (3.5 in)
Tail length 35 mm (1.4 in)
Weight 8 g (0.3 oz)
Color These bats are a glossy light to dark brown, somewhat paler on the belly. The wings, feet, ears, and snout are black.
Distribution and Status The little brown bat is widespread throughout North America and is frequently the most common bat in an area. It ranges from the northern limits of the boreal and mountain forests of Canada and Alaska south to California, Texas, the Gulf states, and along the central highlands of Mexico to the Federal District at elevations up to 2 317 m (7,600 ft). The bat has been found in numerous kinds of habitats but some source of water and forests (both deciduous and coniferous) are essential requirements. One recent study listed 88 species of myotis bats from North and South America, Europe, and Asia. Another list recognized 94 species, including representatives from Australia. There are about 26 species in North America, many of which resemble the little brown bat so closely that careful study is necessary to tell them apart.
Food This bat eats flying insects such as moths, midges, caddisflies, and mayflies as it patrols back and forth over a watercourse or forest edge at night. The insects are located by the returning echoes of the bat's high-pitched calls. The tail membrane is used like a net to scoop up the insects. Small bugs are swallowed during flight but the bat perches in a tree to eat larger ones. Prey size is in the range of 3 to 10 mm (0.1 to 0.4 in) and 2 to 4 g (0.07 to 0.1 oz) of insects are eaten each night.
Reproduction and Growth Males produce sperm as early as May, however mating does not occur until August and September, while swarming in and around the place of hibernation. Some individuals copulate in the winter during periodic arousals from hibernation. Both sexes breed (while landed) with many individuals. The male emits a special call when mounting, which seems to cause the female to cease struggling. The sperm are nourished by the uterus wall until the eggs are released on emergence in the spring. Fifty to

60 days following fertilization, one baby (twins are rare) is born weighing almost 2 g (0.07 oz) — one-quarter the weight of the mother. Births in a nursery colony usually all occur within several weeks, as early as mid-May in the south, early June to mid-July in the north. The pink baby has a fine silky coat of hair, the eyes and ears open in a few hours, and milk teeth have erupted. It does not have control of body temperature until 10 days, hence the selection of hot sites for nurseries where the offspring can grow rapidly. At the tender age of only 3 weeks, the juvenile has developed a brown coat, its permanent teeth are present, and it begins to fly and catch its own insect food. Some females mate successfully their first autumn, but most postpone breeding until a year later, as do all males. Bat mortality is highest during the first winter for many fail to accumulate sufficient fat reserves to last through the dormant period. From the second summer on however, survival is remarkably high—related to the low birth rate. A life span of 10 years in common and one banded individual lived for 31 years under natural conditions.
Remarks This species is small with a wingspan of only 25 cm (9.8 in). The fur is soft and silky, reaching 1 cm (0.4 in) along the back. As in other bats, a flexible rod of cartilage is attached to the heel to help support the delicate tail membrane. About one dozen kinds of calls have been identified, functioning in social, mating, and feeding activities. Bats flying on a collision course emit a special call described as a honk, since its serves to warn the other bat to move out of the way. Far beyond the range of human hearing, the hunting calls are sent out at about 20 pulses per second and speeds up to 50 per second as prey is detected and approached within one m (3.3 ft).

The little brown bat's body temperature fluctuates remarkably — an adaptation to conserve energy. The animal readily enters torpor even in summer when the air temperature surrounding its roosting site falls below 39°C (102.2°F). Rather than burning up calories to maintain a high body temperature, the bat just cools down. Roosting sites are carefully selected to offer shelter, seclusion, and a suitably high temperature. When the nights fall below 15°C (59°F) the bats gather and sleep against each other to take advantage of the combined body heat, whereas on warm nights the bats roost individually. Day and night roosts may be in buildings, tree hollows, under wood or rock piles, and in August and September, in caves. Nurseries are found in buildings or trees where the air is hot. Caves that remain at 0°C (32°F) or above are used for hibernation, but these are not available everywhere so the bats must do with buildings or trees. A relative humidity of over 90 percent is required to prevent excessive dehydration while torpid. Hibernation lasts from early October to mid-May in the north, November to March in the south. The actual time of entry and emergence is largely dependent on the weather. The bats arouse periodically to drink, urinate, and balance various components in their blood and cells. The animal can go up to 90 days without arousing; too many wakenings for any reason, including disturbance by the presence of people, utilize excessive fat reserves and threaten starvation before spring. When arousing, heat is rapidly produced in a number of deposits of brown fat and is transferred to the circulatory system, just like

a furnace and hot water radiators in a house. About 30 percent of the body's fat stores are used up by spring and the maximum period of hibernation for this species is 165 days.

Little brown bats are not territorial and in fall their calls serve to attract others to congregate in roosts. They are generally tolerant of each other, feeding in close proximity and sleeping or hibernating with their bodies in close contact. Much time is spent grooming the fur and membranes. These bats are frequently host to large numbers of fleas, lice, and other parasites, probably related to their repeatedly gathering in large numbers at the same roosting sites. The main predators are owls, snakes, mice, raccoons, and skunks, but pesticides in their insect food, starvation, flooding, and accidents are far more important mortality factors.

I and several assistants once investigated a limestone cave in northern Manitoba where an Indian trapper had reported seeing hibernating bats. Lowering ourselves down on a rope through a crack in the limestone bedrock, our headlamps shone beams of light over the pale brown walls. Although it was a little scary, we crawled on our bellies through a narrow tunnel to reach further rooms. It was freezing outside, but the cave air was moist and fairly warm at 5°C (41°F). Piles of shelled spruce cones indicated that red squirrels used the cave, and bones of hare and fox told us that these animals sometimes fell in and died here. Then we spotted them — brown frosty patches of bats on the walls. Others slept singly where cracks in the rock offered a toehold. The lights and noise woke about 12 of the 500 bats, and they began flying back and forth in the tight quarters. While I waited under the cave entrance for my turn up the rope, the bats flew past me, some of them brushing my clothes with their wings. It was quite a relief to reach the surface and see the green spruce forest and the bright sun again. We left the bats to resume their winter slumber, pleased to be able to report on one of the farthest north hibernating sites in North America, and the first record of bats overwintering in the province.

On another field trip in southern Illinois, I was a member of a class which was identifying and studying various species of bats in an abandoned mine. Stumbling over piles of rocks that had fallen from the ceiling, and slipping in the mud on the floor, we finally located the section of the mine where thousands of bats were hanging from the walls and roof. Amid the little brown bats were an occasional Keen's bat *(Myotis keenii)*, a big brown bat *(Eptesicus fuscus)*, and the tiny eastern pipistrelle *(Pipistrellus subflavus)*. Suddenly we heard a rumbling sound which turned out to be a train passing nearby. Everyone jumped to the walls of the mine in case the vibrations should loosen more rock from above. The next morning a strong earthquake rattled the countryside along the Mississippi fault, and I shuddered to think what would have happened to us had we been underground. The tremors must have disturbed the hibernating bats as well.

Little Brown Bat

Bats by the thousands hung like brown curtains and patches against the white chalky limestone walls of the old cave. It was quiet down here, fourteen meters (46 feet) below the surface. An overwhelming sense of timelessness permeated the musty atmosphere, a feeling that nothing had changed for a million years. The only visitors were little brown bats which had sought refuge here each winter for countless ages. Only a hint of light could be detected from the distant cave entrance — no more than a narrow crack in the ground. The temperature at the end of the blind chamber was 8°C (46.4°F), where it had hovered for most of the winter. Water droplets from the moist, still air condensed on the sleeping bats' fur, turning them into silvery-gray ghosts. The bats had returned to their favorite cave from hundreds of kilometers away, to hibernate from October to May — the long winter period when it was far too cold to live outside and no insect food was available. Most of the females, except some yearlings, had mated last September during swarming activities inside and at the cave entrance.

In the middle of one clump of bats wedged in a crack, a male bat began to stir. Slowly at first, then with more vigorous stretches, the creature was trying to arouse. Heat produced in the muscles and from brown fat deposits began to elevate its body temperature from 9° to 34°C (48.2° to 93.2°F). When sufficiently warmed the bat dropped from its perch, flew around in circles, then alighted by a clear pool where it quenched its thirst. Instead of returning to its former roost, it chose another cluster of individuals farther back down the tunnel where it was slightly warmer. In spite of the cold and the fact that all the other bats were torpid, the male scrambled on top of an adjacent bat and tried to copulate, without success as it turned out, for it was another male. Undeterred by its error in the dark the persistent bat moved on, and after several successful matings it once again fell asleep, cooled down, and became dormant.

Six months later about one hundred females from the colony hung upside down with their hind feet from the rafters of a cottage attic. It was June, and time for a hundred baby bats to make their debut. The air in this nursery was stifling hot — a condition that would promote the rapid growth of the little creatures. When each female was ready to give birth, she turned head up, supporting herself by the thumbs. The first baby to appear was gently cradled in its mother's tail membrane, where it was licked clean. The blind and helpless newborn managed to attach itself to a nipple with its tiny teeth and lips, and was then enveloped in the long webbed wings of its mother. Within two weeks, every female was caring for its offspring.

After sunset the mother bats pushed their babies onto a perch, fluttered to the opening in the roof, crawled out, and soared away to their favorite feeding grounds. Several hunted for insects attracted to a street light in town while others worked back and forth along a stream. Clouds of midges formed an easy target and the little brown bats knocked the tiny flies into their tail membranes with a swipe of the wings, then somersaulted through the air like acrobats as they bent over and snatched up the tiny prey with their mouths. Occasionally, a bat swooped low to skim emerging mayflies from the water's surface and pond weeds. One bat approached a fast-flying moth, and latching onto its target with echolocating cries at a distance of one meter (3.3 feet), the bat plucked the hairy insect out of the air. Chewing rapidly, the bat then decided the moth was not to its liking, for it spit the insect out again. The bats swept the air of about seven insects per minute, and after a feeding frenzy of only fifteen minutes their bellies were full. While the males and nonbreeding females perched singly in their night roosts in trees and buildings, the mother bats returned to the attic to nurse their offspring. The adults digested their meals within an hour, and after midnight, they foraged one more time.

At three weeks of age the young bats finally emerged to try their wings. They flew awkwardly at first, attempting to keep up with their mothers who were actively foraging. They spent most of the first few evenings hanging from a tree, watching for insects to fly within range. Then one night, the bat families returned to the attic nursery to find the entrance hole sealed tightly with a board. The bats circled around and around in confusion, touching the board but not landing. One exhausted little bat swooped too low and was snagged by a prickly burdock growing alongside the house. Fortunately the repairs to the roof had been done at night and after the young had gained the power of flight, otherwise the nursery colony would have perished. The bat families dispersed to locate their own day roosts in the woods along the river.

Meadow Jumping Mouse and Woodland Jumping Mouse

It looked like an evening shower was coming as a bank of dark gray clouds slipped over the low sun. No sooner had the cloud's shadow dimmed the light over the meadow when a ball of woven grass began to shudder. Through the leaves appeared the twitching nose and blinking eyes of a meadow jumping mouse. It crawled out of the makeshift door and stretched its back and enormously long hind legs. Hopping from front to hind feet, it bounced along between the grass stems that seemed as big as trees to the mouse. It followed no particular trail but wandered here and there, looking for a beetle or a sleeping butterfly to eat. Then standing on its hind legs and balancing with the long tail, it gnawed through a thick grass stem. Down slipped the stalk, but it caught on the other grasses. The mouse patiently repeated the process until a heap of seven-centimeter (2.8-inch) sections lay neatly piled like tiny logs on the ground. At last the mouse reached the head of seeds, and it sat back on its haunches to gobble them down. A rather wasteful feeder, the mouse allowed many of the seeds to drop to the ground where they were ignored. The dining hour completed, the rodent wandered down to a favorite trail along a brook lined with a luxuriant growth of grass and willows. Pausing to rest for a minute under a small shrub, the mouse grasped its tail by the base with its front paws and passed the whole length through its mouth to be cleaned.

It was much darker under the canopy of trees in the nearby forest. As several singing warblers, an ovenbird, and a wood thrush finally settled down for the night, only the bubbling sounds of a brook disturbed the still air. A gentle rain began to fall, pitter-pattering on the maple leaves and filling the air with a wonderful fresh earthy smell. From under a mushroom-decked balsam fir log hopped another similar-looking mouse, but this one had a white tip on its long tail. The dainty woodland jumping mouse walked and bounded in half-meter (1.6-foot) hops over to the crystal-clear water where it lapped up a drink. A shiny brown salamander splashed away over the wet rocks, startling the mouse for a second. Then it made its way over the mossy forest floor, careful to conceal itself under logs, ferns, and sedges wherever possible. Stopping suddenly, its sensitive nose detected the aroma of its favorite food — an underground fungus called endogone. Digging

rapidly with the delicate front feet, it tore easily though the moist spongy soil. When it reached the fungus, the mouse's tongue picked up several soft pieces and as it chewed its food, the mouse's half-closed eyes showed its contentment.

On rainy nights without any frightening noises caused by the wind, the jumping mice become more active than usual. After several hours of exploring, interrupted by bouts of eating and grooming, the two mice happened to meet beneath the shrubs at the forest edge. At first each thought they had found another member of their own kind, so they approached each other rather eagerly. They certainly had the same shape, long tail, and coat pattern, but since the mice couldn't see colors, they were unable to distinguish that one of them had orange-colored sides and a brown back, while the other was yellow and black. The white tip on the tail of the woodland species had slipped under the leaves but it was doubtful whether this clue would have helped. How could they tell for sure? — by smell! Each mouse stretched forward on its small front feet to make the other's acquaintance. Sniff, sniff, their whiskered noses twitched nervously. The odors were definitely different. Muscles tensed and tails began to jerk as each mouse became more uneasy, not knowing what to do next. Jumping mice usually "freeze" when they sense danger, hoping that predators won't notice them. But what to do now? The mice just sat there, poised face to face, their little sides heaving rapidly and their big black eyes almost bulging out of their sockets. Half-a-minute passed with neither deciding to retreat or attack. Suddenly a twitching tail hit a dry leaf and the sudden rustle decided the issue — the panicked mice exploded almost a meter (3.3 feet) into the air. When they finally landed, their powerful legs bounced the mice away through the underbrush like rockets on a zig-zag course, one heading for the field, the other into the woods. After a dozen or so bounds the mice stopped suddenly, panting from exertion and shaking with fear, to determine if they were being pursued. Several hours of fitful sleeping in their nests passed before the timid little creatures fully recovered. For the rest of the summer they remembered this frightening experience each time they saw their reflection in the brook.

MEADOW JUMPING MOUSE
Scientific name *Zapus hudsonius*
Family Jumping Mice and Birch Mice
(Zapodidae)
Order Rodents (Rodentia)
Total length 220 mm (8.7 in)
Tail length 130 mm (5.1 in)
Weight 20 g (0.7 oz) Up to 37 g (1.3 oz) when
fat and ready for hibernation.
Color The upperparts are black with pale
yellow hairs showing through. The sides are
pale yellow with a scattering of black hairs
while the underparts and feet are white. The
tail is bicolored — white below and grayish on
top.
Distribution and Status Meadow jumping
mice are often common inhabitants of
meadows, old fields, prairie, marshes, stream-
sides, and shrubby growth at the edge of
forests, seldom wandering into dense timber.
Although they prefer wet sites, particularly the
sedge and alder-willow borders of watercourses, they sometimes appear in dry sparse
cover of grass and forbs. This mouse occurs
in the boreal and deciduous forest regions
from Alaska and British Columbia eastward
to northern Quebec and the Maritimes, and
south to Colorado and Alabama. The species
has two close relatives — the western *(Zapus
princeps)* and Pacific *(Zapus trinotatus)* jumping mice of western North America. Also
represented in the family Zapodidae are the
woodland jumping mouse *(Napaeozapus
insignis)* of eastern North America, the Chi-
nese jumping mouse *(Eozapus setchuanus)*,
and 6 to 9 species of birch mice *(Sicista)* of
Europe and Asia.
Food This jumping mouse eats mostly seeds
of grasses, sedges, and other plants but is also
fond of nuts, berries, and fungi. Insects are
especially important in the spring. I have seen
some individuals whose mouths were stained from eating so many blueberries.
Reproduction and Growth Jumping mice
are ready to breed within days after emerging
from hibernation, which means that their
reproductive organs develop during waking
periods in March and April. In the south most
of the mice are sexually active by late April or
early May, delayed to late May in populations
at high elevations or in the north. About 18
days following mating, 5 (range of 2 to 9)
babies are born in a grass nest on the surface
or below ground. The young are undeveloped
and require 25 days before their eyes open
and their coats appear. Weaning and independence occur about a week later. Females produce 2 or 3 litters from May to September in
the south, while those living in regions with
a short summer season have time for only one
litter in July. Some females breed in their first
summer. The mice live an average of 2 years
and a few reach 4 in the wild, while an age span
of 5 years has been recorded in captivity.
Remarks Meadow jumping mice are present in most fields, especially if water is nearby. Mice in their second and third year put on
weight rapidly (up to 2 g or 0.1 oz per day) in
early autumn, and enter hibernation in
September when fat and lazy. However, young
of the year may remain out through October
or even into November, still growing and laying on fat for their 6-month deep sleep. No
food is stored and the mice sleep while rolled
up in a tight ball. They emerge in April in warm
regions, May in cold areas. The males appear
about 2 weeks earlier than females. These
mice are great travelers, changing their home
range frequently and wandering up to one km
(0.6 mi) when dispersing. The home range
varies from 0.2 to 1.1 ha (0.4 to 2.7 a) and
population densities of one to 48 per ha (0.4
to 19.4 per a) have been found. These mice are
excellent swimmers and can dive to one m (3.3
ft) below the surface. They are usually solitary
but are friendly to each other in captivity. My
captive mice slept while huddled up or lying
on top of each other. Though I have caught
hundreds of these mice, only 6 times could I
capture them by hand. At first they scamper
away for one m (3.3 ft) and then freeze, hoping you have not spotted them. If you miss
grabbing them at this point, you may as well
give up, for the mice bound away in rapid one-
m hops in a different direction each time they
hit the ground. The long tail helps them keep
their balance, just like a kangaroo, while escaping. Major predators include owls, hawks,
weasels, skunks, foxes, and raccoons.

While jumping mice are seldom as common
as deer mice or meadow voles that inhabit the
same fields, on occasion they may reach high
numbers. I recall being surprised by their
abundance at a university field station on the
prairie of southern Manitoba. Unloading our
gear we walked through an almost waist-high
field of brome grass when we suddenly saw
a number of jumping mice bounding away. It
was 38°C (100.4°F) on a sunny June day, with
strong winds bending down the grass — not
the type of weather in which I expected to see
these mice active. As I set a row of traps around
the building, two more mice leapt up in front
of me and bounced off the wall at a height of
0.5 m (1.6 ft). Even before I finished the line
a number of mice had been caught. In several
days I and two assistants had collected 69 jumping mice in this and adjacent areas. Realizing
that there were two species of jumping mice
in the vicinity I carefully examined each
specimen, looking for the telltale sign of white
edges on the ears of the western species. After
identifying the large series of the beautiful
rodents we determined there were 56 western and 13 meadow jumping mice—an astonishingly high density for both species. They
provided valuable information on habitat
selection, abundance, reproduction, age,
parasites, and molt.

WOODLAND JUMPING MOUSE
Scientific name *Napaeozapus insignis*
Family Jumping Mice and Birch Mice
(Zapodidae)
Order Rodents (Rodentia)
Total length 235 mm (9.3 in)
Tail length 145 mm (5.7 in)
Weight 22 g (0.8 oz) Up to 32 g (1.1 oz) prior
to hibernation.
Color The upperparts are dark brown with
orange hairs showing through. The sides are
a warm orange with scattered dark brown
hairs, while the underparts, feet, and the tip
of the tail are white. The tail is bicolored, white
below and grayish-brown above.
Distribution and Status This jumping
mouse is generally found in spruce-fir and
hemlock-hardwood forests, but occasionally lives in pure deciduous forest such as beech-
sugar maple and box elder-green ash. The
range extends from Manitoba northeastward
to Labrador and the Maritimes, and southeast-
ward to Ohio and Pennsylvania, then as far
south as Georgia at high elevations (2 000 m
or 6,561.7 feet) in the Appalachian Mountains.
It prefers cool and moist conditions such as
bogs and swamps, and is particularly fond of
sedgegrass borders of brooks in the forest as
well as the shrubby edges of woods. It almost
never ventures outside of woody cover. While
the mouse may become quite common in
some select sites, it is a rather rare species
over most of the range, often appearing in
somewhat isolated pockets.
Food Seeds, berries, nuts, fungi, insects, and
centipedes are the most important types of
food. The leaves and roots of some plants are
eaten as well, but it is mainly oil from seeds
that enables the mouse to add enough fat on
its body to supply its energy needs during
hibernation.
Reproduction and Growth As with other
species of jumping mice, males emerge above

MEADOW JUMPING MOUSE

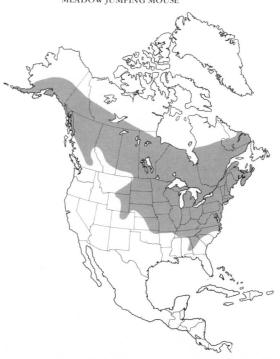

ground and are ready to breed several weeks before the females. Mating occurs soon after the females appear in late May. Five young (range of 2 to 7) are born in an underground den after growing inside the female for 23 days. The mother nurses with 4 pairs of teats. The newborn weigh 0.9 g (0.03 oz), fur is present by 24 days, the eyes open at 26 days, and they are weaned at 34 days. The little mice are slow to develop the coordination and strength required to walk and hop with the long hind legs. Adult weight is attained by 47 days. Two litters per year are normal in the south (mainly in June and August), while one litter is typical for mice living in the north's shorter season. The young do not come into breeding condition until the following spring. Young of the year make up 70 percent of the population by September, though a few of the mice manage to avoid disease, accidents, and predators and live 3 or 4 years. Though this age is exceptionally long for a mouse, it must be remembered that about half this time is spent hibernating in its den.

Remarks The woodland jumping mouse may be easily distinguished from its meadow-dwelling relative by its white tip on the tail, orange rather than yellow sides, and the lack of a premolar. The cheek teeth have a complicated pattern of enamel and dentine ridges which are used in grinding meals into a fine paste. Food is obtained by foraging on the surface, digging in the soil for insects and endogone fungus, and climbing into bushes for insects, nuts, and berries. The animal progresses in a walk or short hop from front to hind feet and does not bound solely on the large hind limbs as do jerboas of the Asian deserts. When frightened it bounds off in hops of around 0.8 m (2.6 ft) but sometimes up to 1.8 m (5.9 ft) — an effective mechanism of escape from weasels, bobcats, owls, and foxes. Should the remarkably long tail become severed through some accident, the mouse cannot control its body in midair, which seriously reduces its chances of escape and survival. The bright colors blend well with dead leaves and with the light flecks that penetrate the vegetation under which the mice live. The borders of the color pattern, passing along the ears, eyes, and mouth, disrupt the outlines of these features, and the dark-to-light gradation from the back to the belly acts as countershading, balancing the effects of light and shadow on the body while in subdued moonlight. A jumping mouse, crouching motionless in its natural surroundings, is a marvellous example of camouflage.

The woodland jumping mouse is more nocturnal than the meadow jumping mouse, but may extend its hours of activity in the morning and evening on the surface during cloudy or rainy conditions. Hibernation begins from mid-September to late October (the latter date for young of the year) and extends, with periodic arousals, until May. The earliest record of emergence is April 16 — a specimen I happened to collect in the snow in southern Quebec. Males are out two weeks before females. No food is stored in the den and the mice lose a third of their weight during the 5 to 8-month-long period of dormancy. Probably related to their powerful legs, these mice cover much ground in an evening (one traveled 107 m or 351 ft in one night). Home ranges are changed frequently and are usually from 0.4 to 3.6 ha (one to 8.9 a). There is considerable overlap in the home ranges of adjacent individuals, and those of males are usually larger than females. Antagonism has only been reported during the breeding season, and at other times and in captivity the mice are highly tolerant of each other. They are among the most gentle and timid of rodents. The few studies that have been conducted on this species revealed densities varying from 0.6 to 59 per ha (0.2 to 24 per a), but an average would be around 8 per ha (3.2 per a).

The scientific name of this mouse translates to "woodland nymph with big feet," which refers to its delicate form, beautiful colors, and enormous hind feet. Most of us have a favorite animal and this little mouse happens to be mine. While a student I studied the ecology of this species from Quebec to the Smoky Mountains and attempted to catch several alive to observe in the lab and to conduct genetic studies. As I walked down a brook at midnight to check my line, I found a trap with the door closed. I was pretty excited since I'd never seen one of these rare animals alive, but knew they were quite abundant there. Peeking into the metal box I saw a golden-colored mouse for a split second as it shot past my left ear. I wheeled around only to catch a glimpse of a woodland jumping mouse bounding off a boulder and vanishing into the night. I could not believe I had let it escape. Luckily, the other traps were full and I left the woods with 9 specimens, each hiding in a bucket of moss. They were so timid I had to house them separately with plenty of litter to hide within, otherwise they would injure or kill themselves by colliding with the cage walls and ceilings. They eventually became rather tame and I learned much about their behavior by sitting quietly and watching them under a dim red light. They needed humid conditions to keep their skin and coat in good condition. Their favorite food was sunflower seeds, on which they grew very fat by autumn. Though they were kept indoors at constant light and dark periods and room temperatures, they seemed to know it was time to hibernate in the autumn. The mice slept for days without moving, and I had quite a time waking one up, even after handling it for several minutes. It looked up at me with its sleepy eyes half open, as if pleading for me to put it back to bed. I couldn't help but speculate on what a tasty energy-rich morsel these mice must make in the autumn for a predator. My captives were so obese and lazy they would have had a hard time escaping anything faster than a turtle.

Strangely enough, searching for such timid creatures as jumping mice can be unnerving and even hazardous. In the southern Appalachians, one must keep alert for poisonous snakes while climbing stream banks and placing traps under boulders and logs. In fact, the first specimen recorded in Virginia was discovered in the stomach of a timber rattlesnake, and another was later found in a copperhead. To add to the suspense, the hill folk of this region take pleasure in "plinking" with .22 rifles while walking along the mountain roads. More than once I had to keep low as rifle slugs smacked into nearby trees. Setting lines of traps in the thick shrubs lining ponds and streams can be full of suspense when bears are in the vicinity. I have inadvertently wandered within close range of a grizzly in the Richardson Mountains of the Yukon, been approached closely by inquisitive black bears in the Mackenzie Delta, and watched polar bears stomp over my study area along the coast of Hudson Bay. While approaching the nest area of gulls, terns, and jaegers in the north I have wished for an umbrella for protection from their dive-bombing attacks, which often ended in a spray of whitewash. In the southern parts of Nova Scotia and Manitoba great numbers of ticks lie in ambush on grass and bushes along the edges of meadows where jumping mice are found. But nothing is more exasperating than attempting to set an oversensitive trigger on a trap while under constant assault by black flies and mosquitoes. All these adversities are more than compensated for when one finally discovers an elusive jumping mouse in a trap.

The best way to observe jumping mice is to walk slowly and quietly through meadows near a watercourse or forest edge in the early

Continued on p.166

WOODLAND JUMPING MOUSE

Raccoon

Early in June a female raccoon and her family of five were dozing in a den located halfway up a basswood tree. The offspring were less than a month old, but already they had grown their bandit masks and sharp little teeth. One youngster decided it was time to eat and began squirming and chattering so that soon everyone was awake. The mother sat upright with her back braced against the den wall. Then she gathered her brood in her arms to help them each reach a nipple. In less than a minute all five youngsters were suckling and purring like little kittens. The air inside the den was warm and the mother began to pant. After a few minutes her eyes began to close and then her head drooped down to her chest. She had traveled far last night and all she wanted to do was fall back to sleep. A sudden noise roused her attention and she stared upward at the den entrance where the light flooded in. Her black nose wiggled left and right, searching for a clue to what was out there. A strange beeping sound reached her ears and she turned over nervously, rousing the whole family. They felt vibrations through the trunk, as if something was climbing the tree towards them. Then a bright light shattered the darkness of the tree hollow and a shiny mirror peered down on them. Each youngster tried to hide under its litter mates and the mother began growling. The intruder was a biologist, come to check on the progress of his study animals who were living along the edge of a new town development. The biologist had put a radio collar on the mother raccoon when she came out of hibernation last March. With the use of special equipment he could locate her anywhere on her home range, which extended about two kilometers (1.2 miles) along the wooded banks of a creek. From experience, he knew not to put his hand down the hole, for the adult raccoon would bite in defense of her young. The examination completed, the man departed, leaving the family to resume their nap.

That evening the mother raccoon decided it was time to leave this den, now that it had been discovered. It was getting rather messy anyway and she knew of several other tree dens not far away. One at a time she picked each baby up by the scruff of the neck and carried them down the tree and off to their new home, the youngsters whimpering all the while. They grew so rapidly over the next several weeks that the offspring could no longer all fit in any of the dens, so they began sleeping under an uprooted tree or in a dense thicket of alders. Previously she had left her family for the whole night, returning at first daylight to nurse them. But now, at ten weeks old, they were strong enough to follow her for short distances to begin with, but then for hours at a time. Occasionally one would become separated, but it always found its own way back to the communal sleeping quarters. Their favorite hunting site was the creek, where they caught fat green frogs and poked around under rocks with their sensitive fingers for crayfish. They drank their fill by lapping with their tongues, or by dunking their front paws and licking off the droplets. Footprints in the mud next morning told of their antics the night before. But for pure excitement, nothing could match a romp down the back lanes in town, turning over trash cans in search of people food. Every item was sniffed and then turned over and over in their delicate hands before eating.

The townspeople were not too happy about these nuisance raccoons and one man went out hunting for them with his dog. The raccoons were asleep beneath the uprooted tree when the female heard the hound barking. Without an instant to lose she roused the offspring with an explosive hum call and a nip for those who wouldn't wake up. She chased them up into the dense canopy of a tuliptree and then quickly departed in a hunched-over gallop through the woods. She was intent on leading the dog away from her family. The hunter never found the young raccoons, but the mother didn't come back. When the leaves turned red and yellow, then tumbled to the ground, the raccoons were almost fully grown. Fat and lazy, they slept by themselves in forks of trees. But when the cold winds blew and the nights were frosty, they all returned to the old tree dens to sleep, piling on top of each other for warmth.

WOODLAND JUMPING MOUSE *cont. from p.163*
morning or evening. In comparison with other small mammals, jumping mice are sufficiently rare that they play a rather minor role in the various ecosystems in which they live. However, their unusual adaptations in habits and body form make them especially interesting members of the North American fauna, well worth searching for in wilderness and agricultural areas throughout much of the continent.

RACCOON
Scientific name *Procyon lotor*
Family Raccoons (Procyonidae)
Order Carnivores (Carnivora)
Total length 850 mm (33.5 in)
Tail length 235 mm (9.3 in)
Weight 9 kg (20 lb); weight is almost doubled when entering hibernation. Northern individuals are much larger (maximum 28 kg or 62 lb with fat) than those in the south such as in the Florida Keys (average 3 kg or 6.6 lb).
Color This animal is a grizzled gray-brown color, with a black facial mask and 5 to 10 black and white rings on the tail.
Distribution and Status The raccoon occurs over a great area from southern Canada (farthest north in the prairie provinces) south through the United States (absent from the central Rocky Mountains) to Panama. The animal is found mainly in wetlands, broad-leaved forests, and in some areas in pine forests. Typical habitats include floodplain forests, hardwood and mangrove swamps, fresh and salt marshes, oak-hickory and aspen groves, and farmlands. Water is often nearby, and in arid regions and the prairie, wooded creek banks offer suitable living conditions. In the mountains, rarely does the animal go above 2 000 m (6,562 ft).

The raccoon has been introduced into the Soviet Union and Europe where it is a pest in some areas and valued as a furbearer in others. Seven species of raccoon have been listed, ranging from Mexico and Caribbean islands to southern South America, but some of these are probably just subspecies (geographic races). It is related to the ringtail *(Bassariscus)*, coatis *(Nasua)*, kinkajou *(Potos)*, and olingo *(Bassariscyon)* of Central America. The raccoon family has been described as a primitive arboreal relict of the ancestors of the dog family, but its origin remains a mystery. Central America appears to have been the site of most of the group's evolution.

Food The raccoon has crushing-type molar teeth which are useful in eating many different types of food, such as grains, berries, acorns, beechnuts, clams, crabs, crayfish, worms, fish, insects, frogs, turtles, snakes, birds' eggs, and mice. Numerous studies have found that plant material forms the bulk of the diet when the whole year is considered.
Reproduction and Growth Although there is some evidence of pair formation, usually a male seeks out and mates with several females. The 2 animals remain joined for a long period — from one-half to over one hour. In the south mating occurs from January to March and most young are born in April. In northern areas mating is delayed somewhat — February to June, with May being the peak month for births. An average of 4 (range of one to 7) young are born 63 days following fertilization. The young weigh 70 g (2.5 oz) at birth and are covered in short fur. They squirm and cry while waiting to nurse from the mother's 4 pair of mammae. Their eyes open by 3 weeks and

weaning occurs from 2 to 4 months. Young raccoons weigh up to 7 kg (15.4 lb) by autumn, yet usually remain with their mother over winter. They are full grown in their second year. Females commence breeding at 10 months, while males are 2 years old before they have the opportunity to father the next generation. Most raccoons live 2 or 3 years but there are records of 16 years in the wild and 20 years in captivity.
Remarks This well-known animal is recognized immediately by its striking black mask, tapering head, hunched back, and barred fluffy tail. The fingers and toes are long and the soles are naked, leaving human-like footprints in the mud or snow. The forepaws and whiskered snout are extremely sensitive to touch, and along with the keen nose are used in locating sources of both plant and animal food. Curiosity is a trait developed in early life and raccoons are constantly smelling, manipulating, and biting objects that they encounter in their nightly ramblings. There are 40 teeth in the jaws, rather similar in shape to those of the wolf family. As a rule, the adults lead a solitary life-style, the exceptions being a female and her offspring, an occasional gathering due to attraction to some food supply, or communal winter den (containing up to 23 individuals). Home ranges vary tremendously in size from 0.2 to 4 946 ha (0.5 to 12,217 a) depending on the availability of food and cover, but average around 40 ha (99 a). Males generally cover more ground than females. The ranges of males do not overlap to any great extent but may contain parts of the ranges of females and their young. This species shows no strong territorial behavior. Populations have been reported as high as 175 per 43 ha (106 a); more commonly there would be 1 to 5 raccoons on this same area. When it comes time to leave the den family, raccoons disperse an average of 16 km (10 mi) from home before settling in a new region. The remarkable dispersal abilities of this species were revealed recently by one raccoon which traveled from Minnesota to Manitoba in 3 years—a straight-line distance of 266 km (165 mi).

Once a home range is defined, activity centers around feeding sites, such as watercourses, and a number of dens which are usually about 440 m (1,444 ft) apart. During the warm season, only one or 2 days are spent at each den, which may consist of a tree hollow (often at a height of 3 m or 9.9 ft), overturned tree, rock crevice, building, or an abandoned burrow or muskrat house. As the weather becomes cold, the raccoon spends more time in its den, and when snow covers the ground and cuts off most sources of food, the animal falls into a deep sleep, but not hibernation, for the body temperature and heart rate remain at normal levels and quick arousal is possible. Body heat is produced utilizing the thick deposits (up to 2.5 cm or one in) of fat, and conserved by the long fur coat and layer of fat. The animal pulls its extremities and face into the belly and frequently huddles with other individuals to maintain warmth. Snow seems to be more important than cold in initiating winter denning, since raccoons are not adverse to venturing out in temperatures as low as -17°C (1.4°F).

The raccoon is an excellent swimmer and on emerging, it shakes itself dry much like a dog, sometimes falling off balance in the process. It is also quite vocal, emitting a chattering sound to maintain contact with others, a distress call when a youngster becomes

separated, purring when content, and barking, hissing, growling, snorting, and squealing when defending itself from attack. This species is active through most of the night, but has occasionally been seen feeding during daylight hours.

Raccoons have extended their range northward, aided by recent agricultural changes. The combining of small family farms into single enterprises, and the use of ever-larger machines have resulted in more abandoned buildings and considerable grain spilt in the fields and stored in bins. Raccoons are able to survive in severe northern climates only because farmers have inadvertently provided them with homes and extra food. However, the young often fail to live through their first winter, since they may not find a suitable den or build up enough fat. I found one of these youngsters in the snow, almost frozen to death, at a temperature of -30°C (-22°F). Raccoons are adaptable creatures, which, unlike most animals, have done well living near people. The fur of this animal is long and durable, and so has become popular for coats and trim. Trapping, automobiles, starvation, disease, and predators such as hawks, owls, bobcat, red fox, coyote, snakes, and alligator keep numbers of raccoons down, but sometimes they become very abundant.

Strangely enough, raccoons almost prevented me from continuing a career in mammalogy. In carrying out my field-research requirements for a graduate degree, my advisor and I devised a quadrat study to live-trap, mark, and release small mammals in several habitats in southern Quebec. I carefully laid out the wooden stakes marking off an area in a beech-maple forest, then set parallel lines of live traps baited with the old standby of peanut butter, rolled oats, and bacon fat. Excitement and anticipation (from months of planning and literature research) rose to a peak level as I ran to the study area the following morning to check the traps. The first contained mouse droppings, but no mouse! The second aluminum trap lay completely disassembled (not an easy task), obviously by someone who was an expert at working with their hands. Finding only a mouse tail in the third trap, my spirits began to plummet. Not until reaching the end of the second line did I begin to suspect that all my hard work had been sabotaged by a masked bandit. The raccoon must have followed my scent up and down the rows of traps, pilfering the bait or live contents. With youthful persistence, I set a trap for my competitor, and sure enough, a large angry raccoon was waiting for me the next morning. Reluctantly I let the rascal go (almost losing my fingers), knowing that its kin must be around as well, and it would only be a matter of time until they too ate all my data. In the bunkhouse that evening, as I summarized the week's events in a notebook and pondered my next research strategy, I happened to gaze out the window and there, hanging down from the roof, was a raccoon's head staring at me. Was this the same individual, hooked on my bait recipe? I couldn't be certain, but the animal sure brought enough friends to keep me company all night.

RIVER OTTER
Scientific name *Lutra canadensis*
Family Weasels (Mustelidae)
Order Carnivores (Carnivora)
Total length males 125 cm (49.2 in);
females 110 cm (43.3 in)

Tail length 45 cm (17.7 in); 40 cm (15.8 in)
Weight 8 kg, maximum 14 kg
(17.6 lb, maximum 30.9 lb);
7 kg (15.4 lb)

Color The river otter has a beautiful dark-brown, glossy coat with grayish-white on the lips, throat, and cheeks. The hair is lighter brown or silvery on the underparts. Otters from southern areas are a lighter color and have shorter and less-dense coats.

Distribution and Status The river otter has a surprisingly large range, facilitated by its aquatic habits. It occurs some distance out on the tundra from Alaska to northern Quebec, and all the way south to the southern United States. Here it is separated from its close relative, the southern otter *(Lutra longicaudus)* in Mexico, by desert country. The otter is an adaptable creature requiring only clean water and the presence of some kind of aquatic prey. Otters are found in lakes and streams on the tundra, mountains, plains, forests, swamps, deserts, brackish estuaries, and marine coastlines. Human activities, fouling of the water, and overtrapping have caused a decline of the species over the last several centuries so that the river otter is now absent from much of the interior of the continent, from the Canadian prairies south to Texas, and from Pennsylvania west to California. Recent reports from North Dakota, Iowa, and Nebraska indicate that the animal may be re-establishing itself in some areas. Otters are still common in the northern half of the range and in the Gulf States. There are 8 species of river otters (genus *Lutra*) with a combined range of North and South America, Europe, Asia, and Africa.

Food Fish are the mainstay of the otter's diet, including not only slow-swimming species (suckers, minnows, catfish, bass), but fast ones as well (trout, pike). Preferred fish are in the size range of 3 to 25 cm (1.2 to 9.8 in) in length. Crayfish are another delicacy, followed by a long list of other creatures—insects, worms, snails, mussels, turtles, snakes, frogs, birds, mice, chipmunks, and rabbits. Even vegetation is accepted such as algae, pondweed, aquatic bulbs and roots, blueberries, and rose hips. A young muskrat or beaver is occasionally taken. Since the otter's esophagus is quite long and narrow, food must be chewed finely before swallowing.

Reproduction and Growth Otters usually mate in the water but occasionally on land, soon after the female gives birth. The estrous or heat period lasts for about one month, generally in March through May, but as early as January in the south. The male holds the back of the female's neck in its jaws, and while she wails loudly the whole time, the 2 are joined for 10 to 24 minutes, several times a day for a few days. The embryos cease their development until the next spring and are born 50 days later — a full year after conception. The den may be under the roots of a tree, a log, in a thicket or rock pile, but most often in a bank — the remodeled den of a muskrat or beaver. The 2 or 3 (range of one to 6) offspring weigh about 132 g (4.7 oz) and are fully furred. The father is driven away until the young are half a year old. The babies' eyes open at 4 to 5 weeks, they begin to play in the nest soon after, but it is 3 or 4 months before they reluctantly leave the den and take to the water. The young otters are at first afraid of deep water and must be dragged in by the mother. They are weaned at this time and leave home about 3 months later. Both sexes become sexually mature at 2 years. The female produces her first litter at age 3; however, males may not be successful at competing for a mate until 5 years old. This species lives an average of 6 years, a few survive to 14 years in the wild, and there is a record of 23 years in captivity.

Remarks The otter's head is flat and broad, with a short muzzle and long touch-sensitive whiskers that aid in catching food and in feeling along the river bottom or the walls of dark burrows. The chest and lungs are large, the nostrils and tiny ears can close to keep out water, and the feet are wide and webbed — all adaptations for an aquatic way of life. Northern otters have rough callouses on the pads of the hind feet which give extra traction on ice and wet rocks. The long tail is thick at the base and tapers at the end. It is used as a prop when the animal sits up in its characteristic begging pose and as a rudder when turning sharply underwater. It also flexes with the whole muscular body when the animal swims as quickly as possible (up to 12 km or 7.5 mi per hour). Generally the otter cruises along slowly by paddling with all 4 legs. It swims rightside up, upside down, on its side, or spiraling through the water. Its breath can be held underwater for only 4 to 8 minutes. While it looks clumsy on land it can easily outrun people as it humps along with the tail extended. On slippery surfaces, such as wet grass, snow, and ice, the otter glides along, usually on its belly with legs either tucked back or forward to help steer and push.

Otters are generally solitary (unless courting or with young), though they may congregate in certain areas for food or at waterfalls and breathing holes in the ice. In favorable habitat they average one otter per 2 to 5 km (1.2 to 3.1 mi) of shoreline, but adult males spread out 20 to 30 km (12.4 to 18.6 mi) from each other. Otters will travel over 100 km (62.1 mi) in watercourses to find food or in dispersing to new quarters, and often cover 15 km (9.3 mi) in one night during normal activities. They are active anytime of the day or night and do not hibernate in winter.

Otters are noted mostly for their curiosity and various maneuvers which are difficult not to interpret as play — behavior not associated with most of the weasel family. They will push and balance a floating stick around with their nose or drop and retrieve pebbles in a pool for 10 minutes at a time. Favorite games are romping in the shallows or sliding down river banks, the more individuals the better. They communicate with each other above and below water with whistles, snorts, chirps, and chuckles. When angry or attacked they growl or scream with their teeth exposed, and are quite capable of defending themselves against animals the size of a dog. The greatest problems for otters are habitat destruction and trapping by humans as well as predation by bobcats, lynx, cougars, wolves, coyotes, bears, alligators, and birds of prey. They are quite safe while in the water.

RACCOON

RIVER OTTER

River Otter

The raucous alarm call of a kingfisher broke the quiet atmosphere of an autumn morning. The big-headed bird flapped over the stream and disappeared into the mixed forest as the bow of a canoe came into sight from around the bend. Two canoeists paddled noiselessly, pausing every once in awhile to scan the scene with binoculars for any sign of wildlife. By looking up in the tree tops for the kingfisher, they didn't notice two tiny eyes and a bulbous nose lying in the water at the edge of the bank. Through a screen of drooping grass, the river otter watched and waited impatiently for the human intruders to glide away. Now, back to the business of finding a meal. In a smooth forward roll the otter dove to the stream bottom, leaving a trail of bubbles to find their way back to the surface. The otter paddled hard with its webbed feet to maintain a head-down position, while the whiskered snout grubbed around in the sediment. Finding nothing on this dive, the otter spiraled towards the rocky shallows. With raccoon-like dexterity of its paws, the animal turned over flat rocks until it spotted a crayfish waving its pincers in defense. Snap went the otter's wide jaws and within seconds bits of crayfish, shell and all, were on their way down to its stomach.

The otter climbed up the bank, shook off a mist of droplets, and rolled over and over in the grass to dry its coat. Scent from another otter caught its attention, and it sniffed all around where soil and grass had been scraped into a little pile. The site marked the boundary between the two animals' home ranges. This otters' agreement helped reduce conflicts that might arise at certain times of the year if they entered too far into the other's section of the stream. But these two individuals were friends and often spent hours playing follow-the-leader, tag, wrestling over a fish, and sliding down the grassy bank into the water. There was little reason to be over-possessive, for both animals could easily catch their fill of fish, frogs, and insects during their daily travels of about ten kilometers (6.2 miles).

As the autumn leaves fell and were buried by several snowfalls, thickening layers of ice and snow separated the aquatic and terrestrial worlds of the otters. But winter seemed to pose little hardship, as the two creatures curled up asleep during the worst blizzards, snug in their dens deep within the stream bank. The first otter centered its activity near the inlet of a spring, the second around the base of a waterfall — the only sites where patches of open water persisted. The animals continued to dive for fish and bottom life, traveling several hundred meters (yards) along the stream. To reach such distances they located pockets of trapped air under the ice, then returned to their den or hole in the ice. On other days they wandered through the surrounding forests or tunneled and played hide and seek together through deep snowdrifts. To the otters it seemed even winter was a time for exploration and fun.

Late one afternoon the two otters paused for a rest during one of their overland excursions. While the older individual attempted to snooze in the last rays of the sun, the younger otter was just too full of energy to sit still. For twenty minutes it chewed and groomed an ear of its partner, who put up with the disturbance with a remarkable show of patience. It finally retaliated by jumping on the antagonist's back and the two characters soon disappeared over a hill in the direction of their homes. As the larger otter returned to the river bank, it found two coyotes sniffing and lapping up water from its haul-out hole in the ice. Realizing its avenue of escape was cut off, the otter snorted in fright. In an instant the coyotes began leaping toward the stranded otter. The otter dove down the bank on its belly and suddenly remembered the waterfall. With the two predators floundering in the deep drifts that had blown in from the forest, the otter alternated two or three bounds with long glides on its belly, sometimes adding a final push with its hind feet. In a hard-packed section the coyotes overtook the otter, and it spun around growling and baring its teeth. The coyotes jumped back in surprise, the otter turned and ran, and the chase was on again. With the animals reaching speeds of thirty kilometers (18.6 miles) per hour, the waterfall soon came into view. The lead coyote was concentrating so intently on the otter's thick tail that it didn't notice it was approaching thin ice. As the otter glided gracefully into the water, the coyote staggered off balance on the cracking ice and slipped helplessly under the dark surface. The second coyote pranced back and forth for half an hour, whimpering and growling at the disappearance of its companion.

Dwayne
Forty

Mammals of the
Deciduous Forest

This biome is characterized by a dense growth of broadleaf trees, generally 25 to 40 meters (82 to 131.2 feet) tall, which lose their leaves in the cold winter season. Sufficient light penetrates below the canopy to support rich shrub and herb layers. In fact, the undergrowth is often so dense that it is difficult to penetrate. Temperate deciduous forest occurs in much of Europe, eastern China, Japan, and in Chile, but it reaches its greatest development in southeastern North America.

There are dozens of forest types found here, but the dominant ones are beech-maple-hemlock in the northeast; aspen-oak and maple-basswood-birch in the northwest; oak-hickory in the west, adjacent to the grasslands; tulip-oak and oak-chestnut in the Appalachian region, though the chestnut was destroyed by blight and has been replaced by other trees like the tulip tree and sweet gum; and magnolia-oak forest in the southern United States. Deciduous forest occurs from sea level to 1 000 meters (3,280.8 feet) in the Appalachian Mountains, and is succeeded at higher elevations and in the north by birch-hemlock-spruce forest. Large areas of deciduous forest in southeastern United States have been logged or burned, and have given way to fast-growing pines. Along the Gulf Coast, mixed broadleaved forests contain both deciduous and evergreen species. Within each climax or mature forest type of the Deciduous Forest Biome are one or more early successional forests containing a variety of other trees. Lining ponds, watercourses, and floodplains are several kinds of distinct forest communities such as cottonwood-willow, white cedar, pondcypress, and baldcypress-swamp tupelo-red maple.

Annual precipitation ranges from 70 to 150 centimeters (27.6 to 59.1 inches), and is consistantly and abundantly available for plant growth during the growing season. The frost-free period is 120 days in the north, 300 days in the south. Mean monthly temperatures from north to south vary from -12°C to 15°C (10.4°F to 59°F) in January, and 21°C to 27°C (69.8°F to 80.6°F) in July. Snow accumulates to over one meter (3.3 feet) in the north but is absent in the south.

Animal life is abundant in this community, supported by a rich growth of plants and a deep, brown, humus soil in mature forest. Species of this biome must adapt to the marked seasonal changes. Abundant herbivores are white-tailed deer, woodchuck, gray squirrel, white-footed mouse, ruffed grouse, katydids, and box turtle. Carnivores and insectivores are represented by the black bear, bobcat, striped skunk, red fox, short-tailed shrew, ovenbird, red-eyed vireo, great-horned owl, hairy woodpecker, timber rattlesnake, copperhead, red-backed salamander, and wood frog.

Short-tailed Shrew

It was springtime in the beech-maple forest. The last snowdrifts hid from the sun in hollows and on the north side of trees, while the spongy brown soil swelled with the ice-cold meltwater. The gurgling sounds of a crystal-clear brook would soon be joined by melodic calls of warblers, vireos, and thrushes. Although they had avoided each other all winter, two shiny black short-tailed shrews took up residence under a moss-covered log. Over the next few nights the male followed the female everywhere, captivated by her irresistible scent. The two kept up an almost constant chatter of clicks and squeaks. Musk from their flank and anal glands became evident in the forest air as the breeding season began.

One morning the male shrew headed out along a familiar trail to the edge of a field, guided by its whiskers and the lingering odor (from a belly gland) that it had left here from a previous trip. Entering the grassy field its keen nose detected the scent of meadow voles. Here and there were green droppings and piles of cut grass stems — certain signs that the mice were still nearby. The passage of their tiny feet over the years had worn a groove into the soil between the grass stems which led to a hole in the ground. The shrew became highly excited and jabbed its pointy head in all directions in search of clues to the voles' whereabouts. Being the same size as a vole, the shrew slipped easily down the burrow, much to the surprise of the resident meadow vole. Without hesitation and with great speed the shrew attached its jaws onto the vole's shoulder, but the vole succeeded in throwing off the attacker and scurried out into the grass. The shrew twittered in eagerness, continually poking its nose from side to side in an attempt to locate its prey. A poison in the shrew's saliva greatly weakened the vole and it struggled off about a meter (yard) away and then lay down panting. When the shrew finally tracked down its quarry, the victim was too weak to fight. The shrew noisily ate half the vole in one meal, and then carried some of the soft brown fur in its mouth back to the log to line its own nest.

The pair of shrews produced a litter of six in early May, and by late June these offspring as well as the parents were all reproducing. As the numbers of short-tailed shrews increased over the summer, the dispersing young experienced difficulty in locating suitable vacant homesites. Frequent fighting was apparent from the red sores and scars on the shrews' faces and bodies. The problems were worsened by lack of rain. The shrews sought living quarters with a comfortably high humidity, and as the soil dried out on south and west slopes, the animals concentrated their activities along the creek bank and in other limited low-lying sites where air in the tunnels was still moist. The male shrew was two and one-half years old now and was tiring under the stress of evicting intruders from his territory in addition to courtship and mating duties with each passing female. Even the red tips of his teeth had all worn away from chewing countless insect skeletons and soil-covered worms.

When the old shrew made its way down the trail to the meadow, it was to be its last excursion. Again the strong aroma of the voles hung in the dark corridors enveloped by overhanging swards of last season's grass. Its hunting instinct remained as strong as ever as it darted boldly from place to place across the meadow. Unknown to the shrew, it was now being stalked by another hunter of equal voracity but greater stealth and power. A long-tailed weasel burst on the scene and pinned the startled shrew down with its rounded front paws. Before the shrew could twist itself around in its loose skin and deliver a bite, the weasel clamped its powerful jaws down around the shrew's neck. Like a patient snake with its prize the weasel crouched down and waited for the shrew to stop struggling in its mouth, its black eyes gleaming with the excitement of a successful attack. The weasel finally arose and bounded away, the shrew's body hanging limply from each side of its jaws. Back in the forest, along the creek, a vigorous young short-tailed shrew expropriated the area around the moss-covered log.

SHORT-TAILED SHREW

Scientific name *Blarina brevicauda*
Family Shrews (Soricidae)
Order Insectivores (Insectivora)
Total length 123 mm (4.8 in)
Tail length 25 mm (1 in)
Weight 18 g, maximum 30 g
(0.6 oz, maximum 1.1 oz)

Color The fur is slate gray or black, slightly paler below. A brown tinge is sometimes present.

Distribution and Status The short-tailed shrew is found in a variety of deciduous, coniferous, and mixed forests, shrub thickets, bogs, marshes, and meadows, reaching its greatest abundance in areas with moist, soft soil with a high content of humus. It is the most common shrew in much of eastern United States and adjacent Canada and extends from James Bay to the Gulf of Mexico and as far west as Saskatchewan and Colorado. Recent studies indicate that there are at least 3 separate species represented within the range of this shrew—the northern short-tailed shrew *(Blarina brevicauda)* over the northern regions, Elliot's short-tailed shrew *(Blarina bylophaga)* in the southwest (Oklahoma, Kansas, Missouri and Arkansas), and the southern short-tailed shrew *Blarina carolinensis)* in the southeast (eastern Texas to Florida and North Carolina). An isolated population occurs in Aransas County of Texas, likely left behind in a pocket of suitable habitat following a northward shift in the range after the Ice Age.

Food This large shrew lives on insects, worms, spiders, centipedes, mice, salamanders, baby birds, nuts, fungi, and other plant material. It has been known to paralyze snails with its poisonous bite and keep them stored alive underground for a future meal. The shells are then dumped on the surface in little piles.

Reproduction and Growth In late February the testes of the males begin to swell to a large size but they remain inside the body cavity, making it difficult to determine the sex without internal examination. Although shrews are generally solitary, it appears that short-tailed shrews may pair and remain together for some time during the breeding season. The female's ovaries are stimulated to release the eggs by the act of copulation, and about 19 days following fertilization of the eggs (21 days after mating), an average of 5 (range of 3 to 10) young are born in a grass and fur-lined nest situated around 30 cm (one ft) below ground. The first births appear in April and second and third litters are produced up to September and occasionally into October (southern part of the range). The babies weigh 0.8 g (.03 oz) and put on weight rapidly with frequent feedings from the mother's 6 mammae. They soon gain sufficient strength and agility to play and wrestle in the nest and begin activity on the surface at the tender age of 17 days. As soon as their teeth erupt at 22 days they commence eating solid food and shortly disperse. Females can breed as early as 6 weeks, but males are not ready until 12 weeks. Short-tailed shrews seldom survive for more than one year but a small percentage attain an age of 2 years. Captives have almost reached 3 years.

Remarks The short-tailed shrew is the heaviest and strongest shrew in North America. It is a high-strung, voracious little beast, as anyone will agree who has seen one hunt down and kill a mouse. The skin is remarkably thick, tough, and loosely attached to the body. The limbs are rather short and end in pink, clawed feet. Its mouth is armed with an impressive array of 22 sharp, red-tipped teeth that resemble a saw blade. As in other shrews the incisors are enlarged and protrude to form a set of pincers, useful in picking up and piercing prey. Mobilizing this dental apparatus is a massive set of jaw muscles. The head tapers sharply into a pink nose supported by a flexible piece of cartilage attached to the nasal bones. The ears are barely visible in the velvety, mole-like fur, but the tiny eyes are readily apparent within a bare patch of skin. Hearing is acute and possibly involves echolocation, while eyesight is poor — the shrew having difficulty in seeing food almost in front of its nose. Insects and other prey are found by the senses of smell and touch with the sensitive vibrissae or whiskers on the snout. This species is well known for its poisonous bite due to the secretions of the paired salivary glands lying near the upper jaw. The poison leaks into the puncture wound of the bitten prey and affects the heart rate, blood pressure, and the nervous system controlling breathing. This secretion causes considerable pain for days in humans.

The shrew constructs its own tunnels with its strong limbs and forward thrusts of its snout. As in most small mammals, it usually takes care to stay out of sight and will readily use available cover of vegetation, logs, rocks, brush piles, and snow, as well as the runways of other creatures. Wherever it travels it leaves its calling card of musk rubbed off on the ground from glands on the belly and sides — the latter marked with a line of white hairs. While its body suggests a more underground existence than most other shrews, it is still frequently active on the surface at any time and any season. Generally, the shrew alternates three-quarter-hour bouts of activity with hour-and-a-half periods of sleep; however, it moves around more at night. The home range averages about 0.5 ha (1.3 a) but can be as large as 2 ha (5 a). Numbers may fluctuate drastically over the years from 1 to 30 per ha (0.4 to 12.2 per a) and populations as high as 120 per ha (48.6 per a) have been recorded in hardwood forests. A high humidity level of the soil seems to be necessary for the long-term health of the animal. Major predators are the red fox, ermine, long-tailed weasel, striped skunk, ground squirrels, snakes, hawks, and owls. It is considered a beneficial forest inhabitant because of its diet of insects, many of which are injurious to timber.

As a young mammalogist, this was one of the first species I collected in my trapline. Initially I thought it was a mole — a common error made by most people when they see a shrew. Checking a field guide, it keyed out to be a short-tailed shrew, much to my surprise. Later, I kept several of these shrews in captivity for months and they were quite remarkable to watch. They worked their way nervously over the floor of the cage, sometimes climbing up the sides and along the wire top. When they met, they uttered twittering squeaks as if they were displeased at seeing each other. The shrews' favorite snack was minnows, which they held in their paws, passing the fish into the mouth like a hot dog. The sharp teeth crunched loudly through the bones and scales until there was nothing left.

VIRGINIA OPOSSUM

Scientific name *Didelphis virginiana*
Family New World Opossums (Didelphidae)
Order Marsupials (Marsupialia)
Total length 85 cm (33.5 in)
Tail length 38 cm (15.2 in)
Weight males 3.8 kg, maximum 6.4 kg
(8.4 lb, maximum 14 lb);
females 2.4 kg (5.3 lb)

Color The underfur is light gray with long black- and silver-tipped guard hairs. A darkish band is usually present along the back, and a yellow stain from gland secretions is sometimes seen on the chest of males. The ears are black with white edges, and the head is white or gray. The tail is black at the base. A black phase is common in opossums from the southeastern United States south to Costa Rica.

Distribution and Status The opossum is presently found from southern Ontario, Min-

SHORT-TAILED SHREW

nesota and Wyoming south to Costa Rica. It has been introduced in the west, and now occurs from southern British Columbia to southern California, and in Arizona and Colorado. There have also been importations to New Zealand where the population is now estimated at over 30 million animals. The opossum is able to thrive in numerous types of habitat but it favors deciduous forest near a watercourse. Literally dozens of different kinds of forests are acceptable, including pine-hardwoods. The animal is less common in marsh, swamp, grassland, mesquite shrub, agricultural land, and suburban areas. In Mexico and Central America it occurs from sea level to over 3 000 m (9,843 ft) and from wet to dry environments.

The genus *Didelphis* originated in South America. Related species are the southern or black-eared opossum *(D. marsupialis)* from Mexico and the Caribbean Islands to Argentina, and the white-eared opossum *(D. albiventris)*, widespread in South America. Until recently the Virginia and the southern opossum were thought to represent one species, but it is now known that the 2 are distinct. The Virginia opossum appears to have evolved from the latter within the last million years and become widespread following the last (Wisconsinan) Ice Age. A further northward expansion has occurred in historic times from Ohio and West Virginia into southern Canada. The northern limit of the range shifts southward again during excessively cold winters.

Food Part of the success of this species is due to its ability to eat many kinds of plants and animals. The bulk of its diet is composed of insects (especially beetles and grasshoppers), earthworms, berries (such as persimmon and cherry), nuts, acorns, corn, grass, mice, small rabbits, frogs, and snakes. Carrion and maggots are relished and cannibalism is not unusual. Opossums may become numerous in and around towns, often competing with raccoons and dogs for tidbits in garbage cans.

Reproduction and Growth The opossum has the most amazing reproductive habits of any North American mammal. Being a marsupial, it raises its young in a maternity pouch, which can be opened or closed, and which contains 9 to 17 (average of 12) nipples arranged in an arc. The female comes into heat for 17 to 38 hours during which period both sexes are attracted to each other by their scent. The male approaches, clicking his teeth continuously, grasps the female's neck in its jaws, and mounts her back. The 2 then roll over on their right side (upright or left-side positions don't seem to result in successful matings) and they remain united for about 20 minutes. The female then rebuffs further attempts by the male. Her ovaries release around 25 eggs and only 13 days following fertilization, up to this many worm-like embryos are born, all within 12 minutes. Each weighs only 0.13 g (0.005 oz) and measures one cm (0.4 in) in length. The blind and naked babies work their way, hand over hand with the aid of tiny claws on the fingers, along the 6-cm (2.4-in) path over the mother's belly fur to reach the pouch. The lucky ones attach themselves to a teat and begin to suckle milk, but others become lost in the jungle of hair or arrive too late to find a free teat. The teat expands within the newborn's mouth so that it becomes securely locked on. A sparse coat appears at 50 days and at 60 days they begin to leave the pouch and crawl around in the mother's fur. Their eyes open at about 65 days. Weaning commences at about 100 days when they weigh 160 g (5.6 oz), but they continue to hitch rides on the mother's back until they become independent at 3 or 4 months of age. Females become sexually mature as early as 6 months, males at 8.5 months. Growth continues through life. The normal life span is under 2 years (maximum of 3 years) in the wild, but up to 7 years in captivity.

In some ways, giving birth to embryos at such an early stage of development seems primitive compared to more modern "placental" mammals which nourish their young for longer periods through a special tissue called the placenta. However, if a female loses a litter, she quickly has another without much stress on her body, since few of her resources are needed to produce another set of newborn. Two litters per year are the norm over most of the range, however one litter is more common towards the northern extremities of the range. Onset of breeding is in December to January in the central part of the range (and perhaps in Central America as well) and January to February in northern regions. The second breeding peak occurs in June. Females still receptive as late as August (especially in the south) are thought to be having only their first or second litter of the year.

Remarks The opossum is a member of a primitive order of mammals called marsupials — widespread in Central and South America and in Australia. Almost all other mammals in this book belong to orders of placental mammals, referring to the placenta — a special organ which unites the developing baby with the mother's uterus. The opossum's brain is small, about one-fifth the size of a cat of equal weight. Another primitive characteristic is the large number of teeth, totaling 50. The penis, which lies behind the scrotum, ends in a fork which fits into the two-horned vagina. The large toe is unusual because it lacks a nail and can grasp somewhat like our thumb. Its tail is long and prehensile, meaning it can curl around objects for support like a fifth leg. In preparing a den, the opossum passes leaves from mouth to front feet to hind feet to tail and then walks home with the coiled tail full of the nest material. Astonishingly, this originally tropical animal has spread to the cold northern states and Ontario, where it becomes torpid and lives off its fat during the winter. It is the only member of its family capable of storing large quantities of fat, and individuals can survive a 45 percent drop in weight by spring. The naked tail and ears are often shortened in these northern individuals, the result of frostbite.

The control of body temperature doesn't begin until the age of around 55 days in a young opossum, and is unusually variable even in adults. It generally ranges from 32°C to 38°C (90°F to 100°F). High temperatures are avoided by nocturnal activity but when heat stressed, an opossum pants, sweats from glands in the feet and tail, and spreads saliva over its body. Daytime retreats include hollow trees and logs, hay stacks, culverts, buildings, rock and brush piles, and even squirrel and bird nests. A different den is used every couple of days and these average 300 m (984 ft) apart. Winter dens in the north are underground burrows excavated and abandoned by other animals. Opossums are not territorial and frequently change their home range. In fact, some appear to be solitary wanderers. Studies have shown short-term home ranges of 5 to 18 ha (12 to 45 a). The animals do not follow trails but simply forage in any direction, averaging one to 3 km (0.6 to 1.9 mi) in a night. Population density may reach one per 1.6 ha (4 a) in prime hardwoods habitat, while one per 43 ha (107 a) is typical in agricultural land.

This species is not a rapid or agile climber, but is surefooted. It swims well both below water and on the surface. Females become aggressive with each other only during the breeding season, while males occasionally engage in fierce fights. Standing face to face they lunge and bite until one retreats or is killed. As yet unexplained is the opossum's incredible resistance to the venom of such poisonous snakes as rattlesnakes, copperheads, and water moccasins — snakes that it sometimes eats. The main causes of mortali-

Continued on p.178

VIRGINIA OPOSSUM

Virginia Opossum and Bobcat

As the fading evening light turned the forest into darkness, something began to stir deep within an old hollow beech tree. A ghost-like figure with moist blinking eyes emerged cautiously from the hole, its black ears still crinkled from being slept on. The opossum proceeded slowly along a branch, securing a foothold on the smooth gray bark by means of numerous tiny ridges on the soles of the feet. Extending up on its hind feet, the opossum reached out to pluck a beechnut free of its stem. The gnawing of numerous sharp teeth soon sent the shells pitter-pattering to the ground below. Continuing with its meal, the animal seemed to glow from the unruly white guard hairs that stuck out all over its body.

Not far away another creature of the night was awakening. Out from a rocky lair gingerly stepped a bobcat. Moving over to a favorite scratching post, the cat arched its back and dug its front claws into the wood, pulling first with one forelimb then the other. A big yawn completed the stretching exercises. Its muscles warmed up for action, the frisky animal bounded down the trail, its hind feet almost overtaking the big front paws. Every so often the bobcat stopped to sniff the ground and to back up and spray the ground or a stump with urine and scent — a thick brownish substance produced by the paired anal glands. Soon it came across a big warty toad, which it tumbled over and over with a paw. The cat had learned when it was a kitten that this amphibian was not good to eat because of its bad-tasting skin. Quickly tiring of the game the hunter pressed on with a more intent look in its eyes. Just as it sat down to scratch a pesky flea with its long hind leg, the bobcat heard faint sounds of something dropping through the leaves. The cat glanced upward, its whiskered lips parted slightly, and a strange low sound rose from its throat. A quivering of its stubby tail revealed the hunt was on.

The opossum continued feeding in the tree, its eyes almost closed in contentment. The sharp rasp of claws on bark caused the animal to jerk suddenly, as if in great pain. The near-sighted creature looked around to see what had disturbed its mealtime. With ears lowered, the cat approached its intended victim until the two animals were face to face. The opossum backed up along the branch, steadying itself with the opposable big toes and long prehensile tail. With an impressive threat display, the opossum rapidly clicked its canine teeth together, then opened its pointy mouth widely. Growls turned into screeches and saliva began drooling out the corners of its jaws. Not the least intimidated the bobcat suddenly batted the opossum off its perch with two lightning-quick blows of its forepaw. Down the opossum dropped, six meters (20 feet) to the ground below where it landed with a thud on its back. It bounced in the leaves then lay still, its eyes staring blankly and its tongue hanging out. The cat peered down to check that its prey was not escaping, then descended quickly and approached its prize. As if expecting the opossum to jump up and run away, the cat pawed the animal repeatedly and bent low several times to sniff it. The opossum had defecated and a foul-smelling greenish substance oozed from its anal glands. The strong smell caused the bobcat to blink its eyes and blow its nose clear, then surprisingly it wandered off looking quite confused. Five minutes passed, then remarkably, the opossum began to stir. Its eyelids opened slowly and it looked around. Eventually assured that the cat had disappeared, it scrambled back to the safety of the tree den. The animal's fainting spell and odor had saved its life. An hour later it forgot the whole ordeal and was back on its perch, feeding on beechnuts.

ty of opossums are coyotes, foxes, dogs, bobcats, raccoons, great-horned owls, shooting hunting and trapping, and moving vehicles. Large opossums sometimes kill and devour smaller ones.

I once found a large opossum lying by the side of the road in southern Illinois. Thinking it had been killed by a car, and that it could be prepared into a museum specimen, I placed the animal in the truck. Minutes later, I noticed the animal stirring, as if it were trying to wake up. But each time I handled it, the opossum passed out again. Realizing the creature still had a chance to live, I put it back into the forest. I never knew whether it had been critically injured by a passing car or just badly frightened. As I drove away, I had a funny feeling of being outsmarted by a so-called "dumb animal." Later I was surprised to read that in spite of its relatively small brain, this creature rated higher than dogs in some learning tests.

BOBCAT
Scientific name *Lynx rufus*
Family Cats (Felidae)
Order Carnivores (Carnivora)
Total length males 83 cm (32.5 in);
females 77 cm (30.3 in)
Tail length 16 cm (6.1 in); 15 cm (5.7 in)
Weight 10 kg, maximum 30 kg
(22 lb, maximum 66 lb);7 kg (15.4 lb)
Color The dense, short, and soft hair is yellowish-brown with black spots and black-tipped guard hairs. The underparts are lighter and spotted as well. The cheek ruffs, sides, forehead, and top end of the tail are streaked with black.

Distribution and Status This cat occurs coast to coast, and from southern Canada all the way down to the state of Oaxaca in southern Mexico. It is an adaptable creature, capable of living in deciduous and mixed forest, swamp, desert, and even agricultural woodlots, unlike its relative the lynx which shuns the proximity of people. It is especially fond of rocky terrain and much of its activity and rest periods center around ledges. Typical habitats are forests of spruce, cedar, fir, and aspen in the north, thickets of palmetto-briar and hardwood bottomlands in the south, and chapparal and pine woodland in the west. Distribution in the north is limited by deep snow, which hinders its movements and hunting ability. The destruction of forests has decreased the bobcat's range, particularly in northern regions.

Food Like many predators, the bobcat is an opportunistic hunter, taking almost any animal it comes across and can overpower. Major food items are rabbits, mice, squirrels, and deer (usually carrion), but fish, lizards, insects, and even grass are accepted, the latter, perhaps, as roughage to clean out the digestive tract.

Reproduction and Growth The courtship of bobcats involves ambushing and chasing, finally ending in one to 5 matings. The male uses the neck grip on the female to protect himself when the 2 are joined. Each individual may breed with several others of the opposite sex, and there are often additional males waiting their turn. Females come into heat up to 3 times a year and males produce sperm year-round, so that young can be born in any month. However, over major portions of the range, pairing and breeding occur most often from February to March. Generally 3 (one to 7) haired young are born about 62 days later in April or May, hidden in a rocky crevice or hollow log. The father bobcat is driven away by the mother, but on rare occasions he returns after the young are weaned to assist in their feeding. Females not bred in the spring produce young from late August to October. The breeding peak commences as early as December in the south and 2 litters per year are possible. The babies weigh about 300 g (10.6 oz) and are furred and blind. They gain around 10 g (0.4 oz) per day, the eyes open at 10 days, exploring begins at 4 weeks, and weaning at 8 weeks. The kittens travel with their mother for 3 to 5 months and disperse from early to midwinter. Females are sexually mature at one year, the males at 2. A bobcat would be fortunate to survive 5 years in the wild, but there are records of 12 years. The maximum life span under captive conditions is a surprising 32 years.

Remarks The bobcat is largely nocturnal, solitary, and extremely secretive. Hence it is seldom seen by people. I have only been able to spot one individual, as it leisurely picked its way across a brown grassy field in California. Relying on the senses of sight and hearing, the bobcat hunts by stealth and a quick burst of speed rather than long pursuit. It bites rapidly and repeatedly with the long canines, and the sharp retractable claws rip open blood vessels and the windpipe of animals as large as deer and sheep. Hunting success is often 20 to 40 percent and a pair of bobcats has been known to cooperate in bringing down prey. In search of food, this species may cover 3 to 11 km (1.9 to 6.8 mi) in a 12-hour period. It is sometimes active during the day as well. Home ranges of adjacent animals frequently overlap, and depending on the terrain, habitat, and food availability, may vary from 0.6 to 200 sq km (0.2 to 74 sq mi). The ranges of males average larger than those of females. Trails are marked with scent and urine about once every km (0.6 mi). Population densities of .05 to 2.7 per sq km (0.02 to one per sq mi) have been reported. Unlike the lynx, bobcats are not known to fluctuate in numbers to any great extent, probably related to the more dependable and varied sources of food. The main causes of death are trapping and shooting by humans, starvation, and predation from coyotes, cougars, and owls.

BOBCAT

EASTERN CHIPMUNK

Scientific name *Tamias striatus*
Family Squirrels (Sciuridae)
Order Rodents (Rodentia)
Total length 265 mm (10.4 in)
Tail length 100 mm (3.9 in)
Weight 100 g, maximum 142 g
(3.5 oz, maximum 5 oz)

Color The eastern chipmunk is an attractive reddish- or grayish-brown color with white underparts. Five black stripes along the back are separated by white and gray stripes. Two alternating dark and light stripes pass through the eye region. The rump is bright reddish-brown, a feature that distinguishes this chipmunk from its smaller cousin, the least chipmunk.

Distribution and Status As its name implies, this common chipmunk is an eastern species found from the southern parts of Manitoba to Quebec, then south to Oklahoma and the northern borders of Louisiana and Florida. It has been introduced in Newfoundland. Deciduous forests such as oak-hickory, beech-maple, and beech-magnolia (both mature and second growth) are its favorite haunts, where it seems to congregate around rock and brush piles. Chipmunks also frequent deciduous-coniferous forests and extend out into the prairie region by way of forested river valleys and woodlots of oak-aspen-box elder.

In spite of comprehensive studies on the anatomy, fossils, chromosomes, and biochemistry of chipmunks, it is still not clear whether the group originated in North America or Asia. About 24 species are known, including the Siberian chipmunk *(Tamias sibirius)* — a dweller of coniferous and mixed forests, brushland, and semidesert from Siberia to northern China and Japan; 20 species of western chipmunks (*Tamias* or *Eutamias* species) of mainly coniferous forests from western Quebec to the Yukon and south through the Coast and Rocky mountains to northern Mexico; and the eastern chipmunk.

Food This stout chipmunk devours seeds, nuts, fruit, fungi, and buds from many herbs, shrubs, and trees. Most important are acorns, hazelnuts, beech nuts, hickory nuts, choke-cherries, raspberries, and maple seeds. Also included in the diet are all sorts of small animal life from insects, worms, salamanders, and frogs to mice, birds, and eggs. Each fall witnesses a frantic period of hoarding food for the winter, a habit which led to the chipmunk's name *Tamias*, meaning steward. Nuts are carried in the animal's spacious internal cheek pouches and later pushed out and buried by the front feet. The chipmunk uses a well-developed sense of smell and memory to locate its larders.

Reproduction and Growth Over most of the range the mating season extends from late February to early April, and from late June to early July. In the north, breeding commences in April and there is time for only one litter per year. Females are receptive for a period of 3 to 10 days. The average number of young is 4 (range of one to 9) which are born 31 days after conception. Each weighs only 3 g (0.1 oz). Nursing occurs from the female's 8 mammae. The babies begin to grow hair at 5 days and their eyes open at 31 days. The youngsters appear above ground at age 5 to 7 weeks, at which time they are weaned. They reach adult size by 3 months, when they leave home. Some spring-born females produce a litter by the summer, while others, plus males, reach sexual maturity the following spring. Two or 3 years is the average life span in nature, though they have been known to live up to 10 years in captivity.

Remarks This alert woodland creature is so brightly colored and entertaining in its antics that people can't help but pause and watch it for awhile. It is a common sight along forest trails and edges, campgrounds, and even in residential woodlots, sitting motionless and chirping loudly over 100 times per minute for up to 10 minutes. When alarmed by people, foxes, bobcats, weasels, snakes, or hawks the chipmunk emits a sharp trill and dashes for cover underground. While most rodents are nocturnal and secretive, this charming small mammal is strictly diurnal and easily seen, particularly during its peak periods of activity in midmorning and midafternoon. It spends most of its time foraging on the ground, but can climb easily into bushes for berries and nuts and has been seen occasionally in trees at heights of up to 18 m (60 ft).

Population densities in good habitat often reach 10 to 37 per ha (4.5 to 15 per a). Over the year the home range averages about 0.5 ha (1.2 a) but may shrink to 0.1 ha (0.3 a) when food is abundant. While home ranges frequently overlap, these solitary creatures are quick to defend the area around the main burrow, which extends underground to a depth of one m (3.3 ft) and a length of 4 to 10 m (13.1 to 32.8 ft). Food-storage and escape burrows are considerably shorter. The main burrow features several chambers for food, nests, and toilets. The earth from excavation is scattered around the surface so that no mounds are present to give away the entrance. The young disperse around 73 m (239.5 ft) or less before setting up their home.

The chipmunk remains active all winter in the south, but it goes into deeper and longer periods of torpor in progressively colder regions so that the species is generally not seen from late October to early April. This species does not produce as heavy a layer of fat as most hibernators, and it wakes up every week or so to eat from its larder and to excrete wastes. The animal hibernates curled up in a ball with the head tucked into the belly (which helps reduce evaporative water loss from the nose and lungs) and the tail wrapped over the head and shoulders. Males emerge about 2 weeks before the females.

I was once trying to determine when various hibernators first appeared above ground in the spring. Traps were set on April 15 in the deep snow of the low Appalachian Mountains that run along the Quebec-Vermont border. The next morning I was pleased to catch an eastern chipmunk, obviously just emerged; or so I thought! It turned out to be a pregnant female which must have been active for at least 2 weeks.

EASTERN CHIPMUNK

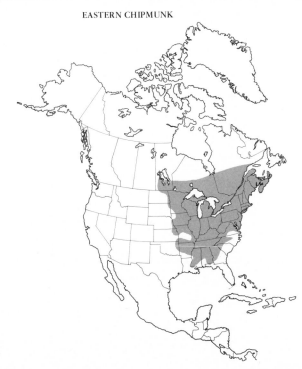

Eastern Chipmunk

Although it was only midafternoon, the forest creatures began to quieten down, as if night were coming. A solid bank of swiftly moving clouds overtook the sun and the low rumble of distant thunder echoed through the valleys and shook the ground. Up the hillside swept hot gusts of wind, at first fluttering the leaves and then animating whole branches of an immense oak which stood above the forest canopy on the ridge top. Perhaps from the plummeting atmospheric pressure, the animals had sensed the approaching storm and quickly sought shelter. As curtains of rain began to fall, a blinding flash of lightning branched earthward, followed instantly by a tremendous clap of thunder. The trunk of the tall oak exploded amid a brilliant flash of fire, and the top half of the tree came crashing down. The animals of the area were stunned with fear from the incredible violence of the storm, and it was not until rather late the next morning that they ventured forth once more.

A gaily colored chipmunk scampered over to the fallen oak and became highly excited on finding thousands of acorns within easy reach. But no sooner had it begun to gather the nuts, when a neighboring chipmunk showed up with the same idea. Emitting a piercing trill the resident chipmunk shot after the intruder, intent on teaching it a lesson. Over rocks and along logs they dashed with tails held high and erect. Then a strange thing happened. As the intruder reached its home area it began to feel bolder, while the first chipmunk became increasingly insecure in the unfamiliar surroundings. The chase slowed, stopped for a few seconds, and then reversed direction! Finally the two competitors called a truce at some invisible border between their home ranges. They sat three meters (9.8 feet) apart, forepaws folded on their chests, scolding each other until their show of bravado was spent. With one last "chip" accompanied by a jerk of its body, the first chipmunk turned around and scampered back to the oak.

Over the next few weeks the resident chipmunk worked long hours harvesting hundreds of acorns.

Carrying a nut in each cheek pouch, it stored them in hiding places, some underground for winter use, others under logs and in the leaf litter. Each was carefully concealed to avoid discovery by other acorn-eating animals such as deer, raccoons, and opossums. Next spring one of these forgotten acorns sprouted and with shiny lobed leaves began its long climb to reach the space in the forest canopy left by the parent oak. As the young oak grew rapidly into a sapling, it seemed to reward the chipmunk for planting it by providing a safe place to hide from a long-tailed weasel that hunted through here periodically. A particular branch also offered the rodent a nice place to stretch out and rest on warm afternoons. In return, the chipmunk ate caterpillars, gall-forming insects, and fungi that attacked the oak.

As the years passed, generations of chipmunks found food and shelter from both the decaying and live oaks. The stump became a favorite location to sit when dining, and it was always littered with discarded pieces of nuts, pits, mushrooms, and insects. The log, repeatedly marked with musk from the chipmunk's scent glands, was a convenient personal highway and food-storage depot. Successive descendants of the original chipmunk expanded the tunnel system among the spreading roots of the living oak tree, which took its place in the sunlight twenty meters (65.6 feet) overhead. These burrows provided secure and dry quarters for baby chipmunks in the spring and a cool retreat on hot summer days, while the insulating layer of fallen leaves helped keep the frost from reaching their hibernating chambers in winter. Over the years hundreds of chipmunks spent the greater part of their lives sleeping, hibernating, and foraging under the tree's protection. As the oak reached its second century, angry thunder rolled through the hills and shook the ground, sending the forest creatures fleeing for cover.

Eastern Cottontail

On a warm evening in May, a family of night hawks could be heard calling and "buzz diving" after moths and other insects flying high over the city. The street lights flashed on up and down the block of houses, spreading their powerful beams over the front yards and outlining a little brown animal with a rusty-orange neck. The female cottontail sat upright with its broad ears spreading like radar dishes over its head. Both nose and fuzzy tail twitched nervously as her big eyes adjusted to the increased illumination. Deftly she clipped a long jagged blade of dandelion with her protruding front teeth and with a rolling motion of her jaws the leaf slowly disappeared into the side of her mouth. She paused eating momentarily as a car sped by. In the back of her consciousness she vaguely remembered a frightening event when as a youngster crossing the road, a car had passed right over top of her as she froze in fear. Voices and laughter of people partying on a nearby patio were of no concern to the cottontail and she continued working over the lawn in short hops in search of tender greens.

A while later she slipped through a picket fence and into a fantastic place, for here was a storehouse of tasty treats all lined up in neat rows — carrots, lettuce, spinach, cabbage, and corn. But before indulging in her favorite pastime — eating — she had a special chore to take care of. She hopped through the long grass, stopped to look around, and then with gentle nibbles of her soft lips and strokes of her front paws, she uncovered five beautiful baby rabbits curled up in a grassy nest lined with warm fur she had plucked from her sides. The blind offspring raised their big wobbly heads to nurse as she stood over them and offered her eight nipples. She spent a minimum of time with her family, preferring to sleep elsewhere and returning only once or twice in each twenty-four hour period to nurse. A light rain began to fall and as soon as she had finished her maternal duties of feeding and cleaning the sparsely haired babies, she carefully concealed them with nest material and slinked away with her ears flattened along the back to avoid detection and to ensure the secrecy of her nest site.

The cottontail had just crawled back between the fence boards and into the garden yard when she was bowled over by some powerful black creature. Unknown to her, she had been watched by a hungry cat perched on top of a fence post. The rabbit let out a shrill scream as the cat's jaws sought her neck and its forelimbs grabbed with piercing claws. Rolling over onto her back from the force of the attack the cottontail lashed out with her only weapons of defense — her strong back legs. Her long claws raked down the cat's belly and knocked the cat loose. Stunned by the unexpected blow the cat staggered backwards with a mouthful of rabbit fur. In a flash the cottontail executed several three-meter (9.8-foot) leaps then dashed away on a zig-zag course that left the cat bewildered after a feeble attempt to pursue its speedier quarry. Following a well-traveled route the cottontail sought refuge in some dense shrubbery, where it remained for the rest of the night. The following day it was the youngsters that would become threatened.

Back from vacation, the man stood on his back porch, gazing at the long grass. He wasn't looking forward to cutting the lawn, but it had to be done. As he pulled out the lawnmower from the shed he was surprised to see a rabbit jumping through the grass and into the prickly hedge. It quickly disappeared and the man turned on the engine. With the lawn half finished he caught sight of something in the grass, and stopped the mower just in time. Parting the dense growth with his hands, he found the nest containing the little cottontails. At their early stage of development they seemed so vulnerable. The man decided that this spot would just have to wait to be cut, and he carefully concealed the nest and finished his task.

Over the next week the man checked on the progress of his rabbit family as soon as the mother departed. Fuzzy hair soon turned the pink bodies brown, and their eyes opened in about six days. A few days later they developed the strength to hop around and began to nibble on grass, clover, and dandelion leaves. At two weeks of age the young cottontails joined their mother in the shrubbery and the man was able to finally finish the yard work. Even though the cottontails were still small the mother returned less and less often to care for them, leaving the young rabbits to fend for themselves. She was already pregnant again and building another nest in a neighbor's grass who happened to be on vacation. True to the reputation of rabbits, this cottontail would produce 35 young by the end of September.

Dwayne
Harty

EASTERN COTTONTAIL

Scientific name *Sylvilagus floridanus*
Family Rabbits and Hares (Leporidae)
Order Rabbits, Hares, and Pikas
(Lagomorpha)
Total length 440 mm (17.3 in)
Tail length 50 mm (2 in)
Weight 1.3 kg, maximum 1.5 kg
(2.9 lb, maximum 3.3 lb)

Color This species is an attractive brown color with black-tipped hairs and a rusty patch on the back of the neck. The underside is pure white. The tail is dark brown above and white below, which gives rise to the name "cottontail." Unlike their relatives, jackrabbits and hares, cottontails do not turn white in winter, reflecting a southern origin where snow is absent or on the ground for only a short time.

Distribution and Status The eastern cottontail occurs over a surprisingly large area for a rabbit — from Saskatchewan and Quebec south to Columbia and Venezuela. It has been introduced in many areas and now occurs from southern British Columbia to Oregon. Cottontails may be found in desert, swamp, prairie, deciduous and mixed temperate forests, and tropical arid and rain forests. Optimum sites are overgrown fields, forest edges, shrubby thickets, and hedgerows. It is found from sea level to as high as 1 200 m (3,937 ft) in the mountains of Kentucky.

Fossil remains of the eastern cottontail are frequently found in caves and other deposits from the Pleistocene (within the last 2 million years). Apparently it was not abundant during the time of the early settlers, but soon flourished with the advent of agriculture. The animal extended its range northward in New England and the Canadian prairies during the early 1900s. Within the last 20 years populations have declined due to intensive farming, which has left sparse cover and little to eat. Cottontails have shown a remarkable ability to adapt to the urban environment and are commonly found in city lanes and gardens.

There are 14 species of cottontails *(Sylvilagus)* — all found in North America and a few continuing on into South America, such as the forest rabbit *(Sylvilagus brasiliensis)* from Mexico to Argentina. Northern relatives of the eastern cottontail are the New England cottontail *(S. transitionalis)* of the northeast, desert cottontail *(S. audubonii)* of the southwest and Mexico, Nuttall's cottontail *(S. nuttallii)* of western United States, brush and pygmy cottontails *(S. bachmani* and *S. idahoensis)* of the west, and swamp and marsh cottontails *(S. aquaticus* and *S. palustris)* of the southeastern United States. Cottontails are closely related to hares and jackrabbits *(Lepus)* and the volcano rabbit *(Romerolagus diazi)* of central Mexico.

Food Over its wide range the eastern cottontail is known to feed on many hundreds of different plants. Choice herbs in the diet are bluegrasses, timothy, quackgrass, red clover, wild carrot, wild rye, dandelion, ragweed, and horsenettle. Woody species are also eaten and predominate during the winter in areas where snow covers the ground. Frequently listed species in food studies are willow, alder, aspen, birch, red maple, apple, chokecherry, red raspberry, blackberry, and staghorn sumac. Corn, soybeans, wheat, alfalfa, and other crops are heavily used when available. Cottontails produce two kinds of droppings — hard dark ones and soft green ones. The latter are eaten before they touch the ground, providing additional nutrients such as vitamin B.

Reproduction and Growth As in most species of mammals, the male cottontail comes into breeding condition before the female. About 4 weeks prior to the renewed growth of vegetation, the female is ready to mate, stimulated into condition by increasing daylight and warming temperatures. At this time she secretes an alluring scent (called a pheromone) which attracts male suitors. Generally the dominant male in the area breeds with most of the local females, which remain in heat until mated. During courtship the two animals squeal, chase, charge, jump over each other, and box, followed by actual mating. The whole sequence may take up to 7 minutes. The eggs within the female's ovary are released 10 hours later (consequently called induced ovulation).

In the northern extremes of the range (i.e., Canada) cottontails mate from March to early September, February to late September at the latitude of New York, January to November in Alabama, and year-round from Texas and farther south. In the warm southern half of the range the breeding peaks are triggered by rainfall and temperature. Over much of its distribution a female cottontail produces an average of 35 young per year, with litters averaging 5 young in the north and 3 in the south. Ranges of 3 to 8 litters per year and one to 12 young per litter have been recorded. First and last litters of the year tend to be smaller than those in mid-season. High soil fertility, and hence nutritious plant food, greatly affect the female's health and fertility.

The eastern cottontail seems to follow a strategy of minimal investment of maternal care and energy in each litter, but compensates by producing plenty of young. The embryos develop for 28 days (range of 25 to 35 days) and are born blind, helpless, only finely haired, and weighing around 40 g (1.4 oz). The nest is usually a shallow depression about 12 cm (4.7 in) deep and 14 cm (5.5 in) across, hidden in the grass or shrubs. Sometimes 2 females place their young in the same nest. The female generally breeds within days after birth, and she returns only once or twice a day to nurse the newborn from her 8 mammae. The young grow rapidly (2.5 g or 0.01 oz per day) and soon begin to crawl. Their eyes open from 4 to 8 days of age, after which time the little ones start to nibble plants. They leave the nest at the tender age of only 12 to 16 days and are weaned, although they continue to associate with their mother for some time after. Juvenile females may produce one or more litters their first summer. Juvenile males may become sexually mature during this time as well, but generally they do not contribute significantly to the breeding pool of individuals until the following year. The average life of a cottontail is 15 months, but some have survived for 5 years in the wild and 10 years in captivity.

EASTERN COTTONTAIL

Remarks The eastern cottontail is a small compactly built rabbit with a silky coat which is kept clean by dusting (rolling in dry soil) and frequent grooming. Saliva-moistened front paws are drawn in unison from the ears to the nose and the hind feet comb the sides. The animal leads a solitary life, most often coming out at dusk and dawn to forage, but activity may occur anytime. Glades, paths, and roadsides are attractive sites for looking for food, and brush or thickets provide essential cover. The home range averages about 2 ha (4.9 a) but can vary from 0.08 to 42 ha (0.2 to 103.7 a). Home ranges are generally largest in winter and overlap is common except for females with young. In winter individuals that bred in the summer have a strong affiliation to their home range, while non-breeders and juveniles do not. Cottontails do not exhibit cyclic fluctuations in numbers as do snowshoe hares. Population density averages around 8 per ha (3.2 per a) with a range of 0.02 to 20 per ha (0.008 to 8.1 per a). Abundance is controlled by a number of factors such as food quality and abundance, dense escape cover, and weather conditions.

Cottontails move about by hopping a few cm to one m (in to 3.3 ft), then they stop, sit up on their hind legs, and look around. Dominant males show their confidence by raising their rump and ears, scratching the front paws on the ground, and by rubbing the corner of their eyes on nearby vegetation. Submissive individuals crouch down with ears lowered. In defense of the nest from another intruder a female grunts, reclines with raised chin and ears laid back, followed by a charge and boxing match. When a predator approaches, a cottontail either remains motionless for long periods, slinks away on its belly, or dashes away at speeds up to 45 km per hr (28 mi per hr). It does not hesitate to dive into dense brush and brambles, or to swim across lakes and rivers to escape a pursuer. People, red and gray foxes, coyote, house cat, bobcat, raccoon, weasels, hawks, owls, eagles, and crows are the main predators. A popular game animal throughout much of the range, cottontails are hunted for sport, food, and fur. Six million have been collected in one year (1958) alone in Missouri. The species is also subjected to numerous diseases and parasites such as tularemia, and Rocky Mountain spotted fever, some of which are transferable to humans.

As a youngster I used to trail these rabbits along the city lanes of my home town. I could never understand how they managed to survive with so many dogs and cats around. Many years later while I was a university student, I and classmates conducted a census of cottontails in an Illinois woodlot as part of a wildlife management course. With spotters standing along 3 of the surrounding roads, the rest of us marched abreast into the woods, hollering and thrashing through the brush, creating as much commotion as possible. Soon we saw several cottontails jumping up from their beds and stealing off under cover of the foliage. When we finally reached the opposite end of the woods, our spotters had tallied a remarkable 26 rabbits crossing the road. Yet a few people walking through the same forest would likely not have seen a single rabbit.

WHITE-FOOTED MOUSE
Scientific name *Peromyscus leucopus*
Family New World Mice and Rats, Gerbils, and Hamsters (Cricetidae)
Order Rodents (Rodentia)
Total length 175 mm (6.9 in)
Tail length 80 mm (3.2 in)
Weight 22 g (0.8 oz)
Color White-footed mice go through 3 distinctive fur coats as they mature, in addition to the usual summer and winter coats. Baby mice soon become light gray above and white below. At 6 weeks dull brown hair begins to grow along the sides and in several weeks this spreads over the back and head. The orangy-brown or grayish-brown adult coat comes in during autumn for spring-born mice; perhaps not until the spring molt for individuals born later in the season. The long tail is dark brown above and white below. The large ears are gray.
Distribution and Status This bright-eyed, big-eared mouse lives in deciduous forests, woodlands, and shrubby growth throughout eastern and central North America. Its range is vast for a mouse, extending from southern Saskatchewan and Nova Scotia in the north to Arizona and Mexico in the south. Such a large array of habitats are occupied that only a few can be listed here: willow-cottonwood floodplain forest along the lower Mississippi, maple-beech forest in the northeast, oak-hickory-basswood forest in the Midwest, cottonwood forest lining creeks in the prairies, bushy slopes in the southwest, and poor tropical rainforest of zapote, gumbo limbo, cecropia, and strangler fig in eastern Mexico.

In much of east-central North America, the white-footed mouse and deer mouse occur in the same vicinity, but the former is typically found occupying warmer and drier deciduous forest, while the deer mouse tends to prefer cooler and wetter deciduous, mixed, or coniferous forest. West of Pennsylvania the prairie form of the deer mouse is restricted more to grassland, leaving wooded habitats to the white-footed mouse. Such segregation is not as definite however for the white-footed

mouse's closest relative — the cotton mouse *(Peromyscus gossypinus)* of the southeastern United States. The 2 mice are frequently found in the same forests and will even interbreed in captivity. The white-footed mouse is believed to have evolved from an ancestral species of *Peromyscus* in relatively recent times (late Pleistocene), at which time this genus became prominent throughout North America.
Food The white-footed mouse is fond of seeds from hundreds of kinds of plants. Cherry seeds, acorns, beechnuts, basswood and hickory nuts, chestnuts, and pine seeds are particularly important. Berries, insects, small mammals, nestling birds, and snails also form part of its diet. Excess food is gathered and stored underground or under logs and rocks for winter use, as this mouse does not hibernate.
Reproduction and Growth In the southern half of the range these mice may breed anytime of the year, annually producing 4 or 5 litters, each with one to 7 young. In the shorter warm season of the north, there is time for only 2 or 3 litters, which appear from April to October. Here, the rodent must spend more energy and time collecting and storing food, and keeping warm, instead of breeding. The female often comes into heat again shortly after giving birth. The babies develop inside the female for about 3 weeks and are born blind and hairless. Nests may be placed in a tree hollow, stump, or underground. At about 3 weeks of age the young are weaned from their mother's milk, and they begin to follow their mother or father on nightly trips to forage. During these forays the young learn what foods to eat and where to find them. If the female is pregnant she soon leaves this family to prepare a new nest. Young females from spring litters can breed later in the season at 7 weeks of age. The maximum life span is 4 years but few live more than one year in their native haunts.
Remarks The white-footed mouse, along with its close cousin the deer mouse, are among the 2 most common and widespread small mammals in North America. These

Continued on p. 188

WHITE-FOOTED MOUSE

White-footed Mouse

The white-footed mouse had the best of two worlds. During the night it spent hours in the forest investigating logs, checking out holes in the ground, and climbing through bushes and trees. There were so many enticing objects to examine and tasty things to eat in the woods. However, the mouse was also fond of a nearby cabin left empty for half the year, for it was quiet and dry inside. Swellings on both sides of the mouse's belly revealed that she would be giving birth before too long. In fact, the expectant mouse was finding it harder lately to push her way through the opening she had chewed in the porch wall. From here it was an easy climb along the boards inside the wall to reach the attic or any room she cared to roam. A few little black droppings showed where the dainty mouse had traveled throughout the cabin during the winter and spring. The kitchen was her favorite spot, since here was a regular supply of oat, corn, and rice seeds, though they were all flattened or puffed and stored inside boxes. She was a much tidier eater than that gray squirrel in the attic, whose acorn shells periodically fell through a crack and littered the floor.

The mouse tired quickly during her nightly forays with the extra weight of her young. It was time to prepare the nest. Several nights later she was carrying some soft grasses in her mouth to add to her nest under a stump, when a great horned owl glided silently overhead. The mouse's big black eyes bulged out and her sides panted in fear as the owl made a terrible sound. She changed her mind about the outside nest, dropped the grass, and headed directly toward the cabin. Once inside, she sat upright on her hind limbs and groomed her pointy snout and ears with strokes of her dew-dampened front feet. As if suddenly coming up with a solution to the problem of a nest, the mouse bounded off to the bedroom. Pulling at the bed mattress with her teeth, she freed a mouthful of stuffing and ran to the bathroom. It took ten trips but finally she had enough soft bedding for the nest. The next weekend, the people returned to their cabin and began cleaning up for the summer ahead. They saw the mouse droppings and squirrel shells and wondered if these two rascals were the same ones who had visited the cottage last year. The squirrel heard the people talking and decided it was time to leave, but it was too late for the mouse. She had just given birth to a pink baby the size of a jelly bean, and five more were on the way.

That evening the children began brushing their teeth at the sink and one of them happened to open the mirrored door on the cabinet. There, blinking in the bright light, was the mouse curled up inside an old shaving mug. The children shouted to their parents to come and see, as the mouse sat up, shaking in fear, her pink babies hanging from her teats. Although she wanted to run away, her instinct was to remain in the nest to protect her young. After everyone had taken a look at the mice, the father gently closed the cabinet door and left the little family alone. The next morning the children couldn't resist peeking inside, just to see how their new boarders were doing. To everyone's surprise, the mug was empty.

WHITE-FOOTED MOUSE *cont. from p.185*

species are often difficult to tell apart, especially as juveniles. The white-footed mouse is an important source of food for many forest animals such as foxes, owls, weasels, and snakes. Even though a female mouse can produce from 12 to 20 young a year, and some of these breed in the same year, only a few succeed in living more than one year due to predation, disease, and accidents. In fact, on the average, when each pair of adults die, they are replaced by only 2 of their young, so that the population size remains about the same from year to year. These mice don't often undergo as large fluctuations in numbers as do many kinds of voles. Population densities in various habitats commonly range from 3 to 30 per ha (1.2 to 12 per a). Each mouse occupies a home range of from 0.2 to 0.8 ha (0.5 to 2 a), frequently overlapping those of other white-footed mice. This species is not known to be highly territorial. Although intensity of use of specific areas of the home range may shift over time, particularly in response to food availability, the actual shape and size of a mouse's home range is remarkably stable. In fact, many mice remain in the same area for their whole life. In seasonally cold regions, the home range shrinks in winter and expands again at the onset of spring breeding. Being curious little creatures, white-footed mice sometimes take extended excursions outside their usual range, likely finding their way home by their scent left along the path. Trails are not used as consistently as in the case of voles. The mice will take advantage of cover (logs, brush, low vegetation, and rocks) but do not hesitate to strike out across open stretches of sand and other bare ground or fields. Once snow covers the ground, ease of travel and economy of energy dictate increased use of burrows and trails, but even then one can often see a white-footed mouse's delicate tracks coursing over many meters (yards) on the surface. Activity is strictly nocturnal, with peak periods just after dusk and before dawn.

The basis for the white-footed mouse story came from an actual incident in my wife's cottage in southern Quebec. The female sat hunched over her babies in a nest within a shaving mug, and although shaking slightly with fear she refused to abandon them. As in most mammals whose den has been discovered, she moved the young away to safer quarters at the first opportunity, through an exit hole gnawed in one corner of the cabinet. I raised several litters of these mice and was impressed by the care and devotion displayed by the females toward their young. The white-footed mouse occurred here at the northern edge of its range and the species' well known attraction to buildings was perhaps even more important in providing shelter from cold winters. It doesn't seem to hesitate occupying the abandoned homes of other animals as well, for it frequently inhabits old bird nests and tree hollows many meters (yards) above the ground.

GRAY SQUIRREL

Scientific name *Sciurus carolinensis*
Family Squirrels (Sciuridae)
Order Rodents (Rodentia)
Total length 480 mm (18.9 in)
Tail length 230 mm (9.1 in)
Weight 525 g, maximum 800 g (18.5 oz, maximum 28.2 oz). The largest races occur in the north, the smallest in Florida.
Color The upperparts are gray with some brown hairs on the head, ears, and back. The undersides are white, occasionally with patches of rusty-brown. The tail is brownish-gray edged in white. In winter the coat becomes much longer, and white hair appears behind the ears. The soles of the feet also grow hair at this time of the year.
Distribution and Status The gray squirrel is a common inhabitant of deciduous and mixed forests from southern Quebec to Florida in the east, and west to the edge of the prairie from southern Saskatchewan to Texas. It prefers more densely timbered regions than the fox squirrel *(Sciurus niger)* which is usually eliminated in areas more than 70 percent wooded. Typical gray squirrel habitats are oak-hickory, oak-pine, live oak-sweetbay, bur oak-aspen, beech-maple, elm-box elder-ash, and magnolia forests. It has been introduced in numerous areas in North America (e.g., west coast, Montana, Nova Scotia), though its recent arrival in Manitoba and Saskatchewan appears to be the result of natural spread as well as introductions. The gray squirrel has also been exported to England, Ireland, Australia, and South Africa.

There are approximately 28 species of squirrels in the genus *Sciurus*, of which 15 are found in North America, most of the others are in South America, and several others occur in Europe and Asia such as the widespread European red squirrel *(Sciurus vulgaris)*. The gray squirrel closely resembles the common fox squirrel of east-central North America and the western gray squirrel of the west coast states. Also found on this continent are the neotropical montane squirrel *(Syntheosciurus)* known only from 3 specimens

and found in the cloud forests of Panama and Costa Rica, 2 species of neotropical pygmy squirrels of Central America and 2 species of red squirrels and 2 species of flying squirrels that are covered elsewhere in this book.
Food The gray squirrel is a good example of how an animal's diet changes throughout the year. Winter is the hardest time of the year to find food, especially in the northern regions where snow covers the ground. The squirrels eat nuts stored in the fall and gnaw on twigs, bark, and any seeds they come across. Spring and early summer bring green buds, catkins, flowers, and seeds of trees like elm, maples, magnolias, and willows. Food is abundant in summer with fruit and berries like apple and cherry, hazelnuts, mushrooms, bird eggs, and insects. When the oil-rich nuts like acorns, walnuts, hickory nuts, butternuts, and beechnuts ripen in the autumn, the squirrel puts on a layer of fat that helps it through the early part of the lean winter. Corn and soybeans are subsistance foods in some regions, and bones and antlers are often gnawed for minerals.
Reproduction and Growth In the south the gray squirrel may breed throughout the year, but most young are born in February and August. In central and cold northern regions the mating season is in February and June, with the peaks of births occurring in March and July. A number of males court a female in heat and the former sometimes fight to determine dominance. The winner then pursues the female through the trees until the two are sufficiently stimulated to mate. The male departs in search of other mating opportunities and plays no role in raising the family. Females are pregnant for 44 days. Yearlings produce only one litter while older individuals normally have 2 annual litters, each with an average of 3 (range of one to 9) young. The newborn are blind, naked, and weigh 16 g (0.6 oz). Fur appears by day 14, the eyes open at 31 days, and they remain in the nest for 6 weeks. Nursing continues from the mother's 8 mammae until 8 or 9 weeks, but the juveniles are still dependent for at least 12 weeks. They disperse

GRAY SQUIRREL

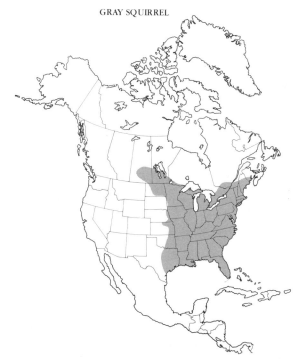

when almost full grown at 6 months. Both sexes mature at 10 or 11 months of age. In spite of a mortality rate of about 50 percent a year, a few squirrels survive and continue to reproduce at age 13. Captives have lived an astonishing 23.5 years.

Remarks The gray squirrel is an attractive woodland creature with a well-furred and flattened tail. Held in a graceful arc over the back while sitting, the tail is a critical balancing rod while the animal bounds and dashes over the ground or executes spectacular leaps through the tree tops. Interestingly the tail hairs are only replaced in August, although the remainder of the body molts in both spring and autumn. The limbs are long and well developed with sharp curving claws — typical adaptations of climbers. The senses of sight and hearing are keen and are used in detecting predators such as people, hawks, owls, bobcats, and ground-dwelling carnivores. When alarmed the gray squirrel's first strategy is to remain motionless on its perch until the danger passes. If discovered it quickly retreats to the opposite side of the tree, and then generally breaks away through the tree tops at such speed that it is difficult for a running person to keep up with it. Although described as a tree squirrel, it spends considerable time foraging on the forest floor, but seldom strays far from the security of the nearest tree – unlike the fox squirrel which wanders hundreds of meters into the open. When the gray squirrel locates an acorn or other nut on the ground, it picks it up in its mouth, jumps a short distance, digs a hole with its forepaws, deposits the nut, and then covers it up with soil and leaves, tamping it down with the nose. Some of these buried treasures are forgotten (and many of these sprout), but the rodent depends on these caches during periods of food shortage such as winter and early spring. Squirrels have been observed locating acorns under 30 cm (11.8 in) of snow, presumably by smell and memory.

This species is active mainly during the early morning and late afternoon in warm weather, and during midday (the warmest hours) on cold days. Occasionally individuals have been seen during moonlit nights, especially in autumn when dispersing or gathering food crops. There is no hibernation period but the animal remains within its nest in a hollow tree during inclement weather. There are usually several such dens that are occupied throughout the year, as well as several leaf nests — large structures of branches and leaves built high in the tree canopy. Home ranges are rather small for such an active squirrel — usually 0.5 to 1.8 ha (1.2 to 4.5 a), with those of males averaging slightly larger than females. Population density is often around 0.5 to 3.5 per ha (0.2 to 1.4 per a), but has been reported as high as 50 per ha (20.2 per a). When dispersing or changing to a new home range, the squirrels frequently move 16 km (9.9 mi) and one was found to have traveled 65 km (40.4 mi). While there have been reports of population outbreaks and consequent movements of large numbers of gray squirrels during this century, none can match the mass exoduses reported in the 1700s and 1800s. Apparently millions of squirrels covered great distances together in search of unoccupied range and new food sources. Such emigrations caused great excitement locally and often involved extensive damage to crops. Even today this species runs counter to the interests of people by eating vegetables and grains (especially corn), gnawing orchard and ornamental trees and shrubs, raiding bird feeders, and nesting in buildings. When the latter happens even a naturalist's patience is put to the test, for the squirrels can create considerable commotion while scampering through the attic and walls, not to mention the holes chewed through the eaves. Just how upset homeowners can become was vividly displayed early one morning while I lay in bed. Astonished to hear what I thought were shots from a .22-calibre rifle, I leapt to the window and peered out with sleepy eyes. As a slug ricocheted with a buzz off a nearby tree limb, I spotted a gray squirrel beating a hasty retreat through the treetops. Then who should appear, running through my backyard in floppy slippers and pyjamas and wielding a rifle, but a neighbor from a few houses down. I expect the squirrel had disturbed his sleep once too often.

The gray squirrel is a popular game animal and over 40 million are shot each year in the United States. Some of the meat is eaten but the fur has limited commercial value. These squirrels are common in city parks where they are a great source of pleasure to people who watch and feed them. It is not advisable to hold food in the hand, for the rodent can mistakenly bite a finger quite badly. An occasional individual can become quite aggressive and may even charge people. I once saw a gray squirrel performing a most amazing routine. It repeatedly ran up the base of a tree and then back-flipped to the ground.

GOLDEN MOUSE

Scientific name *Ochrotomys nuttalli*
Family New World Rats and Mice, Hamsters, and Gerbils (Cricetidae)
Order Rodents (Rodentia)
Total length 175 mm (6.9 in)
Tail length 75 mm (3 in)
Weight 20 g, maximum 30 g
　　　　　(0.7 oz, maximum 1.1 oz)

Color This mouse's soft long hair is a rich golden-brown color on the upperparts and white or light orange on the undersides. The feet are white.

Distribution and Status The golden mouse occurs in the southeastern United States from Virginia and central Florida as far west as Missouri and Texas. It may live in a variety of brushy and forest situations such as brierpatches, hedgerows, pine and oak woodlands, cedar thickets, live oak stands, hardwood swamps, rocky ravines, canebrakes, and even cool hemlock-moss forests on mountain slopes. Preferred sites are those with a heavy undergrowth of honeysuckle, greenbrier, grapevine, and blackberry. Its closest living relatives are the deer mice (*Peromyscus* spp), which it closely resembles.

Food The main food of these mice is seeds from dozens of plants like cherry, sumac, dogwood, blackberry, greenbrier, and oaks. Some insects are devoured as well. Food is carried in expandable internal cheek pouches. Feeding platforms and nests often contain hundreds of seed husks, showing that the animals like to retreat to their favorite hideaways when eating.

Reproduction and Growth In the northern regions of the range pregnant mice have been found from March to October, while in the south the species may breed in any month of the year, but more often in the autumn and winter, and seldom during the hot summer. At 25 to 30 days after mating, generally 2 or 3 young are born per litter (range of one to 5). The male is forced out of the nest at this time and he takes up residence in a spare nest in the trees or on the ground. Two or 3 litters a year occur under normal conditions, although one captive female actually produced 17 litters in one and a half years. The newborn weigh around 2.7 g (0.1 oz), brown hair appears on day 5, and their eyes open at 2 weeks. The young mice change from a diet of milk from their mother's 6 mammae to seeds at an age of 3 weeks. They reach adult size at 10 weeks, but like other mice they continue to grow slowly the rest of their life. Life expectancy is 0.5 to 3 years in the wild, but one captive female was still capable of breeding at 6.5 years and another lived a remarkable 8.5 years.

Continued on p.194

GOLDEN MOUSE

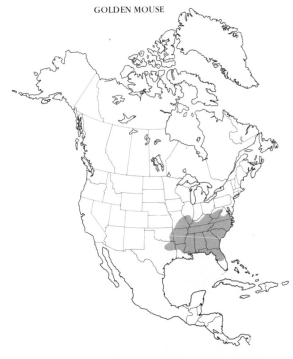

Gray Squirrel

As soon as it was light the gray squirrel awoke in her den high up in an oak tree. She gently nuzzled her five offspring, noticing the sweet scent and heat arising from the tiny bodies, just now becoming clothed in short, fine, gray hair. As they squirmed and waved their arms and legs at the disturbance, she covered them over with soft nest material of shredded grass and plant down. Then up to the entrance she leaped, thrusting her head out the hole for a brief surveillance of the lush green tree canopy and the forest floor dotted with a variety of spring flowers. This scene and the remainder of her half-hectare (1.2-acre) home was ingrained in her memory, for she had lived in this part of the forest for twelve years and successfully raised twenty litters for a total of sixty young.

Off to the left she heard a swishing sound and caught sight of another squirrel rebounding back in springy branches following a leap from one tree to another. Normally she would have ignored her neighbor's approach, but with young in the nest, she coveted this tree as her own. Darting out onto her favorite perch she began rapidly calling "kuk-kuk-kuk," jerking her beautifully plumed tail over her back with each bark. The visiting squirrel paused to rub its chin and cheeks in a branch in the adjacent tree, then proceeded forward in spite of the warning. With only two meters (6.6 feet) separating them, the female began to chatter her teeth and she charged and struck the visitor on the chest with her forepaws with such force that the unfortunate animal lost its balance and fell. As quick as a flash the squirrel twisted its body upright in midair and grasped for a branch, but there was none within reach. Down it dropped eleven meters (36.1 feet) to the ground where it bounced on the spongy soil. After regaining its breath, it headed for home, none the worse for the experience.

With that nuisance out of the way she descended to the ground and began searching the leaf litter for acorns buried the previous autumn. She had harvested far more of these nuts than she could eat at the time, and had instinctively cached a supply in tree hollows and at individual places underground. Using her keen sense of smell she located an acorn that had started to sprout, and dug it free with her clawed forepaws. Rather than eat the meal on the spot, she carried it into the nearest tree, for she never felt entirely secure on the ground. Over the next hour of foraging she traveled two hundred meters (656.2 feet) and filled her belly with nuts, a leathery fungus

growing on a tree, a caterpillar, and some buds. Then she returned to her den where she nursed and slept for most of the day.

It was quiet that evening in the oak forest, which suited the squirrel as it lay stretched out on a limb. She had finished nursing and cleaning her pesky young family and sought some time to doze on her own. As the light began to fade, the flute-like call of the wood thrush echoed through the ravine. She wiped a mosquito off her nose with her paw and yawned, then made her way back to the den where she curled up with the baby squirrels for the night. A sudden rustling outside in the dry leaves indicated some animal was nearby. Out popped her head from the hole and her large black eyes searched the ground for some time before spotting something moving through the underbrush. A raccoon rambled to the base of her tree and it stood up on its hind legs, sniffing the air with its pointy snout. The raccoon could smell something interesting, and having an inquisitive nature it just had to find out what it was. Hand over hand the hunched-back bandit made its way up the tree, its claws hooking onto furrows in the bark. The excited squirrel came out of the hole, and hanging by her hind feet she checked on the progress of the intruder. A decision was needed quickly — would she stay with the defenseless babies or save herself by leaping to the next tree?

As the raccoon neared the den about ten meters (32.8 feet) above the ground, the startled squirrel scampered to a higher perch and scolded the trouble-maker, her bushy tail flailing with each bark. Staying a few meters out of range she was trying to draw the predator's attention to herself. The young squirrels whimpered as the raccoon's paw extended down toward them, but they were just barely out of reach. For over a minute the raccoon tried to solve the dilemma, then frustrated, it backed down the trunk and waddled off in search of other prey. The squirrel quickly returned, and finding her family unharmed she picked one baby up in her mouth and carried it away through the treetops to another secret place. She repeated the trip four more times until all were safe in the second den. Finally she could rest with her offspring nestled along her belly. It had been an eventful day.

Golden Mouse

In the dim light of the moon a small mouse dashed along the swampy woodland floor, its four limbs a blur and its tail held straight back. Sticking out both sides of its mouth were several blades of grass. It seemed in a hurry to reach some distant place and hardly bothered to stop and sniff a greeting to another mouse, which had popped its head out of a nearby log. Half a minute later it paused to catch its breath under the shadow of a big leaf. The ringing of hundreds of cicadas was almost deafening and somewhere off in the night a pair of barn owls called to each other. Grabbing onto a greenbrier stem with the skill of a trapeze artist, up climbed the mouse into the thorny maze, curling its tail loosely around the vines for balance. At a height of two meters (6.6 feet) the mouse stopped again for a few seconds, its gold-colored sides heaving from exertion. Searching around with its large bulging black eyes, the mouse selected a particular spot in the fork of a tree and began to weave the grass amid the tangle of vines. Just like a songbird the golden mouse was constructing a nest high above the ground where it would be safe from most of the local predators like the gray fox and striped skunk. Not even a bobcat or owl would try to penetrate through these sharp thorny brambles, though a long-tailed weasel might. Down went the mouse for more grass, and after many trips over three hours, a ball-shaped structure took form.

Nest-building was tiring work and after one o'clock in the early morning the mouse joined two other mice inside the hollow log. Stirring again at four, the diligent worker left its sleeping partners and continued with its project. At one point it plucked several blue greenbrier berries and ate them while sitting atop the new nest platform. After two more hours of gathering and weaving grass with its mouth and front paws, the mouse pushed its way into the ball, turned around several times inside, then retired. It would be a week before the twenty-centimeter (7.9-inch)-wide nest was completed, for shredded bark and broad tree leaves had to be worked into the roof to shed rain, and a soft bed of plant down and feathers needed to be gathered and tucked in place. The mice inside the log were content to have their nest on the ground, although they often climbed up to a number of feeding platforms in the vines to eat their seeds. These dining sites had obviously been used for some time since they were littered with empty husks and shell fragments of pits and nuts.

For the next two weeks spring rains poured down with such intensity that the nearby river swelled to overflowing. As the muddy debris-filled water spread over the floodplain the larger forest creatures like deer and raccoon left for higher land, but the golden mice had to stay behind, for their short legs could not carry them far and they didn't know which way to retreat. The water soon flooded the hollow log, causing the two mice to scramble up on a dead branch where they sat shaking with fright, unsure what to do. High in the forked tree, the third golden mouse lay curled asleep. The wind and rain drops buffeted the round nest, but it remained warm and dry inside. That evening the two wet and exhausted mice followed a scent path up the greenbriers to the big ball of grass and leaves. One by one they poked their heads through a makeshift grass door, sniffing hesitantly as if to ask whether they might come in. Though the owner did not seem particularly pleased to have these wet characters in its bed, it did not drive them away. The visitors licked and groomed until fairly dry, then all three fell asleep, their soft bodies intertwined. For weeks they lived together, feeding on greenbrier fruit and acorns that floated within reach, until the waters receded back into the river channel. A gray layer of silt covered the ground to fertilize the rich assortment of plants that soon began to grow. It wasn't long before there were three grassy nests in the vines.

GOLDEN MOUSE *continued from p.189*

Remarks The golden mouse appears to move more slowly and carefully than its deer mice relatives, which may be because of its arboreal or climbing habits, where rushing might cause a fall. Grasping a branch with only its tail or with tail and hind feet, the animal can reach out like a monkey to grab food. If chased out of its nest by a snake or other predator, the mouse usually climbs to the top of the tree. More time is spent on the ground in summer, and it has been noted that in Texas the mice are not as prone to climb. The rounded nests may be situated as high as 5 m (16.4 ft) above the ground, while the more-numerous and less-bulky feeding structures are found in branches up to the 15-m (49.2 ft) level. Some nests have been discovered inside strands of Spanish moss draped from live oaks and bushes. This species is strictly nocturnal (night active), with activity peaks several hours after dark and before light. It is somewhat colonial and is often found in local areas and not in other seemingly similar habitats. More sociable than most mice, up to 8 have been found in the same nest. Since golden mice forage in the vertical dimension of shrubs and trees, they seem not to require as large a home range as other ground-dwelling, seed-eating mice. Often they remain in an area of only .05 to 0.6 ha (0.1 to 1.5 a) and are not very protective of the site, for home ranges overlap considerably. Population densities range from 0.5 to 74 per ha (2.5 a). These mice are quite docile and make fascinating pets.

Along with a mammalogy class of students, I set traps in a bottom land forest of southern Illinois hoping to capture golden mice. The next morning we anxiously checked each trap, and there, in the second-to-last one, was a beautiful gold-colored animal — the first golden mouse I had ever seen! Knowing a rare animal's exact habitat requirements is essential in finding it.

RED FOX

Scientific name *Vulpes vulpes*
Family Wolves, Foxes, and Dogs (Canidae)
Order Carnivores (Carnivora)
Total length 100 cm (39.4 in)
Tail length 33 cm (13 in)
Weight males 5 kg, maximum 7 kg (11 lb, maximum 15.4 lb); females 4.5 kg (9.9 lb). Red foxes in Eurasia range from 3 to 14 kg (6.6 to 30.9 lb).
Color There are several color phases of red fox — silver (black with silver frosting), black, cross (grayish-brown with black on the back), bastard (bluish-gray), and Samson (lacking guard hairs). However, the most common is the reddish-brown or yellowish-red coat which is generally darkest along the back. The lips, chin, chest, belly, inside of the ears, and tail tip are white. The legs and the back of the ears are black. The winter coat is a darker red. The pups are at first grayish-brown, turning to a pale yellowish-brown at 7 weeks, and by 14 weeks they attain the reddish coat of the adults.
Distribution and Status The red fox has one of the largest distributions and habitat ranges of the world's land mammals. In North America it is found from Alaska, Baffin Island, and Newfoundland in the north to California, Texas, and Georgia in the south. It is also native to Eurasia, extending from Scandinavia to north Africa and eastward to Siberia and China. Originally the New World red foxes were thought to be a distinct species *(Vulpes fulva)*, but they are now considered the same as in the Old World. This fox appears to have been scarce in the unbroken hardwood forests of southeastern United States during early settlement times and red foxes from Europe were introduced into this region and New England around 1750. In the 20th C the animal has extended farther southeast as well as north and now occupies Baffin Island (since 1919). It has been introduced to Vancouver Island and to Australia (in 1868) where it spread rapidly.

This fox favors diverse habitats with forest or shrub cover interspersed with meadows. It avoids extensive dense forests. It is common-ly found in coniferous and deciduous forest edges, prairie, swamps, marshes, alpine and arctic tundra, desert shrubland, and cropland. Its elevational range is from sea level to 4 500 m (14,763.8 ft). It can adapt to the presence of people and frequently inhabits urban sites such as golf courses and parks. There are about 10 species of *Vulpes*, represented in North America, Europe, Asia, and Africa. Two species—the swift fox *(Vulpes velox)* of the plains and the kit fox *(Vulpes macrotis)* of the American southwest — are considerably smaller than the red fox.

Food The red fox devours a great variety of small animals, including mice, rabbits, ground squirrels, opossums, muskrats, pocket gophers, woodchucks, marmots, carrion (especially deer), pheasants, quail, grouse, songbirds, eggs, and insects. A meat diet is more prevalent in the winter. In summer and autumn, fruit, grasses, and grains (such as corn and wheat) are taken in considerable quantities.

Reproduction and Growth Males begin to produce sperm as early as October and November, and sometimes become aggressive with each other where their territories meet. A strong bond is often formed between a male and female, which may last for years. The mating season in the south extends through December and January, whereas in northern regions it is delayed from February to April. The female comes into heat for one to 6 days and about 52 days (range of 49 to 56 days) later, an average of 5 young (range of one to 13) are born in an underground den. Most births occur from March to May — timed to coincide with the appearance of plentiful food in the spring, yet early as possible following winter to give the pups a maximum development period before the cold season sets in. The pups weigh from 71 to 119 g (2.5 to 4.2 oz) and have a coat of silky fine fur. Their eyes open at 8 days, they can walk at 3 weeks, but activity is restricted to inside the den for 4 weeks. Both parents care for and feed the young, the mother providing milk from 8 mammae. The family may move to a second or third den;

RED FOX

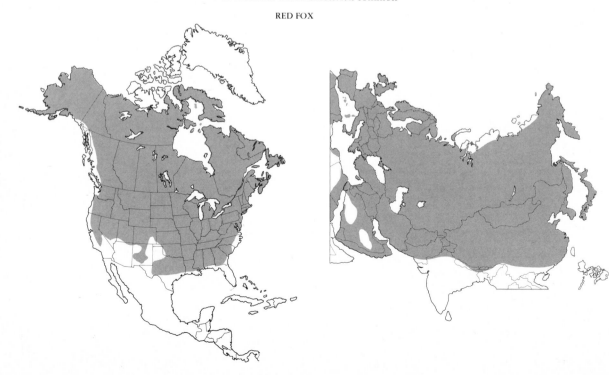

sometimes the litter is separated into two groups. The young foxes travel with a parent to learn foraging techniques and at 10 weeks begin to move about on their own, by which time they are weaned. They reach full size at 6 months and disperse from mid-September to early October. Juveniles are capable of breeding for the first time at 10 months of age, but not all do. Few red foxes reach 4 years of age under natural conditions; however, some have survived to 12 years in captivity.

Remarks The red fox is a most attractive creature with pointy ears and muzzle, and long lustrous fur. The rounded and bushy tail is used to help balance the animal while running and leaping, and folds over the face when the fox is curled up asleep in cold weather. The legs are long and agile, with 5 toes on each front paw and 4 on the back. Prominent claws are present and are kept worn down by contact while running and by scratching the ground. A large gland on top of the tail base gives off a strong musk which sometimes rivals that of a skunk. A relatively large number of teeth (42) are specialized for functions of grasping, stabbing, shearing meat, and pulverizing plant material.

The red fox has a reputation for intelligence and its senses of sight, hearing, and smell are acute — all factors that have enabled the species to adapt to living in farm and urban areas in spite of its shy and nervous nature. It communicates and expresses its moods with a variety of sharp yaps, barks, howls, and screeches. The fox runs on its digits and is a tireless trotter. Speeds of 48 km (29.8 mi) per hour have been recorded. It can also leap over obstacles 2 m (6.6 ft) high and swim long distances.

Red foxes are active mostly at night but it is not unusual to see them hunting during the day as well. They often keep to worn runways, traveling 8 km (5 mi) in a night. A home range may be occupied for life and follows topographical features or forest edges. Ranges have been reported between 58 and 162 ha (143.3 to 400.1 a), occupied by a male and one or 2 females with young. The male is territorial and marks his claim by scent. The red fox either excavates its own den or renovates a burrow of a badger or woodchuck. Dens are situated in good cover with water nearby, and in places not likely to be discovered by humans. The tunnels extend up to 3 m (9.8 ft) deep and 10 m (32.8 ft) long, have up to 19 entrances (usually only around 3), and are used for generations. When it comes time for the family to break up, juvenile males disperse an average of 40 km (24.9 mi), females 10 km (6.2 mi), and there is a record of a male traveling 394 km (244.8 mi) from home. Population density averages one fox per 4 sq km (one per 1.5 sq mi), but can reach much higher levels during somewhat regular fluctuations every 8 to 10 years.

The main mortality factors affecting foxes are trapping, shooting, collisions with automobiles, predation (by coyotes, bobcats, eagles), and diseases (e.g., rabies, distemper, mange). The reputation of this animal has changed from a "raider-varmint" to a valuable furbearer and controller of rodents. Fox fur has recently been in high demand for coats and trim; 421,705 pelts were processed in the United States and Canada in 1977. Fox farming and selective breeding have resulted in a variety of new strains.

My most memorable sighting of this beautiful species occurred in southern Quebec as I was sitting quietly in a mature beech-maple forest. My chair was a log at the side of a path that led away over a hill. Just as I was about to rise, my eye noticed a movement on the left, though there was no sound. As I remained motionless who should come trotting along the trail but a red fox. Dangling from each side of its pointy jaws were a young woodchuck and a meadow vole. The successful but tired hunter drew within 5 m (16.4 ft) before it caught sight of me, or smelled me, and leapt away. On several other occasions I have discovered caches that I believe were made by red foxes, consisting of snowshoe hares covered with leaves and soil.

STRIPED SKUNK

Scientific name *Mephitis mephitis*
Family Weasels (Mustelidae)
Order Carnivores (Carnivora)
Total length 550 mm (21.7 in)
Tail length 220 mm (8.7 in)
Weight males 2.6 kg, maximum 5.5 kg
(5.7 lb, maximum 12.1 lb);
females 2 kg (4.4 lb)

Color The striped skunk is shiny black, with a white stripe on the forehead and 2 broad white stripes running from the back of the neck to the base of the tail. The hairs on the tail are white at the base. Some individuals also have a white stripe on the outside of the front legs or a white patch on the chest.

Distribution and Status The striped skunk is a common animal over much of its large range which extends from the southwestern corner of the Nortwest Territories to central Quebec in the north, and south to northern Mexico in the states of Baja California, Durango, and Tamaulipas. Its elevational range varies from sea level to 4 000 m (13,123.4 ft). Habitats are diverse and include mountain and boreal coniferous forest, dozens of deciduous-forest communities, parklands, prairie, meadows, swamps, marshes, deserts, brushy ravines, rocky outcrops, and agricultural lands.

The skunk subfamily is first recognized in the fossil record in the early Oligocene (37 million years ago) in North America. Close relatives are the hooded skunk *(Mephitis macroura)* from the southern United States to Nicaragua, 5 species of hog-nosed skunks *(Conepatus)* from Colorado to Argentina, and 2 species of spotted skunks *(Spilogale)* from British Columbia to Mexico. Another relative, the zorilla *(Ictonyx)* of Africa, shows a remarkable resemblance in body form and ecology to the spotted or striped skunks of North America.

Food Striped skunks are omnivorous, which means they eat a wide variety of both plants and animals. They are fond of insects (grasshoppers, crickets, wasps, beetles), mice, bird's eggs, frogs, snakes, carrion, and berries, and will even devour buds, nuts, roots, and grain. Animal material is more prevalent in spring and summer, vegetation in autumn and winter. With such a varied menu, skunks seldom starve.

Reproduction and Growth The breeding season runs from mid-February to mid-April over most of the range, perhaps earlier in southern extremes and later in the far north. Males become restless, inquisitive, and aggressive during their search for females. Females come into heat for a few days and if not mated, do so again after 30 days. When approaching each other the male sniffs the female to check her condition, then grasps her by the back of the neck in his jaws. Mating takes about one minute during which time the female sometimes tries to bite the male. The two then separate and go their own way, the male to find other females, the female fighting off the advances of any additional suitors. The embryos probably undergo a rest period before resuming growth, for the time of pregnancy varies from 59 to 77 days. The female prepares a nest of leaves about two weeks prior to birth. Most litters are born in mid-May and average 4 young in a yearling female's first litter, and 6 (range of 2 to 10) in subsequent years. A second annual litter occurs rarely. The young weigh around 32 g (1.1 oz) and are covered in fine fur. Their eyes open
Continued on p.200

Continued on p.200

STRIPED SKUNK

Red Fox

As the yellow school bus made its way down the gravel road, the children inside suddenly gathered around the windows on one side of the vehicle to watch the antics of several creatures in the field. About fifty meters (164 feet) away a pair of red foxes were intent on tracking down a vole hidden under the cover of snow. Every few seconds a fox leapt high in the air and upon landing, dug furiously with its front feet. Unsuccessful so far, the hunters lowered their pointy ears to the surface and listened for the faint scratching sound of the vole moving through the lattice-like lower layer of old snow. The bus disappeared in the distance as the foxes burrowed towards each other, trapped the rodent, and pinned it down with a furred foot. The female snapped up the meadow vole and swung away from her mate, giving her an opportunity to swallow her meal. The male pranced around and nibbled at her lips, whining pathetically at missing out. In his eagerness he pushed her over in the snow but quick as a flash she was up and away. The two hunters then bounded through the snow drifts along the forest-edge, their round fluffy tails rising and falling with each jump.

As the red foxes entered the woods, the steady breeze vanished, no longer rippling across their long soft coats. Without warning the lead fox stopped short, causing the second animal to ride up over its back. At their feet was a trail of a snowshoe hare — a depressed highway through the snow, dappled here and there by brown woody droppings. While the female began a slow stealthy stalk along the trail, the male quickly circled far in advance until he discovered the same trail about sixty meters (196.9 feet) distant. He crouched behind a big maple tree and waited.

The female fox trotted forward, dipping her black nostrils to the surface occasionally to inhale the tantalizing scent. She knew a snowshoe hare had passed this way within the last few hours. The hare was nibbling the bark off a sapling when it realized it was not alone. In the fading light its white coat was almost invisible against the snow. The female fox wandered in so close to the hare that it bolted down the trail. Each time the fox came close to capturing the hare, the path led through a tangle of shrubbery and the hare gained some distance. Suddenly a second hare broke from cover and dashed along the same route. Just as they reached the big maple, the male fox leapt out and deftly grabbed the first hare by the throat. Before it finished its death scream the female caught the other hare. Rather than eat their hard-earned prizes, the foxes stashed them in a nearby snowbank and wandered off into the night.

Three weeks later the snow had vanished from the fields, leaving only the floor of the maple forest covered in a white blanket. Even here, the rays of the sun warmed up the tops of rocks and brown stumps, melting the snow back a little more each day. High in the top of a tree a crow uttered contented gurgling sounds in its throat. The big black bird had just returned from the south and was enjoying the warm sun on its wings and back while it surveyed the surrounding scene as if it owned the place. Its sharp eyes caught sight of something red moving quickly through the woods. The male fox came running into view, obviously in a hurry to reach some distant place. Its dainty paws landed on a narrow trail that had been kept clear by the frequent passage of the fox, white-tailed deer, and snowshoe hares. The crow, being a curious old bird, decided to follow the fox. As the white-tipped tail disappeared around a bend the crow spread its wide wings and swooped down off the perch. From tree to tree the bird followed in silence except for the gentle swishing sounds made by the air flowing over its wing feathers. The fox never suspected it was being watched from above.

Twenty minutes later the fox stopped, looked around, and began sniffing and digging in a snow drift with its front feet and claws, soon exposing the two snowshoe hares it had cached. The clever fox seemed to know that food would be scarce in early spring and had stored excess food in a number of hidden sites. Picking up a hare in its pointy mouth, the fox carefully covered the remaining carcass by kicking snow on it with its hind feet and then bounded off for home. The hare would provide food for both the fox and its mate, who would give birth in several weeks to puppies deep inside a den.

No sooner had the fox left the cache site when the crow glided down to the ground and hopped over to the disturbed snow. Scratching with its scaly feet and probing with the stout beak, the crow found the treasure. While it fed, two other birds lined up in the nearby shrubs for their turn — first a blue jay, then a black-capped chickadee. That night a deer mouse and a short-tailed shrew were attracted by the odors and they too filled their little bellies with meat. The deer mouse even made several trips for the hare's fur to line its nest. Three days later, when the fox returned, only bones and hair remained. The fox had unknowingly helped feed dozens of hungry forest creatures.

Striped Skunk

As soon as it was pitch black outside the skunk family began its nightly rounds through the oak and hickory forest. The moonlight reflected off their white stripes as the animals wobbled down a grassy bank and across a field. Several weeks earlier there had been four offspring. One careless youngster failed to avoid a speeding car along the highway, while another was carried off in the talons of a great-horned owl when it wandered off to chase a snake. Although small and still being nursed, the two remaining juveniles were able to keep up with their mother as she searched the woods and farmlands for food. During the day the family retired to one of sixteen different burrows scattered over their home range. They memorized the exact routes to each one so that they could retreat underground quickly if danger threatened. They used each burrow for two or three days as a center of foraging activities, then moved on to another site.

First stop tonight was the grainfield where tasty grasshoppers abounded. The youngsters smacked their tiny jaws on the thick-bodied insects, rejecting the long scaly legs which dropped to the ground. The mother skunk jumped forward and pounced on a deer mouse, pinning it against a fallen fence post. The young skunks watched her technique with keen interest. Before long the field of grain began to sway in the breeze and clouds blocked out the moonlight. The skunks' large black eyes could still see well in the dark, and their keen noses and ears continually tested the air for new enticing scents and sounds amid the ringing of crickets. Along the edge of the field the skunks discovered a large beetle which was quickly snapped up by one of the youngsters. The beetle must have secreted a bad-tasting substance for it was just as rapidly spit out again. Undeterred, the adult rolled the insect over and over with her paw until the smelly material was all rubbed off in the dust. As soon as she finished, the other offspring moved in and gobbled it up. About an hour later the trio's fortune greatly improved with the discovery of a pheasant nest. Each youngster grappled with a separate egg, but neither leaping on it with their front feet nor biting succeeded in cracking the hard shell. When they tired of these efforts they noticed their mother licking out the contents of her egg. After investigating the empty shell they observed her egg-cracking procedure — backward kicks with the front feet until the shell fractured against a rock. It was then an easy task to open it the rest of the way by gnawing on the broken end.

Rain began to fall, slowly at first, then steadily, but it didn't bother the skunks at all; the drops just rolled off their long shiny fur coats. Several brilliant flashes of lightning suddenly lit up the white backs of the skunks like a spotlight, and with the thunder shaking the ground and rolling away down the countryside, the three frightened animals ran for the nearest den as fast as their short legs could carry them. Safely inside, they licked their coats dry with their pink tongues, finishing with their flowing tails.

When the storm finally passed they were anxious to be underway again, and this time the mother skunk headed for the garbage dump. As any skunk soon learns, a dump can always be counted on for a great meal because people throw away all kinds of food. Some chicken meat here, bacon fat there — in fact there were so many different odors it was difficult to know what to eat next. One of the youngsters investigated a jam jar and eventually forced its head inside to lick up every bit of the sweet, sticky contents. That done, the animal tried to back out, but the jar held tightly behind the ears. Its front legs strained and the back legs pushed, but the jar stuck like glue. The youngster rolled over onto its back and began to panic, while the other skunks went on with their business, oblivious that another accident might claim a third member of the family. Short of air, the excited skunk did what all skunks do under emergencies — it let loose a burst of musk. Staggering to one side the little skunk happened to fall against a boulder, which fortunately smashed the jar into several pieces. Free at last the animal rushed to its mother for comfort. Now even skunks are not fond of their powerful scent and they quickly departed to the shelter of a nearby burrow, ending a rather eventful night for the family. No other animal visited the dump for several days after that, except a few crows and gulls whose senses of smell and taste were not bothered by skunk fumes.

at 2 to 3 weeks and by 4 weeks the youngsters are capable of shooting musk. The female nurses them with her 10 to 14 mammae (usually 12 are present) until the offspring are 6 to 8 weeks old. By this time they follow her on foraging excursions and become fully independent by autumn. Both sexes begin to breed in their second year. Generally at least half the skunk population in the autumn is less than one-year old; however, some survive to 6 years of age in the wild and there is a record of a 13-year old in captivity.

Remarks Most people are familiar with the striped skunk from reputation or by observing them as roadkills along the highway. Otherwise they are not often seen. Although a member of the weasel family the striped skunk has a stocky body, wide rump, a markedly triangular head, and a bushy tail. The nose and ears are prominent and 34 teeth are present in the jaws. The front legs are shorter than the hind legs and the animal walks on the naked soles of its feet. The stout curving claws, especially large on the front digits, are used for digging. The skunk is not fast enough to outrun quick prey, but it still captures them by stalking and ambushing. It walks at 1.6 km (one mi) per hour and can race for short distances at 16.1 km (10 mi) per hour. When disturbed the striped skunk initiates a complex warning and defensive routine. If unable to retreat the animal faces its antagonist, arches its back, and stamps the front feet while backing up. It clicks its teeth, hisses, and flares the tail which makes the skunk look larger and more formidable. If pressed the skunk then bends its body so that both head and rump face the adversary and two nipples project out from the anal region. Muscles surrounding the large musk glands contract rapidly and force out two streams of scent from the nipples with great accuracy to 3 m (9.8 ft). The fine mist or larger droplets can reach a target up to 5 m (16.4 ft) away and the stench carries for over 2 km (1.2 mi). The powerful scent is extremely irritating to the eyes (but does not result in permanent blindness) and causes violent nausea.

Skunks emerge at sunset and retire at dusk, but occasionally they are active during daylight hours. They utilize from 2 to 22 dens, generally shallower than 50 cm (19.7 in) in summer and from one to 6 m (3.3 to 19.7 ft) deep and 2 to 15 m (6.6 to 49.2 ft) long in winter. The nest chamber is lined with grass and leaves and the one to 5 exits are blocked in cold weather. The skunk may dig its own den (preferably on a slope) or use the abandoned burrow of other animals such as badgers, foxes, jackrabbits, armadillos, woodchucks, muskrats, and ground squirrels. Over cold regions of the range this species enters a dormant period — 50 to 120 days in Canada and 62 to 87 days in the central United States. Since the animal's body temperature remains at normal levels, this cannot be described as hibernation. Males are more active during mild spells than are females, and in warm southern regions the skunk remains active year round. Freezing temperatures reduce activity but some individuals come out to forage when the thermometer dips to -17°C (1.4°F). In most cold areas skunks lose about 33 percent of their body weight (mostly fat) from autumn to spring, but this loss may climb to 65 percent at northern extremes.

Skunks are usually solitary but may join a communal den during the winter. These average one adult male and 6 females. Adult males are intolerant of each other throughout the year. While juveniles travel about 40 m (131.2 ft) in a night, adults normally cover 0.4 to 0.8 km (0.2 to 0.5 mi) and even up to 1.5 km (0.9 mi) during this period. Males searching for females in spring often move 2.4 km (1.5 mi) from their regular hunting grounds, while dispersing young in the fall have been known to reach 22 km (13.7 mi) from their area of birth. Home ranges are surprisingly large — from 100 to 370 ha (247 to 913.9 a) for females and somewhat larger for males. Population densities fluctuate but usually range from 0.4 to 27 per sq km (1.1 to 73 per sq mi). Numbers are kept in check by coyotes, foxes, bobcats, lynx, cougars, eagles, and great-horned and barred owls. Hundreds of thousands die each year from being struck by cars, and through diseases such as rabies and leptospirosis. Striped skunks are beneficial to farmers by eating injurious insects and rodents, but they sometimes raid poultry houses and also eat game birds. Their fur is used in the garment industry but it does not claim a high price.

This was one species that we always tried to avoid when setting traps for other mammals to add to the museum collection. Once, as our collecting team approached a study quadrat set in a stately forest of red pine near the Minnesota-Manitoba border, I knew our luck had run out. Even before we got out of the truck the pungent musk of a trapped skunk came drifting through the open windows. Our specimen was quickly sealed inside 3 plastic bags and then placed in a styrofoam cooler. We returned to the museum and left the cooler in the freezer room. When I arrived home my family promptly suggested I change clothes in the garage! My assistant received a telephone call from a security guard that the stench of skunk was growing stronger throughout the exhibit galleries, so he rose from bed and removed the culprit from the museum. The next morning, a rather irate museum director spent a heated hour trying to track down the skunk so he could throw the smelly creature out. He never did find it but he issued strict orders never to bring a particular black and white animal into the museum again.

WOODCHUCK

Scientific name *Marmota monax*
Family Squirrels (Sciuridae)
Order Rodents (Rodentia)
Total length 600 mm (23.6 in)
Tail length 130 mm (5.1 in)
Weight 3 kg (6.6 lb). Up to 6.3 kg or 14 lb when fat and entering hibernation.
Color The upperparts are brown, with black- and white-tipped hairs giving a grizzled appearance. The belly is rusty-red and the feet, tail, and forehead are dark brown or black.
Distribution and Status The woodchuck occurs in a broad zone across the continent from Alaska to Labrador, Idaho, and Oklahoma to South Carolina. Though it lives in the regions of coniferous and deciduous forests, it is more often found along the edges and in meadows rather than deep inside the woods. It favors for its home a pile of logs or stones at the edge of a field, or dry quarters underneath buildings. The woodchuck is a common species, particularly in the east. It is one of the few mammals that seems to have benefitted by the change from forests to farmland, and it is no doubt more abundant now than in former times. The woodchuck has 10 relatives, including the yellow-bellied marmot *(Marmota flaviventris)* widespread in western mountain ranges, hoary marmot *(Marmota caligata)* from Alaska to Idaho, Alaska marmot *(Marmota broweri)* of northern Alaska, Olympic marmot *(Marmota olympus)* of Washington, and Vancouver marmot *(Marmota vancouverensis)*. Eight other species are spread throughout Europe and Asia.

Food Woodchucks are grazing animals that grow extremely fat by eating grass, clover, dandelions, asters, goldenrod, buttercups, alfalfa, and hundreds of other plants including crops. In spring they browse on the buds and bark of shrubs and saplings such as dogwood and cherry. Water is obtained by drinking, licking dew, and from the moist food.

Reproduction and Growth Males are ready to breed as soon as they come out of hibernation, with the warming of the soil in spring. If populations are high, the males may fight and bite each other. Mating occurs when the females appear several weeks later. After a period of one month, 4 (range of one to 9) babies are born, usually in April or May, but later in June in the far north. The newborn are naked, blind, and weigh about 26 g (0.9 oz). Hair develops at 2 weeks, they can crawl at 3 weeks, and their eyes open at 4 weeks. They nurse from the mother's 8 nipples while she stands over them. The young are on their own as early as 6 weeks due to the aggressive actions of the mother. They reach breeding age when 2 years old, except a small percentage of females that bear young at one year. Full size is attained in 2 years. Some of these tough animals may live for 6 years in the wild and 10 in captivity. A normal life span under natural conditions is only 2 or 3 years.

Remarks A woodchuck, standing like a brown stump in a field, is a common sight in many areas of the east. With this picture in mind the animal seemed totally out of place when I found one living under an abandoned cabin of a native trapper at York Factory in the dwarf-spruce forest on the edge of Hudson Bay. This individual, with its thick-set body, short strong legs, inconspicuous ears, and eyes placed high on its broad head, was as wary as its southern kin, although it had probably never seen another human.

This species is the most solitary of the marmots, usually chasing away any other woodchuck that is careless enough to wander into its territory. On rare occasions a female and male or several females may live together in the same den. The home range is quite small for the size of the creature, and is generally within 0.4 to 3 ha (one to 7.4 a). Males disperse farther away from the home den than females, which frequently take up residence adjacent to their mother. Population densities range from 2 to 15 per sq km (5.4 to 40.5 per sq mi).

The woodchuck can run surprisingly fast considering its stout body and short legs, and can even swim across rivers over one km (0.6 mi) wide. It is active mainly in the morning and late afternoon, but when the weather is cold it appears at midday. On rare occasions it has been seen out at night. The animal becomes obese (about 20 percent of its weight is fat) in the autumn and often moves from its meadow home to a burrow it excavates on a well-drained slope in the nearby forest. It curls up and become torpid in a plugged, grass-lined chamber situated 5 to 7 m (16.4 to 23 ft) under the surface and below the frost line. Northern woodchucks hibernate for up to 9 months of the year, while those in the warm south can get by with less than 6 weeks of torpor or perhaps none at all. The animal emerges occasionally during warm spells, but more snow or cold weather quickly drives it below again. It emerges in the spring having lost approximately one third of its body weight.

Bobcats, red and gray foxes, coyotes, wolves, hawks, and snakes are all important predators of woodchucks. It is also hunted as a game animal, trapped for its fur, and destroyed as a pest because it feeds on grain and vegetables or digs holes in inappropriate places.

When I was a teenager, my collie dog and I made a game of sneaking up on an old woodchuck. One day we spotted him in the middle of the field and by running our fastest we were able to cut him off from his burrow. Knowing we had outwitted him this time, he crouched low and froze as we approached ever so slowly to one side, being careful not to walk directly at him. When we were only 3 m (9.8 ft) away, the woodchuck totally startled me and my dog by charging us. With body flattened, teeth gnashing, and growling like a mad dog, the little guy put on such an attack that both of us quickly retreated. Then seeing his chance the woodchuck sped away to his burrow. I'm sure his whistles were meant as laughter as he disappeared safely down the hole. I looked around hoping nobody had seen me running away from a rodent.

One of the saddest sights I have seen during years of observing wildlife, occurred along the edge of a highway. As so often happens, a family of woodchucks had taken up residence in the roadbank and 2 offspring had just been killed by a passing car. With a show of great dedication, the mother tried again and again to raise the little brown bodies from the pavement, retreating only a short distance each time another car sped by. As a biologist I know that it is wrong to attribute human emotions to lower animals, but it was a touching sight nevertheless. I could not resist puzzling

over what the mother woodchuck was "thinking." With her watching me, I placed the bodies some distance from the road and left the scene, hoping she and her remaining family would not return to this dangerous spot.

BLACK BEAR
Scientific name   *Ursus americanus*
Family   Bears (Ursidae)
Order   Carnivores (Carnivora)
Total length   150 cm (59.1 in)
Tail length   10 cm (3.9 in)
Weight   males 140 kg, maximum 300 kg (308.6 lb, maximum 661.4 lb); females 110 kg (242.5 lb)
Color   As its name implies, this bear's long, coarse fur is black, except for the brownish snout. Occasionally a brown-colored cub may appear along with its black litter mates. This brown phase is more common in the west. Rare white and blue phases occur along the northwest Pacific coast.
Distribution and Status   The black bear is the most common and widespread of North America's 3 species of bears, occurring from Newfoundland to Alaska and south to Florida, central Mexico, and California. In general terms it inhabits forests, swamps, and shrub thickets, but occasionally wanders onto the tundra and alpine meadows, especially if grizzlies no longer occur in the area. Except in parks, where it becomes accustomed to people, the black bear is shy and prefers inaccessible country. It is able to sustain itself in a remarkable variety of plant communities; for example, beech-maple and spruce-fir forests of the northeast, black spruce-jack pine forest in the taiga of northern Canada and Alaska; redwood-sitka spruce-western hemlock forest of the Pacific coast region, lodgepole pine-ponderosa pine and spruce-fir forests of the Rockies, oak-hickory and oak-pine forests of the midwest United States and of Mexico, chaparral and pinyon-juniper woodland of the southwest, and cypress-gum and oak-pine of the southeast United States.

The presence of large carnivores and the interests of people are seldom compatible, and

consequently the black bear has suffered population and range reductions, particularly in the south. It has been eliminated from much of the midwestern and eastern states. I could find no recent estimate of numbers for the whole of North America, however during the 1970s, supposedly 170,000 black bears existed in the United States (excluding Alaska) and the total annual kill over the whole range was 30,000.

The ancestors of the black bear may well have been the now-extinct Eurasian Etruscan bear *(Ursus etruscus)* of Pleistocene times (within the last 2 million years). It evolved into the Asiatic black bear *(Ursus thibetanus)* and the bear stock that crossed over the Bering land bridge into the New World during the mid-Pleistocene and which later became the North American black bear.
Food   Though the black bear prefers animal food such as carrion, colonial insects, and any creatures it can catch, most of its diet is vegetation — berries, nuts, grass, sapwood, buds, and grain.

Reproduction and Growth   Female bears come into heat every second year in June or July, occasionally late May or mid-August. The release of the eggs is stimulated by the mating act. The embryos cease developing at an early stage, to resume again in late November or early December. Usually 2 cubs (one to 5) are born in late January to early February, while the female is still torpid. The gestation or developmental period is 7 to 9 months, but most growth occurs in the last 6 to 8 weeks prior to birth. The young are extremely small — only 20 cm (8 in) long and 300 g (10.6 oz) in weight — and undeveloped at birth and could easily fit in a child's hand. The black coat appears in several weeks but the eyes do not open until 6 weeks of age. The family emerges from the den from late March to early May. The cubs need their mother's milk until midsummer and are self-sufficient by autumn; however, most remain with the mother until the following spring or summer when the mother comes into heat and adult males appear on the scene. Full size is reached at 4 years of age. Sexual maturity of females may occur from 2 to 7 years, but usually within 3 to 5 years. Lack of food crops such as berries and acorns delays sexual maturity or results in smaller litter size or even postponement of breeding. Males begin to mate at an age of 5 years, but only live for an average of 3 to 5 years, females for 5 to 8 years. Few reach 10 years and the maximum life span is 26 years in captivity.
Remarks   The black bear, although closely related to grizzly and polar bears, has a distinctive profile and face. It relies on its acute sense of smell to locate food and survey its surroundings. While it looks rather clumsy, especially when fat prior to hibernation, it can easily outrun a person as well as climb and swim with ease. The weight is carried on the soles of the rounded feet which are armed with stout, nonretractable claws. Strangely enough, the old callused layer of skin on these pads is shed while the bear snoozes through the winter. The animal is powerfully built with heavily muscled limbs and a huge head featuring 42 teeth. The first things I noticed while examining anesthetized bears was the incredible hardness of the limb muscles and how often the teeth showed decay.

The black bear is a solitary creature except
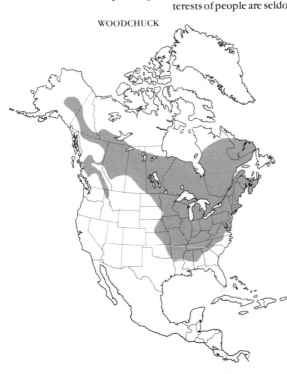
WOODCHUCK

Continued on p.206

Woodchuck

As the sun's warming rays peeked over the hill, the band of mist hanging over the meadow began to slowly dissipate into thin air. At one end of the field lay a big pile of rocks which had, over the years, become overgrown with vegetation. Burrows riddled the mound in all directions, some descending for three meters (9.8 feet) and opening under rocks and tufts of grass and weeds. Well worn paths through the plant cover and fresh tracks in the light brown soil of the main exit indicated that this site was at this time home to some medium-sized animal. A musky odor in the vicinity and a thick black dropping clearly marked the owner's claim.

A mother woodchuck woke up in her nest chamber below and crawled lethargically over the eight meters (26.2 feet) to the entrance. The bright sunlight streamed into the entrance, causing her to blink her half-closed eyes. She climbed up on the highest rock, flopped onto her belly, and stretched out like a bather in the sun. The warm rock felt good and she opened her mouth in a big yawn, revealing her enormous front teeth and thick pink tongue. The hair on her undersides was thin and eight large nipples showed that there were young woodchucks underground. Elevating her stout body onto her hind feet she looked over the meadow, then up into the sky, staring intently for several minutes without moving. She had to be sure there was no animal sneaking up through the grass or hawk soaring overhead, for today she would take her family on its first trip away from the safety of the den. The six youngsters were over a month old now and were beginning to add plants to their former diet of milk. The woodchuck waddled back down the hole, her brushy rust-colored tail the last to disappear into the darkness. Guided by her snout whiskers she encountered her five offspring which were most anxious to nurse. Ignoring their pleas she enticed them to the entrance where once again she surveyed the surroundings with great care.

Satisfied that all was clear, she proceeded to sneak quietly along her favorite trail for ten meters (32.8 feet), then "froze" suddenly in her tracks. One by one, each young woodchuck followed in her footsteps until they came up behind her. This strange way of stop-and-start traveling kept the family spaced out, so they wouldn't attract attention or all be lost to a coyote if one should appear. In time the caravan reached the edge of the woods, and while the youngsters nibbled on leaves on the forest floor, the mother ascended a small tree to look around. Now climbing up is tough enough for a fat short-legged creature like a woodchuck, but getting back down is a real problem. After a few minutes she tried coming down head first, but that didn't work. Then she turned backwards, but her feet and claws wouldn't hold. They were great for digging in soil but not for grasping onto bark and branches. She became frustrated and began to worry about the youngsters below who had wandered some distance away along the edge of the meadow in search of tasty leaves. She chattered her teeth in fright as a pair of red-tailed hawks appeared suddenly overhead. "Ps-s-s," the hunters called to each other as they spotted the plump brown bodies in the grass, though the hawks were yet a hundred meters (328.1 feet) away.

No time for practise now! The mother woodchuck shot down the trunk head first, hitting the ground with a thud. Quickly falling in line, the family ran back along the trail at full speed while both hawks seemed to fall out of the sky. The race was on. If they could just reach the rocks, the woodchucks would be safe. Mother dashed inside the burrow, sending the dirt on the mound flying. One youngster in, then two, three, four . . . Releasing her pent-up excitement she emitted a sharp quivering whistle, then crawled over the youngsters as if to count them. Did she know one was missing? By the time she poked her muddy black nose out of the hole again, three young fuzzy hawks, almost as big as their parents, were sitting on the edge of their tree nest, eating breakfast.

Black Bear

On a beautiful late-summer afternoon a family of people followed a path through the woods towards a clearing. It was berry-picking time and the children's voices showed their keen anticipation as the edge of their favorite harvesting grounds came into view. No one noticed a log at the side of the trail, ripped open and strewn about. The grass in the meadow was pressed down here and there, and the parents talked about the possibility that someone might have beat them to the berry crop this year, although they had kept this site a secret. As they gazed across the raspberry patch, they again failed to see at their feet several piles of dung which resembled black mud filled with seeds. No doubt about it, somebody had been picking berries here already.

The family began to load their buckets with the red fruit and wandered slowly toward the far end of the clearing. With frightening suddenness a deep "woof" sound filled the air and they were shocked to see the black head and broad shoulders of a bear rise up out of the bushes. The children screamed and began running but their mother quickly called to them to stop and move slowly. The bear shuffled and peered with its weak eyes, trying to see what had disturbed its nap. Together the people began to backtrack at a slow pace so as not to provoke an attack. The big animal sniffed the air repeatedly, then with a snort, dropped down on all fours and took off at a gallop away through the woods. The people finally reached their car, still trembling, but excited over the adventure. Next time, the father exclaimed, they would be sure to make a lot of noise before entering the area, to give any feeding or sleeping bears an earlier chance to depart.

About two months later, large rounded tracks in the frost led from the aspen forest, through a stubble field, and ended at a hay stack. The maker of the tracks was nowhere to be seen. Through the chilled October air the honking of Canada geese could be heard, and soon the long-necked, black and white birds glided in by the thousands, anxious for a breakfast of grain. What a racket! A large brownish-black nose and two beady eyes poked out of a hole in the hay stack. The noisy geese had awakened the black bear and he grunted his displeasure. Though his sleepy eyes could not see the geese clearly, he recognized their calls. Nothing to be alarmed about. The flock of geese didn't hear the grunt, but several alert birds certainly spotted the big black head sticking out of the hay stack. Suddenly the frightened

honkers took wing and retreated amid great commotion to the other end of the field, leaving the bear to resume his slumber.

It was dark by five o'clock that evening. The bear emerged from his bed, yawned, then tested the air with his keen nose. For the next two hours he ambled on in the night, covering five kilometers (3.1 miles) in search of something to eat. Powerful front legs and stout claws ripped through a mound of thatching ants, but none swarmed to the surface in defense of the nest; they had all retreated deep underground for the winter. Mice, chipmunks, and migrating flocks of songbirds had cleaned up his favorite berry patches, he and several raccoons and white-tailed deer had devoured almost every acorn the oaks had produced, and the farmer had removed all the honey from the rows of white boxes tucked neatly along the edge of the forest grove. The frustrated bear stood up on his hind legs and scratched deep cuts into the powdery bark of an aspen tree with his front paws. Suddenly remembering where he had fed on a deer carcass left by hunters, he arrived at the scene to find several coyotes finishing up the last morsels. A quick charge sent the scoundrels retreating into the woods, tails between their legs. It was almost dawn before the bear at last found something to eat — a pile of spilled grain beside a steel storage bin. He need not have been too concerned about the small size of supper, for he was fat from gorging all summer and fall. In fact, as the autumn temperatures dropped, the bear had begun to sleep in and was less motivated to forage far from the den.

On the way back to the den the bear entered a bog, where he scraped together a pile of moss with swipes of a forepaw, and then picked it up in his mouth. This soft material was just the right lining for his bed. While the bear was safely sleeping in the haystack, the temperature plummeted well below freezing and it started to snow. The bear's temperature slowly dropped by 8°C (15°F), its heart rate from forty-five to ten beats per minute, and breathing slowed to two breaths per minute. In this state of torpor the animal would be oblivious to the intense chill and storms to come, protected by a thick layer of insulating snow and straw. There would be no bear tracks in the snow until next spring.

BLACK BEAR *continued from p.201*
when breeding, raising young, or when a number are attracted to a plentiful source of food. It is intelligent and shows great interest in exploring and examining new objects, especially if they smell edible. When cornered or challenged, it displays a variety of threatening gestures including a moan, blow, extension of the lips, and lowering of the head and ears, followed by a charge, swiping blows with the forearms, and finally savage biting with the long canines. Humans, the grizzly, and packs of wolves are the only predators capable of bringing down adults, but the cubs sometimes stray too far from their mother and are killed by male black bears, cougars, and alligators. Generally she sends her offspring up a tree if danger is perceived. Many thousands of black bears are destroyed annually by hunters, trappers, and because they are a pest to agriculture and at campgrounds.

This species is most active for several hours just after dark and before dawn, but it is not unusual for it to be out hunting in the day or all night. Foraging increases during late summer and autumn, when the animal may put on one kg (2.2 lb) of fat per day in preparation for winter torpor. Individuals have been known to travel 160 km (99.4 mi) to reach a new source of food. As temperatures approach freezing, the bear becomes less active — a prelude to denning. The adults enter torpor first, in October in the north and as late as January in the southern United States. Dens may be a cave, burrow, thicket, tree cavity, under a fallen log, hay stack, or simply a hollow in the snow. The animals don't eat, drink, urinate, or defecate during the winter, the intestine being blocked by a plug of digested food until spring. In the north, the black bear shows no regular arousal periods as do true hibernators (e.g., ground squirrels); however, in southern regions individuals sometimes become active on warm winter days. The body processes (metabolism) slow down by 50 percent and the animal emerges from mid-March in the south to early May in the north, with a 25 percent loss of weight from fat utilization. Food is

relatively scarce at this time of year, consequently the bear roams widely. Home ranges of males vary from 500 to 5 200 ha (1,235 to 12,844 a), while those of females are much smaller at 235 to 520 ha (581 to 1,284 a). The ranges of males seldom overlap, while those of females may overlap both males' and other females' ranges. Population estimates have been reported at one bear to every one to 14.5 sq km (0.5 to 6.5 sq mi).

One summer when I was a student biologist I assisted as a member of the staff of the Quebec Wildlife Service in capturing troublesome bears and moving them into remote country. The bears were attracted to a bait of meat and honey, trapped, anesthetized, then transported to their new home. Our first customer was a young individual weighing about 100 kg (220.5 lb). Once drugged and unconscious it was carried out of the forest on the shoulders of a burly technician. As soon as it was eased into the back of a pickup truck it suddenly woke up full of life and came charging towards us, growling and snapping its teeth. Without apparent concern, the technician lifted his leg and booted the bear so hard in the nose that it passed out again. Then he hog-tied the animal so it couldn't move until we were ready to release it. In my broken French I asked him how he came to handle bears so well and he told me he had raised one as a pet. This was not the kind of technique generally taught in wildlife management courses, but it sure worked!

WHITE-TAILED DEER
Scientific name *Odocoileus virginianus*
Family Deer (Cervidae)
Order Even-toed Ungulates (Artiodactyla)
Total length 185 cm (72.8 in)
Tail length 20 cm (7.9 in)
Weight males 90 kg, maximum 192 kg (198.4 lb, maximum 423.3 lb); females 60 kg (132.3 lb) Florida Key white-tailed deer weigh only 25 kg (55.1 lb)
Color The deer's coat is reddish-brown in summer and grayish-brown (and longer) in winter. The underparts, muzzle, eye rings, in-

sides of the ears, and the legs are white. The fawn is reddish-brown with white spots on the back and sides.
Distribution and Status The white-tailed deer occurs across southern Canada, throughout the United States (except for the extreme southwest), Mexico, Central America, and into South America to Brazil, Bolivia, and Peru. Populations in the southern continent were formerly thought to be a distinct species. The animal has been introduced to Prince Edward Island and Anticosti Island in eastern Canada, and to Finland, Czechoslovakia, and New Zealand. The adaptability of this ungulate is remarkable, for it finds suitable living conditions in steamy tropical jungles, hot arid deserts, prairie thickets, and mixed forests of cold northern and mountain regions. Its range has increased northward in the last century, probably due to opening of the forests. Extreme cold combined with deep snow, which immobilizes deer and cuts them off from their food supply, probably limit further expansion in the north. Over much of its range this deer prefers broken forests containing both broadleaf and evergreen forest. It frequently forages along forest edges, stream banks, and in second-growth forests, avoiding dense or mature forests or spruce bogs where there is little nutritious food available at ground level.

This species evolved in North America and has no close relatives in Eurasia. It has always been a much sought-after big game animal for food and hides and was exterminated from large regions during the 1800s. Only a half million survived by 1900. With protection and improved habitat conditions (due to such factors as logging and farm abandonment), populations have blossomed to a recent estimated 12.5 million in the United States and 2.5 million in Canada. There are no estimates for Mexico and Central America, but the species is killed for food at every opportunity and much habitat is badly overgrazed by livestock. Over 2 million white-tails are taken by hunters each year in the United States.
Food The deer's diet changes as various plants become available during the year. In summer literally hundreds of kinds of leafy plants, such as grasses, asters, ferns, and goldenrods are eaten. Berries, acorns and other nuts, and mushrooms are favorite items in the fall, while in the winter the buds and twigs of shrubs and trees, such as dogwood, raspberry, cedar, ponderosa pine, birch, rhododendron, mountain mahogany, and aspen predominate. These winter foods are not as nutritious or abundant as the summer fare, and deer often lose considerable weight by spring. Corn, soybeans, apples, grapes, and alfalfa are only a few of the crops highly attractive to deer.
Reproduction and Growth The shortening days of fall trigger the breeding season in the white-tailed deer. The bucks become aggressive and thrash the bushes with their antlers, which greatly increases the size and strength of their neck muscles in preparation for sparring matches with other bucks. Territories are patrolled, marked by stripped saplings and scrapes of soil scented with urine and glandular secretions. Battles sometimes break out among the bucks resulting in injuries from the sharp hooves and antlers. A buck may mate with up to 4 does, courting each for a week. In the northern half of the range the does come into heat several times (for 24 hours in a 28-day estrous cycle) from October to December. She

BLACK BEAR

must nourish herself and the one to 4 (usually 2) developing young during the severest part of the year. The number of young produced each year is largely dependent on the amount and quality of the winter forage. The pre-birth period of growth ranges from 195 to 212 days. The fawns are born in May or June (rarely in April and as late as September). The breeding season is later and more variable in Mexico with most mating occurring from January to February; fawns have been reported from April to September. White-tails in the tropics may reproduce during any month of the year, but generally bring forth their young at the time that improves their chances of survival (e.g., rainy season). Newborn weigh from 1.5 to 3.5 kg (3.3 to 7.7 lb), are covered in short fur with a camouflaging pattern, and can stand in a few hours. Vegetation is added to the diet of milk within a few days, running is possible at 3 weeks, and weaning occurs around 4 months. Females associate with their mother for 2 years while males depart at the end of one year. Most does and bucks become sexually mature at 1.5 years of age, but it is doubtful if many young bucks are strong enough to win a mate. Does in excellent health may breed as early as 6 months. Deer have lived to be 20 years old in captivity, but in the wild the average life span is 3 to 5 years, with few surpassing 10 years.

Remarks The white-tailed deer is characterized by a long bushy tail (up to 28 cm or 11 in), thin legs, conspicuous ears, and antlers (in the male) which branch from one main beam. These bony structures begin to grow in April and are under the control of the pituitary gland (located at the base of the brain) which is stimulated through the visual system by increasing daylight. Antlers first appear in bucks one year old and each annual set becomes larger until age 4 or 5. Development is also known to be related to diet. The growing antlers are covered by a layer of hairy skin whose blood vessels nourish the bone cells. In autumn, this skin dries up and is rubbed off against woody vegetation. The end of the rut is marked by a drop in the male sex hormone

testosterone which results in the shedding of the antlers from December to March.

This deer has 32 teeth (no upper incisors or canines) with sharp grinding surfaces. Two years are required before all teeth are fully erupted and since they do not continually grow, they eventually wear down to smooth surfaces. The 4-part stomach contains bacteria and protozoans (simple microscopic animals) which help to break down the vegetation chemically into forms usable by the deer. About 3.5 kg (7.7 lb) of food are needed each day. Deer have an uncanny ability to select the most nutritious vegetation or parts of plants.

Activity peaks of deer occur at dusk and dawn. The size of the home range varies widely, with availability of food resources being the major determining factor. Females travel over an area of 15 to 140 ha (37.1 to 345.8 a) while males cover 75 to 485 ha (187.5 to 1,198 a). Densities of 2 to 4 per ha (0.8 to 1.6 per a) have been recorded. In northern and mountainous regions of deep snow and severe weather, deer move 16 to 32 km (9.9 to 19.9 mi) to seek shelter among coniferous trees. These deer yards may attract a few families or up to several hundred deer from late December to mid-April. Generally, however, this species does not gather into large herds. Males are solitary, while the family unit consists of a doe, yearling daughters, and fawns.

Deer are secretive and elusive creatures with acute senses of hearing and smell. Three sets of glands between and above the hooves serve to communicate the passage of a deer along a trail to others of its own kind. The animals can run at speeds up to 64 km (40 mi) per hour and jump 10 m (32.8 ft). When alarmed an individual snorts and bounds away with its large tail raised and waving side to side, flashing a warning to other deer. People are the main predators, killing over 2 million deer annually. Cars also cause considerable mortality — 25,000 per year in Pennsylvania alone. Dogs now kill more deer than original predators, namely wolf, coyote, cougar, and jaguar.

Once when my assistant and I had split up to check our traplines I heard some big animal

crashing through the woods. As I stood still, hoping my assistant hadn't upset a bull moose in rut, a white-tailed buck broke through the shrubs and almost ran me down. He didn't even see me until I moved at the last second. On another occasion, a friend and I were driving along an icy road when 3 deer appeared on our left. Instead of running away, they continued parallel to the road, intent on crossing it in front of us. We slowed down as the first, then the second, deer slid across the icy road on all 4 hooves, managing to regain their balance in the snow-filled ditch. The third deer followed swiftly and looked like it too would succeed, when its front legs suddenly swept out of control to one side and down it went on its shoulder. The right antler snapped off on contact with the pavement. After the deer swept into the ditch, we doubted it would survive such a crash. But seconds later the dazed animal stood up on quivering legs and rejoined its companions, looking somewhat worse for wear with only one antler rising from its sore head.

WHITE-TAILED DEER

White-tailed Deer

About thirty meters (98.4 feet) apart, two white-tailed deer fawns lay motionless on a bed of cool moss and leaves. Miracles of camouflage, their reddish-brown coats dappled with white circles seemed to disappear in the pattern of shade and sunspots on the forest floor. Each was unaware of the other, as they patiently awaited the return of their mother. Five hours had passed since they had felt the comfort of her soft soothing tongue and warm milk. Ever alert and stepping deliberately without a sound, the doe was at this very instant moving toward her offspring. She chose to approach upwind, the breezes wafting an array of woodland scents over her black moist nostrils. Everything appeared to be in order, but exactly where were those fawns bedded down? She knew they were close by, but her large expressive eyes had difficulty distinguishing stationary objects.

Lowering her nose to the ground and with ears directed forward, she sniffed and listened for any sign of their presence. Becoming aware of the dull ache from the pressure of milk in her mammae, she called softly. The two fawns instantly arose from their thickets and ran over on stiff, wobbly legs to greet her. Almost frantic for nourishment the two young deer bunted the doe with their snouts until they secured a nipple, almost knocking her off balance in the process. Their little tails, held erect and wagging back and forth, indicated that milk was flowing. While nursing continued for five minutes, the doe licked their hind ends the whole time until she could detect no odor of their waste products. With an instinctive urge to cleanse her offspring, she couldn't possibly have anticipated that her diligence would soon save their lives. The fawns finally backed away to catch their breath as the doe swept her wide tongue over her nose. Her long funnel ears strained to detect any unusual sound amid the hum of crickets from the nearby field and the last flute-like trills of wood thrushes as they prepared to roost for the night. The three walked together for ten minutes, the doe clipping several leaves from a mountain maple in passing. As if saying goodnight, the doe briefly groomed each fawn's head with her tongue and the two then wandered off some distance and curled up to sleep.

The young deer were awake as the sky lightened in the east. At two weeks of age they had just begun to nibble on a variety of green plants, learning which ones were sweet, sour, or bitter. Suddenly they froze in a flattened position as a family of blue jays came gliding overhead, piercing the calm atmosphere with their harsh cries. Something had alarmed these birds and the cause soon came lumbering into view. A powerful black bear stopped to dig out a couple of last year's acorns from the leaf litter. Wandering ever closer the huge predator was unaware of the potential meals lying only a short distance away. For five minutes the panic-stricken fawns were on the verge of jumping up and dashing away, but fortunately they stayed put, for they would have been easily overtaken by the bear. As the fawns' hearts pounded wildly the bear smacked its lips and nodded its big head in the air, testing for food fragrances with its keen sense of smell. A mosquito landed on a fawn's face but the young animal dared not move to flick it away. Only a slight quiver of an eyelash revealed the irritation from the biting insect. With excrutiating slowness the bear shuffled off through the woods and as soon as it was out of sight, the mother crept up to gather her offspring. Quietly and in single file, she led them away from danger to another part of her range. In several weeks the rapidly growing fawns would be strong enough to escape any bear and most other predators.

Mammals of the
Grasslands

Grassland is easily recognized by the predominant growth of grass, lack of trees, and limited growth of shrubs. Most grasslands occur in continental interiors, in extensive zones between desert and forest, and are largely determined by intermediate moisture conditions and by fire, both tending to prevent the encroachment of forest into the grassland community. It is represented on each continent, though known by different names — prairie and plains in North America, pampas of southeastern South America, steppes of Eurasia, veld of South Africa, and Canterbury plains of New Zealand.

On the Great Plains of North America, rainfall decreases from east to west, resulting in the formation of several grassland types — tall-grass prairie (blue stem, drop seed) in the humid east, running from Manitoba to central Texas; mixed-grass prairie (needle grass, June grass, and grama grass) from Saskatchewan to west Texas; and short-grass prairie (grama grass, buffalo grass) in arid regions bordering on desert, east of the Rocky Mountains. Separate from this huge sea of grass are two other associations —bunch-grass prairie (wheat-grass, fescue) in the northern Great Basin, from southern British Columbia to Oregon; and California prairie (needlegrass, bluegrass) in the central valley of California, where the growing season occurs during the rainy winter period.

Tall grasses are in the 3 to 1.5-meter (9.8 to 4.9-feet) range, mid-grasses 1.5 to 0.5 meters (4.9 to 1.6 feet), and short grasses less than 0.5 meters (1.6 feet). Among the grass grows a profusion of forbs which flower for periods through spring and summer. Since precipitation is often sporadic and scarce, grasses have extensive root systems to soak up the moisture before it evaporates into the dry, warm, and windy prairie air. Grasses grow quickly when the warm spring rains come, sprouting from underground buds or from seed. During the cold or dry parts of the year, the leaves and stems die back and turn brown. The soil maintains a rich nutrient cycle from the large crop of vegetation added to the humus each year. Moist prairie soils are deep and black, while in arid regions or in well-drained sites the soil is thin and brown. Turf-forming grasses and bunch or clump-forming grasses are typical of moist and arid conditions, respectively. The topography of grasslands is flat or gently rolling.

Annual precipitation averages 100 centimeters (39.3 inches) in the east, 10 centimeters (3.9 inches) in the west. Deep snow is uncommon, but blizzards with high winds cause extensive drifting. Wind chill and the sand-blasting effect of sharp snow crystals are important stress factors on organisms. The frost-free period extends for only 100 days in the north, while frost is rare or absent in the south. Mean monthly temperatures range from (north to south) -18°C to 16°C (-0.4°F to 60.8°F) in January, 21°C to 32°C (69.8°F to 89.6°F) in July.

The Grassland Biome is an exceptionally productive community, capable of supporting greater concentrations of large grazing animals than any other biome. Prehistoric and modern people have taken advantage of this fertility, the latter replacing the native vegetation and animals with cultivated crops and livestock. Prior to and during the last Ice Age, North American grasslands were inhabited by as great a fauna of large mammals as is found in Africa today.

Common herbivores are bison, pronghorn, white-tailed jack rabbit, black-tailed prairie dog, deer mouse, greater prairie chicken, sharp-tailed grouse, and grasshoppers. Typical carnivores and insectivores include coyote, badger, swift fox, long-tailed weasel, burrowing owl, ferruginous hawk, western meadowlark, prairie rattlesnake, spadefoot toad, and tiger beetles.

White-tailed Jackrabbit

On a quiet prairie farm the setting sun cast lengthening shadows of bare willow stems over the clean sparkling snow. The breeze scooped up and twisted the crystals into whirlwinds which carried the snow from the fields and dropped it just inside the row of trees growing around the farm buildings. One by one, white-tailed jackrabbits appeared from snow caves hollowed out of the drifted landscape. They stretched their long legs and soon began dashing here and there, as if preparing for an important race. Then as if someone had called the participants to order, fifteen jackrabbits arranged themselves in a circle, each facing inward. It was the strangest sight — all these large white rabbits holding a meeting in the moonlight. They sat perfectly still for a minute, waiting for something to happen. Noses twitched and eyes looked straight ahead. Their bodies tensed with excitement until one animal could stand it no longer and raced away around the outside of the circle. Its partner on the left bounded off in close pursuit until the two finally took up their original positions again. Then two different animals took their turn dashing around the circle. Although this tag game looked like fun, it was really quite serious business for the jackrabbits. These courtship activities marked the beginning of the breeding season and served to prepare both sexes for the mating act. For half an hour the chases went on until the animals were rid of their extra energy. Then, one at a time, the jackrabbits wandered away over the fields, searching for grain among the rows of stubble.

Two weeks later, a large male jackrabbit was making his way across a field when he stopped suddenly in his tracks. Bending down, his nostrils sucked in a tantalizing scent most assuredly left behind by a female. The perfume stimulated him to high excitement, and in true bloodhound style, with nose to the ground, he began to track her. The invisible trail led over the crusted snow and bare patches of soil, then along a fence. Browsed shrubs and a few fresh woody droppings showed where the female had been only hours before. At the far end of the fencerow he found her. Hesitantly he approached, as if afraid she would bound away at any second. They sat down on their haunches and checked each other over. Without warning she leapt at the male and boxed so expertly with her front limbs that the male was forced to retreat. But the male's strong mating urge brought him back again. When she advanced towards him this time, he executed a fine leap completely over her. Taken with this maneuver, the female jackrabbit hopped over the male. The acrobatics continued for several minutes, the two "freezing" in crouched position briefly after each hop, and releasing a small spray of urine while in midair. The male decided this was enough of the preliminaries and tried to mount her from behind. Not yet sufficiently aroused, she raced away in a zigzag course, the male hot on her big heels. After running half a kilometer (0.3 miles) she finally stopped, crouched, and submitted to the frantic, out-of-breath male. Although they had been preparing for this union for weeks, the act took only a few seconds.

After some minutes the male tried to remount but the female jackrabbit would have no more of him. The big male displaced his frustration by suddenly nibbling on a bush, and when that didn't help much, he vigorously rolled over and over on his back, as if cleaning his coat was essential at that moment. When he regained his feet and composure, she had vanished. With the sun coming up, he retraced his route back home.

WHITE-TAILED JACKRABBIT

Scientific name *Lepus townsendii*
Family Rabbits and Hares (Leporidae)
Order Rabbits, Hares, and Pikas
(Lagomorpha)
Total length 600 mm (23.6 in)
Tail length 90 mm (3.5 in)
Weight 3.5 kg, maximum 4.5 kg
(7.7 lb, maximum 10 lb)

Color The white-tailed jackrabbit is grayish-brown with a mixture of black hairs. The belly, feet, and tail are white, while the ears are black on the tips. In the northern part of its range, where a snow cover persists in winter, the animal molts into a white coat so that it is almost impossible to see while sitting motionless on snowy fields.

Distribution and Status This long-eared jackrabbit lives in the central region of North America from Saskatchewan to New Mexico, California to Illinois. During this century this species extended its range to the north (Manitoba) and east (Wisconsin), but has declined in some southern regions. It is a creature of the grassy plains, sagebrush flats, and cultivated fields, though in the mountains of the west it occurs in open pine woodlands. Along the forested periphery of its range, it also inhabits clearings in the woods and along river banks. It closely resembles the black-tailed jackrabbit *(Lepus californicus)* whose range overlaps but is largely farther south.

Food Many kinds of green plants are eaten, such as wheatgrass, blue grama, winter wheat, dandelion, sedge, Indian paintbrush, goose-foot, clover, alfalfa, and corn. In winter, rabbitbush, willow, sage, winterfat, and other shrubs are important food sources. Jackrabbits select plants in the resting or early growth stages that are relatively rich in protein. As in other members of the family, this species devours its own droppings, gaining additional proteins and B vitamins produced by intestinal bacteria.

Reproduction and Growth Four peaks of breeding activity occur from late February to mid-July through most of the range, although a shorter season and only 3 litters probably exist in Canada. Mating stimulates the release of eggs within the female and the one to 8 (average of 4) embryos require 41 to 47 days to develop. The young weigh around 100 g (3.5 oz), are furred, with eyes open, and are capable of moving about in hours. For the first few days they keep close to the form or nest — actually a depression less than 10 cm (4 in) deep, scooped out in the grass or soil, and generally under a bush or tree. Tender plants are added to the diet of milk during the second or third week, and the rapidly growing youngsters are on their own by one month. Adult size is reached by 14 weeks of age, but breeding does not occur until the following spring. Each adult female produces an average of 15 young in a year, but less than half survive one year of age. Maximum life span is unknown.

Remarks The white-tailed jackrabbit is intermediate between the snowshoe hare and the antelope jackrabbit *(Lepus alleni)* of the Southwest in the length of the body, ears, and feet. Its hind foot measures 148 mm (5.8 in) and powered by the strong limbs carries the animal at speeds up to 64 km (40 mi) per hour. Hops reach lengths of 3 m (10 ft). Jackrabbits are also excellent swimmers and don't hesitate to take to the water to avoid predators. They need all their wits and speed to avoid coyotes, foxes, bobcats, hawks, great-horned owls, and human hunters. Activity begins in the evening and continues for periods till morning. Trails are sometimes noticeable where the animal travels to and from its feeding grounds and nesting quarters. The home range of males is slightly larger than females, but averages around 90 ha (222 a). Population density averages 4 to 8 per sq km (10 to 20 per sq mi), but has been reported as high as 140 per sq km (350 per sq mi). Die-offs frequently occur when numbers are high, and diseases, such as tularemia, Colorado tick fever, equine encephalitis, and botfly infections, break out.

Jackrabbits illustrate several interesting adaptations to the hot and dry prairie. The body temperature is allowed to rise from 37°C (98.6°F) to 41°C (105.8°F), thereby reducing the need to cool the body by evaporation of moisture. The large ears, richly supplied by blood vessels, act as radiators of excess body heat. To avoid the sun, the animals seek the shade of vegetation or rarely a burrow. During dry periods urine is concentrated and droppings are dry, which helps in the conservation of body water. In winter, the animals molt into a thicker coat and take refuge in deep burrows dug into a snowdrift.

I recall driving along a stubble field and spotting a very large rabbit trying to hide in a rather small alfalfa bush — the only cover for a long distance. The animal had eaten out the inside of the plant, and with its large ears flattened over its hunched body it probably thought it was safely concealed. Little did it know that its rear end and fuzzy white tail were sticking outside the bush. I decided to see how close I could approach before the rabbit would run away. I knew that when approaching an animal it was important never to look it in the eye, and to walk slowly to one side, not directly towards it. Closer and closer I moved in sideways, looking off in the distance. Out of the corner of my eye I could now see its half-closed yellow eyes watching me, and the nervous look on its face. Then, at a distance of only 4 m (13.1 ft), it burst out of its shelter and bounded with remarkable speed across the furrowed field. I yelled, "Stop!" and the inquisitive rabbit halted on command, rising onto its long hind legs for a second look. Then, having had enough of my antics, the rabbit galloped off like a tiny horse until it was only a grayish speck on the horizon.

WHITE-TAILED JACKRABBIT

OLIVE-BACKED POCKET MOUSE

Scientific name *Perognathus fasciatus*
Family Pocket Mice, Kangaroo Rats, and Spiny Mice (Heteromyidae)
Order Rodents (Rodentia)
Total length 130 mm (5.1 in)
Tail length 60 mm (2.4 in)
Weight 10 g, maximum 13 g (0.4 oz, maximum 0.5 oz)

Color The upperparts are a pale sandy-yellow with black and olive hairs throughout, except for a circle around the eyes and a thin border along the sides. It has a yellowish-white patch around the ears, and the underparts and feet are white.

Distribution and Status This tiny animal is found in dry sandy soils with a relatively sparse growth of grass and brush. Typical habitats are grama grass-needle grass; spear grass-Junegrass-winter fat; sagebrush and wild rose thickets; and open ponderosa pine woodlands with scattered grass, prickly pear, and yucca. Generally uncommon and sporadic in distribution, it can become abundant under ideal conditions of weather and food availability. Highest populations occur in alfalfa and grainfields such as wheat, oats, and rye, where the mice have no difficulty finding various kinds of weed seeds that sometimes can be scarce in native prairie. Overgrazed pastures are also favored due to the abundance of weedy plants. This species of pocket mouse occurs from Alberta to Manitoba in the north, and south to Utah and Colorado. There are approximately 24 other species of pocket mice found throughout the southern half of North America.

Food The diet is composed of seeds from numerous kinds of grasses, weeds, and shrubs. The introduced Russian thistle is a characteristic plant of the pocket mouse's habitat and the seeds are an important food. Other favorites are bugseed, tumbleweed, knotweed, pigweed, lamb's quarters, June grass, and needlegrass. Seeds are located with the help of the sensitive nose and the sifting front feet, and are then carried back in the cheek pouches to underground storage chambers. The pocket mouse doesn't just wait for seeds to fall but actively climbs into herbs and low shrubs to reach them. Insects are relished as well. Since these mice have evolved in a dry climate, they are able to survive on a limited ration of water. Sufficient moisture is obtained from licking dew or raindrops, and by chemically extracting water from their food.

Reproduction and Growth The breeding season runs from March to July in the south and from April to August in the north. About 25 days after mating, 5 (range of 2 to 11) young are born in a grass-lined nest below ground. The female's 6 mammae provide the newborn with milk. Most females soon become pregnant again when their first young are about half-grown. Though this species can live 4 years in captivity, few survive for more than 2 years in the wild.

Remarks This tiny attractive mouse moves about by hopping from its hind feet to front feet; because of its small size it is a rather slow runner compared to other mice. Although seemingly a gentle, mild-mannered rodent it is extremely protective of its territory and food caches and will drive away any intruding pocket mouse. It therefore leads a solitary lifestyle. The home range is small, perhaps 0.5 to one ha (1.2 to 2.5 a). Population densities of 1.2 to 5 per ha (0.5 to 2 per a) have been reported, but I have captured up to 20 per ha (8 per a) in several choice locations in sandy grainfields.

This species may become active shortly after sunset when it is still light, but generally it waits until dark before emerging. I have found that individuals often fill up their cheek pouches within 20 minutes of foraging and then retire. I presume they appear on the surface later in the night but with limited attempts I have not been able to find many that are active after 2 a.m. They quite likely spend around 20 hours per day underground. Unexpectedly, the first olive-backed pocket mouse I ever collected was a juvenile foraging at dawn in a sandy blowout on October 22, when the temperature was at the freezing point. While on the surface these mice are easy prey for owls, weasels, skunks, foxes, coyotes, grasshopper mice, and snakes, and badgers can easily dig them out of their shallow burrows.

After mid-October the cold weather and snow drive the thin-coated mice below ground for the winter where they alternate bouts of hibernation with arousal. Seeds harvested in the autumn provide all the energy needs, since the animal does not accumulate large fat deposits like most other hibernators. When climatic conditions improve in their home region (March in the south, April in the north), the mice emerge once again.

These mice often seem to ignore baited traps and therefore not much is known about them even though they may be quite common in some sites. My assistants and I tried for years to collect them in order to study their biology and distribution in the prairie region of Manitoba. Because of limited trapping success we decided to try our luck at catching them by hand. And so it was that we began our strange nightly antics that startled many people passing by in cars. After dark the 3 of us walked side by side for hours along country roads and through weedy pastures and stubble grainfields. The center person carried a lantern and when a pocket mouse was spotted a wild chase began.

"There's one!"
"Quick, over here!"
"Where'd he go?"
"Got him!"

Can you imagine 3 adults diving and scrambling on all fours after a speedy little mouse the size of your finger? We bumped heads, cracked knees, grabbed toads, even caught other kinds of mice, but eventually we became experts and seldom did a pocket mouse escape our pursuit. On some rare nights we caught over 20 individuals. Biologists do some pretty strange things when they are studying animals.

I have kept many of these beautiful little mice in captivity for years and can recommend them as excellent pets. Even people who are generally repulsed by rodents find them charming. The mice tame quickly and soon learn to accept sunflower seeds from a hand. They constantly move their larder from one corner of the cage to another, pushing the seeds out of their fur-lined cheek pouches so fast that the eye cannot follow the actions. A layer of cornmeal is a perfect material for the cage bottom, for the mouse can burrow and dust bathe in it. In the fields pocket mouse tunnels are about the size of one's little finger. I found one nest chamber packed with a handful of grass and seeds, about 0.4 m (1.3 ft) below the surface. Burrows may extend over an area of 7 m (23 ft) and descend below the frostline to a depth of 2 m (6.6 ft).

I once kept at home a silky pocket mouse *(Perognathus flavus)* from Arizona to observe the creature's habits. It was shortly nicknamed "Mouse Wrigley" by my young son. The mouse seemed to enjoy playing "cat and mouse" with both the boy and our cat — from the safety of a glass aquarium. One afternoon I received a distressing call at work that Mouse Wrigley was dying, since it lay on its side and

Continued on p.220

OLIVE-BACKED POCKET MOUSE

Olive-backed Pocket Mouse

If there was anything the pocket mouse could not stand, it was soiled fur. The tiny sand-colored animal generally looked tidy and clean, but after a busy two hours of gathering seeds in the dirt it definitely needed a bath. First it nibbled off bits of mud stuck to its feet, followed by a thorough licking between the toes. It washed both its face and behind the ears with its moistened front paws. Something felt itchy on its back — perhaps a flea or a hair out of place. Up rose a hind foot and it scratched so fast that the foot became a blur. Next the sides were gone over with the tongue and finally the hind legs, each one stretched forward to the mouth. A quick shake to dry and the job was done. Next on its cleaning routine were the fur-lined cheek pouches. Each long delicate pouch was pulled inside out by its hands, and after a rubbing and licking, a muscle snapped the pouch back inside the cheek. These grooming sequences were carried out several times each day and night in the safety of its burrows.

Lying within the mouse's skin were numerous glands that secreted an oil. Constant combing and licking spread this oil over each hair, which waterproofed and conditioned the fur. When excess oil began to mat its coat the mouse experienced an overwhelming urge for a dust bath. Picking a nice sandy spot free of vegetation, the pocket mouse began shoveling out the soil — forward with its delicate paws and backward with the hind feet. Soon a saucer-like depression took shape and the mouse poised itself on the edge, ready to dive in. Closing its eyes and laying its cheek on the ground, the mouse slid over on its right side and regained its feet in a flash. Then it rolled on the left side. It continued alternating side rolls until the dusty sand had scraped away the oil from everywhere but the belly. Keeping a favorite stroke for last, the mouse pushed forward on its belly and pulled its body along with the front feet. The stretching and belly rubs felt so good that the rodent repeated the movement six times. Sand bath completed, the little mouse sat back on its hind feet, shook off the loose dust, and squatted down to rest. Then off it hopped into the night in search of tasty seeds or perhaps a juicy beetle. By dawn the mouse was safely asleep in a small chamber about one-half meter (1.6 feet) below ground. The several entrances to the burrow were cleverly blocked and concealed under sagebrush. However, all around were signs of the mouse's nightly antics — little tracks running here and there, and tiny dead-end holes excavated for seeds by the front feet, and the loose soil kicked away by the hind feet.

With the constant rubbing against tunnel walls and rough plant stems, the mouse's coat began to show signs of thinning and wear. Over a two-week period during June a glossy new coat replaced the old faded fur, with an obvious molt line passing over the body. Each new hair grew in a backward direction so it would not catch on objects and be broken off as the mouse moved forward. On cold nights, the mouse fluffed up its coat by contracting a little muscle at the base of each hair. The erect hairs trapped an airspace which acted like an insulating blanket.

The olive-backed pocket mouse spent more time grooming its fur than people do washing and brushing their hair. Although the little mouse didn't realize all the benefits of grooming, its healthy coat protected it from wetness, sunburn, and scratches, and helped prevent heat and water loss from its body, as well as offering camouflage coloring.

Thirteen-lined Ground Squirrel and Richardson's Ground Squirrel

After long hours of driving across the prairies a family of tourists stopped to stretch their legs beside the road. At the slam of the car doors the cows fenced within the nearby pasture stopped grazing to inspect these noisy intruders. On the other side of the road, the steady prairie breezes rippled like waves through the ripening grain field that extended off to the horizon. It was a warm day, and bright; the kind of afternoon that makes one want to take a snooze in the shade. "Not much to see around here, is there?" exclaimed the father to his kids, who were anxiously watching all the grasshoppers jumping at their feet. They climbed back into the car and drove off in search of a more exciting place. Little did they know that their every move had been closely observed by dozens of prairie inhabitants.

Camouflaged by thirteen alternating stripes of brown and yellow running along the back, several thirteen-lined ground squirrels had been standing motionless in the grass, hands resting on their chests. After the people left, the squirrels dropped down on all fours and continued foraging in a slinky fashion by way of well-worn trails along the roadbank. Here and there were holes in the ground where the ground squirrels could dash to safety. The earth from these underground tunnels had been scattered so that it was difficult to see any sign of the diggings. Each animal kept to itself, though they were not bothered by other "thirteen-liners" passing through their home range. They were not even frightened by trucks and cars that occasionally sped by only a few meters (yards) away. One energetic and slightly foolish ground squirrel had even dug a burrow under the pavement that exited up through the asphalt.

Nearby, spaced throughout the overgrazed pasture, large mounds of brown earth revealed a colony of Richardson's ground squirrels. Often known as gophers, these animals were twice the size of their striped roadside cousins and were colored like the sandy soil upon which they stood. They took turns watching for foxes on the ground and the pair of red-tailed hawks that circled high overhead on the updrafts of warm air. These squirrels seemed to enjoy the company of their own kind and were constantly visiting, grooming, or calling to each other. They foraged over the ground, nibbling on weeds or pouncing on insects. The people had missed seeing all these prairie inhabitants because they didn't observe carefully or realize what kinds of animals lived there.

The peaceful scene was soon to be interrupted once more. Off in the green wet slough, about eighty meters (262.5 feet) away, was yet another grassland dweller whose favorite pastime was stalking and devouring ground squirrels. The female long-tailed weasel moved through the grass toward the colonies with the sinuous flow of a snake, thrusting her blunt, whiskered snout in the direction of each interesting scent. Then bounding rapidly along the roadside ditch for several minutes, she reached the area where the musk of ground squirrels clung heavily to the ground. As she rose on her hind limbs above the level of the grass, she spotted a thirteen-lined ground squirrel staring fixedly at her. She dashed forward, bent on capturing the squirrel before it could reach its burrow. A shrill alarm call pierced the air and every thirteen-liner within earshot immediately disappeared. The weasel arrived too late and then appeared confused over which of the dozens of holes to investigate.

Suddenly the little predator heard another alarm call, only this one was a long whistle. Stretching high to see above the grass she stared intently toward the pasture where numerous Richardson's ground squirrels were all standing in alert position on the mounds. Although her eyesight was too poor to see them clearly from this distance, she decided to investigate. As she broke into the open pasture a movement on her left caught her attention. A female ground squirrel was frantically retrieving one of her young that had crawled away from the den. Picking up the soft squirming body in her mouth, the mother dashed back home with the weasel in pursuit just one bound behind. Without warning, one of the large male ground squirrels slammed into the weasel's slim body, bowling it over. Growling and snapping its impressive incisors, the male chased the weasel back into the grass. The outcome of the attack would have been quite different had the weasel's much larger mate been present. The excitement of the afternoon's events was soon forgotten, and twenty minutes later both thirteen-lined and Richardson's ground squirrels were out filling their bellies again.

Dwayne Harty

OLIVE-BACKED POCKET MOUSE
cont. from p.215

hardly breathed. When I arrived home the family was quite upset at the obviously poor condition of the little pet, and holding its limp body in my hand I didn't expect it to survive the night. To our great surprise and joy the mouse made a miraculous recovery by morning and was again teasing the cat by hopping back and forth in front of its nose. The pocket mouse had simply become torpid — an energy-saving habit that can occur at any temperature or season.

THIRTEEN-LINED GROUND SQUIRREL

Scientific name *Spermophilus*
tridecemlineatus
Family Squirrels (Sciuridae)
Order Rodents (Rodentia)
Total length 270 mm (10.6 in)
Tail length 100 mm (3.9 in)
Weight males 165 g (5.6 oz);
females 140 g (4.9 oz)

Color This ground squirrel has one of the boldest color patterns of all North American mammals. The yellowish body is marked along the back by 7 dark brown or blackish stripes which enclose numerous yellowish dots or squares. Between the brown stripes are 6 yellowish ones, bringing the total to 13; hence its common name. A black band runs along the edge of the tail. Individuals from dry southern regions are paler than their northern kin.

Distribution and Status This active and common ground squirrel lives in grassland country from the southern parts of the prairie provinces, through the Great Plains to Texas and the Gulf of Mexico, west to Arizona, and east to Ohio. The animal has extended its range into agricultural areas that were formerly forest, although it is confined to fields, fence rows, and road banks. It avoids wet sites and tall grass, yet needs more cover than the Richardson's ground squirrel. Cemeteries and golf courses provide suitable habitat in urban areas. Another close prairie relative — Franklin's ground squirrel *(Spermophilus franklinii)* — is restricted to shrubby grassland and the forest edge.

Food Thirteen-liners like to eat animal material in the form of insects (particularly crickets and grasshoppers), birds, lizards, small mammals, and even carrion of their own kind. However, grass (brome grass, blue grama, crested wheatgrass), leaves (amaranth, milk-vetch, clover, white sweet-clover) and seeds are usually the most important items, generally amounting to at least 90 percent of the diet. Also attractive fodder are seeds, seedlings, and fruit of domestic crops such as wheat, oats, barley, rye, peas, beans, strawberries, and squash.

Reproduction and Growth These squirrels are ready to mate within the first few weeks out of hibernation in the spring. Males travel widely in search of females, sometimes fighting with each other. Mating occurs above ground, and 28 days later an average of 8 young (range of 5 to 13) are born in early April in the south, and late May or early June in the north. The mother nurses from 10 mammae. The newborn weigh 4 g (0.1 oz), develop a fur coat by 25 days, and their eyes open by day 28. Soon after, they emerge from the den and begin to feed on their own. Some females produce a second litter in early summer in the southern part of the range. They disperse within several weeks of their coming aboveground, and usually set up home within 100 m (328.1 ft). Sexual maturity occurs at 11 months. Only about one in 10 survives the first year, the others falling to predation by coyotes, foxes, weasels, hawks, roadrunners, and snakes, and to disease and accidents.

Remarks This species is a mid-sized ground squirrel with a slim body, fairly long flattened tail, and short limbs. The eyes are large, the external ears barely project from the head, and the coarse fur lies flat in a backward direction along the body. The animal is quick and slinky in its movements — almost weasel-like as it creeps through the grass, pausing periodically to rise up and survey its surroundings. Large numbers of seeds are collected and carried in the internal cheek pouches, causing the face to swell noticeably. These treasures are then cached in shallow holes, clumps of grass, or in underground chambers.

Thirteen-liners are strictly diurnal and are most active in late morning on sunny days. Cold, wet, or windy weather restricts their surface activity. Although generally found on the ground, they sometimes climb into shrubs while foraging, and are able to swim across watercourses. The main vocalization is a high-pitched alarm whistle or trill — difficult to trace to its source and an obvious adaptation to avoid detection by predators. Juveniles emit a peeping call and are quickly located and retrieved by the mother.

Burrows are of 3 main types — hiding, nesting, and hibernation, some of which extend up to 6 m (19.7 ft) in length and 1.8 m (5.9 ft) below the surface. These underground corridors are usually situated in well-drained sites — an advantage in flat regions of grasslands susceptible to flooding. The several entrances are neatly concealed and reveal no mounds of soil. Connecting these holes are well-trampled trails through the grass. The hibernation den is filled with dried grass and is plugged with a long core of soil.

In spite of thirteen-liners often occurring in colonies, the individuals lead a rather solitary existence, except during the breeding season. Home ranges are generally between 0.7 to 4.7 ha (1.7 to 11.6 a), with those of males being larger than females' ranges. Population densities average around 5 per ha (2 per a) but can range from 2 to 25 per ha (0.8 to 10.1 per a).

Thirteen-lined ground squirrels hibernate from late September to late March or early April in the north and from October to February (occasionally as late as early April) in the south. The animals curl up in a tight ball while torpid, with the face buried in the belly and the tail wrapped around the head and shoulders. Breathing drops from 200 to 2 breaths per minute, the heart rate from 150 to 15 beats per minute, and body temperature falls from 36°C (96.8°F) to a degree or 2 above that of the chamber. Arousal occurs every 12 days or so, accounting for a significant drain on fat reserves. Individuals lose up to 40 percent of their weight by spring. Following an unusually warm, rainy spell in December in southern Manitoba, my assistant found 2 thirteen-liners running down a country road in -10°C (14°F) weather. These individuals may have been flooded out of their hibernation den, or just became lost during a brief foray outside, and their feet, ears, and tails were frozen solid.

Like most ground squirrels, this species has long been considered an agricultural pest for its habit of eating grain. As if to balance this bad reputation the animal devours huge numbers of insects that cause much more damage to crops than the squirrel does. It also turns over and aerates the soil through its digging activities.

THIRTEEN-LINED GROUND SQUIRREL

RICHARDSON'S GROUND SQUIRREL

Scientific name *Spermophilus richardsonii*
Family Squirrels (Sciuridae)
Order Rodents (Rodentia)
Total length 285 mm (11.2 in)
Tail length 75 mm (3.0 in)
Weight 400 g (14.1 oz). Individuals may weigh up to 655 g (23.1 oz) before hibernation.
Color The upperparts are pale yellow with black hairs, giving a grizzled effect. The head, eye rings, legs, and belly are a pale orangy-yellow. The animal is often beautifully camouflaged as it stands erect on its sandy earth mound.
Distribution and Status This medium-sized ground squirrel inhabits prairie, mountain valleys, pastures, and grassy roadbanks from the prairie provinces south to Minnesota, South Dakota, and Montana. Adjacent populations extending from Montana to Nevada and Colorado were recently recognized as a distinct species — the Wyoming Ground Squirrel *(Spermophilus elegans)*. These two species probably arose from the same stock which became segregated during the Ice Ages of the Pleistocene when the range shifted southward as far as New Mexico.
Food The diet is composed of seeds, leaves, and roots of many prairie plants such as grass and broad-leaved species (sunflowers, pigweed, wild onions), as well as grain (oats, wheat, rye). Insects such as grasshoppers are also eaten and meat, including other dead ground squirrels, seems to be a delicacy. Large volumes of seeds are stored underground, which serve as nourishment during cold, wet weather, or in the spring when food is scarce.
Reproduction and Growth Males are in reproductive condition when they emerge from hibernation and their testes reach maximum size within 2 weeks. Females come out one or 2 weeks after males and mating commences within 3 to 5 days. The breeding season extends for 3 to 5 weeks in March and April. Courting pairs usually mate underground, lying on their sides for 3 minutes with the male clutching the female's back. Each may later search out additional

partners. After developing for 22.5 days, 5 to 8 (range of 3 to 13) young are born, each weighing 7 g (0.3 oz). They are naked until 4 to 7 days, the adult coat grows in by 22 to 28 days, their eyes open from 21 to 25 days, and they are able to control their body temperature at 30 days of age — the time they begin to wander out on the surface for the first time (late April to early June). While underground the young nurse from their mother's 5 pair of mammae, and on leaving the den they begin to nibble on greens. Only one litter is produced each year. Both males and females become sexually mature at one year of age. While a few of these ground squirrels are known to have survived 6 years in the wild, the average life span is only 2 years. Males, which travel more extensively than females, usually perish at an earlier age.
Remarks This ground squirrel has a stout body, wide and flattened head, and large bulging eyes which provide excellent vision. Glands present at the corners of the mouth, under the ears, and along the back secrete substances that aid in individual recognition and in marking the home range. Calls include whistles, chirps, churs, squeals, and the teeth are chattered as well. The squirrels are active for periods throughout the day in spring and fall, but often retire below ground at mid-day in summer to avoid the heat. Burrows are also used during cold weather (particularly in winter), to sleep, breed, and escape predators. These excavations extend from 4 to 15 m (13.1 to 49.2 ft) in length and descend for 2 m (6.6 ft) or more (below the frost line) and open into a number of chambers.

The home range of each squirrel is small — often less than one ha (2.5 a). Males may establish a breeding territory if females are numerous, while females that are pregnant or with young will drive away others from the burrow area, particularly males and unrelated females. Young males disperse 3 to 10 km (1.9 to 6.2 mi) in late June or July when 8 to 12 weeks old, but young females frequently remain at the site of their birth. The mother-daughter bond may last throughout life. Population densities average 1.4 to 5.3 per ha

(0.6 to 2.2 per a), and occasionally reach as high as 27 per ha (10.9 per a). The sudden appearance of juveniles on the surface temporarily raises the density up to 60 per ha (24.3 per a).

While some members of a ground squirrel colony are active aboveground for 7 months of the year, certain individuals restrict this period to as little as 3 months. The sequence of entry into hibernation is adult males from late June to July, adult females from July to August, juvenile females from late August to September, and juvenile males from September to early October. Such timing depends on the time required to breed, grow, and accumulate fat reserves for the winter. It seems most unusual that males begin their hibernation period in mid-summer, when the weather and food supply are favorable. During the first 2 months of hibernation, torpor lasts from 2 to 8 days followed by a 12-hour warming and arousal period. Brown fat stored within the chest cavity and around the shoulders is utilized during these warm-ups. The animals urinate but rarely eat or drink while awake. By mid-winter the periods of torpor last around 19 days, then drop to about 6 days in late winter. Depending on the latitude and correlated with soil and air temperatures, the ground squirrels begin to emerge from February to April, with males active one or 2 weeks before females.

While many people believe it is springtime when horned larks, robins, crows, or geese return on their northward migration, I don't look to these or even the unreliable talent of the woodchuck for signs of warmer days. On the prairie, I know spring has arrived when Richardson's ground squirrels poke their heads out of snowdrifts, marking the end of the squirrels' (and many people's) winter hibernation. During unusual mid-winter thaws these creatures sometimes emerge and run around in the snow, as occurred on January 12 in Manitoba while I wrote this account. A few days before, and then after, the temperature hovered from -10° to -25°C (14° to -13°F).

These animals have been a serious pest to grain farmers on the prairies from pioneer days to the present. Poison and bounties have been used to reduce their numbers, but the "gophers" always manage to maintain their numbers. During 1890 in one Manitoba municipality, 40,000 gopher tails were turned in by youngsters for a bounty of 3 cents each. Certain populations of Richardson's ground squirrels (along with other kinds of small mammals) have been known to harbor a number of dangerous diseases such as plague (caused by a flea-transmitted bacteria), Rocky Mountain spotted fever (carried by a tick), and tularemia. The badger, coyote, foxes, weasels, skunks, snakes, and hawks eat these ground squirrels by the millions.

RICHARDSON'S GROUND SQUIRREL

American Badger and Black-tailed Prairie Dog

The sun peeked over the rolling hills on the southeastern horizon, spreading light over the sagebrush, prickly pear cacti, and craters of light brown earth thrown up here and there in the short grass. As the morning advanced, numerous stocky rodents appeared on top of the mounds, calling and greeting each other at the start of another busy day in prairie dog town. It had rained last night, and several members of the colony began repairing eroded den entrances by bunting the mud walls with the top of their snouts. A prairie dog with a muddy nose paused in its work to glance over at two youngsters grappling and kicking in play. Suddenly one squeaked in pain from a bite and dashed off home, threading its way through dozens of other prairie dogs foraging in the grass. The adults took turns watching the skies for hawks and then the ground for other creatures that might be sneaking up behind the shrubs. Within half an hour there were prairie dogs spread over the landscape as far as the eye could see.

Suddenly an alarm call pierced the air as one sentinel spotted movement within some low sagebrush. Four black and white striped faces peered through the gnarled stems and gray leaves. The badger family had been watching since before daybreak, hoping to catch a sleepy or unwary prairie dog too far from its burrow. Within a second of the alarm, every prairie dog in the colony repeated the call with a backward thrust of the head, and then raced towards a burrow and disappeared below ground. The mother badger and her three young made a feeble effort at chasing them, but the town was deserted by the time the four short-legged stalkers waddled up to the mounds. Since the badgers' ambush had failed, the only strategy remaining was to dig out their prey. Selecting one mound the mother positioned the young badgers at each of the nearby den entrances and then she began ripping into the main burrow with powerful strokes of her clawed forelimbs. The left front and right hind leg worked together, alternating with the other two limbs. The sandy soil flew back in a shower of dust, and the flattened body of the badger seemed to sink out of sight. Below ground, she was guided along the correct tunnel by her keen sense of smell, and she snorted loudly from time to time to clear her nostrils and to take in the fresh aroma of prairie dog. A thin moveable membrane protected her eyes from the gritty dust while fringes of hairs kept the soil particles from entering her ear cavities. After burrowing for ten minutes the badger backed out and checked on her offspring to ensure that they had not wandered off. The young lay on their bellies, ready to pounce, their noses only centimeters from the holes.

One and a half meters (4.9 feet) below, two prairie dogs circled nervously in the nest chamber as soil came trickling down the tunnel. For fifteen minutes the badger persisted with its steady descent, her broad hind feet kicking the soil up and over the edge of the crater. Suddenly the roof of the nest chamber collapsed under the heavy weight of the badger, and with a snap of her jaws she clamped down on a prairie dog, catching it in mid-squeal. The powerful grip broke the rodent's back and neck, and it slumped limply from either side of the predator's mouth. Quickly emerging from the deep hole and depositing the prairie dog on the surface, the badger once again checked the anxious youngsters, then crawled down to finish the job.

The other prairie dog managed to flee up an escape tunnel where it crouched in fear, its teeth chattering loudly. The scrape-scrape sounds came closer as the mother badger continued digging, pressure receptors on the end finger bones informing her just how much force to apply to the hard ground without shattering her long shovel-like nails. Closer and closer she came, while the prairie dog shuffled ever farther along the tunnel. Soon it could see daylight ahead. A black pointy nose snuffed just below and the alarmed prairie dog shot out of the burrow right into the face of a young badger. Seconds later all three youngsters were biting and pulling on the kicking brown ball of fur. In their great excitement they emitted a powerful musk from their anal scent glands.

This time the badgers were successful in capturing their prey, but on other occasions the prairie dogs had outsmarted them by retreating down deeper or blocked side tunnels. Although over three hundred prairie dogs would be born that summer, the colony remained at about the same level as in previous years. The meal finished, the adult badger shook some soil from her shaggy coat while the young ones washed their faces. Then off they went to find a den where they could sleep the rest of the day.

AMERICAN BADGER

Scientific name *Taxidea taxus*
Family Weasels (Mustelidae)
Order Carnivores (Carnivora)
Total length 80 cm (31.5 in)
Tail length 14 cm (5.5 in)
Weight males 8 kg, maximum 12 kg (17.6 lb, maximum 26.5 lb); females 6 kg, maximum 8 kg (13.2 lb, maximum 17.6 lb). Badgers in the southwestern United States and Mexico are the smallest.

Color The long coarse hairs are cream-colored with black tips, giving an overall grizzled color. From a distance the animal appears yellowish-brown to silvery-gray. Brown to black fur occurs on the tail tip, the feet, behind the eyes, and 2 patches extending from the nose to the back of the neck on either side of the white streak on the forehead. In southern individuals the white stripe continues to the rump. The underparts are light brown or white.

Distribution and Status The badger is an animal of open country, and is found in grassland, sagebrush plains, parklands, alpine meadows to 4 268 m (14,002.6 ft), hot or cold deserts, and farmlands. It avoids densely forested regions but occupies glades. It occurs from Ohio and the southern parts of Ontario west to British Columbia and extends southward through the western two-thirds of the United States to Puebla in central Mexico. There is a recent report of a small population in southern Yukon Territory. While numbers of the animal have now stabilized over most of its large range, it is spreading in Ohio and the northern prairies and decreasing in Ontario and British Columbia.

Ancestral badgers resembled martens *(Martes)* and are known from Europe and Asia. The line leading to the American badger split from the main stock of badgers during the early Pliocene (about 4 million years ago) and crossed the Bering land bridge soon after. A possible predecessor of the recent badger was *Pliotaxidea*, a small species widespread in North America. During the periods of glacial retreat the American badger occurred farther north and east than at present, since fossils have been found in central Alaska, Pennsylvania, Maryland, and Kentucky.

Close relatives are the Eurasian badger *(Meles meles)* from the British Isles to Iran and southern China, the hog badger *(Arctonyx collaris)* from China to Sumatra, 2 species of stink badgers *(Mydaus)* from southeast Asia, and 3 tree-climbing species of ferret badgers *(Melogale)* also from southeast Asia. The aggressive honey badger or ratel *(Mellivora capensis)* from Africa, Arabia, and India closely resembles the badgers but in reality is only distantly a kin.

Food The diet is mostly small mammals such as prairie dogs, ground squirrels, pocket gophers, cottontails, chipmunks, kangaroo rats, and mice. Birds, reptiles, and insects are also eaten.

Reproduction and Growth The mating season extends from August to September, when males search out females in heat. Occasionally two males engage in fierce fighting, the winner remaining to court the female. The mating couple frequently roll over on their sides, with the male on the female's back and his jaws grasping the nape of her neck to protect himself. The fertilized eggs in the female's womb cease cell division at an early stage and rest until late winter or early spring. Depen-

ding on the latitude, they are triggered into regrowth by the mother's hormones stimulated by the changing amount of daylight. Although the period of pregnancy lasts 7 to 10 months, the actual developmental period is only 6 weeks. An average of 3 (range of one to 7) young are born as early as February in the south and as late as June in the north. Over much of the range births occur mainly in March and April. The female chooses a deep natal den where she can care for her young undisturbed. She nurses them from 8 mammae and defends her family courageously if necessary. The youngsters' eyes begin to open at 4 weeks. Soon after, they begin to gnaw on the flesh of small animals brought into the den by their mother. Weaning occurs at 6 weeks when they appear aboveground for the first time. They can fend for themselves when two-thirds grown and disperse at an early age of 10 to 12 weeks. About one-third of the females breed the same year when about 4 months old, the remainder and all the males wait until the following summer and autumn. The average lifespan is around 4 years, however, some are known to have reached 14 years in the wild and 26 years in captivity.

Remarks The badger has a stocky flattened body, short limbs, and a wedge-shaped head ending in a tough, black nose pad. The tail is short but quite bushy. The animal walks on the soles of its feet; the front feet have partially webbed toes and long curving nails. The badger's maximum speed for short distances is only 19 km (11.8 mi) per hour. It is such a powerful digger that it can literally sink out of sight in less than 2 minutes and has been known to penetrate asphalt roads and rip apart concrete floors. Badgers sometimes dig up to 40 holes while searching for a ground squirrel, prairie dog, or pocket gopher, frequently moving 250 to 500 l (66 to 132 US gal) of soil in the process. The success rate for prey capture by excavation is a surprising 73 percent, but considerable energy is expended.

The shaggy fur wears well considering the abrasion it is subjected to, and along with the thick skin helps protect the badger from the bites of other large predators. The marked facial stripe and patches may serve as warning (similar to the striped skunk) to aggressors, in species recognition, and in light reflection on food while foraging on dark nights. The anal glands produce a strong musk which is used to mark the borders and trails of the home range and to stimulate breeding behavior in other individuals. The skull of the badger is massive and contains 34 teeth including long canines for grasping and biting prey, and shearing cheek teeth which cut meat into pieces small enough to be swallowed.

A solitary creature, the badger wanders over a home range of about 2.4 sq km (0.9 sq mi) for the male, and 1.6 sq km (0.6 sq mi) for the female. Occasionally the range is as large as 17 sq km (6.3 sq mi). Overlapping of home ranges is common, except those of males. A juvenile was found to have dispersed 110 km (68.4 mi) from its natal den; however, this long distance is quite exceptional. Population densities are generally within 0.5 to 6 per sq km (1.4 to 16.2 per sq mi). This species is mainly active at night, but it does not hesitate to be out during daylight hours as well. It is most active in summer, least so in winter. When temperatures drop below -15°C (5°F) the animal retires to a burrow. There may be up to 50 burrows within the home range of a single animal. The badger appears to use a different burrow each night, often leaving its droppings in the tunnels. Winter or breeding burrows are used for many weeks and can be 10 m (32.8 ft) long and 3 m (9.8 ft) deep, with several entrances, blind tunnels, and a nest chamber lined with grass. Such burrows are essential to the survival of badgers in the north, for they would die of exposure or starve on the surface. The animals do not truly hibernate but enter a deep sleep during cold weather, remaining below ground from mid-October to mid-April at northern extremes. The body temperature may actually drop by 9°C (16.2°F) and the heart by 50 percent to 25 beats per minute. Over 30 percent of the body weight may be fat in the autumn, and about 25 percent is utilized during dor-

AMERICAN BADGER

mancy. Badgers in central regions of the range sleep for short periods in winter, while those in the southern United States and Mexico remain active year round.

This member of the weasel family is so large and fierce that few predators attempt to bother it. When attacked, it backs into a hole, flattens its body, bares its teeth, and growls and hisses menacingly. Occasionally one falls prey to a black bear, grizzly, coyote, or eagle.

BLACK-TAILED PRAIRIE DOG

Scientific name *Cynomys ludovicianus*
Family Squirrels (Sciuridae)
Order Rodents (Rodentia)
Total length 390 mm (15.4 in)
Tail length 85 mm (3.4 in)
Weight 1 kg, maximum 1.4 kg
(2.2 lb, maximum 3.1 lb)
Color The upperparts are light brown with black- and white-tipped hairs showing through. The underparts, feet, and cheeks are pale brown or white. The coarsely haired tail is brown with a black tip. The animal is camouflaged against the sandy soil of the plains.
Distribution and Status This prairie dog inhabits short-grass prairie, avoiding wet sites, dense brush, and tall grass. It selects flat lands or gently rolling hills which provide a long-range view of approaching predators. It is found from North Dakota, southern Saskatchewan, and Montana south to northern Mexico and central Texas. Decades of eradication programs have greatly reduced the ranges and numbers of this and other species of prairie dogs. In 1905 there were an estimated 800 million black-tailed prairie dogs in Texas alone, which has been reduced to 2.25 million in recent times. The only population in Canada was discovered late in 1927 near Val Marie, Saskatchewan. It has grown over the years to include about a dozen separate towns.

Although often confused with ground squirrels *(Spermophilus)*, prairie dogs are quite distinct and are found only in North America. The black-tailed prairie dog has 4 other close relatives — the Mexican, white-tailed, Utah, and Gunnison's prairie dogs (*Cynomys mexicanus, leucurus, parvidens,* and *gunnisoni*, respectively).
Food Prairie dogs eat low-growing weeds, grasses (such as bluegrass, wheatgrass, and grama grass), sage, prickly pear cacti, and insects such as cutworms, grasshoppers, and beetles. When plant leaves have mainly been cropped, the animals then dig up the roots. They become incredibly fat in late summer and resemble footballs standing on end. One naturalist roughly estimated that 32 prairie dogs ate as much plant material in a day as one sheep, and 256 ate as much as a cow.
Reproduction and Growth Prairie dogs breed only once a year. Mating occurs in February or March in the south and in April in the north. Almost 30 days later, 5 (range of 2 to 10) young are born deep underground. A baby prairie dog weighs about 55 g (1.9 oz), the first fine coat appears at 13 days, the eyes open and it first begins to call at 35 days. Milk is provided by the mother's 8 mammae until the young appear on the surface and begin eating vegetation at 6 weeks. They are weaned within the next week and are half grown by June. Dispersal to nearby vacant burrows occurs soon after. Full size and sexual maturity are reached the following year. The average lifespan is 3 years under natural conditions, while captives have survived to 8.5 years of age.
Remarks The prairie dog is a robust (largest in the rear), short-legged rodent with a flattened tail and a wide head characterized by big black eyes and small ears. It was named because of its barking habit, which helps to keep the colony together and to warn other members. Interestingly, the scientific name *Cynomys* means "dog-mouse." Each time the animal barks, it pushes the front part of its body right off the ground. Sometimes dozens of these animals all "jump-yip" at the same time, as in a chorus, which appears to be territorial behavior. Prairie dogs are famous for their towns or colonies that spread over enormous areas under ideal conditions. In the days before these animals were poisoned as pests on range lands, the towns may have covered thousands of square kilometers and contained many millions of individuals. More recently, towns are generally under one sq km (0.4 sq mi). Prairie dogs form small social units called coteries of 2 to 35 animals, often family members. They defend their territory against outsiders. A number of coteries form a ward (2 to 4 ha or 4.9 to 9.9 a in size) which is usually somewhat isolated from other wards by topographical features. The home range of a single prairie dog is small — only 0.2 to 0.6 ha (0.5 to 1.5 a). Population densities have been recorded from 12 to 75 per ha (4.9 to 30.4 per a).

These animals play, groom, and nuzzle each other, and sometimes call for help to drive off other prairie dogs from nearby coteries. An individual frequently stretches out flat on its belly with arms extending upward to the sun. As it runs the short tail is waved quickly back and forth, but all motion freezes when it stops to check for danger. During eating, the prairie dog cuts a plant, sits back on its haunches, and holds the blade in one hand to its mouth, like a person eating an ice cream cone.

Prairie dogs spend most of the morning and late afternoon above ground when the weather is fine. The high mounds, thrown up from their extensive burrow systems, serve as lookouts and keep out water from heavy rains or floods. Burrows provide refuge from predators and inclement weather. Each burrow has several openings and a maze of tunnels extending from 4 to 34 m (13.1 to 111.6 ft) in length and from one to 5 m (3.3 to 16.4 ft) in depth. During cold, wet periods, these animals remain below. In the months when the prairies are covered with snow, prairie dogs enter a deep sleep and live off their fat, since no food is stored below ground. Prairie dogs are preyed upon by eagles, hawks, burrowing owl, black-footed ferret, badger, bobcat, foxes, coyote, and rattlesnakes.

BLACK-TAILED PRAIRIE DOG

Black-tailed Prairie Dog

Northern Pocket Gopher

The strengthening spring sun finally began to have some effect on the half meter (1.6 feet) of snow blanketing the prairie valley. The horned larks and bluebirds had arrived a week ago — a sure sign that spring was on its way. They fluttered along the melting roadside and nearby bushes, searching for seeds and fluffing their feathers against the cool breeze. It had been a long cold winter for animals like deer and coyotes that had had to face the elements every day. Three meters (9.8 feet) below the ground and out of reach of the frost's cold grasp, a pocket gopher lay curled up asleep in its grass-lined nest chamber. With a thin coat and sparsely haired tail, this tube-shaped animal had no interest in exposing itself to the cold world above, although it had been locked below ground for six months. In fact, since it rarely emerged and moved about on the surface only on dark nights even during the warm months, wintertime was not really much different than summer for this creature of the soil. The frozen upper layer of ground did, however, severely curtail its burrowing activites in search of succulent rootstocks and bulbs.

Without any external clues to guide its periods of sleep and activity, the pocket gopher's internal "clock" caused it to stir, for the animal had been asleep for three hours. Rolling from its side to its stubby feet, the gopher yawned widely, exposing the full length of four enormous chisel-like teeth. Along each side of the mouth was a slit in the skin that led to a spacious fur-lined cheek pouch. Since the maze of tunnels was pitch black the animal always kept its tiny eyes shut. Wide awake at last it rambled along a tight passageway, took the right fork, and entered its toilet chamber. After relieving itself the pocket gopher felt hungry, but it had recently devoured the remaining food in the storage rooms. Climbing up to the surface its four bare feet contacted the hoar frost that had formed on the burrow floor. The gopher's powerful front claws scraped away the frozen plug of soil that had sealed the main door since last October. Granular snow crystals came tumbling down, causing the creature to shake its massive head. Then it began to tunnel through the snow on the surface of the ground where it found stems and leaves to eat. A faint light filtered down through the snow cover, but even this low intensity was uncomfortable to the gopher's sensitive eyes. Becoming chilled after five minutes, the animal backed up in the tunnel, feeling its way along by its tail, and returned to its familiar world below.

Heat rising from the earth's core and from the sun above melted the frozen ground within a week. Now free to construct new tunnels the gopher dug extensively in the top layer of soil where it located and ate rootstalks until its belly was full. Excess soil from these new excavations was pushed back into the snow tunnels, which along with those formed in early winter would be left lying like earth snakes on the grass when the snow eventually disappeared. A few days later, on a warm afternoon, the pocket gopher was awakened by a strange dripping sound coming from a distant tunnel. Pausing to scratch a flea with its hind leg, the gopher began to investigate this invasion of its solitude. Halfway there, it suddenly felt freezing cold water and mud trickling over its soft pink feet. The animal ground its teeth loudly in fright. Perhaps it could solve the flood by blocking off the tunnel. It dug furiously into the earthen wall and packed the loosened soil into the hole with its wide palms and nose. But soon water came seeping in from several directions. With nowhere to hide the frightened gopher reluctantly made its way to the surface and out into the dazzling daylight. Lost and helpless in the slush, the gopher wandered for three hours before being spotted by a long-tailed weasel, still in its white coat. The gopher was so numb with cold that it was unable to put up much resistance and it squealed loudly before dying from a bite on the neck. The weasel dragged the heavy body across the field and under some branches, where it was soon joined by its mate. The weasels ate their fill and lined their nest with the soft gopher fur.

As spring advanced, green shoots of grass pushed their sharp tips through the gopher mounds and earthen cores. The plants were invigorated by the fresh soil and gopher wastes and their greenness stood out among the surrounding vegetation. Then one night in July the vacant burrow system was visited by a young pocket gopher, recently chased out of its home burrow by an impatient mother. It had traveled about ninety meters (295.3 feet) down the roadbank and had now discovered the mounds. Old scent and an open burrow were good signs for the newcomer, for a resident gopher is always careful to plug the entrance. The youngster quickly entered and began investigating the subterranean passages. Apparently this old home was ideal for the young animal, for ten minutes later damp soil blocked the front door.

NORTHERN POCKET GOPHER

Scientific name *Thomomys talpoides*
Family Pocket Gophers (Geomyidae)
Order Rodents (Rodentia)
Total length 230 mm (9.1 in)
Tail length 65 mm (2.6 in)
Weight 140 g, maximum 210 g
(4.9 oz, maximum 7.4 oz)

Color The upperparts are dark grayish-brown — the color of soil. The belly is grayish-white while the throat, feet, and tail are white. A black patch is present behind each ear.

Distribution and Status This northernmost member of the pocket gopher family occupies the prairies and mountain meadows from British Columbia to Manitoba in the north and south to California, New Mexico, and Nebraska. It appears in a variety of habitats such as dry sandy sagebrush plains, deep moist soil near watercourses, shrub thickets, open deciduous and coniferous woodlands and forests, roadbanks, and cultivated fields. There is usually a ground cover of grass.

When several species of pocket gophers occur in the same vicinity, the northern pocket gopher is often forced into poor habitats such as soil filled with stones or roots from shrubs and trees. This animal exhibits an extraordinary degree of variation among populations which has led to the naming of many dozens of subspecies (almost 60 are presently listed). Some of these have been found recently to be full species. The pocket gopher family occurs throughout North America and into northern South America. It is represented by about 35 species, perhaps 9 of which belong to the same genus *(Thomomys)* as the northern pocket gopher.

Food During the summer, the leaves and stems of various broad-leaved plants comprise about three-quarters of the diet and the remainder, roots and bulbs. Prickly pear cactus, clover, and dandelion roots are choice foods. In winter the gopher lives on the roots and rootstalks of plants that store well underground. The animal may pull down plants into the feeding tunnels or emerge for brief periods at night to forage on the surface. Plants are cut into 5-cm (2-in) sections and carried back in the cheek pouches to the burrow. About 160 g (5.6 oz) of vegetation are devoured daily.

Reproduction and Growth The breeding season may extend over the whole year in southern areas, with one or 2 litters produced. However, over most of the range including Canada, one litter is the norm. Females come into heat (the estrous period) in March and pregnant females are found from April to early August. The testes of males are greatly enlarged and descended from March to early August. Individuals of the opposite sex locate each other by digging into adjoining tunnels or by traveling over the surface. Shortly after mating they return to their solitary life-style. The gestation or developmental period is 19 days, following which 4 (range of one to 6) young are born in a grass-lined nest. Each weighs only 3 g (0.1 oz) and 26 days pass before their eyes, ears, and cheek pouches open. They are weaned at 40 days when about one-third grown, and several weeks later the family becomes so aggressive that the youngsters disperse. Full size is reached when about 6 months old, while sexual maturity occurs at one year. The average lifespan is 3 years but some survive to 5 years in the wild.

Remarks This strange creature is seldom seen by people because it comes above ground only for a few minutes at night. Even so, pocket gopher bones are sometimes common in disgorged pellets of owls. The tunnel entrances are kept plugged to keep out weasels and snakes and to maintain stable conditions of temperature and humidity. The usual sign of this animal is a series of earth mounds, often arranged in a line. Burrow systems may total well over 150 m (492.1 ft), with shallow feeding tunnels and lower chambers at a depth of 2 m (6.6 ft) and occasionally even 3 m (9.8 ft). In regions subject to flooding, the gopher sometimes builds extra-large mounds on the surface 2 m (6.6 ft) across and 0.7 m (2.3 ft) high and creates a nest chamber and storage facilities inside. The home range is about 126 to 172 sq m (150 to 200 sq yd) and population densities range from one per 0.2 ha on poor habitat to 128 per ha (0.5 to 51.8 per a) in choice sites. Individuals have been known to disperse one km (0.6 mi) from home and swim 300 m (984.3 ft) across a river. The animals prefer to live by themselves and tolerate company in their tunnels only during the breeding season. However they seem colonial because of the close proximity of their homes. Owls, snakes, weasels, and badgers are the main predators.

The pocket gopher shows many remarkable adaptations for a life underground — small ears and eyes which close tightly to keep out particles of soil, whiskers and short touch-sensitive tail to guide the gopher through the tunnels in either direction, long sharp claws and strong front limbs for digging, enormous front teeth to bite hard earth and for chewing plants, and a tube-shaped body to fit the round tunnel. The pocket gopher receives its name because of its huge fur-lined cheek pouches which act as "shopping carts" to carry pieces of food back to its storage chambers.

The hip or pelvic bones of a pocket gopher are rather narrow in order to permit the movement of the animal along its tunnels. A remarkable change occurs in the pelvis of pregnant females. The front connection is dissolved under the influence of a hormone relaxin which is secreted by the ovaries, and this allows passage of the large babies through the birth canal. A quick examination of the pelvic bones of pocket gophers reveals which ones have bred.

My field crew and I have caught hundreds of pocket gophers with special traps that must be placed carefully inside the tunnels. Locating a tunnel is sometimes difficult for the gopher is careful to seal the exits with a long plug of packed soil. Once the traps are set, the surface hole is lightly covered with plant debris to permit some fresh air to enter the shafts. The gopher generally arrives within a few hours to close its door, and at least half the time it is caught. I have never seen an untrapped pocket gopher running around on the surface, but one half-frozen individual was brought in by a farmer who had found it lost and wandering through the snow. Its tail was cut, suggesting it had been forced out of its burrow by another gopher. Several young animals have appeared in our mouse traps set in the grass, indicating that the gophers were feeding on the surface while dispersing.

On one particular study quadrat set in a prairie-shrub habitat, we could see hundreds of gopher mounds pushed out on the grass. Pausing for lunch, I sat down and began opening a sandwich bag when I heard a strange scraping sound. At first I thought it must have been my stomach that was noisily anticipating the arrival of food. But when the sounds continued I realized it was coming from underground. I happened to be sitting just above a pocket gopher busily digging out its lunch of grass rootstalks.

NORTHERN POCKET GOPHER

SAGEBRUSH VOLE

Scientific name *Lagurus curtatus*
Family Voles and Lemmings (Arvicolidae)
Order Rodents (Rodentia)
Total length 128 mm (5 in)
Tail length 21 mm (0.8 in)
Weight 32 g (1.1 oz)

Color This rodent is the palest vole on the continent, camouflaging well with the light-colored soil, sagebrush, and parched grass of its surroundings. The long fluffy fur is ashy-gray, with yellowish-buff on the ears, nose, and flanks. The sides are paler, blending to the silvery-white belly, feet, and tail, which also has a faint gray line on top. The juvenile coat consists of gray-tipped hairs.

Distribution and Status The rare sagebrush vole inhabits the Great Basin and northern Great Plains from Washington east to Saskatchewan, then southward as far as eastern California to New Mexico. Local colonies are found in sagebrush and scrub and semiarid short-grass prairie. Topography varies from flat plains to rolling hills and canyons 300 to 3 800 m (984.3 to 12,467.2 ft) in elevation. Soils are generally dry and sandy, but sometimes rocky. Typical habitat consists of bunch grasses such as crested wheatgrass interspersed with sagebrush, rabbitbrush, or greasewood. Highest populations occur in a cover of heavy grass and shrubs, but the voles may also be present in only sparse grass with bare ground. Three closely related species called steppe lemmings are native to central Eurasia.

Food The sagebrush vole lives in arid areas supporting relatively few kinds of plants; however it appears to find most of these acceptable as food — even sagebrush. In spring and summer grass shoots, leaves, and immature seed heads of grasses are eaten, but not, surprisingly, the ripened seeds found so attractive by many other small mammals in the same areas, such as pocket and deer mice. As the seasons progress, various legumes, bulbs, and leaves of herbs like prairie club moss, and the leaves and flowers of sagebrush are eaten. Green vegetation may be pulled into the burrows for short-term use but food is not stored for winter. At this time, the bark and twigs of sagebrush and the underground parts of various grasses and herbs become important. The animal can go without water to drink for long periods, relying on the moisture in its food. It will lap up dew, raindrops, and snow when available. It requires less water than other North American voles and lemmings.

Reproduction and Growth The breeding season may extend year round in the south, from March to December in central regions, and is restricted to the warmer months from April to September in the north. In areas that experience great summer heat and drought, breeding ceases as the testes of males decrease in size. The growth of new vegetation in spring and autumn stimulates reproduction. At least 3 litters are produced per year, but the maximum number is unknown. Four to 6 (range of one to 13) naked and blind babies are born after a gestation period of 25 days. Before the young are weaned and independent at 18 days, the mother often searches for a male and becomes pregnant again. The father is kept away from the nest, for he might destroy and devour the offspring. Young females become sexually mature after 47 days, males after 60 days, and both are full grown by 3 months. Life expectancy is one year, although a small percentage of voles survives to 2 years.

Remarks The sagebrush vole resembles a lemming or bog lemming with its short tail and limbs, and stocky build. In fact, its relatives in Eurasia are called steppe lemmings for this very reason. The soles of the feet are partially haired. Scent glands, present on the hips of males, mark the trails and burrows and serve to communicate the presence of particular individuals.

These voles are sporadic in distribution, usually found in small colonies representing several interbreeding families. Occasional outbreaks in numbers occur over wide areas, generally associated with a mild dry winter and a warm wet summer and autumn. The presence of a colony is identifiable by trails through the grass and dozens of holes under sagebrush which lead to underground burrows lined with clippings of grass and sagebrush leaves. These burrows run horizontally less that 50 cm (19.7 in) below the surface and connect up to the tunnel systems of other voles in the colony. Here and there are blind tunnels for resting, feeding, and escaping predators such as burrowing and short-eared owls, bobcat, coyote, badger, and long-tailed weasel. When local food sources are depleted, or when the colony site becomes too wet during the spring thaw or excessively dry from the summer sun, the voles may move to another nearby area.

Sagebrush voles may be out anytime during the night or day, but peaks of activity occur for several hours at sunset and sunrise. Like other voles, they do not hibernate but continue their busy lives under the snow. Wind is not to their liking however, and they remain below in such weather conditions. Perhaps the wind interferes with their delicate sense of hearing — the main sense for detecting predators. Since these rodents are relatively scarce and seldom found in good agricultural land, they are not considered a pest as are many other voles. A potential threat to humans are the fleas that live in the vole's fur and nest, since they harbor the bacteria that cause a serious disease called sylvatic plague.

I have attempted to collect sagebrush voles in suitable habitats during short stops in Utah, Nevada, Washington, Montana, and Saskatchewan, but without success. Repeated failures to locate this and a few other small mammals just increase the challenge to try again. It's worth the travel and effort just to walk the trapline on a beautiful prairie morning, and to smell the sweet, pungent aroma of sage leaves rubbed in one's fingers.

SAGEBRUSH VOLE

Sagebrush Vole

Pale gray wisps of sagebrush and occasional outcrops of black rock relieved the monotonous sea of short bunch grass that was parched yellow by a long summer of sunshine. The broad expanse seemed devoid of life — not even a songbird fluttered across the sky all day. While the sun paused then sank behind the low hills, a burrowing owl walked boldly from a tunnel, leapt forward into the air, and flapped its way over the valley. It landed lightly on a dead twisted sagebrush and sat perfectly still, listening and watching. At the base of a nearby sagebrush, six holes in the sandy soil led to indistinct trails that radiated off in several directions. The owl did not have long to wait. Its round head swiveled in the direction of a grayish rodent dashing along one of the trails. In a flash the owl opened its wings and dove with extended talons toward the sagebrush vole. But the vole's keen ears heard the rasping sound of the talons leave the perch, and it darted, just in the nick of time, under one of several circular brown objects lying on the ground. The owl swooped past, circled, and descended, then stood beside the piles of dried bison droppings. With a long outstretched leg the hunter flipped over each patty, anticipating a vole huddled under one of them. Instead, under the last hollowed-out patty, a blind tunnel about twenty centimeters (7.9 inches) deep lay exposed, at the bottom of which sat the owl's meal. The burrowing owl blinked its big eyes and shuffled its feet, as if in bewilderment at what to do next. Finally realizing it had missed this chance, the owl returned to its former perch. On the ground beneath lay several disgorged owl pellets, full of white bones and gray fur.

The owl sat patiently till long after sunset, an occasional roll of thunder disturbing its attempt to listen for the gentle rustling of voles or deer mice in the grass. The black prairie sky turned bright as day in flashes of spectacular lightning. The thunder seemed to rumble on long after the bolts fingered down to earth, and the ground began to tremble. The alarmed owl retreated to its burrow, not knowing what was about to happen. Soon the bawls of bison could be heard amid the heavy pounding of many thousands of hooved feet. Another flash of lightning illuminated a black curtain of frenzied animals, stampeding over the hill and filling the valley. The horde swept by for ten minutes, leaving every shrub and blade of grass flattened and punched into the ground. The collapse of animal tunnels suffocated and entombed the owl, but most voles were able to survive because they were partially protected by the thick spongy nest of grass and bark fibers. Digging furiously, the larger voles were able to reach the surface, freeing almost all the colony of eighteen.

A slight drizzle washed some of the dust from the valley air by morning. There was nothing but fragments of leaves and bark for the stressed rodents to nibble on. Over the next few nights most of the voles left the trampled area singly and in small groups, and found refuge in a rocky slope. This rough terrain had deterred the bison, and bunches of grass, sagebrush, and rabbitbrush were still present among the boulders. While the voles set about constructing new tunnels, the last two members of the colony arrived by following the scent left by others. They were females, each carrying a single pink baby in their mouths. They returned again and again from the old tunnels until all thirteen babies were safely retrieved and tucked down in a rock crevice. The two mothers nursed young from either litter in the communal nest.

By the end of a week the vole colony had returned to a normal schedule of activities. While still nursing and caring for their present offspring, the two females and several others became receptive to the amorous approaches of the males. Soon all adult females were pregnant. Cooler autumn days and the renewed plant growth from rains had stimulated breeding. In spite of the natural disaster suffered by the voles several weeks ago, the survival of the colony seemed assured.

Swift Fox and Deer Mouse

It was one of those clear summer nights on the prairie when a million bright and faint stars were visible in the heavens. Pitch-black crickets skulked through the short grass, pausing to grind out a merry tune by rubbing their legs together. In the warm air, several small bats patroled back and forth over a sandy, little-used roadway. Down below on the edge of the road, a tiny set of four tracks revealed that a big-eared deer mouse had passed here this night and would likely soon return, for the morning light was just beginning to show in the east. No self-respecting deer mouse is ever found out after light, so it was not long before the grayish-brown critter came bounding along its personal highway. The last two hours had been spent scrounging in the needle and buffalo grasses for seeds and tasty grasshoppers. Pausing to rest on its hind feet, it glanced upwards with protruding black eyes — not to appreciate the stars or the fancy maneuvers of the bats, but to gaze eagerly at a wild rose bush covered with plump red fruit. Like a practised acrobat, with a long tail for extra balance, the mouse worked its way quickly up among the branches, and biting off a rose hip it descended head-first to the ground. It sat there, a picture of pure contentment — the fruit rotating in its white paws and its sharp incisors sending chips of white and red pulp flying all over. The mouse was after the seeds tucked deep inside.

In the center of the road, only a meter (3.3 feet) away from the dining deer mouse, lay another set of larger tracks. Their maker — a male swift fox — had spent the last two hours scrounging in the grass for tasty grasshoppers and plump deer mice. Not far away the fox's black nose sniffed in the musky odor of the mouse where it had left its scent and urine at the edge of the road. With head lowered, eyes and huge ears trained dead ahead, the hunter trotted on silently, padded feet on cool sand.

Having devoured the rose seeds, the deer mouse was now bent over busily extracting a nasty rose spine from its hind foot. The mouse's sharp reflexes reacted instantly to a rustling sound from behind. The fox's jaws snapped shut on the spot just vacated by the mouse as it jumped into the cover of rose bushes and grass. The fox was not daunted by a mouthful of sand, and in one graceful arc through the air it landed with its two front paws, pinning the mouse's tail. The rodent twisted left and right, then rolled over on its back, exposing its white belly and kicking feet. The fox picked up the squirming prize in its mouth and headed for home in the early morning light.

Meanwhile, back at the fox den, the female fox lay curled half-asleep on top of the knoll, basking in the first rays of the sun. Her head rose periodically to check on her four pups that were romping in the grass below. At the appearance of her mate, she rose excitedly and trotted off to greet him. Within seconds the pups joined in the reunion, anxious to see what their father had brought home this time. Dropping the live mouse to the ground, the adult fox jumped back to avoid the melee. Somewhere under the pile of scrambling furry bodies the mouse managed to escape being trampled on and bitten with needle-sharp teeth. The father fox had brought home this prey to give the weaned pups practise in catching their own food, but he wasn't too impressed with their progress. The deer mouse was getting the better of them as they fought each other for the lead in pursuing the quarry.

The largest pup finally threw the others off, swept up the exhausted deer mouse, and bounded off toward the road. The other three pups seemed to think this was a game and they took after their sibling amid a chorus of yelps. The lead pup swerved around an oak tree and was cut off by another pup. The deer mouse was wet with saliva and one forearm dangled loosely, but it gained the strength to sink its long incisors into the pup's lip. More in surprise than pain the fox opened its jaw and was bowled over by the three attackers. The mouse used this moment of confusion to climb up the rough bark of the oak, out of reach of the yapping pack below. The two adults trotted over to investigate what the frantic calls were all about, but it was too late. The mouse sat shaking under a shiny oak leaf, high in a branch overhead. Three nights later, a fresh set of tiny tracks, showing only three feet, traced a course down the sandy road to the familiar rose bush.

Deer mouse

SWIFT FOX

Scientific name *Vulpes velox*
Family Wolves, Foxes, and Dogs (Canidae)
Order Carnivores (Carnivora)
Total length 80 cm (31.5 in)
Tail length 28 cm (11 in)
Weight males 2.4 kg, maximum 3 kg
(5.3 lb, maximum 6.6 lb);
females 2 kg (4.4 lb)

Color Just the opposite of the dark-tinted red fox, the swift fox is a mixture of pale colors that blend with the yellow parched grass and light-colored soils of the plains. The upper parts are buffy-gray; the sides, legs, and tail are orangy-tan, while the undersides are white.

Distribution and Status The swift fox was originally common from southern Alberta to southwestern Manitoba, and south to eastern New Mexico and northern Texas. Its exact distributional limits will never be known, for the species was wiped out or became rare in most parts of the range within half a century after the arrival of Europeans on the plains — an inadvertent victim of poison set for wolves and coyotes, and of habitat alterations by farming and livestock grazing. By 1900, only a few populations survived in the United States, and the last record in Canada was in Saskatchewan in 1928. A remarkable recovery began in the 1950s, probably related to less severe predator-control programs. New sightings and road kills were reported from most states where the species formerly occurred, as well as in Saskatchewan by the 1970s. The species has been (or shortly will be) reintroduced in a number of areas in both countries.

Short-grass and mixed-grass prairies are the native habitats of this beautiful fox. It has had to adapt to agricultural landscapes and practices, and is now found in cultivated fields, pastures, and road banks. Where the short-grass prairie grades into desert grassland in New Mexico and Texas, the swift fox comes into contact with the kit fox *(Vulpes macrotus).* Limited interbreeding has been reported, indicating the close relationship of these tiny foxes. The 2 have often been considered a single species, but are now believed to be distinct. The kit fox has longer ears situated closer together, a narrower snout, greater distance between the eyes, and a considerably longer tail. There are 9 other relatives (Genus *Vulpes*) spread throughout Eurasia, Africa, and North America including the red fox *(Vulpes vulpes).*

Food Although the diet of the swift fox has not been studied in detail, it appears to concentrate on mammals such as cottontails, jackrabbits, deer mice, pocket mice, and kangaroo rats. Ground squirrels are not commonly taken since they are active only in the day, while the fox is mainly nocturnal. Like many other predators, this fox is an opportunistic hunter and will devour ground-nesting birds, reptiles, amphibians, fish, and many kinds of insects, particularly grasshoppers and beetles. Excess prey is stashed under the snow or other cover. Analysis of stomach contents also reveals the common presence of carrion and vegetation such as grass and berries.

Reproduction and Growth Some accounts note that the swift fox is solitary outside the breeding season while other studies suggest that male and female are mated for life. There are even instances of 2 females associated with a single male. Perhaps all these associations are common under various circum-stances. Mating occurs from late December to early February in the southern range, with the young born from late February to early April. In northern regions the breeding season commences about one month later, with births in April and early May. One litter of 3 to 6 offspring is produced annually in an underground chamber which may or may not be lined with some material like grass. The pups are covered in short wooly hair, their eyes and ears open at 10 to 15 days, and weaning occurs at 6 to 7 weeks. The father may assist in the care and training of the offspring. Most pups come out of the den by early summer and reach adult size by late summer. They disperse from September to October and become sexually mature in their first winter. Few foxes live more than 5 years in the wild but one survived 13 years in captivity and a kit fox is reported to have reached over 20 years.

Remarks This appealing species is the smallest family member of the prairie quartet — swift fox, red fox, coyote, and gray wolf. It is a delicately formed fox characterized by enormous ears and bushy tail. The coat consists of a thick soft underfur and a sparse growth of longer guard hairs. The foot pads are heavily furred as well.

Occasionally found out of the den during the daytime, the swift fox is primarily nocturnal. It enjoys curling up in a sunny spot, particularly during the warmer midday hours of the winter. Communication with other foxes is accomplished by depositing scent along with urine and droppings, and by a range of calls including yaps, whines, growls, and various throaty sounds. A nightly trot of 10 km (6.2 mi) is not unusual over a home range around 25 km (15.5 mi) wide. The animal's life is centered around a den in which it spends more time than do other North American foxes and wolves. It may dig its own den or modify an existing burrow of a prairie dog or other animal, as long as the diameter is under 25 cm (9.8 in) — a size which precludes predators such as a coyote, wolf, or dog. The den is often used for many years and generally features several small nesting chambers and 2 to 9 entrances, each marked by a mound of earth. Bones of prey are commonly present in the side tunnels. Temporary shelters with a single entrance are scattered on the home range and are used for escape. Dens are often located on well-drained terrain but are also common in cultivated fields, pastures, banks, and fence rows, sometimes only 100 m (328.1 ft) from human habitations.

As its name implies, the swift fox literally streaks over the ground at 40 km (29.8 mi) per hour. Although it can run and dodge quickly when pursued, the fox must find refuge in an underground shelter in short order for it cannot maintain this pace as long as a coyote. The swift fox is noted for its rather unsuspicious nature, which has contributed in large part to the animal's disappearance over most of the range. It was easily trapped, shot, poisoned, and struck accidently by cars. The fur was never of much value in the fur trade.

Reintroduction of swift foxes has been carried out or is in the planning stages in a number of states and provinces. Several pairs of captive foxes are placed in a large prairie enclosure to prevent their running away into the surrounding countryside. It is only their offspring that are released, hopefully to remain in their familiar quarters. With so many animals being exterminated from their homelands it is extremely satisfying to see a marvellous species like the swift fox being successfully returned to its former territory with the assistance of wildlife biologists and the support of rural communities and the general public.

SWIFT FOX

DEER MOUSE

Scientific name *Peromyscus maniculatus*
Family New World Mice and Rats, Gerbils, and Hamsters (Cricetidae)
Order Rodents (Rodentia)
Total length (This mouse varies so greatly in size that ranges are given) 121 to 222 mm (4.8 to 8.7 in)
Tail length 46 to 123 mm (1.8 to 4.8 in) (grassland and forest subspecies, respectively)
Weight 15 to 30 g (0.5 to 1.1 oz)
Color The upperparts of the pelage show remarkable variation in color and generally match the background. Palest forms occur in desert and short-grass prairie, becoming progressively darker in dense forests and black lava fields. Color ranges from orange, pale grayish-brown, brown, to black. Deer mice from the Badlands of South Dakota are a bright yellowish-orange — among the most beautifully colored animals in North America. As the colored tips of the guard hairs wear off the gray underfur shows through. The underparts and feet are white and the tail is sharply bicolored (dark above, white below) and ends in a brush of stiff hairs. The ears are gray. The deer mouse goes through 3 molts in reaching the adult coat. Youngsters are a slate-gray color.
Distribution and Status The deer mouse is the most widely distributed small mammal on the continent, extending from Labrador and the Northwest Territories south to Oaxaca, Mexico. It is absent from the southeastern United States, where it is replaced by the oldfield mouse *(Peromyscus polionotus)* and the cotton mouse *(Peromyscus gossypinus)*. It has spread to hundreds of offshore islands as well. Over its enormous range the deer mouse occurs in numerous diverse habitats such as boreal forest, montane forest, pine forest, deciduous forest, to the edge of both alpine shrub tundra (4 343 m or 14,248.7 ft elevation in California) and subarctic woodland, chaparral, brushlands, savanna, grasslands, desert scrub, beaches, croplands, and pastures. Although this mouse frequents the shores of watercourses, it avoids sites that

are wet or flooded for long periods. An adventuresome rodent, it is usually one of the first mammals to invade disturbed areas such as logged or burned forest, drying floodplains, plowed or grazed agricultural land, and even recently cooled lava fields.

Peromyscus is a North American genus of mice represented by 49 to 61 species (the species status of many of them is unknown), including mostly tropical and many island forms. It is not uncommon to catch 2 to 4 species in a single trapline in many areas; some of these, like the white-footed mouse *(Peromyscus leucopus)*, are so similar in appearance to the deer mouse that experts often have difficulty identifying them, especially if the mice are not fully grown.
Food The deer mouse is basically a seed eater and is most abundant in places like fence rows and the edges of grainfields where plenty of seeds are available through much of the year. The mouse gathers these on the ground or climbs nimbly into bushes or even tall trees to reach seeds and nuts. When grasshoppers, beetles, caterpillars, and spiders are abundant in summer, these invertebrates may form over half the diet. Some green vegetation is also devoured, but the mice never overgraze the leaves, bark, and roots of plants as do many voles. Fruit and mushrooms are relished in season. As autumn approaches seeds, which are collected and carried in the mouse's internal cheek pouches, are cached in underground chambers for use in winter. The animal also stores food in the form of body fat. Water is lapped up when available on the ground and as dew, but mice dwelling in arid regions must survive long periods with the limited water obtained from their food. Sometimes the deer mouse reingests its droppings, which provides further nutrients.
Reproduction and Growth Deer mice produce 3 or 4 litters a year over most of the range, reduced to one or 2 at northern and high-elevation extremes. In southern and central regions births occur in every month of the year, with peaks in January to April and June to November (south), and March to October

(central). Breeding is restricted from April to September in the north and on mountain tops. The 4 (one to 9) young are carried for a term of 22 days, which can be increased to 27 days if the mother is still nursing a previous litter. Females may come into heat soon after giving birth. One captive female actually produced 42 young in 11 litters within one year.

The baby mice are usually born underground or inside a hollow log or tree. They are pink, hairless, and weigh only about 1.6 g (0.06 oz). They squirm and suckle almost immediately, their eyes open at 14 days, running occurs at 2 weeks, and weaning at 4 weeks. The father may return to help care for and train the family. Most offspring leave home by 5 weeks, but northern subadults may remain with the female during the cold winter months. In spite of dispersal of young to nearby sites, there is much inbreeding. Females usually mate at about 7 weeks (occasionally as early as 32 days) and males from 4 to 8 weeks. The average lifespan is one year, but in captivity deer mice continue to reproduce up to 4 years and live for 8 years.
Remarks The deer mouse is an attractive, alert creature with bulging black eyes, impressive ears, and an elongated snout with flaring whiskers on either side. The pelage is silky soft and particularly long and dense in northern mice in winter. About 69 subspecies (geographic races) are presently recognized, reflecting the considerable variation in body form, function, and behavior arising through natural selection to local conditions. At opposite extremes are forest mice with large-sized bodies, ears, tails, and feet; and grassland-desert mice with short features. While most pairs or groups of adjacent subspecies show intergrading characteristics where they meet and breed freely, certain pairs (e.g., forest and grassland forms in east-central North America) remain distinct, suggesting various mechanisms have developed that prevent interbreeding. In fact, the latter subspecies would be recognized as full species were they not believed to be genetically tied through a common circle of other nearby subspecies. Perhaps in time, should breeding cease through the intervening subspecies, the pair will have reached species status.

The burrow, which may be dug entirely by the mouse or be simply a renovated hole, may extend up to 10 m (32.5 ft) with various branches and is generally about 10 cm (3.9 in) below the surface. The mouse spends most of the daylight hours sleeping in the nest, but come darkness it engages in long treks over its home range of 0.5 to 2 ha (1.2 to 4.9 a). With high speed it runs, bounds, climbs, and swims until it is familiar with much of the area. While the mouse takes advantage of cover such as logs, rocks, banks, and vegetation, it does not restrict its travels to well-defined runways as do voles. The mouse pauses to nibble a tidbit here and lap a quick drink there, preferring to return to eat a few hours later rather than gorging at one time. When it chances to meet another deer mouse, the 2 stretch forward, cautiously touching noses. Submissive gestures are closing the eyes and folding the ears. If frightened or tense, they freeze, drum the ground with the front feet, or quiver their long tails. Aggression is displayed by wide-open eyes, erect ears, plus threat squealing. Generally peace is established through mutual grooming, sometimes leading to sexual mounting if the 2 are male and female. Should a fight

Continued on p.238

DEER MOUSE

Black-footed Ferret

The green sea of grass stretched away to the horizon, broken only by hundreds of brown earthen mounds that resembled tiny volcanoes. Here and there white-tailed prairie dogs could be seen chasing each other or grazing in the short grass. While most of these pudgy animals went about their evening business, three individuals suddenly stood up straight as bowling pins and watched something intently. About twenty meters (65.6 feet) away, a rounded black and white head extended out of a prairie dog burrow and surveyed the busy scene. The three inquisitive rodents mustered up their courage and began creeping toward the masked creature that had invaded their town. With only three meters (9.8 feet) separating them, the black-footed ferret suddenly dropped below ground, sending the prairie dogs jumping backward in fright. First one brave prairie dog, then the others, approached the edge of the burrow where they sniffed the strong musk of the ferret. Then, dangerously turning their backs to the mound, they began furiously digging and kicking soil down the hole. Ten minutes later the burrow was completely sealed and they ran back to join the others, perhaps thinking they had rid the colony of the menace.

Around eleven o'clock that night, the earth plug shuddered, then collapsed. Out backed the ferret, hauling soil tucked between its forelimbs and chest. Repeating this procedure a dozen times, the ferret left a two-meter (6.6-foot)-long trench of earth leading away from one side of the burrow entrance. As it kicked the last of the soil away, four more heads popped out of the hole to see what mother ferret was doing. Coax as she might, her offspring would not come all the way out. Although half grown, they were extremely nervous at leaving the security of their den which angled downward to a nest chamber four meters (13.1 feet) below the surface.

The adult ferret disappeared into the night and returned a half hour later, dragging the heavy limp body of a prairie dog by the neck. Although the prey had long since stopped struggling, the hunter seemed hesitant to release her hold. Panting heavily from exertion, her teeth were still deeply imbedded in the creature in a powerful death grip and her eyes gleamed with the excitement of the kill. Perhaps satisfied that the animal would not escape, or that no other predator was around to steal what she had won, the ferret finally relaxed her jaws, leaving the prairie dog to slump in a heap. Several drops of hot red blood appeared from the puncture wounds and the odor stimulated the ferret to lick them up. But instead of ripping open the belly and feasting, she lifted the heavy body and dropped it down the hole, then stretched out on her belly along the worn trough. She could hear her offspring hissing and tearing the prairie dog apart. Feeding her large hungry family for the past two months had left her exhausted. It was time they learned how to hunt for themselves.

By three o'clock in the morning all five ferrets had eaten their fill and were now resting, curled around and on top of each other. Not long after, the female's head again appeared at the entrance, watching and sniffing for five minutes to ensure that all was safe. Then she emerged and called to the four youngsters, but still they would not come all the way out. Tiring of this hesitancy the female grabbed each little ferret in turn by the scruff of the neck and rudely pulled it into the outside world. Then off she led them, bounding gracefully in single file, to another burrow where the youngsters would learn how to dig out prairie dogs.

By early August, the ferret family had cleaned out their local food supply which made it necessary to move farther along the edge of the prairie dog colony. The young were almost full grown now and appeared sleek and bright in their new coats beside their rather thin and bedraggled-looking mother. She pushed them away when they tried to nurse. Soon they hunted and played less often together and sometimes slept in separate burrows. By September the female was alone, having completed her task of raising a family for this year. But instead of regaining her health she became too ill to venture far from her burrow. The landowner had used poison in an attempt to control the prairie dogs and the ferret had eaten several of the contaminated rodents. She died curled up in her burrow, unaware that her four offspring had dispersed to safe colonies in an adjacent grassland refuge.

DEER MOUSE *continued from p.235*

break out, the 2 mice push with the paws and then rush and bite each other. Sometimes they lock belly to belly and roll about, biting and kicking all the while until one breaks free and runs away.

Forest-dwelling deer mice are expert climbers, as I once found out on releasing one from a trap. Instead of running away over the ground, this individual headed for a balsam fir and then scooted straight up the trunk till I lost sight of it at a height of 7 m (23 ft). Placing other deer mice in bushes, I watched them use their long tails as a balancing rod and as a fifth leg for support.

These mice do not exhibit regular population cycles like some voles and lemmings, but often reach high densities. Because of their abundance and wide occurrence, they form a major part of the diet of many carnivores. While 3 years is an exceptionally long life for a wild deer mouse, captives have survived over 8 years. Interestingly, life expectancy of mice living in alpine regions is longer than mice inhabiting lower elevations on the same mountains. A lower rate of life processes (metabolic rate) in the alpine mice may be an adaptation to the lower temperatures and shorter growing season of their food plants, and therefore, of the animals.

BLACK-FOOTED FERRET

Scientific name *Mustela nigripes*
Family Weasels (Mustelidae)
Order Carnivores (Carnivora)
Total length males 530 mm (20.9 in); females 500 mm (19.7 in)
Tail length 128 mm (5 in); 125 mm (4.9 in)
Weight 600 g, maximum 1 078 g (1.3 lb, maximum 2.4 lb); 550 g, maximum 854 g (1.2 lb, maximum 1.9 lb)

Color This ferret is handsomely colored with a yellowish-brown coat and striking black markings across the white face, ears, terminal third of the tail, and the legs. The underparts are lighter than the sides. The top of the head and along the middle of the back are brown. Males have a blackish-brown stripe on the belly. Young animals are a slightly lighter color than adults. The black mask is thought to disrupt the image of the ferret's head while sticking out of its burrow, so that prey or predators have difficulty in perceiving the ferret's face. The black color may also relieve strain of the night-sensitive eyes from bright sunlight reflected from light-colored soil or snow.

Distribution and Status The black-footed ferret formerly occurred over a large region (40 million ha or 160,000 sq mi) of short and mixed grassland from Alberta and Saskatchewan south to Arizona and Texas. In fact, its range was closely related to the distribution of the black-tailed prairie dog *(Cynomys ludovicianus)*. Typical habitat was flat or gently rolling hills of clay or silt which supported buffalo grass, needle grass, blue grama, western wheatgrass, and a variety of forbs. Although occasional sightings are still reported from many sections of the range (e.g., Saskatchewan, North Dakota, and Montana), there seems little doubt that most of the surviving population of this endangered species now lives in Wyoming and South Dakota. A 1984 population estimate of the colony near Meeteetse, Wyoming was 129 individuals. This species was never common and it remains

one of the rarest mammals in North America. The closely related polecat *(Mustela eversmanni)* of the Eurasian grasslands is not endangered and has actually increased its range in recent years. During the Ice Age the polecat spread from Siberia into Alaska, but has since disappeared on this continent. The polecat and black-footed ferret may, in fact, be the same species, and are almost identical in size and color.

Food The ferret's long thin body and large front claws are well suited to hunting prairie dogs in their subterranean burrows. It is generally believed that ferrets are so dependent on prairie dogs (including the black-tailed, white-tailed, and Gunnison's prairie dogs) that they cannot establish permanent populations outside prairie dog range, although single ferrets were sometimes found far from prairie dog colonies. Ferrets are known to eat mice, thirteen-lined and Richardson's ground squirrels, cottontails and jackrabbits, birds and their eggs, snakes, and insects.

Reproduction and Growth Black-footed ferrets are solitary animals and it is only during the spring breeding season that the 2 sexes come together. Mating occurs, presumably underground, in March or April and an average of 4 (one to 5) babies is born 42 days later in May or June. There is no delay in embryo development (delayed implantation) as occurs in many other members of the weasel family. The young are nursed from the mother's 6 mammae. The male may remain in the area but does not assist in raising the young. It is a full 2 months (early July) before the half-grown ferrets venture aboveground. The offspring reach adult size by the end of August and leave home shortly thereafter. Both males and females become sexually mature at one year of age and may live for 5 years in nature, 12 years in captivity.

Remarks The black-footed ferret is mainly active aboveground for several hours after dark and then again before sunrise. It digs out prairie dogs at night and kills them with a swift bite to the neck. On some nights, particularly if the weather is bad, the ferret comes to the

surface for only a few minutes or remains in its den for days at a time. During spring and fall, diurnal activity increases and the animal spends hours basking in the sun on top of its burrow. It does not hibernate in winter and individuals have been seen out in temperatures as low as -28 °C (-18.4 °F). A ferret sometimes slides down snowy hillsides on its belly and travels under the snow. When prairie dogs are hibernating (December to March) in their sealed burrows, the ferret is forced to dig out its prey. As much as 50 l (4 gal) of soil might be excavated to the surface in a single night. Average nightly excursions cover 2.2 km (1.4 mi), which increases to 5.9 km (3.7 mi) in the breeding season. This species has been known to disperse 8 km (5 mi) from its home.

The normal gaits are walking and a bounding gallop. The ferret is not especially fast, for prairie dogs occasionally outrun them. The ferret can jump 2.5 m (8.2 ft) in one bound, which sometimes lands it on a prairie dog's back. Young ferrets are playful and enjoy leaping back and forth, chasing, wrestling, and turning somersaults. A ferret can hiss, chatter, and even bark. Its sense of hearing and smell are acute, but it has difficulty locating prey by sight until the prey moves. Droppings are generally deposited in an underground chamber, but urine marks are common at the den entrance.

The ferret was first described in 1851, though the native people of the plains were long familiar with it. With the tilling of the soil and extermination of prairie dogs, the black-footed ferret has almost become extinct. Other causes of mortality are trapping, auto traffic, birds of prey, coyotes, bobcats, badgers, rattlesnakes, and disease such as distemper and tularemia. There are fewer than 20 specimens known in museums. The life history of this species is poorly known because of its scarcity and subterranean habitat. Unfortunately, attempts to breed it in captivity have ended in failure. Since eradication of prairie dogs continues on private lands, the only chance for survival of this fascinating species seems to be to establish the animal in refuges and parks where sizeable colonies of prairie dogs occur.

BLACK-FOOTED FERRET

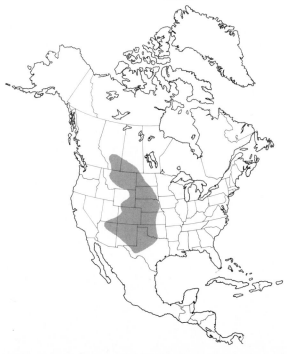

PRONGHORN

Scientific name *Antilocapra americana*
Family Pronghorn (Antilocapridae)
Order Even-toed Ungulates (Artiodactyla)
Total length males 140 cm (55.1 in);
females 135 cm (53.2 in)
Tail length 11 cm (4.3 in); 10 cm (3.9 in)
Weight 50 kg, maximum 70 kg
(110 lb, maximum 154 lb);
40 kg (88 lb)

Color The upperparts and tail are tan, while the underparts, rump patches, and 2 throat bars are white. The mane, snout, and horns are blackish in both sexes, and the buck sports a black triangle under each ear. The young are grayish-brown with a white rump and develop adult coloration at 3 weeks.

Distribution and Status Pronghorns were originally found over most of west-central North America from Alberta to Manitoba south to Baja California, central Mexico, and eastern Texas. They now remain on only a fraction of their former range in dozens of small isolated units. Major populations occur in Oregon and in a broad belt running from Saskatchewan south to New Mexico. The species has been introduced with some success in Washington. Pronghorns live in short-grass and mixed-grass prairie, desert grassland, and sagebrush-grassland from sea level in the south to northern alpine meadows up to 3 400 m (11,555 ft) elevation. Key habitat factors include rolling hills and a proper mixture of forbs, grasses, and shrubs, with vegetation covering over half the ground. Most live in regions with annual precipitation of 25 to 35 cm (9.8 to 13.8 in). They commonly roam over dry alkaline plains, badlands, sagebrush flats, and pastures.

Pronghorns are thought to have numbered 40 million when Europeans arrived on the grasslands. Hunting, fencing, and loss of habitat drove the population down to precariously low levels in the early 1900s — 13,000 in the United States, 2,400 in Mexico, and 1,300 in Canada. Enforced hunting regulations, sanctuaries, and returned habitat have enabled this graceful prairie dweller to rebuild its numbers to the point where hunting is per-

mitted in some regions, with an annual harvest of 40,000. The total population has stabilized at 500,000, but the species is still declining in Mexico. Herds of pronghorns, some numbering over 1,000, can be seen in numerous parks and refuges, and highway travelers are often delighted to see individuals standing on adjacent hillsides in many parts of the west. The pronghorn is the last surviving member of a North American family which was widespread and abundant during the Pliocene and Pleistocene (within the last 5 million years). Extinct relatives from at least 13 genera had a variety of pronged, spiraled, and multiple sets of horns.

Food At least two-thirds of the pronghorn's diet is composed of forbs such as clover, lupin, wooly senecio, and cut-leaf daisy. It is particularly fond of flowers and fruits. Sagebrush, rabbitbrush, cedar, prickly pear cactus, and other shrubs are browsed year-round but are more important in winter, along with dry leaves and grasses like blue and side-oats grama. Crops such as wheat and alfalfa are sometimes eaten as well. The animal's 32 teeth are high crowned and continue to grow throughout life — adaptations to the gritty food. Since grass seldom plays a dominant role in the diet, pronghorns do not seriously compete with cattle, but sheep leave little for pronghorns to eat. They will drink if water is available, but they can also obtain sufficient moisture from their forage except in the severest of droughts.

Reproduction and Growth Groups of adult males break away from the winter congregations in early spring, and some bucks begin to stake out territories with piles of droppings, and urine and scent marking as early as March. The rut lasts from July to early October in the south, mid-August to mid-September in the north, though bucks produce sperm through most of the year. A courting buck performs an elaborate ritual of prancing, head swinging, erecting its mane and rump patches, lip smacking, whining, and emitting scent from glands on the back and under the ears. Dominant bucks select the best forage sites and

protect their territory or harems of females from other males. Disputes between bucks involve staring, wheezing, teeth grinding, and fights using their pronged horns. About 252 days after conception, twins (occasionally one or 3) are dropped to the ground while the female is in standing position. While the fawning season starts as early as February in the south, most are born in May and June in the north. The fawns weigh 2 to 5 kg (4.4 to 11 lb) at birth, are able to stand and nurse from the doe's 4 mammae within one hour, and can run quickly at 3 days. The doe hides them separately in the grass, hopefully to avoid detection from predators. The bond between the doe and the fawn remains strong throughout the winter, but the youngsters like to gather by themselves to chase and play. A few females breed at 5 months of age, although most wait until 15 months. Yearling males are capable of breeding, but likely do not have the opportunity since they must compete with older and stronger bucks. Mortality rates are high for the fawns, but many pronghorns survive 7 to 10 years in nature, and occasionally up to 15.5 years in the wild and in captivity.

Remarks The pronghorn is a thickset animal with thin legs, pointy ears, pronged horns, and a striking color pattern. Long black eyelashes offer the prominent eyes some protection from the intense glare of the sun. While it has excellent vision and can detect movement at a distance of over 6 km (3.7 mi), it often has problems identifying the object, and will frequently approach for a closer look — a habit that was well known to native hunters. The pronghorn is North America's swiftest land animal and anyone who has ever witnessed the flight of a herd will never forget the experience. When alarmed the animal is capable of reaching speeds up to 86 km (53.4 mi) per hour for short bursts, with leaps of 3.5 to 6 m (11.5 to 19.7 ft). A herd can gallop at 48 km (29.8 mi) per hour for as long as 6 km (3.7 mi). The lungs and windpipe are relatively large to facilitate a rapid exchange of oxygen for carbon dioxide waste. Much of the weight while running is borne by the front hooves which contain pads of cartilage to cushion the shock and reduce noise. Only the third and fourth digits are present, no dew claws as in deer. The animal frequently shakes its body after running. Speed, shrubby cover, and depressions in the terrain are used to avoid predators such as wolves, coyotes, bobcats, eagles, and people.

The coat is composed of a wooly undercoat and coarse brittle guard hairs which can be raised or lowered to permit the escape or conservation of body heat. Particularly erectile are the 10-cm (3.9-in) long hairs of the mane as well as those of the white rump patches which flash a warning to other pronghorns many kilometers away. One of the most unusual features of this amazing animal is the set of horns that is formed and shed annually. Each winter the skin covering the 2 blade-like bony outgrowths of the skull begins to lay down a new layer of horn and hair beneath the old set. A front prong develops in the male (usually absent in the female) and by late summer the horns reach a length of 20 to 40 cm (7.9 to 15.8 in) in males and less that 12 cm (4.7 in) in females; some females are actually hornless. Following the rut the underlying skin loosens from the horn and it falls off (generally in October or November). Horns begin to grow as early as 2 months of age in

Continued on p.244

PRONGHORN

Pronghorn

As far as the eye could see, brown grass and patches of gray sagebrush covered the rolling prairie landscape, the gnarled bushes matching the color of the somber sky. The chill autumn air had sent most creatures south or underground. The only movement was an occasional wave of the grass in response to the wind. Suddenly, far off on a distant hill, something began to stir. As if by magic, patches of the brown and white ground took the shape of miniature horse-like creatures, no more than a meter (3.2 feet) high. Within seconds eighteen pronghorns were on their feet. Each animal's big black eyes watched intently as a tumbleweed bounced down a hillside and was snared by the sage. Perhaps it was the call of several coyotes or the falling temperature, but the herd was becoming increasingly restless. As they began grazing, shivers ran along their coats.

Before Europeans had come to the grasslands, the pronghorn herds had migrated southward about eighty kilometers (50 miles) to reach winter range at lower elevations. There, over a thousand head had found sufficient forage under the thin snow cover. But this was now cattle country, and numerous woven-wire fences effectively blocked pronghorn herds from their traditional paths. Though each animal could easily jump over the fences, they never dared to try. Such barriers had never existed in the featureless sea of grass and bush where the species had evolved. The animals were forced to crawl or dive under a fence if pressed by a predator.

The pronghorns fed for two hours, then bedded down in a valley to ruminate their meals. In the black of the night the wind began to howl around them and snowflakes whirled past, catching in their long sweeping eyelashes. Each animal automatically adjusted the position of its coarse, air-pocketed guard hairs to slow the loss of precious body heat. Beside each doe lay its young of the year, fully weaned but still dependent on its mother for security and guidance. Although the young were alarmed at the storm's fury, the adults had experienced wind and snow before. But this was not to be a typical blizzard.

By morning thirty centimeters (12 inches) of snow had accumulated on the ground — a critical depth that signaled problems of movement and feeding for the herd. The storm had struck so quickly that the dominant buck had no opportunity to lead his band into the shrubby growth of an adjacent valley two kilometers (1.2 miles) away. The pronghorns remained bedded down as the drifting white granules engulfed each animal. The air was so thick with blowing snow that they could not see one another. The adults' temperature dropped 3°C (5.4°F), the calves' even lower. For two days the blizzard raged on, until the whole countryside seemed to suffocate under the white blanket. Farmers were unable to leave their ranches to rescue cattle, which were perishing from exposure.

When the clouds finally blew away, exposing a delicate blue sky, the land was white and totally quiet. Within the valley, only twelve pronghorns rose on their thin legs, shaking off the snow from their coats. Each doe nudged the snow from her offspring and attempted to push it up on its feet, but the fawns continued to lay curled up, frozen and lifeless. Resigned to their losses, the does finally followed the deep trail broken by the bucks as they staggered up to the crest of the hill to look for food. Their struggle to survive the effects of the blizzard had just begun.

Bison

About four and one-half million years ago, in the broadleaf evergreen forests of southern Asia, there lived a large, horned mammal called *Proleptobos*. This ox-like creature gave rise to another browser *Leptobus* about three and one-half million years ago, which spread throughout southern and central Eurasia, and survived until the relatively recent Pleistocene Ice Age. This race was probably the direct ancestor of groups of wild cattle known as *Bos* and *Bison*. This radiation occurred at a time of expansion of coniferous forest at high latitudes and mountains, and of grassland (steppe) in temperate regions, to the detriment of broadleaf forests upon which many big herbivores originally depended. With numerous competitors for food and the existence of large predators, these cattle responded by increased development in both body size and horns (useful in combat and a determining factor in social rank).

Two million years ago, animals identifiable as *Bison* evolved from *Leptobos*, including *Bison sivalensis* — an inhabitant of woodlands and forest openings. Expanding its range throughout Europe and Asia, this species split off another evolutionary line leading to *Bison priscus* and *Bison alaskensis* — the former two of which were contemporaries in Siberia. During a glacial period of the Northern Hemisphere about one and one-half million years ago, a land bridge hundreds of kilometers wide formed between Siberia and Alaska. This arose as a result of vast amounts of sea water being tied up as glacial ice (lowering sea level up to 100 meters or 328 feet), and perhaps regional uplift of the land and the accumulation of glacial deposits of soil and gravel. Since *Bison sivalensis* and *priscus* were already adapted to living in a cold climate supporting coniferous woodland and shrubland, these species traversed the Bering land bridge over many generations and entered Alaska — marking the first appearance of bison in the New World.

The land bridge was once again submerged by the sea as the glaciers melted back, while the bison herds rapidly occupied the western and central regions of the continent. In time (about 1.2 million years ago) *Bison sivalensis* evolved into two new North American species. *Bison latifrons* — the giant bison — was the largest bison of all time and sported a two-meter (6.6-foot) spread of horns which curved inward at the tips. It inhabited northern forests and woodlands, along with such a fascinating fauna as the American mastodon, wooly mammoth, stag moose, Jefferson's ground sloth, woodland muskox, saber-toothed cat, and dire wolf.

Also large in body size but with smaller horns and denser growth of hair was the more southern *Bison antiquus*. It lived in grassland and savanna (occasional trees spread amid grass) in the company of the Columbian mammoth, Yesterday's camel, Shasta ground sloth, American lion, Scott's horse, large-headed llama, and bone-eating dog. This species' distribution was enormous, ranging from Beringia (the land bridge and Alaska) all the way south to the tropical savanna of Mexico. During this period populations of *Bison priscus* and *Bison alaskensis* spread far to the south, with ranges extending from Asia to Mexico.

The Wisconsinan glacial period (at a maximum around 30,000 to 20,000 years ago) was a disastrous time not only for bison but for almost all large mammals in the Northern Hemisphere. It was a period of rapid changes in both climate and vegetation. The final blow for many species was hunting by native people who had relatively recently wandered over the Bering land bridge. *Bison latifrons, priscus,* and *alaskensis* all became extinct (around 25,000 to 15,000 years ago), while *Bison antiquus* survived in the Great Basin and the southwest, coming close to extinction (especially from 11,000 to 9,500 years ago). With the subsequent expansion of grassland, bison numbers rebounded again, and *Bison antiquus* became *Bison bison* (the modern bison) around five thousand years ago.

For many thousands of years plains and forest tribes of native people relied on bison as the main provider of meat, robes, and other needs. Along with drought, fire, and winter storms, this hunting pressure kept bison numbers somewhat lower than full potential, but there still existed untold millions on the continent, particularly on the plains. Then a new factor appeared from the east which would alter the future of the species forever. People with firearms began decimating bison for meat and hides, culminating in many millions killed between the 1860s and 1880s. In these few short years the thundering herds vanished and the prairie sod was turned into farms and pasture. No longer would bison graze and fertilize the native prairie and forest glades, feeding a host of other living things including native populations.

PRONGHORN *continued from p.239*

males, whereas those of females do not appear until their second year. Maximum horn size is achieved by the fourth or fifth year.

Pronghorns are active any time but peaks of grazing occur after dusk and before dawn. When food is readily accessible in summer they move only 100 to 800 m (328 to 2,625 ft) in a day. With forage more difficult to find in winter, the animals frequently must travel 3 to 10 km (1.9 to 6.2 mi). Summer and winter range may be in the same general region or as much as 160 km (99.4 mi) apart. Most herds occupy a home range of 2 to 9 sq km (0.7 to 3.3 sq mi), while a male's summer territory averages from 0.2 to 4.4 sq km (0.07 to 1.6 sq mi). A herd may shift its home range over the year to take advantage of water and forage. Population densities of 0.6 to 3.3 per ha (0.2 to 1.3 per a) have been reported in good habitats. During the autumn and winter, loose herds (including individuals of all ages and both sexes) congregate, sometimes reaching upwards of over 1,000 head. It is not unusual to see pronghorns bedded down or grazing in proximity to cattle and mule deer.

When one considers the many extinct members of the pronghorn family (typified by such incredibly bizarre sets of horns) that once inhabited the North American plains, one wonders how the modern pronghorn managed to survive. Whether in Texas, Wyoming, South Dakota, or Alberta, each time I see a pronghorn, I can't help but think I'm looking at a living fossil.

BISON

Scientific name   *Bison bison*
Family   Cattle, Sheep, and Goats (Bovidae)
Order   Even-toed Ungulates (Artiodactyla)
Total length   males 350 cm (137.8 in);
females 210 cm (82.7 in)
Tail length   45 cm (17.7 in)
Weight   males 570 kg, maximum of 1 000 kg (1,256.6 lb, maximum 2,204.6 lb); females 450 kg (992.1 lb)
Color   The bison's front quarters and head are covered in long, dark brown woolly hair, while on the hindquarters the hair is shorter and lighter brown. The horns, hooves, and nose are black. The calf is reddish to orangy-brown for the first 3 months.
Distribution and Status   Bison formerly occupied most of central North America from south-central Northwest Territories to northern Mexico, and New York to California. There are 2 races — the plains bison dwelling in the prairie, semidesert grassland, and aspen parkland in the east and south; and the wood bison of the western mountains and the north, which inhabits coniferous woodlands, aspen parkland, and grass-sedge meadows.

Bison first appeared in the fossil record in the late Pliocene (about 3 million years ago) of India and China, their remains showing a close relationship to oxen *(Bos)*. Early kinds of bison inhabited Beringia (the wide corridor connecting Siberia with Alaska) and they entered North America at numerous times during the first half of the Pleistocene (2 to 1.5 million years ago). The most recent invasion by this route occurred only 20,000 years ago at the end of the Wisconsinan glaciation. Of the many kinds of bison that inhabited Eurasia and North America, such as the giant bison *(Bison latifrons)* and western bison *(Bison antiquus)*, only 2 species have survived. The wisent *(Bison bonasus)* formerly lived throughout much of Europe and possibly Asia, but was exterminated from its last 2 retreats-- in Poland in 1919 and the Caucasus in 1925. Fortunately the wisent was preserved in zoos and has been reestablished in both reserves, where it inhabits woodland and grassland.

Estimates of numbers of North American bison when settlers first arrived range from 50 to 75 million. Under the most deplorable hunting practices, bison were reduced to less than 1 000 animals by 1890, most of which lived in Canada and including 300 wood bison. Only Yellowstone National Park (Wyoming) and Wood Buffalo National Park (Alberta and Northwest Territories) continued to have wild-ranging herds, however plains bison were introduced and interbred with the native wood bison at both sites. A pure-blood herd of wood bison was discovered in a remote area of spruce forest and meadows in the Wood Buffalo reserve in 1957. The relationship between these 2 North American races is still under study.
Food   Food preferences of bison are quite variable among different herds and within the same herd through the seasons, however grasses predominate in the south and sedges in the north. Avens and other forbs (the main food of pronghorns) usually form less than 20 percent of the diet, while such shrubs as willow, sagebrush, Utah juniper, saltbrush, and prickly pear are browsed heavily by some herds. Important grasses include buffalo grass, blue grama, needle and thread grass, western wheatgrass, and reedgrass; choice sedges are slough sedge, sun sedge, and baltic rush.
Reproduction and Growth   The rut extends from mid-July to late September, and rarely, even later. Most mature bulls join the herds of cows and juveniles at this time. Searching through the group, a bull approaches a cow to examine her readiness to mate, sometimes prodding with his head to make her remain still. He sniffs her hindquarters and urine, then curls his upper lip and extends his neck which seem to be part of the odor-testing procedure. Females exhibit a 3-week estrous cycle which reoccurs until they become pregnant or the rut is completed. Cows still nursing last year's calves mate late in the season, which results in their bearing 2 calves in 3 years. The bull tends a receptive female for a few minutes to several days, rigorously keeping other bulls away. Most

BISON

matings are achieved by prime bulls from 6 to 9 years of age, and generally at night.

About 285 (range of 270 to 300) days later, the single calf (twins are rare) is born, most often from May to July but occasionally as early as March and as late as October. The 14 to 18-kg (30.9 to 39.7-lb) offspring stands within a few minutes to 1.5 hours and begins to suckle (in 6-minute bouts) almost immediately. It is able to run in 3 hours and is closely guarded by its mother. Weaning occurs from 7 to 12 months. Devouring around 5.5 kg (12.1 lb) of forage per day, the juvenile gains 0.5 kg (1.1 lb) per 24 hours. While some bulls and cows begin to breed as yearlings, most do not do so until 2 to 4 years of age, and continue until 15 years old. Adult size is reached at 4 years for bulls and 6 years for cows, but growth continues slowly thereafter until 7 and 9 years, respectively. Although bison have lived to 41 years in captivity, few surpass 20 years under natural conditions.

Remarks The bison is the heaviest land mammal in North America. Typical features are the broad forehead, short neck, shoulder hump, and short curved horns. The tail and legs are short, the hooves are rounded, and a distinct beard is present. The coat on the head, shoulders, and forelegs is shaggy, with a dense underfur, while the hindquarters are covered with short, straight fur. The cow has a smaller hump, thinner neck, and more slender horns which curve inward more than those of the bull. Food is bitten off with the lower incisor teeth and the upper lip, and the total of 32 teeth show considerable wear with age from the abrasion of chewing grass and attached soil particles. The stomach has four chambers, and bacteria and other microorganisms are present in the gut which assist in the breakdown of plant material. These animals are capable of a number of vocalizations such as grunts, bleats, snorts, roars, and sneezes. They also stamp their feet and grind their teeth loudly.

Bisons are gregarious creatures. There is much variation in herd size and changes in composition also occur through the year. The matriarchal herd consists of cows, yearlings, calves, and perhaps a few old bulls, and generally numbers from 10 to 60. Although bulls are sometimes solitary, they often form small bands. The breeding herd is formed by the union of one or more matriarchal and bull herds during the rut, usually between 20 to 50 animals. At times, herds may merge to total thousands of individuals. Social status begins to develop as early as 2 weeks of age and male calves are usually dominant over female calves — a characteristic which continues throughout life. Bulls (especially those over 4 years old and in rut), and cows accompanied by calves, often express their status through fighting — butting and hooking horns. Broken ribs are common and sometimes individuals are killed. Young are playful (chasing and butting), and while some remain shy, others become increasingly aggressive over the years and have been known to kill other large mammals like elk or to charge people. Almost any disturbance, such as the appearance of people, may trigger fighting between herd members, or cause a stampede, reaching speeds up to 60 km (37.3 mi) per hour.

A bison herd on the plains may use an area of 30 sq km (11.1 sq mi) in summer and 100 sq km (37 sq mi) in winter. An average of 3 km (1.9 mi) is covered in a day. Migrations were typical of many herds in search of more suitable climatic conditions, forage, water, shelter, or to avoid insects. Such movements consisted of short elevational shifts for some populations, while others undertook extensive annual treks of over 250 km (155.3 mi) in southern Canada each autumn and spring.

Bison feed mostly during the day; the night is spent resting or traveling, and occasionally grazing. The head, rather than a hoof, is used to sweep away snow. The animals do not hesitate to enter chest-deep water to reach emergent vegetation. Horning and rubbing on rocks, shrubs, and trees can actually inhibit the invasion of woody plants into grassland, while grazing and trampling favor the regeneration of preferred short-grass species over tall bunch-grasses. Bison also enjoy wallowing in dry or muddy sites which appears to relieve skin irritation, groom the fur, or have some sexual significance. In their travels, bison frequently follow established trails and do not hesitate to cross large, swift rivers. There are reports of bison attempting to cross thin ice and breaking through. As the herd continues ever-forward, the lead animals are pushed into the icy waters and drown. Apparently hundreds or even thousands of bison have perished in this manner in the course of a day. Wolves, grizzlies, and people are the main predators, while certain infectious diseases such as anthrax, tuberculosis, and brucellosis are a constant threat to whole herds. Severe winter weather occasionally leads to the death of individuals when combined with other factors such as poor health or inadequate forage.

Standing near an adult bison or watching an entire herd thunder across the prairie is a memorable experience. I remember climbing with my wife to the top of a high peak in the Wichita Mountains in Oklahoma, only to find the narrow trail blocked by the largest bull I had ever seen. He was lying down in the sun when he spotted us on the edge of a cliff as we searched for an alternate route. When he stood up and began pawing the dust, we decided not to challenge the king of the mountain; we retreated a little faster downhill that we had climbed up.

On several occasions officials from Riding Mountain National Park in Manitoba called the museum to inform us that a bison from their herd had died and was available for our research collection. One bull was hit by lightning, while another had been gored in a fight. A field crew was dispatched to pick up the latter specimen, and although it had frozen while on the ground, it still smelled rather strongly. On arrival at the museum loading dock, a winch was used to pull the enormous carcass from the van. Much to the amusement of onlookers, the bull's stiff legs shifted position and crashed through the van window. We had some difficulty convincing the insurance company how the accident really happened!

Mammals of the
Desert

Deserts are hot, arid regions that range from nearly lifeless wastelands to rich biological communities. Bunch grasses, succulents, bushes, and shrubs are characteristic, and even trees thrive where water can be reached by their long tap roots. Extensive deserts are found in southwestern United States and northwestern Mexico, southern and western South America, northern and southern Africa, Arabia, central Asia, and west-central Australia. Deserts cover one-fifth of the land surface and occur in warm areas where there is insufficient soil moisture (often less than 13 centimeters or 5.1 inches of precipitation annually) to support grassland. Many are on the lee side of mountains that strip the prevailing air masses of their water vapor. While some deserts may not receive any rain for over a year, others experience one or more annual rainy seasons. However, the evaporation rate far exceeds the precipitation rate (from 10 to 50 times), so that water actually is drawn up from the soil, leaving formerly dissolved salt or alkali as deposits on the surface in some places. The relative humidity is around 25 percent or lower at noon, but may reach the dew point during cool nights, forming a source of water for organisms in this parched landscape. When periods of drought are broken by a shower, desert plants quickly suck up the water through extensive, shallow root systems. Cloudbursts result in a rapid run-off to lower ground, since the hard-baked ground cannot absorb all the precious water. Plants and animals have developed numerous methods of conserving water and coping with the intense solar radiation which may average 90 percent of potential sunshine under the cloudless skies. Topography ranges from 86 meters (282.2 feet) below sea level (in the Mohave Desert) to high plateaus and mountain slopes at 1 830 meters (6,003.9 feet). The frost-free period is as short as 120 days in the north to a full year in the south. The mean monthly temperature in January ranges from 2°C to 21°C (35.6°F to 69.8°F) and in July from 21°C to 27°C (69.8°F to 80.6°F).

Arid regions of North America consist of the relatively cold Great Basin Desert in the north, and three hot southern deserts — Chihuahuan, Sonoran, and Mohave. The Great Basin Desert is the largest and extends from northern Arizona and northwestern Colorado to southern Oregon and Montana, at elevations over 1 220 meters (4,002.6 feet) between the Sierra Nevada - Cascade ranges and the Rocky Mountains. An annual precipitation (including snow) of 10 to 28 centimeters (3.9 to 11 inches) gives rise to monotonous gray-green stands of sagebrush, shadscale, and saltbrush. The second largest is the Chihuahuan, from southeastern Arizona and Texas southward into Mexico, mainly on the high plateau between the Sierra Madre Occidental and the Sierra Madre Oriental. Annual precipitation ranges from 8 to 51 centimeters (3.2 to 20.1 inches). Common plants are creosote bush, tarbush, mesquite, sotol, and an agave called lechuguilla. The Sonoran is third in size and encompasses most of Arizona, northwestern New Mexico, and south through the Mexican states of Sonora and Baja California. It is the most varied in life forms among the American deserts and includes the giant saguaro cactus and the boojum tree. Creosote bush, bur sage, palo verdi, yucca, and ocotillo are common plants, as are many annual plants that suddenly appear after winter and summer rainy seasons, amounting to 5 to 36 centimeters (2 to 14.2 inches) of rainfall each year. The Mohave Desert lies in southeastern California, southern Nevada, and into the western parts of Utah and Arizona. It is extremely arid, with only 6 to 13 centimeters (2.4 to 5.1 inches) of rainfall a year. The vegetation is sparse and consists mostly of creosote bush, bur sage, and the giant yucca Joshua tree.

Desert animals avoid high temperatures by night activity, burrowing, or finding a shady spot. Many have evolved the ability to cope with little or no free water. Typical herbivores of the desert are mule deer, mountain sheep, kangaroo rats, pocket mice, antelope jackrabbit, Gambel's quail, gopher tortoise, and crickets. Common carnivores and insectivores include the coyote, kit fox, spotted skunk, red-tailed hawk, roadrunner, crested lizard, sidewinder rattlesnake, gila monster, tarantulas, and ants.

Spotted Skunk and Brazilian Free-tailed Bat

The park naturalist thanked the audience for attending her evening talk on desert wildlife, and the crowd responded by clapping in appreciation for all the new facts they had learned. As the visitors wended their way from the amphitheatre back to the campsites, a young couple remained behind to ask the naturalist how they might see some of the creatures shown in the slide presentation. They had traveled for days to reach this famous park and were anxious to take in all it had to offer. They did not know that before morning they would indeed have their wish. But meanwhile they decided to retire early, so they could cover the next day's hiking trail before the sun became too hot. Soon they were sound asleep, stretched out in their sleeping bags beside a little creek.

About eighty kilometers (49.7 miles) away another set of travelers was also intent on reaching the park that night to take in its rich resources. As if by clockwork the group began their preparations within the great hall at the identical time. They had made this journey many times before and knew how far they had to go. The hall was a limestone cavern situated sixty meters (196.9 feet) below the desert floor and the travelers were free-tailed bats — about ten thousand of them, clustered in huge patches on the ceiling and walls of the cave. Having slept all day, the bats began to stir and squabble, jostling each other for more space with their wings and toothy jaws. Like jet planes leaving base, the bats dropped from their perches and began wheeling around the chamber, warming up their cool muscles and checking out their radar systems. More and more took flight, till the room was a dizzying scene of flapping missiles, somehow avoiding collision with each other and the cold white walls. The fluttering of their wings created a tremendous rushing sound, much like an underground stream, and the temperature and humidity in the chamber began to increase slightly from the hectic activity. Several baby bats, still incapable of flight, tumbled to the floor, but no mothers seemed to care. Then, as if some leader had issued an order, the stream of bats flowed out along a corridor which led to the surface. As they departed, new recruits took wing, so that the air remained full of circling bats.

The light from the setting sun was still present in the western sky as the advance column of bats burst forth from the sunken cave entrance. Around and around in tight counter-clockwise circles they whirled, gaining altitude all the time as if being pushed up from below. The cone-shaped cloud rose sixty meters (196.9 feet) into the sky, then dissipated at the top as the bats spun off in small groups and headed towards their favorite hunting grounds for the night.

Back at the campground two playful and mischievous bandits awoke inside a hollow cottonwood tree and began chattering at each other in anticipation of adventures they might have that night. When their pointy heads popped out of the entrance to look around, a white patch between their eyes reflected in the moonlight, marking them clearly as spotted skunks. Almost as nimbly as squirrels they chased each other around the tree trunk and then, taking advantage of the thick furrows in the bark, they descended to the ground. With each step their rumps swung from side to side — a motion picked up by the plume-like, white-tipped tail. The trail along the creek led directly to the campsite of the sleeping couple where the skunks hoped to find some leftovers from supper.

Sniffing here and there, one skunk began tugging at the woman's hair while the other ran over the man's stomach. Amid shrieks and frantic manipulations to undo the sleeping-bag zippers, the campers tried to extricate themselves and locate the flashlight. To their horror, the beam suddenly highlighted two black and white striped skunks who were rather upset over all the commotion. One skunk assumed a horseshoe position, facing and aiming its rear at the noisy people. The second skunk's tail quivered over its head while its front feet stamped an alternating warning beat on the ground. Realizing full well what might happen any second, the couple began to back away slowly, caterpillar style, still trapped in their bags. At this strange sight, the closest skunk kicked up into a perfect handstand on its front limbs, with the long flowing white hairs of the tail drooping gracefully over its head. But the elegance and grace of this ballet were completely unappreciated as the couple beat a hasty retreat out of range and under the safety of an overhead light. The timing was most unfortunate, for at this very moment five of the free-tailed bats arrived on the scene and began scooping up flying insects that were attracted to the light. The couple reacted by racing for the safety of their car where they spent the remainder of a fitful night. The original park residents continued their foraging as if nothing unusual had happened.

SPOTTED SKUNK

Scientific name *Spilogale putorius*
Family Weasels (Mustelidae)
Order Carnivores (Carnivora)
Total length males 50 cm (19.7 in); females 47 cm (18.5 in)
Tail length 20 cm (7.9 in); 17 cm (6.7 in)
Weight 700 g, maximum 1.2 kg (1.5 lb, maximum 2.6 lb); 500 g (1.1 lb)

Color The coat is basic black with several horizontal white stripes running along the shoulders and neck, and several others (often broken into spots) in a vertical position on the sides. A white patch is always present on the forehead, and another below and in front of each ear. The end of the tail is white. No 2 skunks have the identical pattern of stripes.

Distribution and Status The spotted skunk has been recorded from southwestern British Columbia, Minnesota, and Pennsylvania, south to Costa Rica. It is notably absent from the New Mexico-Texas border region, the central Mississippi River area, and a number of coastal regions. Desert, short-grass and tall-grass prairie, woodland, and shrubland are all suitable habitats for spotted skunks, but seldom are they found penetrating dense timber (e.g., spruce-fir zone) or wetlands. They are fond of shrubby desert canyons and gulches, fields, cropland, and fence rows, often taking up residence under farm buildings. Individuals have been reported at elevations as high as 2 200 m (7,217.8 ft).

In the past, eastern and western populations of spotted skunks were thought to be distinct species (*Spilogale putorius* and *Spilogale gracilis*, respectively). The rare pygmy spotted skunk (*Spilogale pygmaea*) is the only close relative and lives in southwestern Mexico (Sinaloa to Oaxaca). Skunks are found only in the Americas. Other species found in North America include the striped skunk (*Mephitis mephitis*), the hooded skunk (*Mephitis macroura*), and 3 species of hog-nosed skunks (*Conepatus* spp.).

Food This skunk's diet is anything but specialized and includes a host of animal and plant material. Important items listed in food studies are small mammals (mice, woodrats, small rabbits), birds (eggs and nestlings), insects (grasshoppers, scorpions, beetles), reptiles, amphibians, fish, any carrion it comes across, fruit (cactus, grapes, mulberries, persimmons), nuts, and corn. There is an interesting report of a spotted skunk repeatedly kicking a chicken's egg backward from under its body until it broke against a wall.

Reproduction and Growth This species shows some remarkable differences in reproductive biology in various parts of the range. In eastern North America males become fertile as early as January, but most matings occur in March and April. Following a prebirth (gestation) period of 50 to 65 days, 5 (range of 2 to 9) young are born in May or June. In the western half of the range the mating season seems to occur in September and October, and the embryos (averaging 6) undergo a long rest period (180 to 200 days) before continuing their term next March or April. Thirty days later (April to June) the young are born. In Mexico and Central America births (averaging 4 young) may occur in any month, and some females produce 2 litters in a year, generally in the spring and summer.

The baby skunks weigh 22 g (7.8 oz), are covered in fine hair with the markings visible, and they cry continuously to be fed. The eyes open at 31 days, they begin playing at 36 days, can shoot musk at 46 days, and are weaned at 55 days. Full size is attained around 4 months, males become sexually active as early as 5 months, and females become pregnant at 9 or 10 months of age. Longevity in captivity is 10 years and 3 years under natural conditions.

Remarks The spotted skunk is slender, agile, and more weasel-like than the other larger skunks present on this continent. With short rounded ears, pointy snout, and dark eyes hidden against the black fur, it has an intelligent, alert expression. The glistening fur is dense and long, especially the white tail hairs. On each foot are 5 toes ending in sharp curving claws, those of the front feet being the longest. Thirty-four teeth line the jaws and are used for chopping food into small pieces. The animal is capable of making a variety of grunts and screeches, and is apparently quite playful in games such as chasing crickets. Dens are selected in rocky crevices, deserted burrows, brush piles, tree hollows, or under buildings, and a number of skunks may be found sleeping together. The home range is about 64 ha (158.1 a) but in spring the males wander as widely as 10 sq km (3.7 sq mi). More nocturnal than the striped skunk, the spotted skunk is seldom seen in daylight. In northern regions with a cold winter skunks become inactive for long periods and live off fat reserves. They do not truly hibernate, for their body temperature does not fall appreciably.

The spotted skunk's claim to fame is its repeated, 5-second-long handstands, demonstrated especially when it must aim high with its scent to protect itself. Generally, the animal discharges when on all fours, the white tail distracting the foe which receives the irritating and nauseating musk directly in the face. Owls, coyotes, foxes, and bobcats are the major predators while others fall victim to diseases such as rabies, distemper, and tularemia. Trapping pressure is light because of the low demand for the skunk's small coat. Rarely are spotted skunks struck along highways, a fate which befalls millions of striped skunks each year. Spotted skunks are easily tamed and like to feed on scraps from the table. While occasionally running into trouble in the chicken coop, this skunk is actually beneficial as far as humans are concerned, for it helps to keep mice and insects under control around farms and cabins.

BRAZILIAN FREE-TAILED BAT

Scientific name *Tadarida brasiliensis*
Family Free-tailed Bats (Molossidae)
Order Bats (Chiroptera)
Total length 100 mm (3.9 in)
Tail length 38 mm (1.5 in)
Wing span 300 mm (11.8 in)
Weight 12 g (0.4 oz)

Color The fur is dark brown or grayish-brown, with hairs that are white at the base. The underparts are lighter. Some individuals are bleached pale brown from the ammonia fumes present in the roost. White hairs or patches are frequently present on many bats.

Distribution and Status This is probably the most abundant bat in North America with its northern range extending to Oregon, Nebraska, and North Carolina. Strays have turned up still farther north in Illinois and Ohio. It has yet to be recorded in the Yucatan Peninsula of Mexico, but otherwise is distributed throughout the southern half of the continent including the West Indies, then south in a crescent-shaped range down the Andes Mountains to Chile, Argentina, and eastern Brazil (absent from most of the Amazon basin).

Over such an enormous region, the bats obviously roost and forage in many habitat types. Important natural communities are desert, short-grass prairie, pinyon-juniper and oak woodlands, meadows, and the edges of deciduous forest. They may be found from sea level to 2 800 m (9,186.4 ft) in elevation. A remarkable feature of this bat's seasonal distribution is the relationship between roosting sites and migration patterns. It is essentially a cave dweller in central North America (Nebraska

SPOTTED SKUNK

to Mexico, Arizona to Texas), where it congregates in incredible numbers from March to November (April to October at northern extremes). A total population of 100 million bats has been estimated for Texas, with 20 million in Bracken Cave (near San Antonio) alone. Carlsbad Caverns (New Mexico) may have originally housed 9 million and Eagle Creek Cave (Arizona) 10 million. Numbers of bats have declined drastically in some caves during recent decades, perhaps from pesticide poisoning obtained through insect food. While some bats remain behind in the caves, most migrate south in large flocks to northern or tropical Mexico — a distance of over 1 700 km (1,056.4 mi) for some individuals.

Conversely, in eastern and western parts of the range, free-tailed bats roost in buildings or tree hollows (in flocks up to 50,000) and most remain there year-round, hibernating during cool spells. A relatively small proportion of the population migrates southward.

The Brazilian free-tailed bat is one of 9 species in the genus *Tadarida*, with a combined range of North and South America, Europe, Asia, Africa, the Middle East, and Australia.
Food   The diet consists almost entirely of small moths under one cm (0.4 in) in size, which the bat detects using echolocation and sight, and sweeps up using its tail membrane. The bat often devours a third of its weight in insects each night, sometimes up to one-half.
Reproduction and Growth   These bats breed from late February to mid-April and individuals within a population generally mate at the same time so that births all occur within a short period. Bats that winter in Mexico usually arrive into the United States already pregnant. Females congregate in maternity colonies at low elevations while many males roost elsewhere, such as buildings or under bridges. The gestation period is 77 to 84 days, and the single young (twins are rare) is almost always present in the right horn of the uterus. June and July are the main months of birth. The young are born rump first, which may take 2 minutes to an hour. The female continues

to hang from the hind feet and assists the birth process if necessary by using her mouth. Offspring weigh about 2.7 g (0.1 oz) and are 25 mm (one in) long, blind, and naked. Each drinks about 0.85 g (0.03 oz) of milk a day. Milk is so abundant in the pair of mammae that it often oozes out, and even adult females have been found with milk in their bellies, which they must have obtained by suckling other females. The females leave the young bats hanging in squirming masses on the walls and ceiling of the roost and their activity helps keep them warm. Their body temperature can reach 42°C (107.6°F) even though the surrounding temperature is many degrees cooler. Returning females do not search out their own offspring; they nurse any youngsters that approach. If any young bats fall to the floor they are abandoned and soon perish. Flight is developed at 5 weeks. Females become sexually mature at 9 months, males at 18 months. Life expectancy remains unknown, but has been estimated at up to 18 years.

Remarks   This is a strange-looking bat with a naked, mouse-like tail extending beyond the tail membrane. It has wide, flaring ears that almost meet on top of the head and a deep vertical groove on the lips. The black eyes are sunken in a fold between the lips and ears. The fur is short and velvety, and is groomed by stroking with foot bristles and double claws on the hind toe. Thirty-eight sharp teeth line the jaws, and the canines are particularly large in males. The compact body and narrow wings are evidence that this bat is a swift, long-range flyer. When individuals are handled a strong musky odor is noticeable.

The evening and morning flights of the Brazilian free-tailed bat have become quite a tourist attraction at a number of caves. I was certainly impressed when I witnessed their emergence at Carlsbad Caverns in New Mexico. While some bats leave individually or return after only a short period of foraging, generally most bats depart the cave in bursts or in a continuous column which may last for hours. Five thousand to 10,000 bats leave the

entrance each minute and they fly in circles at about 55 km (34.2 mi) per hour. As the black column rises into the air or drifts at an angle over the landscape, the bats double their speed and break away singly or in small groups. Most reach their feeding grounds within 80 km (49.7 mi) (many Carlsbad Cavern bats fly to the Pecos River 65 km or 40.4 mi away), but some roam as far as 240 km (149.1 mi). When hunting, the bats fly at a height of 4 to 30 m (13.1 to 98.4 ft) and slow speeds of 16 to 24 km (9.9 to 14.9 mi) per hour. Just before sunrise the majority of the bats return at a leisurely pace to roost; late arrivals plummet straight down on folded wings from up to 300 m (984.3 ft) high and over 100 km (62.1 mi) per hour.

Predators of free-tailed bats during flight include owls, hawks, falcons, and Mississippi kite, while skunks, raccoons, opossums, and rat and coachwhip snakes attack them in roosts. Bat droppings and carcasses build up deep layers of "guano" on the cave floors, and these nitrate-rich deposits are mined as a source of fertilizer (formerly they were used to manufacture gun powder). Researchers who enter roosting caves must endure foul air (ammonia and carbon dioxide), slippery guano on the ground, and bats brushing and crawling over them. Though the bats seldom bite people, the hazard of contracting rabies from the airborne virus is a serious possibility. Immunity should be obtained by injections prior to the visit.

Brazilian free-tailed bat

BRAZILIAN FREE-TAILED BAT

Desert Pocket Mouse

For millions of years the mountain range of white gypsum stood glistening in the sun, as though it would withstand the elements forever. Imperceptively however, grains and pebbles showered down to the base of the mountains, testimony to the erosive powers of intense sun, running water, expanding ice, and persistent wind. Funneling in through passes, the prevailing winds picked up the white sand and drove it like a low mist over the flat desert floor. When it finally tired of this game the wind vanished, adding its load to the growing dunes. Occasionally wind storms returned to shift the abandoned piles of sand, and the massive creations moved in slow motion like giant amoebas, overriding each other and the desert vegetation in their paths.

The desert scrub was home to a variety of small mammals, including desert pocket mice — delicately built rodents, colored remarkably close to the brown sand on which they foraged for seeds each night. The mice sometimes left their little tracks over the ripples and slopes of the advancing edge of the white sands, but since there were no plants to provide food and shelter, the mice returned to their home burrows in the brown sand. Over the years certain protected areas of the white dunes finally stabilized sufficiently to allow yucca, grass, and other plants to gain a root-hold. As the vegetation gained in dominance, some of the pocket mice successfully invaded the new habitat and began to reproduce there. But their numbers remained lower than in the adjacent brown desert for a very obvious reason — their dark bodies showed up clearly against the white background, making them more susceptible to the kit foxes, coyotes, and owls that hunted along the dunes' perimeter with some regularity.

Perhaps it was only a matter of time, but one of nature's miracles finally happened. Half a meter (1.6 feet) down in the white sand a female pocket mouse gave birth to four tiny pink babies. Although they all looked the same at first, the firstborn took on quite a distinctive appearance when the juvenile coat grew in. Instead of the regular yellowish-brown color on the upperparts, this unusual offspring was definitely paler. This mutation in coat color had appeared on rare occasions in families of pocket mice living on the brown sand, but these pale mice had rarely lived to a breeding age because they were easily spotted by predators. On the white sand, however, the young pale female stood a slightly better chance of survival than its darker siblings. In fact, she was the only member of the family left alive when breeding season arrived the following spring. When she passed on her genes for pale coat color to several of her offspring, the grand experiment was underway. Ever so gradually, generation after generation, her descendants became progressively whiter and spread throughout the white sandhills. Now it was the original yellowish-brown pocket mice that were at a slight disadvantage. On the average, they failed to survive or to contribute as many young to the next generation as their whitish kin.

Several centuries of natural selection had dramatically generated a new population of desert pocket mice, beautifully adapted to blend in with their dazzling white world. Occasional interbreeding of white and brown mice along the edge of the dunes, as well as a rare appearance of a darker mouse in a litter of white, indicated a flexible strategy built into the genetic system of the mice, almost as if anticipating a need to meet future environmental changes.

DESERT POCKET MOUSE

Scientific name *Perognathus penicillatus*
Family Pocket Mice, Kangaroo Rats, and Spiny Mice (Heteromyidae)
Order Rodents (Rodentia)
Total length 200 mm (7.9 in)
Tail length 110 mm (4.3 in)
Weight 20 g (0.7 oz)
Color The yellowish-brown to yellowish-gray upperparts are sprinkled with black hairs and the underparts are white. The long tail is similarly colored, except for the tuft which is gray. Desert pocket mice in White Sands National Monument (New Mexico) and similar areas near El Paso (Texas) and Samalayuca (Chihuahua, Mexico) are white, closely matching the light-colored sand.

Distribution and Status This locally common mouse is known from southern California to the Trans-Pecos region of western Texas, and then south to the Mexican states of San Luis Potosi and Sonora. Its local distribution is tied closely to loose thin soils of sand (mixed occasionally with a little gravel), silt, and clay. It rarely enters packed gravel or rocky sites. The annual precipitation within its range is less than 30 cm (11.8 in), often considerably less, and is concentrated in one or 2 brief rainy seasons. This weather regime can only support desert scrub and dry grassland. As its name implies, this species inhabits some of the hottest and most arid habitats found on the continent, below 1 600 m (5,249.3 ft) elevation. Over most of this region creosote bush and saltbush form an evenly spaced, monotonous quilt of green, with plenty of bare soil showing between the vegetation. Other plants commonly found in this community are mesquite, catclaw, blackbrush, ocotillo, prickly pear cacti, and grama grasses.

The genus *Perognathus* contains 25 species, generally adapted to arid conditions, and found from British Columbia to Manitoba all the way to southern Mexico. The rock pocket mouse *(Perognathus intermedius)*, often found nearby the desert pocket mouse, is so similar in appearance that the skull must be examined to distinguish between the two. The family originated in North America, and one of the 5 genera (spiny pocket mice of the genus *Heteromys*) invaded forests of northern South America following the joining of the continents.

Food The desert pocket mouse is mainly a seedeater (granivore), with mesquite, creosote bush, broomweed, snakeweed, and various grasses being utilized extensively. Since seed production is seasonal, the mouse spends much of its time foraging (sometimes collecting thousands of seeds in an hour) and storing the kernels underground for use when food is scarce. Green shoots and insects are also eaten, providing important sources of protein and moisture. This and other species of pocket mice are able to extract and conserve sufficient water from their rather dry food — a critically important adaptation for their successful exploitation of desert environments.

Reproduction and Growth In the relatively cool northern half of the range, these pocket mice begin breeding in late February. Pregnancies peak in April and again in June and August as adult females raise a second litter and their spring-born young reach sexual maturity by summer. Four is an average litter size, with a range of 2 to 6. Young appear aboveground for the first time in May. They soon disperse to search for unoccupied range, for they are strongly territorial and intolerant of each other. Studies reveal that almost the entire population turns over each year, so that it is exceptional for an individual to live for 2 years. Surprisingly, pocket mice frequently survive 4 to 6 years in captivity, and a few have surpassed 8 years. Predation and the stresses imposed by the desert surely take their toll of pocket mice.

Remarks This is a medium-sized pocket mouse with a coarse coat, which usually lacks the rump spines present on a number of its look-alike relatives. The snout gives rise to a fine brush of whiskers, the eyes are prominent, and the ears are slightly pointed. Helping to balance the mouse while it hops or scampers over the ground is a long tail which is both crested and tufted on the end. The mouse often sits on its long, naked-soled hind feet, sifting through the sand ripples for seeds with blurring-fast movements of the tiny front limbs. Food items are quickly transferred to the fur-lined cheek pouches, and when the head begins to swell to double size with the load, the mouse returns to its storage chambers where the seeds are pushed out by the front feet. The home range seldom exceeds 0.3 ha (0.7 a) in size and the mouse digs a number of burrows in banks or under vegetation to escape from foxes, coyotes, badgers, snakes, and owls. The main burrow is rather shallow and easily dug up by predators, but the mouse often escapes by retreating down and blocking one of the many side tunnels. During cold weather or when food is scarce the pocket mouse becomes torpid inside its blocked burrow, lessening its need for energy and improving its chances of surviving until the situation improves.

The first time I made the acquaintance of the desert pocket mouse was along a mesquite-lined dry river bank at Terlingua, near Big Bend National Park in southern Texas. I remember becoming rather scratched from the thorny shrubs and I also had to keep an eye on the hundreds of bees seeking the sweet-smelling flowers. My efforts at placing the traps in just the right spots were rewarded with a fine series of the mice. It was fortunate I arrived to check the traps at an early hour, for the midmorning heat and the ants would have quickly spoiled the specimens.

Along with two other students and my professor, I once attempted to collect a few white pocket mice beside the boundary of the White Sands National Monument in southern New Mexico. After an exciting day roaming through and photographing this marvellous place, we hopped into our sleeping bags set up on cots to avoid such night creatures as rattlesnakes and scorpions. The full moon and billions of stars reflected off the white sand with such brilliance it seemed as if someone had left the lights on. Although I have slept for months in a tent in the arctic I have never experienced such cold as I felt that night. As soon as the sun went down the desert radiated its heat, built up to a daytime temperature of about 43°C (109.4°F) back into the atmosphere. By midnight I was folded up into a hypothermic ball, shivering to keep warm. My luck ran out when the bottom legs of the cot finally collapsed with my tossing, and inside the slippery nylon bag, I glided off the cot onto the cold white sand. To make matters worse we discovered the next morning that we had missed catching the famed white pocket mouse and had to settle for viewing a mounted specimen in the interpretive center. The next day we camped alongside the Kenzin Lava Flow and collected white-throated woodrats, Ord's kangaroo rats, western harvest mice, northern grasshopper mice, cactus mice, and several rock pocket mice. These pocket mice were taken among the black lava boulders, and I was fascinated to see their grizzled black color — so different from the brownish-gray typical of this species.

DESERT POCKET MOUSE

ORD'S KANGAROO RAT

Scientific name *Dipodomys ordii*
Family Pocket Mice, Kangaroo Rats, and
Spiny Mice (Heteromyidae)
Order Rodents (Rodentia)
Total length 265 mm (10.4 in)
Tail length 155 mm (6.1 in)
Weight 70 g, maximum 94 g
(2.5 oz, maximum 3.3 oz)
Color The long silky pelage is a yellowish-buff on the upperparts, with scattered black hairs along the back. The underparts as well as the flank stripes, upper lip, and around the ears and eyes are white. The snout whiskers arise from a black patch. The long thick tail is dark above and below, separated on the sides by white stripes. Juveniles are grayer, lacking the bright colors of the adults.
Distribution and Status Ord's kangaroo rat has the widest distribution of all 24 species of kangaroo rats, extending from Saskatchewan and Washington south to central Mexico. It is mainly restricted to sandy soils which permit easy burrowing. Sand dunes, blowouts, banks in farm and pasture lands, and dry floodplains are typical habitats where it becomes very abundant. Gravel, clay, and loamy soils are avoided. Plant cover may be quite variable, including grassland and shrub communities, but there are always plenty of bare patches of ground where the rat can bound unimpeded by vegetation.
Food This rat is predominantly a seedeater, gathering them on the ground or in low shrubs. Seeds of mesquite, ragweed, sunflower, creosote, dropseed, Russian thistle, grass, and grain may make up 90 percent of the diet in autumn and early winter. Vast quantities are stored underground where a slight covering of mold seems to make them more palatable and perhaps more nutritious. Fruits and insects such as beetles, moths, caterpillars, and ants, plus the leaves of sweet clover, sagebrush, grass, and thistle are eaten in great quantities when seeds are unavailable from late winter to early summer.

Reproduction and Growth The female comes into heat for 6 days, during which time she is courted by one or more males. Following much chasing and nudging, the couple mates repeatedly for several minutes, the male protecting himself by grasping the female's neck between his long incisors. The gestation period is 30 days and an average of 3 (one to 6) babies are born underground in a nest lined with plant fibers. The young remain in the nest for over a month, but reach adult size in 6 weeks. Females may begin breeding as early as 2 months of age. Kangaroo rats generally have 2 or more litters a year, but postpone breeding under adverse conditions such as drought and shortage of food. The breeding season varies greatly over the range, with births in June and July in Canada, May to September in the central United States, and August to February (cool part of the year) in the southern states. Captives have lived up to 10 years although the average life span in nature is 2 years and few live to 5 years.
Remarks This kangaroo rat is a remarkable rodent adapted to life in the desert and arid grasslands. The large size of its head is accentuated by 2 inflated bony ear capsules, which may be related to the delicate sense of balance needed during locomotion. The powerfully developed hind legs, with haired soles for traction on loose sand, can catapult the animal in 2-m (6.6-ft) hops at speeds up to 20 km (12.4 mi) per hour. With the help of the bushy-tipped tail, the rat can position itself in midair for a quick change in direction. A pursuer may also be distracted by the flashing white tail tip and flank stripes. Dust baths are an essential part of grooming the fur which otherwise becomes matted with excess conditioning oil produced by a large gland situated on the back between the shoulders.

This animal is known for its ability to survive without drinking free water, though it will lap up dew or raindrops when available. It obtains moisture from its diet and by oxidizing food substances like fats and carbohydrates. Water is conserved by several means. Minimal water is lost in the dry feces and urine, which is so concentrated by the kidneys (4 times more efficient than human kidney) that a drop on drying will leave crystalized urea. The rat avoids the heat of the day by sleeping in its blocked tunnel, where the soil moisture lessens water loss through evaporation from the lungs and skin. Therefore, there is no need to lose valuable water to cool the animal by sweating. Surprisingly, the regulation of temperature seems poorly developed, for the animals may enter torpor below 21°C (69.8°F) and are stressed above 27°C (80.6°F). In the north, these rats become dormant (but do not truly hibernate) for many months in the winter. In southern populations they remain active year-round, even emerging in spite of a thin cover of snow. Their main enemies are foxes, coyotes, badgers, skunks, owls, and snakes, some of which are mainly dependent on this rodent for food.

Kangaroo rats are night-active creatures and tend to restrict their movements even when the moon is bright. During severe drought a few individuals have been seen out in daytime. They may travel 300 m (984.3 ft) in several rounds of foraging, but the home range is surprisingly small—most activity occurs within 0.1 ha (0.3 a). Population densities are generally within the range of one to 20 per ha (0.4 to 8.1 per a).

I have often found this species to be the most abundant mammal in an area in sand-dune habitats from Saskatchewan to the Mexican border. Sometimes there seemed to be a kangaroo rat living under almost every bush and bank. I once brought one of these beautiful animals home alive to learn more about its interesting habits. It rapidly became tame and would sit quietly in my hand. I later gave it to a colleague who frequently let it have the run of his room. When after several years the rat died of old age, my friend found one of its nests tucked inside the amplifier box of his stereo set.

ORD'S KANGAROO RAT

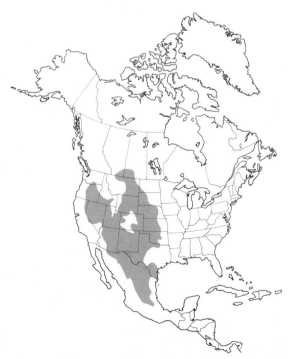

Ord's Kangaroo Rat

The night began like any other for the kangaroo rat. It twitched awake and arose almost painfully in the nest, as if some internal alarm clock had given a noisy wake-up call. The rat's long whiskers then guided the sleepy animal step-by-step up the slanting dark tunnel until it reached a plug of sand that acted as a front door. Delicate clawed paws rapidly scraped the sand under its body and then the hind feet kicked the loose grains back down the tunnel. The kangaroo rat's big head filled the den entrance, and its bulging black eyes began to survey the nearby dunes. The moonlight's glow reflected off the light-colored sand and the rodent seemed hesitant to emerge, perhaps hoping for the brightness to fade, for it felt insecure in the light. Once out, the rat hopped from tiny front feet to enormous hind feet across the bare sand to the shelter of a mesquite bush. As the animal paused in the shadows to ensure it hadn't attracted any unwanted attention, its outline formed a perfect semicircle. Satisfied that it was alone, it began the routine business of searching and sifting through the sand for seeds.

As the rat toiled in a hunched-over position, a cool breeze began to ruffle its silky fur. Suddenly it detected a faint sound coming from the other side of the bush. Cautiously it hopped over to investigate, front feet tucked against its chest, the long tail trailing behind. There sat another kangaroo rat, boldly gathering seeds and stuffing them into its cheek pouches. Both rats claimed this bush as private property and neither felt like giving it up to the other interloper. Since each kangaroo rat lived on its own small home range and had to harvest and store sufficient seeds to see it throught the rest of the year, each treated the appearance of another member of its own or a related species as a thief and a threat to its survival.

The kangaroo rats displayed mild irritation by grinding their teeth and drumming the sand with their hind feet. Neither retreated. They approached until almost nose to nose and began bumping each other with their shoulders. This contact seemed to arouse their hostility even further and the rats then scratched at each other with their front claws. The two miniature boxers stood upright and circled, jabbed, and butted, looking for a weak point in the other's defenses. Squealing warnings, the combatants resorted to their major weapon. One rat rocked back on its tail and in one quick motion kicked forward with its hind feet. The blow struck the other rat on the chest and sent it tumbling over the edge and down the side of the dune. In seconds the two were at it again, leaping up and kicking in midair like miniature kangaroos. Tufted tails swung frantically in an effort to balance the flying bodies.

These two feisty characters were not the only ones to claim this piece of the desert floor. Their pounding feet were sending vibrations through the sand, which attracted the interest of a rattlesnake. Across the bare sand glided the thick-bodied reptile, ever closer to its favorite prey — kangaroo rats. The snake coiled up under the mesquite bush, bent its neck into striking position, and patiently waited for a careless rat to bound within range. The skirmish ceased for a few seconds while the rats caught their breath, and it was only then that they spied the slight movement of the snake's forked tongue. With the terrifying face of the rattler only one meter (3.3 feet) away, the rodents instantly forgot their spat, whirled their striped flanks in the direction of the snake, and began kicking up a sandstorm. The snake jerked backwards as each burst of sand hit its face. Unable to see its potential meal any longer, the rattler withdrew from its tight coil and slithered off into the night.

The exhausted kangaroo rats sat under the mesquite breathing heavily. Each had had enough excitement for one night, and somehow signaling a truce, they retreated to their home dens. The following morning a black darkling beetle coursed a lacy trail over the myriad of rat and snake tracks, almost tumbling into some of the deeper paw prints. By noon the warm desert winds whistled around the mesquite, smoothing the dune's surface and erasing all signs of the incident. Soon all was ready to record the next night's adventures.

Dark Kangaroo Mouse

High on a western mountainside snow began to melt on the boughs of pinyon pines and junipers, and droplets trickled into ever-larger rushes of water that filled the usually dry creekbeds to overflowing. The ground was so hard and rocky that little moisture seeped into the soil; most of it ended up in several small shallow lakes in the valley below. The foothills and desert floor were covered in a patchwork of gray sagebrush, all of the same size and so evenly spaced the bushes seemed to have been carefully planted. Warm spring rains and the snow melt triggered an explosive growth of grass and annual flowers in the bare soil between the shrubs, as seeds lying dormant for one or more years suddenly came to life. There wasn't a moment to lose, for this region averaged only fifteen centimeters (5.9 inches) of precipitation a year and it fell mostly in the spring. Other kinds of living things had also been sleeping in the ground for months, but these had been hibernating to escape the freezing temperatures of winter. Not only ants, spiders, crickets, and beetles, but an attractive mouse with an enormous head, well developed hind feet, and a long tail — the dark kangaroo mouse.

Just after dark, the mouse pushed away the soil that had sealed the entrance to its burrow and began hopping among the bushes. The bottom and sides of its hind feet were fringed with white coarse hair, which helped prevent slipping while traveling up the loose sides of dunes. Its favorite place to search for seeds was in between the ripples of sand and under bushes, for the wind had sorted and dropped all kinds of treats there. The mouse dug rapidly in the sand with its front feet and sniffed with its whiskered nose. If a good deposit of seeds was located the mouse picked them up with its paws and stashed them into its fur-lined cheeks for storage until it was back safely underground. When active on the surface throughout the night, the kangaroo mouse stopped frequently to look around with its big black eyes and to listen for coyotes, snakes, or owls. Its sense of hearing was acute, due partly to the expanded bony ear chambers at the back of the skull — the reason its head seemed all out of proportion to the rest of the tiny body. If alarmed it bounded away on its hind legs in a most erratic fashion.

The mouse was very particular that everything be just right before it wandered away from its burrow. Bright moonlight, rain, snow, wind over thirteen kilometers (8.1 miles) per hour, or blowing sand all drove it below ground. Even the tiny little pocket mouse that lived in the same area could chase the kangaroo mouse away after a brief confrontation of sand kicking. The only times it showed aggression was when it pounced on a grasshopper or beetle, or met another kangaroo mouse near its burrow. Rising onto its big hind feet it rushed, kicked, and sprayed sand into the other mouse's face while squealing at high pitch. Then it dashed to its den where it soon fell asleep from exhaustion, lying on its back. During the day this desert dweller retreated to its cool burrow, always being careful to plug the doorway.

By midsummer the lakes evaporated, leaving behind a white cracked layer of alkali. The grasses and flowers turned brown and withered under the daily exposure to an unforgiving sun. The gray-green sagebrush seemed to shimmer in the air as the valley turned into a furnace each day. The kangaroo mouse was not dependent on free water to drink, since it obtained its needs from food and by conserving moisture within its body and from its wastes. But when foraging was unsuccessful and its food caches were all exhausted, the little mouse began to lose weight. The consequences of prolonged drought are the major problems all desert creatures must cope with, but somehow the kangaroo mouse knew what to do. It blocked its burrows to shut out the hot, dry air, then curled up to sleep with its nose tucked into its belly. The mouse's temperature dropped to that of the surrounding soil as it entered a kind of summer hibernation called estivation. Stirring only once a week or so to check on outside conditions, the animal slept for a month, surviving on the fat stored in the thickened middle section of the tail. When it finally ventured out again the days and nights were cooler, and a number of plants had resumed growth. Time to fatten up that tail again and to store additional seeds, for the winter hibernation period was not far off.

DARK KANGAROO MOUSE

Scientific name *Microdipodops mega-cephalus*

Family Pocket Mice, Kangaroo Rats, and Spiny Mice (Heteromyidae)

Order Rodents (Rodentia)

Total length 160 mm (6.3 in)

Tail length 85 mm (3.3 in)

Weight 14 g (0.5 oz)

Color The upperparts are blackish or grayish-brown, sometimes with a reddish tint. The underparts are white, although the hairs are gray at the base. The tip of the tail is black.

Distribution and Status The dark kangaroo mouse is found in desert scrub of sagebrush and shadscale within the Great Basin Desert of Nevada, Utah, Oregon, and eastern California. It is a fairly rare rodent, preferring fine gravel or sandy soil and dunes within an elevational range of 1 200 to 2 000 m (3,937 to 6,561.7 ft). Closely resembling this species is the pale kangaroo mouse *(Microdipodops pallidus)*, also present in Nevada and adjacent California. Since there is no fossil record, the ancestors of this North American genus are unknown, but a closer relationship has been speculated with pocket mice *(Perognathus)* than with kangaroo rats *(Dipodomys)*.

Food These mice subsist on a variety of seeds from desert plants, but seek succulent leaves for added moisture. Insects are relished as well and are particularly important in summer.

Reproduction and Growth Reproduction is strongly influenced by seed production of plants which in turn depends on soil moisture accumulated from the previous autumn and winter. Two litters are usually produced from late March to late September (mainly in May and June), each averaging 4 (range of one to 7) young. The offspring remain within the 2 m (6.6 ft) of underground tunnels for many weeks before they venture outside. Most kangaroo mice do not survive for more than one or 2 years, however captives have lived for 5.5 years.

Remarks The dark kangaroo mouse is a flattened little rodent with the large head forming half the body length. The ears are rounded, the black eyes protrude, and great sprays of whiskers arise from either side of the mouth. The hind feet are strong and greatly elongated for hopping quickly over open terrain, while the front feet are small and carried close to the chest. The tail is long and widest at the middle and serves for both functions of balance and fat-storage. No tuft of hairs is present on the end as in kangaroo rats. The fur is long, soft, and silky. The animal hibernates to avoid the unfavorable winter period from late October to early March, and is active at night during the rest of the year. However, lack of food may cause it to estivate — a kind of summer hibernation which allows it to survive on a low-energy budget until food availability improves. Home ranges are rather large, averaging 0.7 ha (1.7 a) for males and 0.4 ha (one a) for females. There is considerable overlapping of home ranges and only the vicinity of the burrow is defended. Kangaroo mice are solitary and generally aggressive with their own kind, but are gentle and easily maintained in captivity. These desert mice do not lose much water in their wastes or from evaporation from the skin and lungs. They spend most of their lives in burrows where it is relatively cool and moist — lessening the demand for precious water. Under these conditions they find sufficient moisture in dry seeds and kangaroo mice may never actually drink water, though dew is available on cold nights.

This is one species that has persistently eluded my attempts to catch it. Arriving at a site in Nevada where the kangaroo mouse had previously been reported, I and my companion were excited to find numerous holes dug into the hard-packed soil under the desert shrubs. Dozens of traps were set accordingly. With great confidence we bedded down in our van to await the morning and the rewards of all our efforts. Disappointment mounted as trap after trap remained set. Not a mouse or rat of any kind was found in the area. For some reason (perhaps a failure of the seed crop) rodent populations had crashed from the fairly high numbers of the recent past as evidenced by the abundant signs. The only living creature we found was a fat rattlesnake coiled up neatly under a bush — obviously a better mouser than we were.

SPOTTED GROUND SQUIRREL

Scientific name *Spermophilus spilosoma*

Family Squirrels (Sciuridae)

Order Rodents (Rodentia)

Total length 220 mm (8.7 in)

Tail length 70 mm (2.8 in)

Weight 125 g (4.4 oz)

Color The upperparts are a grayish- to cinnamon-brown color, paler on the sides, and white on the undersides. The tail is similar in color to the back, slightly paler underneath, and with a black tip. Numerous square or round spots are scattered at random or in loose rows along the back and sides. The color of the spotted ground squirrel is quite variable, often matching the soil to an admirable degree.

Distribution and Status From south-central South Dakota to the central Mexican state of Jalisco, and from Arizona east to central Texas, this pretty little ground squirrel is found in desert grassland and desert scrub, up to about 2 200 m (7,217.8 ft) elevation. Generally the soil is dry and sandy but occasionally clayey or rocky, with open ground among the vegetation. Typical habitats include yucca-grass sandhills, sagebrush-grass, desert scrub of creosote-blackbrush, mesquite and cacti, pinyon-juniper woodland, and overgrazed range. This species is but one of 36 kinds of ground squirrels in the genus *Spermophilus*, which occurs throughout North America and Eurasia.

Food The squirrel nips green shoots and gathers the seeds of numerous annual and perennial desert plants such as grass, sunflowers, wild gourd, salt bush, mesquite, and tumbleweed. Cactus stems and fruit provide additional moisture, for water is a scarce commodity in this animal's home. Grasshoppers,

DARK KANGAROO MOUSE

beetles, and a host of other insects are relished, as well as meat when a carcass is available. Because of its arid-country preferences, the spotted ground squirrel only rarely has an opportunity to feed on crops.

Reproduction and Growth The mating season begins within 2 or 3 weeks of emergence from hibernation. Males pursue females in lively chases, with most couplings occurring below ground. About 28 days after fertilization an average of 7 (4 to 12) young are born in a grass-lined den. Each weighs around 4 g (0.1 oz) and the ears and eyes are closed. They nurse for 5 weeks from the mother's 5 pair of mammae, and then finally come aboveground to nibble on solid food, at which time they have reached 50 g (1.8 oz). Three weeks later they wander off and become independent. One litter is the norm in northern populations. The presence of young in late summer farther south in the United States and Mexico has been interpreted as a second litter. Perhaps some of these are the offspring of late-breeding yearlings. The expected life span is one or 2 years, but they no doubt survive much longer under captive conditions.

Remarks This is a relatively small ground squirrel, about the size of a large chipmunk. The ears are short, the tail is slender, and the coarse hair is rather sparse. Studies have shown that relatively little moisture escapes through the skin and lungs — an obvious advantage to a desert dweller. The spotted ground squirrel usually remains close to its many burrows, where it retreats to avoid temperature extremes beyond 10 to 34°C (50 to 93.2°F). During periods of drought, intense heat, or when food is scarce, the animal is able to estivate; that is, it becomes dormant for many days in an attempt to survive until favorable conditions return. Likewise, the animal becomes fat and enters hibernation to pass the cold season. Adults disappear below ground from late August to September, while young need more time to build up energy reserves and generally retire from late September to November. As with most hibernators, they arouse every week

or two for a few hours to adjust various body functions. Emergence occurs from March to April, with a much shorter hibernation period in the south. Perhaps they are active year-round in Mexico.

These ground squirrels spend about two-thirds of their aboveground time foraging for food; the rest of the day involves activities such as alert behavior, sunbathing, resting in the shade, sand-bathing, grooming, and eliminating wastes. Found aboveground only during daylight hours (diurnal), activity is controlled by environmental conditions — wind, rain, and excessive heat or cold drive them into their burrows. In most regions they are shy and relatively uncommon but can become conspicuous and common in highly favorable habitat. An average density is 2 to 7 per ha (0.8 to 2.8 per a), with a home range of one to 5 ha (2.5 to 12.4 a) with males ranging the farthest. Home ranges overlap and individuals protect a territory only in the vicinity of the main burrow.

SOUTHERN POCKET GOPHER

Scientific name *Thomomys umbrinus*
Family Pocket Gophers (Geomyidae)
Order Rodents (Rodentia)
Total length 225 mm (8.9 in)
Tail length 65 mm (2.6 in)
Weight 175 g (6.2 oz)
Color This widespread species ranges in color from black, brown, golden, to whitish, slightly paler underneath. The coat color often resembles the soil — dark in rich black soils with abundant humus, light in pale-colored soils (e.g., sand) with low organic content.

Distribution and Status The southern pocket gopher ranges from Oregon and Colorado all the way south to the Mexican state of Veracruz. Some mammalogists consider the northeastern populations as a distinct species named the Townsend's pocket gopher *(Thomomys townsendii)* and populations from the rest of the United States as Botta's pocket gopher *(Thomomys bottae)*; the

southern pocket gopher, in the strict sense, would then be present only in Mexico. This complex situation exists because the 3 populations seem not to interbreed in some areas, and to do so in others. They have obviously evolved to the threshold of becoming new species. There are 5 to 9 species in this genus, depending on the particular authority's interpretation of presently known facts. A total of about 35 species within 5 genera of pocket gophers are known. They occupy much of the continent from southern Canada to Panama.

The southern pocket gopher (in the combined sense) occupies an enormous region and therefore could be expected to live in a variety of habitat types. It has been reported in desert scrub, cedar-ocotillo woodland, oak-cottonwood floodplain, oak woodland, yellow pine woodland, and mountain meadows. The soil may be rich loam to sand, or even rock, as in lava fields. It can become remarkably abundant at times in choice locations.

Food Pocket gophers are strictly vegetarians and this particular species devours tender roots, bulbs, and aboveground parts of many plants such as sunflowers, lupines, lilies, thistles, and cacti. Individuals often find their way into agricultural fields where they cause havoc with clover, alfalfa, potatoes, and orchard trees by girdling the roots. Since their food consists of succulent greens, there is no need to drink water.

Reproduction and Growth Two annual litters and year-round breeding occur in the south, while one litter per year is born in late spring in the north. The gestation period is only 18 days and the number of young averages 5 (range of 2 to 11). The newborn are 5 cm (2 in) long with loose, wrinkled skin, and the teeth are still hidden in the gums. Milk is provided by the mother's 4 pair of mammae and the young are weaned by 6 weeks of age. Sexual maturity is attained after the age of 3 months, and they leave the mother's burrow by autumn when they are nearly full size. Pocket gophers usually live less than 2 years, but some reach 4 years in nature.

Continued on p.264

SPOTTED GROUND SQUIRREL

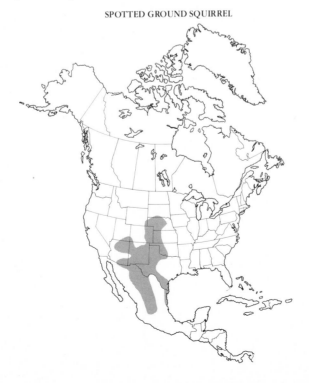

Spotted Ground Squirrel and Southern Pocket Gopher

Under a full desert moon a coyote trotted down the mountainside and out onto the desert floor, careful not to impale its toe pads on cactus spines. Then all was quiet except for the steady trill of crickets. The unsuspecting coyote suddenly leapt high into the air as the earth shuddered under its very feet. The confused animal ran around in circles, trying to figure out what had happened. With head cocked to the ground it could hear a steady scraping sound coming from underground. Finally realizing there was no meal about to show itself, the coyote wheeled around and ran off, but not before a hind paw stumbled into a tunnel in the sandy soil. Below, only a few meters (yards) away, a southern pocket gopher lurched in fear at the sound of something invading its serene world.

For the past half hour the gopher had been mining its way through the sand in search of succulent roots. Long claws and short, powerful arms loosened the packed sand until a thick tough root blocked the way. With head turned to the side, an enormous set of chisel-sharp incisor teeth cut through the wood with ease. Since the lips closed behind these teeth, the mouth remained clear of sand throughout the whole procedure. When the pile of loosened sand under the belly began to restrict digging movements, the gopher performed a twisting forward roll, ending up facing the other direction. Encircling the mound with its big hands and chest, the pocket gopher, propelled by the hind feet, shoved the soil in a smooth motion along the tunnel. Rather than fill an old tunnel the animal decided to deposit the soil on the surface, and while it was clawing up at an angle, the coyote's foot penetrated the gopher's tunnel system.

At first the pocket gopher was afraid to investigate the intrusion. It just crouched low with its big front paws tucked under its chin and its teeth grinding. Warm dry air reached its nostrils, causing its nose to twitch. The pocket gopher could not rest until its home was secure once again. Within minutes the damage was repaired by a thick plug of soil. The pocket gopher then scurried along a slanting tunnel leading two meters (6.6 feet) downward to a nest chamber, where it curled up to sleep.

The following morning a sandy-colored squirrel with white spots on the back appeared in the area for the first time. It streaked from bush to bush and seemed to disappear from view each time it stopped, so well camouflaged was its coat. Once it rose on its hind legs and let loose a high-pitched bubbling call,

resembling a songbird more than a squirrel. No answering notes came back. The spotted ground squirrel seemed to have found a new home. There were prickly pear cacti here to provide moisture and plenty of seeds on the dry tufts of grass. It began to dig a hole in the bank of a dry creek bed under the cover of bushes.

By late morning the sun beat down so strongly that the air began to wave. The ground squirrel's feet became tender from contact with the hot sand. As the desert temperature at ground level rose past 50°C (122°F), the squirrel began to seriously overheat and it searched for a shaded spot to rest. It felt too uncomfortable to worry about the strong musk of coyote that filled the air. Then it detected the odor of moist soil, which held the promise of a cool and damp retreat. Quickly locating a fresh mound of sand, the squirrel searched in vain for an opening. It began to pant under the stress of an elevated body temperature. With all its remaining strength, the squirrel dug into the mound, kicking the sand back through the air with the hind feet. The plug of sand gave way more easily than the packed surrounding material, and within a minute the squirrel broke through into a cool tunnel. Now another strange odor indicated the presence of some other creature down here in the darkness. Although it was nervous, the squirrel couldn't go back into the bright furnace aboveground. Its built-up body heat began to escape through its skin and sparse coat, and its rate of breathing slowed down to normal.

All of a sudden the squirrel sensed the presence of another animal shuffling toward it. The pocket gopher had returned to close the burrow once more. When each realized they were no longer alone, the two subterranean warriors prepared to do battle, for neither one was about to abandon its ground. Teeth grinding and voices growling, the two rodents clashed with teeth and claws. Realizing it was overpowered, the squirrel backed up past the open chimney and into the recently vacated old tunnel system. Accepting this retreat as a draw, the pocket gopher sealed up its side of the burrow. From that point on the two creatures became the best of neighbors — the squirrel feeding above ground during the day, the pocket gopher restricting its activities aboveground to mostly at night. A truce based on mutual avoidance permitted their coexistence in the same little spot on the desert floor.

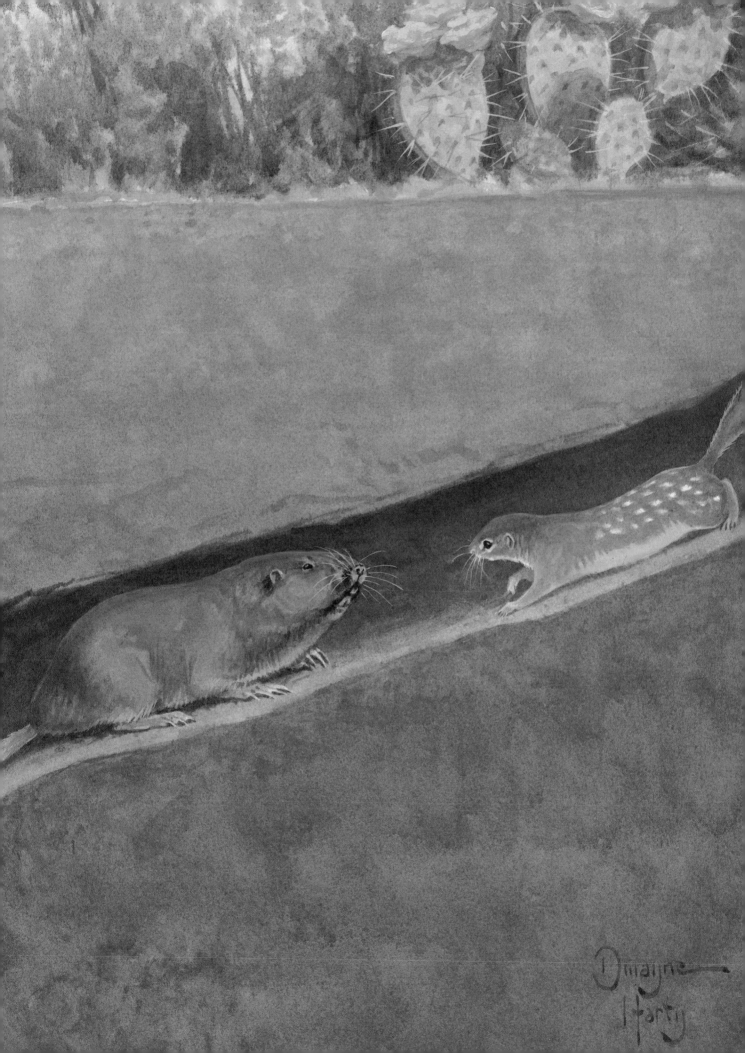

Remarks Pocket gophers represent a family of fascinating rodents which have evolved and remained in North America. Without a doubt they are among the most highly adapted burrowing mammals (fossorial) on this continent. Interestingly, a number of other unrelated mammals in far-flung regions of the world closely resemble pocket gophers and provide classic examples of how natural selection has molded or directed the evolution of creatures living under similar subterranean conditions (convergent evolution). Examples are lesser mole rats (rodent family Spalacidae) of South Africa, the Middle East, and eastern Asia; African mole-rats (rodent family Bathyergidae) of Africa; mole-rats (rodent family Cricetidae) of eastern Asia; bamboo rats (rodent family Rhizomyidae) of southeast Asia; coruros (rodent family Octodontidae) of Chile; tucu tucos (rodent family Ctenomyidae) of South America; mountain beaver (rodent family Aplodontidae) of western North America; Cape golden mole (insectivore family Chrysochloridae) of South Africa; marsupial mole (marsupial family Notoryctidae) of Australia. Photographs of these mammals and many other beautiful examples of convergent evolution can be seen in *Walker's Mammals of the World*.

People are amazed when shown a pocket gopher, for it is unlike any creature they have ever seen before. The head is about one quarter the length of the body, with tiny ears and eyes and an enormous set of incisor teeth arching out of the mouth. These upper and lower teeth are self-sharpening by abrading against each other and grow throughout life (about 30 cm or 11.8 in per year) at the same rate as they wear down at the tips. The single premolar and

3 molars in each side of the jaw are rooted (cease growing), and hence wear down from grinding on earth-covered plant material. The cheek pouches are also remarkable features and are used solely for transporting food, never soil. These spacious "shopping carts" reach all the way back to the shoulder, and are emptied by relaxing the outer "drawstring" muscles and pushing the contents out with the knobby palms. While inside out, the fur-lined pouch is wiped clean, and retractor muscles pull it back inside the cheek.

Although each pocket gopher prefers to live alone (except during the brief mating season or a female with young), they are often distributed in semi-isolated colonies, separated by unsuitable terrain or rivers. These groups frequently have evolved anatomical differences from adjacent groups as a result of little or no opportunity to interbreed and an unusual ability to adapt physically to local conditions. In fact, pocket gophers exhibit more variability than any other kind of mammal in North America. Consequently, they have received much attention in genetic and speciation studies.

Pocket gophers dig feeding tunnels 3 to 9 cm (1.2 to 3.5 in) wide within 0.5 m (1.6 ft) of the surface, as well as deep tunnels leading to grass-lined sleeping quarters, food-storage chambers, and latrines. Their subway may run up to 180 m (590.6 ft), broken into a number of side branches. The animals are constantly digging new tunnels and closing off old ones. Surface mounds can be thrown up at the rate of 4 in a day, but these appear more often at certain times of the year, such as spring. A typical home range may be 150 sq m (1,614.6 sq ft), and population levels as high as 50 to 130 per ha (20.2 to 52.6 per a) are known. Ac-

tivity occurs anytime during the night or day, but the limited surface appearances to push out soil or collect food are generally restricted to nighttime. Pocket gophers' main predators are owls, badgers, coyotes, foxes, and weasels. While destroying some crops and occasionally weakening earthen banks, pocket gophers are beneficial in aerating and turning the soil over vegetation which increases soil fertility, and by improving drainage.

I can recall walking up to a roadside bank to check a gopher trap set the night before. At least half the time when trapping these animals, the gopher either blocks the trap with a plug of soil or fails to show up at all. After moving aside the thin cover of grass, I pulled gently on the wire connecting the 2 traps. I was pleased to feel some resistance, and, in short order, a fine specimen was dug out. Then the second trap was drawn out of the other fork in the burrow. Instead of being still set, as expected, it had sprung and caught the skin of a ground squirrel. Still very much alive, the animal growled convincingly, causing me to jump back in surprise. Seeing its chance, the squirrel leapt free of the trap, burrow, and me, and quick as a flash disappeared in the thick grass. I had caught a few pairs of pocket gophers in a single burrow during the mating season, but never knew that a ground squirrel would take up such an unfriendly roommate. I figured it was only a matter of time till this strange union would come to an end.

SOUTHERN POCKET GOPHER

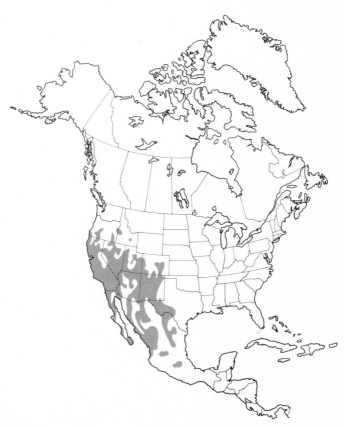

NORTHERN GRASSHOPPER MOUSE

Scientific name *Onychomys leucogaster*
Family New World Mice and Rats, Gerbils, and Hamsters (Cricetidae)
Order Rodents (Rodentia)
Total length 150 mm (5.9 in)
Tail length 40 mm (1.6 in)
Weight 45 g, maximum 52 g
(1.6 oz, maximum 1.8 oz)
Color Adult mice occur in several phases — gray or a range of grayish-brown to reddish-brown. Individuals dwelling on black lava or cinder are grayish-black. There is a gray juvenile coat and a subadult coat before the similarly colored adult coat is attained in the autumn. Some researchers have thought that old mice may turn gray again. The lower half of the animal is white, as is the tip of the bicolored tail and a patch in front of each ear.
Distribution and Status The northern grasshopper mouse lives in desert scrub, short-grass and mixed-grass prairie, and sage and other brushlands, and is mainly restricted to sandy or other thin soils. More recently, the edges of grainfields have become a favored habitat, with their abundance of seeds and insects. The distribution is surprisingly large and extends from Washington, Alberta, Manitoba, and Minnesota in the north, to the Mexican states of Sonora and Tamaulipas in the south.

It has only 2 close relatives — the southern grasshopper mouse *(Onychomys torridus)* of the Mohave, Great Basin, and Sonoran Deserts, and Mearn's grasshopper mouse *(Onychomys arenicola)* of the Chihauhuan Desert. These 3 species are the sole survivors of a diverse group of North American rodents that appear to have lost out to the related but highly competitive line of deer mice *(Peromyscus* species). In fact, the three grasshopper mice may have survived to the present only because of their specialized diet of animal material, to some degree avoiding competition with the host of other desert and grassland rodents that rely on vegetation, particularly seeds.

Food As far as diet is concerned, this mouse has taken the place of shrews and moles of more moist regions in the reliance on insects and other small animals for food. From 75 to 90 percent of the stomach contents are animal material, such as grasshoppers, beetles, crickets, caterpillars and moths, spiders, scorpions, lizards, and even small mammals and birds. Deer mice, pocket mice, small kangaroo rats, and harvest mice are ambushed, killed, and devoured. With its short legs and heavy build, the grasshopper mouse is unable to out-run most of these rodents. Numerous kinds of seeds are eaten throughout the year, but especially in the winter when insects are scarce. The mouse has a prodigious appetite and can consume half its weight in food during the night. As with other rodents of arid regions, it can exist on the moisture obtained from food.

Reproduction and Growth Three and perhaps occasionally 4 litters are born to adult females in the southern part of the range, spread out over a long season from February to October. In the north, 2 litters are the norm, from May to August. The courting and mating behavior has been described as the most complex of any North American rodent, characterized by circling, grooming, mounting, rolling on the sides while coupled, and requiring up to 3 hours to complete the whole sequence. Numerous successive matings, involving the locking of the pair's sex organs for up to a minute on each act, are required to ensure pregnancy. Females carry the young for about 30 days, and up to 47 days if development is slowed by having to nurse a previous litter. Another period of heat or estrus commonly occurs from hours to a few days following birth. The number of young per litter average 4 (range of one to 6), each weighing 2 g (.07 oz). Their eyes open at 10 days, at which time there is some control of body temperature. They nurse from the female's 6 nipples until the age of 3 weeks. Grasshopper mice reach

sexual maturity later than most other mice, requiring 3 months for females, 4 months for males. While the young are dependent, the female aggressively defends them, even from human disturbance. The offspring disperse by the time the next litter is born and have a life expectancy of 4 years in captivity, probably 2 years in nature.

Remarks The similarity of this mouse to the deer mouse is quite obvious, but so are a number of differences such as a short, tapering, fat tail; heavier body; larger feet; and shorter and more densely furred ears. For some unknown reason (perhaps related to their specialized diet) this species is not as common as most other rodents in the same region. Only occasionally is it abundant, to the usual detriment of other small mammals. Active only at night, but throughout the year, the grasshopper mouse leads a solitary life outside the breeding season. It ranges over a large home area of one to 3 ha (2.5 to 7.4 a) and frequently wanders away in search of better hunting grounds. An aggressive creature, it is capable of giving a nasty bite and dislikes being handled. Snakes, long-tailed weasels, foxes, coyotes, badgers, and several kinds of owls are the major predators.

The first live grasshopper mouse I saw was trapped while I was on a student field trip in Arizona. I had the misfortune of having it as a caged roommate for a few nights, and it kept me awake by constantly gnawing on the steel bars. When we took it back to the lab, it whistled every time I entered the room. After many unsuccessful attempts to locate this rare species in Manitoba, I found a single locality where it was abundant. The mice were living in a sparse sandy field of rye and in an adjacent overgrazed horse pasture. Most of the 48 specimens were caught coming out of renovated burrows of thirteen-lined and Richardson's ground squirrels. The hefty mice were so powerful that sometimes they carried the trap away and escaped. Although I saw several racing for their burrows, I was able to catch only 2 subadults by hand, and subsequently kept them for a year in captivity. One farmer told me that he trapped one of these critters in his henhouse where it had killed a number of newborn chicks. I'm not certain he agreed with me when I mentioned the benefits of having these insect-eating mice on his property.

NORTHERN GRASSHOPPER MOUSE

Northern Grasshopper Mouse

No sooner had the moon sailed behind a bank of cloud when the warm still air was pierced by a high shrill whistle. Half hidden under a catclaw shrub, a desert cottontail suddenly stopped chewing on a leaf, intent on locating the direction of the sound. After several seconds of quiet, its jaws resumed a circular chewing motion. About ten meters (32.8 feet) away a thickset mouse scurried around a hole at the base of a small mesquite. The brown-colored grasshopper mouse rose on its hind legs, revealing a pure white underside, and again emitted its strange whistle. Perhaps it was warning other grasshopper mice to stay away, maybe trying to attract a mate, or just whistling to release pent-up energy from being cooped up all day. Dropping to all fours again, it moved off on its short legs, pausing frequently to sniff the ground with its pink nose, or to listen for the songs of night-active insects.

As the mouse approached a sprawling prickly pear cactus, its bright eyes spotted movement under a dried cactus pad which lay curled on the sand. Without hesitation the mouse darted after a pale-yellow camel cricket, still peacefully waving its antennae. Two clawed paws shot forward, pinning the insect to the ground. A quick nip removed its head. The mouse sat back on its haunches, and holding the plump cricket in its paws, it proceeded to crunch through the hard skeleton. Soon, two discarded spiny legs dropped to the ground and the mouse disappeared in the darkness.

One hour later the mouse reached the edge of its home range, bordered by a brushy hillside. Reinforcing its ownership of the area, it dug out a shallow hole and rubbed its belly on the mound, depositing a musky secretion from the anal glands. For the past several nights the mouse had busied itself in this area by gathering the seeds of mesquite and other thorny plants and caching them in an underground chamber. Descending the tunnel at a forty-degree angle, the mouse expected to encounter a plug of earth which it had placed there to prevent the pilfering of its winter storehouse by insects. But the tunnel had been cleared by some larger creature, and the mouse's ears detected that the thief was still below.

The grasshopper mouse's countenance changed dramatically. With ears trained forward, black eyes bulging, and hair on the forehead and nape raised, the owner of the tunnel moved down the dark corridor in short jerky movements. All sound ceased from the seed chamber. The mouse's quivering whiskers dislodged some sand grains and they slid over its paws. Uncertain as to what other animal was trapped down there, the grasshopper mouse was not about to rush in. There was no frightening scent of snake, weasel, or pocket gopher, just a faint but familiar odor of mouse. No moonlight could reach the chamber, for it lay at the end of a fifty-centimeter (19.7-inch)-long curving tunnel. Becoming bolder by the second, the grasshopper mouse entered the dark room, where it could hear rapid breathing and the nervous twitch of a tail. Nothing happened for a full half minute. Then, orienting by a keen sense of hearing, the grasshopper mouse lunged across at the Mexican spiny pocket mouse. Four pairs of legs scrambled for support among the loose seeds. Squeals from both mice were deafening in the close quarters, as the pocket mouse desperately sought to gain the exit. The heavier grasshopper mouse used its weight to flatten the pocket mouse, and one savage bite with long incisors sliced through the pocket mouse's neck and spinal cord. The victor huddled over its prey like a miniature wolf and began its feast, internal organs first.

It was twenty minutes before the mouse backed out of the tunnel, pulling the spiny-haired skin with only a leg and the tail attached. The grasshopper mouse had solved the problem of competing for seeds by eating the competition. The moon reappeared from behind the clouds, flooding the desert scene with an eerie light. A far-off coyote let loose with a lonesome wail, as another little predator rose on its hind feet to whistle, its white chest and belly stained bright red.

Western Harvest Mouse

A gray plume of smoke rose straight up from the peak of a mountain and then leveled off and dissipated under the influence of strong air currents. For almost a century the old volcano had remained quiet, allowing a mantle of desert scrub, grassland, and oak-pine woodland to reestablish on its slopes and valleys. The ground shuddered periodically, indicative of the monumental pressures building up in the earth's crust below the mountain's base. That night a powerful explosion rocked the countryside, and an orange and red creek of molten lava trickled over the crater's edge and slowly snaked its way down the slope. Yellow flashes lit up the blackness as dry trees burst into flame from the intense heat. By day the destruction to the plant cover was obvious. Wildlife had perished or retreated to lower elevations, imparting a tense silence to the air.

In the desert below, a little ball of plant fibers tucked within a clump of grass continued to vibrate long after the shock waves had ceased. Inside sat a juvenile harvest mouse, quite stressed from the mountain's eruptions. If this was what it was like to live on its own, the mouse wanted to be home again, huddled safely with its mother and siblings. Only two weeks ago the harvest mouse's life was a carefree round of playing, nursing, and sleeping among the warm bodies of its family. But at three weeks of age it could not resist the urge to explore farther and farther away. Then one night it simply became lost and its home ties were abruptly severed.

The harvest mouse centered its activities around a yucca plant, amid tufts of grass and bushes. For the first few days its slept fitfully, curled up in a hot shallow burrow it had discovered in the stony ground. Instinctively, it began to construct a nest in a patch of thick grass. Without instruction or assistance from a parent, the young animal cut blades of grass with its sharp incisors and twisted them around until a ball-shaped structure began to take shape. Working for a few hours after dark and then again before sunrise, it paused occasionally to eat some grass seeds. These it picked off the ground or reached by ascending the stems, which easily supported its light weight. The mouse ate while it was perched in the grass, propped up by its long tail, or it climbed the stalk, cut off the seed head, let it drop, and then dined back on the ground.

When the grass nest reached a diameter of about twelve centimeters (4.7 inches), the mouse burrowed its way inside from below, using forefeet and snout. Repeated twisting and shoving finally hollowed out a chamber only slightly larger than the mouse's body, but something seemed to be missing. Remembering the soft feel and warmth of its original quarters, the rodent went searching for nest lining. By chance it came across some mature thistles which it recognized as suitable material, for its mother had used the same soft fluffs in her nest. It required ten trips, carrying the thistle down in its mouth, to finally complete the task. No sooner had it fallen asleep in its new home when the volcano began to awaken.

For the next three weeks grayish-white ash settled over the vegetation, rocks, and ground like a blanket of dirty snow. The ash coating smothered many plants, and most animals disappeared, succumbing to starvation and lack of moisture, or traveling away from the valley. The harvest mouse spent almost all its time sleeping soundly in its nest, preferring not to run through the fine, choking powder. Over the next few weeks the wind blew the ash into low areas and drifts under bushes and rocks. The mouse entered a deep sleep or torpor — an adaptation of some desert creatures to lower food and water requirements during periods of hostile environmental conditions. When it finally awoke, it was able to find and live on only a couple of grass seeds a day, due to its small size and warm insulating nest. When the rains came to freshen the earth and to trigger dormant seeds lying in the ash-fertilized soil, the harvest mouse was one of the few animals to have survived the ordeal.

WESTERN HARVEST MOUSE

Scientific name *Reithrodontomys megalotis*

Family New World Mice and Rats, Gerbils, and Hamsters (Cricetidae)

Order Rodents (Rodentia)

Total length 135 mm (5.3 in)

Tail length 62 mm (2.4 in)

Weight 12 g, maximum 16 g (0.4 oz, maximum 0.6 oz)

Color The harvest mouse is grayish-brown on the upperparts, with a darker area running along the top of the head and back. The flanks and cheeks are orangy-brown and the undersides a grayish-white. The tail is bicolored. An orangy-brown spot on the chest is common in some regions. The juvenile coat is a dull gray, subadults are somewhat browner, but not as bright as adults. As with most small mammals, adults molt in the spring and autumn.

Distribution and Status A surprisingly large range for a small mouse, this species is found from southern British Columbia to Indiana in the north, to Baja California and Oaxaca in southern Mexico. This wide distribution is accommodated by the adaptation of various populations to quite different habitats. Among the more important are several kinds of grasslands from arid plains to mountain-meadows, salt marshes, weedy patches along fence rows, grainfields, and old fields; sagebrush and other shrublands; desert communities; and pine-oak woodland. Topography ranges from 77 m (252.6 ft) below sea level in California's Death Valley to mountain slopes in Mexico up to an elevation of 4 000 m (13,123.4 ft).

There are 19 species of this New World genus of harvest mice, representatives of which occur from southern Canada throughout most of the United States, and south into northern South America. One or more of these species may be found in the same general region as the western harvest mouse (though often in separate habitats), and individual specimens may be exceedingly difficult to identify. Of course, the mice would have no problem in distinguishing their own kind.

Food This harvest mouse depends on seeds as a basic food, particularly those of grasses like fescue, bluestem, side-oats grama, brome, and foxtail. Grass shoots, clover, legumes, and many other forbs augment the diet and provide moisture when free water or dew is unavailable. The harvest mouse is remarkable for its ability to drink sea water or other waters high in mineral salts. Spiders and insects such as grasshoppers, beetles, moths, and caterpillars are also eaten, especially in the summer when they are most abundant.

Reproduction and Growth The breeding season extends over the whole year in warm southern areas of the range, where females may have up to 7 litters annually. In central regions such as the southern United States, breeding is largely restricted to a period from April to October, often with a pause during the hot, dry weather of June to August. At northern extremes, breeding occurs only during the warmer months from May to August, where 2 or 3 litters are the norm. Females may come into heat shortly after giving birth, and there is generally no shortage of mature males to accommodate them. An average of 4 (range of one to 9) offspring are born 23 days after mating. Development of the 1.5-g (.05-oz) babies is rapid, for their eyes and ears are open by 12 days, at which time they begin to walk and eat solid food. Weaning is complete in 20 to 24 days and they disperse. Sexual maturity is attained at 4 to 8 weeks for females, 5 to 8 weeks for males. The reproductive capabilities of harvest mice are astonishing. Captives have been known to bring forth 14 litters totaling 58 young in just one year. The weight of a litter may surpass half the weight of the female.

Remarks This is a small, slim rodent with large naked ears, long and thin sparsely haired tail, and grooved upper incisors — a feature which gives rise to its generic name *Reithrodontomys* (meaning groove-toothed mouse). It resembles the introduced Old World house mouse more than its close relative the deer mouse. It is a common species, averaging 4 to 10 per ha (1.6 to 4 per a), but occasionally reaching numbers as high as 60 per ha (24.3 per a). The home range is about 75 m (246.1 ft) across and there is much overlap among individuals, for the mouse is relatively sociable. The day and much of the night are spent in the nest, with the main activity periods just after sunset and before sunrise.

Several nests are constructed in grass or thickets, sometimes aboveground in a shrub, or underground in winter. A bird nest is often renovated. The well-insulated nest reduces heat loss from the tiny animal's body by as much as 25 percent, while huddling in the nest with other individuals in cold weather assists heat conservation even further. Runways may be constructed, however the mice frequently use those of other small mammals. Almost like a miniature monkey in the trees, the harvest mouse travels above the ground through grass stems and other vegetation. A population of harvest mice changes over annually, for few individuals live more than one year. The major predators are snakes, owls, long-tailed weasels, skunks, coyotes, foxes, and bobcats.

My first introduction to the western harvest mouse came while I was on a student field trip in Illinois. This tiny species is very rare and known in only a few localities in Illinois and Indiana, where it appears to be expanding its range in the last several decades. We all set traplines in an old field with plenty of weedy bushes, and the next morning we anxiously drove up to the site. I caught several deer mice and a prairie vole, then a small rodent which I took at first to be a house mouse. Before the end of my line I had caught yet another. As I approached my professor, I jokingly quipped that I had two harvest mice for his collection. But I don't think he believed me until he checked the grooved incisors and then seemed very pleased. Strangely enough, those were the only two specimens taken on the whole trip.

Mammalogists can become very excited about catching a common species like a harvest mouse if a specimen represents a range extension or if the animal is rare in the region. Perhaps it is the challenge of locating a secretive small mammal through intimate knowledge of its habitat requirements. My collecting of a number of harvest mice in Arizona seemed fairly routine, among the dozens of unusual and colorful mammals of that region. But finding it at the northern tip of its range in Illinois or the Okanagan desert of British Columbia was most satisfying.

WESTERN HARVEST MOUSE

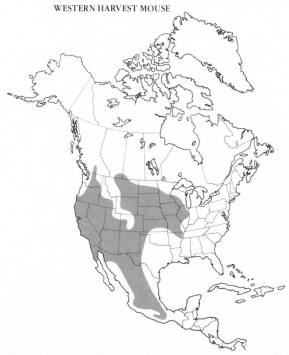

COYOTE

Scientific name *Canis latrans*
Family Wolves, Foxes, and Dogs (Canidae)
Order Carnivores (Carnivora)
Total length males 120 cm (47.2 in); females 118 cm (46.4 in)
Tail length 38 cm (15 in); 34 cm (13.4 in)
Weight 14 kg, maximum 34 kg (30.9 lb, maximum 75 lb); 11 kg (24.2 lb). Northern coyotes are larger than southern ones; e.g., 18 kg (40 lb) versus 11 kg (24.2 lb).
Color The long hair is grizzled gray with a touch of red. Black-tipped hair is present along the back, shoulders, and end of the tail. The lips and underparts are paler or white. Northern individuals are grayer compared to the reddish coyotes of the desert. At first the pups are dark gray, somewhat paler on the head and belly, and with a white spot on the chest. Within several weeks they become dark brown.
Distribution and Status Originally a western species, the coyote has shown a remarkable ability to expand its range in the east, north, and south. It now occurs naturally from the arctic coast of Alaska as far south as Costa Rica and east to New Brunswick and Louisiana. Scattered records in every southeastern state are the result of numerous releases by people. The coyote is an adaptable creature, capable of living from the cold northern coniferous forests to the prairie, desert, temperate and tropical deciduous forests, tropical savanna, and farm and pasture lands. In most regions it selects open hilly country. It is still common in many regions in spite of centuries of persecution.
Food Coyotes eat deer, pronghorn, elk (especially the young), rabbits, rodents, ground-nesting birds, reptiles, amphibians, fish, insects, and various fruits (persimmons, cherries, grapes, juniper, prickly pear cactus) and seeds (mesquite). At least 90 percent of the diet is mammal flesh, though much of it is carrion, particularly in winter. Poultry, sheep, and cattle (usually young, old, or sick animals) are also attacked occasionally. Pups chase down and devour large numbers of insects,

which not only provide good nourishment, but also hone their hunting techniques. An adult can devour 5 kg (11 lb) of meat in one meal. A source of water is essential, and individuals will travel long distances to drink.
Reproduction and Growth Coyotes frequently have a long courtship period of 2 or 3 months and a close bond may result so that the pair breeds in succeeding years. The female experiences one period of heat per year which lasts about 10 days, and occurs from January to March. The mating act takes up to 25 minutes since the 2 animals are locked together. Approximately 63 days later, an average of 6 young (range of one to 19) are born in an underground den. Occasionally 2 females raise their litters in the same den. The haired pups weigh from 240 to 275 g (8.5 to 9.7 oz), their eyes open at 14 days, and weaning occurs at 5 to 7 weeks. Yearlings and the father often help feed the young by regurgitating food for them after they are 3 weeks of age. If the den is approached by people or becomes soiled, the adults will transfer the family to new quarters, as far as 8 km (5 mi) away. The young usually disperse at the age of 6 to 9 months, when they are almost the size of their parents; however, the family occasionally remains together for the first winter. If food is abundant yearling females may breed, otherwise both sexes mate the following year. Coyotes have lived up to 18 years in captivity, 14.5 years under natural conditions, but few survive more than 6 to 8 years. The coyote has been known to breed with the gray wolf, red wolf *(Canis rufus)*, and even large dogs.
Remarks The coyote is an easily recognizable animal with its yellow eyes, long thin legs, and luxurious coat consisting of coarse guard hairs and fine underfur. Northern coyotes have a long soft coat, especially in winter, while that of southern individuals is short and bristly. This species generally does not begin to shiver until the temperature drops below -10°C (14°F). The long flowing tail acts as a balancing organ and a gland on the top surface near the base produces a secretion that serves in individual recognition. The snout is long

and thin compared to a wolf, and the jaws contain 42 teeth. Vision, smell, and hearing are keenly developed. Gait, stance, position of the tail and ears, baring of the teeth, and calls (bark, howl, squeal, yap) are indicative of moods and rank. Social position begins to develop as early as 5 weeks of age when the pups play and engage in fighting. Coyotes are less sociable than wolves but do form groups (often members of a family), perhaps in response to such factors as defense and prey size. The coyote maintains a series of dens in secluded locations, either dug themselves or a renovated burrow of some other large creature. Each den extends from 2 to 7 m (6.6 to 23 ft), has several entrances, and is used from year to year.

This species patrols regular pathways over its home range, traveling about 6 km (3.7 mi) per night, with a top speed of 32 km (19.9 mi) per hour. The size of the home range varies considerably depending on the habitat, terrain, and food availability. A pack may cover 14 sq km (5.2 sq mi), but even a pair sometimes covers up to 30 sq km (11.1 sq mi). A pack may defend a territory, however a pair does not seem to do so. Young usually disperse from 20 to 50 km (12.4 to 31.1 mi) from their birthplace, but can reach 160 km (99.4 mi) on occasion. One individual is known to have traveled over 400 km (248.6 mi) in 8 months in Arizona.

Coyotes often pair up to hunt large animals like deer. Sometimes they give up after a chase of only 50 m (164 ft), while on other occasions they may pursue their quarry for 5 km (3.1 mi). They bite and tear out pieces of hide from the deer until it falls to the ground. Mice and squirrels are captured by stalking and pouncing. Urban coyotes sometimes kill cats and dogs. Coyotes may be active anytime during the day or night, but are more so at sunset. A long list of parasites, both internal and external, and various diseases are known to infect this species. Wolves, cougars, and eagles occasionally prey on coyotes, while coyotes, in turn, do not tolerate foxes or bobcats in their range and will try to kill them.

I recall sighting coyotes on 2 occasions which showed their surprising lack of concern for people in cars. As I turned a curve on a mountain highway in Alberta, there sat a regal-looking coyote right at the side of the road, as if to greet passersby. At the other extreme, I was driving up to a desert wash in Arizona when the skinniest-looking coyote I had ever seen trotted slowly past in the opposite direction, completely ignoring me. The animal reminded me of the cartoon character Wily Coyote.

COYOTE

Coyote

A dog lay sleeping at his post in the yard, too exhausted from a hard day's work herding cattle to even notice the ranch lights go out. In the bright moonlight, the dark form of a hairy tarantula shuffled toward the building, searching the ground for insects. The quiet scene was suddenly shattered by loud howling and yapping which echoed off the surrounding hills. The dog jumped to his feet and the hair rose slowly along the back of his neck. He knew there was an unwanted visitor — a coyote — in his valley.

It was several days before they met face to face. The female coyote was trying to chase down a speedy roadrunner, which took flight just as she was about to snap her jaws around the bird's scrawny neck. When the coyote spotted the dog, she came to a sliding halt on the gravel, while the dog approached boldly with stiff-legged steps. The fur on both animals' backs stood on end and their tails were held high. They snarled at each other, exposing shiny white teeth behind their curled upper lips. At ten meters (32.8 feet) the dog charged the coyote, and although the coyote was smaller, she was quicker and easily outdistanced the dog. Excitedly, the dog paced his way back to the ranch, pausing frequently to lift his leg and mark his territory with a spray of urine.

Throughout the autumn the coyote frequently passed by the ranch. The dog knew of her presence from her odor and calls, and he began to enjoy trailing her. Since there were no other coyotes or dogs in the valley, they sought each other's company, though always remaining at some distance. Then one winter day, as they approached, the coyote no longer dashed away but crouched low and tucked her tail under her body. The dog rushed up with his tail wagging high. Nose to nose, then nose to tail, the two cautious animals finally became acquainted. The coyote flattened her ears, rolled over on her back, and began to whine with a grin on her lips. Their courtship had begun and during the following month the two companions frequently hunted together, sometimes staying out all night. In February, their behavior changed once more. As the coyote came into heat, the dog became very interested in her urine marks and droppings, and he ripped up the ground with his hind feet and claws. In his excitement, he tried to mount her but she whirled around and snapped at him. After repeated attempts at mating for over a week, she finally lifted her tail to one side and the two joined. A minute later, the dog changed position so that they faced opposite directions, but they remained tied together for fifteen minutes.

After each sojourn together the dog returned to the ranch while the coyote slept under the cover of bushes, retreating to a den only when the weather was uncomfortable. She used and kept clean about a dozen dens, some situated on rocky slopes, a cave in a canyon wall, and an abandoned building. The dog was fed each evening by the rancher, however the coyote had to be self sufficient. Early morning and late evening she patroled her runways, hoping to flush a rabbit or rodent, or to discover a clutch of quail eggs. On one occasion when the two animals were hunting together, she pounced on a kangaroo rat. Playfully tossing it into the air and catching it repeatedly, she teased the dog by turning away each time he tried to participate in the game. Suddenly a jackrabbit burst away from under a sagebrush and the frustrated dog immediately bounded after it. The coyote calmly gulped down the long-tailed rat and then lay down behind some brush. The jackrabbit easily outdistanced its pursuer but the dog persisted on the hot trail, barking all the while. Just as he was tiring he broke into a clearing only to find the coyote with his jackrabbit, still kicking, in her jaws. She had known that this prey frequently circles when being chased, and she had simply positioned herself to intercept the animal. This time she allowed the dog to feed first before finishing up the remainder of the carcass.

Over the following months the pair became expert hunting partners, greatly increasing the number of successful attacks compared to both foraging on their own. Their newly developed food-gathering strategy would stand them in good stead, for there would soon be some strange-looking young coyotes running through the valley.

Mammals of the
Woodlands and Shrublands

Included here, for sake of convenience, are several biomes and lesser communities that lie between tropical rainforest and savanna (trees dispersed in grassland) or desert. These are found in many warm, arid regions, but are best developed in southwestern United States, Mexico, Central America, Argentina, India, Australia, and in many African countries. Woodlands consist of trees, anywhere from 2 to 20 meters (6.6 to 65.6 feet) high, spaced so that they do not touch or form a canopy as occurs in a forest. In North America, pure stands or combinations of pines, junipers, and evergreen or deciduous oaks are typical. Prevalent examples include oak woodland (Oregon to Arizona), pine woodland (North Carolina and Florida west to Texas), western juniper woodland (Oregon to California), pinyon pine-alligator juniper woodland (Great Basin to Mexico), oak-juniper woodland (Arizona and Texas to Mexico), and pine-oak woodland (Mexico).

Thorn woodland is found in Sonora and Sinaloa, Mexico and is dominated by shrubs and bushes like acacias and mesquites (under 6 meters or 19.7 feet) which have thorns and small leaves or leaflets, and also by spiny succulents such as cereus cacti and agaves. Chaparral (from the Spanish "chaparro" for scrubby evergreen oaks) is an evergreen hardwood woodland present from Oregon to California and features small trees, shrubs, and bushes such as scrub oak, poison oak, manzanita, mountain mahogany, snowbush, cottonseed bush, chamise, and coffee berry. It is this arid shrubland that frequently burns with such devastating results to vineyards, ranches, and houses in southern California. Desert scrub grows from Arizona and New Mexico well into Mexico and is distinguished by such plants as creosote, mesquite, palo verde, catclaw acacia, western ironwood, ocotillo, yuccas, agaves, and cacti. Lastly, oak bushland occurs in the southern Rockies.

The climate of these various communities is arid, with precipitation falling either on a sporadic basis or, more frequently, after a prolonged dry season. This results in a predominance of plants that either lose their leaves or prevent excessive water loss by having small leaves covered in wax. Winter snowfalls are common in the north and at intermediate elevations in the south. Annual precipitation varies in different regions but is generally between 10 and 30 centimeters (3.9 to 11.8 inches), but occasionally as high as 90 centimeters (35.4 inches). Mean monthly temperatures range from 4°C to 24°C (39.2°F to 75.2°F) in January, 21°C to 38°C (69.8°F to 100.4°F) in July.

Woodlands and shrublands occur in valleys, foothills, and on steep mountainsides. In some communities the soil is a rich loam, with a buildup of humus from grass and tree leaves, but more often the soil is thin and rocky, supporting a sparse cover of grass. However, even barren ground bursts forth with numerous annual plants when the rains arrive.

Herbivores of woodland and shrubland are mule and white-tailed deer, peccary, brush rabbit, variegated squirrel, kangaroo and cotton rats, various relatives of deer mice, banded quail, scrub jay, inca dove, white-fronted parrot, and cicadas. Common carnivores and insectivores include the ocelot, badger, armadillo, coyote, opossum, hognose skunk, screech owl, roadside hawk, tyrant flycatcher, gila woodpecker, horned lizard, rattlesnakes, and ants.

Southern Pygmy Mouse and Hispid Cotton Rat

A bristly growth of low bunch grass covered the rolling hills, dotted here and there by scattered trees and broken by dry creek beds (arroyoos) lined with thorny acacia shrubs. Concealed amid the tangle of green grass, a maze of six-centimeter (2.4-inch)-wide runways stretched out in an interconnecting system. Like highway reststops, neat piles of cut stems lay in the path at intervals, and latrines, loaded with green and brown droppings, were situated at strategic points just off the trail. These signs, of two different sizes, revealed that two or more kinds of small mammals utilized this freeway.

As the intense, late-morning sunlight streamed down over the fields, bits of grass shuddered periodically, squeaks were heard, and occasionally rodents could be seen racing through sections of sparse cover. Under the shelter of a thick clump of grass, a tiny northern pygmy mouse paused and, in its nervousness, began washing its ears and face with circular, forward strokes of the front limbs. The mouse had traveled ten meters (32.8 feet) in an hour of foraging, and was about to retrace its route back home to the nest when its rounded ears detected a rustling sound. The little figure crouched low and trembled slightly in anticipation.

Suddenly the pathway was filled with the blunt face and stocky forequarters of a hispid cotton rat, many times its size. The pygmy mouse whirled around and disappeared down the trail, leaving the large rat momentarily startled. In a fighting mood at discovering a competitor on its personal grounds, the cotton rat charged after the pygmy mouse, gaining on it rapidly with its longer stride. The mouse's bulging eyes glimpsed the oncoming cotton rat over its shoulder. In a split second the mouse dove into the wall of grass, forcing its narrow body through spaces where the pursuer would have difficulty following. While the cotton rat sniffed and searched the spot where its quarry had vanished, the pygmy mouse circled for home on another trail.

This scene was repeated with increasing frequency throughout the summer. An exceptionally rainy period had produced a luxuriant growth of grass, and this abundant fresh food stimulated a rapid rise in rodent populations. Under crowded conditions, the cotton rats became more intolerant of pygmy mice and killed them and their nestlings at every opportunity. Wounds on the ears, tail, and body of all cotton rats were evidence of the daily conflicts among themselves as well. Under this constant threat, the pygmy mice ceased breeding and began to depart from the fields, taking up residence in less favorable brushy sites nearby.

Then one morning, a number of people appeared and commenced clearing the land to plant corn. Turned out of their burrows, nests, and trails by plows and hoes, the cotton rats scattered. Since adjacent fields were already occupied by other cotton rats, most of the displaced individuals perished over the next several months. By winter, spindly corn stalks stood over a layer of weedy plants whose seeds had lain dormant in the red, clay-like soil or had blown in from adjacent areas. Pygmy mice crept back into the fields, unhindered by cotton rats who were too timid to venture into the sparse cover. The plantation was abandoned the following year and clumps of grasses and a few shrubs appeared. The pygmy mice were joined by seed-eating spiny mice and harvest mice. Then, one by one, cotton rats invaded the fields again as the native vegetation grew dense enough to hide them. In five years they once again reached plague numbers.

SOUTHERN PYGMY MOUSE
Scientific name *Baiomys musculus*
Family New World Mice and Rats, Gerbils,
and Hamsters (Cricetidae)
Order Rodents (Rodentia)
Total length 125 mm (4.9 in)
Tail length 50 mm (2 in)
Weight 8 g (0.3 oz)
Color In different areas of the range, the upperparts range from light brown, reddish-
brown, to almost black, while the underparts
vary from pinkish-brown to white. The young
are more grayish. Populations from humid
regions are darker than those from arid areas
— a phenomenon noticed in many other
species and named Gloger's rule.
Distribution and Status The southern
pygmy mouse occurs from central Mexico
south to northern Nicaragua. It is most commonly found in grassy areas with a cover of
brush, shrubs, rock, or scattered trees. The
mouse's small size and adaptable ways allow
it to take advantage of numerous habitats
derived from human activities. Some of these
are active and abandoned plantations of corn,
sugar cane, coconut, and oil palm, rock and
cactus fences, and ditches overgrown with
cane grass and mesquite shrubs. Specimens
have been collected in rocky semidesert to
lush, grassy stream banks with an overstory
of cypress, willow, fig, and bamboo.

Its only close relative, the northern pygmy
mouse *(Baiomys taylori)*, is located from
southeastern New Mexico and eastern Texas
south to central Mexico. Where the 2 kinds
overlap, one species is usually far more abundant than the other. In this region the northern
pygmy mouse prefers the arid temperate
highlands, leaving the arid tropical lowlands
to its southern cousin. The northern species
prefers grassier sites. The 2 are believed to
have originated from a single ancestral stock
which became separated on either side of a
volcanic region in central Mexico during the
Pleistocene Ice Age. Now that the 2 groups
have reunited and there is no evidence of interbreeding, they merit recognition as distinct
species.

Food The bulk of the diet is plant material,
including leaves, bark, seeds, and nuts;
however, some insects are eaten as well.
Reproduction and Growth As might be
expected for a tropical rodent, the pygmy
mouse is capable of breeding at any time of the
year. The reproductive rate appears to decline
in winter and spring, and this can generally
be related to dry conditions and dormant food
plants. A litter averages 3 young, but may range
from one to 4, and requires 20 to 25 days from
fertilization to birth. The newborn weigh only
1.2 g (0.04 oz), yet they are eating soft green
leaves and fending for themselves within 3
weeks. Both parents care for them during this
period. In one month they attain 80 percent
of the adult weight. Females begin to conceive
at 28 days, while males are not capable of
mating successfully until 70 days old. Caged
mice have survived for 3 years; however, few
would reach even one year in their native
countryside due to the rigors of natural existence and a host of predators.
Remarks Pygmy mice closely resemble tiny
deer mice, but the ears are more rounded. The
gray juvenile coat begins to molt at about 40
days and the adult fur grows in by 60 days.
Although this species may be active at any
time, its peak periods occur at dusk and dawn.
The home range is remarkably small, often less
than 30 m (98.4 ft) across. The southern pygmy
mouse can become locally abundant in one
area and absent in other suitable locations.
Nests of shredded grass are tucked in grassy
swales, under rocks and loose bark, or beneath
the ground. Pygmy mice are gentle and peaceful creatures, easily kept together in captivity.

HISPID COTTON RAT
Scientific name *Sigmodon hispidus*
Family New World Mice and Rats, Gerbils,
and Hamsters (Cricetidae)
Order Rodents (Rodentia)
Total length 285 mm (11.2 in)
Tail length 115 mm (4.5 in)
Weight 150 g, maximum 225 g
(5.3 oz, maximum 7.9 oz)
Color The upper parts are blackish, with the
yellow- or light brown-tipped guard hairs imparting a grizzled effect. The underparts are
grayish-white.
Distribution and Status This species is the
most widespread of the cotton rats and occurs
from southern California, Nebraska, and
Virginia in the north, all the way south to Peru
and Brazil. The rodent has been expanding its
range northward in North America, rebounding from its displacement into extreme
southern United States and Mexico during the
last Ice Age. In this century it spread rapidly
into the northern Great Plains (160 km or 99.4
mi in Kansas in only 14 years), west into
Arizona along grass-lined watercourses, and
into eastern forested regions via fence rows
and road banks. The California population is
believed to have been isolated during the last
major glacial advance, when the main species'
range shifted south and east, leaving this remnant population in a refuge along the Colorado
River.

In south-temperate and tropical regions the
hispid cotton rat replaces the voles *(Microtus)*
of north-temperate, boreal, and arctic zones
as the dominant rodent of grassy habitats. It
is often abundant in tall or low grass of prairie,
swamps, salt marshes, stream borders, grass
under creosote or mesquite, forest edges, and
pine woodland. Disturbed sites are attractive
as well, such as ditches, cultivated and old
fields, and pastures. There are 7 or 8 species
of cotton rats distributed from the southern
United States to northern South America, and
likely several additional species will be
recognized from within present groups.
Food Over its enormous range the hispid
cotton rat makes use of many hundreds of dif-

SOUTHERN PYGMY MOUSE

ferent plants as food, utilizing leaves, roots, fruit, and seeds. Sedges and grasses such as bluestem, grama, and brome are most important, but forbs like sweet clover, goldenrod, wild rose, and dandelions are also accepted. Cotton rats relish cultivated crops and do considerable damage to sugar cane, cotton, corn, peanuts, watermelons, squash, sweet potatoes, and other plantations. Grasshoppers, beetles, crayfish, crabs, and eggs and chicks of ground-nesting birds have also been reported in their diet.

Reproduction and Growth The breeding season is restricted to the period from April to October at the northern extremes of the range but may occur during any month from the southern United States southward. Reproduction declines during the dry season or in years of low rainfall. Females become receptive to males within hours after giving birth, and come into heat again about every 8 days. Some produce at least 5 litters a year under favorable conditions (9 litters a year have been reported in a captive cotton rat). Following fertilization, the one to 15 embryos require 27 days for development prior to birth. In southern regions such as Costa Rica, litters average only 2.8 young, while litters are larger in the north—3 in Texas, 9 in Kansas—seemingly in response to the abbreviated breeding season. The newborn weigh 7 g (0.2 oz), are covered in fine brown hair, and are so well developed they are capable of moving around in a few hours. The eyes open within 3 days and the mice gain about 2 g (0.07 oz) per day, nursing from the 8 to 12 (usually 10) mammae of the mother. They appear out of the nest as early as 4 days and eat greens by one week. The female may tolerate several litters in her nest, but the male occasionally devours them if they are left unguarded. The offspring begin mating successfully at 40 to 50 days, and reach full size in 100 days.

Remarks The hispid cotton rat is quite a large, heavyset rodent with short limbs and a shaggy coat which almost conceals the rounded ears. The tail is thick and sparsely haired and has been found to be an important organ of temperature control, acting as an exposed surface for radiation of body heat. The teeth are high crowned and flat topped, with S-shaped folds covered in hard enamel for grinding tough and gritty plants and insects.

This species may be active anytime, although peak periods often occur after dusk and before dawn. Temperature, light, food availability, and the reproductive cycle can influence an individual's activity patterns. While the cotton rat forages through the grass, it eventually develops a system of concealed runways which are kept clear by the frequent passage of its feet and by cropping with its sharp teeth. Little piles of cut stems reveal where the rat logged a grass or sedge plant to reach the nutritious new growth on the tip. The nest may be situated on the surface or underground and consists of a shredded ball of grass. Coarse grass on the outside helps shed the rain, while the fine lining insulates against temperature extremes. Cotton is a favorite lining when available. Often the entrance is situated on the south side of the nest, which helps warm the contents and avoids drafts from cool north breezes. Burrows descend below the frostline in northern regions.

The home range is generally under 0.5 ha (1.2 a). Typical movements in 24 hours for males are 17 m (55.8 ft); 6 m (19.7 ft) for females. Populations of hispid cotton rats often fluctuate from a low of one per ha (0.4 per a) in winter and spring to 20 per ha (8.1 per a) by autumn. Occasionally they reach numbers of 70 per ha (28.3 per a), whereupon crowding and other stresses result in increased susceptibility to disease and predation. Many kinds of hawks and owls rely on cotton rats as their basic food supply, while snakes, alligators, mink, fox, and other carnivores hunt them regularly as well. Cotton rats compete with domestic livestock for pasture, devour crops, and may harbor diseases (like rabies) and parasites which can infect humans and livestock. On the plus side, they have been used in the laboratory for the study of nutrition and of diseases such as poliomyelitis and diptheria. Yet even when bred in the la-

boratory, they maintain their timid-aggressive nature, frightening easily but biting the hand that feeds them. Over much of its large range, the hispid cotton rat continues to play a major ecological role for a small mammal in native and altered habitats of North America.

I became familiar with the hispid cotton rat while collecting in grassy areas in Texas and New Mexico, and with the yellow-nosed cotton rat *(Sigmodon ochrognathus)* in grass-woodland in southern Arizona. A fellow graduate student who began studying the chromosomes of hispid cotton rats from different parts of the range was astonished to find 3 chromosomal types. Each represented a distinct species since there was no evidence of interbreeding where their ranges overlapped in Arizona and western New Mexico, and in southwestern Mexico. No doubt there are many more such "hidden species" to be discovered among North American mammals.

HISPID COTTON RAT

Coati

It was still early in the morning, yet the sun was already heating the hillside of black rocks exposed among the dry bunches of blue grama grass. The only shade to be found was under the Mexican pinyon pine and alligator juniper trees that were spaced widely and evenly, as if planted in error by foresters over this rough countryside. Suddenly there was movement of some large animal in one of the trees, and a strange-looking creature dropped to the ground on all fours. It moved like a raccoon, but its head, body, and tail were all greatly elongated. With the long banded tail held vertically, the animal swung its pointy up-curved snout around to test the air, then grunted. At this signal, a host of these reddish-brown creatures descended from the trees like a troop of baboons. Within a minute three large and twelve smaller animals were assembled, grunting and peeping loudly. The band of coatis was ready to commence its daily activities.

At first following the dominant female in single file and then spreading out, the other two females and offspring began foraging for food. While some coatis turned over rocks with their clawed paws in hopes of uncovering a mouse, most of the band sought insects or spiders in the soil. The young animals seemed more interested in playing and they chased and jumped on each other with great energy and quickness, screaming all the while. Several coatis spied a juniper covered with bluish-gray berries, and they ascended into the branches like monkeys to feed on the fruit. The group moved slowly downhill and soon entered an open woodland of evergreen oaks. With fifteen noses snorting in the leaves for enticing odors, it sounded as if pigs were running loose. When a coati smelled beetle larvae or some other underground creature, it dug deeply into the soil with the long blunt claws of the front feet. Then the flexible snout, which projected far beyond the lower jaw, was thrust inside to help guide the excavation. If the animal's head disappeared into the hole, it closed its eyes to keep out the dirt. As well, the small rounded ears lay back and a screen of coarse hairs sealed the ear canal. Usually the coati was rewarded for its efforts, as could be seen by its chewing jaws. The other animals continued to shuffle along slowly through the leaves and grass. Sometimes a grasshopper would take flight and an adult coati would expertly knock it out of the air with a paw. The youngsters were not as quick, but two or three gamely pursued the flying insects and soon lost sight of the band. Realizing they were lost, the little coatis let loose with plaintive peeping until one of the mothers came to the rescue and rounded them up again. Just before noon the animals stopped foraging and began to groom themselves and each other with their tongues, teeth, and claws. They spent the hot afternoon lazing about or sleeping in the shade of the oaks.

A few hours later the coatis rose to their feet at the sound of rustling leaves, and a large, powerful male coati appeared. Not intimidated, the three females growled and bared their blade-like canines, and the lonesome male bolted from the scene. The group departed in the opposite direction, still downhill. The vegetation changed to a chaparral of bush oaks less than two meters (6.6 feet) high. Here the animals were attracted to numerous small acorns lying on the ground or still growing on the branches. The dried nuts cracked open with a pop under pressure of the cusped cheek teeth. One coati scraped open an old log, and out scuttled a yellowish-white scorpion with stinger and pincers held aloft in defense. The coati rolled the scorpion over and over with its paw, until only the unprotected juicy body remained.

By late afternoon the troop had traveled almost two kilometers (1.2 miles) and were now on the edge of a mesquite scrub. Here and there between the bushes, white-spined cholla cactus and prickly pear pads grew out of the stony ground. A lizard streaked away like a shadow from beneath the fallen flower stalk of a bluish-gray agave. One coati twitched in anticipation of chasing it, but the lizard was too fast and disappeared from view. Suddenly there was great excitement as a kingsnake was pulled out of a rodent burrow. The meter (3.3-foot)-long snake was quickly pinned down and bitten on the head. Almost every coati was able to grab a bite as the dangling snake was whipped around and pulled into pieces.

That evening the band of tired coatis made their way back uphill to the oak woodland where they retired for the night, draped over forks in the trees. Not even a noisy flock of jays prevented them from drifting off to sleep, for it had been a full day. They had traveled through four plant communities and over eight hundred meters (2,624.7 feet) in elevation.

COATI
Scientific name *Nasua nasua*
Family Raccoons (Procyonidae)
Order Carnivores (Carnivora)
Total length males 120 cm (47.2 in);
females 100 cm (39.4 in)
Tail length 60 cm (23.6 in); 50 cm (20 in)
Weight 8 kg, maximum 11 kg
(17.6 lb, maximum 24.3 lb);
6 kg (13.2 lb)
Color Coatis are quite variable in color, both within a group and even the same individual during successive molts. Red and black phases are common, but the usual color varies from brown to brownish-red, often with a yellow wash over the chest and shoulders. The face is masked with brown, accentuated by white spots around and behind the eye. A thin white streak extends from the white muzzle along either side of the snout to the eyes. The ear tips and patch behind each ear are yellowish-white, as are the chin and throat. The underparts are yellowish to dark brown, becoming black on the feet. The brownish-red tail is marked by 6 to 10 indistinct bands.
Distribution and Status The coati originally occurred from the American-Mexican border and southern Texas all the way south to Peru, Argentina, and Brazil. Within several decades in the early 1900s it spread northward into Arizona and then into adjacent New Mexico. An occasional coati has been found in southeastern California. Some of these northernmost records are thought to be wanderers or captives which have been released. Coatis are able to live in vastly different habitats from wet jungle at sea level (where they are most abundant), pinyon-juniper and oak-pine woodlands at elevations up to 2 500 m (8,202 ft), oak forest, chaparral, mesquite grassland, and desert scrub. They often remain in the vicinity of trees or rocky canyons.

A closely related species, the Cozumel Island coati *(Nasua nelsoni)* is restricted to an island off the east coast of the Mexican state of Quintana Roo. The slightly smaller mountain coati *(Nasuella olivacea)* dwells in the Andes of Columbia, Ecuador, and Venezuela.

Food The mainstay of the coati's diet is invertebrates such as insects, worms, scorpions, centipedes, and spiders. It will also attack and devour any small animal it can catch such as mice, rats, squirrels, birds and their eggs, lizards, and snakes. Certain plants are commonly eaten, especially tubers and bulbs which are dug from the ground. Dozens of kinds of nuts and fruit are relished, including acorns from many types of oaks, manzanita, juniper, madrone, and prickly pear cactus. When dealing with larger tropical fruits, the coati scrapes the pulp free with the claws and then laps it up with the tongue.

Reproduction and Growth The breeding season lasts about a month, beginning as early as January in the southern part of the continent, and as late as April in the southern United States. During this period, the solitary adult males attempt to join the troop of females and subadults, but remain clearly subordinate to the female leaders. The male rubs his belly on the ground and marks objects with urine and musk from the anal glands. This behavior is increased in frequency at the appearance of a competing male. The 2 face off, raising their rubbery noses, baring the teeth, lowering the ears, and shrieking loudly. Generally the bluff works, but fights sometimes break out and lead to serious wounding by the 2.5-cm (one-in)-long canines. The hind feet can also do damage by scratching kicks with the sharp claws.

Following the mating act, the male resumes his private life-style while the female becomes pregnant for about 74 days. Near the end of her term, the female leaves the group and bears her 2 to 7 young in a nearby tree nest, rocky ledge, or cave. The offspring weigh about 150 g (5.3 oz) and are covered in dark gray hair with faint markings. They begin exploring away from the nest at 3 or 4 weeks, but are quickly discovered by the mother who is kept busy carrying them back in her mouth. At 5 weeks the new family rejoins the group, so that the number of coatis seems to increase dramatically during this period. The young continue to suckle for months even though

they are eating solid food they have caught themselves. They remain close to mother until she gives birth to another litter the following spring. Reaching full size by 15 months, they attain sexual maturity at age 2. The males depart, leaving the females to carry on within the group.

Remarks The slender and long-tailed coati does not closely resemble its cousin the raccoon, and is in fact a much smaller animal. The fur is long and coarse, except on the head and legs where it is quite short. A soft curly under-fur protects the coati from the cold, for the temperature can drop to surprisingly low levels on mountainsides even at southern latitudes. Individuals occurring on slopes in the United States often suffer frostbite on the end of their tails. The long tail is used for balance when the animal is moving on the ground and climbing, and as a prop when standing on the hind legs.

Coatis are unusual in their preference for daytime activity and in their social gatherings of up to 50 animals, often related females and their young. The group ranges over a region of perhaps 40 ha (98.8 a) in good habitat and as much as 300 ha (741 a) in country without much food, and covers several kilometers per day. Home ranges of bands frequently overlap and following some threat display, the members usually proceed to feed side by side without trouble. Coatis have even been observed peacefully eating fruit in trees alongside howler monkeys. The coati is not a fast runner. It rambles at a top speed of 27 km (16.8 mi) per hour and tires quickly. It seeks refuge in rock cover or in trees, where it is an adept climber. Enemies include eagles, hawks, big snakes, cats, and people, who kill it for meat and to protect crops. Rabies and distemper have been known to decimate populations (e.g., in Arizona during 1960-1961). Life expectancy is 14 years, but this is probably seldom achieved under natural conditions.

My first experience with a coati was in, of all places, a university campus in downtown Montreal, Quebec. While hurrying to class one

COATI

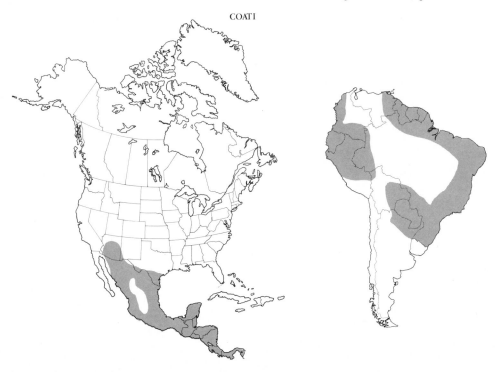

afternoon, I stopped to watch a strange-looking mammal being led on a leash by its owner. The coati was permitted to run free and headed straight for an old elm tree. This creature could teach a squirrel a thing or two about climbing, for it ran easily and confidently to a height of about 25 m (82 ft). I couldn't stay to learn how one coaxes a young playful coati out of a tall tree. This species is often displayed on a leash or in a cage at tourist spots in Mexico.

The last coati I met made off with my lunch! While my wife and I were camping in the spectacular Chiricahua Mountains of southern Arizona, we left some food on the table and returned to the car to obtain other supplies. We didn't concern ourselves with the excited hollering of nearby campers until we turned around to see a large coati leap up on the picnic table. With the coolness of a practised thief, this masked character proceeded to demolish the better half of a package of weiners before I could convince it to leave. It finally departed in a slow gallop, snorting through its long nose and probably planning its next sneak attack.

RINGTAIL

Scientific name *Bassariscus astutus*
Family Raccoons (Procyonidae)
Order Carnivores (Carnivora)
Total length males 800 mm (31.5 in); females 730 mm (28.7 in)
Tail length 380 mm (15 in); 350 mm (13.8 in)
Weight 1 kg (2.2 lb); 0.9 kg (2 lb)
Color This remarkably patterned animal is a grayish-tan with black-tipped guard hairs particularly on the head and along the back. The underparts are yellowish-white. The large eyes are accentuated by white circles. The cheeks and lips are white and 2 dark spots occur on each side of the snout. The lovely tail sports 6 to 9 black bands (incomplete below) alternating with narrower white bands, and ends in a black tip.
Distribution and Status This relatively unknown species occurs from Oregon, Wyoming, Kansas, and Arkansas south to Baja California and Chiapas—the most southern state of Mexico. It is typically found in rocky canyons, cliffs, talus slopes, and other rough country, from sea level to 3 300 m (10,827 ft)

in elevation. Selected habitats range widely from mesquite desert, brushy arroyos, chaparral, oak woodland, pinyon-juniper woodland, riverbank forest of willow, cottonwood, sycamore, and walnut, and to some extent, montane pine forest. The closely related cacomistle *(Bassariscus sumichrasti)* lives in the trees of dense forests from southern Mexico to Panama. The ringtail displays a remarkable resemblance in both shape and color to the ringtailed lemur *(Lemur catta)* — a primate from Madagascar. Interestingly, the lemur also lives among rocks in savanna or woodland.

Food The bulk of the diet is small mammals such as mice, kangaroo rats, wood rats, pocket gophers, and cottontails, but birds and their eggs, snakes, lizards, beetles, grasshoppers, crickets, spiders, and even scorpions are also accepted. Carrion of wild and domestic animals is devoured, as is poultry on occasion. Plants may make up a quarter of the food supply (especially important in the autumn) in the form of the fruit and seeds of juniper, hackberry, persimmon, manzanita, madrone, oak, mistletoe, cactus, and corn. Nectar from agave flowers is also consumed. Although the ringtail lives in semiarid landscapes, it is seldom found far from some source of water. This supply may be intermittent, since the animal is capable of surviving drought by concentrating the urine, thereby conserving body moisture.

Reproduction and Growth Ringtails live alone or they may pair, but it is not known how long this relationship lasts. Mating occurs from February to March and after 53 to 60 days development in the womb, usually 3 or 4 (range of one to 5) young are born. The period of births extends from April to July, with most in May and June. There is only one litter per year, but if a litter is lost the female mates again. The 28-g (one-oz) young are covered in sparse white hair and the tail shows bands of dark pigment where the back bands of hair will appear. The infants squeak and whimper constantly unless sleeping or suckling. Their eyes and ears open at 30 days and the teeth erupt at about this time as well. The father is kept away from the den for the first 3 weeks, after which he

is allowed to join the family. The little ringtails nurse from the mother's 4 nipples until 4 or 5 weeks of age when they change over to solid food caught by both parents. The female then concerns herself with the training of her offspring, and they become full grown and independent in the autumn or early winter.

Remarks This is a slender member of the raccoon family, notable for its fluffy banded tail, wide eyes, and pointy nose. Although its legs are short, it is active and agile in bounding over the ground and in climbing trees. Pads and semi-retractile claws offer excellent traction on any surface, and the animal is capable of running up almost vertical walls of rock. In negotiating narrow ledges, the body is balanced on the front feet while the back feet are worked into position. Leaps of 3 m (9.8 ft) are possible. The tail fluffs up much larger than the body when the animal is excited, sometimes arching over the back. Vocalizations include chitters, chirps, barks, growls, spits, and screams — a call for every occasion. When alarmed, the ringtail releases a smelly musk from the anal glands. This scent and urine are used to mark the animal's home range which, depending on the availability of food, may cover from 50 to 200 ha (123.5 to 494 a). Home ranges often overlap, and males tend to wander more widely than females. Prey animals are caught by ambush, and if missed on the first rush are not pursued for any distance.

Ringtails are common in many areas, but they are seldom seen because of their nocturnal habits. Most activity occurs in the middle of the night, to a lesser extent at dusk and dawn. Occasionally the animal may rest at the den entrance in daylight. Like its relative the raccoon, the ringtail will occupy old buildings in the vicinity of people. In fact, miners in the American Southwest used to keep them almost as pets, since they were interesting to watch and were great "mousers." The dens and resting sites are usually found in caves, rock piles, abandoned burrows, underbrush, in hollow trees, and even in stone walls separating fields. The average life span is unknown but is probably under 10 years. In captivity one individual lived for 23.5 years.

RINGTAIL

Ringtail

While many night creatures had been active for several hours, it was after midnight before the ringtail woke up. Its nest chamber, hidden under rocky debris at the base of a sandstone cliff, was still warm from solar heat built up in the orange-colored rocks. The ringtail lay on its back amid a floor covering of leaves. The slim creature rose on tiptoes and stretched its muscles in anticipation of the night's excursion. The long tubular and barred tail arched gracefully over the back and floated down again as gently as a feather. The animal sat back, scratched an itchy spot on the neck with a hind foot, and then proceeded to wash its face and ears with paws moistened by saliva. Becoming more active by the second, the ringtail dashed along the narrow space between two rock slabs and emerged from a crack just large enough to permit the passage of its body. No coyote or bobcat could reach the ringtail once it had gained entrance to the den.

The ringtail bounded lightly from boulder to boulder without a sound, crossed the savanna of grass and scattered live oaks, then descended to the canyon floor. In the dark shadows cast by the overhead crown of tall cottonwoods, willows, and sycamores, the pupils of the animal's eyes opened widely, gathering in the reflected moonlight. Seeing as well as in daylight, the ringtail headed toward the faint gurgling sounds of a shallow creek. Taking care not to wet its feet, the cat-like creature leaned forward and lapped up the water by repeatedly flicking its tongue. Pausing every few seconds, the ringtail looked around nervously and directed its ears like antennae toward the sudden hooting of a screech owl. Then it was off again on padded, hairy soles, seeming to flow over the ground like a windblown tumbleweed till it came to a quick halt near the base of a cliff. Having traveled about two hundred and fifty meters (820 feet) from its den, the ringtail had just come across the fresh scent of a white-throated wood rat. With tail held straight out, the ringtail flattened its ears and body and began to stalk its quarry. The wood rat was busy gnawing on a red fruit of a prickly pear cactus, oblivious of the snakish form slinking toward it. The wood rat bobbed its whiskered snout high into the cool night breeze, perhaps suspecting not all was as it should be. With split-second precision, a blur of gray shot out from behind a bush, and snapping jaws with stabbing canines caught the wood rat in mid-squeal. It could only manage a few strong kicks before it lay limp in the ringtail's mouth.

Rather than eat in the open, the hunter dragged its prey within the cover of rock rubble only a short distance away. While pulling out the belly contents, the ringtail braced itself against an unsteady rock, and with dull, knocking sounds, a number of boulders tumbled down over the animal, sealing it in a small cavity. The ringtail panicked and ricocheted from wall to wall, bumping its head and shoulders before it calmed down. All night the ringtail paced and turned in its cramped quarters, searching for a way out. In fright it had released a powerful-smelling musk from the anal glands, which drifted with the animal's barking call over the surrounding valley.

By morning the ringtail was exhausted and dehydrated from the shock of being trapped. It slept fitfully for short periods, alternating with bouts of digging, jumping, and nibbling the remains of the wood rat. Although weakened, the animal continued to leap upward, finally managing to gain a hold on a crevice with its extended claws. Its flattened head pushed forward, assisted by the scrambling hind feet. Slowly the long thin creature crept along the passageway on its short legs. Any space the head passed through, the rest of the ringtail could follow. It would be difficult to back up again, but the ringtail thought only of moving ahead. Then the ordeal was over as suddenly as it had begun. The escape artist was free of the rock tomb. It raced back home in broad daylight, the fluffy tail sailing along behind. The ringtail did not appear at the entrace to the den till the following morning. It curled up to rest in the early-morning sun, obviously still not recovered from the near-fatal accident.

Nine-banded Armadillo and Ocelot

Along the brush-lined riverbank some animal was hard at work scratching in the dry leaves. Half-hidden under the vegetation, the shelled creature paused once in awhile, puffing and snorting like a little pig. Was this a turtle digging a den in the bank for a clutch of eggs? Instead of a flattened reptile, out strode what looked like a scaly football — a nine-banded armadillo foraging for food. Encased in brown armor, the tank-like animal displayed surprising mobility as its short legs carried it into a grassy clearing. Here it smelled something attractive and began to dig out a cone-shaped hole with the large claws on the front feet. For the next five minutes the armadillo busied itself uncovering and swallowing whole, about a dozen beetle larvae, leaving the area littered with little excavations.

The armadillo then returned to the bank and commenced gathering a mixture of grass and leaves to reline its nest. A week earlier this female had given birth to four tiny replicas of itself, and the offspring had soiled their old nest. The forefeet raked the fresh plant debris into a neat pile, but instead of carrying it in her mouth, she squatted and clamped the material between her belly and the top of her hind legs. With a curious shuffle, the armadillo zigzagged backwards several meters and disappeared down a burrow, guided by her tapering bony-ringed tail.

High above in a nearby tree, another creature was on the prowl. A magnificent young ocelot bounded from limb to limb without the faintest sound, hoping to surprise a snoozing iguana or fowl settling down to roost. Its graceful lithe movements and alert expressive face were in sharp contrast to the plated armadillo, now nursing her young below ground. While hunting, the spotted cat used its keen hearing and prominent eyes to locate prey, whether on the ground or in trees. Suddenly the ocelot froze in a crouch, its twisted body following the curving contours of a branch. The soft chirp of a sleepy bird had revealed its position to the approaching cat. From each padded toe a needle-pointed claw curved out of its furry sheath and sank into the gray, lichen-crusted bark. A rapid lunge and the bird was pinned down by the cat's front feet before it could unlock its legs from the perch. A quick bite on the head dispatched the bird, and the ocelot painstakingly plucked every feather before devouring the meal in two big chunks.

The last of the feathers floated downward through the warm evening air, just as the pointy nose of the armadillo reappeared aboveground. Craving the berries that grew in bushes along the edge of the field, the armadillo plowed a furrow through the grass and then rose on its hind limbs, braced by the tail. It grunted and sniffed the air while turning its head slowly, as if relying on its nose to locate the fruit, although the meal was only a short distance from its tiny weak eyes. Meanwhile, the ocelot had watched this strange creature's antics with great interest and now decided to investigate more closely. The cat backed down the trunk until two meters (6.6 feet) from the bottom, when it abruptly turned around and leapt to the ground in one quick motion.

The snapping of a twig was heard by the armadillo's funnel-like ears and the animal ceased moving. The ocelot stalked from behind so that the armadillo was unaware of its presence. As the cat strained forward to smell this musky rock, the armadillo unexpectedly jumped straight up into the air, smashing its hard shell into the cat's nose and canine teeth. The ocelot jumped back in great surprise, while the squeaking armadillo ran quickly for the thorny cover of the riverbank brush. Recovering and accepting the challenge, the ocelot galloped after the leader, but it had difficulty penetrating the bushes. The armadillo dug furiously with its front feet, stopping only to arch and kick back the earth in the cat's face. Within a minute the tunnel-maker had almost disappeared from view. Seeing it was escaping, the ocelot jumped in and grabbed the tail in its jaws. But pull as it might, the armadillo would not budge from the hole, for it had wedged its shelled and scaly surface against the soil and roots. The ocelot finally released its hold, backed up while looking somewhat confused, and then continued on its way. The armadillo was left displaying its exceptional ability to hold its breath, for it did not back out of the hole until fifteen minutes later.

NINE-BANDED ARMADILLO

Scientific name *Dasypus novemcinctus*
Family Armadillos (Dasypodidae)
Order Sloths, Anteaters, and Armadillos (Edentata)
Total length 70 cm (27.6 in)
Tail length 30 cm (11.8 in)
Weight 5 kg, maximum 7.7 kg
(11 lb, maximum 17 lb)

Color The armadillo is dark brown with a patchwork of ivory spots, becoming more prevalent on the sides. The belly and underside of the tail are light colored, and the long, banded tail ends in a dark tip. Tufts of hair arising between the scales are gray or brown, while hairs on the ears, neck, legs, and belly are light brown or yellowish-white.

Distribution and Status This species has the widest distribution of any edentate — from New Mexico, Kansas, and South Carolina south to Argentina and Uruguay. It has also reached the Caribbean islands of Trinidad, Tobago, Grenada, Margarita, and Mexiana. The armadillo was first reported in the United States by the famous naturalists Audubon and Bachman in 1854, along the Rio Grande of southern Texas. Perhaps due to a warming climate the animal was in the process of extending its range to the north, east, and west, so that by 1934 it had spread thoughout the southern half of Texas and into Louisiana. By this time several introductions in peninsular Florida began another expanding population center which united with the main species range in the 1970s. Under the added influence of overgrazing and predator control, the armadillo has now reached New Mexico, Colorado, Kansas, Tennessee, and South Carolina.

Armadillos are found in many types of habitat — semidesert, grassland, fields, orchards, bottomland forest, sand-pine scrub, slash pine-turkey oak and other deciduous forests, evergreen broadleaf forest, cloud forest, tropical rain forest, savanna, and thorn scrub. They prefer areas with moist soil which provide easy digging for insect life and worms. In arid regions the animals are restricted to the edges of watercourses. Cold winters in the north periodically kill armadillos even when they are curled up in a nest.

There are about 20 species of armadillos, all but 2 restricted to South America. The nine-banded armadillo has 5 close relatives, including the hairy long-nosed armadillo *(Dasypus pilosus)*. This strange animal, from high elevations in the Peruvian Andes, is covered by a shell and long dense fur. An extinct armadillo *(Dasypus bellus)* was common over the southeastern United States during the Pleistocene Ice Age.

Food The armadillo probes its snout in soft moist soil and rotten logs in search of small animals, which make up over 90 percent of its food. Beetles, crickets, grasshoppers, scorpions, ants, termites, worms, slugs, and snails are important items, as well as occasional crayfish, amphibians, reptiles, birds and their eggs, and small mammals. One quick swipe of the tongue can bring into the mouth 72 ants, while 40,000 may be swallowed whole in one meal. Larger prey is broken up by the 32 peglike premolars and molars (incisors and canines are absent). Fruit and seeds are also eaten, including plums, blueberries, persimmons, mulberry, citrus, juniper, pine, and fungi. Considerable plant debris and soil are ingested along with food items. The animal likes to drink water.

Reproduction and Growth The armadillo has one of the most unusual methods of reproduction to be found among mammals. The female becomes receptive for 4 days during the period of June to August and mates with a male who often occupies the same burrow. Males are known to produce sperm year-round. The female may stand on all fours with the male above and behind, or she may lie on her back. One week later the fertilized egg reaches the uterus or womb, but enters a resting stage. Sometime in October or November the embryo implants into the uterus wall and starts to divide, but instead of forming the organs of a single individual (as occurs in other mammals), the embryo divides into 4 cells, each of which begins to develop into a separate baby armadillo. The result is identi-

cal quadruplets. After continuing growth for 70 to 100 days, the 4 (rarely 2 to 6) offspring are born from February to April. Each weighs about 85 g (3 oz) and looks like a miniature adult. The shell is soft, but the eyes are open and they can walk in a few hours. The female nurses them from 4 nipples and within a few weeks she leads them away from the nest to forage, protecting them aggressively should a predator appear. Weaning occurs around 3 months of age although they usually remain with the female for several more months. Sexual maturity is attained at one year, but full size and hardening of the shell requires 3 years. Life expectancy in the wild is about 4 years, and individuals have survived 8 years in captivity.

Remarks Much like a turtle, the armadillo is enveloped in a bony external skeleton that is braced, but not joined, to the hips and vertebral column. The shell or carapace consists of shoulder and hip shields with 9 (sometimes 8 to 11) overlapping bands in between. The tail is likewise encased in 12 to 15 bony bands, and a third shield lies atop the head. The bands and shields are formed of connected bony scales or scutes, covered with a thin leathery skin. Tufts of hair project from behind these scales and also appear on the undersides, the scaly legs, and the base of the tail. The large ears are black, pebbly, and shaped like funnels. The head narrows to a pink, pig-like snout. The eyes are small and don't seem to see other creatures until within a few meters. The legs are short and strong for digging, the front feet being armed with 4 big claws (the middle 2 the stoutest) and the hind feet with 5. Altogether, the armadillo is a fantastic prehistoric-looking animal.

In spite of the heavy armor and short legs, an armadillo can easily outrun a person until it escapes into a burrow or thorny brush. It has also been known to walk submerged along the bottom of a creek, but usually prefers to swim at the surface. It continually improves the buoyancy of its heavy body by swallowing air.

Other unusual but internal features are a common pouch in the female which serves as both vagina and urethra, a bladder which

NINE-BANDED ARMADILLO

stores the sticky saliva, a worm-like tongue, and a pair of anal glands which can be pushed out to release a musky scent when the animal is alarmed. The metabolic rate is low and temperature control is relatively primitive; it may take several days for an individual to warm up again after it has been subjected to cold. In fact, it has been estimated that an armadillo can last only 10 days at 0°C (32°F), even when sleeping in a nest, for it has little insulation and cannot feed in frozen ground. It is most active at night or dusk and dawn (occasionally on a cloudy day) when the temperature is within 20 to 25°C (68 to 77°F). Panting or shivering occurs if the animal is hot or cold.

An armadillo spends much time sleeping in its burrow, sometimes in company with another armadillo, cottontail, skunk, or mouse. The burrow is usually located on a hillside or in a brushpile and extends for 2 to 8 m (6.6 to 26.2 ft), ending in a grass-lined chamber. It may use a number of burrows spread over its home range, which averages 10 ha (24.7 a). The coyote, dog, black bear, and bobcat occasionally eat an armadillo, in spite of its curling up to protect its belly. Accidental collisions on highways take a heavy toll. People destroy them as well because their burrows weaken dikes and create a hazard for livestock. Armadillos are roasted and eaten in some areas. Though I have witnessed a number of road-killed specimens, I was quite unprepared for my first observation of a living armadillo. Settling down in a campsite in Texas, we heard a rustling in the leaves. A few seconds later an armadillo trotted past, grunting away as if it were unaware of our presence.

OCELOT

Scientific name *Felis pardalis*
Family Cats (Felidae)
Order Carnivores (Carnivora)
Total length males 110 cm (43.3 in);
females 100 cm (39.4 in)
Tail length 40 cm (15.8 in); 35 cm (13.8 in)
Weight 14 kg, maximum 16 kg
(30.9 lb, maximum 35.3 lb);
11 kg (24.3 lb)

Color The thin short fur is variable in background color, even among individuals from the same region. Generally forest-dwellers are orangy-yellow, while shrubland forms are grayish-yellow. The underparts, cheeks, whisker pads, and partial eye rings are white. The whole body is covered by a large number of black or brown stripes, spots, and black-bordered blotches. The back of the ears are black, as are the tail rings. Every ocelot is marked with its own pattern, which does not even match from one side to the other. This beautifully colored and spotted coat blends the animal into its surroundings of shadows and spots of sunlight and moonlight coming through the trees and shrubs.

Distribution and Status The range of the ocelot extends from Arizona, Texas, barely into Arkansas and Louisiana, thence southward (except in the interior corridor of Mexico) to Peru, northern Argentina, and Uruguay. Although once a common cat, it is now endangered from overharvesting in some parts of the range and is extremely rare in the United States. The ocelot is found in a considerable variety of habitats, from rocky shrubland, savanna, and woodland, to deciduous and tropical rain forests.

There are many other spotted relatives of the ocelot in Asia, Africa, and South America, including the margay *(Felis wiedii)* whose range closely approximates that of the ocelot. The margay is slightly smaller and is highly arboreal.

Food Ocelots feed on small mammals such as mice, rats, hares, and agoutis as well as birds, lizards, snakes, and invertebrates (mostly insects). Monkeys, lambs, calves, and poultry are occasionally taken as well.

Reproduction and Growth Ocelots may pair and remain together for years. Reproductive habits are not well known, but ocelots are thought to breed throughout the year in the tropics. In northern Mexico and southern United States the mating season occurs from July to September, and 70 days later (September to November) 2 to 4 young are born in a hollow log or rocky den lined with soft vegetation. They are blind and lightly covered with hair. The female nurses them, then soon begins to deliver solid food like mice and other small prey. When the youngsters are strong enough they accompany the adults on their forays, thereby learning through example the techniques and strategies of a feline predator. If danger threatens, the whole family retreats to the safety of a tree. The offspring mature at 12 months of age, by which time they have dispersed.

Remarks The alert face, graceful body, and colorful coat combine to make the ocelot one of North America's most attractive mammals. Highlighting its many expressions are the 2 large brown eyes, whose pupils open widely in the dark and constrict to narrow spindles in bright light. As in other cats, the eyes are set in a forward position, permitting binocular vision (the focusing of both eyes on the same object). This ability enables excellent depth perception and intensifies the image by superimposing signals on the light-receptive retina of both eyes. Of great value in night perception is a crystalline layer behind the retina which reflects the faint light back again through the rods of the retina. It is this tapetum which is responsible for the eerie eye-shine of night-prowling mammals. The senses of hearing, balance, and touch with the whiskers are well developed, whereas the ability to smell is not as keen as in the wolf family. These features are all important elements in the ocelot's role as a night hunter of quick terrestrial and arboreal prey.

An ocelot frequently sleeps on a tree bough or may retire inside a hollow log or cave. It hunts during the day or night, seeking to flush prey while walking briskly. The body is sup-

Continued on p. 292

OCELOT

Giant Anteater

A brownish-black cat crept stealthily through some bushes and out into the short dry grass. It was morning and the jaguarundi was wending its way back to its den after a long night of hunting. Bounding along the edge of the bushes it leapt gracefully onto a fallen log. Though it had scarcely made a sound, the cat was suddenly startled by the movement of something alongside the tree trunk. As the cat crouched low, ready to attack or bound away, it watched an enormous bushy tail move to one side, uncovering a long snout with sleepy black eyes. The cat growled at this strange animal, for it had never come across a giant anteater before. The anteater bolted to its feet, emitting a hiss from its tiny mouth. The inquisitive jaguarundi backed away, jumped to the ground, and circled for a closer look. At its approach, the anteater rose up on its hind feet and shuffled around to face the cat. Standing over a meter (3.3 feet) high, and with huge arms and claws ready to strike a fatal blow, the anteater was an equal match for any predator — even a jaguar. The jaguarundi wisely retreated and disappeared from the scene.

The anteater stood there for some time, still upset at being so rudely awakened. Although it could not see very far with its tiny eyes, it carefully sniffed the air and listened for sounds of the cat in case it was still trying to sneak up from behind. Confident it was alone, the hairy animal dropped down on all fours and moved slowly off through the grass. With pointed snout, vertically flattened tail held erect, and striking color pattern, the anteater was indeed a strange-looking animal. Perhaps it would have appeared more like a normal creature if it walked backwards, with its head concealed in the bushy hair. The several scythe-like claws folded back out of the way, so the animal walked on the knuckles and sides of the front feet. The anteater kept its nose just clear of the ground, obviously searching for food with a keen sense of smell. Pausing frequently, it dug in the soil and appeared to find a few beetles or other insects.

Suddenly it changed direction and headed for a mound of brown earth that was projecting above the surrounding grass. With as great excitment as an anteater can muster, the animal circled the mound, constantly testing it with its nose. Then, with an inward stroke of its powerful right arm, the anteater's claws scraped into the clay which had been baked hard by the sun. Several strokes later the claws tore open a branching network of tunnels swarming with fat white termites. The anteater poked its snout inside, and the long worm-like tongue which was covered in sticky saliva, slithered rapidly out and in, catching hundreds of termites as well as earth particles. Once the insects were inside the anteater's mouth they were ground up against hard bumps on the cheeks and roof of the mouth. Digging deeper toward the base of the termite colony, the claws reached the nursery which was filled with eggs and larvae. Again the tongue went to work, sweeping up the squirming termites that were trying in vain to carry the young to safety. Within twenty minutes the mound lay scattered and most of its former contents of fifteen thousand termites were being digested in the anteater's stomach.

Next to eating ants and termites, the anteater's favorite pastime was sleeping. The heat and glare of the noon sun sent most creatures scurrying for shade, and it was not long before the anteater ambled over to a dry creek and curled up against the bank. With its head buried between thick arms and the tail acting as an umbrella, the anteater drifted into a light sleep. Each unusual sound or new smell brought the rounded snout poking out through the pile of fur.

OCELOT *continued from p.289*
ported on the toes and not the soles of the large feet. A pair of ocelots may hunt together, communicating by soft mews. The animal does not hesitate to enter water and is an excellent swimmer.

The ocelot is sometimes kept as a pet and is notable for its gentle disposition and attractiveness. However it can grow into a powerful animal capable of causing damage to households, and can become rather smelly from its body odor and from spraying urine — a habit from nature whose function is to mark the territory. Ocelots have lived 17 years in captivity. A number of years ago I received a call from a woman who was most upset at the death of her pet ocelot. She wished to donate the specimen to the museum and offered to pay the cost of mounting it in a lifelike position. When the carcass arrived, I was astonished at its great size and muscle development. That put an end to my long-time wish of securing an ocelot for a pet.

GIANT ANTEATER
Scientific name *Myrmecophaga tridactyla*
Family Anteaters (Myrmecophagidae)
Order Sloths, Anteaters, and Armadillos (Edentata)
Total length 200 cm (78.7 in)
Tail length 80 cm (31.5 in)
Weight 20 kg, maximum 23 kg (44.1 lb, maximum 50.7 lb); females average slightly smaller than males
Color The coat is grayish-brown or grayish-black, sporting a prominent black blaze with a white border that extends from the throat and chest to either side of the back. White fur continues down onto the forearms and reappears as a patch on the front and sides of the wrist. The young is similarly colored and marked, and when it clings tightly to the mother's back it almost disappears due to the complex color pattern and long hair. Perhaps the black and white patch is an example of warning coloration (like the striped skunk), permitting easy recognition and avoidance by

predators. When an anteater folds up to sleep under the long hairy tail, the animal blends into the background and is difficult to see.

Distribution and Status The giant anteater's range extends as far north as Belize and Guatemala (almost to Mexico) and south to northern Argentina and Uruguay. It is a relatively common animal in savanna and dry and humid woodlands where ants and termites abound. This species originated in South America and spread into North America by way of the Panamanian land bridge. It has only 3 close relatives — 2 tamanduas *(Tamandua tetradactyla* and *mexicana)* and the two-toed anteater *(Cyclopes didactylus)* — the latter 2 species reaching southern Mexico.

Food Like the pangolins of Africa and Asia and the echidnas of Australasia, the giant anteater has become specialized to feed on ants and termites. Other foods include beetles and their larvae, worms, and some fruit such as berries. Anteaters lick dew and rain drops from leaves but don't appear to drink often.

Reproduction and Growth Anteaters lead a solitary life-style and come together briefly for the purpose of mating. The single young develops for about 190 days before it is born, generally in spring but sometimes in autumn. The female stands while giving birth, and soon after being licked clean, the baby crawls up on its mother's back. The 1.7-kg (3.8-lb) offspring comes down to nurse from 2 nipples, which draw milk from mammary glands extending from the chest to the abdominal region. Although the youngster can move at a slow gallop by one month, it still prefers a free ride on mother for yet another month. It frequently emits a short shrill whistle to communicate with its mother. At 2 years of age the offspring is full grown and weaned. It either leaves or is forced away from its mother who is likely ready to give birth again.

Remarks The giant anteater is one of nature's more fanciful creations, and it can be mistaken for no other animal. Sweeping down from the high and narrow arched back is a prehistoric-looking elongated head with tiny eyes and small ears, covered with short hair.

At the other end of the animal is probably the bushiest tail of any mammal, with coarse hair up to 40 cm (15.8 in) long arising mainly from the top and bottom of a scaly tail. While there are the usual 5-clawed toes on the hind feet, only 4 toes can be seen on the front feet (the fifth is internal). The second and third claws reach a length of 10 cm (3.9 in) and are used expertly to rip open insect nests, in defense, and to comb the fur. The skin is thick and tough, useful in warding off the bites and stings of insects.

There are no teeth in the jaws to grind up the hard skeletons of ants and beetles. Their function has been replaced by rough surfaces of the mouth and the strong grinding action of sand, pebbles, and the stomach walls. Copious amounts of sticky saliva are produced when the animal begins to feed. The rounded tongue is about 60 cm (2 ft) long and 1 cm (2.5 in) wide. It flicks in and out at rates up to 160 times per minute. With such an effective insect catcher, the anteater may consume 30,000 ants or termites in one day. The tongue retractor muscles and the extensive salivary glands are situated in the chest rather than in the head like all other mammals. There is some indication that the large hairy tail may be used to sweep swarming insects into a pile for easy gathering and to brush them off the body.

Giant anteaters are active during the day or night, but near people they become nocturnal. Rather than remaining in a specific home range, they wander widely in search of insect prey. Most of the time is spent sleeping against a tree or in shallow burrows. They do not hesitate to swim across rivers and are able climbers, but are not inclined to do so. The anteater has few enemies, for it is capable of defending itself against a cougar or jaguar. Any person or predator coming too close is hit or grasped with the strong arms and claws. It cannot bite, since the mouth is only a narrow opening and teeth are lacking. This docile creature never attacks and generally runs away from danger with a lumbering gait, fighting only when pressed.

GIANT ANTEATER

COLLARED PECCARY

Scientific name *Tayassu tajacu*
Family Peccaries (Tayassuidae)
Order Even-toed Ungulates (Artiodactyla)
Total length 90 cm (35.4 in)
Tail length 3 cm (1.2 in)
Weight 20 kg, maximum 27 kg
(44 lb, maximum 59.5 lb)

Color Peccaries range in color from light gray, brown, to black, with a grizzled effect from the 4 to 6 white or yellowish bands on each bristly hair. The coat is darkest along the back and lighter on the underparts and sides of the head. A light band, running from the breast to the back, is usually present. This accounts for the name "collared peccary." The young are reddish-brown with a blackish stripe down the back and a distinct collar.

Distribution and Status The collared peccary ranges from the southern regions of Arizona, New Mexico, and Texas south to northern Peru and Argentina. It is absent from Baja California and the high central plateau of northern Mexico, and has been introduced in Cuba. This is an animal of both temperate and tropical regions, reaching its highest densities in shrubland along the coasts and its lowest in desert country. It is found in mesquite-ironwood desert scrub, mesquite and manzanita-scrub oak thickets, juniper and pine-oak woodlands, thorn forests, and tropical evergreen and tropical deciduous forests. The northern distribution is undoubtedly controlled by desert conditions and periodic snowstorms and cold weather, resulting in the death of whole populations from exposure and starvation. In Arizona it reaches elevations of 1 900 m (6,234 ft) in alligator juniper and ponderosa pine - Douglas fir forests.

The family of peccaries evolved in South America and spread into North America several million years ago. Until recently, only 2 species were known — the collared and the white-lipped peccaries *(Tayassu pecari)* — the latter occurring from southern Mexico to northern Argentina and traveling in herds of 100 or more. A fossil species, called the Chacoan peccary *(Catagonus wagneri)*, was unexpectedly discovered alive in the Chaco region of Paraguay in the early 1970s.

Food The collared peccary is omnivorous, meaning it eats both plants and animals. However, vegetation is far more prevalent in the diet and consists of roots, bulbs, greens such as grass and forbs, nuts, and berries. Items eaten, of course, depend on what is available in each habitat. In desert areas succulent cactus pads and fruit, and lechuguilla (an agave or century plant) supply the necessary nourishment and water. In shrublands and woodlands nuts of oaks and pines, beans of mesquite and catclaw, and berries of manzanita and juniper are most important. In tropical forests, palms, figs, zapote, and hundreds of other trees and shrubs provide fruit. Cultivated crops are taken on occasion, as are birds, reptiles, insects, and carrion. Peccaries prefer to drink about 1.5 *l* (50.7 fl oz) of water daily, but subsist on 0.5 *l* (16.9 fl oz). They can survive about 6 days in the desert without water or succulent forage. As with most other mammals, the quality and abundance of food are the main factors controlling population level and territorial size.

Reproduction and Growth In tropical regions the young are born during any month of the year, but in northern Mexico and adjacent United States births are usually restricted to the spring and summer. Survival of young is highest following the rainy season when new vegetation has appeared. Most births occur from May to July in Texas, July to August in Arizona. Females begin periods of estrus or heat in late autumn and throughout the winter until they become pregnant, generally by mating with the dominant male who keeps other males away during the several-day courtship. About 115 days after fertilization the female seeks privacy from the herd and gives birth in a sheltered spot. Newborn range from one to 4, but twins are most frequent. More than 2 seldom survive, and strangely enough, although the female has 4 pairs of mammae, the front one or 2 pairs do not secrete milk. She cleans and nurses her offspring while in a standing position, and the next day leads them back to the protection of the herd. Weaning occurs at about 6 weeks. The young are fierce fighters but continue to accompany their mother for over a year. Females may commence breeding as early as 33 weeks, males at 46 weeks if they have the opportunity. Their permanent set of teeth appears at 84 weeks. The average life span under native conditions is unknown, but individuals have lived for 25 years in zoos.

Remarks The peccary is obviously related to the true pigs, as evidenced by many similar features including the pink flattened snout. The head is proportionally large, the legs are short, and the tail is hardly noticeable. There is no insulating underfur, just a coat of bristly hair, longest from the crown to the back. Four digits are present on the front feet and only 3 on the rear feet; however, the weight is carried on paired hoofed toes on both front and back. The premolars and molars are low crowned and rounded, not unlike human teeth which are also adapted for an omnivorous diet. Whereas the upper canines of a pig recurve upwards, the peccary's grow down and wear against the lower canines to form formidable stabbing weapons. The upper canines grow to a length of 3.5 cm (1.4 in) in an adult, but wear down to half this length in an old individual.

Peccaries are social creatures, gaining comfort and security from marauding predators by gathering in related family herds, generally numbering 5 to 15 but sometimes up to 50. Some old boars prefer a secluded life and are called "jabali solitario" by the Mexicans. Composition of the herd is stable, with few individuals moving in or out. It is based on a hierarchy with the largest male dominant, but with some males subordinate to certain females. The herd forages over an area of 50 to 800 (average 200) ha (124 to 1,976 a; average 494 a), and since it defends this area from other peccary herds the home range is the same as the territory in this case. Activity periods are largely controlled by temperature. The animals are active at dusk and dawn (crepuscular) and

Continued on p.296

COLLARED PECCARY

Collared Peccary

During most of the night a chorus of grunts and snorts rose from a series of low hills that were covered in scrub oak and mesquite. By early morning all was quiet. Shallow holes, black droppings, and thousands of small rounded hoof prints in the dry soil revealed that a large number of grazing animals had passed through the area. Not far away, in a shaded canyon, a band of peccaries lay bedded down among the rocks, the reddish-brown offspring contrasting with the grizzled-black adults. As the air began to wave in the heat, a few young peccaries rose periodically to play or suckle, if they could convince their mothers to cooperate. Most adults were passed out, panting heavily while on their sides, managing but a flick of an ear or flinch of their hide in response to pesky buzzing flies.

As night fell the temperature refused to fall below 35°C (95°F), but the depressing heat was not about to delay the herd's activities. Up on all fours, the first peccary displayed the species' stocky body, enormous tapering head, and short, almost-dainty legs. Like a school of excited fish, they mulled around at close quarters until twenty- three animals had gathered. Based mainly on its size, each individual knew its social rank in the hierarchy and confirmed its attachment to the group by reciprocal grooming with other members. Standing head to tail, a pair of animals commenced rubbing their heads and eye glands over each other's hind legs, rump, and prominent musk gland situated on the back. Repeated grooming of alternating couples throughout the night resulted in the transfer of a common scent mixture to each peccary. On occasion an animal backed into the brush or grass, and with up and down movements of the hindquarters, applied its musk to the vegetation, thereby marking the site as part of the herd's territory.

Close-knit and harmonious as the herd appeared at this moment, fresh cuts and bruises on ears and pink noses reflected mounting aggression among a number of older males and females. In charge of the herd was a vigorous male, until recently supported by the majority. But increasingly, members appeared to grow impatient of the frequent disruptive encounters; they would rather sleep and dine on acorns and manzanita berries. Without a final skirmish or even a glance back, the herd split almost evenly and wandered off to forage. Breaking up into subgroups was a common occurrence, perhaps serving to reduce tension and to improve feeding conditions by spreading the animals over a wider area of the range. However, as the seasons passed and the early winter breeding period approached, the two groups showed no inclination to rejoin their relatives, as had often happened in former years. Another leader had emerged in the breakaway group, and allegiances of his associates were with him and not the original boar. Once segregated for the breeding period the two herds never mingled again, for their claim to territory and social relationships had evolved to the point of independency. From this time individuals seldom trespassed more than a hundred meters (328 feet) into the other territory, and if caught there, they were quickly routed with great displays of bravado, loud grunting, and, if need be, slashing tusks. A new herd had arisen.

COLLARED PECCARY *continued from p. 293*
nocturnal during the hot summer, and more diurnal in winter when they huddle for warmth during cold nights. Spring and autumn are transitional times and feeding bouts may occur anytime, but usually less in midday.

At least 15 calls, related to aggression, submission, alarm, and contentment, have been described. When aroused or defensive a peccary repeatedly opens and closes its jaws, baring its canines and clapping its teeth. With eyes closed to mere slits, the animal charges and bites. On occasion, people have been attacked, dogs killed, and even jaguars seriously injured by peccaries. They may form a defensive circle like tiny muskoxen. If left alone, peccaries are timid creatures, electing to run away rapidly and to hide in dense vegetation. Their main predators are jaguars, cougars, smaller cats, coyotes, and people. In the last several centuries this species has been overhunted for food, hides, and sport in most of its North American range. The animal is therefore rare in many areas where it was formerly common.

Mammals of the
Tropical Forest

Regions providing continuously high temperatures and plentiful annual rainfall are clothed in a dense tropical forest or jungle. The largest of these magnificent forests occur in the Amazon Basin of South America and north into Mexico, and in southeast Asia, stretching from India to Japan and Indonesia. Other areas include west-central Africa, New Guinea, northeastern Australia, and numerous Pacific Islands. Being close to the equator, the lengths of days and nights are relatively uniform throughout the year.

In the tropical forest of southern North America, the mean monthly temperature varies only from 18°C to 32°C (64.4°F to 89.6°F) and rainfall ranges from one to over 2 meters (3.3 to 6.6 feet). (Equatorial rainforests average 4 m or 13.1 feet of rain each year.) The relative humidity is kept high, 60 to 100 percent, by sudden afternoon thunder showers. Humidity increases at higher elevations, so that above 1 000 meters (3,280.8 feet) there is an almost constant fog and drizzle. Where rainfall is over 1.5 meters (4.9 feet) and well distributed throughout the year, a luxuriant broadleaf evergreen forest develops. Vegetation is tiered with three or more heights of trees ranging from 14 to 62 meters (45.9 to 203.4 feet), a layer of shrubs and tall herbs, and another of low herbs. The crowns of trees form such a dense canopy that less than one percent of sunlight reaches the forest floor. Under such shady conditions, herbs and shrubs are sparse in most areas and walking is easy — quite unlike the common perception of dense jungle undergrowth. There is a low evaporation rate and little air movement within the forest. The treetops are hotter by day and cooler by night than the forest floor.

The tall trees often lack branches for most of their length, are broadly buttressed at the base, and are coated in epiphytes — plants such as lichens, mosses, ferns, orchids, and bromeliads. Thick vines or lianas hang between adjacent trees. Leaf growth, flowering, and fruiting continue throughout the year, some species flowering as often as 6 times annually, others once in 40 years. In contrast to northern forests, where a few species are extremely abundant, the tropical forest consists of scattered individuals of hundreds of species. Soils contain little humus because leaf decay is rapid, and organic and mineral salts are quickly washed away under torrential rains. Most of the nutrients are tied up in living plants. Typical rainforest trees are ironwood, zapote, banak, cecropia, Honduras mahogany, masica, bogamani, roble, flora de mayo, rubber trees, tree ferns, palms, and figs.

In disturbed areas or at higher elevations, the trees become shorter, fewer layers are evident, and undergrowth becomes dense. Where rainfall is more seasonal, or drops as low as 10 centimeters (3.9 inches) some months, a tropical deciduous forest is formed. During this dry season, most of the trees lose their leaves.

Tropical forests are also rich in animal life, particularly arboreal and flying species. There is no need for adaptations to cold (so important in northern animals), food and water requirements are easily met, and breeding may occur throughout the year unless restricted by a dry season. However, competition for living space and certain popular foods can be intense. Common herbivores are brocket deer, tapir, agouti, howler monkey, toucans, parrots, green iguana, and termites. Carnivores and insectivores include the jaguar, coati, capuchin monkey, anteater, black vulture, geckos, boa constrictor, tree frogs, and ants.

Common Vampire Bat

Deep within the recesses of an abandoned mine, a colony of fifteen vampire bats began fidgeting and chattering, somehow sensing the fact that it was now dark outside. Hanging from hind feet, several bats reached up with their long clawed thumbs and climbed onto a rocky ledge. Two of these active individuals faced each other, raised high on all fours, and commenced exchanging blows with folded wings. With surprising agility the two combatants sparred and jabbed until one was forced off the ledge, whereupon it soared away, perhaps to seek refuge in another friendlier colony. Still excited, the dominant male bobbed its head up and down, looking much like a prizefighter with its slit lower lip, "cauliflower" ears, and pug nose. Though the bats recognized each individual of the colony they did not appear to mind the loss of the recently departed member. All were anxious to leave their day roost for a night of foraging in the jungle. Before taking flight the bats relieved themselves, then flapped away through the maze of shafts, guided by their pulsed calls and returning echoes.

The male bat flew straight and swiftly along a familiar aerial pathway, adding his scanning song to the myriad of noises arising from the black canopy of forest below. Buzzing, fat-bodied moths and other insects floated past, but the vampire ignored them for it was after bigger prey. Having traveled about eight kilometers (5 miles), the bat fluttered earthward toward a pasture where a herd of cattle lay bedded down. The little hunter circled lower and lower, emitting a different investigative call that was above the hearing range of the sleeping cows. Hovering at close range the bat seemed to be searching for a particular animal. Pits in the bat's wrinkled face could detect the warmth rising from the cattle, and its keen nose located the cow of its choice. Wings slowed, flight stalled, the bat touched down on the brown hairy hide as lightly as a mosquito. It paused briefly to determine whether the cow had sensed its landing, then walked carefully along its back, supported by the soft pads on the wrists and soles of the hind feet. The vampire's black eyes flashed in the moonlight as it gazed upward to the cow's massive head. Up the neck it scampered, using the long thumbs to grasp the matted hair. The vampire had finally arrived at its destination — the cow's ear — a tremendous feat of navigation in the vast, featureless jungle landscape.

The cow flicked its ear several times, causing the vampire to crouch in readiness to leap into flight. When all was still again, the bat directed its attention to the base of the ear where the hair was thin. Half-hidden scars revealed that this was a return visit. With tongue and scoop-like lower incisors the bat attempted to lift off a scab, but it stuck tightly to the surrounding hairs. Side-stepping to a fresh site, the vampire used its two upper incisors to gouge out a piece of skin. The scalpel-like cut was so smooth and swift that the cow slept through the operation as if it were anesthetized. Scarlet-red blood began to ooze slowly from the wound, and the bat then curled the sides of its tongue downward to form a tube with the groove on the lower lip. In and out movements of the tongue kept the liquid flowing through the bat's makeshift straw.

After twenty minutes the bat's belly began to swell noticeably, as it filled with the warm meal. The flow of blood slowed and the bat used this opportunity to urinate. Poking the wound with its tongue, the vampire continued to feast for another ten minutes. By this time its belly was so distended that when the bat jumped into the air it could only fly about ten meters (32.8 feet) before it was forced to the ground. Seeking the shelter of a leaf, the bat crawled under it to digest its dinner. An hour later and a third lighter, the bat leaped into the air and flew to a temporary roost under a bridge. Who should be hanging there already but the male with which it had fought earlier in the evening. Just before dawn two black figures arrived at the mine entrance and disappeared below ground.

COMMON VAMPIRE BAT

Scientific name *Desmodus rotundus*
Family American Leaf-nosed Bats
(Phyllostomidae)
Order Bats (Chiroptera)
Total length males 80 mm (3.2 in);
females 85 mm (3.4 in)
Tail length no tail
Wingspan 500 mm (19.7 in)
Weight 28 g (1 oz);
34 g, maximum 40 g
(1.2 oz, maximum 1.4 oz)

Color The upperparts are dark grayish-brown, the undersides silvery-gray. Several color phases exist, with a tinge of red, orange, or gold.

Distribution and Status The common vampire bat is a species of tropical and subtropical climates and is found from the Mexican states of Sonora and Tamaulipas in the north to Chile, Argentina, and Uruguay in the south. It is also present on Trinidad and Margarita Islands in the West Indies. This bat occurs from open arid regions to closed humid jungle. Although it is absent from the high Mexican Plateau, specimens have been found at elevations of 2 300 m (7,546 ft) in the Sierra Madres of southern Mexico and 3 800 m (12,468 ft) in the Peruvian Andes.

The common vampire and 2 close relatives — the white-winged vampire *(Diaemus youngi)* and hairy-legged vampire *(Diphylla ecaudata)* — are the only living mammals subsisting on an exclusive diet of blood. Several larger extinct forms were present in Texas, Florida, and Cuba during the Pleistocene.

Food The common vampire appears to feed mostly on mammals, while the other 2 species accept birds as well. Domestic animals such as horse, donkey, cattle, sheep, goat, pig, and poultry are attacked frequently in many regions, but small and midsized mammals are natural prey. Sleeping people are occasionally fed on as well. The bat generally alights on its victim, but sometimes it lands on the ground nearby and then scrambles onto its host. The extremities, ears, lips, nipples, neck, shoulders, and hips are favorite sites. About 10 to 20 ml (0.3 to 0.7 fl oz) of blood are extracted during the meal which may last for up to 40 minutes. Strangely, the victim is seldom wakened by the bat. The wound continues to ooze for some time as a result of several anticoagulants present in the bat's saliva. A number of bats may line up to drink from the same wound, or they may all feed in different places on the host at the same time. Vampires dine nightly, or at least every second night after a large meal, and begin to starve after only several days without food.

Reproduction and Growth The breeding season occurs throughout the year, females producing one or 2 annual litters, each with a single young. The embryo enters a resting phase early in its development so that the gestation period is extended from 5 to 7 months. The ligaments of the pelvic girdle stretch to allow the passage of the baby bat, rump first. It weighs around 6 g (0.2 oz) and is well haired. The eyes open on the first day and tiny milk teeth help attach the bat to its mother's nipple. The newborn clings to the mother for the first month (except when she is away feeding) and by the end of the second month it is beginning to fly on its own. The mother regurgitates blood into the offspring's mouth at 4 months, and thereafter it learns to drink blood from the mother's incision. However, milk is still suckled from the mother until the youngster is 10 months old. Should the mother disappear, another female in the colony will adopt the abandoned young.

Remarks The common vampire is a medium-sized bat. The muzzle is short, a leaf-like ridge is present around the flat nose, and the lower lip is deeply grooved. The tail is absent and the membrane between the hind legs is naked and narrow, and does not extend to the ankle as in most bats. There are 20 teeth, including 2 upper knife-like canines and 2 enlarged upper incisors, which are used to open the skin of prey animals. The well-developed upper arms support the bat when walking, running, hopping, and leaping into the air. With legs held vertically, the bat resembles a giant spider as it clambers over the rocks. Strong claws are present on all digits.

Vampires navigate and locate their prey by echolocation of sound pulses (0.6 to 1.6 milliseconds duration) emitted through the mouth. The sounds are of low intensity and frequency compared to many other bats, serving to find prey without waking it. The senses of smell and sight have not deteriorated in this animal with specialized hearing, and it supposedly sees in the dark as well as a rat.

The vampire's internal organs also show some interesting modifications related to a blood diet. The stomach is extremely long, spiraled, and capable of expanding to a remarkable size to accommodate the liquid meal. Before the bat has finished drinking, digestion is well advanced, for excess water and non-nutritive elements of the prey's blood are absorbed, circulated to the kidneys, and eliminated from the body within minutes. Bacteria in the digestive tract assist in the chemical breakdown of the meal.

This species roosts during the day in caves, mines, hollows and buttresses of trees, and in buildings where colonies generally number 20 to 100 bats, occasionally up to 5,000. The composition of the colony includes both sexes and often the same individuals for years, though some bats shift from one colony to another. In some caves the smell of ammonia from the decaying excretions of the bats makes it necessary to use gas masks before it is possible to enter. Over 20 species of other bats have been found roosting with vampires. Soon after dark the vampires strike out on regular flyways in search of a host, flying up to 20 km (12.4 mi) in several hours. Some individuals have been known to travel home in 2 nights when released from a distance of 120 km (74.6 mi).

These bats are subject to a number of diseases (from viruses and trypanosomes) which are often transmitted during contact with other bats in the colony and, of course, through their biting of victims. The spread of paralytic rabies from vampires to domestic animals is so severe in some regions that efforts at raising herds have had to be abandoned. Attempted methods of bat control have

COMMON VAMPIRE BAT

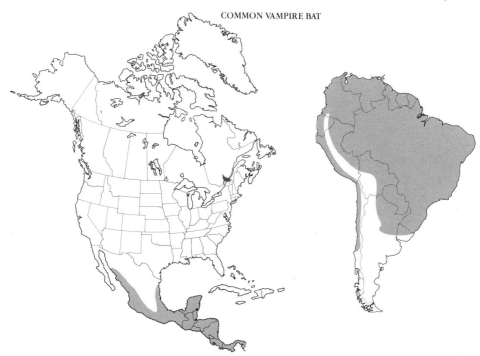

ranged from napalming and bombing of roosts to applying a poisonous paste on cattle, but vaccination seems to be the most successful technique. The volume of blood lost to vampires is usually not serious for a large healthy animal, but the wound may become infected with screw worms and the larvae of other parasitic insects.

Infected bats often succumb to diseases like rabies. Other causes of mortality are accidents, predation by snakes, mammals (including other kinds of bats), and predatory birds like owls. Some vampires have been known to survive 12 years. As repulsive as these bats are to people, vampires are in reality no different than other animals (including ourselves) and plants that survive by extracting nourishment from other living organisms. In fact, the daily drawing of blood from cattle herds is a method of food production still practised to this day by certain African tribes. Difficult as it is for us to accept, there is no good or bad in nature. Viewing vampires objectively, they display some of the most fascinating adaptations to be found in the animal kingdom.

SPOTTED PACA

Scientific name   *Agouti paca*
Family   Agoutis and Pacas (Dasyproctidae)
  Some biologists place the pacas in
  their own family (Agoutidae).
Order   Rodents (Rodentia)
Total length   700 mm (27.6 in)
Tail length   25 mm (1 in)
Weight   8 kg, maximum 10 kg
  (17.6 lb, maximum 22.1 lb)

Color   The upperparts and sides are a warm brown color, darkest along the back. Along the sides, from neck and shoulders to the flanks, run 4 rows of white spots and lines, the inner 2 being the most united. The underparts are whitish or light brown.

Distribution and Status   The spotted paca is found from southeastern San Luis Potosi of Mexico south to Paraguay and southern Brazil. It has also reached Cozumel Island off the Yucatan Peninsula, and has been introduced into Cuba. This animal is restricted to tropical

forest, both evergreen and deciduous. Occurring in a variety of habitats from lowlands to middle elevations on mountainsides, its favorite sites are along densely overgrown banks of watercourses. The mountain paca *(Agouti taczanowskii)* is a close relative from the northern Andes Mountains of South America. Thirteen other similar species of agoutis *(Dasyprocta* spp) and acouchys *(Myoprocta* spp) are known from Mexico south to South America.

Food   Pacas are vegetarians, utilizing leaves, stems, roots, and fallen fruit and nuts from many kinds of tropical plants. Avocados, mangos, and papayas are frequently eaten, as well as plantation crops like corn, sugar cane, cassava, and yams.

Reproduction and Growth   The relatively constant climate of the tropics enables pacas to breed during any season. Two litters are produced in a year, each with a single young or twins, so that the annual average is 2.5 young. The elaborate courtship of the male may be responsible for triggering the breeding cycle in the female. Pairing of the sexes occurs only for the purpose of reproduction; mating accomplished, the male resumes a solitary lifestyle. The gestation period is remarkably long at about 118 days. The young weigh around 710 g (1.6 lb) at birth and their eyes are open. The mother remains in the burrow with her newborn during the day and returns frequently during nightly foraging to nurse the young from her 4 nipples. It is not long before the offspring begin to accompany the mother, thereby learning where to feed and how to avoid predators. A paca is half-grown at 14 weeks. The expected life span under natural conditions is unknown, but individuals have survived 16 years in zoos.

Remarks   The spotted paca is a large stocky rodent with short but strong legs. On the 4 front and 5 hind digits are blunt pink claws used for digging out food and burrows. Its most unusual features are resonating chambers for amplifying growls, housed inside, of all places, each expanded cheek bone. These 2 chambers are connected to the mouth cavi-

ty by tubes, through which pass the vibrating columns of air, set in motion by the larynx. As in other rodents, pairs of upper and lower incisor teeth are backed by a space and then a series of high-crowned premolars and molars for grinding plant material into a paste. The pelage is stiff, lies close to the body, and lacks the dense, short, insulating underfur characteristic of mammals of north temperate and arctic climates.

Pacas spend most of the day in burrows that they excavate in river banks, slopes, and under rocks and tree roots. The several exits are usually blocked with leaves. The animals form pathways through dense vegetation when traveling to feeding grounds in an attempt to avoid owls, cats, and other predators. When frightened, they seek refuge in water or their burrows. The home range averages about 5 ha (12.4 a) and population estimates range from 12 to 50 per sq km (32.4 to 135.1 per sq mi). The ranges of males and females overlap, but males become defensive with other invading males, particularly if food is scarce. In captivity, behavior varies greatly among different individuals, some being playful, shy, obstinate, or aggressive.

Throughout their range pacas are subjected to constant hunting and trapping by local people, not only for the damage they cause to crops but also because pacas are a tasty and valuable source of protein. Considering the paca's wide distribution and importance to the jungle ecosystem, surprisingly little is known about it.

SPOTTED PACA

Spotted Paca

As the day drew to a close a brightly colored gecko walked down the smooth bark of a Mexican rubber tree and disappeared behind a sweeping buttress, which supported the great trunk in the clay soil. The tree rose majestically, without branches, through the shrub story at six meters (19.7 feet), and past the dense canopy of subordinate trees at twenty meters (65.6 feet), before bursting into a full crown. Every tree branch was covered with a gray or green coat of lichens, mosses, and other ephiphytes, and the whole jungle seemed to be tied together and to the ground below by a profuse network of woody vines or lianas. Only dim light and flecks of moonlight managed to penetrate to the barren forest floor, which was littered with decaying brown leaves. An animal suddenly appeared from nowhere and commenced foraging on the wet ground. When it paused, it seemed to vanish again, so perfect was its camouflaged coat of brown with white spots. Looking much like a miniature hippopotamus, the male paca walked along on its short legs, changing direction frequently. Every once in awhile the mature fruit of a mango came tumbling down from above, and the thick-bodied rodent tried to locate it with nose and eyes. Since mangos were a favorite food of dozens of birds, mammals, iguanas, and insects, the fruit was almost instantly gobbled up each time a tree produced its crop. The search was finally rewarded. Knocking the ants off its meal, the paca picked up a mango in its front paws, sat back on its haunches, and buried its long incisors into the juicy pulp.

It wasn't long before another paca arrived on the scene, this one a female. Although occupying separate burrows, the two pacas knew each other and proceeded with the usual greeting. At first they stared with bulging eyes and then approached more closely, snouts and whiskers twitching. Nose to nose, nose to rump, the two animals quickly learned as much about each other's conditions as if they had carried on a conversation. The female's appetite for mangos was not entirely consistent with the male's rising ardor. She moved away to sniff the spot where the male had just fed. The male followed in little hops and kicks. While the female did her best to ignore this suitor, the male began to playfully ambush and attack her. Each time she jumped away, while emitting an impatient snort. The courtship increased in intensity and continued for half a minute before the male paca attempted to mount her from behind. She whirled around and the two sat growling face to face. Suddenly she broke free from the encounter and ran away. The hoof-like claws of the male sent leaves flying as he galloped off in pursuit.

A brocket deer stood in the river shallows, nibbling quietly on tender leaves. Its big ears swerved abruptly towards angry growling sounds coming from the forest, and its legs bent low in anticipation of fleeing. As the two pacas emerged from the dense bank vegetation and splashed noisily into the weed-choked water, the tiny deer bolted and in two spectacular leaps gained the cover of the trees. Showing great persistence, the male paca paddled after the female, the two gasping for air with upraised snouts. Unseen on the far shore, three brown knobs, projecting slightly above the green scum, slipped beneath the water. A slight wave rippled through the weeds in the direction of the swimmers. From below, their stroking legs slowly propelled the two plump bodies across the surface of the water. Just as the female paca's feet touched the muddy bottom, an open-mouthed alligator exploded from the depths. Its jaws snapped on the rump of the male paca, whose piercing squeal sent flocks of parrots and smaller birds flapping away through the jungle. The force of the wave from the reptile's attack pushed the female paca right up on the shore, and she disappeared in the bushes. The alligator backed into deep water, thrashing its head and the paca back and forth until it stopped struggling. The great jaws opened and closed several times, positioning the paca's body within its mouth. Then, with a bend of the alligator's neck, the paca was gone.

Brown-throated Sloth and Mantled Howler Monkey

The native hunter stood motionless for over a minute in the early morning shade, searching the treetops and listening for any signs of game. Something greenish-brown was just visible among the leaves, about fifteen meters (49.2 feet) high in the canopy. Thinking it was an ant or termite nest, the hunter moved on without making a sound. Oblivious to its close call, the sloth slept on, hanging comfortably upside down by its long, clawed limbs. Even at close range it was hard to realize that this mop was a living creature. The head was hidden between the forelimbs and the stump of a tail projected out like an amputated limb. The yellowish-brown coarse hair was soiled green by algae, and dozens of little moths scrambled in and out of the coat. No wonder it went unnoticed.

Suddenly its calm world was shattered with the arrival of eight toucans that landed in the same tree and let forth a piercing chorus, which not even a sleepy sloth could ignore. Slowly a small round head appeared and turned an amazing one hundred and eighty degrees in the direction of the big birds that were busy gulping down fruit through their enormous colorful bills. As the guests flew off to check out another tree, the sloth decided it was time to eat as well. One arm loosened its hold on the horizontal branch, reached out, and pulled in a bundle of leaves. Lacking incisor teeth for nipping the stems, the sloth's horny lips rasped the leaves free. Every movement was in slow motion, even chewing. Hand over hand, the animal made its way to the end of the branch, pausing at intervals to feed. Reaching a spot exposed to the sun the sloth dozed off again, and in twenty minutes its body temperature rose five degrees.

For a week the sloth had been filling its belly with new leaves from the outer canopy of two adjacent trees. Now it was time to make the tiresome descent to the ground to relieve itself of stored wastes, for it preferred not to carry out this function from above. Grabbing hold of a liana or woody vine, the animal began backing down. It took fifteen minutes to reach its destination, and the sloth commenced to dig a shallow hole with the hind feet. Its business concluded, the sloth covered the site with leaves, and in an awkward, spread-eagled position, hauled itself a few meters over the forest floor to the base of a cecropia tree. As it began the long climb back up it could hear the roaring calls of an approaching band of howler monkeys.

It was now midmorning, and having fed in the trees where they spent the night, the monkeys were in an exuberant mood as they traveled through the forest canopy to find a new source of favorite leaves and fruits. The troop consisted of four adult males, nine adult females, and eight juveniles and infants. Less agile and reckless than their smaller relatives, the spider monkeys, the howlers moved deliberately from branch to vine, holding on with several feet until the next step was secure. In a bout of playfulness one juvenile pinched the rump of another, and the two shot off along a vine covered with ferns and sharp, pineapple-like plants. Under their combined weight the rotten vine snapped, and the lead monkey was suddenly left grasping in air. A shriek instantly arrested the attention of the band, and they watched in horror as one of their family plummeted from such a fatal height. In reflex action the little monkey spread out its limbs and tail like a skydiver, and halfway to the ground its tail struck a branch. Instantly the touch-sensitive tail tip wrapped around the woody stem, and with a graceful arc, the monkey swung into a safe position. It sat there for a moment, flicking its head to compose itself, while its mother wailed for it to rejoin the group. "Cluck, cluck," the dominant male called, impatiently urging the members to regather and move on.

A short time later, the troop froze at the rasping sound of claws on bark. Crouching low, each adult quickly scanned the surrounding forest for signs of a jaguar, harpy eagle, or perhaps an unwelcome visit of another band of howlers. The juveniles scrambled alongside the infants who were clutched onto their mothers' chests. The dominant male moved forward to investigate, pausing every few steps to let out a powerful roar, which swelled his throat to enormous size. Soon the other males and then the females joined in, creating a ruckus that echoed off the surrounding jungle hillside. Then, from around a tree trunk, a strange face with a black mask slowly appeared. The big male howler bounded over for a closer look, becoming more and more confused over what sort of creature this was. For five minutes the monkeys jumped around the sloth, roaring continually at a deafening level. Finally venting all their fear and excitement, the howlers left the sloth to continue its journey to the treetop, never realizing that this animal was a competitor for the very food sources the monkeys were searching for.

BROWN-THROATED SLOTH
Scientific name *Bradypus variegatus*
Family Sloths (Bradypodidae)
Order Sloths, Anteaters, and Armadillos (Edentata)
Total length 625 mm (24.6 in)
Tail length 68 mm (2.7 in)
Weight 4.5 kg (9.9 lb)
Color The dense coat is an overall yellowish- or brownish-gray color; often a greenish cast is present due to algae living on the hairs. The face is white with a dark brown patch through the eye. Females have a brown stripe down the back, while males exhibit a back patch of short, yellow hair, split by a narrow band of brownish-black.
Distribution and Status This sloth is found in tropical rain forests, particularly along forest edges and river shores, from eastern Honduras south to Bolivia, northern Argentina, and southern Brazil. Some South American populations are endangered, and habitat destruction may soon jeopardize the species in North America. There are 2 other species of three-toed sloths *(Bradypus)* and 2 species of two-toed sloths *(Choloepus)* that occur in the northern half of South America; one species of the latter reaches as far north as Nicaragua.

These strange-looking creatures are the 5 surviving members of the superfamily of sloths that orginated in the South American continent. From there various forms spread into the West Indies and well into the North American Midwest during the Pleistocene (within the last 2 million years). These included giant ground-dwelling sloths *(Megatherium)* the size of elephants, and smaller West Indian ground sloths (Family *Megalonychidae*), several species of which became extinct as recently as the period of European arrival.
Food The sloth has been described as the most important vertebrate consumer of tree leaves (known as a folivore) in the tropical forest. In one study, sloths were estimated to devour 2 percent of the total leaf production in a Panama forest. Moving to a new tree on the average of once every 1.5 days, the sloth picks young leaves, fruit, buds, and tender twigs of only certain kinds of trees — the ones that it learned to eat while with its mother. Therefore, unrelated sloths living nearby feed largely on different tree species and this helps to prevent over-utilization of the forest. Some trees, like the common cecropia, are highly preferred by sloths.

Reproduction and Growth Brown-throated sloths breed at any time of the year in most regions, with higher rates during certain periods if there is a dry season. The sexes come together briefly to mate, then return to their independent life-style. Six months pass before the single young is born, weighing about 350 g (0.8 lb). The young is fully haired, the eyes are open, and teeth have already erupted from the gums. Quickly learning to drink milk from its mother's 2 mammae, at only 2 weeks it begins to nibble bits of vegetation from the parent's lips, thereby developing a taste for certain tree leaves. By one month of age the offspring can survive on leaves alone, but it often continues to nurse considerably longer, up to 6 months. The little sloth remains clutched to its mother for 6 months; if it falls the mother ignores its pleas for help and it likely perishes. Prior to the next birth, the parent abandons her young on the present home range and moves away to dwell on a second, adjacent area. Full size is attained at 2.5 years, sexual maturity at 3 years. Longevity in nature is unknown. One wild sloth lived 11 years, and perhaps 20 or 30 years is possible.

Remarks The first things one notices about this unusual creature are the upside-down position while resting and feeding, and the shaggy, dense coat. The 6-cm (2.4-in) long hairs hang downward towards the back (in the opposite direction of all other animals), which helps to shed dew and rain. A short, fine underfur provides insulation, which at first would seem so unnecessary for a life in the constantly warm jungle. However, the sloth has a variable body temperature that is related to a low rate of biological processes (metabolism), and the consequent need to save energy. A range of 24°C to 33°C (75°F to 91.4°F) has been recorded when sleeping at night and exposed to the sun, respectively.

The head is small and round, with inconspicuous eyes and ears. A unique feature of the sloth's long neck is the presence of 8 or 9 vertebrae (7 is the mammalian standard) which provides great rotation, as in owls. These extra vertebrae appear to be derived from the first 2 chest vertebrae, since they are attached to tiny ribs. A total of 18 teeth are present (even though the order name Edentata means toothless) — no incisors, but sharp triangular canines, and continually growing, well-enameled cheek teeth for grinding plant material. The stout tail might be mistaken for the head by an attacking predator. The limbs are long and powerful (especially the forelimbs) and armed with scythelike claws on the 3 digits (representing the second to fourth fingers). The canines and claws may be used against an attacker and can inflict a serious wound; however, only the careless are in any danger, for the sloth's defense movements are rather slow. The sloth has evolved to such a degree for an arboreal, suspended, or sitting life-style that its bones and muscles simply cannot support the animal on the ground. It seldom is caught there, but when it is, it must pull itself along on its belly with its arms, in paraplegic fashion, until it reaches a tree. The digestive tract is long and complicated (5-chambered stomach) — an adaptation to break down the hard-to-digest cell walls of plants.

The sloth is famous for its incredibly slow rate of movement that averages 38 m (125 ft) per day, but it can "hustle" if pestered. Surprisingly, it swims well and has been known to cross wide rivers. Around 15 hours a day are spent sleeping, while feeding occupies most of the remainder — in periods during the night or daylight hours. It changes trees about every second day, but has been known to remain in a favorite tree for over a week. A high population of 5 to 8 per ha (2 to 3.2 per a) has been recorded in Panama, each occupying a home

BROWN-THROATED SLOTH

range (with overlap) of around 2 ha (4.9 a).

Grooming the coat is not a sloth's strong point and it can become quite messy from the attached youngster's body wastes, a coating of algae, and many kinds and numbers of moths, beetles, and mites which spend much of their life hiding in the fur. These free-loading insects have amazing life cycles and are dependent on the sloth for survival. For example, the sloth moth leaves its host momentarily to deposit its eggs on the sloth's droppings, and quickly returns to hitch a ride back up the tree. The eggs develop through larval and pupal stage, and the newly emerged moths fly away to find a sloth and complete the cycle.

Major predators of the sloth are harpy eagles, big cats, snakes, and people. It is eaten by certain tribes and left alone by others. It is astonishing that such a slow and seemingly vulnerable animal has not gone the way of its extinct ground-dwelling relatives. Protective concealment, its defensive actions, and more importantly, its incredible ability to recover from even terrible wounds, have no doubt played major roles in its survival.

MANTLED HOWLER MONKEY
Scientific name *Alouatta palliata*
Family Capuchin, Howler, and Spider Monkeys (Cebidae)
Order Human, Apes, Monkeys, and Lemurs (Primates)
Total length 112 cm (44.1 in)
Tail length 61 cm (24 in)
Weight males 6.5 kg, maximum 9 kg (14.3 lb, maximum 19.8 lb); females 4.5 kg (9.9 lb)
Color The coat is black with a brown to yellowish mantle extending from the shoulder to the flank. The young are silver to golden brown.
Distribution and Status The mantled howler is distributed from the Mexican states of Veracruz and Oaxaca south to Ecuador. It lives in mature rain forest, scrub forest, woodland, and in secondary or disturbed forests. In the adjacent Yucatan Peninsula,

Belize, and Guatemala lives the closely related and similar Lawrence's howler monkey *(Alouatta pigra)*, and 4 additional species of howlers occur in the northern half of South America. Both species are endangered from hunting and deforestation in Central America.

Monkeys are thought to have originated in North America and Eurasia when these continents were joined during the Cretaceous Period (over 65 million years ago), and soon spread to the African continent. Whether monkeys reached South America by "island hopping" (accidently rafting through a chain of interconnecting islands) from North America, or from Africa when these 2 southern continents were closely aligned during the Cretaceous, is still an open question. It is known, however, that monkeys became extinct in North America in the Oligocene (24 to 37 million years ago), and have only recently (within the last 3 million years) returned to the tropical zone of this continent from adjoining South America.
Food The mantled howler's diet contains a larger percentage of leaves (about 65 percent) than any other New World monkey. Highly selective, it chooses parts of leaves from certain trees — a practice based on nutritional quality and a lower concentration of unwanted substances (tannins and alkaloids). Young leaves and flowers are usually preferred, but in areas with a marked dry season the monkeys resort to mature leaves and fruit.
Reproduction and Growth This species may bring forth young at any time of the year. Females have a sexual cycle of 13 to 24 days, and when receptive, are mated repeatedly by the dominant male and occasionally by males of lesser rank. Six months (180 to 194 days) later a single young is born, weighing 400 g (14.1 oz) and covered in silver to golden-brown hair. Clinging to the mother's chest, the infant periodically nurses from 2 mammae. As it becomes stronger, it usually rides on its mother's back. At 12 weeks the adult coat is attained, but lactation continues as a supplement to solid food for up to 2 years. During this period it becomes more and more in-

dependent. Females become sexually active at 4 or 5 years of age, males at 6 to 8, but the latter do not have much opportunity to mate until they rise in status within the troop. On the average, a female bears a young every 23 months. Females generally leave the group between 15 and 36 months of age; the males later at 24 to 40 months. Normal life spans in nature are unknown, but howlers have lived 20 years in captivity.
Remarks This powerfully built monkey is the largest member of its family. The prominent muzzle, enlarged throat pouch, and shaggy beard accentuate the size of the head. A pair of front-facing bright eyes and a bare face with well-developed facial muscles provide for a wide range of expressions. The nostrils open to the side. Next to humans, howlers are the most intelligent animals of the New World as a result of their large and complex brain structure. They are also capable of seeing colors due to the presence of cones distributed among the rods in the retinal layer of the eye. The arms and fingers are long and end in flat curving nails. Although the first toe is opposable to the other toes (and is useful in grasping branches), the thumb is not. The howler can walk with ease on the ground but seldom does so. Used like a fifth arm, the thick, muscular tail is prehensile and naked on the bottom third, forming a touch-sensitive friction pad for swinging and grabbing functions. The hands and feet are also hairless with an individual pattern of ridges and grooves on the skin, just like the personalized fingerprint of humans. The jaws contain 36 teeth which are remarkably similar in appearance to those of humans. The brightly colored penis hangs freely and is used in display behavior. Eyesight is the highest developed sense in conveying information about the surroundings.

The roaring call of howlers is perhaps the loudest sound produced by any animal in the world, carrying one to 3 km (0.6 to 1.9 mi) in dense forest and 5 km (3.1 mi) over water. The males begin the concert at daybreak, often joined by females. Almost any excuse will cause a roaring response — rain, other monkeys, planes, people, just prior to retiring at night, or even to express well-being. These calls serve to communicate the presence of different troops of howlers, so that direct contact (and perhaps fighting) is reduced. The high-volume roar sounds like "a-hu, a-hu, a-hu," emitted with the lips funneled and the expanded neck pouch (including modifications of the larynx and hyoid bone) acting as a resonating or amplifying chamber.

Howlers live in bands of 2 to 50, but if 2 bands come together the group may reach 65 or more. Adult males are always dominant over females but are outnumbered by the latter, which are accompanied by infants and juveniles. The troop defends its present position against other monkeys, but shares a common home range which may vary widely in size from 3 to 76 ha (7.4 to 187.7 a). They generally move 200 to 1 200 m (656 to 3,937 ft) in a day. As many as 1,040 howlers per sq km (416 per sq mi) have been recorded in Panama. These monkeys never seem to attack humans, but they roar and may throw objects at intruders.

MANTLED HOWLER MONKEY

Jaguar and Capybara

Seconds after a brilliant flash of lightning lit up the blackened evening sky, a pounding clap of thunder rolled over the coastal jungle hills. The air soon filled with a driving rain. Beneath some dense bushes an old jaguar jolted from its snooze with the intensity of the storm. Water ran in steady little streams from the drip tips of the broad leaves, splashing down on the big cat's face. He lowered his ears and half shut his eyes to keep the water out. The droplets particularly bothered him when they struck his long white whiskers, causing the great head to roll from side to side. Knowing there were no drier sites, he prepared to stay put and wait out the weather.

Some distance away a family of capybaras, wading knee-deep in a pond and unconcerned by this bout of rain, continued to feed on aquatic plants. Resembling miniature hippopotamuses, their favorite pastime was eating, and no daily shower was about to send them scurrying for cover. Leaving at least one sentry to watch, they took turns submerging their blunt snouts and emerging with stringy weeds dangling from their mouths. The capybaras' coats were so sparse that the skin could be seen through the wet hair. In obvious contentment, the animals moved off along the shallows, emitting clicking sounds. Bellies full, the group reached the shore and entered the jungle, leaving behind cylindrical droppings and deep prints where the hoof-like toes sank into the mud.

Later, although the rain had finally stopped, water vapor formed curtains of mist that drifted slowly through the warm evening air. A big clean padded foot suddenly squished into the mud, erasing the capybara tracks. The jaguar's nose dropped low to sniff the musky odor of its favorite prey. With its great sides heaving, several low grunts rose from its throat, "uh," "uh," "uh." The experienced predator knew the capybaras would likely be back in a few hours, and he crouched down beside the trail to wait.

Was it the vibrating tips of delicate whiskers or its keen ears that first detected the oncoming capybaras? Powerful leg muscles tensed in crouch position and the tail quivered ever so slightly. The jaguar's spotted coat was invisible amid the dapples of moonlight coming through the tall trees. The ambush was set. In single file, with the dominant male at the front, the unsuspecting capybaras trotted towards the water. The big cat's body exploded from concealment as the capybaras approached within three meters (9.8 feet). Sharp whistles and the sounds of desperately thrusting feet broke from the grass and thicket, followed in an instant by noisy splashing. Then all was quiet until the hunter let loose with a tremendous roar, revealing his frustration. In his prime he would have been thrashing the life out of a fifty-kilogram (110.2-pound) prey, but now the aging cat just stood there alone, spattered with mud and panting heavily.

The capybaras had sought the refuge of the pond where they remained submerged in the depths for about two minutes. Then, one by one, they rose to the surface, concealing their ears, eyes, and nose amid the floating plants. An hour passed before they regrouped and sneaked away in the shadows. All night they froze each time the jaguar roared as it continued in unsuccessful pursuit of a meal. A week later, in the bright morning sunlight, the jaguar stood in the grass at the pond's edge, watching the same band of capybaras grazing without apparent concern only forty meters (131.2 feet) away. The whiskered lips curled upward, uncovering the yellow, worn canine teeth, and he coughed a low growl as his eyes turned away. The jungle master was nearing the end of his time.

JAGUAR

Scientific name *Panthera onca*
Family Cats (Felidae)
Order Carnivores (Carnivora)
Total length 2 m, maximum 2.6 m
      (6.6 ft, maximum 8.5 ft)
Tail length 60 cm, maximum 75 cm
      (23.6 in, maximum 29.5 in)
Weight males 100 kg, maximum 158 kg
      (220.5 lb, maximum 348.3 lb);
      females 75 kg, maximum 82 kg
      (165.3 lb, maximum 180.8 lb)

Color Usually an attractive golden color, the background color may range from pale yellow to light brown. Reddish-brown individuals occur and black jaguars are not uncommon. The undersides are white. Irregularly shaped markings or rosettes create a striking pattern along the sides and back, each made up of a ring of dots on a somewhat darker patch of hair, with another single spot in the middle. The remainder of the body and the extremities are heavily marked with black spots of various sizes. Even in black individuals the spots and rosettes are slightly visible when the light catches the coat at the right angle. The jaguar's disruptive coat pattern is a beautiful example of camouflage.

Distribution and Status Although the jaguar is often thought of as a jungle cat it is found in many other areas as well, originally ranging from California to Texas (absent from the Mexican Plateau) all the way south to the Strait of Magellan in South America (absent from the southern Andes Mountains). This species is most abundant in tropical forests, but is also found in woodland, shrubland, savanna, grassland, and even desert. It ranges from sea level jungle to high mountain pine forests, generally not far from water. Cover requirements may be as little as grass thickets and rocks barely high enough in which to hide.

Hunting pressure has reduced population numbers and distribution in many regions, but it is still common over much of South America's wilderness. The last individual known in California was shot in 1860, and the resident population was lost to the rest of the United States in the early 1900s. Occasional wanderers have appeared since then (e.g., 1971 in Arizona), but they are usually killed on sight. There may now be fewer than 1,000 individuals in all of Mexico. At the opposite end of the range, it is now rare in Argentina and restricted to the north part of the country. Following the Ice Age, the jaguar occurred throughout the southern United States and was especially common in Florida. The closest living relatives of the jaguar are the lion, leopard, snow leopard, and tiger (all in the genus *Panthera*, but considered under *Felis* by some mammalogists).

Food The jaguar and other large cats of the jungle fill the role of dominant predators, as do the coyotes and wolves of the temperate and arctic regions. The jaguar stalks and ambushes deer, capybaras, tapirs, peccaries, agoutis, mice, and snakes on land; fish, crocodillians, and frogs in the water; and monkeys and birds in the trees. It even roams the ocean shores for sea turtles and digs up their eggs. Sometimes the big cat takes livestock and there are cases of attacks on humans, but it has seldom been described as a "man-eater" as have several of its Old World relatives. After devouring about 3 kg (6.6 lb) of meat, the animal covers the remainder of the carcass with plant debris and returns to it later.

Reproduction and Growth Generally solitary creatures, the sexes come together when preparing to mate. The male may stay on to help raise the cubs, unlike the cougar male which must be driven off if the young are to survive. In the north of the range, mating occurs mainly in January and February, with births 93 to 105 days later in the spring. However, in the tropics, young are born anytime. The average number of young per litter is 2, with a range of one to 4. They weigh 700 to 900 g (1.5 to 2 lb) at birth and are fully furred in a spotted brown coat. The eyes open at 7 to 13 days. Reaching the size of a house cat at 6 weeks, the big-footed young may weigh 45 kg (99.2 lb) at one year. Full growth and sexual maturity occur at 3 or 4 years of age. Some jaguars are known to have survived 15 to 18 years in their native environs, and one captive finally died of old age at 22.

Remarks Largest of the New World cats, the jaguar's muscular body and formidable facial expressions reveal great physical power. The head is massive with small ears and eyes that are sometimes hard to locate among all the black spots. The fur is short and stiff. The animal is at home splashing and cooling off in the water, stalking through forest or thicket, or stretched majestically along a limb high in a favorite tree. It announces its home area by marking with urine and by loud roars, made possible through an elastic band of tissue in the voice box which is absent in smaller cats. Other sounds in its repertoire are grunting, mewing, purring (exhaling only), hissing, and spitting. A typical home range of a male is 60 sq km (24 sq mi), 30 sq km (12 sq mi) for a female. As in other species of cats, individual jaguars sometimes wander far and wide and are known to have followed landmarks such as rivers for 800 km (497 mi). When hunting, the jaguar prefers an ambush strategy and is clever enough to position itself in front of an advancing troop of monkeys, coatis, or peccaries. It is also a patient stalker, and dispatches its prey with a powerful swipe of its clawed paw or a crushing bite. Adults have few enemies other than people and poisonous snakes, while, in addition, young are susceptible to predation by crocodillians and large snakes, such as the anaconda and boa constrictor.

Presently classified as an endangered species, conservation measures in many countries have slowed its decline; however, there seems little doubt that encroachment of peo-

JAGUAR

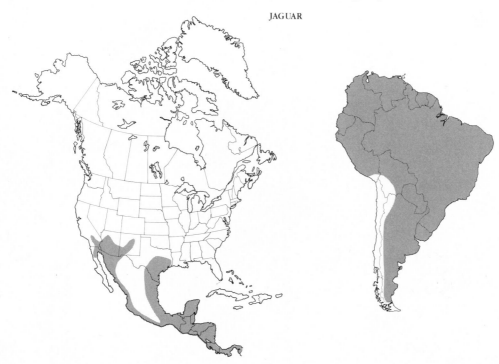

ple on its wild lands will continue to reduce both numbers and distribution. In Brazil alone 15,000 were killed annually during the 1960s. Its valuable coat, destruction of livestock, and the fear it instills in local people are 3 problems most difficult to overcome in saving *el tigre*, as it is called in Spanish.

CAPYBARA

Scientific name *Hydrochaeris hydrochaeris*
Family Capybara (Hydrochaeridae)
Order Rodents (Rodentia)
Total length 120 cm (47.2 in)
Tail length no tail
Weight males 50 kg (110.2 lb);
females 60 kg (132.3 lb)
The subspecies or race in Panama is much smaller, averaging only 27 kg (59.5 lb).
Color These animals are reddish- or grayish-brown above, yellowish-brown below. Black hair is often present on the face, rump, and outer sides of the legs.
Distribution and Status Capybaras live from Panama south through the northern two-thirds of South America, from Ecuador east of the Andes to northeastern Argentina. The species invaded North America about 2 million years ago, and probably occurred much farther north than at present. It frequents the overgrown margins of streams and ponds, and invades swamps and grassy clearings. The only surviving member of the family, the capybara resembles a giant guinea pig on long legs. In fact, the nearest relatives are the guinea pigs or cavies (Family Caviidae) of South America.
Food These are herbivorous creatures, dining on grass, fruit, and the bark of saplings and shrubs. They have become a pest in some agricultural areas, regularly devouring squash, melons, corn, rice, and sugar cane. They have even been seen in fields grazing alongside cattle.

Reproduction and Growth As in many tropical animals the capybara may breed at any time of the year, but reaches a peak before the rainy season (often in April and May). The developmental period of the embryos is 104 to 111 days and one litter of 5 (range of one to 8) is born annually. The fully haired newborn are large and well developed for a rodent, weighing 0.9 to 1.5 kg (2 to 3.3 lb), and they nurse for 16 weeks from the mother's 5 pair of mammae. Amazingly they are able to follow their mother about, and even eat plants, within a day of their birth. Sexual maturity and adult size are attained at 15 months. Capybaras have a life expectancy of 8 to 10 years in their natural habitats, and up to 12 years in captivity.

Remarks The capybara is the largest living rodent and has a pig-like shape quite unlike that of other North American rodents. The stocky body is sparsely covered in long coarse hair, becoming shorter on the limbs. The nostrils, eyes, and prominent ears are situated on top of the head, so that the animal can remain submerged with only these sense organs exposed to gather information about possible predators. The muzzle is thick with a split upper lip; in adult males a bare raised spot on the snout marks the site of large oil glands. There are 20 ever-growing teeth, including the large clipping incisors in front and the highly ridged and cemented cheek teeth for grinding plant material. The front feet have 4 digits, the hind feet 3, each partially webbed and ending in hoof-like claws. The animal can run with surprising speed and swim easily on the surface or below water.

The *carpincho*, as it is known in South America, has been described as semiaquatic since it is often found feeding or taking refuge in water. Its ecological role has been likened to the pygmy hippopotamus of Africa. However, most activity occurs on land. It sleeps during the day and moves about in the evening, at night, and in the morning. When

persecuted by people it becomes more nocturnal. The basic social unit is the family, but groups of 20 are common and up to 100 have been seen together on one occasion. A vigorous hierarchy of dominance is maintained, as a result of fierce fighting. Newcomers are usually rejected by the group, amid much grunting and barking.

The capybara is sought by people as an important source of food, hide, fat (used by pharmacies), and also because of its raids on crops. In some areas of South America the animal is raised on farms. Other important mortality factors are disease and predation by the jaguar, cougar, ocelot, snakes, and crocodilians. In spite of these pressures, the capybara remains widespread and common over much of its range.

CAPYBARA

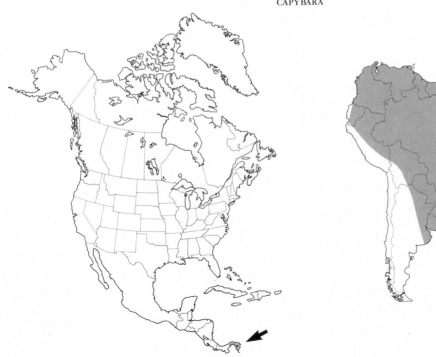

Hispaniolan Solenodon

With the sun setting over the Caribbean island, a large green iguana pulled itself laboriously into a gumbo limbo tree and clawed hand over hand until it reached a favorite spot on a horizontal limb. Squatting and stretching out its chubby limbs, a hiss of air escaped from its nostrils. So anxious was it to sleep, the iguana did not notice a colorful, ringed snail glide by on a highway of its own slime, busily grazing on the algae covering the branch. Not even the noisy calls of roosting birds and singing insects could keep its big rounded eyes from closing and its plated chin from sinking to the perch.

A short distance away an extraordinarily long, whiskered snout poked out of a hollow log, began wriggling like a worm, then suddenly withdrew. Perhaps it was not yet dark enough, for the creature did not reappear until ten minutes later. Then, out waddled what looked like a giant shrew, at least half a meter (1.6 feet) long. Zigzagging slowly across the forest floor as if unsure of its directions, the male solenodon finally located what it was looking for. It leaned forward over a small pool of rainwater and began to lap up a drink with its tongue, the strange nose curving away from the surface. Satiated, the animal headed off again, walking stiffly on the front feet and hind toes. It paused once in awhile to root in the leaf litter, but seemed to find nothing of interest.

The solenodon's actions stopped suddenly, as if it had heard some important signal. From the cover of bushes appeared a female with her family of two yearlings and two young offspring. They had located the male by its high-frequency clicks that it continuously uttered whenever it moved. The solenodons relied on a keen sense of smell and a system of radar-like echolocation instead of vision while traveling about. The two adults softly whistled a greeting as if excited to see each other, and they began to nuzzle. Anxiously the male directed his snout under the female's arm, where a scent gland was located. He continued to push his way underneath, almost knocking her over. During this whole period the offspring tried to keep as close to their mother as possible, whimpering for attention.

The solenodon family was so occupied that it failed to notice the approach of two invaders to their island home. A pair of mongooses surrounded the solenodons, darting in and out with great speed. Finally aware of their presence the family broke away, shrieking in alarm. Before each solenodon could escape, a mongoose caught up from behind and delivered a bite to the neck with blinding speed. The wounded animals dropped twitching to the ground, while the predators wheeled around to pursue the other fleeing individuals. The adult male solenodon turned to face its attacker and attempted to bite and administer its poisonous saliva into the mongoose's body, but each time its jaws snapped harmlessly in the air. Its tiny eyes and slow reflexes were no match for these agile foreign hunters. There was no time to hide in the burrows that provided some safety from the island's native predators — snakes and owls. The carnage had awakened the iguana high above, and it peered down with its head cocked and eyes wide open. How could any solenodon, iguana, or other midsized animal, sheltered in isolation for millenia, cope with this new threat?

HISPANIOLAN SOLENODON

Scientific name *Solenodon paradoxus*
Family Solenodons (Solenodontidae)
Order Insectivores (Insectivora)
Total length 52 cm (20.5 in)
Tail length 22 cm (8.7 in)
Weight 1 kg (2.2 lb)
Color The long coarse pelage varies from reddish-black to brown, somewhat lighter on the undersides. A white spot is present on the back of the neck, which changes in size and shape over the course of a year.
Distribution and Status The Hispaniolan solenodon is found only on the island of Hispaniola, now called Haiti and the Dominican Republic. It lives in tropical deciduous and semideciduous forests, often in brushy and stony areas, and around plantations as well. Another similar species, the Cuban solenodon *(Solenodon cubanus)*, lives on the adjacent island of Cuba. Solenodons and other island life have survived to the present age by virtue of their isolation for many millions of years from the constantly changing panorama of medium- and large-sized North American predators, and perhaps by the relatively constant tropical climate. No one is certain whether their ancestors are of North American or African origin. The family appears closely related to the tenrecs of Africa. One proposed view is that ancestral solenodons reached the Greater Antilles around the time (180 million years ago) when North America split from Africa and the 2 former land masses drifted away to the east.

Fossils of an extinct giant solenodon have been discovered in Cuba, and it is thought to have survived into the late Pleistocene (within the last million years). Another related family, represented by about 6 species of West Indian shrews *(Nesophontes* spp*)*, is thought to have become extinct following the arrival of the Spaniards.

As with so many other island species, solenodons are highly susceptible to predation from new forms of life introduced accidently or purposefully by people. Rats arrived with the earliest explorers, and the Asian mongoose was released in 1872 to kill off snakes and rats. Not long after, cats and dogs became feral (wild). Under the onslaught of these predators, populations of both the Hispaniolan and Cuban solenodons declined rapidly. In fact, the Cuban species was thought to be extinct until it was recently discovered in eastern Cuba. With added pressures of habitat destruction, the outlook for survival of these primitive creatures is questionable.

Food With the aid of its sensitive nose and whiskers, the solenodon searches the soil, leaf litter, and rotting logs for insects, other invertebrates, and small reptiles. If digging is required, the clawed front limbs come into use. Some fruit and green vegetation are also devoured. Unusual as it sounds for an insectivore, the solenodon may raid poultry and plantations, although it might be more interested in soil organisms than vegetables like sweet potatoes. When finding a worm or larvae, it rubs off the dirt with its hands.

Reproduction and Growth Solenodons are able to breed during any season and usually 2 litters are born in a year. The male seems always ready to mate, and its belly is often moist with scent to stimulate a female. The pair rubs bodies, pausing often to sniff, and when sufficiently stimulated, the male crawls underneath and encircles the female's belly. The developmental period of the young is unknown, but one to 3 are born in an underground nest. They are naked, except for whiskers and scattered guard hairs, and a full coat comes in by 2 weeks. Solid food is eaten by 18 weeks, although suckling continues for some time from the mother's 4 mammae. Several successive litter mates often remain with the parents so that up to 8 solenodons may be found in a burrow. Life expectancy in the wild is unknown, but captives have survived for 11 years.

Remarks The solenodon resembles a giant shrew, and is, in fact, among the largest of the order of Insectivores. The pelage consists of short, dense underfur and long, stiff guard hairs. The feet, scaly tail, and ears are almost naked. So, too, are the thighs and lower back, but these are covered with hairs from adjacent areas. The long jaws support 40 teeth, including grooved, second lower incisors that transmit a poisonous saliva capable of killing midsized animals, even another solenodon. Actually, the name solenodon means "grooved tooth." The animal walks in a waddling fashion, supported on the soles and toes of the front feet and the toes of the hind feet. It can run with surprising speed, bounding from front to hind feet. Able to climb, it hesitates to jump down, probably because of poor eyesight.

Solenodons are mainly nocturnal and retire to a burrow, cave, or tree hollow during the day. Here they sleep piled on top of each other. During the night, individuals are generally active for about half an hour, then they rest for several hours. Sometimes solenodons collect objects like snail shells and place them in the nest. Like other insectivores, these creatures communicate and navigate by emitting and listening to returning echoes of high-frequency sounds (9,000 to 31,000 cycles per second, and 0.1 to 3.6 milliseconds in durations). They also shriek if alarmed, or wheeze, twitter, and whimper. Since their hearing is so sensitive, a sudden loud sound sends them into panic and they dash away.

As might be suspected of such rare and secretive species, little is known about the ecology of solenodons. In nature they are preyed upon by snakes and owls, and within the last century, by introduced mongooses, cats, and dogs as well. Much that is known of their behavior comes from observations of the animals in zoos. Some fight on first meeting (occasionally to the death), others are friendly and inseparable, and certain individuals become attached to their keeper, coming when called and climbing up to the shoulder. Oddly, they have never been seen to bathe or lick themselves, restricting their grooming activities to simple scratching. In total, they are most unusual mammals.

HISPANIOLAN SOLENODON

Cuban Solenodon

Hispaniolan Solenodon

MEXICAN MOUSE-OPOSSUM

Scientific name *Marmosa mexicana*
Family New World Opossums
(Didelphidae)
Order Marsupials (Marsupialia)
Total length 330 mm (13.2 in)
Tail length 175 mm (7 in)
Weight males 100 g (3.5 oz);
females 85 g (2.9 oz)

Color The coat is yellowish-gray to chestnut-brown above and white or pale yellow underneath. A prominent black marking surrounds each big black eye and extends to a point down the snout. The tail looks naked and scaly, but is sparsely covered with fine hairs and is faintly bicolored, darker above.

Distribution and Status This mouse-opossum occurs from the Mexican states of Tamaulipas and Oaxaca south to western Panama. It lives in lowland rain forest, tropical deciduous forest, and woodland. The range overlaps with several other kinds of mouse-opossums, and a total of 47 species (some difficult to distinguish) are presently recognized, most of which occur in South America. Certain of these species might be better included in a new genus other than *Marmosa*, but much remains to be learned about the relationships and ecology of these fascinating pygmy marsupials.

Although opossums formerly occurred widely throughout North and South America, they became extinct in the former sometime in the late Tertiary Period. The family reinvaded North America only several million years ago, just before or shortly after the 2 continents became joined.

Food This animal shows flexibility in its eating habits, but its preference is clearly for insects. Earthworms, mice, birds and lizards and their eggs, carrion, and fruit are eaten regularly, and in agricultural areas the mouse-opossum doesn't hesitate to feed on bananas, mangos, and sugar cane.

Reproduction and Growth Male and female mouse-opossums are attracted to each other only when the latter comes into heat (called estrus), which happens for about 2 days in an 18- to 30-day cycle. Breeding may occur in any month in some regions of relatively constant environmental conditions, but is restricted to certain periods if there is a dry season. Following preliminary gestures of becoming acquainted, in which the sense of smell is important, the male grasps the back of the female's neck in his jaws, secures his position on top by seizing some nearby object with the tail, and begins to mate. The penis is split on the end, corresponding to double canals of the vagina. The 2 remain attached for a remarkably long time — from 50 minutes to 5 hours.

After only 14 days in the uterus, an average of 9 (maximum of 14) young are born in a premature state. The limbs are only tiny buds and the eyes have developed only as dark spots under the skin. Most of these babies manage to locate and become attached to a circle of teats (up to 19), where milk is actually forced into the mouth. Since the passageways for food and air are separated, suckling and breathing can both occur simultaneously. The young remain attached for about one month and are hauled around, sometimes dangling precariously, while the mother leaves the nest to forage. When their eyes finally open, the young begin to move around on the mother's body, first on the side, then on the back. At this point she often leaves them alone in the nest, but at 45 days, when their coat is complete, they begin to wander from the nest themselves. If the tree nest is disturbed, the whole family opens their mouths up to a 90 degree angle and hisses. Weaning occurs at 53 to 70 days and the family soon breaks up. The young become sexually active after 6 months of age and females become barren at the ripe old age of 18 months. While a new litter is possible every 77 days, some females no doubt only breed once in their life in areas where the breeding season is restricted by the seasons. Life expectancy in the wild is only one year, but some live longer, and up to 5 years in captivity.

Remarks This delicate little opossum is reminiscent, both in appearance and in ecological role, of the pygmy marmoset of South America or the dwarf lemur of Madagascar. The triangular-shaped head features rounded, naked ears, a bristly snout, and bulging eyes accentuated by the black markings, which likely serve to reduce the amount of reflected moonlight entering the eyes. A crease on the pink nose separates the nostrils. There is no pouch, but the birth canal and urinary system open into a common pouch called a cloaca, as in other marsupials. The limbs are used while climbing and scurrying on the ground. They are aided by foot pads and claws on all 5 digits except the hind toe, which is opposable to the rest of the foot. Acting as a fifth leg, the prehensile tail helps stabilize the body, carries nest material, and permits the animal to hang down when reaching for food. The fur coat is short, smooth, and shiny, and does not extend onto the basal part of the tail as occurs in many other species of mouse-opossum. Yellow or orange stains may be present around the female's teats, or on the lower throat region of the male — the site of glands used to mark the animal's presence on branches. The Mexican mouse-opossum leads a solitary life and is fairly intolerant of other individuals on its home range of about a quarter ha (0.6 a). Some individuals seem to be nomadic. Strictly nocturnal, it does not necessarily return to a nest, but simply seeks daytime cover in a tree hollow, bird nest, or beneath a log or rock. Foraging occurs on the ground and in trees. It generally tries to escape by climbing. Although of small size, the mouse-opossum is a courageous fighter, rearing up on its hind legs and, with ears lowered, snapping and hissing at intruders of any size. It can also utter a high-pitched chatter.

MEXICAN MOUSE-OPOSSUM

Mexican Mouse-opossum

The last wails from a troupe of howler monkeys signaled the end of another intensely hot and humid day in the forest. Searching for a comfortable perch to spend the night, a brilliantly colored songbird landed beside a ball-shaped nest of leaves and twigs that was neatly constructed in a tangle of moss-covered vines. But before the sleepy bird could lock its toes around a vine, a fierce little head popped through the roof of the nest. The animal's pointy snout snapped open and a startling hiss erupted from its throat. Not the kind of neighbor the bird wanted for the evening, it departed as fast as it could flutter off. Obviously upset from being jostled awake, the mouse-opossum crawled the rest of the way out of the nest and began to clean its face and ears with great diligence. As it sat up on its hindquarters a number of tiny forms could be seen squirming in the belly fur. Unprotected by a pouch (as in the larger Virginia opossum), the nine diminutive babies of the mouse-opossum simply hung there, each attached to a separate life-sustaining nipple. Suddenly a beetle flew within reach and, quick as a wink, the mother deftly picked it out of the air with her jaws. She turned the struggling insect over in her delicate fingers and bit off its head. Only the spiny legs and hard wing covers escaped the mashing of fifty sharp teeth, and the insect remains soon dropped to the jungle floor.

The mouse-opossum had set up home only forty meters (132 feet) from the edge of a banana plantation, and it was this ready source of fruit that had attracted her to reside in the area. She began a hand-over-hand route through the vines and trees toward the edge of the forest, steadying herself with an opposable set of hind toes and a long prehensile tail, which seemed to snake around everything it came in contact with. Concentrating with her large glistening eyes on a nearby branch of the next tree, the mouse-opossum prepared to jump across the gap. But while she landed safely on the other side, one of the embryos caught on a rough piece of bark and the tiny infant tumbled two meters (6.6 feet) to the ground. The mother mouse-opossum was unaware of her loss and continued on her way. Then she stopped, turned her head, and adjusted her ears like a set of antennae. She could faintly hear a rapid clicking sound amid the constant background buzzing of insects. She began to descend to the ground on a swaying vine, homing in on the clicking, which was far above the range of human hearing. Remarkably, she located the infant, which was still waving its limb buds in the air, and tucked it to her belly, where its mouth quickly located an unoccupied teat. Within a short time the teat expanded in the infant's mouth, securing it in place once again.

The rest of the night was uneventful, the mother filling her belly with banana paste and the young ones being pumped full of milk. Morning found the mouse-opossum curled up asleep in a bunch of green bananas, four meters (13.1 feet) up the stalk. But once again she was jostled awake, only this time her cover of bananas was cut free and loaded on a truck so quickly that she had no time to escape. She cowered in fright during the long bumpy ride, having no idea what was happening, nor of her impending journey. When things finally quietened down and became dark she ventured forth, but finding a totally foreign world, she retraced her steps to the only familiar object — the bundle of bananas. With bits of debris she fashioned a nest among the stiff green fruit and stayed inside, coming out only to nibble on a banana or to relieve herself. During the ensuing three weeks the mouse-opossum was subjected to stifling hot conditions. When her body temperature rose to 35°C (95°F), she wet herself down with saliva and panted. Later, on board an ocean liner, the temperature dropped to 13°C (55.4°F), and the little creature became dormant.

Her long voyage ended in a northern port, thousands of kilometers away from her native home. A surprised worker in a fruit company warehouse was literally attacked by this strange little critter. The story appeared in the local newspapers, and a biologist from a nearby museum arrived to capture and take care of the visitor from the tropics. Madame Marmosa, as she was now known, became quite tame, and along with her offspring, provided new information about her poorly known species.

Baird's Tapir

As night closed over the jungle like a heavy curtain, the daytime opera of birds and monkeys hushed, leaving the scene to buzzing insects and the periodic cry of some unknown creatures. At various but precise degrees of darkness, numerous kinds of bats came out of hiding from beneath tree bark and curled leaves, anxiously fluttering through the warm, moist evening air in search of night-blooming flowers, fruit, and big moths. But this night was quite different from others, at least for one terrified orphan, huddling silently between the buttress roots of a tall tree. The animal's body was covered in spots and stripes, which rendered it almost invisible against the patches of moonlight reaching the forest floor. At the deep roar of a distant jaguar, the youngster jumped in fright and rose up on its forelegs. The light revealed a most remarkable head — tubular ears, tiny sunken eyes, and a snout ending in what could only be described as a shortened version of an elephant's trunk. The trunk sniffed the air and actually lengthened, then shortened again an instant later. No doubt about it, the little tapir was really lost.

Only last night the tapir accompanied its huge mother down the hillside to their favorite swamp. The trail was worn so deeply through the underbrush that at times they seemed to be trotting along a tunnel. After feeding on water plants off and on for several hours, the family of two made their way to a nearby wallowing hole. The youngster wanted to play and began jumping around and butting its mother, but she was only interested in a refreshing mud pack, perhaps to gain some relief from the numerous ticks and stinging insects trying to penetrate her thick hide. As she stepped onto the soft ground, her flexible toes, each ending in a little hoof, spread out in the mud in an effort to support her great weight. Then over and over she rolled, kicking her feet in the air like a horse. Meanwhile, the young tapir wandered off to locate the source of a sweet odor detected by its nostrils. Walking slowly with head lowered, the little fellow worked over every leaf, stump, and rock with its amazingly flexible trunk, hardly bothering to use its eyes at all. The adult tapir paused for a moment and sat up on its hindquarters, as mud slipped down her broad sides. Realizing that she was now alone, the

low ridge of hairs on her mane rose slightly and she called to her offspring. Always obedient, the wanderer quickly rejoined her and the two moved off down the trail. The tapirs stopped to browse each time their keen noses found certain leaves, fruit, and seeds. They selected only particular plants, sometimes tasting and spitting one out. When food was just out of reach of clipping incisors or rasping tongue, the tapirs rose on their hind feet and used their snouts to pluck it free.

After resting for two hours, the family began foraging again along a familiar worn trail. They were halfway back to the swamp when, without warning, a flash of white struck the mother tapir on the neck. The same instant a heavy vine-like object dropped over the tapir's back with a thud. Then a tremendous struggle erupted, as the tapir sought to free herself from the tightening coils of a powerful boa constrictor. Wheezing loudly, the tapir swung back her head, trying to throw off or bite the snake with her sharp front teeth. Failing this, the tapir thrashed off into the undergrowth, the snake taking the full force of sturdy branches and tearing thorny vines. Meanwhile, the young tapir had panicked with the furious action, and galloped away as fast as its legs could carry it. Finally it could go no farther and it collapsed at the base of a tall tree. Out of breath and with heart pounding, the tapir buried its head among the roots and stayed put all night. The following day it ventured into the surrounding forest several times, but finding neither its mother nor a familiar trail it returned to its resting place, obviously stressed.

During the second night on its own, the youngster's ears heard the approach of some big animal and it prepared to dash away if discovered. Fear turned to excitement as a soft call floated in from the darkness. The mother tapir had been too great a match for the snake, and knocking it off, she had followed the scent of her offspring to its present location. After much nudging, she led the way to a secluded resting site where they could recover from their close brush with death.

BAIRD'S TAPIR

Scientific name *Tapirus bairdii*
Family Tapirs (Tapiridae)
Order Odd-toed Ungulates (Perissodactyla)
Total length 200 cm (78.7 in)
Tail length 8 cm (3.2 in)
Weight males 250 kg (551.2 lb);
females 275 kg, maximum 315 kg
(606.4 lb, maximum 694.4 lb)
Color The tapir's skin and sparse cover of hair are black to reddish-brown, somewhat paler below. The ear tips are rimmed with white. The young are reddish-brown and covered with rows of horizontal spots and stripes of a creamy-white color.

Distribution and Status Baird's (or Central American) tapir is found from southern Mexico to Columbia and Ecuador where it inhabits wooded and grassy areas with permanent water nearby. Typical plant communities that provide its requirements are tropical rain forest, tropical deciduous forest, mangrove swamp, and bamboo thickets on mountainsides as high as 3 500 m (11,483 ft). Its closest relatives are the Brazilian or lowland tapir *(Tapirus terrestris)* and the mountain tapir *(Tapirus pinchaque)* of South America, and the Asiatic or Malayan tapir *(Tapirus indicus)* of Southeast Asia. This strange distribution pattern is believed to have developed in the following stages — the family originated in Asia, spread to North America, then sometime in the late Pliocene or early Pleistocene (about 2 million years ago), several kinds of tapirs were able to reach South America, perhaps by swimming from island to island. Baird's tapir was the last to reach the southern continent and has not been able to penetrate as far south as its 2 other cousins. With the cooling trend of the Pleistocene, tapirs were lost from much of the Northern Hemisphere, leaving only 4 species to survive to the present day in the 2 tropical zones.

With heavy hunting pressure and extensive habitat destruction, Baird's tapir has all but disappeared from Mexico and is largely restricted to parks in most other Central American countries. It, as well as the other 3 species, have all been placed on the Endangered Species List, and the outlook for survival of Baird's tapir is not bright.

Food Tapirs eat aquatic plants, grass, and broad-leaved plants, including leaves, seeds, fruit, and buds. Their strong teeth crack open all but the hardest seed and nut coats, and these are either spit out or swallowed whole. Some of these tough seeds pass through the intestines undamaged, while others may germinate and then become digestible while in a special sac off the intestines called the cecum. In some areas tapirs have become agricultural pests, conducting nightly raids on corn and other grain crops. In one experiment, a tapir accepted 150 kinds of plants and rejected 300 others, showing that, like most herbivores, well-developed senses of smell and taste are used in selecting among the many possible food plants in its environment.

Reproduction and Growth A female tapir comes into heat for a few days each 50 to 80 days throughout the year. Her urine marks are examined by the male with a lip-curling and tongue-rolling procedure similar to that of deer. When sexually receptive, the pair initiates a ritual of circling, pausing side by side to sniff each other's rump area, and snapping at the other's hind legs. Amid wheezing and whistling, the pair mates several times, then the female drives her partner away by biting him. Following a gestation period of 390 to 400 days, one (rarely 2) young is born. As soon as she cleans it off, the little tapir rises to its feet and searches for the udder (2 mammae present). The mother usually lies on her side to make the udder accessible, and if the youngster is having trouble, she pushes it in the right direction with her snout. For the first several weeks she conceals her spotted and striped offspring in a secluded thicket while she travels to her feeding grounds, reminiscent again of deer. The rapidly growing calf remains with its mother for 8 to 12 months (then two-thirds adult size), by which time she has generally become pregnant again. On the average, a tapir produces young every second year, with the birth not restricted to any particular season. Tapirs have been known to defend their calves by biting furiously if they cannot escape. These animals become sexually mature at an age of 3 or 4 years, and may live 35 years in zoos.

Remarks The tapir's appearance resembles that of many prehistoric forms of large herbivorous mammals, and in fact, it is a true "living fossil." In details of the feet and skull, it shows the primitive conditions that became specialized in the tapir's related surviving families — the horse (Equidae) and rhinoceros (Rhinocerotidae). Today, tapirs are the largest land animal of the American tropics.

The first thing one notices about a tapir is the short fleshy trunk with nostrils at the tip. This remarkable organ can move in and out and in any direction, and is used constantly to explore the ground, objects, or air. As well, it is used to pluck leaves just out of reach of the teeth. The head itself is long, curved downward, and flattened from side to side, with prominent ears and tiny sunken eyes. The heavy, hog-like body is supported on short strong legs. There are 4 hooved digits on the front feet and 3 on the hind feet. The hide is extremely thick (one to 3 cm or 0.4 to 1.2 in) and tough, almost a leathery shell along the back, which must protect the animal from predators, jabbing vegetation while running through brush, and from insect bites. The short, bristly hair is sparsely distributed, but forms a low mane along the neck and shoulders.

Tapirs can run quickly (faster than people), are good swimmers and divers, and are surprisingly good climbers up steep hillsides. They generally walk with the head down, but throw it high when galloping. Splashing and wallowing are frequently engaged in. Unsociable creatures, it is rare to see more than 3 together, and most times they prefer their own company. Although capable of fighting and slashing with their incisor teeth, adults usually just avoid each other and do not aggressively defend their worn trails and waterholes from others. They are shy and when frightened, they run away to hide. While mostly nocturnal, they come out during the daylight hours if not persecuted. Orphans and even captive adults become docile, enjoy being patted or scratched, and will even follow their owner around like a dog. All but the mountain tapir adapt well to zoo life. Their main predators are the big cats, crocodilians, snakes, and people who hunt them for meat and hides.

BAIRD'S TAPIR

Mammals of the
Warm Oceans

Most of the earth's surface is covered by temperate and tropical oceans — the cradle where life originated from complex chains of molecules. The ocean floor is an ancient, diverse landscape with plains, slopes, trenches, and volcanic mountain ranges running for thousands of kilometers. Coral reefs — the amalgamated skeletons of countless polyps — are also major topographical features along the coasts and islands from Florida south through the Caribbean, where water temperatures remain above 21°C (69.8°F), the water is clear, and less than 76 meters (249.3 feet) deep.

Powerful currents, driven by wind drag and the Coriolis force from the earth's rotation, act like giant rivers, transporting vast quantities of water, mixing waters of different temperatures, dispersing vital chemicals, and warming or cooling lands. The Gulf Stream and North Equatorial currents predominate in the Atlantic; the North Pacific and California currents in the Pacific. Water temperature decreases with depth. Often the warm surface is separated from cold deep water by an abrupt layer called the thermocline. Surface waters of the tropics and arctic change little through the year (2°C or 3.6°F difference in monthly averages), but considerably more (up to 10°C or 18°F) at mid-latitudes. In winter, south-temperate and tropical surface waters range from 7°C to 32°C (44.6°F to 89.6°F) from north to south; in summer, 13°C to 32°C (55.4°F to 89.6°F).

The coastline of North America is over 160 000 kilometers (99,422 miles) long. The tidal or littoral zone experiences twice-daily exposure and submergence as a result of one to 7-meter (3.3 to 23-foot) tides, and fluctuations in salinity, temperature, and wave action. Each type of shore bottom is host to a particular fauna — barnacles, limpets, and sea urchins on rock; mollusks and polychaete worms in sand; and the lugworm and innkeeper worm in mud. Attached to the littoral and offshore or sublittoral zones are many kinds of seaweeds (mainly algae) which form the marine equivalent of forests. Some of these seaweeds grow 12 meters (39.4 feet) long and create a quiet refuge from the pounding Pacific surf which strikes the rocky coastline unabated by ridges or islands. Seed plants — eelgrass, turtle grass, and marsh grass — are also represented along coastlines. The ocean floor consists of the continental shelf which descends to a depth of about 180 meters (590.6 feet), the continental slope which drops to an average of 1 830 meters (6,003.9 feet), and the abyssal plain, averaging 4 000 meters (13,123.4 feet) but continuing to a maximum depth in the Pacific Marianas Trench of 11 033 meters (36,197.5 feet).

The open sea or pelagic zone consists of an upper euphotic layer where light penetrates to about 200 meters (656.2 feet) depth, the bathyal zone below to a depth of 1 830 meters (6,003.9 feet), and the abyssal zone descending to the sea floor. In the surface waters, tunas, ocean sunfish and whale shark feed on smaller fish and plankton — tiny drifting organisms. Plants such as sargassum and microscopic phytoplankton live mainly in the upper 15 meters (49.2 feet) and support directly or indirectly all other marine life. However, the production of phytoplankton is discontinuous — some waters turning green or brown with their abundance, while other vast regions are virtual "deserts." The limiting factor is nutrients — nitrates and phosphates — which continually sink to the depths in the form of detritus from dead organisms. Where upwhellings of currents from below, or rivers entering the sea, deliver this fertilizer to surface waters, phytoplankton growth is immediate. In most warm oceans there is little mixing because the continually warm upper layer prevents the cold, lower, and nutrient-laden water from rising. This is the reason why warm oceans are generally less productive than antarctic and arctic waters, where upwhellings are more prevalent.

Animals of the bathyal zone live in a cold, dark or twilight world. Some actually migrate to the surface to feed at night. Common creatures living here include jellyfish, deep-sea squid, octopus, shrimp, halibut, Greenland shark, and viperfish. Abyssal animals dwell in total darkness, at 1°C (33.8°F) constant temperature, and under tremendous water pressure (one atmosphere for every 10 meters or 33 feet in depth). Here swim tripod fish, rattail, luminescent angler fish, and amphipods, while sea cucumbers, brittlestars, sea lilies and sea urchins dwell on the bottom ooze.

Sea Otter and Northern Sea Lion

The afternoon sunlight flooded through the upper regions of the sea, energizing a vast forest of brown kelp. These giant algae plants arose from sturdy holdfasts cemented onto the rocky floor and spiraled upward in graceful gelatinous ribbons to the surface where they were kept afloat by thousands of gas-filled bladders. The fronds swayed back and forth, caught in the eternal rhythm of the waves. The heavy sound of surf pounding on the rocky reef did not seem to bother schools of rock bass and other fishes winding through the kelp in search of food. Suddenly the fish scattered from sight as a silver missile spun down through the water and landed on the ocean floor at a depth of forty meters (131.2 feet). It was a sea otter, paddling rapidly with its webbed hind feet to overcome the natural buoyancy of its air-pocketed fur coat. With touch-sensitive whiskers and hands it rooted among the rocks for a starfish, clam, or other form of marine life. Finally discovering a sea urchin, the otter picked it up and shoved the spiny creature in its mouth. Rapid snapping of the otter's jaws soon reduced the urchin to a pile of shell fragments, and the soft contents were swallowed in short order. Rather than surface immediately, the otter then scratched free several clams and tucked them, along with a rock, into a loose fold of skin under its left arm. Having now been below for fifty seconds, the otter made its way back to the surface with forearms folded along its chest.

The otter's sudden appearance at the surface was duly noted by several gulls floating nearby as well as a sleepy sea lion, yawning with its nose pointed straight up. The otter rolled over on its back and began banging the clams, one at a time, against the rock which lay balanced on its chest. As each clam cracked open, the otter scooped out the insides with its projecting lower incisor teeth and swallowed it whole, its head bobbing up and down in contentment. Then, with two gracefully smooth rolls of its sleek body, the otter washed the food scraps from its chest, then wrapped itself within the kelp and drifted off to sleep, knowing that it would not drift away in the current.

Now it was the northern sea lion's turn to feed. With a bellow which could be heard over the roar of the surf, the massive creature clumsily shifted its weight from front to hind flippers. With each lunge, shock ripples ran through the blubber and muscle of its powerful shoulders and neck. Awkward as it was on land, the one-tonne (1.1-ton) creature hurled its bulk off the rocks, and in a nine-point dive, entered its true realm with hardly a splash. Unlike the true seals, which use the hind flippers for a power stroke, the sea lion propelled itself with the front flippers, literally flying through the water like a huge penguin. Surfacing frequently, the sea lion flared its nostrils to take in air, then shut them again the instant the nose slipped under water.

By the time the sea lion had gone fifteen kilometers (9.3 miles) offshore the sun had set. In the darkening water the plankton commenced rising toward the surface, followed by fish and other carnivores. Fulfilling its role at the top of the food chain, the sea lion darted after fish and squid, gobbling down smaller creatures below, surfacing to devour larger fish. It was morning by the time the sea lion returned to the reef, its digestive tract sixty-kilograms (132.3-pounds) full of food.

Its home range was not as the bull had left it. Approaching the hauling-out grounds, a floating black substance coated its face, and the rocks were so slippery that the sea lion had great difficulty climbing out along the usual route. A spill from a passing tanker had left an oil slick along many kilometers of the Pacific shoreline. With the return of daylight, the sea lion departed from its traditional home, moving north to find unpolluted range. The sea otter fared less well. Its coat, covered in black grease, lost its insulative qualities, and the otter, chilled to the bone, had no choice but to ground itself on the shore. Weakened from exposure, the blackened otter lay helpless on the beach sand, along with a multitude of birds of the sea and shore. Conservation officers arrived in the afternoon and began washing as many of the pathetic-looking creatures as possible. Bulldozers scraped the mess of oil-soaked straw into piles, as the otter was placed in a special cage, loaded on a truck, and driven away. One week later, cleaned and health restored, the otter was released to the sea in a nearby colony, hopefully to be spared in the future from the oily threat.

SEA OTTER

Scientific name *Enhydra lutris*

Family Weasels (Mustelidae)

Order Carnivores (Carnivora)

Total length males 145 cm (57.1 in);
females 140 cm (55.1 in)

Tail length 30 cm (11.8 in); 28 cm (11 in)

Weight 35 kg, maximum 45 kg
(77.2 lb, maximum 99.2 lb);
25 kg, maximum 33 kg
(55.1 lb, maximum 72.8 lb)

Color The luxurious coat ranges from reddish-brown or dark brown or almost black. With age, the head, neck, and shoulders become grizzled with white.

Distribution and Status The sea otter is native to coastlines and offshore islands in the great Pacific arc running from central Baja California (Mexico), north to British Columbia and Alaska, then west through the Aleutian, Pribilof, and Commander Islands, and south along Kamchatka, Kuril Islands, and Sakhalin (Soviet Union) to Hokkaido (Japan). Colonies tend to remain within 16 km (9.9 mi) of the coast and most activity occurs within one km (0.6 mi). No migratory movements are known. Occasional wanderers have traveled over 300 km (186.4 mi) from home. The species lives in water depths usually under 40 m (131.2 ft), but sometimes as deep as 55 m (180.5 ft); one was trapped at 97 m (318.2 ft). Otters are found in areas with a rocky or soft bottom, often in sites with rich beds of kelp, although concentrations have been seen in the Bering Sea where kelp does not grow. Natural barriers appear to be sea ice in the north and warm water in the south. The animals have never been reported in freshwater lakes or rivers.

The sea otter has been one of the world's most valuable furbearers, which has led to severe hunting pressure throughout its range ever since colonies were discovered. It was hunted to near extinction in the late 1800s, and by the time the animal received protection in 1911, only 1,000 to 2,000 individuals were known from secluded sites in northern regions. Few were actually seen until the population began to increase dramatically in the 1960s. The California population was long thought exterminated, but 50 to 100 individuals apparently survived near Monterey. This colony has now spread along 300 km (186.4 mi) of the coast and presently numbers over 2,000. Various transplants have been attempted with some successes and failures. British Columbia now supports about 100 otters near Vancouver; Washington and Oregon fewer than 50; 120,000 in Alaska waters; and the world population may now exceed 150,000 — a marvellous conservation success. The sea otter appears to have evolved from an earlier genus of sea otter *(Enhydriodon)* known from India, the North Atlantic, and the North Pacific.

Food High activity and rapid heat loss from a life in cool water require the sea otter to eat a relatively large amount of food. In fact, the animal needs to process from 20 to 25 percent of its weight in food each day. Such a heavy food intake in a colonial species places a considerable drain on the local resources of the sea, and occasionally the otters deplete their food supply. Mollusks such as abalone, clams, and snails are a major food source, supplemented by sea urchins, crabs, starfish, fish (often sluggish bottom species), and a host of other small sea creatures. Food is eliminated from the digestive tract in only 3 hours after eating. Apparently the otter cannot digest seal or bird tissues or kelp. Water is obtained from its food and sea water. Food is collected in shallow water, generally less than 40 m (131.2 ft) and is eaten where it is found or is carried to the surface. Its well-known habit of cracking open the shells of prey likewise can occur at the bottom or surface.

Reproduction and Growth The male otter is capable of breeding throughout the year, and when he detects a female coming into heat, he follows her every move. The constant companions feed, float in the kelp, and haul out for the night, often centering their activities around a particular rock. The mating period lasts for about 3 days during which several copulations occur, each lasting around 20 minutes. The male is driven away or is abandoned soon after, and continues on his way, perhaps to serve another female. Only the female cares for the young, and will adopt orphans.

Following fertilization, the egg undergoes a rest period of several months, then implants in the womb and continues its growth. The single pup is born 8 to 12 months after conception. Although births may occur in any month, most are in late May and June in northern regions and December to February in the south. The pup is born on land or in the water and is well developed — a dense fur coat is present, the eyes are open, and the teeth are erupting. It weighs 2 kg (4.4 lb) and measures 56 cm (22 in) in length. The guard hairs give the newborn a wooly appearance. The pup is cleaned, dried, and nursed while lying on its mother's chest. Milk is provided from 2 mammary glands. The mother spends much time feeding and caring for her offspring, and it is doubtful if she could raise 2 pups at a time if twins were born. With all this attention, pup survival is relatively high, but most females produce only one young every second year. When off foraging, the mother otter leaves the pup bobbing at the surface, buoyed up by the air trapped in its fur coat. One month passes before the pup develops the strength and coordination necessary to dive. At first it collects useless but attractive items on the bottom (e.g., pebbles, empty shells), and its mother begins to feed it solid food. It soon learns what to pick up or chase on its diving expeditions. Females begin to breed at 4 years of age, males mature at 5 or 6, but several more years pass before they are able to court and mate successfully.

Remarks The smallest of all marine mammals, the otter closely resembles the river otter with its tubular streamlined body, blunt head, and short limbs. The tail, however, is flattened horizontally and does not taper as much as in the river otter. The rounded ears, which stand erect when above water, fold down when the animal submerges, perhaps helping to keep out the water. The front limbs have retractable claws, useful for grooming and scratching out food items, yet tuck out of the way when the sensitive fingers are employed in searching for food. This sense of touch is important in prey location, since the otter's eyes are not as well adapted to seeing in the dim light underwater as are seals.' The hind feet are webbed and broad and used to propel the animal through the water with up and down strokes — at about 9 km (5.6 mi) per hour underwater, 1.5 km (0.9 mi) per hour on the surface. The front limbs, tail, and sinuous body assist in maneuvering. Dives are generally less than one minute in duration, but if necessary the animal can hold its breath for 4.5 minutes. Incredibly graceful in the water, the sea otter hunches along awkwardly on land.

The sea otter also differs from the rest of the weasel family by its lack of anal scent glands, having teeth with rounded cusps rather than sharp cutting edges which it uses for crushing hard prey, and having only 2 (rather than 3) pairs of lower incisors. The liver, lungs, and kidneys are remarkably large and appear to be related respectively to the need to digest huge amounts of food, to assist buoyancy and diving, and to eliminate salt from the blood.

This species depends on fur for insulation

SEA OTTER

rather than a thick layer of blubber, as in most marine mammals. Each guard hair is surrounded by about 70 underhairs (2.5 cm or one in long), which, along with trapped air, prevent the chilling water from reaching the skin. The fur is constantly being groomed and is dried after exiting from the water. Should the fur become soiled by pollutants, the otter quickly suffers from cold exposure and may perish. An adult otter supposedly has around one billion fur fibres covering its body — the densest coat of any marine mammal. Blood flow in the webbed feet is automatically controlled to conserve or increase body heat loss, depending on the internal temperature of the otter. When cold, the animal's dark coat and system of veins in the top of the feet help absorb heat from the sun.

Males and females occupy different areas of coastline, and females seldom enter male home ranges. Males of all ages have been known to concentrate (up to 200 individuals) along certain beaches, but at other times definite territories about 30 ha (75 a) in size are set up, patrolled, and defended by kicking and splashing. Female territories are double the size of male's, often at sites protected from heavy wave action. Competition for space, food sources, and the opportunity to breed appear to control the size, spacing, and composition of otter colonies. Females that are pregnant or with pups shun the company of other individuals.

Sea otters communicate by whistles, growls, hisses, screams, and soft grunts and cooing when contented. A baby otter emits a high-pitched gull-like cry when distressed and trying to contact its mother. The otter's main predators are killer whales, sharks, eagles, and of course, people. While the species is now protected from fur trappers, competition with fishermen for abalone, clams, and fish has resulted in strong political pressure for reducing the numbers of otters.

If there is one animal that seems to enjoy itself in any activity, it must surely be the sea otter. My first sighting of these fascinating animals was off the magnificent cliffs of Point Lobos near Monterey, California. About 80 m (262.5 ft) from the surf-pounded shore were half-a-dozen otters frolicking in the kelp beds. Lying on their backs, nipping at each other, and then disappearing below, I wondered what adventures they were having. I wished I had brought along scuba gear so that I could have joined them. On another occasion, I and two friends were standing on the Monterey wharf, when we spotted a mother otter and pup. Apparently she was teaching it how to dive and locate prey on the bottom. They dove down together, but the pup always returned empty handed after only 15 seconds and bobbed around like a cork until mother returned with breakfast. She loudly chomped the shelled creature apart and the 2 fed together in obvious enjoyment. We could have watched their harbor antics for hours, but we had to continue on our trip south. A few days later, at Sea World, we had the opportunity of watching several otters at close range, and we marvelled at their fluid movements of spirals and rolls while they were swimming.

NORTHERN SEA LION

Scientific name *Eumetopias jubatus*
Family Eared Seals (Otariidae)
Order Carnivores (Carnivora)
Total length males 340 cm, maximum
400 cm (133.9 in, maximum 157.5 in);
females 240 cm (94.5 in)
Weight 900 kg, maximum 1 089 kg
(1,984.1 lb, maximum 2,400.8 lb);
275 kg, maximum 318 kg
(606.3 lb, maximum 701.1 lb)
Color The coat is yellowish- to reddish-brown, while the flippers are dark brown. The pups are also dark brown.
Distribution and Status This largest of the sea lions is found from San Miguel Island off California north to Alaska, then west through the Aleutian and Pribilof Islands, and south again along Kamchatka and Kuril Islands (Soviet Union) to the Sea of Okhotsk. Following the breeding season, some individuals move farther north in the Bering Sea to St. Lawrence Island. The northern sea lion lives on islands and secluded coastlines of either rock or coarse sand. Ice in the north and warm water in the south appear to limit distribution; in fact the recent decrease in California colonies is believed to be related to an increase in water temperature. Although herds undergo extensive migrations in summer and autumn, much remains unknown of their movements. Occasionally individuals swim far up rivers. The major concentrations are found in summer throughout the Aleutian and Pribilof Islands. Current population estimates are 50,000 in the Soviet Union, 200,000 in Alaska, 5,000 in British Columbia, 600 in Washington, 2,000 in Oregon, and 7,000 in California (world total 264,600).

The northern (or Steller) sea lion is closely related to 4 other species (but placed in different genera) — Australian, New Zealand, South American, and California sea lions. The family of eared seals originated from land-dwelling, dog-like carnivores about 25 million years ago (late Oligocene) in the basin of the North Pacific. The 5 recent species first appear in the fossil record about 3 million years ago.
Food The dominant foods are squid and fish such as flounder, herring, sculpin, halibut, greenling, lumpfish, and sand lance. Octopus, crabs, clams, and dozens of other kinds of marine invertebrates have also been found in the stomach of sea lions. Occasionally, a sea bird or young seal is captured and eaten. To meet its needs, a sea lion devours about 14 percent of its body weight per day. However, the bulls give up eating for around 60 days while staked out on their territories. The digestive tract is an astonishing 80 m (262.5 ft) long.
Reproduction and Growth In early May the bulls arrive at the breeding grounds and begin to jostle for prime territories along the beach. Hissing with open mouth, neck fencing, and biting savagely, the dominant bulls prevent the younger and weaker bulls from entering their area, which averages 225 sq m (2,420.6 sq ft) in size and may extend into tidal pools. The cows, about one-third the size of the bulls, arrive several weeks later and give birth within a few days (from mid-May to mid-July). Delivery occurs on land and takes about 30 minutes. The mother cleans the pup off, picks it up by the loose skin on its neck, and places it in a suckling position. At the tender age of one hour, the 20-kg (44.1-lb) pup is able to walk and hopefully avoid being squashed

by adult seals. By the end of the day it can swim weakly. Unlike the fasting bulls, the cows spend 9 to 40 hours feeding in the sea and return to nurse their own pup only, which they recognize by its odor. After practising swimming in tidal pools for 6 weeks, the pup is lured into the open sea where it soon learns to catch its own food by observing its mother. The bond between the 2 is close and lasts for at least one year; some 3-year-old sea lions have been seen trying to nurse.

About 12 days after giving birth, the cow comes into heat and wanders into the harem of a bull of her choice. Climbing atop the bull, she may bite him to gain his attention; then she coyly lumbers away. Mating lasts about 16 minutes and may be accomplished on the beach or in shallow water. Having eaten nothing for 2 months, mated with up to 30 cows, performed hundreds of threat routines, and engaged in perhaps a dozen brutal battles, the exhausted bull master leaves his noisy harem of cows and pups in August for the serenity of the sea. The cows remain in the rookery until September or October. During this time, the fertilized egg in the cow's womb has been resting. At 3.5 months it implants in the wall of the womb and begins to grow. Pregnancy, including the resting stage (called delayed implantation), takes 11 months. Females become sexually mature at an age of 3 or 4 years and produce one pup a year until about 14 years old. While males mature at 4 or 5 years, they do not attain full strength and become proficient breeders until 9 years, and continue to about 15. Maximum life span in the wild is 22 years.
Remarks Female sea lions are beautifully streamlined for smooth passage through the water. The enormous males are massively developed in the forequarters and neck to support the heavy creature when it rises on its front limbs on land and to permit powerful swimming strokes of the front flippers. True seals, like harbor and ringed seals, cannot rise on their front limbs and the thrust during swimming is achieved mainly by the hind flippers. As in other seals, the upper limb bones of the sea lion lie within the body. The flippers are lengthened beyond the bones and nails with pieces of cartilage, connected by a web of tough skin. The animal grooms its short, coarse coat with its hind flippers. A thick mane is developed on the neck of bulls. Insulation against the cold water is obtained through a thick layer of blubber, since there is only a sparse underfur lying beneath the guard hairs. If the animals become chilled on land, they tuck their flippers under their bodies and huddle to reduce the loss of body heat. Should they become too warm on land, they sweat and wave their flippers or enter the water.

Sea lions have large eyes, small pointy ears, and long (50 cm or 19.7 in) whiskers, which perhaps help in locating food through the sense of touch. The blunt teeth are adapted for grasping prey, but they can also tear pieces of flesh from large creatures. Feeding activity occurs during the night and in the morning. Sea lions feed either singly or in groups, depending whether the prey is solitary or schooling like some fish or squid. Hunting occurs within 25 km (15.5 mi) off the shore and at maximum depths of 183 m (600.4 ft). Most of the colony hauls out on the shore for the afternoon. In stormy weather sea lions tend to remain together in the water just beyond the breakers.

Continued on p.328

Sperm Whale

The warm Gulf Stream spread out into the mid-Atlantic, sliding overtop deeper cool waters and flowing ever-onward in a great circle to the north-African coast. From here it would swing back again to the West Indies as the North African Equatorial Current. Encouraged by the wind, the ocean surface rocked slowly with each passing wave, reflecting the somber, overcast sky of early dawn. The scene appeared devoid of any life — no birds in the sky, nor fish in the upper two hundred meters (656.2 feet) or pelagic zone. Suddenly, a great square head erupted from the water and let out a blast of moisture-laden air. The sperm whale's momentum carried its ponderous hulk in a graceful, slow-motion arc, half out of the water, leaving its tail flukes to mark the spot with a patch of white foam. Then another, and another whale surfaced to breathe, until an entire school of twenty-two sperm whales cruised in formation, following the lead of the bull master. The cows and young were considerably shorter and slimmer than the bull, whose massive head formed one-third of its whole length. The harem kept together by means of a continuous emission of rapid clicking noises and by their eyes, set out on bumps on the sides of the head. Almost in unison, the whales reappeared every ten to fifteen seconds to fill their huge lungs with air.

After blowing about sixty times, the bull pointed its blunt snout downward, causing its mighty tail to stand vertically in the air for a few seconds. Once below, the tail began a powerful steady rhythm of up-and-down strokes, propelling the creature on its long journey to the ocean bottom. As if on signal, the other whales turned tail up and followed their master into the depths. Swimming at ten kilometers (6.2 miles) per hour, the bull passed beyond the range of light penetration at about five hundred meters (1,640.4 feet). The rest of the herd remained above this level to chase fish and meter (3.3-foot)-long squid, but the bull was after bigger prey. Every ten meters (32.8 feet) in depth added another atmosphere of water pressure, and the crushing force constricted the whale's lungs and nasal passages. In fifteen minutes the sperm whale approached the ocean bottom at twenty-five hundred meters (8,202 feet). No other species of mammal in the whole world could reach such a depth and return alive.

In the pitch blackness of the deep, the bull perceived the presence of the clay-covered floor by returning echoes of clicks emitted at seventy per second from the front of its blunt head. All during the descent, the whale maintained neutral buoyancy by controlling the flooding of its five-meter (16.4-foot)-long nasal tubes with water. The cold water also chilled and solidified the five tonnes (5.5 tons) of oil present in front of the skull, increasing its density. The following ten minutes the whale hung motionless in a horizontal position, scanning its hunting grounds with a series of sonar calls. Something big moved into range, and at a distance of one hundred meters (328.1 feet), the sperm whale began its stalk. Reaching top speed, it soon spotted a faint glow in the darkness — a luminous giant squid. Although the ten-meter (32.8-foot)-long squid was a speedy swimmer, the whale was upon it before it could escape. Just prior to impact the whale's slim lower jaw opened and snapped shut on the soft flesh of the squid. The force of the attack carried the two through the water, with the squid's long tentacles draped tightly over the whale's head. For twenty minutes the fight raged, the whale chomping down repeatedly while the squid tried to defend itself with bites from its beak and powerful suckers. When the squid ceased struggling and released its hold, the whale proceeded to swallow the whole slippery mass at one time. A few pieces of tentacles drifted off unnoticed and sank slowly to the bottom to nourish some other deep-sea creatures.

By now, the sperm whale had been below for a full hour. Its meal completed, it headed straight back up the way it had come. An increased flow of warm blood to the head changed the wax back to a lighter oil, providing added lift for the exhausted whale. As it approached the lighted zone, it could hear the familiar whistles and wheezes of its companions. Having held its breath for eighty minutes, the bull frantically soared past the others who obediently followed him to the surface. Once again the mighty sperm whale breached clear of the water, blasting stale air from the single nostril and falling back into the sea with a tremendous splash. Satiated with food and fresh air, the black hulk ceased swimming and stood almost vertically on its tail, with its nose at the surface. Soon it fell asleep with only the raw circular wounds from the squid's suckers to mark its incredible journey to the deep.

NORTHERN SEA LION *continued from p.325*

The rookery is a most noisy place, with bulls roaring, coughing, and grunting, cows barking, and pups bleating. Barren cows, bachelor males, and yearlings haul out in an area adjacent to the territories of the breeding bulls and their harems. The main predators of the northern sea lion are people, killer whales, and big sharks. Large numbers of sea lions have been destroyed at times to protect fishing interests.

SPERM WHALE

Scientific name *Physeter macrocephalus*
Family Sperm Whales (Physeteridae)
Order Toothed Whales (Odontoceti)
Total length males 15 m, maximum 20 m
(49.2 ft, maximum 65.6 ft);
females 11 m, maximum 17 m
(36.1 ft, maximum 55.8 ft)
Weight 36 t, maximum 38 t
(39.6 tons, maximum 41.8 tons);
20 t (22 tons)
Color This whale is black or dark gray and somewhat paler below. The young are gray. White blotches are often present on the lips, head, hump, navel, flank, and tail, generally increasing with age. Old males may become white. Albinos (as in the story of Moby Dick) are known as well. Diatom algae growing on the skin of bulls give them a greenish color while in the arctic, but this plant life soon dies off in warmer waters.

Distribution and Status The sperm whale plies all oceans of the world and prefers to hunt along ocean trenches, the edges of continental and island shelves, and other deepwater sites 1 000 m (3,280.8 ft) or more, where currents bring nutrients up from the ocean floor. Due to separate migration patterns, only limited interchange occurs between populations in the Northern and Southern Hemispheres. In autumn, sperm whales in the Northern Hemisphere migrate southward into tropical waters and thousands have been seen congregating around the Cape Verde and Canary Islands. In the spring, males migrate farther north than females and young, often entering arctic waters (Davis Strait and the Alaska coast). Movements may be influenced by the moon cycle. North Atlantic sperm whales range widely, while there appears to be 2 or 3 fairly distinct stocks in the North Pacific.

This species was formerly common (perhaps 2 million), but has been greatly reduced in numbers after centuries of intense hunting for its oil. Only rough population estimates are available because of its deep-water habits, but there are thought to be about 200,000 in the Southern and 175,000 in the Northern Hemispheres. The species is classified as endangered and is now under full protection. It still remains the most abundant of the giant whales. Its closest living relatives are the pygmy and dwarf sperm whales (genus *Kogia*), both confined to warm waters of the world.

Food The most important food resources for the sperm whale are cephalopods — namely squid, cuttlefish, and octopus. Squid often forms up to 90 percent of the diet and can amount to one t (1.1 ton) a day. Whale bellies have been opened to reveal as many as 28,000 small squid, or an 11-m (36.1-ft)-long giant squid thought to weigh about 184 kg (405.6 lb). However, most squid are under 2 m (6.6 ft) in length, including deep-water forms. Other items commonly devoured are jellyfish, lobster, skate, shark up to 4 m (13.1 ft) long, barracuda, albacore, and deep-sea angler. All but the largest prey are swallowed whole. Surprisingly, the sperm whale swims along the sea floor, plowing through the sediment with its lower jaw and scooping up some sand and other debris along with bottom life.

Reproduction and Growth Breeding schools congregate in winter, with the polygamous bulls each gathering 10 to 40 females. Mating occurs from January to July with a peak in April, at the start of the northward migration. After developing inside the womb for 14 to 16 months, a single calf is born while the mother stands vertically with her head out of the water. She is often surrounded by other females who assist in pushing the

NORTHERN SEA LION

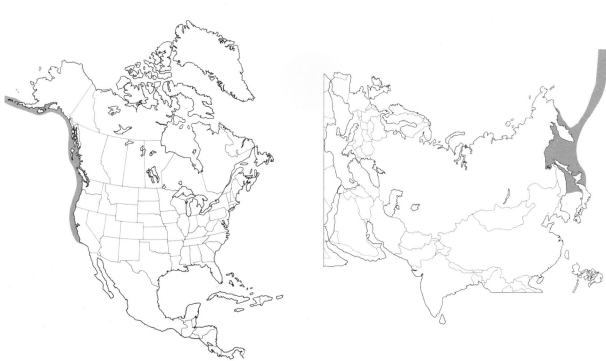

newborn to the surface to breathe. The offspring is 4 m (13.1 ft) long, weighs about one t (1.1 ton), and shortly learns to slip its toothless lower jaw into the mother's mammary groove, whereupon milk is pumped into its mouth. Weaning occurs at one or 2 years of age but occasional nursing may continue for several more years. Females become sexually mature at 7 to 12 years when around 9 m (29.5 ft) long. Males often take longer, 9 to 18 years and around 12 m (39.4 ft), and may not have an opportunity to gather a harem and mate until about 25 years old and some 14 m (45.9 ft) in length. Full size is attained at 28 years in females, 35 years in males. The life span of the sperm whale is believed to be 77 years.

Remarks The huge blunt head of the sperm whale is distinctive, and contains the largest brain in the animal kingdom — 8 to 10 kg (17.6 to 22.1 lb). In fact, the head accounts for one-third the length and over one-third the weight of the whole whale. Sitting atop the skull lies an enormous spermaceti organ consisting of up to 5 t (5.5 tons) of free oil and cells filled with oil, which functions in buoyancy control and directing sound waves. The relatively small narrow jaw fits into a groove far back on the head, and is lined with several dozen teeth, each about 20 cm (7.9 in) long. Teeth also occur in the upper jaw, but not all of them erupt from the gums. Since food is swallowed whole, the teeth serve to grasp or immobilize slippery prey. Sperm whales don't have teeth until 10 years old, so they don't seem to have trouble feeding without them.

Female sperm whales are slimmer, shorter, and have relatively smaller heads than males. The dorsal fin is lacking in this species, replaced by a series of 5 or 6 bumps along the back. Many females develop a callous on the first, largest bump, the purpose of which is unknown. This region also houses another

reservoir of oil. The flippers are short and weak, and serve to brake and maneuver. The whale is powered by the muscular tailstock, terminating in the widest tail flukes of all whales. Deep wrinkles and pleats run lengthwise down the body, and the head is deeply scarred with scratches from fighting and sucker marks. The sperm whale also claims the thickest skin of any animal — a full 36 cm (14.2 in) including the blubber. No body hair has been found at any stage of life.

A single S-shaped nostril leads to the left nasal passage and connects to several air sacs, the right nasal passage, and the lungs. While the functions of this system are not completely clear, it may help control buoyancy and nitrogen absorption at great depths, and produce and direct sound waves used in echolocation and communication. A wide range of sounds are possible — knocks, clicks, squeaks, and even roars which carry for many km underwater. It has been suggested (but not proven) that a powerful blast of sound waves may be able to stun prey.

Sperm whales often swim slowly at around 6 km (3.7 mi) per hour, but can reach a top speed of 40 km (24.9 mi) per hour. They sometimes float and rest at the surface, sleep vertically with the nose above water, or lie on their side with a flipper and tail fluke sticking out. Their dives to depths of at least 3 200 m (10,498.7 ft) is truly phenomenal, not even closely matched by any other sea mammal.

Females, juveniles, and calves remain in a closely knit school, joined in the breeding season by one to 5 bulls. Young males finally leave and form bachelor herds which the older males tend to abandon for long periods, preferring to be on their own in northern waters. Bulls can become aggressive when courting, and savagely bite and ram each other. There are also reliable cases of sperm whales,

singly or in groups, attacking and even sinking ships, apparently after being wounded by whalers or after accidental collisions. Congregations usually range between 20 to 40 whales, occasionally up to 80, and records of 1,000 and almost 4,000 have been reported.

Strandings in shallow water are not uncommon in this species and usually involve herds of females and young; bachelor schools seldom strand. Apparently one individual becomes trapped due to fright, injury, or sonar confusion. Cries for assistance quickly attract others, since sperm whales exhibit strong supportive behavior for their schoolmates. The tragic response continues, one whale at a time, until the whole school becomes trapped. The only solution biologists have come up with to halt this chain of events is to shoot the stranded whale, thereby preventing further distress calls.

One last item about this most fascinating creature is a waxy material called ambergris, which forms from intestinal wastes sticking to indigestible materials like squid beaks. Ambergris, either removed from a dead whale, or found in the water, was highly prized as a perfume fixative, but it has recently been replaced by synthetics.

SPERM WHALE

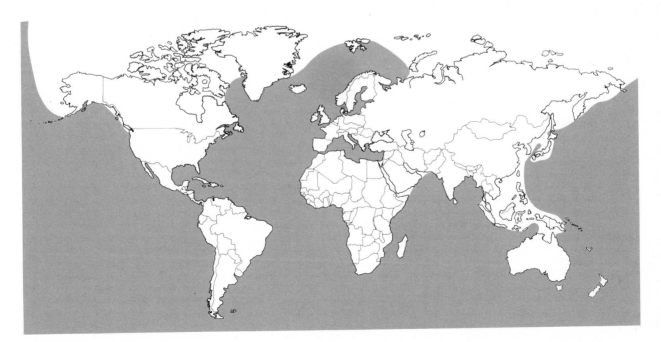

Harbor Porpoise

It was a warm spring day along the coast. People flocked to the beaches to refresh themselves in the salty breeze after being cooped up for weeks by the recent cool and rainy weather. Several couples sat in lounge chairs in front of telescopes, watching the sea birds and some small whales that broke the surface periodically with their black shiny backs a kilometer (0.6 miles) offshore. A motorboat passed nearby the herd and one of the passengers remarked that she thought the animals were porpoises because they lacked the beaked face so characteristic of dolphins. As well, these porpoises kept their distance from the boat and didn't leap clear of the water, unlike dolphins which love to race under the bow wave of a speeding craft and to frolic and flip in midair. The timid creatures disappeared from view for up to ten minutes, then resurfaced every twenty seconds to breathe, rolling smoothly without a splash. Each individual harbor porpoise took several quick breaths of air through the blowhole, loudly puffing on the exhale and whining while inhaling. The group of eleven porpoises included adult females, young, and immature animals, leaving the older males to travel together on their own. The water was filled with whistles and clicks as the porpoises called continually to each other. Rather than gliding through the water in a synchronous ballet, it was every porpoise for itself, with individuals shooting around every which way, including the path of others, whereupon they glanced off each other, touching ever so lightly.

Suddenly, as if a command had been issued, the creatures turned toward the shore in unison and began moving faster in an even column. A school of fish had been detected by the porpoises' echo-locating calls at a distance of one kilometer (0.6 miles) and at forty kilometers (24.9 miles) per hour they rapidly closed in on their unsuspecting prey. With marvellous precision the torpedo-shaped animals swept around and under the school of mackerel, preventing the fish from breaking away to safety. The sea's surface rippled from the powerful thrusts of the porpoises' tailstocks as they took turns penetrating the silvery mass with their spade-shaped teeth snatching a fish on every pass. For twenty minutes the feeding frenzy continued until each animal had swallowed its fill, then they broke formation and let the surviving mackerel swirl away.

Then, without warning, a terrible thing happened. Perhaps one of the porpoises had seen a killer whale or some other danger, but an alarm call was given and two of the panic-stricken mammals burst towards shallow water. People on the beach stopped their activities and watched with astonishment as the porpoises propelled themselves onto the shore and began flopping helplessly among the rocks. The animals actually seemed to be trying to get out of the water. As several men began lifting and pushing the creatures back into deeper water, the animals' underwater distress calls attracted one of the offshore porpoises and soon it stranded as well. This sequence continued until all eleven were in trouble. A couple of the unfortunate porpoises were even roped and towed far offshore with boats, but they tragically returned to their beached herd. By now, the animals were lying half out of the water, flapping their tail flukes uselessly and whining through their blowholes. They were having great difficulty breathing since their weight, no longer supported by the buoyant sea water, pressed down on their lungs. A few hours later, the eleven bodies lay like black logs scattered along the shore. The saddened crowd gathered around the beautiful but mysterious creatures and asked a marine biologist who had arrived on the scene what would cause such a tragic event. The answer was that no one really knew. Maybe the porpoises were afraid of something offshore, or were trying to help a panicked companion, or perhaps they just became confused by the gently sloping bottom — a flaw in the behavior of an otherwise intelligent sea mammal.

HARBOR PORPOISE

Scientific name *Phocoena phocoena*

Family Porpoises (Phocoenidae)

Order Toothed Whales (Odontoceti)

Total length 150 cm, maximum 180 cm (4.9 ft, maximum 5.9 ft)

Weight 45 kg, maximum 90 kg (99.2 lb, maximum 198.4 lb)

Color The animal's top half, flippers, and tail flukes are grayish-black while the underparts are white. A grayish area is present on the side of the body and a thin gray line passes from the angle of the jaw to the flipper. The newborn is slightly darker.

Distribution and Status The harbor or common porpoise is the most abundant cetacean in many regions, but its numbers have declined from heavy hunting pressure. Its range is enormous in both the Atlantic and Pacific Oceans. In the north Atlantic it is found as far south as Virginia (rarely to North Carolina) then north along the continental shelf and east to Europe into the Barents Sea (off the Soviet Union) and south to Senegal, the Mediterranean, and the Black Sea (an isolated population). In the Pacific it ventures as far south as Baja California, north to Alaska, across the Bering Sea and south along the coast of Asia to the Sea of Japan. North American populations summer in the northern part of the range, then migrate south to Maine-Virginia (and perhaps out to sea in the west Atlantic) and to British Columbia to Baja California. They seldom live in waters over 15°C (59°F); however, they are not deterred by brackish water (mixed fresh and salt) since they occasionally explore rivers such as the Columbia; one porpoise was reported 320 km (198.8 mi) upriver in Holland. It is most abundant in estuaries and coastal shallows less than 32 km (19.9 mi) offshore. The harbor porpoise has 3 close relatives — the gulf porpoise or Vaquita *(Phocoena sinus)* of the Gulf of California, the spectacled porpoise *(Phocoena dioptrica)*, and the black porpoise *(Phocoena spinipinnis)* of South America.

Food The diet consists of fish such as herring, mackerel, whiting, hake, cod, pollack, sardine, caplin, shad, and shark, as well as squid and shrimp. About 5 kg (11 lb) of food are ingested per day, generally of a size less than 25 cm (9.8 in) in length.

Reproduction and Growth A long-lasting bond develops between the members of a pair of harbor porpoises which is rare among cetaceans. During courtship the 2 swim side by side, the male caressing the female with its flukes and nuzzling her with his snout. Both animals emit squeaking and grinding sounds as they mate, generally during the months of July and August. Ten to 11 months later a single calf is born weighing 5 kg (11 lb) and measuring 75 cm (29.5 in) in length. The female retires to a secluded cove where she rolls on her side at the surface to assist the nursing and breathing of the calf. The newborn has several bristles on each side of the snout (leftovers from their hairy ancestors that lived on land) but they are soon lost. The young animal grows rapidly, its teeth erupt at 5 months, and weaning occurs at 8 months. Full size is reached at 1.5 years. Females become sexually mature at the astonishingly early age of only 14 months, while males require 3 years. Since a female produces one calf each year, she is pregnant for almost her whole life. The life span is rather short in this species, generally 6 to 10 years, although an occasional individual may surpass 13 years.

Remarks The harbor porpoise is the smallest cetacean in the world — a fact quite likely related to its great abundance and wide distribution. It is a stout animal with short flippers and a low triangular dorsal fin, which has bumps on its leading edge. The eyes are rather tiny and the tailstock is markedly keeled. The jaws contain 92 short, spade-shaped teeth (unlike the conical teeth of dolphins) which grasp slippery prey but are not often used for chopping up food, since it is usually swallowed whole. The stomach is 3-chambered and the first 6 vertebrae (of 68) are joined to form a strong rigid neck. The animal's thick layer of blubber (up to 40 percent of total weight) insulates against excessive heat loss to the cold water as well as provides a source of stored energy.

Porpoises and their relatives have excellent hearing underwater, which they use for locating obstacles, food, and each other. In their system of echolocation, high-pitched clicks are produced at about 1,000 per second in the nasal passages and are beamed forward off the dish-shaped skull and through the lens-like "melon" — an oil-filled cavity which constitutes the large bump on the forehead. These directed sounds travel much farther though water than in air (since the denser water is a better transmitter) and bounce off objects in their path. These echoes return to the dolphin, are picked up through the oil-filled lower jaw, and transmitted to the inner ear. The porpoise's brain interprets these messages so that the animal can actually "hear" the shapes and movements of objects in their surroundings.

These sea mammals prefer to school in small groups of 2 to 5 individuals, sometimes up to 15, and rarely to several hundred when on migration. They are vocal and friendly both among themselves and with members from other groups. They are known to support an injured or sick individual at the surface so it can breathe. Activity occurs during the day and night between bouts of rest. They seem to enjoy basking in warm surface waters. Major causes of death are hunting by humans, killer whales and sharks, entrapment in fish nets, stranding, and insecticide poisoning. In the past this species was difficult to catch and maintain in aquaria; the animal often died of shock during capture or succumbed to stress and disease within 2 years. With recent improvements in capture and maintenance techniques, survival has greatly improved and the animals have proved to be as trainable as dolphins.

HARBOR PORPOISE

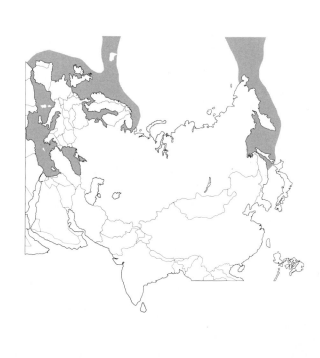

NORTHERN ELEPHANT SEAL

Scientific name *Mirounga angustirostris*
Family Hair Seals (Phocidae)
Order Carnivores (Carnivora)
Total length males 5 m (16.4 ft);
females 3 m (9.8 ft)
Weight 2 500 kg, maximum 3 200 kg
(5,511.5 lb, maximum 7,054.7 lb);
900 kg (1,984.1 lb)
Color The short dense coat is yellowish-gray, somewhat paler on the belly. Pups undergo several molts from black to silver to yellowish-gray.
Distribution and Status The northern elephant seal breeds in the Pacific from Cedros Island off Baja California (Mexico) north to the Farallon Islands near San Francisco. Non-breeding seals regularly occur north to the Queen Charlotte Islands (British Columbia) and there is a record of a stray at Prince of Wales in Alaska, 4 800 km (2,982.7 mi) from the breeding range. Remote sand or gravel beaches on islands and the mainland are selected for breeding and molting, but their sea travels are largely unknown.

This species was all but exterminated in the late 1800s as a result of overharvesting for seal oil. By 1890, the only known survivors were a colony on Guadaloupe Island (Mexico), which numbered about 100 adults and an undetermined but small group of subadults out at sea. Protection was offered just in time in 1922 by Mexico, and soon after by the United States. Populations responded dramatically and many former breeding grounds were recolonized. A recent estimate is over 60,000 in a dozen breeding colonies on islands and the mainland.

The northern elephant seal takes second place as the largest seal, behind its close relative the southern elephant seal *(Mirounga leonina)*. This astoundingly huge pinnipede is much more common (600,000) and widespread, and is found throughout the subantarctic islands and coasts of Antarctica, Africa, South America, and New Zealand.

Food The elephant seal appears to avoid some competition for food resources with other seals and the sea otter by diving to greater depths — often 100 to 300 m (328.1 to 984.3 ft). Prey includes small sharks, skates, rays, ratfish, puffers, rockfish, hake, eels, and squid.
Reproduction and Growth The breeding season commences in late November with the individual arrival of bulls on the rookery of their birth. The cows appear in mid-December, some giving birth within a week, others as late as February. The single pup weighs around 32 kg (70.6 lb), is 1.3 m (4.3 ft) long, and sports a thick black coat, but no insulating layer of blubber. It keeps warm by producing considerable body heat. The mother nurses her own pup (occasionally another if she is asleep or loses her pup) for only 28 days at which time it molts into a silver coat, develops a layer of fat, and weighs an amazing 160 kg (352.7 lb). Within a few days after weaning, the cows come into heat for about 5 days. Unlike some other species of seals, the bulls do not defend a specific territory, but form a hierarchy in which the dominant bull defends his position around his harem.

The cow takes an active role in courtship, stimulating the bull who grasps her by the neck with his canines. Mating lasts a few minutes, and if the cow is swift enough to avoid the attention of the bull master, she may mate again with other bulls nearby. The pregnant cows soon depart from the breeding grounds, some as soon as 34 days after their arrival. Pregnancy lasts 11 months, including a 3-month rest period of the embryo (delayed implantation). The deserted pups gather in groups, living off their fat, and finally leave at around 14 weeks of age in April or May. Pup mortality is high up to this point, with 13 to 26 percent killed by cows biting or trampling them, and especially by falling under the bulls. Females become sexually mature at 3 to 5 years of age, males 4 to 5 years, although they don't achieve sufficient size and dominance to breed until at least 8 years. In fact, the chance of a male

breeding at all is slim, for only about 3 percent of males live to be 8 years old, and even some of these are kept out of breeding activity by stronger rivals. The bull masters may, on the other hand, mate with about 250 cows in the 4 years of their prime. This species is unexpectedly short-lived with maximum life spans of 20 years for males and 12 years for females.
Remarks Elephant seals are characterized by the balloon-like inflatable nose and the incredible size of the bulls — 3 times the weight of the cows, and the largest differentiation of the sexes demonstrated in any mammal. In spite of the weight and the fact that the foreflippers are of little use in supporting the body, this seal can raise the front half of the body at right angles to the ground, and even arch up its hind end at the same time, approaching a U-shape. The nasal sac or proboscis develops only in the male and becomes prominent after the animal reaches 3 years of age. A full 28 cm (11 in) long when inflated with air and the walls distended with blood, the proboscis is used in visual and vocal threats, acting as a resonating chamber for roars. This unusual organ shrinks in size after the breeding season.

Eighteen teeth are present in the skull, with single-cusped cheek teeth and 3-cm (1.2-in)-long canines used during aggressive and defensive behavior. Interestingly, these daggers are only half the thickness of the rival's skin on the chest and neck, so that although blood flows freely during hours of fighting, serious injury is rare.

The coat is composed of short stiff hairs, and since an underfur is absent, protection from the cold is achieved by a thick (8 cm or 3.2 in in places) layer of blubber. The skin and blubber can actually weigh more than the rest of the animal's body. Consequently, the seal cannot tolerate much heat-producing activity while on land during warm days, as it quickly overheats. On such occasions, the dexterous foreflippers scoop up and spray wet sand on the animal's back, while blood vessels in the thin-skinned flippers radiate internal heat away.

The eyes of elephant seals are sensitive to low levels of light while submerged, but since the animals often feed at night, they obviously can locate food without seeing it. The 2 main calls of bulls are the snort and a series of low throaty roars called a clap-threat. The cow produces a loud prolonged threat call as well as a wavering sound used when responding to its pup's shrill distress cry. The only known predators of these big seals are killer whales, large sharks, and people.

NORTHERN ELEPHANT SEAL

Northern Elephant Seal

The Mexican fisherman landed his boat on a remote island off Baja California. He was curious about a strange roaring noise amid the usual sound of the surf. Walking along the shore he came across a colony of elephant seals stretched out like sunbathers on the beach. A number of enormous bulls were surrounded by hundreds of much smaller seals — the cows and their young. Packed into close quarters, some seals were trying to sleep while others were obviously involved in disputes. A few cows were returning from cooling off in the sea, and the fisherman wondered how they ever found their own pups again, for they would not accept and nurse the other pups that pleaded for attention. Many of the seals were just too lazy to move, so they cooled themselves by throwing wet sand over their backs with the front flippers. Here and there on the beach lay a number of pathetic-looking bodies of pups, squashed by adults as they thrashed about, mating and fighting.

Near the center of the rookery two huge bulls were threatening each other, bellowing through inflated nasal sacs that curved down grotesquely over their faces. Elevating the front half of their bodies at a right angle, perhaps to accentuate their size, the bulls bared their canines and roared. When neither backed down, the two began pounding at each other with open mouths, trying to bite the delicate nose and eyes. After twenty minutes, the slightly smaller bull was bleeding from several gashes on its thick wrinkled neck. With a tremendous swing of its head the larger bull slammed into its rival, knocking him off balance. Barely avoiding being rolled upon, the smaller bull succeeded in escaping and waddled off backwards like a giant brown inchworm, scattering the cows and pups in its way. The dominant bull had fought dozens of times, earning the right to mate with about forty cows during the past month.

The fisherman came too close to the herd and many seals panicked and rushed to the sea in an amazing display of awkwardness. A number of bulls and cows were so sound asleep from exhaustion that they were never aware of the man that stood among them. One bull charged a few meters (yards) and the fisherman beat a hasty retreat back to his boat.

Over the following month, the pregnant cows weaned their young and abandoned them on shore, escaping to the sea to regain their strength. Living off the fat built up from the former diet of milk, the pups learned to swim and dive for their own food, and in a month they too departed in small groups, leaving the rookery to the bulls. It was now March, a full four months since the bulls had arrived on this same beach of their birth. Although they had entered the water on occasion, they had not eaten a thing. Considerably thinner and with new scars as reminders of the trials of being a bull master, the dominant male finally eased its heavy body into the surf. All day it swam strongly from land with alternate strokes of its hind flippers. Then, breathing deeply several times in the night air, it dove two hundred meters (656.2 ft) to the bottom, where it seized and swallowed several squid, a ratfish, and three small sharks. Thirty minutes later it came up for air with a full stomach.

For the next two months the bull alternated its time gorging and sleeping at sea. An urge once more came over it to return to the rookery, not to breed again, but to molt. Landing at the same spot, the bull fell promptly into a deep sleep. Great patches of fur and skin flaked off in the succeeding weeks, and the bull protected its sensitive new skin from the blazing sun with flipperfuls of sand. As soon as a fresh yellowish-gray coat appeared, the anxious bull returned to the sea again, having completed its second fasting period of the year. With the breeding and molting seasons behind him, the great elephant seal headed northward, enjoying, finally, the ease of a solitary life in the sea. September found him in Canadian waters, where his strange features caught the excited attention of people on a sailboat. Then, on a small island north of Vancouver, a fisherman landed his craft to investigate a huge brown structure beached on the shore. It was the bull elephant seal, sound asleep and snoring every five minutes when it exhaled.

Blue Whale

The huge dark shadow of a blue whale hung motionless under the surface of the ocean like a disabled submarine. At the corners of the long mouth the tiny eyes, surrounded by several barnacles, moved slowly, surveying the sky and then the depths. The cetacean was halfway along its annual migration route from the arctic feeding grounds to winter quarters in temperate waters. Restless and hungry, the whale began to move forward with powerful upward strokes of the broad tail flukes. Every twenty meters (65.5 feet) or so the colossal animal broke the surface with its head and a blast of mist erupted like a volcano nine meters (29.5 feet) into the air. The pear-shaped cloud dissipated as the whale's back arched slowly and gracefully above the water, followed by the tail flukes. Descending to a depth of sixty meters (196.9 feet) the whale began to cruise at eight kilometers (5 miles) per hour toward a dense cloud of plankton — shrimp-like crustaceans or krill — which it located by emitting clicking sounds and listening for the returning echoes. The great mouth opened and the cavernous pleated throat gulped in a large volume of water and krill, then closed, causing the water to jettison out the corners of the mouth. Thousands of two-centimeter (0.8-inch)-long animals became entrapped in the fibers of baleen plates hanging down like a meter (3.3-foot)-long curtain from the upper jaw. Then the massive tongue moved up to sweep the food off the plates and down the gullet. After feeding for half an hour and consuming about two hundred kilograms (441 pounds), the blue whale headed for the surface to take in fresh air. By the end of the day, forty million krill weighing thirty six hundred kilograms (7,936.5 pounds) were ingested. It was to be one of the last meals for about eight months, for the whale was entering warmer waters where its food was scarce. Fasting for such a long period was no hardship, for the whale had built up enormous reserves of fat during winter feeding, exceeding one-quarter of its total weight.

Three weeks later, this female whale detected a faint moaning sound, and knew instantly it was one of her kind. The whale swam at a steady twenty kilometers (12.4 miles) per hour, occasionally emitting a slowly descending moan which lasted about thirty seconds. A bull blue whale heard her calls and the two giants homed in on each other. A half hour later, the two whales met at the surface, the moonlight reflecting silver off their broad dark backs. For several days they nudged and stroked each other, rolling over and over and exposing their blue and white-mottled bellies to the sky. After coupling several times, the whales parted company forever. Down inside her womb a single fertilized egg, smaller than a pinhead, began to divide repeatedly, someday to grow into one of the heaviest creatures to ever inhabit the earth. At first the embryo looked like any other mammal, with a head, tail, and four limb buds. But by three months the hind limbs had stopped developing, the little teeth disappeared, and a beautiful baby whale took shape, complete with flukes and flippers.

It was almost a year later when the calf was born, measuring seven meters (23 feet) and weighing two tonnes (2.2 tons). Following the tail-first delivery, the female turned around to examine her first offspring and instinctively nudged it to the surface for its first breath of air. Several other companion whales closed in to help, but the female swam in their way, preferring to care for her offspring herself. Swaying gently in the waves, the baby found the mother's nipples and warm rich milk was pumped into its mouth. Feeding bouts had to be fast, for the baby needed to surface every few minutes for air. Ingesting six hundred liters (130 gallons) of thick rich milk per day, the baby whale doubled its weight in a week.

For two years the mother-calf bond was strong, but as the calf wandered farther away to feed, it became increasingly independent. Then one day, as the female was close to giving birth again, they lost each other. Roaming for decades over millions of square kilometers (miles) of ocean, perhaps they would one day recognize each other's moaning calls and swim side by side once more.

BLUE WHALE

Scientific name *Balaenoptera musculus*
Family Rorqual Whales (Balaenopteridae)
Order Baleen Whales (Mysticeti)
Total length 25 m, maximum 31 m
(82 ft, maximum 101.7 ft)
Weight 120 t, maximum 178 t
(132 tons, maximum 195.8 tons)
Color This impressive giant is dark blue-gray with mottled light spots on the back, sides, and belly. The baleen plates are black. Sometimes these whales take on a yellowish cast on the undersides—the result of growths of microorganisms on the skin — responsible for an alternate name, the "sulphurbottom."
Distribution and Status The blue whale inhabits all oceans of the world, including tropical, temperate, and arctic waters. Populations in the Northern Hemisphere migrate northward to arctic feeding grounds in summer (July), while those in the Southern Hemisphere go south to antarctic waters in their summer period (January); hence the 2 populations are separate. A third population of smaller whales occurs in the Indian Ocean. While generally found far out to sea and along continental shelves, it has occasionally been reported within 3 km (1.9 mi) off the shore of Baja California in water only 50 m (164 ft) deep. There are also sightings in the Gulf of St. Lawrence.

The blue whale has been under intense pressure by the whaling industry. The total catch during the 20th C has been about 350,000, with 29,410 killed during the 1930-31 season alone. This species is on the endangered list and has received protection since 1966, but there is still great concern for its survival. Perhaps a century will be required to build up numbers to a safe level. The world population is unknown at present, but it is certainly a small fraction of former numbers. One recent estimate was only about 12,000, with 8,000 in the Antarctic and Indian Ocean, 500

in the North Atlantic, and 1,500 in the North Pacific. Pre-exploitation numbers were estimated at 200,000, 1,200, and 5,000 respectively. Water pollution and possible harvest of krill for human consumption are future threats for this magnificent sea mammal. It is rapidly becoming a commercially valuable species for whale-watching tourists.

Whales evolved from land-dwelling mammals but the fossil record is too incomplete to reveal much about their early origins. Mysticetes (whales with baleen) first appeared in the Oligocene (37 to 22 million years ago), while the ancestors of the modern baleen whales have been recorded from the Pliocene (about 5 million years ago) in both Atlantic and Pacific waters. Five species are recognized in the genus *Balaenoptera* — the blue whale, minke whale *(B. acutorostrata)*, Bryde's whale *(B. edeni)*, sei whale *(B. borealis)*, and fin whale *(B. physalus)*.
Food These whales feed on little shrimp-like crustaceans (euphausiids) of the plankton (a mixture of small animals and plants which live in the upper levels of the ocean), perhaps the only food abundant enough to support such large animals. This tiny sea life, averaging less than 5 cm (2 in), abounds in polar regions in summer as a result of upwelling of cold currents to the surface, which carry nutrients from the ocean floor back up to the sunlit zone.
Reproduction and Growth Mating of blue whales has seldom been witnessed and much remains to be learned about their reproductive habits. Mating is thought to occur every second or third year in temperate or warm tropical waters during winter. One young (rarely twins) is born 11 or 12 months later, at a length of 7 m (23 ft) and weight of 2 000 kg (4,409.2 lbs). Drinking an astonishing 600 *l* (158.5 gal) of milk per day, the young whale gains 90 kg (198.4 lb) a day. The baleen plates are functional at 7 months, when the young-

ster no longer requires feeding from its mother's nipples located one on either side of the genital slit. It has reached about 15 m (49.2 ft) by this time and becomes sexually mature at 19 m (62.3 ft) and about 23 years old (formerly thought to be at 5 years old). Maximum age for this species has been estimated at 110 years, but there is little evidence that most reach even half this age.
Remarks The blue whale is believed to be the largest organism to have ever lived, far surpassing even the biggest aquatic dinosaurs. As befitting this title the animal holds a number of impressive size records, such as the longest penis in the animal kingdom — a full 3 m (9.9 ft) long. A testicle weighs 45.4 kg (100 lb), the tongue 3.7 t (4.1 tons), and the brain 6.8 kg (15 lb). The upper lip gives rise to a continuous row of about 400 triangular-shaped baleen plates 50 to 100 cm (19.7 to 39.4 in) long on each side of the upper jaw whose fibrous bases sieve food items from the water. There are no teeth to catch large fish. Up to 94 grooves run from the lower lip all the way back to the navel, which greatly expand the throat region when gulping water and food. The fins seem almost too small to steer such a hulk; for example the dorsal fin is only 33 cm (13 in) high. In spite of its great length the spinal column contains only 63 thick vertebrae — fewer than most dolphins. It cruises at around 22 km (13.7 mi) per hour but when alarmed can reach 48 km (29.8 mi) per hour, making it one of the fastest cetaceans. The whale is usually found at depths of less than 100 m (328.1 ft) but has descended to 500 m (1,640.4 ft) when harpooned. It frequently surfaces every 10 to 20 m (32.8 to 65.6 ft) followed by 8 to 10 blows for air exchange. Blue whales are generally solitary or occur in groups of less than 4, but on occasion herds of up to 60 individuals have been seen off California. The only predators are people and killer whales, however the whales sometimes become entrapped by ice where they suffocate or starve.

BLUE WHALE

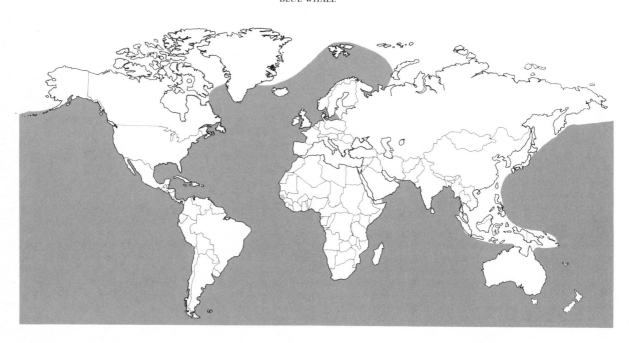

ATLANTIC WHITE-SIDED DOLPHIN

Scientific name *Lagenorhynchus acutus*
Family Dolphins (Delphinidae)
Order Toothed Whales (Odontoceti)
Total length 2.5 m, maximum 3 m
(8.2 ft, maximum 9.8 ft)
Weight males 190 kg, maximum 250 kg
(419 lb, maximum 551 lb);
females 182 kg (401 lb)

Color This attractively patterned dolphin is black or dark gray on the upperparts and flippers, and white beneath. Running along the side is a gray band interrupted by a two-toned yellowish blaze which extends up and backward through the black tailstock. A thin gray stripe is present from the flipper to the eye. This pattern provides for countershading found in many sea mammals and fish and for species recognition when they are schooling or leaping out of the water.

Distribution and Status This sea mammal is found in the North Atlantic from the southern tip of Greenland to the North Sea off Norway, and south to Massachusetts and the British Isles. Occasional strays have been reported as far south of the usual range as Virginia and Portugal. The dolphin inhabits cool waters of the Temperate Zone, between the warm Gulf Stream and the cold Labrador current. In summer it may enter the Arctic Circle. Although it is encountered far from land, it is most common along the continental shelves and offshore waters, even near densely populated areas. The world population is estimated at around 60,000, and is regularly hunted off Newfoundland and Norway. The dolphin family, which includes killer and pilot whales, arose in the late Miocene, about 10 million years ago. There are 33 species presently recognized in the family, and 6 in the same genus as the Atlantic white-sided dolphin, including a western counterpart — the Pacific white-sided dolphin *(Lagenorhynchus obliquidens).*

Food Dolphins are opportunistic feeders, eating a wide variety of sea life of an appropriate size. Fish (particularly herring and mackerel) and squid are pursued in surface and midwaters, and mollusks and crustaceans are scooped up from the bottom. Dolphin herds hunt for prey by sweeping an area in columns of up to 50 individuals, each swimming abreast at distances of about 10 m (32.8 ft) apart. When a school of fish is contacted, the herd surrounds it and feeds for perhaps half an hour until each dolphin is satiated. Apparently dolphins obtain sufficient water from their food, but do take in some saltwater, either intentionally or incidentally while feeding. Excess salt is, of course, eliminated from the blood by the kidneys.

Reproduction and Growth Summer is the mating period for this dolphin and as a female becomes receptive she receives the attention of mature males. Amid biting, tail slapping, and various poses and vocal threats among rival males, one male wins the honors of courtship. The pair swims closely together exchanging body rubs, stroking with flippers, gentle nips, and head bumps. The 2 present their bellies and often touch each other's genital slits with a flipper or snout. Mating finally occurs belly to belly. Long-lasting bonds form between some individuals while others are promiscuous and mate with others in the herd.

The single calf takes 10 or 11 months to develop and is born generally in April or May at a weight of 34 kg (75 lb) and a length of one m (3.3 ft). The mother is attentive to her offspring and if it strays too far away or is otherwise disobedient, she applies pressure with her jaws or lifts it clear out of the water on her belly. The calf begins to eat solid food at about 6 months, but continues on milk for 18 months, after which its attempts to suckle are repelled by the mother. Between the ages of 2.5 to 6 years, at a length of 2 m (6.6 ft), the calf is usually driven away from the breeding herd and must swim alone or with an outside group of dolphins of the same or different species. Eventually it joins a herd with which it remains for a long time, or it may depart and swim with other herds. Sexual maturity is attained at 9 years of age and the maximum life span under natural conditions is at least 27 years for females and 22 years for males (as measured by examining tooth wear).

Remarks The dolphin's robust but streamlined shape and slippery skin allow the animal to swim through the water with a minimum of turbulence and friction. Even the flippers, flukes, and dorsal fin are sharply pointed and directed backward for easy passage. The tailstock is swollen, keeled above and below, and narrows quickly where it joins the flukes. The beak (which distinguishes dolphins from porpoises) is relatively short, and is separated from the melon (oil-filled chamber of the forehead) by a deep groove. There are 30 to 40 small pointed teeth in each side of the jaw (total of around 132), which are used to grasp prey until it can be swallowed whole or to cut pieces of larger prey.

This is an active species, often leaping into the air, but it is not known to turn somersaults or ride the bow-wave of boats like other dolphins, such as the Pacific white-sided dolphin. It is seldom captured or exhibited, partly due to its avoidance of capture boats. Capable of swimming at speeds up to 28 km (17.4 mi) per hour, the dolphin's thrust is achieved by powerful muscles and a flexible vertebral column, consisting of around 80 vertebrae with wide disks in between. The tailstock produces up and down strokes, while turns are executed with the help of the flippers and sideways movements of the body. The dolphin can also swim easily on its side or upside down. It gains stability in the water from the fins and the lungs which lie along the back. Depending on whether it is resting or active,

Continued on p. 344

ATLANTIC WHITE-SIDED DOLPHIN

Atlantic White-sided Dolphin

Every two or three minutes, two smooth, rounded objects rose above the calm surface of the ocean, reflecting the moonlight into the black water. After a short hissing sound of escaping air, the two shapes slipped out of sight once again. Lying just below the surface of the water, a dolphin and a pilot whale were sleeping with half-closed eyes. When it was time to breathe, a downward-stroke of the tail caused the head to rise, allowing the blowhole on the top of the animal's head to exchange stale air for fresh. It was still dark when the male dolphin awoke and began swimming slowly in circles around its lazy companion. It attempted a wake-up call in the form of a squeal, but a squawk came out of the blowhole instead, along with a stream of bubbles that danced their way upward. Apparently it would take a few attempts to clear or tune the nasal passages before the proper song could be produced. However, the squawk had the desired result, and the pilot whale jolted into consciousness.

Fully awake and warmed up, the two creatures headed out to sea with the arrival of dawn. They had traveled together for six months, ever since the white-sided dolphin became separated from its group. Had it broken away to explore on its own or had it become separated during an attack by a shark or killer whale? The cause had long since been erased from its memory. Being more agile than the larger long-finned pilot whale, the dolphin began to leap clear of the water in graceful arcs. Then it disappeared below for a few seconds before shooting past its companion with a great burst of exuberance. Suddenly it braked with its flippers, as if something of great importance was about to happen. Familiar sounds transferred from the saltwater through its oil-filled lower jaws and into its inner ears. Becoming more excited by the second, the dolphin swept upward and began swimming with its head above water. Eyes trained forward, it caught sight of a school of dolphins, a dozen members of which were airborne at any one moment. The flashing pattern of white, yellow, and black sides instantly informed the dolphin that it had found its own kind. The pilot whale followed far behind, obviously not as interested.

As the dolphin sped along underwater, it could hear loud splashing sounds, though the herd was still a hundred metres (328 feet) away. When it joined the group of forty white-sided dolphins, there was great commotion. The water seemed alive with a chorus of whistles, rocketing bodies, and curtains of bubbles. The dolphin had found its family group. Recognizing every individual by its distinctive call, the dolphin swam among the herd, as if trying to find one particular animal. Finally, it met a female head on, and their two bodies slipped smoothly over one another. Together once more, the long-lost mates swirled around and around, bumping with their beaks and touching with their flippers and flukes. They had remembered each other over the long period of separation. A rival male approached the newcomer from behind and bit him on his tailstock. The dolphin retaliated by confronting the rival and clapping his jaws, which produced a series of loud cracking sounds. The threat seemed to be successful, and the rival male disappeared among the other dolphins.

Now the female took the initiative, stroking her mate and bumping him with the soft melon of her forehead. The courtship gained intensity over the next half-hour, while the remainder of the herd rounded up a school of herring and took turns picking off the strays. The pair were now colliding head-on with considerable force. As the male slid by, the female glided her flipper along his sensitive genital area, and when he circled back from below, he turned belly up and the two began to mate. The pilot whale and the dolphin herd continued their feast, oblivious of the reunion.

Caribbean Manatee

A school of sheepshead fish swam into view through the clear water, moving in synchrony with the precision of a military battalion on maneuvers. When the silvery bodies flashed over a large algae-covered boulder, several broke ranks and began to pick vigorously on the rock's surface for microorganisms. Without warning, a paddle appeared and struck at the pesky fish. The boulder was, in fact, a Caribbean manatee, lying asleep on the sea floor. Undaunted, the fish resumed their feeding activities, which the manatee ignored until one fish's rasping teeth came too close to the big creature's eye. A push off the bottom with its flattened tail sent the manatee sailing slowly three meters (9.8 feet) to the surface. Only the two semicircular nostrils projected slightly for a quick breath of air. Hovering just below the surface, the sea mammal let out a long groan as it slowly arched its back and then its belly, followed by a slow headfirst descent which carried it right into the soft silt. Closing its tiny, deeply set eyes, the manatee drifted off to sleep again.

For a month, the manatee had explored the shallows of the sea coast. Grazing mostly on seagrasses, the animal now felt thirsty for fresh water which would restore its salt balance. With flippers folded against its sides, the great tail began moving up and down in a steady beat of thirty strokes per minute, propelling the bulky animal at a cruising speed of ten kilometers (6.2 miles) per hour. The manatee paused only for short naps, and in a few days it detected the taste of fresh water from a lagoon. Having traveled just outside the breakers for thirty kilometers (18.6 miles), it soon entered brackish water, then a narrow outlet of a river where it had to swim strenuously to overcome the current. Finally it glided into a shallow bay, choked with water weed and eel grass. The manatee forced its way into the jungle of submerged stems, and when it surfaced, its snout and shoulders were draped with weeds. An extended flipper pulled the chains of plants towards the bristly lip pads which closed around the vegetation and drew it into the mouth. Standing on its tail on the muddy bottom, the animal noisily devoured fifteen kilograms (33.1 pounds) of food before its belly was full.

During the preceding several weeks the temperatures of the bay had been dropping from a summer high of 30°C (86°F) to the autumn level of 21°C (69.8°F). That night, as the sleepy manatee rose to the surface to breathe every twelve minutes or so, its nostrils detected cold air from an approaching storm. The air temperature plummeted to 10°C (50°F), cooling the shallow waters to 13°C (55.4°F) within a day. Becoming increasingly chilled, the animal tried to keep warm by swimming constantly, its body heat being partially retained by an insulating layer of blubber. Perhaps it was the cold, or maybe the change in diet from marine to freshwater plants, but the manatee developed a severe case of indigestion, resulting in the production of intestinal gas. The bloated creature experienced the greatest difficulty submerging, and by next morning, curious boaters surrounded the helpless manatee. Fortunately it was not struck by speeding propellers, but floating for hours at the surface had exposed its body to the cold air. By the time it regained its proper buoyancy, the manatee had caught a cold. The animal tried to sleep in the slightly warmer water at a depth of four meters (13.1 feet), but it had to rise for air about every minute due to cold stress. At the surface, it sneezed in an attempt to clear its nasal passages. If a warm refuge could not be found within a few days, it would surely perish.

Years of exploration along the coast and in brackish and freshwater bays had taught the manatee the location of warm waters issuing from bottom springs and from factory discharge pipes. Remembering the place where it had spent last winter, the manatee retraced its course down river, then south along the Gulf of Mexico. Fifteen kilometers (9.3 miles) later, it reached a familiar bay where squeals and groans reached its ears. Homing in on the sounds through the cloudy water, the manatee passed through an invisible wall of warm water and was suddenly surrounded by dozens of other manatees. While one embraced the newcomer in its flippers, several others bumped and rubbed with their bodies, then kissed a greeting with their bristly lips. The manatee was finally home with old friends.

ATLANTIC WHITE-SIDED DOLPHIN
continued from p.339

the dolphin breathes 2 to 6 times per minute, and is capable of remaining submerged for only 7 minutes.

Hearing is the most important sense in a dolphin, a fact reflected in the greatest development of the hearing centers in the brain of any group of animals except bats (which also use sonar). Columns of air are set vibrating within the nasal ducts and sacs and beamed forward by the curved skull and melon. At frequencies as high as 150,000 cycles per second (human hearing upper limit is 20,000 cps), the soundwaves bounce off objects and the returning echoes are transmitted to the inner ear, probably through the lower jaws. The ears and hearing centers of the brain are capable of distinguishing direction, size, shape, and to some extent, the consistency of the object. Apparently each dolphin has its own sound that identifies it among its fellow herd members. Series of clicks, whistles, grunts, squeaks, and even silence, all have special meaning to dolphins. Since sounds may be produced in both left and right nasal sacs, 2 sounds or messages may be sent at once. Sound travels 60 times more efficiently in water than in air, so the dolphin's world must be a noisy place indeed, with the calls of a myriad of sea creatures.

The sense of taste is moderately developed, but there is no evidence that the dolphin can detect odors at all, and the smell or olfactory lobes of the brain have disappeared during the animal's course of evolution from terrestrial mammals. Touch plays an important role in a dolphin's social life. The dolphin's eyes can see a long way in air, and some distance underwater, depending to a great degree on the clarity of the ocean. Although set on opposite sides of the head, the eyes can be directed forward to focus on an object, thus giving good depth perception.

After a dolphin has eaten, the fish or squid fill a large pouch at the bottom of the esophagus called a forestomach. Although no digestion occurs here, ingested items are ground into smaller pieces with the aid of a few stones. The food then passes to the true stomach and later to a connecting stomach, where it is mixed with enzymes and digestion proceeds.

White-sided dolphins are usually encountered in schools of from 6 to 50, including both sexes and all age groups, but concentrations of around 1,000 have also been noted. Activities such as feeding or playing (e.g., tossing a fish into the air) may occur during the night as well as the day. Strandings are unfortunately common, occuring singly or in groups up to several dozen. The main predators are killer whales, large sharks, and people.

CARIBBEAN MANATEE

Scientific name *Trichechus manatus*
Family Caribbean Manatee (Trichechidae)
Order Sea Cows (Sirenia)
Total length 3.5 m, maximum 4.5 m
(11.5 ft, maximum 14.8 ft)
Weight 360 kg, maximum 680 kg
(793.7 lb, maximum 1,499.1 lb)
Color This species' color ranges from slate gray to brown, sometimes marked with pinkish patches and pale scars from scrapes and cuts. The true color may be obscured by a thick coating of algae, protozoans (microscopic animals), copepods, and barnacles. The young manatee is blackish-gray, becoming paler with age.
Distribution and Status The Caribbean or West Indian manatee is native to tropical and subtropical rivers, estuaries, and island and mainland coastlines of the Atlantic from Virginia south to Brazil. It is a nomadic and migratory species, sometimes putting out to sea for 15 km (9.3 mi), exploring up river for hundreds of kilometers (230 km or 142.9 mi in Florida, 800 km or 497.1 mi in South America), and in northern areas, retreating to warm springs during cold spells. The manatee usually keeps to depths of 2 to 4 m (6.6 to 13.1 ft), but has been observed in 60-cm (23.6-in) shallows and in dives to 10 m (32.8 ft). Perhaps it is unable to withstand the water pressure at greater depths.

The Florida manatee population is stable at around 1,000 individuals but the animal is declining, rare, or absent from many other regions. Considered an endangered or threatened species, it is protected by several acts in the United States where boating accidents and vandals are the main causes of death. Elsewhere the manatee is hunted for meat, hides, oil, and bones (ivory).

The order of sea cows is thought to have originated from the same ancestors as the elephants, and the manatee family has lived in the Caribbean since Miocene times (24 million years ago). Manatees are known (through fossil evidence) to have occurred from Maryland to Argentina within the last several million years. There are 4 recent relatives, but the Steller's sea cow *(Hydrodamalis gigas)* of the Bering Sea was exterminated by sealers in 1768, only 27 years after its discovery. The Amazonian manatee *(Trichechus inunguis)* is found in the Amazon Basin; the West African manatee *(Trichechus senegalensis)* from the coasts, rivers, and lakes of West Africa; and the dugong *(Dugon dugon)* is a marine species of the Red Sea, Indian Ocean, and Pacific Ocean.

Food The manatee devours about one-quarter of its weight in aquatic vegetation per day. Relatively indiscriminate, it feeds on whatever is available, such as marine seagrasses, water milfoil, eel grass, turtle grass, water weed, water hyacinth, alligatorweed, wild celery, and freshwater and marine algae. On occasion, it hauls its forequarters onto a bank and chews on grasses and mangroves. The animal selects a particular plant in an area, and ignores it in another, but generally shows first preference for submerged, then floating, and lastly emergent plants. Rhizomes, leaf bases, and young shoots are eaten before old mature leaves. Some animals have been seen chewing bottom sediments, perhaps obtaining minerals in the process. Dining rarely on small fish caught in nets, most of the manatee's animal food is ingested accidently, while attached to or concealed in vegetation. Included here are shrimps, amphipods, crabs, crayfish, insect larvae, worms, and starfish. Excessive salt is accumulated within the manatee's body after weeks in the sea, and so it must return to fresh water to drink.

Reproduction and Growth What little is known of this secretive species' breeding habits is fascinating. A cow in heat attracts the ardent attention of one or as many as 17 bulls at one time. Courtship proceeds with much squealing, bumping, and blows with the tail, and may continue for a month. In desperation to escape, the cow sometimes enters shoals as shallow as 60 cm (23.6 in), while the rebuffed males satiate their frustration by performing homosexual activities for hours at a time. Finally the cow is ready to receive a male, and after nuzzling with the lips and rubbing their bodies, the bull turns on its back under the cow, the 2 embrace with their flippers, and they sink to the bottom, where mating lasts for about one minute. Around 400 days later, the cow gives birth to one, or rarely 2, calves, measuring one m (3.3 ft) in length and weighing 11 to 27 kg (24.3 to 58.5 lb). The birth, which may occur during any time of the year, has never been observed, but presumably occurs in a secluded lagoon, away from other inquisitive manatees. Cows have been seen supporting their young at the surface to breathe. Suckling occurs from 2 mammae situated behind the mother's flippers. The offspring begins nibbling algae in a few weeks and continues to nurse for one or 2 years. It becomes sexually mature at 4 to 6 years, when about 2.6 m (8.5 ft) in length. Females generally reproduce every 2.5 years, earlier if they lose their young, and may become foster parents. Longevity has been recorded at 30 years in captivity and may extend to 50 years or more in the wild.

Remarks The manatee is an aquatic creature unable to come on land like seals. The front limbs, with nails present, are shaped like paddles and are used in maneuvering, feeding, scratching, cleaning the mouth, and sexual stimulation. Hind limbs are absent and the hip bones are reduced in size. Thrust for locomotion is achieved through the broad, horizontally flattened tail and adjacent trunk muscles. The manatee's skull has a distinctive shape and it and the other bones are extremely dense and heavy, which provide ballast to oppose the buoyancy of the lungs. While incisor teeth are present, they remain undeveloped beneath a horny plate. Five to 7 functional cheek teeth in each jaw are worn down in the front and replaced in the rear (as in elephants), so that in time, 20 to 30 teeth erupt in each jaw. Sparse fine hairs arise through the wrinkled skin, and the split upper lip supports a series of stiff bristles. The small, sunken eyes are washed frequently with a protective layer of mucus. The ears are reduced to tiny openings. Hearing and a sense of taste-smell are well developed. These sluggish gentle creatures are inquisitive but easily frightened by sudden loud noises.

The manatee spends most of its time resting, alternating with 0.5- to 2-hour bouts of feeding for 6 to 8 hours per day. It may travel 13 km (8.1 mi) in a day to reach feeding grounds, a warm spring, or to explore. When submerged, the animal's heartrate drops from 60 to 30 beats per minute, and the muscular lungs contract to compress the stored air. Individuals have been known to remain below for up to 30 minutes if resting, but 4- to 16-minute periods are the norm when cruising and feeding. Breathing occurs only through the nostrils, as the snout emerges for a few seconds.

Manatees generally prefer a solitary lifestyle, but at times they congregate in certain bays where they socialize, play, and mate. Curiosity is a common trait, and they nudge and chew on any new object they come across, such as a beer can or shiny stone. There appears to be considerable variation in temperament between different individuals. Relatively little is known about these animals because they are frequently nocturnal and they hide from people, often in inaccessible habitats of coastal shoals and murky rivers. Individuals are difficult to maintain in aquaria, and attempts at breeding captives have been unsuccessful. They may be used in the future to crop thick growths of aquatic weeds that often block boat channels. On a visit to an aquarium, as I watched a plump manatee finish off a head of lettuce and then drift slowly off to sleep while standing on its tail, it was difficult to imagine how this creature could have given rise to the mermaid myth through the longing eyes of love-starved sailors.

CARIBBEAN MANATEE

North American Mammals

Checklist

This list of common names covers the native mammals occurring from Canada and Greenland south to Panama and the West Indies. It is adapted from E.R. Hall (1981) "The mammals of North America," J.H. Honacki et al (1982) "Mammal species of the world," and J. K. Jones (1982) "Revised checklist of North American mammals north of Mexico, 1982." This list should be considered provisional, for the status of numerous species and subspecies (geographic races) has still to be worked out. No doubt some species listed here will be found to include a complex of similar species, while others may be distinct only at the subspecific level. A few mammals are known from only a single or several specimens, and continued research will likely turn up entirely new species. A few kinds of mammals have become extinct since the arrival of Europeans, and a number of others are endangered and in need of immediate conservation measures. Unfortunately, habitat destruction, conflict of interest, excessive hunting for sport or as a necessity of life, ignorance, and lack of a national will to protect resources such as wildlife will eventually exterminate many additional species.

For convenience in describing the geographic distribution of each species, the following arbitrary zones and abbreviations are used:

Abbreviations
N   north
S   south
C   central
E   east
W   west
Ar   Arctic
A   Atlantic
P   Pacific
†   extinct
*   species account

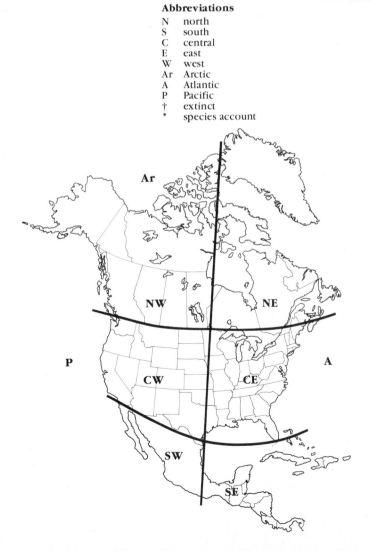

ORDER Marsupials (Marsupialia)
Family New World Opossums (Didelphidae)
  Southern Opossum SE
* Virginia Opossum CE, S
  Gray Four-eyed Opossum SE
  Water Opossum SE
  Wooly Opossum SE
  Alston's Opossum SE
  South American Mouse-opossum SE
* Mexican Mouse-opossum SE
  Grayish Mouse-opossum S
  Pale Mouse-opossum SE
  Panama Mouse-opossum SE
  Brown Four-eyed Opossum SE
  Short-tailed Murine Opossum SE

ORDER Insectivores (Insectivora)
Family Solenodons (Solenodontidae)
* Hispaniolan Solenodon SE
  Cuban Solenodon SE

Family West Indian Shrews (Nesophontidae)
† Hispaniolan Shrew SE

Family Shrews (Soricidae)
* Masked Shrew NC
  Pribilof Island Shrew NW
  St. Lawrence Island Shrew NW
  Mt. Lyell Shrew CW
  Preble's Shrew CW
  Carmen Mountain Shrew SW
  Southeastern Shrew CE
  Vagrant Shrew NW, CW
  Dusky Shrew NW, CW, SW
  Pacific Shrew CW
  Ornate Shrew CW
  Inyo Shrew CW
  Dwarf Shrew CW
  Verapaz Shrew SE
  Large-toothed Shrew SE
* Water Shrew N, C
  Pacific Water Shrew NW, CW
  Smoky Shrew NE, CE
  Arctic Shrew N, C
  Gaspé Shrew NE
  Long-tailed Shrew NE, CE
  Tundra Shrew NW
  Trowbridge's Shrew NW, CW
  Merriam's Shrew CW
  Arizona Shrew CW, SW
  Saussure's Shrew S
  Mexican Long-tailed Shrew SW
  Sclater's Shrew SE
  San Cristobal Shrew SE
  Pygmy Shrew N, C
* Northern Short-tailed Shrew NE, CE
  Southern Short-tailed Shrew CE
  Elliot's Short-tailed Shrew CE
  Mexican Small-eared Shrew S
  Goldman's Small-eared Shrew S
  Goodwin's Small-eared Shrew SE
  Least Shrew NE, CE, S
  Blackish Small-eared Shrew S
  Talamancan Small-eared Shrew SE
  Ender's Small-eared Shrew SE
  Big Small-eared Shrew SE
  Crawford's Desert Shrew CW, CE, SW
  Merriam's Desert Shrew SW

Family Moles, Shrew-moles, and Desmans (Talpidae)
* American Shrew-mole NW, CW
  Townsend's Mole NW, CW
  Coast Mole NW, CW
  Broad-footed Mole CW, SW
  Hairy-tailed Mole NE, CE
  Eastern Mole NE, CE, SE
* Star-nosed Mole NE, CE

ORDER Bats (Chiroptera)
Family Sac-winged Bats (Emballonuridae)
  Brazilian Long-nosed Bat SE
  Greater White-lined Bat S
  Lesser White-lined Bat SE
  Wagner's Sac-winged Bat SE
  Lesser Doglike Bat SE
  Greater Doglike Bat SE
  Thomas' Bat SE
  Peters' Bat S
  Thomas' Sac-winged Bat SE
  Short-eared Bat SE
  Northern Ghost Bat S

Family Bulldog Bats (Noctilionidae)
  Greater Bulldog Bat S
  Lesser Bulldog Bat SE

Family Mormoopid Bats (Mormoopidae)
  Parnell's Mustached Bat S
  Macleay's Mustached Bat SE
  Sooty Mustached Bat SE
  Wagner's Mustached Bat S
  Davy's Naked-backed Bat S
  Big Naked-backed Bat SE
  Antillean Ghost-faced Bat SE
  Peters' Ghost-faced Bat CW, S

Family American Leaf-nosed Bats (Phyllostomidae)
  Brazilian Large-eared Bat S
  Gervais' Large-eared Bat SE
  Schmidt's Large-eared Bat SE
  Hairy Large-eared Bat SE
  Niceforo's Large-eared Bat SE
  Dobson's Large-eared Bat SE
  Large-eared Forest Bat S
  Davies' Large-eared Bat SE
  California Leaf-nosed Bat CW, SW
  Waterhouse's Leaf-nosed Bat S
  Tomes' Long-eared Bat SE
  Long-legged Bat SE
  Spix's Round-eared Bat SE
  Pygmy Round-eared Bat SE
  D'Orbigny's Round-eared Bat SE
  Davis' Round-eared Bat SE
  Bennett's Spear-nosed Bat SE
  Striped Spear-nosed Bat SE
  Spear-nosed Bat SE
  Pale Spear-nosed Bat SE
  Northern Spear-nosed Bat SE
  Fringed-lipped Bat SE
  Peter's False Vampire Bat SE
  Linnaeus' False Vampire Bat SE
  Pallas' Long-tongued Bat S
  Davis' Long-tongued Bat S
  Commissaris' Long-tongued Bat S
  Miller's Long-tongued Bat SE
  Brazilian Long-tongued Bat SE
  Thomas' Long-tongued Bat SE
  Panama Long-tongued Bat SE
  Little Long-tongued Bat SE
  Leach's Long-tongued Bat SE
  Insular Long-tongued Bat SE
  Handley's Tailless Bat SE
  Geoffrey's Tailless Bat S
  Starrett's Tailless Bat SE
  Mexican Long-tongued Bat CW, S
  Trumpet-nosed Bat SW
  Godman's Bat S
  Underwood's Long-tongued Bat S
  Big Long-nosed Bat CW, S
  Little Long-nosed Bat CW, S
  Brown Long-nosed Bat SE
  Allen's Short-tailed Bat SE
  Hahn's Short-tailed Bat S
  Silky Short-tailed Bat S
  Seba's Short-tailed Bat SE
  Sofaian Bat SE
  Yellow-shouldered Bat S
  Anthony's Bat S
  Talamancan Bat SE
  Davis' Bat S
  Tent-making Bat SE
  Heller's Broad-nosed Bat SE
  Greater Broad-nosed Bat SE
  Thomas' Broad-nosed Bat SE
  San Pablo Bat SE
  Little Yellow-eared Bat SE
  Big Yellow-eared Bat SE
  Salvin's White-lined Bat S
  Goodwin's Bat SE
  Shaggy-haired Bat SW
  Guadeloupe White-lined Bat SE
  McConnell's Bat SE
  Honduran White Bat SE
  Jamaican Fruit-eating Bat S
  Big Fruit-eating Bat S
  Hairy Fruit-eating Bat SW
  Honduran Fruit-eating Bat SE
  Highland Fruit-eating Bat S
  Lowland Fruit-eating Bat S
  Gervais' Fruit-eating Bat SE
  Thomas' Fruit-eating Bat SE
  Pygmy Fruit-eating Bat S
  Little Fruit-eating Bat S
  Tree Bat SE
  Cuban Fig-eating Bat SE
  Dominican Fig-eating Bat SE
  Jamaican Fig-eating Bat SE
  Desmarest's Fig-eating Bat SE
  Wrinkle-faced Bat S

  Antillean Fruit-eating Bat SE
  Brown Flower Bat SE
  Buffy Flower Bat SE
  Puerto Rican Flower Bat SE
  Haitian Flower Bat SE
  Cuban Flower Bat SE
  Jamaican Flower Bat SE
* Common Vampire Bat S
  White-winged Vampire Bat S
  Hairy-legged Vampire Bat S

Family Funnel-eared Bats (Natalidae)
  Mexican Funnel-eared Bat S
  Cuban Funnel-eared Bat SE
  Gervais' Funnel-eared Bat SE

Family Smoky Bats (Furipteridae)
  Eastern Smoky Bat SE

Family Disk-winged Bats (Thyroptera)
  Peters' Disk-winged Bat SE
  Spix's Disk-wing Bat SE

Family Smooth-faced Bats (Vespertilionidae)
  California Myotis NW, CW, S
  Small-footed Myotis N, C, SW
  Yuma Myotis NW, CW, SW
* Little Brown (Bat) Myotis N, C, SW
  Cinnamon Myotis S
  Indiana Myotis CE
  Southeastern Myotis CE
  Cave Myotis CW, S
  Peninsular Myotis SW
  Guatemalan Myotis SE
  Gray Myotis CE
  Long-legged Myotis NW, CW, SW
  Black Myotis S
  Elegant Myotis S
  Dominican Myotis SE
  Silver-tipped Myotis SE
  Hairy-legged Myotis S
  Schwartz' Myotis SE
  Riparian Myotis SE
  Montane Myotis SE
  Fringed Myotis NW, CW, S
  Keen's Myotis N, C
  Mexican Long-eared Myotis CW, S
  Miller's Myotis SW
  Long-eared Myotis NW, CW, SW
  Flat-headed Myotis SW
  Fish-eating Bat SW
  Silver-haired Bat N, C, SW
  Western Pipistrelle CW, SW
  Eastern Pipistrelle NE, C, S
  Big Brown Bat N, C, S
  Gaudeloupe Big Brown Bat SE
  Lynn's Brown Bat SE
  Argentine Brown Bat S
  Andean Brown Bat SE
  Northern Yellow Bat C, S
  Southern Yellow Bat CW, S
  Pfeiffer's Hairy-tailed Bat SE
  Jamaican Hairy-tailed Bat SE
  Small Hairy-tailed Bat SE
  Red Bat N, C, S
  Seminole Bat CE
  Tacarcuna Bat SE
  Big Red Bat SE
* Hoary Bat N, C, S
  Evening Bat NE, C, S
  Cuban Evening Bat SE
  Central American Yellow Bat S
  Little Yellow Bat S
  Least Yellow Bat SW
  Slender Yellow Bat S
  Allen's Yellow Bat S
  Spotted Bat CW, SW
  Allen's Big-eared Bat CW, SW
  Mexican Big-eared Bat S
  Rafinesque's Big-eared Bat CE
  Townsend's Big-eared Bat NW, C, S
  Pallid Bat NW, CW, SW
  Cuban Bat SE
  Van Gelder's Bat S

Family Free-tailed Bats (Molossidae)
  Southern Dog-faced Bat SE
  Greenhall's Dog-faced Bat S
* Brazilian Free-tailed Bat C, S
  Peale's Free-tailed Bat S
  Pocketed Free-tailed Bat CW, SW
  Broad-tailed Bat S
  Big Free-tailed Bat C, S
  Little Goblin Bat SE
  Western Mastiff Bat CW, SW
  Shaw's Mastiff Bat SE
  Underwood's Mastiff Bat CW, S

Wagner's Mastiff Bat S
Sanborn's Mastiff Bat SE
Dwarf Mastiff Bat SE
Thomas' Mastiff Bat SE
Black Mastiff Bat S
Miller's Mastiff Bat S
Allen's Mastiff Bat S
Bonda Mastiff Bat SE
Pallas' Mastiff Bat S

ORDER Human, Apes, Monkeys, and Lemurs
(Primates)
Family Capuchin, Howler, and Spider
Monkeys (Cebidae)
  Bole's Douroucouli SE
  Three-banded Douroucouli SE
* Mantled Howler Monkey SE
  Lawrence's Howler Monkey SE
  Capuchin SE
  Titi Monkey SE
  Brown-headed Spider Monkey SE
  Geoffrey's Spider Monkey S
Family Marmosets (Callithricidae)
  Crested Bare-faced Tamarin SE
Family Human and Apes (Hominidae)
  Homo sapiens N, C, S

ORDER Sloths, Anteaters, and Armadillos
(Edentata)
Family Anteaters (Myrmecophagidae)
* Giant Anteater SE
  Tamandua S
  Two-toed Anteater SE
Family Sloths (Bradypodidae)
* Brown-throated Sloth SE
  Two-toed Sloth SE
Family Armadillos (Dasypodidae)
  Central American Five-toed Armadillo SE
* Nine-banded Armadillo C, S

ORDER Rabbits, Hares, and Pikas
(Lagomorpha)
Family Pikas (Ochotonidae)
  Collared Pika NW
* Pika NW, CW
Family Rabbits and Hares (Leporidae)
  Volcano Rabbit SW
  Pygmy Rabbit CW
  Forest Rabbit S
  Brush Rabbit CW, SW
  San Jose Brush Rabbit SW
  Marsh Rabbit CE
* Eastern Cottontail N, C, S
  New England Cottontail CE
  Nuttall's Cottontail NW, CW
  Desert Cottontail CW, S
  Swamp Rabbit CE
  Omiltemi Cottontail SW
  Mexican Cottontail S
  Tres Marias Cottontail SW
* Snowshoe Hare N, C
  Alaska Hare NW
* Arctic Hare N
* White-tailed Jackrabbit N, C
  Black-tailed Jackrabbit C, SW
  Black Jackrabbit SW
  White-sided Jackrabbit CW, S
  Tehuantepec Jackrabbit SE
  Antelope Jackrabbit CW, SW

ORDER Rodents (Rodentia)
Family Mountain Beaver (Aplodontidae)
* Mountain Beaver NW, CW
Family Squirrels (Sciuridae)
* Eastern Chipmunk N, C
  Alpine Chipmunk CW
* Least Chipmunk N, CW
  Yellow-pine Chipmunk NW, CW
  Townsend's Chipmunk NW, CW
  Yellow-cheeked Chipmunk CW
  Allen's Chipmunk CW
  Siskiyou Chipmunk CW
  Sonoma Chipmunk CW
  Merriam's Chipmunk CW, SW
  California Chipmunk CW, SW
  Cliff Chipmunk CW, SW
  Colorado Chipmunk CW
  Red-tailed Chipmunk NW, CW
  Gray-footed Chipmunk CW
  Gray-collared Chipmunk CW
  Long-eared Chipmunk CW

Lodgepole Chipmunk CW
Panamint Chipmunk CW
Uinta Chipmunk CW
Palmer's Chipmunk CW
Buller's Chipmunk SW
* Woodchuck N, C
  Yellow-bellied Marmot NW, CW
  Alaska Marmot NW
  Hoary Marmot NW, CW
  Olympic Marmot CW
  Vancouver Marmot NW
  Harris' Antelope Squirrel CW, SW
  White-tailed Antelope Squirrel CW, SW
  Texas Antelope Squirrel CW, SW
  Espiritu Santo Island Antelope Squirrel SW
  Nelson's Antelope Squirrel CW
  Townsend's Ground Squirrel CW
  Washington Ground Squirrel CW
  Idaho Ground Squirrel CW
* Richardson's Ground Squirrel NW, CW
  Uinta Ground Squirrel CW
  Belding's Ground Squirrel CW
* Columbian Ground Squirrel NW, CW
* Arctic Ground Squirrel N
* Thirteen-lined Ground Squirrel NW, C
  Mexican Ground Squirrel CW, SW
* Spotted Ground Squirrel CW, SW
  Perote Ground Squirrel SE
  Franklin's Ground Squirrel N, C
  Rock Squirrel CW, S
  California Ground Squirrel CW, SW
  Ring-tailed Ground Squirrel SW
  Lesser Tropical Ground Squirrel SW
  Mohave Ground Squirrel CW
  Round-tailed Ground Squirrel CW, SW
* Golden-mantled Ground Squirrel NW, CW
  Cascade Golden-mantled Ground
    Squirrel NW, CW
  Sierra Madre Mantled Ground Squirrel SW
* Black-tailed Prairie Dog, NW, CW, SW
  Mexican Prairie Dog SW
  White-tailed Prairie Dog CW
  Utah Prairie Dog CW
  Gunnison's Prairie Dog CW
* Gray Squirrel N, C
  Mexican Gray Squirrel S
  Collie's Squirrel SW
  Yucatan Squirrel SE
  Variegated Squirrel SE
  Deppe's Squirrel S
  Fox Squirrel NW, C, SW
  Peter's Squirrel S
  Allen's Squirrel SW
  Nayarit Squirrel CW, SW
  Arizona Gray Squirrel CW, SW
  Western Gray Squirrel CW
  Abert's Squirrel CW
  Tropical Red Squirrel SE
  Richmond's Squirrel SE
  Bang's Mountain Squirrel SE
  Alfaro's Pygmy Squirrel SE
  Cloud Forest Pygmy Squirrel SE
* Red Squirrel N, C
  Douglas' Squirrel NW, NC
  Southern Flying Squirrel NE, C, S
* Northern Flying Squirrel N, C
Family Pocket Gophers (Geomyidae)
* Northern Pocket Gopher NW, CW
  Wyoming Pocket Gopher CW
  Idaho Pocket Gopher CW
* Southern Pocket Gopher CW, SW
  Botta's Pocket Gopher CW
  Townsend's Pocket Gopher CW
  Mazama Pocket Gopher CW
  Mountain Pocket Gopher CW
  Camas Pocket Gopher CW
  Michoacan Pocket Gopher SW
  Plains Pocket Gopher NW, C
  Attwater's Pocket Gopher C
  Texas Pocket Gopher CW, SW
  Tropical Pocket Gopher SW
  Southeastern Pocket Gopher CE
  Desert Pocket Gopher CW, SW
  Oaxacan Pocket Gopher SE
  Large Pocket Gopher S
  Hispid Pocket Gopher SE
  Big Pocket Gopher SE
  Variable Pocket Gopher SE
  Chiriqui Pocket Gopher SE
  Darien Pocket Gopher SE
  Underwood's Pocket Gopher SE
  Cherrie's Pocket Gopher SE
  Nicaraguan Pocket Gopher SE

Buller's Pocket Gopher SW
Alcorn's Pocket Gopher SW
Yellow-faced Pocket Gopher CW, SW
Merriam's Pocket Gopher S
Queretaro Pocket Gopher SW
Smoky Pocket Gopher SW
Naked-nosed Pocket Gopher SW
Zinser's Pocket Gopher SW
Llano Pocket Gopher SW
Family Pocket Mice, Kangaroo Rats, and Spiny
Mice (Heteromyidae)
* Olive-backed Pocket Mouse NW, CW
  Plains Pocket Mouse C, SW
  Great Basin Pocket Mouse NW, CW
  White-eared Pocket Mouse CW
  Yellow-eared Pocket Mouse CW
  Silky Pocket Mouse CW, S
  Little Pocket Mouse CW, SW
  Arizona Pocket Mouse CW, SW
  San Joaquin Pocket Mouse CW
  Long-tailed Pocket Mouse CW, SW
  Bailey's Pocket Mouse CW, SW
  Hispid Pocket Mouse C, SW
* Desert Pocket Mouse CW, SW
  Little Desert Pocket Mouse SW
  Dalquest's Pocket Mouse SW
  Sinaloan Pocket Mouse SW
  Rock Pocket Mouse CW, SW
  Nelson's Pocket Mouse CW, SW
  Goldman's Pocket Mouse SW
  Narrow-skulled Pocket Mouse SW
  Lined Pocket Mouse SW
  San Diego Pocket Mouse CW, SW
  Anthony's Pocket Mouse SW
  California Pocket Mouse CW, SW
  Spiny Pocket Mouse CW, SW
* Dark Kangaroo Mouse CW
  Pale Kangaroo Mouse CW
* Ord's Kangaroo Rat NW, CW, SW
  Gulf Coast Kangaroo Rat CW
  Chisel-toothed Kangaroo Rat CW
  Panamint Kangaroo Rat CW
  Stephen's Kangaroo Rat CW
  Big-eared Kangaroo Rat CW
  Narrow-faced Kangaroo Rat CW
  Agile Kangaroo Rat CW, SW
  Santa Catarina Kangaroo Rat SW
  Baja California Kangaroo Rat SW
  Huey's Kangaroo Rat SW
  Heermann's Kangaroo Rat CW
  California Kangaroo Rat CW
  San Quintin Kangaroo Rat SW
  Giant Kangaroo Rat CW
  Banner-tailed Kangaroo Rat CW, SW
  Nelson's Kangaroo Rat SW
  Texas Kangaroo Rat CW
  Phillip's Kangaroo Rat S
  Merriam's Kangaroo Rat CW, SW
  San Jose Island Kangaroo Rat SW
  Margarita Island Kangaroo Rat SW
  Fresno Kangaroo Rat CW
  Desert Kangaroo Rat CW, SW
  Mexican Spiny Pocket Mouse CW, S
  Painted Spiny Pocket Mouse S
  Jaliscan Spiny Pocket Mouse SW
  Salvin's Spiny Pocket Mouse SE
  Panamanian Spiny Pocket Mouse SE
  Desmarest's Spiny Pocket Mouse SE
  Goldman's Spiny Pocket Mouse SE
  Long-tailed Spiny Pocket Mouse SE
  Santo Domingo Spiny Pocket Mouse SE
  Motzorongo Spiny Pocket Mouse SE
  Gaumer's Spiny Pocket Mouse SE
  Southern Spiny Pocket Mouse SE
  Goodwin's Spiny Pocket Mouse SE
  Nelson's Spiny Pocket Mouse SE
  Mountain Spiny Pocket Mouse SE
Family Beaver (Castoridae)
* Beaver N, C, SW
Family New World Mice and Rats, Gerbils, and
Hamsters (Cricetidae)
* March Rice Rat C, S
  Coues' Rice Rat SE
  Key Rice Rat CE
  Nelson's Rice Rat SW
  Nicaraguan Rice Rat SE
  Black-eared Rice Rat S
  Ixtlan Rice Rat SE
  Alfaro's Rice Rat S
  Long-whiskered Rice Rat SE
  Tomes' Rice Rat SE
  Harris' Rice Rat SE

Large-headed Rice Rat SE
Bicolored Rice Rat SE
Concolored Rice Rat SE
† St. Vincent Rice Rat SE
Pygmy Rice Rat S
Dusky Rice Rat SE
Alfaro's Water Rat SE
† Antillean Muskrat SE
† Audrey's Muskrat SE
† Santa Lucia Muskrat SE
Painted Bristly Mouse SE
Mount Pirri Climbing Mouse SE
Chiapin Climbing Rat SE
Fulvous-bellied Climbing Rat SE
Peters' Climbing Rat S
Panama Climbing Rat SE
Tumbala Climbing Rat SE
Watson's Climbing Rat SE
Big-eared Climbing Rat S
Sumichrast's Vesper Rat S
Yucatan Vesper Rat SE
Plains Harvest Mouse C, SW
Sonoran Harvest Mouse SW
Eastern Harvest Mouse CE
* Western Harvest Mouse NW, C, S
Salt-marsh Harvest Mouse CW
Volcano Harvest Mouse S
Sumichrast's Harvest Mouse S
Fulvous Harvest Mouse C, S
Hairy Harvest Mouse SW
Slender Harvest Mouse SE
Darien Harvest Mouse SE
Mexican Harvest Mouse S
Cozumel Island Harvest Mouse SE
Short-nosed Harvest Mouse SE
Nicaraguan Harvest Mouse SE
Small-toothed Harvest Mouse S
Narrow-nosed Harvest Mouse SE
Rodriquez's Harvest Mouse SE
Chiriqui Harvest Mouse SE
Cactus Mouse CW, SW
Eva's Desert Mouse SW
Merriam's Mouse CW, SW
Angel Island Mouse SW
San Lorenzo Mouse SW
Turner Island Canyon Mouse SW
Pemberton's Deer Mouse SW
Dickey's Deer Mouse SW
California Mouse CW, SW
Oldfield Mouse CE
* Deer Mouse N, C, S
Cascade Deer Mouse NW, CW
Santa Cruz Island Mouse SW
Slevin's Mouse SW
Sitka Mouse NW
Black-eared Mouse S
* White-footed Mouse N, C, S
Cotton Mouse CE
Canyon Mouse CW, SW
Burt's Deer Mouse SW
False Canyon Mouse SW
White-ankled Mouse CW, SW
Brush Mouse CW, S
Texas (Attwater's) Mouse C
Chihuahuan Mouse SW
San Esteban Island Mouse SW
Osgood's Deer Mouse S
Aztec Mouse S
Oaxacan Deer Mouse SE
Forest Mouse SW
Southern Wood Mouse SW
Pinon Mouse CW, S
Palo Duro Mouse CW
Rock Mouse CW, S
Perote Mouse SE
Marsh Mouse SW
Plateau Mouse S
Puebla Deer Mouse SE
El Carrizo Deer Mouse SW
Yucatan Deer Mouse SE
Mexican Deer Mouse S
Naked-eared Deer Mouse SE
Mayan Mouse SE
Stirton's Deer Mouse SE
Naked-footed Deer Mouse S
Blackish Deer Mouse S
Todos Santos Deer Mouse SE
Guatemalan Deer Mouse SE
Brown Deer Mouse S
Zempoaltepec Deer Mouse SE
Chiapan Deer Mouse SE
Big Deer Mouse S
Thomas' Deer Mouse S

Yellow Deer Mouse SE
Mount Pirri Deer Mouse SE
Jico Deer Mouse S
Chinanteco Deer Mouse SE
Crested-tailed Mouse SE
Slender-tailed Deer Mouse SE
Michoacan Deer Mouse SW
Florida Mouse CE
* Golden Mouse CE
* Southern Pygmy Mouse S
Northern Pygmy Mouse C, S
* Northern Grasshopper Mouse NW, CW, SW
Southern Grasshopper Mouse CW, SW
Mearn's Grasshopper Mouse CW, SW
Cane Rat SE
Chiriqui Brown Mouse SE
Alston's Brown Mouse SE
* Hispid Cotton Rat C, S
Jaliscan Cotton Rat S
Arizona Cotton Rat CW, SW
Zacatecan (Tawny-bellied) Cotton Rat CW, SW
Allen's Cotton Rat S
White-eared Cotton Rat S
Yellow-nosed Cotton Rat CW, SW
Volcano Mouse S
Eastern Woodrat C
Southern Plains Woodrat CW, SW
White-throated Woodrat CW, SW
Nelson's Woodrat SE
Bolanos Woodrat SW
Turner Island Woodrat SW
Desert Woodrat CW, SW
Arizona Woodrat CW
Bryant's Woodrat SW
Anthony's Woodrat CW
San Martin Island Woodrat SW
Bunker's Woodrat SW
Stephens' Woodrat CW
Goldman's Woodrat SW
Mexican Woodrat CW, S
Nicaraguan Woodrat SE
Tamaulipan Woodrat SW
Dusky-footed Woodrat CW, SW
* Bushy-tailed Woodrat NW, CW
Allen's Woodrat S
Sonoran Woodrat SW
Magdalena Rat SW
Diminutive Woodrat SW
Thomas' Water Mouse SE
Hartmann's Water Mouse SE
Underwood's Water Mouse SE
Goldman's Water Mouse SE
Goodwin's Water Mouse SE

Family Voles and Lemmings (Arvicolidae)
Northern Red-backed Vole N
* Southern Red-backed Vole N, C
California Red-backed Vole CW
* Heather Vole N, C
White-footed Vole CW
Red Tree Mouse CW
* Meadow Vole N, C, SW
Beach Vole CE
† Gull Island Vole CE
Montane Vole NW, CW
Gray-tailed Vole CW
Zempoaltepec Vole SE
Tarabundi Vole SE
California Vole CW, SW
Guatemalan Vole SE
Townsend's Vole NW, CW
Tundra Vole NW
Long-tailed Vole NW, CW
Coronation Island Vole NW
Creeping Vole NW, CW
Rock Vole NE, CE
Yellow-cheeked Vole N
Prairie Vole NW, C
Mexican Vole CW, S
Pine Vole NE, C
Jalapan Pine Vole S
Singing Vole NW
St. Matthew Island Vole NW
Water Vole NW, CW
* Sagebrush Vole NW, CW
Round-tailed Muskrat CE
* Muskrat N, C, SW
* Brown Lemming N
Southern Bog Lemming N, C
* Northern Bog Lemming N, C
* Collared Lemming N
St. Lawrence Island Collared Lemming NW
Labrador Collared Lemming NE

Family Jumping Mice and Birch Mice (Zapodidae)
* Meadow Jumping Mouse N, C
Western Jumping Mouse NW, CW
Pacific Jumping Mouse NW, CW
* Woodland Jumping Mouse N, CE

Family New World Porcupines (Erethizontidae)
* Porcupine N, C, SW
Mexican Porcupine S
† Antillean Porcupine SE
Rothschild's Porcupine SE

Family Capybara (Hydrochaeridae)
* Capybara SE

Family Agoutis and Pacas (Dasyproctidae)
* Spotted Paca S
Brazilian Agouti SE
Mexican Agouti SE
Agouti SE
Coiba Island Agouti SE

Family Hutias and Coypus (Capromyidae)
Garrido's Hutia SE
Desmarest's Hutia SE
Bushy-tailed Hutia SE
Dwarf Hutia SE
Prehensile-tailed Hutia SE
Hutia Rat SE
Land Hutia SE
Brown's Hutia SE
Ingraham's Hutia SE
Dominican Hutia SE
Allen's Hutia SE

Family Spiny Rats (Echimyidae)
Armored Rat SE
Tomes' Spiny Rat SE
Gliding Spiny Rat SE

ORDER Toothed Whales (Odontoceti)

Family Dolphins (Delphinidae)
Rough-tooth Dolphin A, P
Long-snouted Spinner Dolphin A, P
Short-snouted Spinner Dolphin A
Striped Dolphin A, P
Briddled Spotted Dolphin A
Gray's (Pantropical) Spotted Dolphin A, P
Atlantic Spotted Dolphin A
Common (Saddle-backed) Dolphin A, P
Fraser's Dolphin P
Bottle-nosed Dolphin A, P
Northern Right-whale Dolphin P
White-beaked Dolphin A
* Atlantic White-sided Dolphin A
Pacific White-sided Dolphin P
False Killer Whale A, P
* Killer Whale Ar, A, P
Grampus (Risso's Dolphin) A, P
Long-finned (Atlantic) Pilot Whale A
Short-finned (Pacific) Pilot Whale P
Melon-headed Whale P
Pygmy Killer Whale A, P

Family Porpoises (Phocoenidae)
* Harbor Porpoise Ar, A, P
Gulf Porpoise P
Dall's Porpoise P

Family White Whale and Narwhal (Monodontidae)
* White Whale Ar, A, P
* Narwhal Ar, A

Family Sperm Whales (Physeteridae)
Pygmy Sperm Whale A, P
Dwarf Sperm Whale A, P
* Sperm Whale A, P

Family Beaked Whales (Ziphiidae)
Baird's Beaked (N. Pacific Bottle-nosed) Whale P
True's Beaked Whale A
Gervais' Beaked Whale A
Ginkgo-toothed Beaked Whale P
Hubbs' (Arch-) Beaked Whale P
Stejneger's (Northern Sea) Beaked Whale P
Sowerby's (N. Atlantic) Beaked Whale A
Blainville's (Dense-) Beaked Whale A
Cuvier's (Goose-) Beaked Whale A
Northern (N. Atlantic) Bottle-nosed Whale Ar, A
Hector's Beaked Whale P

ORDER Baleen Whales (Mysticeti)

Family Gray Whale (Eschrichtidae)
Gray Whale Ar, P

Family Rorqual (Fin-backed) Whales (Balaenopteridae)
Minke Whale Ar, A, P
Bryde's Whale A, P

Sei Whale A, P
Fin Whale A, P
* Blue Whale A, P
Humpback Whale Ar, A, P

Family Right Whales and Bowhead Whale
(Balaenidae)
Northern (Black) Right Whale A, P
* Bowhead Whale Ar, A, P

ORDER Carnivores (Carnivora)
Family Wolves, Foxes, and Dogs (Canidae)
* Coyote N, C, S
* Gray Wolf N, C, S
Red Wolf C
* Arctic Fox N
* Red Fox N, C
Kit Fox CW, SW
* Swift Fox NW, CW
Gray Fox N, C, S
Channel Islands Gray Fox CW
Bush Dog SE

Family Bears (Ursidae)
* Black Bear N, C, SW
* Brown (Grizzly) Bear NW, CW, SW
* Polar Bear N

Family Raccoons (Procyonidae)
* Ringtail C, A
Cacomistle S
* Raccoon N, C, S
Tres Marias Raccoon SW
Bahama Raccoon CE
Cozumel Island Raccoon SE
Guadeloupe Raccoon SE
Barbados Raccoon SE
Crab-eating Raccoon SE
* Coati CW, S
Cozumel Island Coati SE
Kinkajou S
Bushy-tailed Olingo SE
Chiriqui Olingo SE
Harris' Olingo SE

Family Weasels (Mustelidae)
Marten N, C
* Fisher N, C
* Ermine N, C
Least Weasel N, C
Long-tailed Weasel N, C, S
* Black-footed Ferret NW, CW
* Mink N, C
† Sea Mink A, NE, CE
Tayra S
Grison S
* Wolverine N, C
* Badger N, C, SW
Pygmy Spotted Skunk SW
* Spotted Skunk C, S
* Striped Skunk N, C, SW
Hooded Skunk CW, S
Hog-nosed Skunk C, S
Eastern Hog-nosed Skunk CW, S
Striped Hog-nosed Skunk SE
* River Otter N, C
Southern River Otter S
* Sea Otter P, NW, CW, SW

Family Cats (Felidae)
* Jaguar C, S
* Cougar (Mountain Lion) N, C, S
* Ocelot C, S
Margay CW, S
Little Spotted Cat SE
Jaguarundi C, S
* Lynx N, C
* Bobcat N, C, S

Family Eared Seals (Otariidae)
Northern Fur Seal P, NW, CW
Guadalupe Fur Seal P, CW, SW
* Northern Sea Lion P, NW, CW
California Sea Lion P, NW, CW, SW

Family Walrus (Odobenidae)
* Walrus Ar, A, P, N

Family Hair Seals (Phocidae)
* Harbor Seal Ar, A, P, N, C, S
Spotted Seal P, NW
Ribbon Seal Ar, P, NW
* Ringed Seal Ar, A, P, N
Harp Seal Ar, A, NE
Bearded Seal Ar, A, P, N
Gray Seal A, NE, CE
Hooded Seal Ar, A, NE
* Northern Elephant Seal P, NW, CW, SW
West Indian Monk Seal A, CE, SE

ORDER Manatees, Dugong, Sea Cow (Sirenia)
Family Manatees (Trichechidae)
* Caribbean Manatee A
Family Dugong and Sea Cow (Dugongidae)
† Steller's Sea Cow P

ORDER Odd-toed Ungulates (Perissodactyla)
Family Tapirs (Tapiridae)
* Baird's Tapir SE

ORDER Even-toed Ungulates (Artiodactyla)
Family Peccaries (Tayassuidae)
* Collared Peccary C, S
White-lipped Peccary SE
Family Deer (Cervidae)
* American Elk N, C, SW
* Mule Deer NW, C, SW
* White-tailed Deer N, C, S
Red Brocket S
Brown Brocket SE
* Moose N, C
* Caribou N, C
Family Pronghorn (Antilocapridae)
* Pronghorn NW, CW, SW
Family Cattle, Sheep, and Goats (Bovidae)
* Bison, NW, C, SW
* Mountain Goat NW, CW
* Muskox N
* Mountain Sheep NW, CW, SW
Dall's Sheep NW

Additional Reading

National and regional publications of mammals in North America vary considerably in scope, technical level, and date. While mammals of Canada and the United States are relatively well known, the fauna of Mexico, the West Indies, and the Central American countries remains in an elementary state — in fact, the habits of many species are almost totally unknown and certain animals are represented by only one or several specimens. Some excellent books on the mammals of various political units have been produced in the last two decades. They incorporate years of research by local specialists, beautiful color photographs, and detailed distribution maps. However, many provinces and states have not yet developed popular books and so one must refer to regional, technical, or old works which are of less value for a general audience seeking local information. Rather than list references directed at particular species or groups such as furbearers, I have chosen books that discuss a number or all species of an area — an approach that I hope will give the reader a better understanding of how the mammals of a given region relate to each other and their environment. Most of these books and papers contain bibliographies that cover particular species in more detail. Titles marked with an asterisk are highly recommended to amateur naturalists for broad coverage and illustrations.

NORTH AMERICA (only E. R. Hall covers Mexico and Central America)

* A field guide to the mammals. W. H. Burt and R. P. Grossenheider. Houghton Mifflin Company, Boston. 284 pp. 1976.

* A field guide to animal tracks. O. Murie. Houghton Mifflin Company, Boston, 374 pp. 1975.

American mammals. W. J. Hamilton, Jr. McGraw-Hill Book Company, New York. 434 pp. 1964 (paperback of 1939 edition).

Field book of North American mammals. H. E. Anthony. G. P. Putnam's Sons, New York. 625 pp. 1928.

* Field guide to North American mammals. J. O. Whitaker, Jr. The Audubon Society. Alfred A. Knopf, New York. 745 pp. 1980.

How to know the mammals. E. S. Booth. W. C. Brown Company, Dubuque, Iowa. 203 pp. 1982.

Lives of game animals. E. T. Seton. Charles T. Branford Company, Boston. 8 volumes. 1953 (reissue of 1909 edition).

Mammals — a guide to familiar American species. H. S. Zim and D. F. Hoffmeister. Simon and Schuster, New York. 160 pp. 1955.

Mammals of North America. V. H. Cahalane. MacMillan Company, New York. 682 pp. 1961.

Mammals of North America. R. T. Orr. Doubleday and Company, Inc., New York. 1971.

North American mammals. R. A. Caras. Meredith Press, New York. 578 pp. 1967.

Pictorial guide to the mammals of North America. L. L. Rue III. Thomas Y. Crowell Company, New York. 299 pp. 1974.

Pleistocene mammals of North America. B. Kurten and E. Anderson. Columbia University Press, New York. 442 pp. 1980.

Sportsman's guide to game animals — a field book of North American species. L. L. Rue III. Harper and Row, New York. 650 pp. 1968.

The imperial collection of Audubon animals. J. J. Audubon and J. Bachman (Edited by V. H. Cahalane). Hammond Incorporated, Maplewood, New Jersey. 307 pp. 1967.

The mammal guide. R. S. Palmer. Doubleday and Company, Incorporated, New York. 384 pp. 1954.

The mammals of North America. E. R. Hall. John Wiley and Sons, New York. 2 volumes. 1181 pp. 1981.

Wild animals of North America. National Geographic Society, Washington. 400 pp. 1960.

* Wild animals of North America. National Geographic Society, Washington. 406 pp. 1979.

Wild mammals of North America — biology, management, economics. J. A. Chapman and G. A. Feldhamer (Editors). The John Hopkins University Press, Baltimore. 1147 pp. 1982.

CANADA (national)

Canadian mammals. A. W. Cameron. National Museums of Canada, Ottawa. 81 pp. 1958.

* Handbook of Canadian mammals. C. G. van Zyll de Jong. National Museums of Canada, Ottawa. Volume 1, Marsupials and insectivores. 210 pp. 1983. Volume 2, Bats. 212 pp. 1985.

Large mammals. R. E. Wrigley. Hyperion Press Limited, Winnipeg. Volume 1, 40 pp. 1983. Volume 2, 40 pp. 1985.

Mammals of the Canadian wild. A. Forsyth. Camden House, Camden East, Ontario. 351 pp. 1985. (Also published as Mammals of the American north.)

Small mammals. R. E. Wrigley. Hyperion Press Limited, Winnipeg. 40 pp. 1981.

* The mammals of Canada. A. W. F. Banfield. National Museum of Natural Sciences, University of Toronto Press. 438 pp. 1974.

* Wild mammals of Canada. F. H. Wooding. McGraw-Hill Ryerson Limited. Toronto, New York. 272 pp. 1982.

CANADA (regional)

Animals of the north. W. O. Pruitt, Jr. Harper and Row, New York. 173 pp. 1960.

Mammals of the eastern Rockies and western plains of Canada. A. L. Rand. National Museums of Canada, Ottawa. Bulletin 108:1-237. 1948.

Mammals of the islands in the Gulf of St. Lawrence. A. W. Cameron. National Museums of Canada, Ottawa. 165 pp. 1958.

Mammifères du Québec et de l'est du Canada. J. Prescott et P. Richard. Éditions France-Amérique, Montréal. 2 volumes. 447 pp. 1982.

* The mammals of eastern Canada. R. L. Peterson. Oxford University Press, Toronto. 465 pp. 1966.

* Wild mammals of western Canada. A. Savage and C. Savage. Western Producer Prairie Books, Saskatoon, Saskatchewan. 209 pp. 1981.

CANADA (provinces, territories, other areas)

Alberta

* The mammals of Alberta. J. D. Soper. Hambly Press Limited, Edmonton. 410 pp. 1964.

The mammals of Banff National Park, Alberta. A. W. F. Banfield. National Museums of Canada, Ottawa, Bulletin 159:1-53. 1958.

The mammals of Jasper National Park, Alberta. J.D. Soper. Canadian Wildlife Service, Report Series 10:1-80, 1970.

The mammals of Waterton Lakes National Park, Alberta. J. D. Soper. Canadian Wildlife Service, Report Series 23:1-55. (no date)

British Columbia

* The mammals of British Columbia. I. M. Cowan and C. J. Guiguet. British Columbia Provincial Museum, Victoria, Handbook 11:1-414. 1965.

Manitoba

Animals of Manitoba. Edited by R. E. Wrigley. Manitoba Museum of Man and Nature, Winnipeg. 158 pp. 1974.

Life histories of northern animals — an account of the mammals of Manitoba. E. T. Seton. Charles Scribner's Sons, New York. 1267 pp. 1909. (Reprinted by Ayer Company, Salem, New Hampshire. 1984.)

The mammals of Manitoba. J.D. Soper. Canadian Field-Naturalist 75(4):171-219. 1961.

New Brunswick

see The Mammals of eastern Canada (regional)

Newfoundland

The land mammals of insular Newfoundland. T. H. Northcott. Wildlife Division, Newfoundland Department of Culture, Recreation and Youth. 90 pp. 1980.

Northwest Territories

The mammals of Banks Island. T. H. Manning and A. H. MacPherson. Arctic Institute of North America, Technical Paper 2:1-74. 1958.

The mammals of Keewatin. F. Harper. University of Kansas, Lawrence. 94 pp. 1956.

Mammals of the Mackenzie Delta. A. E. Porsild. Canadian Field-Naturalist 59:4-22. 1945.

Mammals of the Northwest Territories. R. MacFarlane. Smithsonian Institution, United States National Museum, Washington D.C. 764 pp. 1905.

Nova Scotia

The land mammals of Nova Scotia. R. W. Smith. American Midland Naturalist 24:213-241. 1940.

see The mammals of eastern Canada (regional)

Ontario

Mammals of Ontario. A. I. Dagg. Otter Press, Waterloo. 159 pp. 1974.

see The mammals of eastern Canada (regional)

Prince Edward Island

see The mammals of eastern Canada (regional)

Quebec

Les mammifères du Québec. E. J. Duchesnay. Éditions Hurtubise, Montréal. 124 pp. 1972.

Mammifères de la province de Québec. P. Pirlot. Le Naturaliste Canadien 89:129-147. 1962.

Land and freshwater mammals of the Ungava Peninsula. F. Harper. University of Kansas, Lawrence. 178 pp. 1961.

Mammals of the province of Quebec. R. M. Anderson. National Museums of Canada, Ottawa. 114 pp. 1938.

see Mammifères du Québec et de l'est du Canada (regional)

Saskatchewan

Field data on the mammals of southern Saskatchewan. J. D. Soper. Canadian Field-Naturalist 75:23-41. 1961.

A guide to Saskatchewan mammals. W. H. Beck. Saskatchewan Natural History Society, Regina. 52 pp. 1958.

Yukon Territory

Mammal investigations on the Canol Road, Yukon and Northwest Territories. A.L. Rand. National Museum of Canada, Ottawa, Bulletin 99:1-52. 1945.

Mammals of the Yukon Territory. P. M. Youngman. National Museum of Natural Sciences, Ottawa, Publications in Zoology 10:1-102. 1975.

Mammals of the Yukon region. W. H. Osgood. In "Results of a biological reconnaissance of the Yukon River region." W. H. Osgood and L. B. Bishop. North American Fauna 19:1-100. 1900.

UNITED STATES (regional)

* Guide to mammals of the plains states. J. K. Jones Jr., D. M. Armstrong, and J. R. Choate. University of Nebraska, Lincoln. 1986.

Little mammals of the Pacific Northwest. E. B. Kritzman. Pacific Search Press, Seattle. 118 pp. 1977.

* Mammals of the eastern United States. W. J. Hamilton, Jr. and J. O. Whitaker, Jr. Cornell University Press, Ithaca. 346 pp. 1979.

Mammals of the Great Lakes region. W. H. Burt. University of Michigan Press, Ann Arbor. 246 pp. 1957.

Mammals of the Great Smoky Mountains National Park. A.V. Linzey and D.W. Linzey. University of Tennessee Press, Knoxville. 114 pp. 1971.

Mammals of the national parks. R. G. Van Gelder. The Johns Hopkins University Press, Baltimore. 310 pp. 1982.

* Mammals of the northern Great Plains. J. K. Jones Jr., D. M. Armstrong, R. S. Hoffmann, and C. Jones. University of Nebraska Press, Lincoln. 379 pp. 1983.

* Mammals of the Pacific States — California, Oregon, and Washington. L. G. Ingles. Stanford University Press, Stanford. 506 pp. 1965.

Mammals of the Southwest. E. L. Cockrum. The University of Arizona Press, Tucson. 176 pp. 1982.

Mammals of the southwest deserts. G. Olin. Southwestern Monuments Association and the National Parks Service, Globe, Arizona. 112 pp. 1954.

* Wild mammals of New England. A. J. Godin. Johns Hopkins University Press, Baltimore. 304 pp. 1977.

UNITED STATES (states and other areas)

Alabama

A biological survey of Alabama. II The mammals. A. H. Howell. North American Fauna 45:1-88. 1921.

see Mammals of Georgia

Alaska

* Alaska mammals. J. Rearden. Alaska Geographic Society, Anchorage. 184 pp. 1981.

Distribution of Alaska mammals. R. H. Manville and S. P. Young. Bureau of Sport Fisheries and Wildlife, Circular 211:1-74. 1965.

Fauna of the Aleutian Islands and Alaska Peninsula. O. J. Murie. North American Fauna 61:1-364. 1959.

Mammals of northern Alaska. J. W. Bee and E. R. Hall. University of Kansas, Lawrence. 309 pp. 1956.

Arizona

* Mammals of Arizona. D. F. Hoffmeister. University of Arizona Press, Tucson. 700 pp. 1985.

* Mammals of Grand Canyon (Arizona). D. F. Hoffmeister. University of Illinois Press, Champaign. 183 pp. 1971.

The recent mammals of Arizona: their taxonomy and distribution. E. L. Cockrum. University of Arizona Press, Tucson. 276 pp. 1960.

The mammals of the Huachuca Mountains, southeastern Arizona. D. F. Hoffmeister and W. W. Goodpaster. Illinois Biological Monographs 24:1-152. 1954.

Arkansas

* A guide to Arkansas mammals. J. A. Sealander. River Road Press, Conway, Arkansas. 313 pp. 1979.

California

Mammals of California and its coastal waters. L. G. Ingles. Stanford University Press, Stanford. 396 pp. 1954.

Mammals of the San Francisco Bay region. W. D. and E. Berry. University of California Press, Berkeley. 72 pp. 1959.

Review of the recent mammal fauna of California. J. Grinnell. University of California. Publications in Zoology 40:71-234. 1933.

Mammals of Yosemite National Park. H. C. Parker. National Park Service and the Yosemite Natural History Association. 105 pp. (no date).

see Mammals of the Pacific States (regional)

Colorado

Distribution of mammals in Colorado. D. M. Armstrong. University of Kansas, Lawrence. 415 pp. 1972.

Mammals of Mesa Verde National Park, Colorado. S. Anderson. University of Kansas, Lawrence, Museum of Natural History, Publication 14:29-67. 1961.

* Wild mammals of Colorado. R. R. Lechleitner. Pruett Publishing Company, Boulder. 254 pp. 1969.

Connecticut

The mammals of Connecticut. G. G. Goodwin. State Geological and Natural History Survey, Hartford. 221 pp. 1935.

see Wild mammals of New England (regional)

Delaware

see Wild mammals of New England (regional)

Florida

The land mammals of South Florida. J. N. Layne. Miami Geological Society Memoir. 2:386-413. 1974.

Vertebrates of Florida: Identification and distribution. H. M. Stevenson. University Press of Florida, Gainesville. 607 pp. 1976.

Georgia

* Mammals of Georgia. F. B. Golley. University of Georgia Press, Athens. 218 pp. 1962.

Idaho

* Mammals of Idaho. E. J. Larrison and D. R. Johnson. University Press of Idaho, Moscow. 166 pp. 1981.

The recent mammals of Idaho. W. B. Davis. Caxton Printers Ltd., Caldwell, Idaho. 400 pp. 1939.

Illinois

* Fieldbook of Illinois mammals. D. F. Hoffmeister and C. O. Mohr. Illinois Natural History Survey. 233 pp. 1957.

Mammals of Illinois. W. L. Necker and D. M. Hatfield. Chicago Academy of Science, Bulletin 6:17-60. 1941.

The mammals of Illinois and Wisconsin. C. B. Cory. Field Museum of Natural History, Publication 153, Zoological series 11:1-505. 1912.

Indiana

Distribution of the mammals of Indiana. R. E. Mumford. Indiana Academy of Science, Monograph 1:1-114. 1969.

* Mammals of Indiana. R. E. Mumford and J. O. Whitaker, Jr. Indiana University Press, Bloomington. 537 pp. 1982.

Iowa

Distribution and biogeography of mammals of Iowa. J. B. Boles. Texas Tech Press, Lubbock. 184 pp. 1975.

Kansas

Handbook of mammals of Kansas. E. R. Hall. University of Kansas, Lawrence. 303 pp. 1955.

* Mammals in Kansas. J. W. Bee, G. Glass, R. S. Hoffmann, and R. R. Patterson. University of Kansas, Lawrence. 300 pp. 1981.

Mammals of Kansas. E. L. Cockrum. University of Kansas, Museum of Natural History, Lawrence. 303 pp. 1952.

Kentucky

* Mammals of Kentucky. R. W. Barbour and W. H. Davis. University Press of Kentucky, Lexington. 322 pp. 1974.

Louisiana

* The mammals of Louisiana and its adjacent waters. G. H. Lowery, Jr. Louisiana State University Press, Baton Rouge. 505 pp. 1974.

Maine

see Wild mammals of New England (regional)

Maryland

Mammals of Maryland. J. L. Paradiso. North America Fauna 66:1-193. 1969.

Massachussetts

see Wild Mammals of New England (regional)

Michigan

* Mammals of Michigan. W. H. Burt. University of Michigan Press, Ann Arbor. 246 pp. 1957.

Minnesota

Mammals of Minnesota. C. L. Herrick. Minnesota Geological and Natural History Survey, Bulletin 7:1-299. 1892.

Minnesota Mammals. W. Longley and C. Wechsler. Minnesota Department of Natural Resources, St. Paul. 28 pp. (no date).

* The mammals of Minnesota. E. B. Hazard. University of Minnesota Press, Minneapolis. 280 pp. 1982.

The mammals of Minnesota. H. L. Gunderson and J. R. Beer. University of Minnesota 6:1-190. 1953.

The mammals of Minnesota. G. Swanson, T. Surber, and T. S. Roberts. Minnesota Department of Conservation, Technical Bulletin No. 2:1-108. 1945.

Mississippi

A review of Mississippi mammals. M. L. Kennedy, K. N. Randolph, and T. L. Best. Eastern New Mexico University, Portales. 36 pp. 1974.

Mississippi land mammals. J. L. Wolfe. Mississippi Museum of Natural Science, Jackson. 44 pp. 1971.

The mammals of Mississippi. R. P. Ward. Journal of the Mississippi Academy of Science 11:309-330. 1965.

Missouri

* The wild mammals of Missouri. C. W. Schwartz and E. R. Schwartz. University of Missouri Press, Columbia. 341 pp. 1959.

Montana

A guide to Montana mammals. R. S. Hoffmann and D. L. Pattie. University of Montana, Missoula. 133 pp. 1968.

The distribution of some mammals in Montana. 1. Mammals other than bats. R. S. Hoffmann, P. L. Wright, and F. E. Newby. Journal of Mammalogy 50:579-604. 1969.

Nebraska

Distribution and taxonomy of mammals of Nebraska. J. K. Jones, Jr. University of Kansas, Lawrence. 356 pp. 1964.

see Mammals of the northern Great Plains (regional)

Nevada

Mammals of Nevada. E. R. Hall. University of California Press, Berkeley. 710 pp. 1946.

New Hampshire

see Wild mammals of New England (regional)

New Jersey

Checklist, identification keys, and bibliography of New Jersey land mammals. J. J. McManus. New Jersey Academy of Science, Bulletin 19:52-58. 1974.

The mammals of New Jersey. W. Stone. New Jersey State Museum, Trenton. Annual Report for 1907. 1908.

The mammals of Pennsylvania and New Jersey. S. N. Rhoads. Published privately, Philadelphia. 266 pp. 1903.

The mammals of the State of New Jersey: A preliminary annotated list. R. G. Van Gelder. New Jersey Audubon Society, Occasional Paper 143:1-20. 1984.

see Wild mammals of New England (regional)

New Mexico

Mammals of New Mexico. J. S. Findley, A. H. Harris, D. E. Wilson, and C. Jones. University of New Mexico Press, Albuquerque. 360 pp. 1975.

Mammals of the southwestern United States — with special reference to New Mexico. V. Bailey. Dover Publications, Inc., New York. 412 pp. 1971 reprint of 1932 publication (North American Fauna 53).

New York

* The mammals of New York. P. F. Connor. New York State Museum and Science Service. In preparation.

see Wild mammals of New England (regional)

North Carolina

see Mammals of the eastern United States (regional)

North Dakota

A biological survey of North Dakota. V. Bailey. North American Fauna 49:1-226. 1927.

Mammals from southwestern North Dakota. H. H. Genoways and J. K. Jones, Jr. Museum of Texas Tech University, Lubbock, Occasional Paper 6:1-36. 1972.

see Mammals of the northern Great Plains (regional)

Ohio

* A guide to the mammals of Ohio. J. L. Gottschang. Ohio State University Press, Columbus. 176 pp. 1981.

Oklahoma

Faunal relationships and geographic distribution of mammals in Oklahoma. W. F. Blair. American Midland Naturalist 22:85-133. 1939.

The mammals of Harmon County, Oklahoma. R. E. Martin and J. R. Preston. Oklahoma Academy of Science, Norman, Proceeding 49:42-60. 1970.

Oregon

The mammals and life zones of Oregon. V. Bailey. North American Fauna 55: 1-416. 1936.

see Mammals of the Pacific States (regional)

Pennsylvania

* Mammals of Pennsylvania. J. K. Doutt, C. A. Heppenstall, and J. E. Guilday. Pennsylvania Game Commission and Carnegie Museum, Pittsburgh. 288 pp. 1973.

see The mammals of Pennsylvania and New Jersey

Rhode Island

* The mammals of Rhode Island. J. M. Cronan and A. Brooks. Rhode Island Department of Natural Resources. 133 pp. 1968.

South Carolina

* South Carolina mammals. F. B. Golley. Charleston Museum, Charleston. 181 pp. 1966.

South Dakota

Mammals of northwestern South Dakota. K. W. Anderson and J. K. Jones Jr. University of Kansas, Lawrence. Publications of the Museum of Natural History 19:361-393. 1971.

Mammals of the Black Hills of South Dakota and Wyoming. R. W. Turner. University of Kansas, Lawrence. 178 pp. 1974.

see Mammals of the northern Great Plains (regional)

Tennessee

Annotated list of Tennessee mammals. R. Kellog. Proceedings of the United States National Museum 86:245-303. 1939.

see Mammals of Kentucky.

Texas

Mammals of the Guadalupe Mountains National Park, Texas. H. H. Genoways, R. J. Baker, and J. E. Cornely. Proceedings Transcript 4:271-332. 1979.

* Texas mammals east of the Balcones Fault zone. D. J. Schmidly. Texas A&M University Press, College Station. 400 pp. 1983.

The mammals of eastern Texas. W. H. McCarley. Texas Journal of Science 11:385-426. 1959.

* The mammals of Texas. W. D. Davis. Texas Parks and Wildlife Department 41. 267 pp. 1966.

* The mammals of Trans-Pecos, Texas. D. J. Schmidly. Texas A&M University Press, College Station. 225 pp. 1977.

Utah

Mammals of Utah. S. D. Durrant. University of Kansas, Lawrence. 549 pp. 1952.

Vermont

The mammals of Vermont. F. L. Osgood, Jr. Journal of Mammalogy 19:435-441. 1938.

see Wild mammals of New England (regional)

Virginia

Mammals of Virginia. J. W. Bailey. Published privately, Richmond. 416 pp. 1946.

Wild mammals of Virginia. C. O. Handley, Jr., and C. P. Patton. Virginia Commission of Game and Inland Fish, Richmond. 220 pp. 1947.

Washington

Mammals of Washington. W. W. Dalquest. University of Kansas, Lawrence. 444 pp. 1948.

* Washington mammals—their habits, identification, and distribution. E. J. Larrison. Seattle Audubon Society. 243 pp. 1970.

West Virginia

The mammals of West Virginia. F. E. Brooks. West Virginia Board of Agriculture 20:9-30. 1911.

see A guide to the mammals of Ohio.

Wisconsin

* Mammals of Wisconsin. H. H. T. Jackson. University of Wisconsin Press, Madison. 540 pp. 1961.

see The mammals of Illinois and Wisconsin.

Wyoming

The mammals of Wyoming. C. A. Long. University of Kansas, Lawrence. Museum of Natural History 14:493-758. 1965.

see Mammals of the Black Hills of South Dakota and Wyoming.

MEXICO

A guide to Mexican mammals and reptiles. N. P. Wright. Editorial Minutiae Mexicana. 112 pp. 1970.

* Biological investigations in Mexico. E. A. Goldman. Smithsonian, Washington, D.C., Miscellaneous Collection 115:1-476. 1951.

* Mamíferos silvestres de la cuenca de México. G. Ceballos González and C. Galindo Leal. Publicacíon, Instituto de Ecologia de México, 12:1-299. 1984.

Notas acerca de los mamíferos Mexicanos. L. G. Ingles. Anales del Instituto de Biología, Universidad Nacional Autónoma de México 19:319-408. 1959.

Present distribution and affinities of Mexican mammals. W. H. Burt. Association of American Geographers, Annals 39:211-218. 1949.

* Wildlife of Mexico — the game birds and mammals. A. S. Leopold. University of California Press, Berkeley. 568 pp. 1959.

Baja California

Los mamíferos de la Sierra de la Laguna Baja California sur. D. and B. W. Woloszyn. Consejo Nacional de Cienci Y Tecnologia, Mexico. 168 pp. 1982.

The mammals of Baja California, Mexico. L. M. Huey. San Diego Society of Natural History, Transactions 13:85-168. 1964.

Chiapas

Los mamíferos de Chiapas. M. Alvarez del Toro. Universidad Autónoma de Chiapas. 147 pp. 1977.

Chihuahua

Mammals of Chihuahua, taxonomy and distribution. S. Anderson. American Museum of Natural History Bulletin 148:149-410. 1972.

Coahuila

Mammals of Coahuila, Mexico. R. H. Baker. University of Kansas, Lawrence, Museum of Natural History Publication 9:125-335. 1956.

Durango

Mammals of the Mexican state of Durango. R. H. Baker and J. K. Greer. Michigan State University, East Lansing. Publications of the Museum, Biological Series 2:25-154. 1962.

Guerrero

Mammals of the Mexican state of Guerrero, exclusive of Chiroptera and Rodentia. W. B. Davis and P. W. Lukens, Jr. Journal of Mammalogy 39:347-367. 1958.

Michoacan

An annotated checklist of the mammals of Michoacan, Mexico. E. R. Hall and B. Villa R. University of Kansas, Lawrence, Museum of Natural History Publication 1:431-472. 1949.

Oaxaca

Mammals from the state of Oaxaca, Mexico, in the American Museum of Natural History. G. G. Goodwin. American Museum of Natural History Bulletin 141:1-269. 1969.

Puebla

Birds and mammals of the Mesa de San Diego, Puebla, Mexico. D. W. Warner and J. R. Beer. Acta Zoologica Mexicana 2:1-21. 1957.

San Luis Potosi

Mammals of the Mexican state of San Luis Potosi. W. W. Dalquest. Louisiana State University, Baton Rouge, Biological Studies, Science Series 1. 229 pp. 1953.

Sinaloa

Mammals from the Mexican state of Sinaloa. D. M. Armstrong et al. Journal of Mammalogy, Part 1, 52:747-757, 1971; Part 2, University of Kansas, Lawrence, Museum of Natural History, Occasional Papers 6:1-29, 1972; Part 3, Journal of Mammalogy 53:48-61, 1972.

Sonora

Faunal relationships and geographic distribution of mammals in Sonora, Mexico. W. H. Burt. University of Michigan, Ann Arbor, Museum of Zoology, Miscellaneous Publications 39:1-77. 1938.

Tamaulipas

The recent mammals of Tamaulipas, Mexico. T. Alvarez. University of Kansas, Lawrence, Museum of Natural History, Publications 14:363-473. 1963.

Veracruz

The mammals of Veracruz. E. R. Hall and W. W. Dalquest. University of Kansas, Lawrence, Museum of Natural History Publication 14:165-362. 1963.

Yucatan

Annotated checklist of mammals of the Yucatan Peninsula, Mexico. J. K. Jones, Jr., et al. Texas Tech University, Lubbock, Occasional Papers Museum 13, 31 pp. 1973; 22, 24 pp. 1974; 23, 12 pp. 1974; 26, 22 pp. 1975.

Mammalian distributional records in Yucatan and Quintana Roo, with comments on reproduction, structure, and status of peninsular populations. E. C. Birney, J. B. Bowles, R. M. Timm, and S. L. Williams. Museum of Natural History, Occasional Papers, Bulletin 13:1-25. 1974.

WEST INDIES

Catálogo de los mamíferos vivientes y extinguidos de las Antillas. L. S. Varona. Academia de Ciencias de Cuba. 139 pp. 1974.

Mammals of the West Indies. G. M. Allen. Museum of Comparative Zoology, Bulletin 54:173-263. 1911.

The indigenous land mammals of Porto Rico, living and extinct. H. E. Anthony. American Museum of Natural History, Memoirs 2:331-435. 1918.

CENTRAL AMERICA

Biologia Centrali-Americana. Mammalia. E. R. Alston. 220 pp. 1879-1882.

Geographical distribution of terrestrial mammals in Middle America. R. H. Baker. American Midland Naturalist 70:208-249. 1963.

History of the fauna of Latin America. G. G. Simpson. American Scientist 38:361-389. 1950.

Mammals from British Honduras, Mexico, Jamaica and Haiti. P. Herschkovits. Fieldiana Zoology 31:547-569. 1951.

Mammals from Guatemala and British Honduras. A. Murie. University of Michigan Press, Ann Arbor. 30 pp. 1935.

Costa Rica

A list of mammals from Costa Rica. W. P. Harris, Jr. University of Michigan, Museum of Zoology, Occasional Papers 476:1-15. 1943.

Costa Rican natural history. Edited by D. H. Janzen. The University of Chicago Press, Chicago. 816 pp. 1983.

Mammals of Costa Rica. G. G. Goodwin. American Museum of Natural History, Bulletin 87:271-473. 1946.

El Salvador

The Mammals of El Salvador. W. H. Burt and R. A. Stirton. University of Michigan, Ann Arbor, Museum of Zoology, Miscellaneous Publications 117:1-69. 1961.

Guatemala

Mamíferos colectados en Guatemala en 1954. R. M. Ryan. Acta Zoologica Mexicana, 4:1-19. 1960.

Honduras

Mammals of Honduras. G. G. Goodwin. American Museum of Natural History, Bulletin 79:107-195. 1942.

Panama

Checklist of mammals of Panama. C. O. Handley, Jr. In "Ectoparasites of Panama". Field Museum of Natural History. pp 753-795. 1966.

Los principales mamíferos silvestres de Panama. E. Mendez. Zoologo del Laboratorio Conmemorative Gorgas, Miembro de la Comision Nacional de Proteccion de la Fauna Silvestre Panama. 283 pp. 1970.

Mammals of Panama. E. A. Goldman. Smithsonian Miscellaneous Collection 69:1-309. 1920.

OTHERS

* Fascinating world of animals. The Reader's Digest Association Incorporated, Pleasantville, New York. 427 pp. 1971.

Journal of Mammalogy. Published quarterly by American Society of Mammalogists. Shippensburg University, Shippensburg, Pennsylvania.

Living mammals of the world. I. T. Sanderson. Doubleday and Company, Garden City, New York. 303 pp. 1965.

Mammalian species. American Society of Mammalogists. Shippensburg University, Shippensburg, Pennsylvania. 253+ accounts.

Mammalogy. T. Vaughan. W. B. Saunders Company, Philadelphia. 518 pp. 1978.

* Sea guide to whales of the world. L. Watson. Nelson Canada Limited, Scarborough, Ontario. 302 pp. 1981.

* Simon and Schuster's guide to mammals. L. B. Boitani and S. Bartoli. Edited by S. Anderson. Simon and Schuster, New York. 511 pp. 1983.

* The atlas of world wildlife. Rand McNally and Company, New York. 208 pp. 1973.

* The encyclopedia of mammals. D. W. Macdonald (editor). Facts on File Inc., New York. 928 pp. 1984.

* The world of mammals. A. V. Taglianti. Gallery Books, New York. 256 pp. 1979.

* Walker's mammals of the world. R. M. Nowak and J. L. Paradiso. Johns Hopkins University Press, Baltimore. 4th ed. 2 volumes. 1362 pp. 1983.